02-21-01

$ 266.40

42435026

v1

CONTEMPORARY AMERICAN RELIGION

CONTEMPORARY AMERICAN RELIGION

WADE CLARK ROOF

Editor in Chief

VOLUME 1

MACMILLAN REFERENCE USA

AN IMPRINT OF THE GALE GROUP

NEW YORK

Macmillan Reference USA
1633 Broadway
New York, NY 10019

PRINTED IN THE UNITED STATES OF AMERICA

Printing Number

2 3 4 5 6 7 8 9 10

LIBRARY OF CONGRESS CATALOGING-IN-PUBLICATION DATA

     p. cm.
   Includes bibliographical references and index.
   ISBN 0-02-864926-5 (v. 1 : alk. paper)—ISBN 0-02-864927-3 v. 2 : alk. paper)—
ISBN 0-02-864928-1 (2 v. set : alk. paper)
     1. United States—Religion—Encyclopedias. I. Roof, Wade Clark.

BL2525 .C65 1999
200'.973'03—dc21

                                                         99-046712

Contents

Editorial and Production Staff

Project Editor
Scott Kurtz

Production Editor
Peter Rocheleau

Manuscript Editors
William Drennan
Evangeline Legones

Proofreaders
Sal Alocco
Susan Gamer
Julie Marsh
Ned McLeroy
Joseph Pomerance
Gregory Teague

Photo Researcher
Deanna Raso

Compositor
Impressions

Indexer
Cynthia Crippen

Macmillan Library Reference USA

Elly Dickason, *Publisher*

Preface

This two-volume work, consisting of more than five hundred articles on many facets of religious life, is unusual in its approach. *Contemporary American Religion* is intended as a lexicon of popular religious culture, pulling together beliefs, practices, ideas, symbols, traditions, movements, trends, organizations, discourses, and major leaders making up the incredibly diverse religious climate of the United States at the beginning of the twenty-first century. By focusing on popular religious life, we explore terms and categories that ordinary Americans are likely to encounter as they become aware of other religions and spiritual disciplines or even of multiple traditions within their own faith communities. It also means that we pay less attention to official teachings and practices held up by religious institutions as normative and more attention to how those beliefs, practices, and symbols are popularly understood or drawn upon in the context of people's everyday lives. "Lived religion" is more than just an entry in this compendium; the concept points to a vital quality that runs throughout the Encyclopedia—an emphasis on the experiential, imaginative, and behavioral expressions of ordinary religious life.

For several reasons, this more comprehensive look at popular religion is increasingly important. One is the ever-widening religious pluralism in the United States. Since the immigration laws were liberalized in the mid-1960s, religious traditions from other parts of the globe have become increasingly visible and dispersed across the country. In an earlier era, the "Other" as religiously defined was largely in some other place, contained by geographical boundaries; today he or she may be living next door or possibly within one's own family. Muslims from many parts of the world are establishing communities in this country; more than a hundred different ethnic Buddhist traditions now reside here; Chicano and other Hispanic populations are rapidly reshaping American Roman Catholicism. Add to this the revival of metaphysical traditions, nature religions, and indigenous spiritual beliefs of the past quarter-century, and it becomes obvious that the boundaries of religious pluralism are greatly expanding. Involving more than just new players on the religious field, this increased pluralism creates a distinctive psychology, an awareness of differences in belief and worldview that at one level may be befuddling to believers, yet at another level forces them to think through their own commitments. Fear and worry about holding on to a cultural past is one common reaction; openness and acceptance of religious change and diversity is another—both of these trends find expression in the entries found within these volumes.

Another reason for the broad sweep of our purview of American religious culture stems from changes in modern life. A high level of personal autonomy creates an expanded menu of choices. Many people, and especially those not very well grounded in any religious tradition, feel free to explore religious and spiritual alternatives. Many are seekers not in some narrow meaning of that word but in the sense of being curious about how to enrich their lives. Even faithful followers within a tradition are looking for ways of cultivating their spiritual life and learning more about their own heritage. Broadly within American culture, there is concern about the self, about personal growth and well-being. Religious life is understood less as a stable identity and more as a process of development and enrichment. This being the case, it is not surprising that the religious themes people draw upon in their searching will be eclectic—involving psychological, popular spiritual, ideological, mass-media, and traditional religious notions. If we think of religious culture as a script and of the contemporary world as consisting of multiple religious subscripts, then we can appreciate the complexity of people drawing selectively off those subscripts as they arrive at their own conceptions of themselves. Or alternatively, the religious event horizon—not just the number of religious groups, but popular cultural styles and definitions of spiritual need—has expanded, producing a religious landscape with many new alternatives.

Hence in these volumes we have sought to assist students and scholars in understanding this complex and ever-evolving religious situation. Like any encyclopedia, this one can be read in many ways. The alphabetic order in which the entries are listed makes for easy access to a particular topic, and no doubt searching for specific articles using the alphabetic list will be the most common way the volumes will be used. However, the cross-references at the ends of articles and between articles provide help in interrelating the various topics, and the comprehensive index at the end of the second volume further aids the reader in sorting out the material. Much of what is written about in these pages bears some relation to other entries, and usually something is to be gained by examining how and in what ways one topic relates to others. Whatever the uses of these volumes, the large body of information and rich interpretations that they provide will challenge older conceptions of religion and should broaden ways of thinking about religion and culture generally. Additionally, a varied selection of 195 photographs serves to clarify further the significance of the people, places, and concepts discussed.

I am grateful to the associate editors—Catherine L. Albanese, Randall Balmer, Frederick M. Denny, Cheryl Townsend Gilkes, Ana María Díaz-Stevens, Anthony M. Stevens-Arroyo, and Ellen M. Umansky—for their many hours of hard work, generating concepts and topics to include, identifying contributors, and reading and editing the final entries. Without their assistance, this project would not have been possible. Of course, without the help of our many valued contributors, it would not have been possible either.

I appreciate as well the efforts of the publisher and project editor at Macmillan Reference USA, who encouraged the project and guided us through it-respectively—Elly Dickason and Scott Kurtz. Finally, to the reader, I hope the material herein contained not only informs but also encourages your interest in the study of American religion.

Wade Clark Roof

Alphabetic List of Articles

Directory of Contributors

A

Omer Bin Abdullah
Herndon, VA
Da'Wa

Carol Adams
Richardson, TX
Vegetarianism

James Aho
Idaho State University
British Israelism
Identity Christianity

Daniel O. Aleshire
Association of Theological
Schools
Seminaries

Horace T. Allen, Jr.
School of Theology
Boston University
Liturgy and Worship
Prayer

Robert S. Alley
University of Richmond
Freedom of Religion

Rebecca T. Alpert
Temple University
Jewish Renewal
Lesbian and Gay Rights
Movement

Nancy T. Ammerman
Hartford Theological Seminary
Congregation
Secularization

Ray S. Anderson
Huntington Beach, CA
Death and Dying

Edward P. Antonio
Ilif School of Theology
Civil Rights Movement
Missionary Movements

Yaakov S. Ariel
University of North Carolina,
Chapel Hill
Holy Land
Jews for Jesus
Seder, Christian

Boulos Ayad Ayad
University of Colorado, Boulder
Coptic Orthodox Church

B

Edward Bailey
Winterbourne Rectory (U.K.)
Implicit Religion

William Sims Bainbridge
National Science Foundation
Belonging, Religious
Future of Religion
Globalization
Human Rights
Space Flight

Randall Balmer
Barnard College, Columbia
University
Premillennialism

Eileen Barker
London School of Economics
Divine Principle

Steven Barrie-Anthony
Albany, CA
Meher Baba

Judith R. Baskin
State University of New York,
Albany
Chanukah
Jewish High Holy Days
Menorah
Passover
Shivah

Diana Hochstedt Butler Bass
Rhodes College
Communion
Dispensationalism
Faith
Temptation

Dorothy C. Bass
Valpariso University
Practice

John Baumann
University of California, Santa
Barbara
Celtic Practices

Michael Baxter, N.S.C.
Notre Dame University
Catholic Worker

Lori Beaman
University of Lethbridge,
Canada
Child Abuse by Clergy
Divorce, Christian

Mary Farrell Bednarowski
United Theological Seminary of
the Twin Cities
Spirit

Patricia Behre Miskimin
Fairfield College
Religious Persecution

Gustavo Benavides
Villanova University
Mysticism

John Berthrong
Boston University
Confucianism

James A. Beverley
Tyndale College, Toronto
Adventism
Christian Science
Freemasonry
Miracles

Loriliai Biernacki
University of Pennsylvania
Vedas

Khalid Yahya Blankinship
Temple University
Allah

Kathleen Blee
University of Pittsburgh
Ku Klux Klan

Edith L. Blumhofer
University of Chicago Divinity
School
Baptism in the Holy Spirit
Charismatic Movement
Holiness Movement
Pentecostal and Charismatic
Christianity

Cynthia Bourgeault
The Contemplative Society
Salt Spring Island, BC
Centering Prayer

Henry Warner Bowden
Rutgers University, New
Brunswick
Advent
Altar
Christmas
Divinity
Easter
Lent
Trinity

Paul Boyer
University of Wisconsin,
Madison
Second Coming

Brenda E. Brasher
Mount Union College
Cyber Religion
Promise Keepers
Star Trek
Testimony

Marcy Braverman
University of California, Santa
Barbara
Meditation
Transcendental Meditation

Lucy Bregman
Temple University
Human Potential Movement

Daniel Breslauer
University of Kansas
Heschel, Abraham Joshua

David G. Bromley
Virginia Commonwealth
University
Branch Davidians
est (Erhard Seminar Training)
Satanists
Scientology, Church of
Unification Church
Way International, The

Lee Hayward Butler, Jr.
Chicago Theological Seminary
Psychotherapy

C

Bret E. Carroll
California State University,
Stanislaus
Masculine Spirituality
Séance
Secret Societies

Darryl V. Caterine
Dartmouth College
Names and Naming

Patricia Mei Yin Chang
Notre Dame University
Church
Denomination
Sect

Christopher Key Chapple
Loyola Marymount University
Jainism

David Chidester
University of Cape Town
Jones, Jim

James F. Childress
University of Virginia
Euthanasia and Assisted
Suicide

Carol P. Christ
Ariadne Institute for the Study
of Myth and Ritual
Athens, Greece
Goddess

Joseph Chuman
Ethical Culture Society of New
Jersey
Agnosticism
Ethical Culture

Lynn Schofield Clark
University of Colorado, Denver
Angels

Anne M. Clifford
Duquesne University
Creationism

Timothy T. Clydesdale
College of New Jersey
Dobson, James C., Jr.
Focus on the Family
Young Life

Kelton Cobb
Hartford Theological Seminary
Ethics

Sharon L. Coggan
University of Colorado, Denver
Archetype
Dreams
Journeys and Journeying
Rites of Passage

Daniel O. Conkle
Indiana University School of
Law
Religious Freedom Restoration
Act

Jonathan F. Cordero
University of California, Santa
Barbara
Colson, Charles
Sacrilege

Ronald K. Crandall
Asbury Theological Seminary
Church Growth Movement

Michael W. Cuneo
Fordham University
Exorcism

D

Barbara Darling-Smith
Wheaton College, Norton, MA
Sexuality

Erwan Dianteill
Centre d'Etudes des
Interdisciplinaires des Faits
Religieux, Paris
Afro-Cuban Religions
Bricolage

Ana María Díaz-Stevens
Union Theological Seminary,
New York
Calendars
Latino Traditions
Matriarchal Core

Michelle Dillon
Yale University
Afterlife
Annulment
Encyclical
Relic
Sacraments
Vatican

William Dinges
Catholic University of America
Opus Dei

Jay P. Dolan
Notre Dame University
Marty, Martin

Elliot N. Dorff
University of Judaism
Circumcision
Divorce, Jewish
Jewish Observance
Marriage, Jewish
Mikveh

Herbert Druks
Brooklyn College, City
University of New York
Anti-Semitism
Kahane, Meir
Schechter, Solomon

Jorge Duany
University of Puerto Rico
Santos

E

Heather Eaton
St. Paul University, Ottawa
Ecofeminism
Ecospirituality

Theresa Eddins
Virginia Commonwealth
University
est (Erhard Seminar Training)

Nancy Eiseland
Emory University
Religious Communities

Virgilio Elizondo
Mexican American Cultural
Center, San Antonio
Mestizo Worship

Cynthia Eller
Princeton University
Magic
Neopaganism
Priestess

Gracia Fay Ellwood
California State University
Ascended Master
Occult, The
Pantheism
Paranormal
Salvation
Spiritualism
Summerland

Robert Ellwood
Auburn University
Ascended Master
Extraterrestrial Guides
Occult, The
Pantheism
Paranormal
Salvation
Spiritualism
Summerland

Michael O. Emerson
Bethel College, St. Paul, MN
Home Schooling
Rapture
Sociology of Religion

Ronald Enroth
Westmont College
Anti-Cult Movement
Family, The

Larry Eskridge
Wheaton College, Illinois
Campus Crusade for Christ
InterVarsity Christian
Fellowship
Jesus Movement
Navigators
Youth for Christ

Gastón Espinosa
Westmont College
Catholic Charismatic Renewal
Cortese, Aimee Garcia
Romero, Oscar Arnulfo
Rosseau, Leoncia Rosado

F

Tommy L. Faris
Columbia University
Blasphemy
Conversion

Darrell J. Fasching
University of South Florida
Holocaust

Stephen Field
Trinity University, San Antonio
Feng Shui
I Ching

Martha Finch-Jewell
University of California, Santa
Barbara
Body
Williamson, Marianne

Walter E. Fluker
Morehouse College
Thurman, Howard

Robert Fogarty
Antioch College
Communes

Tanice G. Foltz
Indiana University, Gary
Spirit Guides

Tamar Frankiel
Los Angeles, CA
Kabbalah
Quest
Reiki
Sabbath, Jewish
Vision Quest
Visionary

Bryan Froehle
Georgetown University
Marriage, Christian
Parish
Priesthood
Retreat

Robert Fuller
Bradley University
Alternative Medicine
Health
Holistic Health

G

Norman J. Girardot
Lehigh University
Elvis Cults

C. Jarrett Gray, Jr.
Duke University
Womanist Theology

Wendy Griffin
California State University, Long
Beach
Spirituality
Wicca

R. Marie Griffith
Princeton University
Self-Help Movement
Twelve-Step Programs
Women's Aglow Fellowship
  International

H

C. Kirk Hadaway
United Church of Christ
Attendance

David D. Hall
Harvard University
Lived Religion

Thomas D. Hamm
Earlham College
Peace Churches

Phillip E. Hammond
University of California, Santa
Barbara
Church and State
Civil Religion
Conscientious Objection
Prayer in School

Francis Hannafey, S.J.
Fairfield University
Celibacy

David Edwin Harrell, Jr.
Auburn University
Roberts, Oral
Robertson, Pat
Swaggart, Jimmy

Milmon F. Harrison
University of California, Santa
Barbara
African-American Religions
Southern Christian Leadership
  Conference
Word of Faith Movement

John Hart
Carroll College
Black Elk
Native American Religions

Richard Hecht
University of California, Santa
Barbara
Jewish Identity
Religious Studies
Totem

Marcia K. Hermansen
Loyola University, Chicago
Sufism

Maria R. Hibbets
Harvard University
Yoga

Dean R. Hoge
Catholic University of America
Financing Religion

David Hogue
Garrett Evangelical Theological
Seminary
Ministry

Barbara Holdrege
University of California, Santa
Barbara
Enlightenment

Stephen Holler
Thomas More College
Mary

Ralph W. Hood, Jr.
University of Tennessee
Dogmatism
Near Death Experiences

Stewart M. Hoover
University of Colorado, Boulder
Megachurch

Beulah S. Hostetler
Goshen, IN
Mennonites

Fisher Humphreys
Beeson Divinity School, Samford
University
Evil
Heresy

Mary E. Hunt
WATER, Silver Springs, MD
Birth Control
Ordination of Women
Theism

I

Julie J. Ingersoll
Rhodes College
Glossolalia
Reconstructionist Christianity
Televangelism

J

Carl Jackson
University of Texas, El Paso
Ramakrishna Movement
Vedanta Society

Janet L. Jacobs
University of Colorado, Boulder
Crypto-Judaism

Christopher Jocks
Dartmouth College
Native American Church
Peyote

C. Lincoln Johnson
Notre Dame University
Food

Doyle Paul Johnson
Texas Technical University
People's Temple

Mark Juergensmeyer
University of California, Santa
Barbara
Niebuhr, Reinhold

K

David G. Kamitsuka
Oberlin College
Tillich, Paul

Sara Karesh
University of California, Santa
Barbara
Fasting

Dennis Kelley
University of California, Santa
Barbara
Cursillo Movement
Posada, La
Quinceañera, La

James R. Kelly
Fordham University
Humanae Vitae
Vatican II

Omar Khalidi
Massachusetts Institute of
Technology
Mosque

Evelyn Kirkley
University of San Diego
Astral Planes

Pamela Klassen
University of Toronto
Birth

Ronald E. Koetzsch
Fair Oaks, CA
Macrobiotics

Frances Kostarelos
Governors State University
Anthropology of Religion

David Kraemer
Jewish Theological Seminary
Kosher
Midrash
Talmud
Torah

Miles Krassen
Oberlin College
Hasidim

L

Gary Laderman
Emory University
Southern Religion

J. Shawn Landres
University of California, Santa
Barbara
Chastity
Generation X
Kippah
Peak Experience
True Love Waits

John Lardas
University of California, Santa
Barbara
Drugs

Dorothy Le Beau
Saint Meinrad Archabbey and
School of Theology
Merton, Thomas

Luis D. Léon
Carleton College
Ecstasy
Shamanism

Bill J. Leonard
Wake Forest University
Baptism
Baptist Tradition
Deacon
Heaven
Hell
Preaching
Religious Right

Cristine Levenduski
Emory University
Quakers

Peggy Levitt
Wellesley College
Transnational Religion

Ed Linenthal
University of Wisconsin,
Oshkosh
War Memorials

Andrew Linzey
Mansfield College, Oxford
Animal Rights

Charles H. Lippy
University of Tennessee
Millennialism

Charles H. Long
Chapel Hill, NC
Drumming

Sandra B. Lubarsky
Northern Arizona University
Process Theology

Phillip Charles Lucas
Stetson University
Astrology
Church Universal and
Triumphant
Cult
Cult Awareness Network
Divine Light Mission
Heaven's Gate
New Age Spirituality
New Religious Movements
Peale, Norman Vincent
Silva Mind Control

M

David W. Machacek
University of California, Santa
Barbara
Prosperity Theology
Soka Gakkai

Otto Maduro
Drew University
Base Communities
Liberation Theology

William K. Mahony
Davidson College
Avatar
Chakra
Upanishads

Lawrence Mamiya
Vassar College
Black Muslims
Fard, W. D.
Farrakhan, Louis
Muhammad, Elijah Karriem

Christel Manning
Sacred Heart University
Gender Roles
Matriarchy
Patriarchy
Visualization

Herbert Marbury
Vanderbilt University
Wisdom Literature

Stephen Marini
Wellesley College
Music
Rock Masses

Penny Long Marler
Samford University
Attendance

William Martin
Rice University
Christian Coalition
Falwell, Jerry
Graham, Billy
Moral Majority

Martin E. Marty
University of Chicago Divinity
School
Fundamentalist Christianity
Publishing, Religious

Deborah Vansau McCauley
East Orange, NJ
Appalachia, Religions of
Snake Handling

Aminah Beverly McCloud
De Paul University
Muhammad, Warith Deen
Muslim Brotherhood
Nation of Islam

Thomas J. McFarlane
Palo Alto, CA
Quantum Healing
Quantum Physics

John Anthony McGuckin
Union Theological Seminary,
New York
Creeds
Epiphany
Icons

William McKinney
Pacific School of Religion
Mainline Protestantism

Josephine C. McMullen
University of California, Santa
Barbara
Proselytizing

Lara Medina
California State University,
North Ridge
Day of the Dead
Las Hermanas

James J. Megivern
University of North Carolina,
Wilmington
Capital Punishment

J. Gordon Melton
Institute for the Study of
American Religion
International Society for
Krishna Consciousness
New Thought
Ramtha's School of
Enlightenment
Rosicrucians
Solar Temple
Synanon
Tarot
Triple Goddess
Unidentified Flying Objects

Donald E. Messer
Ilif School of Theology
Ecumenical Movement

Katherine Meyer
Ohio State University
Work

Claudine Michel
University of California, Santa
Barbara
Vodun

Donald E. Miller
University of Southern
California
Calvary Chapel
Postdenominational Church

Matthew R. Miller
University of California, Santa
Barbara
Survivalism

Timothy Miller
University of Kansas
Amish
Bruderhof
Shunning

Robin Minahan
Bethel College, St. Paul, MN
Rapture

Mustansir Mir
Youngstown State University
Islam
Islamic Circle of North America
Islamic Society of North
America
Jihad
Qur'an

Kerry Mitchell
University of California, Santa
Barbara
Temperance

Beverly Moon
Fordham University
Eliade, Mircea
Revelation

Douglas Morgan
Columbia Union College
Seventh-Day Adventism

Joseph M. Murphy
Georgetown University
Syncretism

N

Paul R. Nelson, D.C.M.
Evangelical Lutheran Church in
America
Clothing, Religious

Paula Nesbitt
University of Denver
Book of Common Prayer
Episcopal Churches

Diann L. Neu
WATER, Silver Springs, MD
Feminist Spirituality
Sophia

Jacob Neusner
University of South Florida
Bar Mitzvah and Bat Mitzvah
Shavuot
Synagogue
Zionism

Gwen Kennedy Neville
Southwestern University
Reunions

Richard Newman
Harvard University
Spirituals

Mark A. Noll
Wheaton College, Illinois
Evangelical Christianity

O

Roger E. Olson
Bethel College, St. Paul, MN
Born Again Christians
Eckankar

P

Marie Anne Pagliarini
University of California, Santa
Barbara
Mother Teresa

Birger Pearson
University of California,
Berkeley
Jesus Seminar

Andrés Péres y Mena
Long Island University
Animal Sacrifice
Santería

Lloyd W. Pflueger
Truman State University
Bhagavad Gītā

Sarah M. Pike
California State University,
Chico
Apocalypse
Dowsing
Psychic

James Newton Poling
Garrett Evangelical Theological
Seminary
Pastoral Counseling

Margaret Poloma
Southern California College,
Costa Mesa
Brownsville Revival

Amanda Porterfield
University of Wyoming
Myth
Ritual

William Powell
University of California, Santa
Barbara
Martial Arts

Charles Prebish
Pennsylvania State University
Buddha
Buddhism

Stephen Prothero
Boston University
Cremation
Hinduism

R

Nancy Ramsey
University of California, Santa
Barbara
Pantheon
Pentagram
Purification
Sabbat
Warrior

Carl A. Raschke
University of Denver
Jehovah's Witnesses
Rajneesh Bhagwan

Eric Reinders
Emory University
Taoism
Tao Te Ching
Zen

James Richardson
University of Nevada, Reno
Brainwashing

Jana Kathryn Riess
Winchester, KY
Book of Mormon
*Church of Jesus Christ of
Latter-day Saints*
Mormon Temple

Greg Robinson
New York University
Jackson, Jesse

John K. Roth
Claremont McKenna College
Death of God

Jeffrey Ruff
University of California, Santa
Barbara
Healing

Abdulaziz A. Sachedina
University of Virginia
Mecca
Mullah

S

Daniel Sack
Material History of American
Religion Project
Material Religion
Moral Rearmament

Richard C. Salter
Hobart and William Smith
Colleges
Rastafari

Arlene M. Sánchez Walsh
University of Southern
California
Vineyard Christian Fellowship

James Santucci
California State University,
Fullerton
Ashram
Theosophical Society

Kimon H. Sargeant
Pew Charitable Trusts
Seeker Churches

Robert F. Scholz
Holy Trinity Lutheran Church
New York, NY
Lutheran Churches

Mel Scult
New York, NY
Kaplan, Mordechai

Robert A. Segal
Lancaster University (U.K.)
Campbell, Joseph
Gnosticism

Thomas D. Senor
University of Kansas, Fayetteville
Free Will
God

Ilene Ava Serlin
Saybrook Institute
Dance

Drorah O'Donnell Setel
Yale University
Feminist Theology
Starhawk
Women's Studies

Cybele Shattuck
Western Michigan University
Self-Realization Fellowship

Roger Lincoln Shinn
Union Theological Seminary,
New York
Atheism
Existentialism

Peggy L. Shriver
National Council of Churches of
Christ in the U.S.A.
National Council of Churches
of Christ in the U.S.A.
World Council of Churches

Elijah Siegler
University of California at Santa
Barbara
Channeling
Lazaris

David Sikkink
Bethel College, St. Paul, MN
Home Schooling

Mark Silk
Trinity College, Hartford
Journalism, Religious
Judeo-Christian Tradition

Judith Simmer-Brown
Nairopa Institute
Mantra
Nirvāṇa
Tantra

Nikky-Guninder Kaur Singh
Colby College
Reincarnation
Temple

James Spickard
University of Redlands
Religious Experience

Paul Spickard
University of California, Santa
Barbara
Hawaiian Religions
Japanese-American Religions
Korean-American Religions

Anthony M. Stevens-Arroyo
City University of New York
Marian Devotions
Patron Saints and Patron-Saint
Feasts
Popular Religion
Roman Catholicism

Mark Stoll
Texas Tech University
Sanctuary Movement

Jerome A. Stone
William Rainey Harper College
Transcendence

T

Ines M. Talamantez
University of California, Santa
Barbara
Sun Dance
Sweat Lodge

Robert B. Tapp
University of Minnesota
Unitarian-Universalist
Churches

Bron Taylor
University of Wisconsin,
Oshkosh
Deep Ecology
Nature Religion

Sarah McFarland Taylor
University of California, Santa
Barbara
Creation Spirituality
Rave

Christine Thomas
University of California, Santa
Barbara
Bible

Don Thorsen
Azusa Pacific University
Inclusive Language

Robert A. F. Thurman
Columbia University
Dalai Lama
Tibetan Buddhism

Gene R. Thursby
University of Florida
Dharma
Guru
Karma
Sikhism

Jesse T. Todd
Drew University
Self-Mutilation
Spirit Possession
Trance

Emilie M. Townes
Saint Paul School of Theology
Legalism
Love
Suffering
Theodicy

Lou Ann G. Trost
Graduate Theological Union
Eschatology

Richard Brent Turner
De Paul University
Malcolm X
Noble Drew Ali

Thomas A. Tweed
University of North Carolina,
Chapel Hill
Pilgrimage
Shrine

U

Ellen M. Umansky
Fairfield College
Judaism

V

Lonnie Valentine
Earlham College
Pacifism

Bradford Verter
Princeton University
Crowley, Aleister
Devils, Demons, and Spirits
Satanic Bible

Jaime R. Vidal
Iowa State University
Papacy
Rome
Sainthood
Stations of the Cross

Dennis Voskuil
Hope College
Schuller, Robert

W

Margit Warburg
Institute of the History of
Religion, Copenhagen
Baha'is

Earle H. Waugh
University of Alberta
Chanting
Imam

Gisela Webb
Seton Hall University
Bawa Muhaiyadeen

Louis B. Weeks
Union Theological Seminary,
Richmond
Presbyterianism

Renita Weems
Vanderbilt University
Wisdom Literature

Robert Weisbrot
Colby College
Father Divine
King, Martin Luther, Jr.

Melissa M. Wilcox
University of California, Santa
Barbara
*Metropolitan Community
Church*

Rhys Williams
Southern Illinois University
Culture Wars

Sherwin T. Wine
Society for Humanistic Judaism
Humanism

Diane Winston
Princeton University
Salvation Army

Stuart Wright
Lamar University
Koresh, David
LaVey, Anton Szandor

David M. Wulff
Wheaton College, Massachusetts
Psychology of Religion

Y

Fengang Yang
University of Southern Maine
Chinese-American Religions

Charles Yrigoyen
Drew University
Methodism

Z

Barbara Brown Zikmund
Hartford Theological Seminary
Clergy
Ordination

Sandra Zimdars-Swartz
University of Kansas
Virgin of Guadalupe

Gary P. Zola
Hebrew Union College-Jewish
Institute of Religion, Cincinnati
Rabbinate

Laurie Zoloth
San Francisco State University
Abortion
Bioethics

Abortion

Of all of the religious and philosophical issues that mark the contemporary American discourse, and the realpolitik of public policy, there is perhaps none that divides as deeply as the question of the meaning and morality of abortion. How this came to be the case, and how the stance on abortion became the definitive linguistics for religion, politics, and ethics in the popular imagination requires an exploration of historical and textual positions of various religious faiths, of the place and meaning of moral status, of the changing abilities of medical technology, and of the evolving understanding of the role of women in society.

Medical Considerations

Let us begin with definitional medical terminology. As narrowly defined medically, abortion is the interruption and termination of pregnancy prior to the viability of the fetus, by natural or artificial means. Spontaneous abortion refers to the miscarriage of a pregnancy and is characterized by the unexpected loss of function of the uterus; of the placenta to support a term pregnancy; or the unexpected death of the developing fetus and its expulsion from the womb. Elective abortions are planned interventions that remove the embryo or fetus from the womb, along with the supporting placenta. Such abortions are commonly called therapeutic abortions or TAB in the medical literature and are defined as a medical procedure necessary to terminate pregnancy for reasons of maternal physical health, or significant mental anguish that would impinge on health. The moral and

political controversy involves debate only about elective abortion procedures, and centers on when and in what instances, if ever, such procedures are to be used, who can decide on their use, and what criteria define and justify their use. Because abortions take place within the medical context, and are acts that involve both the family and the society, abortion raises issues of both personal liberty and public policy in addition to questions regarding the morality of the act. These range from how to protect medically informed consent to how society ought to allow, fund, regulate, or discipline those who seek abortions, or to sanction or regulate or discipline those who perform them.

But the medical considerations only begin the debate. The debate about abortion is one that is divisive and painfully difficult to resolve, touching on the deepest moral issues of the meaning of the responsibility of one to another, the problem of who we will include in the community, and the persistent issues of power. For all religious traditions, abortion is a crisis, a failure of the public and the private spheres. What is at stake is the moral justification for the act, and what can be done to limit the deep symbolic disruption of this act within a social community and a personal and family narrative. The medical language itself raises critical issues and limits. However, the essential thinness of the description obscures the critical questions of morality and meaning that surround issues of life and death. For that genre of discourse, human societies have turned to religious considerations, and on the issue of abortion the discourse is intensely shaped by the understanding of the body, the issue of forbidden sexual liaisons, the view of health, the definition of personhood, and the role of women. Religions debate the permissibility of the interruption and termination of pregnancy, and the nature of maternal and fetal health itself. For most religious traditions, the medical aspects of the procedure are not central—what is central is the moral meaning of the human fetus; the power of women over reproduction, birth, and lineage; the embodied and terribly fragile nature of human existence; and the paradoxical conundrum that elective abortion presents: that of the regulation of the boundary between death and birth. Similarly, all religious traditions are the carriers of a strong pronatalist position, particularly in contrast to modernity. This pronatalist view creates a lay pastoral norm that in some cases shapes the choice of text used for counseling, but is held in tension with the widespread customary practice of abortion even in faith communities where the act is forbidden.

Moral Status and Contextuality Frame the Discourse

The first, and for some traditions, the final consideration of the question of abortion is the moral status of the embryo from the moment of conception to birth. Moral status is a consideration of the obligations and responsibilities of the human world toward the entity that is in question. If the embryo is considered a fully ensouled human person, of equal moral status as the mother in whose womb the embryo is carried, a carrier of a unique and sacred human life, then to end that life is tantamount to murder, and could only be considered in situations in which one would murder a born human child.

For Roman Catholic traditions, for whom abortion was always considered a serious sin, the key point to be considered is the absolute inviolability of a human life from the moment of conception. Roman Catholic teachings on abortion have changed over time, and in the contemporary period, a debate on the precise timing and exceptions to the absolute prohibition has emerged. For example, the "principle of double effect" is invoked to permit the removal of a cancerous uterus, even when a woman is pregnant, allowing for an "indirect abortion." The 1974 Vatican Declaration on Abortion argues for the inclusion of the unborn in general principle of respect for life, but notes that human reason needs to take note of serious issues that create a dilemma for which there is "no human solution" but addressing underlying political causes that make childrearing difficult for many. Other authors have used the changing understanding of embryology or the principles of liberation to raise serious ques-

An abortion rights advocate and an anti-abortion advocate stand back to back, placards in hand, during a demonstration outside the U.S. Supreme Court building in Washington, D.C., on December 8, 1993. Inside, the Supreme Court was hearing arguments on whether abortion rights advocates may sue protesters who block access to abortion clinics. (Credit: AP/Wide World Photos.)

tions within the general framework of Roman Catholic thought on this topic.

For Jewish theologians, the debate is rooted in context. If the mother's life, or physical or mental health is at risk (including, for some, the situation in which having a severely disabled child, such as a child with Tay-Sachs disease, would threaten her mental health), the abortion is not only be permitted, it is required. Not only does Jewish tradition have a developmental view of the moral status of the embryo and fetus, but also the tradition's focus on life and health for the mother is the primary ground for the debate. The moral status of the embryo in Jewish considerations of abortion is based on age and proximity to independent viability.

In that capacity, there are discussions about the nature and character of the contents of the womb at various stages of embryonic and fetal development. There are other considerations, such as quickening (the development of a spinal cord) and the external visual changes in a woman's body that also warrant differing social responses and a different consideration of the pregnancy. The discussion and commentary take two courses, either that the fetus is a part of the body of a woman and hence does not have an equal moral claim, or a later understanding, put forward by Maimonides, that in the case where a pregnancy is endangering the life or health of a woman, the fetus can be considered a *rodef* (an aggressor—literally, one who pursues), and killing a rodef is a permitted act of self-defense. The decision about the language of the choice is framed by the woman herself (it is she who names the situation as unendurable and thus asserts her moral voice over the voice of the fetus), but the discourse is to be made in conjunction with a spiritual teacher, a rabbi. A discourse not wholly private, nor wholly public, opening the possibility that the discourse is primarily based in the context of a supportive and caring community. Finally, Jewish practice as developed after the Holocaust is shaped by a strong pronatalist view, with a sense of the importance and fragility of each potential life as a powerful feature in this discourse.

Islamic law draws attention to similar issues, seeing abortion as permitted in some circumstances, prohibited in others, with the decision made in the context of the mutual relationship of husband and wife, and the general understanding that life is a gift from God. While discouraging abortion, Muslim law, which in most cases defines personhood as beginning after the fourth month of pregnancy, allows for abortion for specific reasons of life and health within that period. Traditional texts, for example, cite the protection of a nursing mother's ability to nourish her other young infant as a valid reason.

In Buddhist traditional texts, abortion is prohibited as a violation of the principle of not killing. But as many scholars have noted, the practice of abortion within the Buddhist community is widespread, and in Japan the practice includes the formalistic ritual of the *mizuko kuyo* in which offerings are presented and prayers made that the fetus (the "water child" or *mizuko*) will be able to be born again into another corporal body, having sacrificed its life for the greater good of the family.

Protestant doctrine and practice spans a wide range of belief, and in the contemporary period, Evangelical Protestants have led the opposition to abortion as unjustified killing, while liberal Protestants have urged the admission of other appeals to justify abortion. The biblical fundamentalist argument contrasts directly with the liberal arguments for personal autonomy, and the liberationist appeals for broad social justice considerations. At stake are the weight given the context of the act (rape, incest); the health status of the fetus (severe disability); the attendant condition of the family (poverty, deprivation, oppression); as well as endangerment of the mother's health and personal well-being. Further, liberal Protestants have urged full support for those enacting abortion, and for the decriminalization of the act in American jurisprudence.

Contemporary feminist arguments also influence the debate. Access to the entire range of reproductive technology, including birth control and abortion, became linked to the cause of women's liberation from the early 1920s. In the 1970s the debate generated a U.S. Supreme Court case, *Roe v. Wade,* which allowed abortions to be legal in America, under certain restrictions (applicable to the second and third trimester of pregnancy). Feminist arguments include an analysis of both the relative disempowerment of women in the sexual encounter, and in the relative lack of social support for children and those who care for them.

Finally, the debate is quickened by social factors. Contemporary debates have emerged about the problem of population and global ecology and the ethics of childbearing in that context. Other venues in which abortion is debated include new research in which early human embryonic or fetal tissue is used for experimental medical technology, or the use of embryonic preselection prior to IVF pregnancy. Emerging technologies that create situations far afield from those originally imagined by the classic commentaries of religious texts will be the subject of intense discussion and policy debate.

See also ANIMAL RIGHTS; ANIMAL SACRIFICE; BIRTH; BIRTH CONTROL; CHURCH AND STATE; DEATH AND DYING; ETHICS; EUTHANASIA AND ASSISTED SUICIDE; FEMINIST SPIRITUALITY; FEMINIST THEOLOGY; WOMANIST THEOLOGY; WOMEN'S STUDIES.

BIBLIOGRAPHY

Biale, Rachel. *Women and Jewish Law: An Exploration of Women's Issues in Halachic Sources.* 1984.

Bakar, Osman. *Tawhid and Science: Essays on the History and Philosophy of Islamic Science.* 1991.

Connery, John. *Abortion: The Development of the Roman Catholic Perspective.* 1977.

Feldman, David. *Marital Relations, Birth Control, and Abortion in Jewish Law.* 1968.

Harrison, Beverly. *Our Right to Choose: Toward a New Ethic of Abortion.* 1983.

Jacobowitz, Immanuel. *Jewish Medical Ethics.* 1967.

Jung, Patricia, and Thomas Shannon, eds. *Abortion and Catholicism: The American Debate.* 1988.

Keown, Damien. *Buddhism and Bioethics.* 1995.

McCormick, Richard. *Health and Medicine in the Catholic Tradition: Tradition in Transition.* 1984.

Rahman Fazlur. *Health and Medicine in the Islamic Tradition: Change and Identity.* 1987.

Laurie Zoloth

Advent

Regarded as the beginning of each new cycle in the Christian liturgical year, Advent usually occurs during the four Sundays preceding Christmas Day. Taken from the Latin *adventus,* which means "coming," the season has always been utilized as a time of preparation for the Feast of the Nativity of Jesus Christ. Eastern Orthodox churches begin Advent after St. Martin's Day (November 11) and observe a season of approximately six weeks. Most others, including Roman Catholic, Anglican, and Lutheran traditions, inaugurate Advent on the Sunday nearest St. Andrew's Day (November 30) and continue activities until Christmas Eve.

References to Advent in early Christianity describe it as a period of ascetical and penitential preparation for one's baptism, a ritual often culminating at Epiphany on January 6. It first became widespread in Spain during the fourth century and then in Gaul a century thereafter. By the sixth century the season had been sanctioned for use in Rome, where Bishop Gregory I associated Advent with the Incarnation and with the Second Coming as well as with baptism. By the ninth century, Roman influence had caused Advent to be recognized as the beginning of the ecclesiastical year everywhere in Western Europe.

Advent is full of theological meanings that overlap and reinforce each other. Connected with baptism, it reminds the faithful of the coming of Christ in human souls and urges participants to make themselves worthy of such divine indwelling. As preparation for Christmas, it heightens the worshiper's anticipation of not only historical events surrounding physical birth but more generally of God's coming into the world in the flesh as a redemptive event. Advent thus points to Incarnation and Nativity as glory. A great number of American churches in contemporary times still perceive Advent as containing three segments of the salvation process: Christ's first appearance on earth in human form, a renewed sense of his abiding presence in each believer's soul, and his eventual return in triumph to judge the world and redeem his people.

In early times the four weeks of Advent were marked by an atmosphere of penitence and severe soul-searching. This was gradually modified into somber yet joyful expectation of Christ's tripartite presence.

In contemporary America Advent continues to be a time of penance for some, but fasting is no longer required, and most observers embody a sense of joyful expectancy as the new liturgical year begins to unfold once again the drama of salvation. As part of this, many people use Advent calendars in their homes, opening paper panels each day of the season to reveal sacred or decorative images. Evergreen wreaths are popular items, too, in both homes and churches, where four candles are set among the greenery, one for each Sunday of the period. Customs vary, but one traditional usage is that the first three candles are dark blue while the fourth (signifying Mary, the mother of Jesus) is either pink or purple. Once the circle of lighted candles is complete, a central one of white or red is featured to signify the coming of Christ into the world.

See also CALENDARS; CHRISTMAS; LIVED RELIGION; MAINLINE PROTESTANTISM; ROMAN CATHOLICISM.

BIBLIOGRAPHY
Cowley, Patrick. *Advent.* 1960.
MacArthur, A. C. *Evolution of the Christian Year.* 1953.

Henry Warner Bowden

Adventism

In the Gospels and Epistles of the New Testament, emphasis is placed on the promise that Jesus Christ will return to earth again. What is called "the blessed hope" has received varying focus in the Christian church through the centuries. At the end of the first millennium there was a wave of apocalyptic fever. Reformation leaders also believed that they were near the end of time. Through the influence of Jonathan Edwards, America's early Christian communities often adopted the view that the world would get better, leading to a thousand-year time of peace (the millennium) climaxed by the second coming of Christ.

Political tumult at the end of the eighteenth century led to doubts about Edwards's postmillennial views, first in Europe and then in the United States. This set the stage for the birth of Adventism (referring to the Second Advent of Jesus) in the middle decades of the last century. Modern Adventism owes its birth to the writings and ministry of William Miller (1782–1849), a Baptist preacher whose main claim to fame is three false predictions of the visible return of Jesus.

Miller was born in Pittsfield, Massachusetts. He had an evangelical conversion experience in 1816 but did not begin preaching the message of Christ's near return until 1831. A pamphlet on prophecy in 1833 was expanded into book form in 1836, both under the title *Evidences from Scripture and History of the Second Coming of Christ About the Year 1843, and of His Personal Reign of a Thousand Years.* Miller devoted himself to the study of key texts in Daniel, Revelation, and Matthew, combined with application to the major "signs of the times" that pointed to the "end of the age." The bit of uncertainty in the title of his book gave way to specific predictions of the return of Jesus between March 21, 1843, and the same date the next year. Failing this prophecy, Miller confessed his error but then accepted arguments from other Adventists that Jesus would come back to earth on October 22, 1844. That failed prophecy is known as "the Great Disappointment," one of the most famous nonevents in history.

Miller's Adventist views were spread through the periodical *Signs of the Times* and through a network of preachers in Congregational, Baptist, Methodist, and Presbyterian churches, extending from Maine to Michigan. Early Adventist leaders Joshua Himes (d. 1895), Josiah Litch (d. 1886), and Charles Fitch (d. 1844) aided Miller in the urgent task of warning the churches about the coming Judgment Day. In the end Miller acknowledged the dangers of date setting but comforted himself with the positive aspects of preparation for the Lord's return.

As is well known to historians, Miller's approach to Bible prophecy and his focus on the Second Advent of Christ was foundational to the rise of both Seventh-Day Adventism and the Jehovah's Witnesses. The Seventh-Day Adventists, under Ellen G. White (one of the most famous American female religious leaders), labored under the burden of dealing with "the Great Disappointment." They argued that the 1844 date was a correct deduction from Bible study but that Miller failed to understand that it concerned a pivotal event in Christ's ministry in the heavenly realm, not the date of Christ's return to earth.

Charles Taze Russell, the founder of the Jehovah's Witnesses, duplicated Miller's penchant for date setting, though he was never quite so dogmatic as to cite a single day for the return of Jesus. Witnesses have suggested through the twentieth century that the end of the world would take place in 1914, 1918, 1925, the early 1940s, and 1975. Both Seventh-Day Adventists and the Witnesses inherited the sectarian impulses in Miller's later Adventist ideology. Thus both groups have been isolated from mainstream American religious life. The Witnesses, in particular, have been victims of religious and political persecution, especially in the United States during World War I and in Germany under Hitler.

The Adventist message under William Miller is forever linked to his failed prophecies. In a general sense, however, what he would regard as his positive focus on Christ's Second Advent has been a constant theme in American evangelicalism since the start of the twentieth century. Prophecy books are often the best-selling books from evangelical publishers. The classic in modern times is Hal Lindsey's *The Late Great Planet Earth,* a work that has sold millions of copies in both religious and secular bookstores.

See also APOCALYPSE; ESCHATOLOGY; EVANGELICAL CHRISTIANITY; JEHOVAH'S WITNESSES; SEVENTH-DAY ADVENTISTS.

BIBLIOGRAPHY
Numbers, Ronald and Jonathan Butler, eds. *The Disappointed.* 1987.
Weber, Timothy P. *Living in the Shadow of the Second Coming.* 1979.

James A. Beverley

African-American Religions

African-American religion cannot be reduced to any one form or tradition. It is a complex constellation of diverse systems of belief and practice ultimately concerned with the relationship between the sacred and the profane. African-Americans' religion has been central to their survival, developing as a cultural response and adaptation to the conditions of their experience in the New World.

African captives were not homogeneous in origin, tribal affiliation, language, or religion. Yet sufficient similarities existed between their respective cultures to allow a worldview to emerge out of the context of their interaction and collective condition. To appreciate the creativity and adaptability of those first generations of African-Americans, we must first appreciate the perspective they brought with them. This generalized African worldview, particularly as expressed in religion, included: (1) belief in a supreme deity, and a lesser order of spiritual beings (including the spirits of ancestors and of nature), all of whom are imminent, intervening in the affairs of mortals; (2) ecstatic forms of worship, including drumming and ritual dancing, and the belief in spirit possession; (3) oral transmission of culture and emphasis on the collective production of the sacred; (4) close integration of the sacred and the profane, with the religious specialist not holding an exalted position over other members of the community; (5) value and respect for all forms of life, human or otherwise, and an emphasis on living harmoniously with nature; (6) respect and recognition of women as actors in the structures of power, governance, and religious leadership; and (7) em-

Two members of the choir at St. Paul's Baptist Church in Montclair, New Jersey, enthusiastically sing a hymn at a Sunday morning service on February 2, 1997. (Credit: AP/Wide World Photos.)

phasis on the collective over the individual. These factors were part of a general orientation to the world, shaping Africans' approach to the new cultures and conditions encountered in the Americas.

Afro-Christianity and the Black Church in America

While some Africans had been previously exposed to Christianity, the mode of Christianity imposed upon them in the Americas, particularly in the Southern United States, was carefully constructed to shape them into compliant and submissive slaves. By emphasizing certain scriptures and omitting others, many slaveholders used Christianity as an ideological tool of social control designed to help perpetuate and justify the institution of slavery.

To circumvent the control of whites in their plantation churches, slaves held secret meetings at night beneath the brush arbors (called "hush harbors" because the dense foliage contained and quieted the sounds of their worship). These secret services provided emotional, physical, and spiritual catharsis, hope, a sense of solidarity, and affirmation of their intrinsic value as human beings. These meetings were

also used to obtain news from friends and loved ones on other plantations via itinerant slave preachers, and to plot acts of covert and overt resistance as seen in the acts of Nat Turner, Denmark Vesey, Gabriel Prosser, Harriet Tubman, and others who formulated or carried out insurrections and escapes. This was the "invisible institution" of the antebellum South.

The first documented African-American Baptist congregation was founded on a Virginia plantation in 1758, but the emergence of a separate African-American-controlled Christian denomination came, at least partly, in response to continued discrimination within white-controlled churches. In 1787, Richard Allen and Absalom Jones, part of a larger group of free African-American parishioners, were forced to rise from kneeling in prayer on the main floor of the St. George's Methodist Episcopal Church sanctuary in Philadelphia and were asked to assume a place in the church's segregated upper gallery. This incident led to the collective withdrawal of the African-American parishioners and the establishment of the Free African Society. From this society developed the African Methodist Episcopal Church (AME) in 1816, the first independent African-American Christian religious institution, which later developed into a national denomination. It remains the oldest extant African-American-controlled organization in the United States (membership 3.5 million). For similar reasons the African Methodist Episcopal Zion (AMEZ) Church was incorporated in New York in 1821 (membership 1.2 million), followed by the Christian Methodist Episcopal Church (CME) in 1870 (membership 1 million).

Other denominations that comprise the traditional black church and to which the majority of African-American Christians still belong today, are: the National Baptist Convention, U.S.A., Inc. (founded 1895; membership 8.2 million), the National Baptist Convention of America (incorporated 1915; membership 3.5 million), the Progressive National Baptist Convention (founded 1961; membership 2.5 million), the National Missionary Baptist Convention of America (founded 1988; membership 3.2 million), and the Church of God in Christ, an African-American Pentecostal denomination (originally established in 1897; membership 5.5 million). African-American-controlled congregations and caucuses within other Christian denominations are also considered part of the institutional black church.

Self-help, mutual aid, political struggle for social change, and education have always been among the top priorities of the black church as expressed in their founding of a number of the historically black colleges and universities. Mutual aid societies, providing monetary aid or even burial insurance, also served African-American congregants. As a black-controlled institution, the church created one of very few spheres in which African-Americans could exercise their right to vote for their own leaders, either with the ballot or with their feet.

With the mass exodus of African-Americans out of the rural South to Southern and Northern cities in the decades following the Civil War through World War I, numerous variations on the Judeo-Christian theme emerged in the form of urban sects and cults led by charismatic personalities. Many of these were storefront churches, which were part of the Holiness and Pentecostal movements. Other movements included: the Church of God (Black Jews), which taught that the Old Testament Jews were black people, and the cults of self-proclaimed gods Father Hurley (Universal Hagar's Spiritual Church) and Father Divine (Peace Mission Movement).

In the century between emancipation and the end of Jim Crow segregation, the black church became the institutional center of the African-American community. Perhaps the finest hour of institutionalized African-American religion was the civil rights movement of the 1950s and 1960s, which may not have been possible without the pre-existence of the black church as an exploitable network for the mobilization of the masses of African-Americans. For example, the Southern Christian Leadership Conference (SCLC) and the National Conference of Black Churchmen's (NCBC) ministers articulated a Christian-based vision of racial and class justice. They also trained and led the masses in tactical resistance to oppression by directing the financial, organizational, and human resources mobilized through their churches.

Today, African-American congregations and religious organizations can be found among virtually all of the major denominations and Christian traditions, including the Catholic, Episcopalian, and Presbyterian churches as well as various sects. African-Americans are also represented in nondenominational-ecumenical Christian movements. As the black church approaches the twenty-first century, its most pressing issues include: the role of women as ministers; the need to attract younger members into the ministry and as members; violence; AIDS; and the role of the church in helping to foster economic development and revitalization within its communities.

Islam in the African-American Experience

Islam has always been part of the African-American religious experience. Many African slaves had adopted Islam on the African continent and struggled to retain many aspects of their Afro-Arabic cultural heritage in the form of their names, language and writing, dietary customs, holidays and celebrations, as well as clothing customs.

In 1913, Noble Drew Ali (born Timothy Drew) established the Moorish Science Temple of America in Newark, New Jersey. He taught that African-Americans were not the descendants of Ethiopians, as some in the black community taught, but that they were actually descended from the Moors. In 1925 the Temple was moved to Chicago and incorporated as the not-for-profit Moorish Holy Temple of Science. In 1928 Ali published the Holy Koran, which differed significantly from the Qur'an of orthodox Islam. A few months after his death in 1930, one of Ali's followers, Wallace D. Fard, established the Nation of Islam (NOI) with its first temple (mosque) in Detroit. The Chicago branch of the NOI was established in 1933, and in 1934, after the mysterious disappearance of Fard, the Honorable Elijah Muhammad (born Elijah Poole) became the movement's leader.

In 1975, Wallace (Warith) D. Muhammad, son of Elijah Muhammad, became the leader of the movement after his father's death. Under the younger Muhammad's leadership, the movement's name was changed to American Muslim Mission (AMM), and he sought to align the movement's teachings more closely with orthodox, international Islam as well as disavow some of the more radical, nationalistic elements of his father's teachings: that Christianity was the white man's religion, that whites are the Devil incarnate, rejection of Christian, "slave," names, and that there should be a separate African-American nation on the continent of North America, among other things.

In the late 1970s Minister Louis Farrakhan led a splinter faction, which separated itself from the AMM to reclaim the name of Nation of Islam, reviving many of the original teachings of Fard and Elijah Muhammad. Since coming to prominence, Farrakhan has been quite a charismatic and controversial figure, arousing anger in many people with his nationalist, separatist, and anti-Semitic remarks. His apparent power to mobilize many of today's young African Americans was demonstrated when Farrakhan called for the Million Man March which took place in Washington, D.C., on October 15, 1995. It was to be a day of atonement for African-American men of all religious persuasions to come together in brotherhood and unity. The march and the subsequent rally on Capitol Mall, drew large numbers of African-American men and boys (the actual numbers continue to be disputed) across class, religion, and regional lines. It also encouraged a truce among rival gangs and was seen by many as a success.

In addition to the Nation of Islam under Farrakhan, today there are several groups claiming to revive or preserve the Nation of Islam's original traditions or to uphold orthodoxy. These include: Nation of Islam groups led by John Muhammad and Silas Muhammad, respectively; the Nation of the Five Percent (or "Five Percenters") founded in 1964 by Clarence Jowars Smith, who states that only five percent of African-Americans know the truth and are thus able to lead the community; and the African Islamic Mission, an orthodox group originating in 1970s Brooklyn.

Islam remains significant in the African-American experience as it provides an Afro-Arabic identity for blacks while its self-help emphasis is carried on in its educational institutions, community-based economic enterprises, rehabilitation programs in prisons and inner cities, affording a major source of discipline and self-esteem for African-American youth, particularly young males. Today African-American Muslims comprise 1.4 million of the total 5 million Muslims in the United States.

Yoruba-Based Religions: Vodun and Santería (Orisha)

Throughout the Caribbean and South America the structure of slavery under the Spanish made possible the creolization of Yoruba (and Dahomey) West African religious traditions with certain elements of Catholicism. Vodun (or vodou, or voodoo, as popularly known in the United States) is the term used to describe this complex religious system as practiced in Haiti. In Puerto Rico and Cuba it is known as santería or orisha. It is also practiced in Trinidad, Jamaica, and Brazil under still other names. The African belief in the hierarchy of spiritual beings and deities, some of which were responsible for some aspect of life or nature and all having distinct personalities and sensibilities, correlated with the pantheon of Catholic saints and other sacred beings. For example, the snake god of traditional African religion was recognized as similar to Saint Patrick of Catholicism.

Led by the priests—manbo (female) or oungan (male)—participants invoke a particular spirit, or loa, achieving a trancelike state during which one or more spirits possesses, or "rides," one or more worshipers. Communal rites include drumming, dancing, feasting, and sometimes animal sacrifice. While the invoked spirit controls the body and mind of an entranced worshiper, who then displays the characteristics associated with it, that spirit may perform cures or speak to the assembly, dispensing wisdom and guidance or the solution to some question or problem. Because these religions have been associated with various slave uprisings throughout the Americas, practitioners have generally had to operate within underground, secret societies out of fear of official sanction and reprisal from those who view them as Satanic or as catalysts for slave rebellion.

Practitioners of these Yoruba/Dahomey-based religious traditions are generally concentrated in communities with large numbers of immigrants from South America and the Caribbean (New York and Miami). In the Southern United States, particularly Louisiana, vodun has had a long history of mystery, fear, and folklore which has kept it an underground movement for most of its existence there. These rites offer a sense of cultural continuity with a traditional African past, strengthen social bonds, and give a sense of empowerment for many in the immigrant populations who may also be newly arrived members of the African-American community in a racially stratified system.

Finally, conjuration and magic are also part of the multifaceted world of African-American religion still in existence today. Sometimes collectively referred to as hoodoo, its beliefs and practices include: homeopathic healing with herbs and roots, divination with bones or pebbles, influencing the will of others or casting curses on them, and other forms of spiritualism in which a medium consults the spirits of the dead on behalf of a client.

In short, the story of African-American religion is one of creativity and adaptability in the face of circumstances not of their choosing. Their diverse religions and the institutions informed by them have emerged as dynamic collective responses to institutionalized discrimination and exclusion from mainstream paths to social and economic equality. As such, the religion they made helps them to maintain a sense of their existential human value and to survive, the first order of resistance in the African diaspora abroad.

See also AFRO-CUBAN RELIGION; ANIMAL SACRIFICE; CIVIL RIGHTS MOVEMENT; DRUMMING; ECSTASY; FARD, W.D.; FARRAKHAN, LOUIS; ISLAM; JACKSON, JESSE; KING, MARTIN LUTHER, JR.; MAGIC; MUHAMMAD, ELIJAH KARRIEM; NOBLE DREW ALI; SANTERÍA; SECRET SOCIETIES; SOUTHERN CHRISTIAN LEADERSHIP CONFERENCE; SOUTHERN RELIGION; SPIRIT POSSESSION; SPIRITUALISM; VODUN.

BIBLIOGRAPHY

Baer, Hans A., and Merrill Singer. "Toward a Typology of Black Sectarianism as a Response to Racial Stratification." In *African American Religion: Interpretive Essays in History and Culture*, edited by Timothy E. Fulop and Albert J. Raboteau. 1997.

Brandon, George. "Sacrificial Practices in Santeria, an African-Cuban Religion in the United States." In *Africanisms in American Culture*, edited by Joseph E. Holloway. 1990.

Brown, Karen McCarthy. *Mama Lola: A Vodou Priestess in Brooklyn.* 1991.

Cárdenas, Julio Sánchez. "Santería or Orisha Religion: An Old Religion in a New World." In *South and Meso-American Native Spirituality from the Cult of Feathered Serpent to the Theology of Liberation*, edited by Gary H. Gossen. 1993.

Jackson, Bruce. "The Other Kind of Doctor: Conjure and Magic in Black American Folk Medicine." In *African American Religion: Interpretive Essays in History and Culture*, edited by Timothy E. Fulop and Albert J. Raboteau. 1997.

Lincoln, C. Eric. *The Black Muslims in America.* 1961.

Lincoln, C. Eric. "The Muslim Mission in the Context of American Social History." In *African American Religion: Interpretive Essays in History and Culture*, edited by Timothy E. Fulop and Albert J. Raboteau. 1997.

Lincoln, C. Eric and Lawrence H. Mamiya. *The Black Church in the African American Experience.* 1990.

Payne, Wardell J. *Directory of African American Religious Bodies.* 1995.

Raboteau, Albert J. *Slave Religion: The "Invisible Institution" in the Antebellum South.* 1978.

Turner, Richard Brent. "What Shall We Call Him? Islam and African American Identity." *Journal of Religious Thought* 51, no. 1: 25–52.

Weisbrot, Robert. *Father Divine.* 1983.

Milmon F. Harrison

Afro-Cuban Religions

In Cuba, the largest Caribbean island, African religions were introduced by slaves coming from West and Central Africa. Santería is the most famous of Afro-Cuban religions, but it is not the only one. At least three other Afro-Cuban religious traditions can be identified: the cult of Ifá, the Palo Monte, and Cuban Spiritualism. These religions evolved in colonial and postcolonial Cuban society. They influenced one another and were influenced by Spanish Catholicism. They also had contacts with Spiritualism, which penetrated Cuba in the second part of the nineteenth century. It is important to note that these four traditions are not exclusive and that the practitioners still consider themselves as Catholics in Cuba. After Fidel Castro came to power in 1959, some believers left the country and settled in the United States, especially in Florida and around New York, where they continued practicing these four main Afro-Cuban religions.

One Afro-Cuban tradition is Santería. This word originally referred to the popular cult of saints and apparitions of the Virgin Mary in Spain. This designation was also used by Spanish colonials in Cuba because Yoruba slaves, coming from present-day southwestern Nigeria, established a relatively stable link between their deities, called *orishas,* or *òrìsà,* and Catholic saints and virgins. Scholars differ in their interpretations of this phenomenon. Some argue that there was a real identification of African and European spiritual entities on the basis of similarities such as colors or spiritual powers. For instance, Shango, the Yoruba god of thunder and lightning, is linked to Santa Barbara, a female saint who protects people from these same things. Furthermore, in Catholic iconography she is usually dressed in red and white, the symbolic colors of Shango. Other scholars think that this kind of relation was simply meant to hide African beliefs behind Catholic images but had no serious religious implications. These different opinions regarding syncretism are also present today among Santeros (Santería practitioners) themselves. In the United States, followers who reject European influences completely also reject the very word *Santería* and use the Afrocentric expression "*òrìsà* worship."

A second religious tradition derived from traditional Yoruba religion is the cult of Ifá. While Santería is open to men and women, with no discrimination based on sexual orientation, the cult of Ifá is limited to heterosexual men. *Bàbálaos,* the highest initiates in the cult of Ifá, are specialists of divination, and they are also usually in charge of animal sacrifice in Santería initiations. They worship Orula, the *orisha* of human destiny, and use a complex system of 256 divinatory signs linked to a set of myths.

A third Afro-Cuban religion is the Palo Monte, which is derived from traditional Bantu religion from the present-day lower Zaire River area. In Cuba it focuses on the relation between an initiate called a *palero* and the spirit of one or several dead people. Spirits are "fixed" or "installed" in iron pots called *gangas,* where the palero puts sticks, bones (sometimes human bones), stones, and earth. In addition to the spirits of dead people, paleros have adopted Santería orishas, to whom they have given different names and who can also be summoned through the gangas. Paleros do not hesitate to cast spells against enemies, and their material culture does not correspond to European aesthetic standards. That is why in Cuba, as in the United States, Palo Monte is a more secretive and private religion than Santería.

The last Afro-Cuban tradition is Cuban Spiritualism, which is especially popular in the eastern part of Cuba. Even if it is derived from French and American Spiritualism, it shares important similarities with the three previous traditions. There is neither the animal sacrifice nor the ritualized initiation that one finds in Santería, the cult of Ifá, and Palo Monte, but mediums are frequently possessed by spirits of African slaves during collective ceremonies. In this case they give divinatory advice very similar to those given by Santería orishas and Palo Monte spirits. As a relatively simple and cheap religion, Spiritualism is usually the first stage of a career in the field of Afro-Cuban religions. This career often ends in Santería and in the cult of Ifá, which are generally considered the most prestigious of Afro-Cuban religions.

It is very difficult to estimate the number of practitioners of these religions in the United States because they are traditionally secretive and not institutionalized. Nevertheless, there might be several hundred thousand Santeros in the United States, and around seventy thousand in the Miami area. No longer confined to black Cuban immigrants, today Afro-Cuban religions are spreading, especially in the Hispanic population and in the black American population.

See also AFRICAN-AMERICAN RELIGIONS; ANIMAL SACRIFICE; LATINO TRADITIONS; PRACTICE; ROMAN CATHOLICISM; SANTERÍA; SECRET SOCIETIES; SPIRITUALISM; SYNCRETISM; VODUN.

BIBLIOGRAPHY

Bascom, William. *Ifá Divination: Communication Between Gods and Men in West Africa.* 1969.

Brandon, George. *Santería from Africa to the New World: The Dead Sell Memory.* 1993.

Bueno, Gladys González. "An Initiation Ceremony in Regla de Palo." In *AfroCuba: An Anthology of Cuban Writing, Politics and Culture,* edited by Pedro Perez Sarduy and Jean Stubbs. 1993.

Dianteill, Erwan, and Gerard Pigeon. *Seven Lightnings Over California: Don Daniel, a Palero in Los Angeles: A Video Documentary.* 1999 (video).

Palmiá, Stephan. "Against Syncretism: 'Africanizing' and 'Cubanizing' Discourses in North American *Òrìsà* Worship." In *Counterworks: Managing the Diversity of Knowledge,* edited by Richard Fardon. 1995.

Erwan Dianteill

Afterlife

Belief in an afterlife is a feature of all the world's religions, although there are major differences among traditions, both historically and contemporaneously, in how the afterlife is construed. Whereas Western religions emphasize the break between earthly life and the afterworld of death and possible resurrection (eternal salvation), some Eastern traditions believe in the eternal cycle of successive lifetimes. Thus while Christianity has traditionally emphasized heaven and hell as opposing afterlife domains that reward or punish people for what they have "reaped on earth," the doctrine of karma in Hinduism and Buddhism states that a person's current existence is a direct result of one's past existences and a determinant of one's future existences. The Christian tradition does not accept the doctrine of reincarnation. Such differences in how the concept of "afterlife" is understood clearly have quite diverse implications for how adherents of particular traditions understand themselves, their place in the social world, and relations with their fellow human beings.

Within Christianity, some of the theological disagreements between Catholicism and Protestantism extend to include conceptions of the afterlife, particularly regarding the means of salvation. The notion of purification for sins committed is deeply grounded in New Testament accounts and in the writing of early church fathers such as St. Augustine. The doctrine of purgatory, however, was a cause of dissension during the Protestant Reformation. In particular, the Reformers rejected the practice of the church in encouraging the faithful to seek indulgences from church officials as a way of redeeming their own sins and those of the souls in purgatory. This practice contravened the Protestant belief in faith alone, and not prayers for the dead, as the means to salvation. The Council of Trent (1545–1563) reaffirmed the Catholic belief in purgatory as an intermediate state between death and possible salvation with Christ. In contemporary Catholicism, reflecting this theology of salvation, prayers for the dead are a routine dimension of the Mass liturgy, as the gathered community invoke God's mercy for any deceased family members and friends who may be in purgatory.

There is also doctrinal disagreement within Judaism as to what comprises belief in an afterlife. Orthodox Judaism adheres to the traditional rabbinic dogma of corporal resurrection and the immorality of the soul, whereas the Reform movement in America (following the Pittsburgh Platform, 1885), rejects both the idea of bodily resurrection and the notion of either eternal punishment or reward, while nonetheless embracing the more ambiguous concept of personal immortality. Notwithstanding the variety of ways in which different traditions envision the afterlife, it is noteworthy that death is recognized as an important life passage deserving of special rituals, whether evidenced by Christian funerals, the sanctity of *shivah* (period of mourning) and *kaddish* (prayer for the dead), for Jews, the emphasis on communal mourning in Islam, or the rites of ancestor-worship practiced in communities influenced by Confucianism.

No one, of course, can know whether there is an afterlife, and if there is, whether it approximates the scenes so vividly imagined in great literary works such as Dante's *Inferno* or James Joyce's *Portrait of the Artist as a Young Man*. The lack of plausible evidence has not dampened Americans' beliefs in an afterlife. National opinion polls indicate that almost three-quarters of Americans believe in life after death, a proportion that has remained relatively stable throughout the post–World War II period. Similarly, three of four Americans believe in heaven as a place of eternal reward, and although fewer, approximately 50 percent believe in hell. These beliefs do not vary significantly by either age or level of education. As Andrew Greeley points out, "in both 1944 and 1985 college-educated young people (under thirty) and non-college-educated older people (over sixty) were equally committed to the proposition that there is life after death" (Greeley, 1989: 15). It is also noteworthy that, reflecting Americans' comparatively higher levels of religious belief and involvement, they are significantly more likely than Europeans, for example, to believe in an afterlife.

The tenacity of Americans' beliefs in an afterlife is quite remarkable, especially given the tendency of Catholicism and mainline Protestantism to downplay the salience of concrete images of heaven, and especially hell, over the past three decades. The continuing appeal of such beliefs may be understood, in part, in terms of the broader search for personal meaning and purpose in life that seems to have become more public since the 1950s. The emphases on personal seeking and spiritual journeying prevalent in personal religious narratives and in mass media accounts point to the fact that for many people today material well-being is experienced as unfulfilling unless it is accompanied with some sense of a larger, transcendent meaning. It is also evident that while many contemporary Americans believe in an afterlife, the ways in which they construe it are quite diverse, and in many instances it is removed from traditional concepts of heaven and hell. The post–World War II trend toward the decoupling of personal spirituality from institutionalized religion means that people can envision an afterlife that is autonomous of the images of salvation that are enshrined in various faith traditions. For some, belief in an afterlife is nurtured by their strong experiential sense of an enduring personal spiritual connection with a loved one who has died. Whether people understand heaven and hell as actual afterlife domains, or more symbolically as representing the polarities of good and evil, for many, the belief in some form of continuity beyond one's present life serves to give purpose to life events and experiences that otherwise they would find difficult to integrate.

Concern with questions pertaining to the afterlife also helps to orient people to greater awareness of the finite nature of their own current existence and thus encourages them to set priorities with respect to personal relationships, community involvement, or in their attitudes toward nature and the environment. Although traditionally, therefore, the concept of afterlife denoted an emphasis on "last things" and the possible triumph of life over death, for some people today, the spiritual power of belief in an afterlife may help them focus on more immediate issues of personal salvation and growth in this world.

Notwithstanding Americans' embrace of the idea of an afterlife, it is striking that many people resist talking about issues of death and dying. In recent years, however, death has become a more salient part of public discourse. The aging of the American population has forced health practitioners and policymakers to openly discuss dilemmas of end-of-life care and has encouraged individuals and families to discuss practical matters relating to living wills. Beliefs about the afterlife are also tacitly present in current public debates with respect to physician-assisted death, and the assumption shared by some of its advocates that whatever the after-death experience, it will be preferable to the pain and suffering associated with terminal illness.

See also DEATH AND DYING; EUTHANASIA AND ASSISTED SUICIDE; GOD; HEAVEN; HELL; JOURNEYS AND JOURNEYING; NEAR DEATH EXPERIENCES; REINCARNATION; RITES OF PASSAGE; RITUAL; SHIVAH.

BIBLIOGRAPHY

Greeley, Andrew. *Religious Change in America.* 1989.

Roof, Wade Clark. *A Generation of Seekers: The Spiritual Journey of the Baby Boom Generation.* 1993.

Wink, Paul. "Spirituality and Inner Life." *Generations.* 1999.

Wuthnow, Robert. *After Heaven: Spirituality in America Since the 1950s.* 1998.

Michele Dillon

Agnosticism

Agnosticism is the belief that there is insufficient evidence to assert with confidence the existence or nonexistence of God. Although an agnostic outlook was evident in ancient Greek materialism and skepticism, the word itself was coined in 1869 by the noted British biologist and promoter of Darwinism Thomas Huxley. Agnosticism, according to Huxley, is a method of inquiry holding "that it is wrong for a man to say that he is certain of the objective truth of any proposition unless he can produce evidence which logically justifies that certainty." Though agnosticism can pertain to any truth claim, it was immediately applied to belief in God's existence. The word itself stands in contrast to the ancient doctrine of "gnosis"—that positive knowledge of God's existence and His attributes is possible.

Modern agnosticism emerged from two convergent intellectual and religious trends in Victorian culture. The first was the legacy of the eighteenth-century German philosopher Immanuel Kant. Kant proclaimed that the limitations of human sense experience made knowledge of transcendental realities impossible. He argued against belief in God based on evidence and applied reason, but opened the possibility of such belief derived from faith. Many agnostics a century later proclaimed religious beliefs of some kind. Herbert Spencer's "Unknowable" and Matthew Arnold's "Power not ourselves that makes for righteousness" expressed religious reverence for a reality beyond the grasp of human understanding.

Kant's philosophical emphasis supported the growing prestige of science, especially in the decades after the publication of Charles Darwin's *Origin of Species* in 1859. Many defenders of science and empiricism felt that discoveries in biology, physics, geology, and in the new fields of anthropology and comparative religion had destroyed the foundations for belief in a supernatural God. Biblical criticism brought the doctrines of the historical religions, even when liberally interpreted, within the realm of scientific explanation. For these thinkers, including such philosophers and literary figures as John Stuart Mill, Bertrand Russell, George Eliot, and Leslie Stephen, agnosticism supported the scientific naturalism of the day while avoiding identification with either the positivism of Auguste Comte or the atheism of the Marxists.

Agnosticism has had a rich tradition in the United States, often aligning itself with reform movements and the spirit of progressivism. Robert Ingersoll, Civil War captain, lawyer, and captivating orator, preached agnosticism to large audiences while issuing biting attacks on the evils of religious orthodoxy. Mark Twain and Clarence Darrow were among hundreds of figures in the late nineteenth and early twentieth centuries who joined their agnosticism to democratic and humanistic ideals.

Agnosticism is often interpreted as a midway position between atheism and theistic belief. From the standpoint of the traditional religious believer, agnosticism may appear as functionally identical to atheism, or as providing a safe haven for atheists wishing to hedge their bets.

An agnostic response is that both theists and atheists share a common error in making an unwarranted leap into positive assertions about the nature of ultimate reality. Rather than categorically denying God's existence, as atheists do, agnostics maintain that their view more successfully fulfills the demands of intellectual integrity. In addition, agnosticism provides a more promising framework than atheism for the development of humanitarian concerns. Defenders of agnosticism would assert that loyalty otherwise given to a Supreme Being can be readily transferred to the realm of social ideals. Agnosticism also opens the door to a sense of humility, natural piety, and cosmic reverence in its acceptance of mysteries beyond the reach of human powers.

Recent surveys indicate that more than 1.1 million Americans identify as agnostics. Of the 14 million Americans who claim "no religion," it may be assumed that many are agnostics in all but name. Furthermore, if account is made of people who formally affiliate with churches and synagogues for primarily social and not religious reasons, the number of agnostics may be considerably higher. Though contemporary agnosticism lacks the polemical spirit of its formative decades, it is broadly represented among the unchurched, in universities, in the scientific community, and in various humanistic organizations such as the American Humanist Association, the Ethical Culture Movement, the Society for Humanistic Judaism, and the Unitarian-Universalist Association.

See also ATHEISM; CREEDS; DEATH OF GOD; ETHICAL CULTURE; HUMANISM.

BIBLIOGRAPHY

Lightman, Bernard. *The Origins of Agnosticism.* 1987.
Stein, Gordon, ed. *An Anthology of Atheism and Rationalism.* 1989.

Joseph Chuman

Alcohol, Use of.

See Temperance.

Allah

The word "Allah" is derived from the Arabic language and simply means God. As it first received currency as the name for the deity in the Qur'an in the seventh century C.E., the term has always been associated with the religion of Islam, and continues to be used mostly by Muslims or by groups that are offshoots from Islam. Thus, although it is a fairly widely known term, it still tends to be associated by non-Muslims with foreign exoticness, which leads to the mistaken notion of some that Allah is fundamentally a different deity than the Christian or the Jewish God. However, this is inaccurate, for Arabic-speaking Christians and Jews also call God Allah, and God is called Allah in Arabic Bibles. Indeed, Christians in America from Arabic-speaking countries, to the extent that they still use Arabic, continue to refer to Allah. Also, when the Qur'an itself speaks of the Jewish and the Christian conceptions of Allah, it is obviously speaking about the Jewish and Christian God (4:171; 5:18, 64; 9:30). Nevertheless, the claim by some American Christians that because Muslims use the term "Allah," they worship a different deity than the Christians do, remains part of some anti-Muslim Christian polemics.

The History of Allah in America

Still, it is true that Allah originally occurs in English strictly in the context of writings about Islam; its first appearance is dated to 1584. Thereafter, as British and, later, American relations with the Muslim world grew, Allah continued to refer exclusively to a usage of exotic foreigners, inhabitants of the Ottoman Empire and the British colonies, never Europeans or native speakers of English. Interestingly, the term was little used in English, as books on Islam, including all early English-language Qur'an translations, continued to refer to the Muslims' object of worship as God.

Native speakers of English first began to embrace Islam at about the same time that Muslim immigrants began to arrive in English-speaking lands, mainly after 1900. Both natives and immigrants shared an ambivalent attitude toward using Allah as opposed to God for the name of the deity. The word "Allah" appealed to authenticity: It was the original Arabic term in the Muslim scripture, had been cultivated throughout the past history of Islam, and had always held a dominant position across many different Muslim linguistic groups. On the other hand, the term "God" seemed to offer better chances for the acceptance of Islam as a normal part of the spectrum of religion in America by being more assimilationist. Generally, Muslims in the old Muslim countries insisted that the deity should be referred to exclusively as Allah in Muslim English-language publications and discourse. Thus many Muslim Qur'an translations, starting with the first by Muhammad 'Abd al-Hakim Khan in 1905, use Allah, whereas no translation by a non-Muslim used Allah until that of Bell in 1937. But among English-speaking Muslims in non-Muslim countries such as the United States, the term "God" frequently continued to be preferred. The split remains to this day, as about half of the English-language Qur'an translations by Muslims use God, while the other half use Allah. There also tends to be a liberal versus a conservative element to these usages, the more conservative favoring Allah, the more liberal God. But this is not absolute, as the very conservative *Tafseer-e-Usmani* uses God, for example.

While some immigrants, such as the East Indian Ahmadiyyah missionaries who began to arrive in 1920, always preferred using Allah to using God, the rise of native Muslim movements among African Americans undoubtedly gave great impetus to the spread of the use of Allah. This is because of the non-Christian authenticity that was perceived to reside in the term. Probably the African-American usage of Allah began in the 1920s and thus may have been influenced by the Ahmadiyyah missionaries. The earliest definitely dated use of the term "Allah" among African Americans in a publication seems to be in *The Holy Koran of the Moorish Science Temple* of 1927, although it had likely been in use also some time before that. In the Moorish Science Temple's writings, the term "Allah" appears alongside "God." But with the foundation of the Nation of Islam by W. D. Fard in about 1930, Allah began more completely to displace God in the usage. This culminated in the Nation of Islam under the leadership of Elijah Muhammad, who presided over it as the "Messenger of Allah" from 1934 to 1975. Indeed, the Nation of Islam under Elijah Muhammad undoubtedly exerted a crucial influence in popularizing the usage of Allah for God among African Americans and in making that usage more familiar to the rest of the population as well, especially through the media exposure of Elijah Muhammad's chief spokesman, Malcolm X, from 1959.

Though recognition of the term "Allah" thus became much more widespread in America in time, the concept of Allah as received by the people has varied widely according to the doctrines of the groups utilizing the term and according to the degree of knowledge of individual Muslims about Islam. Generally, in the earlier part of the twentieth century, American Muslims were not yet well informed about traditional Muslim concepts, while immigrant Muslims, having no support for their religious practice in America and lacking traditionally trained religious leadership, tended as well to be poorly informed, making them subject to assimilation. Because of these conditions, both groups possibly were influenced by Christian conceptualizations of God. This is particularly manifest in the incarnationist doctrine taught by Elijah Muhammad, who elevated W. D. Fard to the level of Allah in the flesh. Such a belief in the possibility of divine human beings, in itself quite antithetical to mainstream Sunni Muslim belief, still manifests itself among many heterodox groups, such as the Five Percenters, who teach that all male Five Percenters are Allahs. It should be noted, however, that beliefs in divine incarnations in human form have occurred frequently in Muslim history and have been shared as well to some degree by Druzes and Baha'is, neither of whom originated in America.

As the twentieth century wore on, however, the mainstream Muslim concept of Allah became more prominent in American Islam, owing to many factors. More Sunni and Shiite Muslim immigrants arrived after 1950, principally coming from South Asia and the Arabic-speaking world. These included a higher proportion of well-educated people who were less marginal in their original societies than earlier immigrants had been. Likewise, these later immigrants included a higher percentage of religious Muslims, especially after about 1970, when a widespread Muslim religious revival began in the Middle East and elsewhere. Also, a few traditionally trained religious leaders began to arrive.

Meanwhile, Americans who had embraced Islam began to study Arabic, and a traditionalizing Islamization started among them, too. Both immigrants and natives were influenced by the increasingly cheap and easy communication with the ancient centers of Islam, both via telephone and air travel. This facilitated numbers of Americans going to study abroad in traditional or conservative religious academies, especially in Saudi Arabia, Syria, and Senegal, as well as more Americans being able to make their pilgrimage to Mecca, which put them in touch with masses of traditional Muslims. Perhaps the pioneer in this regard was Malcolm X, whose conversion to Sunni Islam in 1964 had, and continues to have, a major impact. Later, the change in the Nation of Islam under Elijah Muhammad's son and successor, Warith Deen Muhammad, to Sunni Islam in 1975 had an even broader effect. All these factors led to a greater standardization of Muslim belief among the largest number of Muslims. By these means the traditional Muslim understanding of the transcendent and incorporeal Allah had become unquestionably dominant by the end of the twentieth century and had even begun to influence such consistently heterodox groups as the revived Nation of Islam of Louis Farrakhan.

Muslim Theological Understanding of Allah

The traditional theology of the Sunni community teaches that Allah is above all one, unique, transcendent, creator, distinct from creation, eternal and permanent, and worthy of worship. Allah has, according to Sunnis, seven essential attributes: life, power, knowledge, will, hearing, sight, and speech. Of these attributes, power means absolute omnipotence, while knowledge, hearing, and sight indicate omniscience. Omnipresence is not stressed to avoid confusing Allah with His creation. Some of the more mystical trends in Islam have emphasized His nearness and presence everywhere (Qur'an 50:16; 57:4), causing others to accuse such mystics of pantheism. The traditional Sunni position explains verses referring to Allah's nearness as meaning He is everywhere near in His knowledge (6:59, etc.), not that He is immanent in His creation.

Apart from Allah's knowledge of His creation, He also relates to it in its past, present, and future stages. In the past, He originated the universe as the prime mover (10:4, etc.), so that all things owe their existence to Him. In the present, He remains active, answering the prayers of those who call on Him (2:186, etc.), generally maintaining the world (35:41) and providing for all creatures (11:6). Most important, in the future on Judgment Day, He will individually judge all human beings and jinni, assigning each eternally to heaven or to hell under His rule, according to their actions in this life.

In some of its descriptions of Allah's actions, the Qur'an suggests a material picture of a celestial court, but all actual imagery of Allah Himself is completely avoided, even though Allah is said to have a hand (3:73, etc.), to come with the angels (2:210, etc.), and to be established over His throne (7:54, etc.). Apart from the mention of the heavenly throne, storehouses (6:50, etc.), and angels, there is little elaboration of the picture and no really descriptive imagery. This trend continues in the Hadith, which contains some further details but offers no possibility of a complete material picture. It also extends to the law, where the portrayal of Allah, the angels, the prophets, and the companions of Muhammad is strictly prohibited. On this point Islam corresponds with Judaism but contrasts sharply with much of Christianity.

Although the nonrepresentation of Allah in any form other than the written word became a solidly established principle of the law, the material terms used in describing Allah in His relation to the world have long been problematic and continue to be the locus of the main continuing theological controversy in Islam. One party, which could be described as Salafi or neo-Hanbali, favors literalist interpretations of texts and has greatly grown in the twentieth century through modern mass education and mass literacy, which encourage the newly educated to read and interpret texts for themselves. The other party tends to look to various forms of traditional authority and seeks figurative interpretations of material expressions such as "the hand of Allah." Such disputes have even appeared in the discourses of African-American Muslims in inner cities. Whether this type of conflict seriously threatens the unity of Muslims in America or not, it at least points to the continuing diversity of conceptualizations of Allah held by different individuals both inside the Sunni majority and outside it.

Muslim Devotion to Allah

While various views of Allah's exact nature may be entertained, it is no doubt true that for most Muslims, Allah remains simply God, Whom they worship and call on in prayer. All Muslim religious practices are primarily directed to worship of Allah. First among these is the five-times-daily worship ritual known as *salat,* in which the worshiper bows and prostrates with face on the ground in the direction of Mecca in Arabia, where the Ka'bah represents Allah's inviolable sanctuary. In the local mosques the direction is indicated by a niche in one of the walls. The niche contains only empty space, reproducing the emptiness of the Ka'bah, for Allah cannot be confined or defined by space or time. In the salat worship, which may be performed individually or in rows in a congregation,

each worshiper repeats Qur'anic verses and other formulas in Arabic and is in a state of direct communion with Allah. In the salat and outside of it, the believer is encouraged to offer individual, private prayers or supplications as well. By these means, as well as by charity payments, fasting, and pilgrimage to Mecca, a Muslim is kept in constant awareness of Allah, providing a certain unity in Islam in spite of all the diversity of individual understanding and experiencing of Allah that exists.

See also BLACK MUSLIMS; FARD, W. D.; GOD; ISLAM; MALCOLM X; MECCA; MOSQUE; MUHAMMAD, ELIJAH; NAMES AND NAMING PRACTICES; NATION OF ISLAM; QUR'AN; THEISM; WARITH DEAN MUHAMMAD.

BIBLIOGRAPHY

al-Ash'ari, Abu al-Hasan 'Ali ibn Isma'il. Al-Ibanah 'an Usul ad-Diyanah (The Elucidation of Islam's Foundation), translated by Walter C. Klein. 1940.

Clegg, Claude Andrew III. *An Original Man: The Life and Times of Elijah Muhammad.* 1997.

Gardet, L. "Allah." *The Encyclopedia of Islam,* 2nd ed.

al-Ghazzali, Abu Hamid Muhammad ibn Muhammad. *The Foundation of the Articles of Faith: Being a Translation with Notes of the Kitab Qawa'id al-'Aqa'id of al-Ghazzali's "Ihya' 'Ulum al-Din,"* translated by Nabih Amin Faris. 1963.

Haddad, Yvonne Yazbeck, and Jane Idleman Smith, eds. *Mission to America: Five Islamic Sectarian Communities in North America.* 1993.

Haddad, Yvonne Yazbeck, and Jane Idleman Smith, eds. *Muslim Communities in North America.* 1994.

McCloud, Aminah Beverly. *African American Islam.* 1995.

Murata, Sachiko, and William C. Chittick. *The Vision of Islam.* 1994.

Turner, Richard Brent. *Islam in the African American Experience.* 1997.

Khalid Yahya Blankinship

Altar

In religions around the world, from prehistoric times to the present, an altar has almost always been regarded as a central locus of worship, a holy place set apart for divine-human interaction. Derived from the Latin word *altus,* meaning "high place," altars have occasionally consisted of earthen mounds or of wood, but most of them have been made of stone, providing a fixed surface on which sacrifices could be offered to supernaturals thought to be important in particu-

The altar at the Mission San Francisco Solano in Sonoma State Historical Park in northern California, ca. 1990.   (Credit: CORBIS/Richard Cummins.)

lar cultures. Jewish altars figured importantly in the Jerusalem Temple of biblical times, and the practice of making both thank offerings and guilt offerings has remained embedded in the Judeo-Christian heritage.

Early Christianity throughout the Mediterranean world featured altars as central foci of worship. Some of them served simply as tables on which believers shared a common meal. Most of them, however, were viewed in a more sacrosanct way: as the place where the Eucharist, Holy Communion, or Mass was celebrated. This perspective became increasingly dominant as local practices developed into ecclesiastical traditions. Consecrated to sacred use by church officials, the altar came to be regarded as a symbol of Christ's presence, a place where his sacrificial death was reenacted as a sacrament beneficial to whose witnessing the liturgical act.

During the Middle Ages altars were placed at the apse, the eastern end, or back of churches, essentially obscuring them from public access. They were placed behind rood screens (screens containing a crucifix) in Western practice and behind an *iconostasis* among the Eastern Orthodox. In this seclusion altars became

quite ornate, offering a medium for displaying crosses, candles, statues, monstrances, elaborate carvings, reliquaries, tabernacles, paintings, and tapestries. The magnificence of these secondary elements often made altars the most notable features in churches built between 500 and 1500.

Protestantism, which emerged in the sixteenth century, often devalued the significance and use of altars in Reformed liturgies. Rejecting the idea of the Mass as a sacrifice, Protestants of many varieties retained only a table, using it to celebrate the Lord's Supper. Most of them also retained the traditional elements of bread and wine, but congregations usually thought of themselves as observing no more than a commemorative meal.

In modern times use of altars persists in both perspectives. Many churches stemming from Calvinist or evangelical traditions make pulpits the center of their worship, and altars survive only as tables, a means of nurturing group solidarity, not a place of sacramental significance. Protestants of Anglican and Lutheran heritage have stayed much closer to perennial attitudes regarding altars in Christian worship, those ideas maintained in Roman Catholicism since the earliest centuries of Christianity.

Changes authorized in 1963 by the Second Vatican Council have occasioned noticeable modifications. Modern liturgical renewal has stressed a simpler altar, a streamlined shape placed centrally amid the congregation, with officiants facing the people. Simple, dignified decoration exhibits a cross and candles with moderate use of images. Less ornate altars, placed much nearer the people and featuring celebrants who do not turn their backs on worshipers, convey once again how the Eucharist is both spatially and theologically central to many contemporary Christians. Modern altars thus replicate the sacrificial connotations that they have projected for thousands of years.

See also CHURCH; LITURGY AND WORSHIP; PREACHING; RELIC; RITUAL; SYNAGOGUE; TEMPLE; VATICAN II.

BIBLIOGRAPHY

Leach, W. H. *The Altar in Your Church: Its History, Purpose, Position, and Adornment.* 1945.

Pocknee, Cyril E. *The Christian Altar in History and Today.* 1983.

Henry Warner Bowden

Alternative Medicine

Scientific medicine made enormous progress throughout the twentieth century. The steady improvement of pharmaceutics, surgical techniques, and biotechnology has given humans control over diseases that would have led to untimely death just a generation or two before. Yet for all the progress that scientific medicine has made, millions of twenty-first-century Americans are still enthusiastic adherents of alternative medicine. Some persons are motivated to explore alternative medicine out of sheer desperation. After all, alternative medicine provides hope for those whose pains (e.g., lingering back pain) do not fall under the purview of conventional medicine or who have a terminal illness and have already exhausted all conventional treatment options. Alternative medicine is, furthermore, less likely to be as invasive or to assault the body with heavy doses of drugs as scientific medicine often does. Alternative medicine is usually less expensive and also tends to establish warm personal relationships between healers and patients, thus appealing to those who are turned off by the bureaucratic impersonality of modern hospitals. Furthermore, alternative medicine is especially prevalent among recent immigrants or ethnic groups who have preserved cultural traditions that do not understand issues of health and illness in the same way as scientific medicine does.

What is striking, however, is the great extent to which Americans have become interested in alternative medicine for spiritual reasons. Beginning in the nineteenth century with unorthodox medical systems such as mesmerism, hydropathy, homeopathy, and mind cure, Americans have found alternative medicine to have spiritually edifying interpretations of mind-body-spirit interaction. After all, most alternative medicine is embedded in belief systems that affirm the existence of energies or forces not recognized by scientific medicine. Health is typically understood to be the result of achieving harmony with these more-than-physical energies. In short, unorthodox healing systems are not only purveying alternative medical treatments, but alternative spiritual philosophies as well. The religious and cultural significance of these "alternative" interpretations of body-mind-spirit interaction often has as much to do with the popularity of alternative medicine as with its ability to heal.

The sheer diversity of healing systems that are lumped together under the category of alternative medicine makes it somewhat difficult to make tidy generalizations about their connection with American religious life. We might begin, however, by suggesting that alternative medicine systems can be arranged along a philosophical or religious continuum. On one end of the continuum are those healing systems that have no overtly supernatural or metaphysical elements. Many dietary, exercise, and botanical healing systems fall into this category. They are considered alternative simply because their therapies have not yet been validated as efficacious by scientific researchers. Yet even though these therapies do not propound belief in more-than-physical energies, they nonetheless frequently invoke attitudes and outlooks that can be classified as belonging to American "nature religion"—that is, alternative medicine systems characteristically profess belief in the recuperative and progressive forces inherent in nature. Believing nature to be the handiwork of God, many alternative therapies suggest that nature, not a credentialed doctor, is the source of all healing. Thus even nonmetaphysical healing systems often articulate a form of moral and religious piety based on belief in the sanctity of nature's own restorative powers.

The other end of the philosophical continuum along which alternative medicine systems might be arranged is more frankly supernatural or metaphysical. These healing groups overtly profess belief in the existence of some invisible, spiritual power capable of promoting healing within the human body. Since the Transcendentalists of the mid-nineteenth century,

American nature religion has also tended to foster the belief that, under special conditions, energies from higher spiritual dimensions can flow into—and exert influences on—our natural universe. The majority of alternative healing systems incorporate some degree of this metaphysical belief. This is especially true of "manipulative" therapies such as traditional chiropractic medicine, acupuncture, Therapeutic Touch, and shiatsu. Many "mind over matter" healing systems such as meditational practices, twelve-step programs, and power-of-positive-thinking therapies also rely heavily on metaphysical beliefs. So, too, do most New Age healing practices, such as those that draw on Eastern religious beliefs in "subtle energies" and those that claim to awaken our dormant psychic abilities to draw on the energies from our astral bodies.

The early history of chiropractic medicine provides an excellent example of how alternative medicine systems provide patients with a spiritually significant way of viewing the world. Daniel David Palmer was a grocer and fish peddler in Iowa before he began the study of the nineteenth-century metaphysical healing system known as mesmerism. Palmer soon learned that he could heal persons by using his hands to apply pressure to their spinal vertebrae. However physical his methods were, Palmer's philosophical explanation was entirely metaphysical. He reasoned that there is an intelligent spiritual force that pervades the entire universe and which he chose to call Innate Intelligence. Disease develops whenever Innate Intelligence is blocked from flowing freely through the human nervous system. The manipulative therapy that Palmer designed was thus understood to be a means of aligning people to make them more receptive to the working of a higher spiritual power. Over the years, the majority of chiropractic physicians downplayed their metaphysical origins to gain both scientific respectability and access to both government- and insurance-sponsored programs. Thus while some chiropractic physicians continue to champion a decidedly metaphysical understanding of the healing process, others have muted the supernatural elements in favor of the more restrained form of nature religion that reverences the revitalizing powers inherent in the natural order. Today more than nine million persons visit chiropractic physicians each year. And while some of these persons go for reasons wholly unrelated to chiropractic's spiritual underpinnings, others are eager to be introduced to a spiritually charged philosophy concerning every person's inner connection with the spiritual power that radiates life and health throughout the entire universe.

What is commonly referred to as the New Age movement has also encouraged Americans to explore alternative medical systems. The various philosophies and practices that make up the New Age movement all endorse an approach to health and medicine that is said to be holistic and that envisions every human being as a unique, interdependent relationship of body, mind, emotions, and spirit. New Agers are for this reason critical of the Western scientific heritage and instead drawn to those Eastern religious and medical systems that teach that humans can potentially open the inner recesses of their psyches to the inflow of a higher spiritual energy (variously referred to as *ch'i, prana, kundalini,* or pure white light). Americans have embraced yoga, t'ai chi, ch'uan, Ayurvedic medicine, shiatsu, acupuncture, and various Oriental massage systems for their advocacy of attitudes and lifestyles geared to bringing persons into harmony with a metaphysical healing energy.

New Age crystal healing serves as an additional example of Americans' fascination with the metaphysical dimensions of alternative medicine. New Age philosophies tend to view God as a "pure white light" or "divine spirit" rather than in the traditional biblical categories of father or king. They further explain that this pure white light continuously flows into, or infuses, each plane of existence—mineral, vegetable, animal, human or mental, and astral. Pure white light is thought to enter into each person's consciousness by passing through his or her spiritual aura, where it is diffused into the seven interior centers or *chakras* that supply the body with power and vitality. Any technique (e.g., massage, color healing, visualization exercises, meditation) that can help persons increase their receptivity to this white light and promote its proper flow through the various *chakras* can thus have medical value. The most popular of these techniques is the use of rock crystals. It is claimed that crystals, because they are almost entirely devoid of color, are almost perfect capacitators of divine white light. They can be placed over a *chakra* believed to be "blocked," or held by a healer who moves them back and forth along the patient's nervous system. Over and beyond their healing power, crystals are thought to be capable of enhancing our spiritual awareness and aligning us more fully to the "Higher Guidance" that is believed to permeate our universe.

These examples draw attention to the fact that alternative medicine systems have become important vehicles of an unchurched American spirituality. The healing practices advocated by alternative medicine systems typically stress the importance of finding personal harmony with nature, becoming receptive to spiritual power, and establishing more emphatic relationships with one's fellow human beings. Spiritual themes such as these are especially attractive to individuals who are sensitive to the excesses of the hierarchical, exploitative, and overly male institutions that have historically dominated Western culture. Those who are attracted to alternative medicines are thus seeking to create a counterculture that provides a remedy for the increasing mechanization, secularization, and depersonalization of modern life (including modern medicine). Adherents of these groups are characteristically white, middle- or upper-middle-class, well educated, and either urban or suburban (except, of course, those who subscribe to medical folk traditions owing to their participation in ethnic or immigrant communities). The ideas advocated by alternative medicine can be found in bookstores in almost every shopping mall in the country, in displays at health-food stores, and in advertisements placed in various "human potential" magazines. Thus, although only a small percentage of Americans rely on alternative healing practices to the exclusion of scientific medicine, a good many others drawn from all regions of the country and all religious denominations have been influenced by their alternative philosophies of body-mind-spirit interaction.

See also CHAKRA; HEALTH; HOLISTIC HEALTH; HUMAN POTENTIAL MOVEMENT; MACROBIOTICS; NATURE RELIGION; NEW AGE SPIRITUALITY; PEALE, NORMAN VINCENT; QUANTUM HEALING; TWELVE-STEP PROGRAM.

BIBLIOGRAPHY

Albanese, Catherine. *Nature Religion in America.* 1990.

Fuller, Robert C. "Alternative Medicine." In *Encyclopedia of American Social History,* edited by Cayton, Gorn, and Williams. 1993.

Fuller, Robert C. *Alternative Medicine and American Religious Life.* 1989.

Gevitz, Norman, ed. *The Other Healers.* 1988.

McGuire, Meredith. *Ritual Healing in Suburban America.* 1988.

Robert C. Fuller

American Humanist Association.

See Humanism.

American Indian Religions.

See Native American Religions.

Amish

The Amish branched off from the Mennonites in Europe in the 1690s under the leadership of Jacob Ammann, who emphasized the shunning (ostracizing) of persons who had been expelled from the church. They came to America primarily in two waves, from 1727 to 1770 and from 1815 to 1860, as part of a larger mass immigration of Germans, settling on farms west and northwest of Philadelphia. As the Amish population has grown, shortages of local farmland have propelled migrations to Indiana, Ohio, and other states. Differences over theological and lifestyle issues have also caused some groups to split away from their cobelievers and move to new areas.

Specific beliefs and practices vary in different localities, but generally the Amish adhere to the Anabaptist tradition forged in Europe in the early 1500s. They are best known to the larger public for their "plain" dress, largely unchanged for three centuries, and their rejection of modern technology (including, usually, motor vehicles and household electricity). Intent on preserving their culture, they speak an unusual German dialect, operate private schools for their children, and avoid excessive contact with the non-Amish, whom they call "the English." Occasionally they come into conflict with secular authority, especially over issues of compulsory education and military service (like other Anabaptists, the Amish are pacifists). In recent decades they have become, in their quaintness, a tourist attraction, and Amish settlements are often thronged with sightseers whose presence is not sought but cannot be prevented.

Differences over lifestyle issues, particularly, have spurred the fragmentation of the Amish into many subgroups, a process further propelled by the fact that local Amish congregations are self-governing and independent. The most traditional are the Old Order Amish, who travel by horse and buggy, farm with horse-drawn equipment, and do not use electricity. A continuum of more liberal groups also exists, including the Beachy Amish and the New Order Amish, both of whom allow for the use of motor vehicles, among other things.

Amish "districts," as local congregations are called, tend to be small—about twenty-five to thirty-five families. Most do not build church buildings, preferring to meet in homes, and none has professional clergy or Sunday schools. Modernization and social change do creep in, but at an exceedingly slow pace. The strong cohesion of the Amish is maintained by family ties, cultural heritage, and the *Ordnung,* the detailed system of regulations governing daily life. One who seriously violates the *Ordnung* is shunned, cut off from the social and religious life of the community (the process is called *Meidung*), until he or she publicly repents.

Conversion to Amish life is rare, and Amish population growth is due almost exclusively to the preva-

An Amish man wearing a traditional vest and straw hat, stands in front of a horse-drawn carriage.   (Credit: © Medford Taylor/Black Star/PNI.)

lence of large families (the average Amish family has seven children) and an ability to retain a strong majority of grown children in the movement, despite the attractions of modern secular life. By the 1990s their numbers had reached more than 125,000, including children.

Young Amish adults who have not yet joined the church often participate in "worldly" activities, in some cases owning cars and engaging in various youthful excesses, including, sometimes, heavy drinking and drug use. However, by their early twenties most submit to church authority, marry, and carry Amish traditions forward into a new generation.

See also BRUDERHOF; MENNONITES; PACIFISM; SHUNNING.

BIBLIOGRAPHY

Hostetler, John A. *Amish Society.* 1980.
Kraybill, Donald B., ed. *The Amish Struggle with Modernity.* 1994.

Timothy Miller

Angels

At the end of the millennium, nearly three of four Americans reported that they believed in angels. While our earliest recorded references to angels date to the Gnostic culture of the first centuries C.E., angels cannot be understood apart from the development of monotheism begun with Zoroastrianism.

Writing in Persia (now Iran) between 1000 and 630 B.C.E., Zoroaster challenged the polytheistic religious traditions of his day, promoting instead an idea of one supreme God and an evil spirit who opposed God. This reorganized a Gnostic belief in a spiritual conflict between good and evil beings. In the centuries following his teachings, the commitment to monotheism grew as the Persian Empire spread into Egypt and Europe, although people continued to worship the Aryan nature gods in popular practices. Eventually, rather than being eliminated, the gods were incorporated into the new monotheism as angels, a demotion that preserved the idea of one supreme God while also accommodating popular practices.

The ancient polytheistic traditions therefore provided important precedents to contemporary angels. The word itself comes from the Greek *angelos,* meaning messenger, making a reference to the Greek god Hermes, who was the divine messenger between humans and the gods. The concept of a "guardian angel" also echoes Greek and Roman beliefs, as it was accepted that every man had his Genius and every woman her Juno. The hierarchy of angels and the assignments of specific tasks to certain divine beings are also borrowed from earlier traditions.

The Hebrews, already a monotheistic culture during the Hellenistic period, came into contact with the ideas of Zoroastrianism after the Babylonian exile. By tradition Yahweh, a remote God, could be reached only through intermediaries; the angels of Zoroastrianism may have seemed to fulfill the same function. Angels emerged later in apocalyptic Jewish writings, notably with the legends that came to be recorded in the Books of Enoch in about 200 C.E..

While Judaism distanced itself from popular angel traditions, Christianity, in its formative stage at the time, incorporated them. Even then, however, some viewed angels as a threat to orthodox faith: The Apostle Paul, for instance, warned against "angel worship" and stressed that Christ, not the angels, was the sole mediator between God and humans.

Despite the controversies, angels remained in popular consciousness, gaining prominence and legitimacy in the medieval period. Parallel writings on the divine nature and importance of angels emerged with the rise of the Jewish mystic tradition Kabbalah, in the writings of the Muslim cosmographer al-Qazwini, in Dante's epic *The Divine Comedy,* and in the philosophical writings of Thomas Aquinas. Aquinas asserted the noncorporeality of angels, arguing that they, like God, are "pure intelligence" and so are not subject to the bodily drives of hunger or lust, claims echoed in Islam. Ironically, it was during this Gothic period that angels came to be depicted in art as corporeal, human, and sensual.

Angels fell out of favor in religious thought and art as emphasis shifted away from the supernatural during the Age of Enlightenment. Demoted once again, angels, now feminized and infantilized, became central to the sentimental art of Victorian England in the nineteenth century.

A group of young Latino children are dressed as angels for a Christmas pageant in New York City, December 1987.   (Credit: © Hazel Hankin/Impact Visuals/PNI.)

This sentimentality combines with more traditionally religious ideas in the representations of angels found in contemporary material goods, books, film, and television. Yet while the visual media reference earlier writings and artwork, through visual codes they also present an idea not commonly accepted within any religious tradition: the conflation of angels with spirits of the deceased. Today, both ghosts and angels are represented similarly (a halo of backlight, an ethereal smile, a white robe), and both serve similar narrative functions, as the deceased must return to earth to perform good deeds to earn his or her rank as an angel (see, e.g., the *Topper* films [1937, 1939, 1941, 1979] *It's a Wonderful Life* [1946], *The Bishop's Wife* [1947, remade as *The Preacher's Wife,* 1996], *Heaven Can Wait* [1978], and *Ghost* [1990]).

In the last decade of the millennium, more than three hundred web sites were devoted to angels; an average of eighteen million Americans a week watched the televised series *Touched by an Angel;* and more than five million books on angels had been sold, most of which were authored by persons without religious training and in many cases outside formal religious institutions altogether. Thus contemporary angels, like their predecessors of earlier periods, seem to be flourishing, particularly outside the formal institutions of religion.

See also DIVINITY; GNOSTICISM; GOD; HEAVEN; KABBALAH.

BIBLIOGRAPHY

Bloom, Harold. *Omens of Millennium.* 1996.
Clark, Lynn Schofield. *From Angels to Aliens.* Forthcoming.
Knapp, Gottfried. *Angels, Archangels and All the Company of Heaven.* 1995.
MacGregor, Geddes. *Angels: Ministers of Grace.* 1988.
Murata, Sachiko. "The Angels." In *Islamic Spirituality,* edited by Seyyed Hossein Nasr. 1987.

Lynn Schofield Clark

Anglo-Israelism.

See British Israelism.

Animal Rights

The modern animal rights movement, which originated in the 1970s, is largely an Anglo-American phenomenon. Its earliest public creed was the "Declaration Against Speciesism" promulgated at the Royal

Society for the Prevention of Cruelty to Animals (RSPCA) symposium "The Rights of Animals," held at Cambridge, England, in 1977: "We do not believe that a difference in species alone (any more than a difference in race) can justify wanton exploitation or oppression. . . . We believe in the evolutionary and moral kinship of all animals and we declare our belief that all sentient creatures have rights to life, liberty, and the quest for happiness."

While some Eastern religious traditions—notably Jainism, Hinduism, and Buddhism—have at least notionally shown some regard for animals, Western monotheistic traditions have been heavily humano-centric in theology and ethics. This may itself help to explain the emergence in the West of a countermovement that is indebted, negatively yet also positively, to Jewish, and especially Christian, traditions.

Negatively, animal rights may be viewed as a reaction to the dominant form of Christian teaching, which has denied moral status and rights to nonhuman sentients. How far this teaching is uniquely or authentically Christian is a matter of debate, but it is beyond dispute that classical theologians—Augustine, Aquinas, Luther, and Calvin, to take just four examples—held that animals were made for human use. Moreover, for the most part of its history, dominant strands within the Christian tradition held animals to be undeserving of moral solicitude.

Key ideas have buttressed this moral indifference. Animals have been held to be nonrational or irrational beings devoid of the *imago dei* that places humanity in a unique and superior position. While Catholic tradition has never denied souls to animals, such souls have been deemed nonrational and therefore strictly mortal. Human "dominion" over animals given in Genesis 1:28 has frequently been coupled with the Aristotelian notion that nature is made for the sake of humanity alone. The result of these intellectual underpinnings has been to render animals all but invisible as a moral problem within Christian theology. Most especially, the largely unspoken but almost unanimous rejection of the idea that animals can have moral rights has fueled a powerful counterreaction.

Paradoxically, however, the modern animal rights movement can be seen as itself a development of certain positive notions within the Jewish and Christian traditions. The idea that there are moral limits to what humans may do to animals is explicit within the Hebrew Bible and rabbinic tradition. Jesus apparently taught that even sparrows (*strouthia*—little birds) were "not forgotten by God" (Luke 12:6). Aquinas held that cruelty to animals is wrong if it encourages cruelty to humans. And the examples of countless saints—from St. Basil the Great to St. Francis of Assisi—testify to subtraditions sympathetic to fraternal relations with other creatures. Indeed, Christian visions of extended benevolence or charity were directly responsible for the creation of the first animal protection society in the world, the RSPCA, in 1824, followed by the American Society for the Protection or Cruelty to Animals (ASPCA) in 1866.

It is doubtful whether the modern animal rights movement could have come into existence without this antecedent religious history, which in some of its subtraditions has fostered notions of a wider interspecies fraternity. In addition to the notion of moral limits, lesser-known religious traditions have also kept alive the notion that animals, as creatures of God, have value in themselves apart from their utility to human beings. Much emphasis in modern animal rights literature has been placed on the idea that sentients possess "intrinsic value"—a notion, it should be noted, that if not essential to a theistic view of the world is clearly compatible with the confession that God the Creator is "merciful over all his works."

Contemporary Jewish and Christian reactions to animal rights are divided. Some believe that the attribution of "rights" to nonhuman (even, in some cases, human) subjects is theologically misguided, since creation is "grace" and creatures can have no rights against their Creator. Animals cannot have rights, it is also argued, because they are incapable of recognizing duties or do not possess the inherent dignity of the *imago dei*. Others regard the increased moral standing of animals as a threat to human uniqueness or moral superiority. Conservative critics have not shrunk from classifying the animal rights movement as essentially "pagan."

Other theologians have seen a continuity of moral concern. The notion of rights is explicable and justifiable, it is argued, if all rights are grounded in the prior right of God the Creator. Viewed from this perspective, animals have rights, sometimes termed "theos-rights," because the Creator has the right to have what is created treated with respect. Some have championed the idea that made in the image of God and given "dominion" mean that humans should specifically reflect God's own love and care for other creatures. Interpreted Christologically, our power over other creatures should be expressed not in terms of mastery but servanthood: As Christ manifested divine power in service so should our "dominion" over other creatures be similarly expressed.

What gives the debate its poignancy is the perceived continuing indifference to animals within contemporary churches. It is true that some church people and theologians have championed the cause of animals, and none less forcefully than Archbishop Donald Coggan, who in 1977 maintained that "animals, as part of God's creation, have rights which must be respected." But many animal advocates still complain of ecclesial blindness. Helen E. Jones, president of the National Catholic Society for Animal Welfare (USA), spoke prophetically in 1967 of how the church should be "a leader in the movement for the protection of animals but it is not even in the procession." Significantly, the NCSAW subsequently abandoned its specifically Catholic identity and became the (now International) Society for Animal Rights. Despite some emerging theological work on animals, it remains true that institutionally churches and synagogues have yet to find creative ways of responding to the increased moral sensitivity to animals that the movement represents.

See also ANIMAL SACRIFICE; BUDDHISM; HINDUISM; HUMAN RIGHTS; JAINISM; JUDEO-CHRISTIAN TRADITION; VEGETARIANISM.

BIBLIOGRAPHY

Lawler, J. G. "On the Rights of Animals." *Anglican Theological Review* 47 (April 1965):180–190.

Linzey, Andrew. *Animal Gospel: Christian Faith as if Animals Mattered.* 1998.

Linzey, Andrew. *Animal Rights: A Christian Assessment.* 1976.

Linzey, Andrew. *Animal Theology.* 1994.

Linzey, Andrew. *Christianity and the Rights of Animals.* 1987.

Webb, Stephen H. *On God and Dogs: A Christian Theology of Compassion for Animals.* 1998.

Andrew Linzey

Animal Sacrifice

The bloodletting of animals at an altar and the Latin word *sacrificium,* meaning "to make holy," establish the link between blood and an opening to the sacred. Animal sacrifice is a recent development in the long history of human culture, since it evolved from agrarian or pastoralist societies. Sacrificial offerings of animals defused from the Egyptians into Western Asia. This Afro-Asiatic development later made an impact on Greco-Roman culture. The ritual activity of spilling animal blood at altars continues from antiquity into the modern era.

Sacrifices were probably conducted as cannibalistic feasts that evolved into rituals. Humans sacrificed one another, as a means of atonement, and to secure a continued association with the departed person. Some examples are the community scape goats at the Beltrane fires of Scotland, Ireland and Brittany, where historical evidence of human sacrifice is often contra-

dictory. Another example, where the historical record is more firmly established, is among New World Mesoamerican civilizations, most notably among the Mayas and Aztecs, who engaged in cannibalistic sacrifices. The Spanish conquistadores, after coming into contact with the inhabitants of the New World, ended these practices by the middle of the 1600s and brought about an increase in animal sacrifices, which are still practiced today. Yet there are other clear examples of human sacrifice that can be found from sources as diverse as ancient Japan to the Teutonic (Icelandic) people.

Substitution of animals for humans in sacrifices can be said to have occurred in some form in the history of most ancient societies. It is conceivable that escalation of animal sacrifices simultaneously diminished the number of human victims. Animal sacrifices began with firstlings, young animals offered to the sacred in gratitude. It was a form of thanksgiving where domesticated farm animals were sacrificed and placed on an altar along with other uncooked foods. In time, these sacrifices became more ritualized as they evolved into communal religious affairs and sacrificial offerings that included doves, fowl, and larger farm animals. Although the pig has not been used as a sacrificial animal by those who can trace their religious roots to Afro-Asiatic civilizations, the wild boar is used for communal rituals by some South Pacific people.

An offering is nothing other than a synonym for a gift. This action evokes a sacred relationship. Animal sacrifice has been described as a means to bribe or propitiate either cosmic entities or a supreme being. In other words, some have interpreted this ritual practice as a bribe, a business transaction, without moral significance, intended to influence nondiscernible entities. These animal sacrifices are categorized into four types of offerings: praise, thanksgiving, supplication, and expiation. A sacrifice of praise expresses homage and involves the veneration of a religious relationship with the sacred. Thanksgiving rituals of sacrifice are conducted because a favor has been granted, such as the birth of a child. The more complicated form of sacrifice is that of supplication because it requires pleading for a specific request through a direct link established with the sacred. This link is intended to help establish protection over a community or individual. Just as important for supplicants are sacrifices to forestall the anger of the god(s). Other animal sacrifices are intended as expiation, where there is a moral fault on the part of the person performing the sacrifice, who intends to placate animist entities that will help the person re-establish a connection with the sacred.

The topic of animal bloodletting has contributed to many interesting anthropological and sociological interpretations. Animal sacrifice has been correctly viewed as a gift to the deities, as a communal meal, as a homage, as a link between the sacred and profane, as a recognition of society, as affirming the present world order, as the result of anxiety due to success, as a substitute for intra-human violence, as a rite of purification, and as a dramatic encounter with the "other."

All major religions have had periods of animal sacrifice. Among Israelites in the Temple of Jerusalem and at the Temple of Onias in Egypt there were animal sacrifices of young bulls (Leviticus 4:3), male goats (Leviticus 4:23), and lambs (Leviticus 4:32). During Passover, the blood of the lamb was caught in basins and passed to the priest who tossed the blood at the base of the altar (Pes. 5: 5–7). Afterward, the lamb was roasted and eaten as part of the Passover Seder. Significantly, non-Israelites also contributed to sacrifices at the Temple, but during the Roman siege the lamb sacrifices had to be discontinued. The Roman destruction of the Temple brought an end to the sacrificial system. Jesus of Nazareth's corporal sacrifice is reenacted at the altar as the Eucharist, where bread and wine represent his body and blood. Some Orthodox Jews would like to re-institute animal sacrifices while others secretly engage in the sacrificial use of fowl on the day of atonement. The dead animals are given away to the poor, as is the custom at Mecca by the Muslims.

Arab Muslim people, Semites themselves, also engage in animal sacrifice, but it is unlike that of the Israelites, since they do not maintain an altar and have no tradition of atoning through sacrifice. The closest thing to sacrifices is found in the slaughter of animals in the valley of Mina, at the annual pilgrimage and the rituals at Mount Arafat near Mecca. The animal's flesh is given away as charity. Bloodletting rituals exist in the popular religiosity of believers in Islam that is unsanctioned by the orthodox.

Many sub-Saharan African areas had similar customs of human sacrifice. Religious animal bloodletting is especially prevalent among believers in Ifá, from the area of Yorubaland, in present-day Nigeria. Fowl and firstlings are the preferred animals for sacrifice. Blood is seen as having a sacred quality and is poured near the altar. This religion has made great strides in the New World and can be categorized as worshipers of ancestor deities, orisàs. Some of those religions that share animal sacrifices are the Cuban Regla de Ocha, popularly known as Santería, Brazilian Cantomblé, and Haitian Vodun, all increasing in presence in the United States.

See also AFRO-CUBAN RELIGIONS; SANTERÍA; SYNCRETISM; VODUN.

BIBLIOGRAPHY

Baal, Jan van. "Offering, Sacrifice and Gift." Numen 23 (December 1976): 161–178.

Evans-Pritchard, E.E. Theories of Primitive Religion. 1965.

Girard, René. Violence and the Sacred, translated by Patrick Gregory. 1977.

Henninger, Joseph. "Sacrifice," translated by Mathew J. O'Connel. In The Encyclopedia of Religion, edited by Mircea Eliade. Vol. 12. 1987.

Jensen, Adolf E. Myth and Cult Among Primitive Peoples, translated by Marianna Tax Choldin and Wolfgang Weissleder. 1963.

Pérez y Mena, Andrés I. Speaking with the Dead: Development of Afro-Latin Religion Among Puerto Ricans in the United States. 1991.

Pérez y Mena, Andrés I. "Puerto Rican Spiritism as a Transfeature of Afro-Latin Religion." In Enigmatic Powers: Syncretism of African and American Indigenous People's Religions in the Americas, edited by Antonio Stevens Arroyo and Andrés Pérez y Mena. 1995.

Pérez y Mena, Andrés I. "Cuban Santería, Haitian Vodun, Puerto Rican Spiritualism: A Multicultural Inquiry Into Syncretism." Journal for the Scientific Study of Religion. 37, no. 1 (1998).

Pérez y Mena, Andrés I. "Spiritualism as an Adaptive Mechanism Among Puerto Ricans in the United States." Cornell Journal of Social Relations. 12, no. 2 (Fall 1977): 125–136.

Smith, Jonathan Z. "The Domestication of Sacrifice." In Violent Origins, edited by Walter Burkert, Rene Girard, and Jonathan Z. Smith. 1987.

Smith, W. Robertson. Lectures on the Religion of the Semites: The Fundamental Institutions, 3rd ed. Reprint, 1969 (first published 1889).

Tylor, E. B. Primitive Culture. 2 vol. Reprint, 1970 (first published 1871).

Andrés Perez y Mena

Annulment

Annulment is the juridical procedure used in the Catholic Church to deal with broken marriages. Although Catholic theology on marriage emphasizes indissoluble monogamy, the Catholic Church has historically affirmed various exceptions to this ideal. From earliest times (New Testament), the "Pauline privilege" allows nonbelievers who subsequently convert to the faith to break their marriage to a nonbeliever and enter a second (sacramental) marriage. New norms enhancing papal power to dissolve marriages (or to remove church impediments to the contraction of sacramental marriages) developed throughout the twentieth century and were codified in the revised Code of Canon Law (1983). Annulments are granted by regional tribunals of the Catholic Church who after a detailed process of deliberation determine that the marriage contracted by the couple in question was not in fact a "valid" marriage. The grounds for nullity are quite broad and reflect Vatican II's (1962–1965) recognition of the psychosocial importance of personally fulfilling relationships. Most annulments are granted on grounds of "defective consent" of one or both partners at the time of the marriage. The absence of full consent may be linked to external pressure to marry (e.g., as a result of pregnancy); to moral or psychological immaturity; to schizophrenia; or to other conditions that inhibit one or both partners' understanding of the emotional and practical obligations of the marriage commitment. Other grounds for nullity include impotence, the existence of a previously valid marriage, ordination, a close blood relationship between the couple, or nonobservance of the correct procedural form for the conduct of the marriage ceremony. Once a marriage is declared null, the partners are free to (re)marry, since in the eyes of the church they have not contracted a previous valid marriage. In some cases, however, the nullity decree granted prohibits an individual from entering a new marriage due to the persistence of a defective condition (e.g., emotional immaturity).

The Catholic Church emphasizes that an annulment is not a divorce. Whereas divorce dissolves a valid marriage, annulment declares that a valid marriage never took place. Nevertheless, annulment can be seen as a response to the increase in civil divorce, providing a channel allowing divorced Catholics and divorced non-Catholics who want to marry Catholics, to remarry with church approval. In practice, annulment is used by divorced Catholics to legitimate a second marriage. Because divorced Catholics who remarry cannot remain full participants in the sacramental life of the church (e.g., they can attend Mass but are prohibited from receiving Communion), they are under pressure to seek to have their first marriage annulled even though both partners may have experienced a happy marriage for many years and/or have children as a result of the marriage. Various opinion polls indicate that more than three-quarters of American Catholics believe that someone who divorces and remarries without church approval can still be a good Catholic. Nonetheless, American Catholics are significantly more likely than divorced Catholics in other Western societies to seek annulments. In 1995, for example, for every hundred American Catholics who divorced, thirty obtained an annulment, whereas the comparable rate for Canadians was fourteen. In light of the fact that marriages break down for a variety of reasons, many of which are unrelated to issues of "defective consent" or other impediments, it may be more pastorally affirming for the church to accept divorced/remarried Catholics as communicants while simultaneously articulating its ideal of lifelong, indissoluble monogamy. In recent years, there has been growing attention to issues related to annulment, brought on by some high-profile cases in the media and public reaction to them.

See also DIVORCE, CHRISTIAN; MARRIAGE, CHRISTIAN; PASTORAL COUNSELING; ROMAN CATHOLICISM; SACRAMENTS; VATICAN II.

BIBLIOGRAPHY

Noonan, John. *Power to Dissolve.* 1972.

Vasoli, Robert. *What God Has Joined Together: The Annulment Crisis in American Catholicism.* 1998.

Wilde, Melissa. "From Excommunication to Nullification: An Assessment of Supply-Side Theories of Religion Through Roman Catholic Marital Annulments." Paper presented at the American Sociological Association Annual Meeting, San Francisco. 1998.

Michelle Dillon

Anthropology of Religion

Since the early 1900s anthropologists have been conducting field research to retrieve, record, classify, and interpret religious beliefs and practices. Early anthropological study of religion was guided by social theory that was informed by evolutionary biology. Thus anthropologists were concerned with the origins of religion and stages in the development of human thought. Social theorists believed that religious ideas preceded scientific thought and practice. In their conception religious beliefs and institutions would give way to the forces of modernization, rational thought, and secularization. However, at the close of the twentieth century anthropologists find that religious beliefs and practices abound throughout the globe in industrial and preindustrial societies. In many modern and modernizing social contexts religious beliefs and practices underlie political and social unrest and development.

Anthropologists are no longer primarily concerned with origins and stages in human thought. An emphasis in contemporary anthropology is on the adaptive functions of religious institutions and on symbols and meanings as they relate to social structure and organization. Anthropological methods emphasize an objective stance by the investigator. In their field research, anthropologists do not evaluate the validity of the beliefs and practices they observe, but seek to provide an insider's explanation of the religious beliefs and practices they observe and record. Anthropologists working in the postcolonial context have been examining the relationship between subject and object in anthropological research and writing as a result of local responses to anthropological texts. Increasingly, anthropologists find members of the groups they study investigating and interpreting their own religious life.

Anthropological approaches to religion have been influenced by Émile Durkheim, Max Weber, and Karl Marx. Durkheim and members of his school focused on small-scale societies. They analyzed cosmology embodied in religious ideas and systems. In religion they found the articulation of a coherent worldview that meaningfully ordered human life. They provided detailed analysis of concepts of time, space, and person in the universe embodied in religious thought. They also sought to understand the functions of religious precepts and tenets in structuring social institutions and everyday social transactions.

Weber conducted a comparative study of world religions. His work directed attention to symbols and the problem of meaning framed in religious cosmology and practice. His discussion of religion embodies analytic constructs used by anthropologists to describe and interpret the actions of religious leaders and believers. Weber also provided models for analyzing religious authority and the making of religious institutions, and he emphasized the relationship between religious thought and practice and the development of economic systems. Weber's work on Protestantism and the emergence of capitalism in America articulates his argument on the importance of religious values in the development of material culture. His emphasis on the significance of religion in shaping industrial capitalism was contested by Marx.

For Karl Marx, religion constitutes a system of beliefs that orients individual to otherworldly concerns and masks the harsh realities of uneven economic development under capitalism. According to Marx, religion provides the basis for individual and group subordination and capitulation to power and authority. In his schema, religion provides the ideological justification for unjust economic distribution and the privileges of the wealthy. However, Marx's position on religion does not entirely accord with the empirical record. In several contexts with prevailing severe social, political, and economic injustice, religion provides the ideological foundation for challenging and resisting authority. One example is the black struggle on American soil for freedom and civil rights in which religious ideas and institutions provided the ideological and material foundations for collective action that challenged and reversed racial discrimination, legal segregation, and economic injustice. Contemporary analysts are inclined to look for the potential in religion to work as a conservative or revolutionary force; religion is one of many interrelated structural factors that influence social order and movements for social change.

Following Durkheim and Weber, social anthropologists conceive of religion as culture. Religion is a pattern of beliefs, values, and actions that are acquired by members of a group. Religion constitutes an ordered system of meanings, beliefs, and values that define the place of human beings in the world. The human capacity to acquire and use symbolic thought in everyday transactions is an essential element of culture. Each social group embodies its own symbolic system that individual members learn. The human ability to create meaningful symbols underlies religious thought and expression. In ethnographic writing, anthropologists seek to describe cosmology and ritual action. Anthropologists are concerned with examining the relationship between religion and other social institutions.

The anthropological enterprise has added greatly to knowledge of variety and complexity of religious expression. The field today faces the challenges of globalization and rapid social change. Anthropologists no longer conduct field work in remote settings untouched by wider social and technological developments. Human solidarity has been greatly influenced by emergent computer technologies, the worldwide expansion of capitalism, and the massive movement of people seeking work in a global economy. Anthropologists working in the United States are refining their theories and research practices to interpret religious innovation created by an atmosphere of religious freedom and tolerance, plurality reflecting diverse religious bodies, interfaith dialogue, questions about the relationship between rational authority and faith statements, and the breakdown of gender and race discrimination that characterize the American religious landscape. Anthropologists seeking to interpret American religious life are using traditional analytical and practical tools established in their discipline as well as forging interdisciplinary study and collaborative work that includes local people in representing their own religion.

See also GLOBALIZATION; PSYCHOLOGY OF RELIGION; RELIGIOUS STUDIES; RITUAL; SOCIOLOGY OF RELIGION.

BIBLIOGRAPHY

Banton, Michael, ed. *Anthropological Approaches to the Study of Religion.* 1968.

Glazier, Stephen D., ed. *Anthropology of Religion: A Handbook.* 1997.

Lessa, William A., and Evon Z. Vogt. *Reader in Comparative Religion: An Anthropological Approach.* 1979.

Morris, Brian. *Anthropological Studies of Religion: An Introductory Text.* 1987.

Frances Kostarelos

Anti-Cult Movement

The emergence of unconventional new religious groups during the late 1960s and into the early 1970s was accompanied by widespread media coverage of these "cults," their supporters, and their critics. The surge of new religious movements (NRMs) that flourished during the 1970s and 1980s consisted primarily of youthful converts who were the successors to the countercultural protesters of the previous decade. In addition to the more extreme elements of the Jesus Movement (such as the Children of God and the Alamo Christian Foundation), various Eastern groups, including the Hare Krishna and the Divine Light Mission, together with eclectic organizations such as the Unification Church, were being labeled "destructive cults" by parents and other critics who claimed that mind-control techniques were being used to subvert and entrap vulnerable youth.

Largely because of allegations made against controversial NRMs by distraught parents, there emerged in the early and mid-1970s various *ad hoc* citizen groups in opposition to cults and in support of "victimized" families. By the end of the decade a powerful grassroots "anti-cult" movement had been formed to lobby public officials and to expose the activities of fringe religious groups described as "totalistic" and "authoritarian" by their opponents. One of the earliest countercult organizations was the Citizens Freedom Foundation, founded in 1975, which later (in 1986) became the Cult Awareness Network (CAN), the largest and best known of the anti-cult groups. CAN was forced into bankruptcy in 1996 as the result of legal action brought against it. An attorney in the case was associated with the Church of Scientology, a longtime foe of anti-cult organizations.

CAN and similar groups disliked the label "anti-cult." They saw themselves supporting freedom of religion while fulfilling several functions that their critics viewed with skepticism: serving as support groups for families and former members; providing information to the public through preventive education; and exposing what they defined as the fraudulent and illegal activities of destructive cults.

The membership of one well-known countercult organization, the American Family Foundation (AFF), consists largely of mental health professionals, scholars, lawyers, and activist laypersons. AFF promotes research on new religious movements and publishes the *Cultic Studies Journal* and a newsletter, *The Cult Observer.* It sponsors conferences on topics relating to NRMs and serves as a resource for the media and the general public. The existence of AFF represents a shift toward professionalization and institutionalization that has characterized much of the anti-cult movement in recent years.

Whereas some anti-cult groups initially tended to be linked by the NRMs to the controversial practice of "deprogramming" (forced removal of members from cults), they have moderated considerably and now advocate voluntary "exit counseling" or "strategic intervention therapy" instead of the involuntary methods used earlier to help people separate from cult experiences. The activity level surrounding various forms of intervention has decreased since the 1980s due largely to the changes that have taken place in the religious groups opposed by the anti-cult activists. Some of these religious groups no longer exist or have experienced dramatic membership declines. Others have evolved into forms more compatible with the larger society and have moved closer to the cultural mainstream.

The controversy surrounding the NRMs and their critics inevitably spilled over into the academic and professional communities. Sociologists and others did not restrict their research and writing to the nontraditional religious groups, but increasingly turned their attention to the dynamics of the countermovements. Scholars and mental health professionals intensely debated the validity of concepts such as "brainwashing" and "thought reform," sometimes bringing the discussion into the courtroom as expert witnesses.

Differences in research methodologies and conceptual frameworks produced two distinct and opposing "camps" regarding how new religious movements and cults should be characterized and how society should respond to their presence in our midst. One camp assumed a largely negative stance toward cultic groups, championing notions of mind control as an explanatory framework for the behavior of some cult members. These scholars were seen by some observers as extensions of the anti-cult movement. Those academics more favorably disposed to new religions were labeled "cult apologists." They rejected the brainwashing model and preferred the more neutral designation "new religious movement" to the term "cult." Both "sides" assumed a crusading spirit that moderated somewhat in the 1990s when representatives of both positions agreed to participate in joint publication efforts and conferences. Nonacademic anti-cult activists remained wary of such developments.

See also BRAINWASHING; CULT; CULT AWARENESS NETWORK; FREEDOM OF RELIGION; NEW RELIGIOUS MOVEMENTS.

BIBLIOGRAPHY

Saliba, John A. *Understanding New Religious Movements.* 1996.

Shupe, Anson, and David G. Bromley, eds. *Anti-Cult Movements in Cross-Cultural Perspective.* 1994.

Singer, Margaret Thaler, with Janja Lalich. *Cults in Our Midst.* 1995.

Ronald Enroth

Anti-Semitism

Dr. Leo Pinsker, a physician and Zionist philosopher living in Odessa, Russia, wrote in the late nineteenth century that anti-Semitism was like a disease or virus. In his book *Auto-Emancipation,* he observed that it was useless to try and persuade anti-Semites to stop hating Jews. It just would not work. It was necessary for the Jews to emancipate themselves, to reestablish themselves in the land of their forefathers, the land of Israel. Now the Jews have reestablished their state of Israel, but anti-Semitism has not disappeared. Six million Jews were murdered by the Nazi Germans and their collaborators, and yet the lies and hatred against Jews continue to exist. The human race has not been able to conquer the virus of anti-Semitism. But for that matter it has not been able to conquer the virus of prejudice and hate that is part of the human personality.

In the United States today there are anti-Semitic forces at work. There are those like Louis Farrakhan (the Muslim minister) and the Ku Klux Klan, who claim that Jews control Wall Street, Hollywood, and the media. It may be that prejudice against Jews in the United States is not as bad as it was when Henry Ford promoted hatred of Jews in the 1920s, with his *Dearborn Independent,* but hatred of Jews is still part of the American scene.

A distraught Lubavitcher Hasid in a black suit and hat stands in front of a boarded-up synagogue in the Crown Heights section of Brooklyn, New York, in August 1991, shortly after the synagogue had been attacked by rioters. The synagogue is the headquarters of the Lubavitch movement.   (Credit: © Robert Fox/Impact Visuals/PNI.)

Anti-Jewish feelings can even be found within elements of the Christian Religious Right. For the most part, its leadership has been supportive of brotherhood and has not been anti-Semitic. They have been most supportive of Israel, and many believe that the existence of Israel will encourage Jesus to return. In particular, the Rev. Jerry Falwell has observed that to be "against Israel is to stand against God." He has contributed handsomely to Israeli institutions and has even led tours throughout Israel. Falwell testified in Congress in favor of the United States moving its embassy from Tel Aviv to Jerusalem, and in 1980 Israeli Prime Minister Menachem Begin awarded Falwell Israel's Jabotinsky Medal. But, at times, some of the leadership of the Christian Right has given expression to some anti-Jewish remarks. At a "Love America" rally Jerry Falwell asserted, "A few of you don't like Jews and I know why. He can make more money accidentally than you can on purpose." Jerry Falwell later apologized for that remark.

But then there are others. While Jerry Falwell has made an occasional anti-Jewish remark, there are others, like Donald Wildman of the American Family Association, who contend that Jews control the media and that the mass media is involved in an organized conspiracy against Christianity and Christian values. Jack Van Impe, an evangelical and fundamentalist writer, wrote in 1979 that anti-Semitism was a punishment for the Jewish people's failure to accept the Messiah and that the "Jews marched toward Hitler's ovens ever since the fall of their beloved city in A.D. 70."

Anti-Semitism does not seem to be a major element of the American Christian scene, but every now and then it raises its ugly head, and we are reminded of times when it was an integral part of American life, when Jews were excluded from their basic right to "life, liberty, and the pursuit of happiness" from professional life, as well as from recreation and residency. It may be that we are living in a more enlightened age. It may be that the United States has overcome some of its prejudices and bigotry, but the virus is still there and may some day develop into more dangerous strains. Of particular concern are certain missionary groups, some Southern Baptists, and groups like the Jews for Jesus, who believe that their mission is to convert the Jews. According to Mark Powers, of Jews for Judaism, there are more than 450 missionary groups who specifically target Jews in the United States, Canada, and Israel. They are reminiscent of the menace which the Inquisition, Nazism, and Communism posed to the existence of the Jewish people and to all freedom-loving peoples. There are also more directly anti-Semitic splinter groups like the Christian Identity Movement, whose numbers are relatively small.

See also HOLOCAUST; IDENTITY CHRISTIANITY; JUDAISM; RELIGIOUS PERSECUTION; RELIGIOUS RIGHT.

BIBLIOGRAPHY

Belth, Nathan C. *A Promise to Keep: The American Encounter with Anti-Semitism.* 1988.

Dinnerstein, Leonard. *Anti-Semitism and the American Jewish Experience.* 1987.

Herbert Druks

Antiwar Movement.

See Conscientious Objection; Pacifism; Peace Churches.

Apocalypse

Apocalypticism is the belief in the end of the world and time as we know them, usually through violent upheaval. It is a contradictory phenomenon characterized by order and chaos, hope and terror, faith and despair. Because of its urgency and violence, apocalypticism is a powerful ideology that can be both destructive and creative. Apocalyptic beliefs can serve as incentives for social change, but they can also result in despair and apathy. Many historical eras and particular cultures, as diverse as Hindu and Hopi, adopt urgent messages or prophetic myths about a cataclysmic end of the world or a large-scale transformation of consciousness. For centuries Western cultures believed that apocalyptic transformations would come about as a result of divine intervention in the human world. In contemporary American apocalypticism, catastrophes are the result of human action as well as divine plan; examples are nuclear annihilation, plagues, and ecological destruction. Americans blend beliefs derived from biblical texts with the post–World War II possibility of nuclear destruction.

Apocalyptic religious movements and individuals draw on past frameworks of meaning to address contemporary problems and issues. "Apocalypse" comes from a Greek word meaning "revelation" or "unveiling," which in the biblical tradition is linked to the unveiling of God's plan and includes such themes as the Last Judgment, an unveiling of each person's ultimate destiny. The biblical texts that inform the Western tradition are Ezekial and Daniel in the Hebrew Bible and the Revelation of John in the New Testament, which offer different versions of the end times. In the biblical imagination, large-scale catastrophes wreak havoc on the earth as God battles Satan before bringing about a new heaven and a new earth.

The Christian apocalyptic tradition identifies images of catastrophe and redemption with the second coming of Jesus Christ and the millennium during which many Christians believe Christ will reign. Millennial ideas emerge in the Christian world when apocalypticism is linked with a numerical theory about the end of the world through interpretations of the Book of Revelation. Christian apocalypticism developed certain characteristics that influenced contemporary American apocalyptic thinking: date-setting; connections between current events or signs—identification of the Antichrist, for instance—and the end times; and the desire for catastrophe that results in purification or redemption. America has played a special role as a "redeemer nation" in the apocalyptic scenarios of European explorers, Catholic missionaries, and radical Protestants (Ernest L. Tuveson, *Redeemer Nation: America's Millennial Role,* 1968). The sermons of Puritan ministers, full of warnings of doom and destruction, predate contemporary televangelist prophets of the apocalypse. Apocalyptic predictions have fueled important political events such as the American Revolution as well as religious movements such as the Great Awakening in the 1740s. Religious movements characterized by apocalyptic thinking flourished in the nineteenth century. Prophet William Miller and his followers gave away their possessions and eagerly awaited Christ's coming in the year 1843. But other religious communities, such as the Shakers (also known as the United Society of Believers in Christ's Second Appearing), took a less passive approach and attempted to institute heaven on earth by establishing utopian communities.

The Civil War marked a turning point in the American apocalyptic imagination. The war itself was experienced as an apocalypse because of the death and destruction it wrought, highlighting the role of Americans as agents of both destruction and redemption, as President Lincoln implied in the Gettysburg Address (1863). Two and a half decades after the Civil War the apocalyptic Ghost Dance movement, which spread among Plains Indians because it promised a violent cleansing of white people from the land followed by peace and cultural restoration, was tragically extinguished at Wounded Knee when more than two hundred Lakota men, women, and children were brutally slaughtered by the 7th Cavalry in 1890. Wounded Knee continues to function as an American Indian apocalyptic symbol of the loss of land and culture under the pressure of colonialism and Christianization.

Just as Wounded Knee has become a symbol for the apocalyptic scale of the destruction of Native cultures and languages, so the bombings of Hiroshima and Nagasaki served as a warning to all Americans of their own destructive power. According to folklorist Daniel Wojcik, atomic fear and fatalism have profoundly marked American culture since the 1950s, beginning

with popular films such as *On the Beach* (1959) and *Dr. Strangelove* (1964). War movies such as *Apocalypse Now* and horror films such as *The Omen* feature an evil Antichrist and allow viewers to vicariously experience apocalyptic chaos from the safety of a theater seat. Other apocalyptic responses to environmental and political problems in contemporary America include radical environmentalists such as Earth First!

At the same time, more specifically religious forms of apocalypticism have permeated the American landscape in the second half of the twentieth century. One signpost of increasing interest in apocalypticism is the best-selling *The Late, Great Planet Earth* by Hal Lindsey (1970). Conservative evangelical Protestants have found that their brand of apocalypticism—premillennialism—reaches a broad audience in postatomic American culture. Premillennialist Christians look toward the Rapture as an event that will save them from the catastrophes about to be unleashed on the world. The growth of other apocalyptic Protestant traditions, such as Pentecostalism, are due in part to the urgency with which many contemporary Americans look to the end times. Apocalyptic Christians watch for signs of the coming apocalypse in political events, disasters such as floods, and diseases such as AIDS.

Late twentieth-century Catholics have their own response to life in the atomic age in the rise of Marian apparitions, in which the Virgin Mary warns of impending doom and destruction, such as Veronica Lueken's visions of the Virgin Mary in Bayside, New Jersey (beginning in 1970). In her messages to visionaries, Mary points to many of the same symptoms identified by conservative evangelical Protestant preachers as signs of the coming apocalypse; abortion and AIDs are two examples of contemporary issues that can be made sense of in an apocalyptic framework. These religious choices provide clear moral guidelines in the midst of what their adherents describe as an evil, decaying civilization. As they imagine that meaningless chaos is taking hold, they can look to the biblical apocalyptic tradition for explanations of current events and social conditions.

Alongside these Protestant and Catholic manifestations of apocalypticism, new religious movements such as the Branch Davidians draw on the Adventist tradition, which originated with the nineteenth-century followers of William Miller, as just one of many examples of the continuity of the apocalyptic imagination in American society. Contemporary survivalist and militia groups are characterized by the same kind of certainty that large-scale destruction will be visited on Americans in the not-so-distant future. Many of these communities and individuals follow the theology of Identity Christianity, which teaches that the world is on the brink of a final apocalyptic battle between Aryan whites and Jews. The New Age Movement provides a contrasting apocalyptic scenario in which a gradual transformation of consciousness will be brought about without the kind of violence anticipated by other expressions of apocalypticism. But the New Age movement carries forward the kind of dualistic thinking that has always seemed to characterize apocalyptic movements. Although New Age is a loosely networked movement with no central doctrine, some New Age writers believe that those who advance into the new era of consciousness are the chosen, while others will remain in utter darkness.

See also DEATH AND DYING; ESCHATOLOGY; IDENTITY CHRISTIANITY; MARY; MILLENNIALISM; NEW AGE SPIRITUALITY; PREMILLENNIALISM; SECOND COMING.

BIBLIOGRAPHY

Boyer, Paul. *When Time Shall Be No More: Prophecy Belief in Modern American Culture.* 1992.

Detweiler, Robert. "Dancing to the Apocalypse." In *Uncivil Rites: American Fiction, Religion, and the Public Sphere.* 1996.

Gould, Stephen Jay. *Questioning the Millennium: A Rationalist's Guide to a Precisely Arbitrary Countdown.* 1997.

Robbins, Thomas, and Susan J. Palmer, eds. *Millennium, Messiahs, and Mayhem: Contemporary Apocalyptic Movements.* 1997.

Strozier, Charles B. *Apocalypse: On the Psychology of Fundamentalism in America.* 1994.

Wojcik, Daniel. *The End of the World As We Know It: Faith, Fatalism, and Apocalypse in America.* 1997.

Sarah M. Pike

Apostacy.

See Conversion.

Appalachia, Religions of

West Virginia put John F. Kennedy over the top in the presidential primaries of 1960. West Virginia saw hard, on-site campaigning by both Kennedy and his principal challenger, Hubert H. Humphrey. The Bostonian Kennedy encountered living conditions in parts of West Virginia he had never known existed in the United States. With the ascendency of Kennedy to the presidency in 1961, the War on Poverty was born with Appalachia as its beginnings and its nexus at that time. At the height of institutionalization of the War on Poverty in the Johnson administration, Jack E. Weller, a United Presbyterian minister who had served as a home missionary in the coalfields of West Virginia since the early 1950s, published a small book, *Yesterday's People: Life in Contemporary Appalachia* (1965). From its first day to the present, this book has served as the defining statement of Appalachia in the collective American consciousness, and in particular of religious life distinctive to the mountain regions of Appalachia. *Yesterday's People* is still in print, with nearly one hundred thousand copies sold.

Along with the publication of Weller's book, 1965 marked the creation of the Appalachian Regional Commission (ARC), which was federally mandated to promote regional redevelopment. To achieve this goal, the ARC took the step of establishing for the first time a political definition of Appalachia based on boundaries by counties, which soon expanded well beyond the areas commonly and historically understood to make up the Appalachian region. For the ARC, Appalachia now ranged as far north as Coharie County in New York State and south to Kemper County in Mississippi. State legislatures pushed to the limits the mandate's boundaries for inclusion, so that more of their states' counties would be eligible for federal funds. Many counties did resist being included in this new Appalachia. Appalachia, after all, meant poverty, "yesterday's people."

The more commonly perceived Appalachia is a region that has shrunk in upon itself over two centuries, concentrated today in the mountains and plateaus of east Kentucky, southwest Virginia, southern West Virginia, eastern Tennessee, and western North Carolina. The implications for Appalachia as a now federally delineated political entity often compel an artificial inclusiveness that obscures people's historical and ongoing perceptions of the region. In its most literal and comprehensive sense, for instance, the religions of Appalachia range in West Virginia alone from a large, national center for the Hare Krishna movement to the Antiochian Orthodox Church. But these are not the traditions people commonly have in mind when thinking about what is special and unique, or at least distinctive about Appalachia's religious cultures, especially in its mountain regions, which largely shape much of its people's history and character.

Two defining features set off Appalachia's religious life. It has, first, the largest regional religious tradition in the United States. This status stands apart from the expanded regional boundaries so recently established by the ARC. It is delimited instead by Appalachia's long-established but never rigid historical boundaries. In addition, its historical breadth makes Appalachia second only to New England as having the nation's oldest regional religious tradition in terms of Christianity in general and American Protestantism in particular. In this article, American Protestantism is broadly understood in terms of denominational categories that historically made up the nation's dominant religious culture with regard to its social, political, economic, and cultural influences until the mid-twentieth century.

The more commonly held perceptions of what is distinctive to religious life in Appalachia and the geographic areas where that distinctiveness is found are what Weller wrote about. And he wrote about it in the context of more than a century of white home missionaries being sent to provide social uplift and to evangelize Appalachia's people. Largely white and already long established in their own Protestant religious cultures, Appalachia's people shared the same earlier heritages as that of the home missionaries sent to help and evangelize them, an anomaly unique in the history of American home missions.

Weller wrote about religion in Appalachia from the point of view of a highly institutionalized and influential national religious culture that was seeing the long, inevitable dissolution of its collective purposes understood in the nineteenth century as American benevolence and in the twentieth as ecumenism and the imperative of the social gospel. For these defining movements of American Protestantism, Appalachia's religious cultures had served and continued as a sign of radical contradiction. They were an affront to a powerful national religious culture that was neither tolerant nor forgiving of the image it saw in the mirror that mountain religious life held up to it. Weller's indictment of the varied yet cohesive religious heritage and culture so vital to the identity of a majority of Appalachia's people was harsh and simplistic, frustrated and exasperated, and above all, uncomprehending.

But Weller was not uncaring. He cared very much. After the publication of *Yesterday's People,* Weller went on to found the Coalition for Appalachian Ministry (CAM), an organization of Reformed-tradition denominations, from various Presbyterian bodies to the Reformed Church in America. CAM sought to train clergy and church workers new to Appalachia about its characteristics that have direct impact on denominations' abilities to be effective in their ministerial efforts in the region. CAM continues in its purpose as of this writing. But through Weller, we hear in the voice of a single individual the national religious culture's historical perceptions of Appalachia, its people, and their religious identity that have continued to prevail to no lesser extent up to the present. The national preeminence of American Protestantism, especially in the guise of denominationalism and all it entailed, had never truly taken hold among an intensely religious people living in the small valleys,

mountain regions, and plateaus of Appalachia. Nor does it today.

If Weller summed up the denominational perspective of Appalachia persisting today, so did Rupert B. Vance sum up the perspective of the academic study of religion toward mountain religious life in his introductory note to Weller's *Yesterday's People.* A sociologist of religion at the University of North Carolina at Chapel Hill, Vance gave voice to the preeminent indictment of Appalachia's religious life current throughout its history and up to the present, that of fatalism. Early nineteenth-century Baptist church historians such as David Benedict had intoned the same charge against the Old School Primitive Baptists, who were predominant principally in the areas historically identified with Appalachia. In the mid-twentieth century, scholars of religion continued the pattern, now including the breadth of mountain religious cultures, especially Old Time Baptists, who consist of a large number of nondenominational or subdenominational traditions that go by a variety of names (Primitive Baptists, Primitive Baptist Universalists, Regular and Old Regular Baptists, Regular Predestinarian, Regular Primitive, United Baptists, Separate Baptists in Christ, and Free Will or Freewill Baptists, to name some but certainly not all).

Most of Appalachia's Old Time Baptist traditions have little to no significant history or presence elsewhere in the United States, except through outmigration. All of them continue today in a Calvinist tradition emphasizing grace and the Holy Spirit, which separated them from what became the dominant religious culture of American Protestantism by the second decade of the nineteenth century, including clear separation from the Southern Baptist Convention when it formed in 1845. This separation persists today in Appalachia over theology, missions, and a hierarchical institutionalism that intrudes into the autonomy and integrity of local church communities. Critics such as Vance explain this form of resistance to the dominant culture as the result of Appalachia's historical isolation, a phenomenon of topography that led to "mental and cultural isolation" summed up in the attitude or condition of fatalism embodied foremost by the religions of Appalachia.

In concert with Appalachia's Old Time Baptists—instead of in opposition to them—are its independent Holiness churches, which are as varied in name and history as the Old Time Baptist groups and which probably make up Appalachia's single largest tradition. It is a tradition that remains unnoted and uncounted in any census of church life in the United States because of a general absence of formal institutional structures and written church records. The religions of Appalachia are largely oral cultures, apart from the notable literacy beyond the functional level of a significant number of its people. Appalachia's independent Holiness churches arose out of the great revival on the Appalachian frontier toward the turn of the nineteenth century. They preceded the clear differentiation of the Holiness and Pentecostal movements not so much in name as in the worship practices and beliefs that became institutionalized through these movements' denominational developments that took place mostly outside of Appalachia during the late nineteenth and early twentieth centuries.

Like their Calvinist counterparts among the Old Time Baptists, today Appalachian Holiness people continue to reject a works-righteousness emphasis that arose early in U.S. church life and theology, largely at the expense of an emphasis on grace and the Holy Spirit as it is given voice especially through expressive and ecstatic worship practices, many of which Appalachia's Old Time Baptists share. But in the national consciousness, in popular culture, the fatalism attributed primarily to religious life specific to Appalachia came to be embodied by one small Holiness group that had also, for much of the twentieth century, become synonymous with Appalachia more than any other—what mountain people call serpent handlers and outlanders usually call snake handlers.

See also BAPTIST TRADITION; BELONGING, RELIGIOUS; DENOMINATION; HOLINESS MOVEMENT; PENTECOSTAL AND CHARISMATIC CHRISTIANITY; PRACTICE; RELIGIOUS COMMUNITIES; RELIGIOUS STUDIES; SNAKE HANDLING; SOCIOLOGY OF RELIGION.

BIBLIOGRAPHY

Dorgan, Howard. *The Airwaves of Zion: Radio and Religion in Appalachia.* 1993.

Dorgan, Howard. *Giving Glory to God in Appalachia: Worship Practices of Six Baptist Subdenominations.* 1987.

Jones, Loyal. *Faith and Meaning in the Southern Uplands.* 1999.

Leonard, Bill J., ed. *Christianity in Appalachia: Profiles in Regional Pluralism.* 1999.

McCauley, Deborah Vansau. *Appalachian Mountain Religion: A History.* 1995.

Rutenbeck, James. *Raise the Dead* (film). 1998.

Weller, Jack E. *Yesterday's People: Life in Contemporary Appalachia.* 1965.

Deborah Vansau McCauley

Archetype

Archetype is a term used in religious and mythic studies to indicate regularly occurring universal patterns witnessed across world religions and cultures. An external expression of an archetype might bear unique qualities characteristic of that specific culture, yet the underlying skeletal form of the motif will be the same in all traditions.

The term is primarily associated with the work of the Swiss psychologist Carl G. Jung (1875–1961). The theory of consciousness that he authored is, in fact, sometimes referred to as the archetypal theory. This term is absolutely central to Jung's entire oeuvre and to the work of those who follow in the Jungian tradition.

Jung self-consciously took the term from the original Greek philosophers of the sixth to fourth centuries B.C.E. These founders of the Western philosophical tradition, known as the pre-Socratics, were originally cosmologists who authored theories regarding the nature and origin of the cosmos. The pre-Socratics were searching for what is labeled in German scholarship the *Urstoff*, the "original stuff" of the universe. The first philosopher, Thales (ca. 625–547 B.C.E.), posited that the Urstoff was water, Anaximines (fl. 545 B.C.E.) thought it was air, and so on. Several terms were employed by these philosophers for this essential substratum of the cosmos, one of which was the term *arche*.

"Arche" is a Greek word that is the source of English words relating to "archaic." In Greek it means "old" but also something more: it signifies "original" or "first." The first words of the Bible, "In the beginning," were rendered in the Greek translation (the Septuagint) as "Arche." The arche is what was there "in the beginning" or "from the beginning."

Later philosophers developed highly complex theoretical systems, building upon the foundation the pre-Socratics had set. Plato (425–367 B.C.E.), in his famous theory of forms, states that the physical, or "phenomenal," world is only an imperfect copy of a higher, nonmaterial realm of perfection, where the forms exist as eternal, immutable, perfect ideas, such as beauty, truth, justice, and so on. One of the terms Plato used for these forms was *archai*.

As Plato's school continued to evolve, the middle-Platonists re-imaged the forms as pure, perfect thoughts in the mind of God, which can emanate out from Him into the physical world. This philosophy was then inherited by Augustine (354–425 C.E.) and other Christian theologians known as the church fathers. Augustine applied the term archetypes to these exemplary thoughts in the mind of God, one of which, the Logos, proceeds out from Him, takes on a human form and becomes the Christ in the theological formulation of the church. This is the philosophical legacy then that Jung purposely petitions in his use of the term archetype.

Types are "typical" patterns. This term also derives from a Greek word, *typos*, meaning an "imprint" or "impression," such as footprints will leave pressed into the wet sand along the sea coast. Archetypes are fundamentally understood, then, to mean "original impressions," or "imprints present from the beginning."

Though Jung borrows the term archetype from the Greek and early Christian philosophers, his concept of what it means is somewhat different. The locus of the archetypes in Jung's system is not some ethereal, transcendental realm of perfection or the mind of God. Jung places them as original impressions within collective consciousness—one of the key features of Jung's theoretical system.

In his autobiography, *Memories, Dreams, Reflections* (1961), Jung recounts an important dream he had in 1909, which first led him to his signature theory of the collective unconscious. In the dream he was in the upper story of a house and proceeded down the stairways to the lower level, then to the basement and subbasement. At each successive level the scene became darker and historically older, until the subbasement appeared as a prehistoric cave shared by animals. Jung felt that this dream represented the structure of the psyche. The ego consciousness is on top, but it is undergirded by successively older layers containing within them the entire history of life. This means that the archaic past is carried within all of us, allowing us to access ancient memory traces from out of the great repository of consciousness.

Onto this field of consciousness the ongoing experience of life has imprinted forms, typically expressed as images. These primal forms in consciousness include not only memory traces from the entire history of life's evolution but also potentialities for future developments. These forms Jung labels the "archetypes," calling them the "living contents of the unconscious," symbolized by the fish and other life (archetypes) which are the "living contents" of the vast, unfathomable ocean (unconscious), or the trees (archetypes), the "living contents" of the forest (unconscious). He describes the archetypes as a priori structures built into consciousness, and says they are equivalent to the "instincts."

By the term *a priori*, Jung means that these structures are present prior to any personal experience the individual may have had. They are built in just as hands and other physical structures are built in by the genetic coding. In a parallel manner, the archetypes are innate structures built into consciousness that will then well up autonomously in dreams, fantasies, pathologies, mythologies, folklore, and religion.

Jung's theory of a priori structures inherent in consciousness would represent the polar opposite of John Locke (1632–1705), the British empiricist philosopher famous for the concept of the *tabula rasa*, the theory that each of us is a totally "blank slate" at birth, and everything in our consciousness is learned a posteriori, "after direct experience."

To call the archetypes instincts is a profound statement. Jung believes archetypal forms encompassing everything from geometric shapes to mythic and spiritual elements are instinctive to life forms, just as the drives to satisfy hunger and to reproduce are. We instinctively produce a vast range of archetypal potentialities, all of which press for expression; as Jung says in the opening statements of his autobiography, "Everything in the unconscious seeks outward manifestation."

Owing to the presence of these archetypal forms, similar motifs show up across the world. The pyramid, a structure built in the ancient world by Sumerians, Egyptians, Indians, Chinese, Meso-Americans, and others is one prominent example. Jung believes this is not due to cultural diffusion, the hypothesis that one group invented the pyramid and travelers to that place learned of it there (a posteriori) and spread it to other places. Certain areas were completely isolated from others until centuries later. Jung believed that direct contact between cultures is not required to produce similar forms in art, architecture, religion, and other media. The pyramid shape has been produced across the world because the form preexists and is held in common by all within the collective unconscious. From there it can well up and be externally expressed at different times in different parts of the world.

This concept of archetypal forms in collective consciousness, according to Jung, is the explanatory mechanism accounting for synchronistic expressions all across the board. Where others might apply the word "coincidence," Jung rejects this concept as by far the more unlikely possibility and places in its stead the term "synchronicity."

Archetypal forms are virtually infinite in number. In the twenty volumes of his *Collected Works*, Jung provides examples and presents the evidence for his claims. A few prominent examples of archetypal forms include the ubiquitous shape of the circle, or mandala, which Jung thinks is symbolic of the key category of "wholeness." Mandalic forms show up in religious symbols and rituals, art forms, the dreams of individuals, and even as a fundamental shape produced by phenomena in nature, such as planets, stars and galaxies, and the structure of atoms, the building blocks of all physical reality.

Specific elements occurring in nature leave impressions upon consciousness as archetypal forms, such as the the snake, which appears in religious and mythic contexts all over the world. Each archetype is holistic, that is, opposite aspects are always represented, as in the fearsome, awful qualities of the snake, as well as its awesome, fascinating side. Other animal forms impress human consciousness and come to expression as the archetype of the wolf, the bear, the horse, the jackal, the bull, the whole range of different birds, and so on. Each such symbol represents qualities that are ultimately ineffable, beyond description, and numinous, or awe producing, as, for example, the wolf archetype represent the essentially untamable quality and the winged horse, the soaring of the imagination in unlimited freedom.

Mythographers and historians of religion are in an excellent position to document archetypal forms, as both religion and myth are considered by Jung to be veritable treasure-houses of archetypal symbolism. All the gods and heroes of mythic lore are precisely archetypal expressions, according to Jung, whether or not they are understood by specific religious adherents to be actually existent beings. Thus gods and goddesses appear in typical patterns in religious contexts all across the world.

We can easily take note of these types: the thunder/lightning/war god such as Zeus, Jupiter, Thor, Indra, and even Yahweh; the dying and rising gods who offer resurrection and eternal life, such as Osiris, Dionysus, Persephone, Attis, Adonis, Baal, and Jesus Christ; and triple-goddess traditions across the world representing variants of virgin, mother, and crone. Specific archetypal motifs will sometimes constellate to form a complex, such as the Oedipus complex, or an archetypal pattern, as in the hero myth found all over the world.

According to Jung, it is because there are underlying patterns in consciousness that are "alive" in the collective psyche that such common themes repeat themselves in religious and mythic traditions and in the lives of individuals as well. Jungians feel that the existence of such common patterns everywhere can not be understood if one does not posit the existence of something like archetypal forms in a collective consciousness.

See also DREAMS; MYTH; PSYCHOLOGY OF RELIGION; RITES OF PASSAGE.

BIBLIOGRAPHY

Campbell, Joseph. *The Hero with a Thousand Faces.* 1956.
Copleston, Frederick. *A History of Philosophy.* Vols. 1, 2, 5. 1946.
Jung, Carl G. *The Archetypes and the Collective Unconscious: Collected Works.* Vol. 9, Part I. 1959.
Jung, Carl G. *Man and His Symbols.* 1961.
Jung, Carl G. *Memories, Dreams, Reflections.* 1961.
Jung, Carl G. *On Synchronicity.* 1959.
Kirk, G. S., and J. E. Raven. *The Presocratic Philosophers.* 1957.

Sharon L. Coggan

Aryan Nation.

See Identity Christianity.

Ascended Master

In several movements derived from the Theosophical tradition (particularly the "I Am" Activity of the Saint Germain Foundation, very active and controversial in the 1930s and continuing today, and the Church Universal and Triumphant), Ascended Masters are the principal mediators of spiritual wisdom and power. They are essentially human beings, from this or other worlds, who have so perfected themselves as to become quasi-divine, free of the limitations of space, time, and the physical body, though they can appear to privileged humans or speak mediumistically through them.

Since the founding of the Theosophical Society in New York in 1875 by Helena Blavatsky, Henry Steel Olcott, and others, Theosophists have believed that certain individuals have been in touch with Masters of the Wisdom guiding the spiritual development of individuals and the world. By the 1920s Theosophical writers such as C. W. Leadbeater had proposed that a hierarchy of Masters, including the Master Jesus (believed to be ascended in conventional Christian theology), and the Master Saint Germain, identified with the mysterious occultist of that name of eighteenth-century France, were essentially transcendent and constituted an invisible government of the world.

In 1934 Guy Ballard, under the pen name Godfré Ray King, published *Unveiled Mysteries* and *The Magic Presence,* foundational books for the "I Am" movement, which he and his wife, Edna Ballard, established. In these works Ballard reported a series of meetings with those he called Ascended Masters, beginning with a meeting with Saint Germain on the slopes of Mount Shasta in northern California, apparently in about 1931. Soon the Ascended Masters were speaking through the founders in sessions that, in the 1930s, drew thousands of attenders filling some of the largest auditoriums in the nation. Themes included: a sense of wonder induced by evocations of these beings operating in a universe of billions of suns and planets; "New Thought" ideas regarding the power of thought and affirmation, an emphasis on the spiritual importance of color; and patriotic motifs. The Ascended Master Hosts of "I Am" expanded well beyond those originally named by Theosophical writers to include many other figures, including Guy and Edna Ballard after their deaths in 1938 and 1971, respectively.

The Masters of "I Am" figured in a significant court case in the 1940s, when the movement's leaders were convicted of fraud for advocating and collecting money on behalf of teachings, including those regarding the Masters, that was false and that they knew to be false. In an important religious liberty case, the U.S. Supreme Court eventually reversed the conviction in 1946, on the grounds that it was beyond the power of the Court to determine the truth or falsity of a religious belief.

Many of the same Masters presented by "I Am" have also taught through the Church Universal and Triumphant, originally founded as the Summit Lighthouse by Mark L. Prophet in 1958, and continued after his death in 1973 by his wife, Elizabeth Clare Prophet. Always more communal than "I Am," this movement has centered around a series of campuses, most recently near Livingston, Montana.

See also CHURCH UNIVERSAL AND TRIUMPHANT; FREEDOM OF RELIGION; NEW THOUGHT; THEOSOPHICAL SOCIETY.

BIBLIOGRAPHY

Braden, C. *These Also Believe.* 1949.
Ellwood, R. S., and H. Partin. *Religious and Spiritual Groups in Modern America.* 1988.

Gracia Fay Ellwood
Robert Ellwood

Ashram

Ashram, an Anglicized form derived from the Sanskrit *âshrama,* denotes a hermitage or an abode wherein individuals practice austerities. A later development associates the term to the four transitional stages of life associated with orthodox, twice-born Hindu males: (1) student, (2) householder, (3) forest hermit, and (4) renunciant.

Although this development is perhaps most widely known among those with some acquaintance with Hindu social teachings, Patrick Olivelle, in a review of ancient Hindu and Buddhist sources, has concluded that *âshrama* originally referred to: (1) a place where the religious life could be practiced, and (2) shortly thereafter and by extension, to the religious lifestyle itself. Only much later, in about the first century

The Satchidananda Ashram Yoga Ville in a forest in Virginia's Blue Ridge Mountains is topped by a light blue dome encircled with overlapping pink curved surfaces. (Credit: © Joseph Sohm/Stock, Boston/ PNI.)

B.C.E., did it develop into the well-known system described in the Book of Manu (*Mânava Dharmashastra*): the four transitional stages of life as given above.

The modern sense of ashram reflects its earliest meaning (in about the sixth century B.C.E.) as a residence for the religious life. As such, it may be considered as a synonym for the term "monastery," also defined as a place dedicated to the practice of religious discipline. Indeed, "monastery" is sometimes used interchangeably with "ashram."

Regarding the second meaning, the religious lifestyle, what is of interest is that in its early phase, and not in the later classical Hindu formulation, the lifestyles were not transitional but permanent choices undertaken by Brahmanical (i.e., members of the priestly or intellectual class of society) householders. In much the same manner, inhabitants of modern ashrams reflect the practice of religious discipline in a manner consistent with the particular religious organization.

Ashrams have been part of the American landscape for well over fifty years. In southern California (Trabuco Canyon, Orange County), the Ramakrishna Monastery, which has been affiliated with the Vedanta Society since 1949, was founded by a disciple of Swami Prabhavananda, Gerald Heard, in association with Aldous Huxley and Eugene Exman, in 1942. This ashram or monastery is inhabited by a small number of monastics who follow a prescribed regimen as defined by the order they belong to, the Ramakrishna Order of India. Candidates for the monastic life must follow four guidelines: (1) devotion to higher ideals, (2) renunciation of ordinary enjoyment and sensate values, (3) a spirit of service, and (4) an affinity and a zeal for sharing. The stages that lead to a full monastic life include (1) a preprobationary period lasting six months; (2) a probationary period lasting at least five years; (3) "trial renunciation" or Brahmacarya, in which the first vows are taken; and (4) after a minimum of five years the candidate is then considered eligible for the vows of final renunciation or Sannyasa.

Other ashrams are located in various parts of the United States. The Kauai Aadheenam (or Kauai's Hindu Monastery), on the island of Kauai in Hawaii, is the headquarters of the Saiva Siddhanta Church, which was founded in 1949 by Satguru Sivaya Subramuniyaswami to promote Shaivite (dedicated to the supreme god Shiva) Hinduism. The monastery was established in 1970 and is the residence of twenty-five monastics or *mathavasi*. Among the activities of the church and the monastery is publication of the newspaper *Hinduism Today,* founded in 1979.

Two ashrams are in the eastern United States: one in Buckingham, Virginia, and the other in South Fallsburg, New York. The first, Satchidananda Ashram–Yoga Ville, was founded to further the instruction and training in a Yogic practice known as Integral Yoga, which follows an eclectic practice of Hatha Yoga, which emphasizes postures, breathing exercises, and relaxation techniques, among other practices.

The ashram in South Fallsburg, New York, is the Shree Muktananda Ashram, the international headquarters for Siddha Yoga Dham Associates (SYDA) and founded by Swami Muktananda in 1979. The purpose of the ashram is to teach Siddha Yoga meditation, a practice that must be taught by an enlightened teacher (Siddha guru) who has the power to awaken the divine energy within the individual.

See also BELONGING, RELIGIOUS; GURU; HINDUISM; INTERNATIONAL SOCIETY FOR KRISHNA CONSCIOUSNESS; MEDITATION; RELIGIOUS COMMUNITIES; VEDANTA SOCIETY; YOGA.

BIBLIOGRAPHY

Flood, Gavin. *An Introduction to Hinduism.* 1996.

The Laws of Manu, translated by Wendy Doniger with Brian K. Smith. 1991.

Olivelle, Patrick. *The Ashrama System: The History and Hermeneutics of a Religious Institution.* 1993.

James Santucci

Association of Vineyard Churches.

See Vineyard Christian Fellowship.

Astral Planes

In occult cosmology, the astral plane is one of several (most often, seven or twelve) planes of existence, along with physical, etheric, causal, and mental. Although humans function within all these dimensions at once, they are usually only conscious of the physical plane. The astral plane is the level beyond the physical, the realm of dreams, spirits, and psychic phenomena, the substance and vehicle for contact between the material and the mystical. Within the astral plane, there are believed to be numerous densities and vibrations, commonly divided into lower, middle, and higher planes, each associated with a distinctive sound and color. After death, people are thought to shed their physical bodies and exist in the astral plane in astral bodies resembling their previous physical ones; from there, they may ascend to a higher plane of existence and/or be reincarnated in a different physical form.

Although many occult traditions believe in astral planes, including Spiritualism, Sufism, and Kabbalah, it is central to at least three: Theosophy, Eckankar, and the New Age movement. One of the earliest interpreters of astral planes was Helena Petrovna Blavatsky (1831–1891), cofounder with Henry Steel Olcott of the Theosophical Society in 1875 in New York City. She posited the existence of Masters or Mahatmas, human and once-human beings who have transcended the physical plane and exist in the astral. These highly evolved adepts, together constituting the Great White Brotherhood, were said to possess extraordinary paranormal powers and manifest their presence through astral projection. Blavatsky claimed that the Masters revealed a tradition of ancient and esoteric wisdom that enabled Theosophists to experience authentic humanity on all planes of existence.

Founded by John Paul Twitchell (c. 1910–1971) in 1965, Eckankar, or the Ancient Science of Soul Travel, teaches techniques thought to enable individual souls to be freed from the limitations of physical being to experience Sugmad, the boundless source of love and mercy equivalent to God in theistic religions. Chelas, as students are called, aim to learn to travel along the Eck, or Audible Life Current, a cosmic current which is depicted as flowing and ebbing in waves from the Sugmad and back again. Through spiritual exercises that are kept confidential from outsiders, chelas are said to learn to apprehend the Eck in sounds and colors, and they journey on it through the planes of existence back to the Sugmad. Although Eckists claim to learn to trek the astral plane, they place greater significance on experiencing higher levels closer to the Sugmad.

Although the term "New Age" incorporates a wide variety of beliefs and practices, belief in astral planes is held by many, if not most, advocates of the New Age. While the astral plane is thought to be experienced spontaneously in dreams or near-death experiences, New Agers actively seek awareness of and movement within it through lucid dreaming and astral projection, also known as astral travel, soul travel, or out-of-body experiences. Both lucid dreaming and astral projection are characterized by reports of bilocation, consciousness of the body remaining in one place, asleep or in a trance, while the soul travels freely in the astral plane. For some in the New Age, beginning soul travelers learn to relax, imagine shadowy-gray astral bodies hovering above the ground, and float toward a white light "doorway" to the astral plane. Advanced soul travelers navigate Earth, the cosmos, and beyond, communicating psychically with the living and the dead, retaining control and memory of their experiences.

See also AFTERLIFE; BODY; CHANNELING; DEATH AND DYING; DREAMS; ECKANKAR; GOD; HEAVEN; JOURNEYS AND JOURNEYING; MYSTICISM; NEAR DEATH EXPERIENCES; NEW AGE SPIRITUALITY; NIRVĀNA; OCCULT, THE; PSYCHIC; SÉANCE; SPIRIT; SPIRIT GUIDES; THEOSOPHICAL SOCIETY.

BIBLIOGRAPHY

Buhlman, William. *Adventures Beyond the Body: How to Experience Out-of-Body Travel.* 1996.

Conway, D. J. *Flying Without a Broom: Astral Projection and the Astral World.* 1995.

Gomes, Michael. *The Dawning of the Theosophical Movement.* 1987.

Evelyn A. Kirkley

Astrology

Astrology is the study of the movements of heavenly bodies—particularly those within our solar system—and the relationship of these movements to human destiny and life. It has been present in various forms in America since the colonial era, and it continues as a significant aspect of our popular and religious cultures during the twentieth century. According to recent national surveys, roughly one-fourth of all Americans ascribe some validity to astrology. Most major newspapers carry daily horoscope features. As many as eleven thousand professional astrologers are at work in the United States, serving more than 20 million clients. Many bookstores have an entire section devoted to astrological books and periodicals. A blending of the insights of astrological symbolism with the field of humanistic psychology has become the most important development in American astrology in the past thirty years. In this "human potential" form, astrology is often grouped together with the set of beliefs and practices referred to as "New Age" religion.

In late nineteenth-century America, a largely unprofessional and traditionbound astrology decided to align itself with the growing influence of science. The assertion that astrology was an exact science became a commonplace of introductory chapters in astrological publications. Astrologers claimed that centuries of empirical observation had led to the discovery of immutable laws that governed planetary influences on human life. The exact nature of these influences was more difficult to articulate, however. Most theorists fell back on the Hermetic doctrine of correspondences, which assumed that the human person was a microcosm of the greater universe, the macrocosm. As planets moved through the zodiac—a zone of twelve equal segments that extends nine degrees on either side of the ecliptic—corresponding energies and roles were stimulated in human beings, inclining them to act in predictable ways. In "mundane" astrology this theory was expanded to include nations, organizations, and institutions, each of which were affected by planetary movements. Although astrologers professed that they were practicing science, they understood the movements of the heavenly bodies to be part of an ordered universe of meaning and purpose. In a sense, therefore, astrology came to occupy border lands between religion and science.

The first popular astrologer was Evangeline Adams, a descendant of two American presidents who practiced her craft in the heart of New York City between 1899 and 1932 and who counted as clients many of the Eastern Seaboard elite. Adams's four astrological books, published by Dodd, Mead & Company, opened the door for a wave of astrological titles distributed by respectable publishers beginning in the 1920s. Elbert Benjamine, Max Heindel, Paul Clancy, and Llewellyn George were other great populizers of astrology during this period, with both Benjamine and Heindel promoting the "science of the stars" within a metaphysical subculture that included Theosophical, Rosicrucian, Spiritualist, and New Thought ideas.

Several national organizations were formed between 1920 and 1940, the most enduring of which has been the American Federation of Astrologers, which was founded in 1938. The federation helped to professionalize a field that had long been associated with fortune-telling and superstition in the public mind. It continues to publish research, certify practitioners, and sponsor national conferences.

During the 1960s, the study and practice of astrology became part of the counterculture's search for spiritual enlightenment. Along with other mantic systems such as Tarot, palmistry, and I Ching, astrology helped counterculture seekers feel connected to a meaningful matrix of correspondences that included the divine, human, and natural worlds. Under the guiding vision of philosopher, composer, and Theosophist Dane Rudhyar, astrology also became a "language of the soul" that could be used in the work of self-transformation.

Rudhyar adapted astrological symbolism to the analytical psychology of Carl Jung. The horoscope, which is a picture of the solar system at the moment of a person's birth, became reinterpreted as a map of the individual psyche. The planets' placements in signs and houses—for example, Mars in Aquarius in the twelfth house—came to reflect all the forces, drives, and functions in the psyche, and "humanistic" astrologers sought to help their clients integrate these different parts of themselves into a harmonious and meaningful whole. Further, the birth chart provides a kind of seed plan for a fully individuated life, including different stages of development and a sense of ultimate purpose. "Person-centered" or humanistic astrology, as Rudhyar's system came to be called, took astrological practice away from its traditional emphasis on the prediction of events and focused it more on helping human beings realize the potentials indicated in the horoscope. Traditional predictive techniques such as progressions—the movement of the planets forward according to the formula one day equals one year, and transits—the daily movement of the planets through the natal horoscope—became methods for timing the various cycles of psychological development throughout a person's lifetime. "Hard" aspects, such as the square (90-degree angles) and the opposition (180-degree angles) became reinterpreted as growth opportunities when repressed and fragmented psychic functions are brought to the conscious level and thus made amenable to conscious integration.

A new generation of humanistic astrologers, such as Stephen Arroyo, Liz Greene, Rob Hand, Zipporah Dobyns, and Donna Cunningham, have helped turn astrology in the direction of astrotherapy, the use of astrology for psychological counseling. Within the astrotherapeutic perspective, nothing is predetermined in human existence. Rather, human beings, as reflections of the cosmic whole, have the innate powers to create their own reality and to realize ever higher levels of material and spiritual empowerment. In this perspective such growth does not come without work, however, and in the main this work is of a psychological nature. Humanistic astrologers have also emphasized the relational dynamics symbolized within horoscopes. Astrologers now regularly cast charts that map the interpsychic forces at play in relationships between lovers, parents and children, and business partners. These "composite" and "synastric" charts are used in family, group, and couples therapy. The advent of personal computing has made the laborious mathematical calculations of traditional astrological practice a thing of the past. The construction of a horoscope can now be done within a few seconds.

Astrology has always had a tenuous relationship with mainstream Christianity, but the stigmatization of astrology by Christians has taken a more severe turn during the twentieth century with the rise of fundamentalism in American religious life. For many conservative Christians, astrology is seen as part of a complex of metaphysical, occult, and magical beliefs that threaten to destroy authentic Christianity in the name of Satan. In spite of its demonization in the fundamentalist subculture, however, astrology continues to grow in popularity both as a tool for self-transformation and as a system of divination.

See also ASTRAL PLANES; NEW AGE SPIRITUALITY; NEW THOUGHT; PSYCHOLOGY OF RELIGION; ROSICRUCIANS; SPIRITUALISM; THEOSOPHICAL SOCIETY.

BIBLIOGRAPHY

Rudhyar, Dane. *Person-Centered Astrology.* 1972.
Greene, Liz. *Relating: An Astrological Guide to Living with Others on a Small Planet.* 1977.
McIntosh, Christopher. *The Astrologers and Their Creed: An Historical Outline.* 1969.

Phillip Charles Lucas

Atheism

Atheism, defined most briefly, is denial of the reality of God. Since there are many concepts of God, there are many varieties of atheism. Athenians accused Socrates of atheism, although (in Plato's *Apology*) he told his judges, "I shall obey God rather than you." Romans referred to Christians as atheists; they rejected the gods of Rome. The seventeenth-century philosopher Spinoza was described as a "God-intoxicated man" and as an atheist. Today somebody occasionally says, only half jokingly, "I am a Catholic atheist, not a Protestant atheist," or "I am a Jewish atheist, not a Christian atheist."

Therefore a revised definition might say: Atheism is the denial of any reality (1) regarded as the core energizing and ordering force of the universe and humankind, and (2) evocative of awe and worship. That

Mrs. Madalyn Murray O'Hair and her two sons, William and Garth, stand in front of the U.S. Supreme Court building on February 28, 1963. Ms. O'Hair's lawsuit led to the 1963 Supreme Court decision prohibiting prayer in public schools. (Credit: AP/Wide World Photos.)

means also the denial of any transhuman moral authority.

Atheism is less frequent than agnosticism, which says of ultimate reality, "I don't know," usually also meaning, "You don't know either." There are strains of agnosticism in all religions.

Modern Western atheism appears in several forms:

1. Scientific atheism explains natural phenomena as the result of matter-energy in motion. Studies of religious beliefs of scientists reveal about the same diversity as in the general public. Albert Einstein understood his beliefs as similar to Spinoza's and occasionally referred to God as *der Alte* (the Ancient). But today's science usually does not introduce God into causal explanations of natural processes. It may echo the French astronomer LaPlace's reply to Napoleon's question about God, "Sire, I have no need of that hypothesis."

2. Logical positivism in the mid-twentieth century defined religion, ethics, and metaphysics as meaningless, because they lacked empirical verification or disproof. Although not quite atheism, since it held that denial of God is as meaningless as affirmation of God, it was effectively a practical atheism.

3. Marxist atheism adopted Ludwig Feuerbach's belief that religion is bound to illusions projected by the human mind. But the real passion of Marxist atheism is its insistence that religion is "the opiate of the people," which supports the privileges of the powerful and solaces the weak in their miseries.

4. Existentialist atheism may express radical faith in God or radical atheism. The driving force of its atheism is rejection of any divine authority that submerges human freedom. Often it adopts Friedrich Nietzsche's declaration that God is dead, a statement usually intended as a cultural observation (the death of belief in God), less often as a metaphysical reality. In the 1960s this belief influenced some Christian theologies, with the crucifixion of Jesus related to the death of God. The social activism associated with Martin Luther King, Jr., and other liberation theologies countered both existentialist and Marxist atheism.

Some believers today welcome atheism as an energizing partner in conversation, since it makes religious commitment an act of will, not conformity to cultural habit. The issues surrounding atheism play out in public controversies about printing "In God we trust" on money, the pledge of allegiance to "one nation under God," and arguments about religion in public schools or symbols of Christmas and Hanukkah in public parks.

See also AGNOSTICISM; CHURCH AND STATE; DEATH OF GOD; ETHICAL CULTURE; EXISTENTIALISM; GOD; HUMANISM; SECULARIZATION.

BIBLIOGRAPHY

Buckley, Michael J. *At the Origins of Modern Atheism.* 1987.

Monod, Jacques. *Chance and Necessity*, translated by Austryn Wainhouse. 1972.

Roger Lincoln Shinn

Attendance

Religion in the United States exists in many forms, but worship attendance at a local congregation is its most traditional and visible expression. The institutional character of religion is a legacy of Protestant colonization and Catholic immigration. Its diversity and voluntary nature, on the other hand, are the products of a unique experiment in political democracy. In the United States, religion is not imposed by virtue of citizenship; it is a choice.

Americans attend churches and other types of congregations (synagogues, mosques and temples). When people say they "go to church," the reference could include a committee meeting, a special concert, a daycare program, a sports event, a troop meeting, or a support group. Ordinarily, however, attendance means (and is measured by) participation in regularly scheduled ritual observances common to a particular religious tradition. Protestant Americans go to a Sunday worship service; Catholic Americans attend a weekend mass, and Jewish Americans, Saturday morning temple.

The "Churching" of America

If institutional involvement in congregations is used as a measure of religiosity, Americans are quite religious. According to Gallup Polls, two-thirds of the adult population claim to be church or synagogue members and report attendance within the past six months. Attendance in most industrialized nations is considerably lower.

Religious involvement was not always so high in the United States. Indeed, at the time of the American Revolution, only about 17 percent of Americans were church or synagogue members. Despite the popular image of a colonial America populated by pious Pilgrims, Roger Finke and Rodney Stark argue that "Boston's taverns were probably fuller on Saturday night than were its churches on Sunday morning."

The rapid growth and westward movement of the American population created difficulties for churches organized around the European model of stable, geographic parishes. While once-established denominations like Congregationalists and Episcopalians struggled to retain adherents, circuit-riding Methodist preachers and a series of frontier revivals stirred religious enthusiasm and industry in the late eighteenth and early nineteenth centuries. With clear evangelistic and missionary aims and without the burden of an educated clergy or cumbersome bureaucracies, "upstart" Protestant churches—especially the Baptist and Pentecostal variety—flourished well into the twentieth century.

Immigration during the last quarter of the nineteenth century slowed the pace, if not the pattern, of the churching of America. At first, there were more Catholic immigrants than established parishes could handle. Also, many immigrants hailed from nominally Catholic nations with lower norms for mass attendance. Through the establishment of ethnic parishes and evangelistic efforts remarkably similar to Protestant revivalism, Catholic adherence and attendance equaled (and later exceeded) that of the Protestant majority.

Since the late 1930s, national attendance trends were based on data from public opinion polls. In 1955 and 1958 Gallup Polls reported that 49 percent of Americans said they had attended church in the previous seven days. No higher poll-based rate of church attendance was reported before or since the 1950s. In 1965 the polls reported a weekly attendance rate of 47 percent and by 1970 the rate had declined to 40 percent.

Why attendance fell after the 1950s is a matter of dispute, but three factors contributed most to the decline. First, the greatest drop in attendance was among Roman Catholics in the years following Vatican II. The changes instituted by the Church gave many Catholics the impression that attendance at mass was voluntary. A second factor related to the overall decline in worship attendance was an expansion of the nonreligiously affiliated population during the 1960s and 1970s—a period when persons claiming "no religion" expanded from around 2 percent to 10 percent of the American population. Finally, there was an erosion of attendance among educated, middle-class young adults from mainline Protestant denominations. After college, many never found their way back to the church.

Church Attendance Today

According to most polls, weekly attendance at religious services did not continue to decline. Instead, it stabilized in 1970 at 40 percent of the population and has fluctuated around that level for the past three decades. This stability in church attendance—in the midst of rapid social and cultural change—has struck many social observers as incongruous, particularly since other measures of religiosity show decline. With membership in many denominations declining and composite measures of religious interest and confidence at near-record lows, could actual attendance today be as high as it was in the early 1970s? Were problems with measuring religious activity in postmodern society interfering with our ability to detect changes in the way Americans express their religiosity (or spirituality)?

A few years ago we began to question the reliance on social surveys to measure attendance in religious organizations. We argued that poll-based estimates of attendance ought to be cross-checked by looking at actual counts of persons attending religious services. In 1992 we teamed up with Mark Chaves to test the 40 percent figure for church attendance. Our initial study, based on attendance counts in one Ohio county and Catholic churches in eighteen dioceses, indicated a much lower rate of religious participation than the polls report. Instead of 40 percent of Protestants attending church, we found 20 percent. Instead of 50 percent of Catholics attending church, we found 28 percent. In other words, actual church attendance was slightly over half the rate indicated by national public opinion polls. Additional research in thirty Catholic dioceses in the San Francisco area provided additional confirmation that actual worship attendance is much lower than suggested by polls.

So what percent of the population attends worship at a church or synagogue during an average week in the United States? Probably somewhere between 22 and 24 percent. An exact figure is not possible because no national attendance count exists.

Interpreting Attendance Trends

Attendance at worship services is an important indicator of religious activity, especially in a society with a heritage of institutionalized religion where participation is voluntary. The level of this activity remains fairly high in the United States, but it is not as high as it once was, and it is not as high as the polls suggest. What is happening here?

Some scholars argue that declines in institutional forms of religion are compensated by increases in nontraditional forms of spirituality. Religion in America is becoming more individual, less institutional, and increasingly innovative. Witness the proliferation of parachurch organizations and quasi-religious groups as well as a surge in publications and seminars that focus more on Eastern, contemplative forms of religion. Like *Habits of the Heart*'s infamous modern, Sheila, contemporary Americans can "be their own church."

Other scholars doubt whether such religious experimentation effectively compensates for traditional institutional involvement. There is no evidence that church attendance declines are numerically offset by participation in highly individualized or nontraditional religion. In addition, there is serious doubt about the social durability of any kind of "Sheilaism." In fact, our data on church attendance indicates that most Americans still identify with traditional denominations, and whether they go or not, prefer to see themselves as churchgoers.

See also CONGREGATION; JUDAISM; LITURGY AND WORSHIP; MAINLINE PROTESTANTISM; NEW RELIGIOUS MOVEMENTS; ROMAN CATHOLICISM; SPIRITUALITY.

BIBLIOGRAPHY

Bellah, Robert, Richard Madsen, William M. Sullivan, Ann Swidler, and Steven M. Tipton. *Habits of the Heart*. 1985.

Finke, Roger and Rodney Stark. *The Churching of America, 1776–1990*. 1992.

Hadaway, C. Kirk, and Penny L. Marler. "The Problem with Father as Proxy: Denominational Switching and Religious Change, 1965–1988." *Journal for the Scientific Study of Religion* 35 (1996): 156–164.

Hadaway, C. Kirk, Penny L. Marler, and Mark Chaves. "What the Polls Don't Show: A Closer Look at U.S. Church Attendance." *American Sociological Review* 58 (1993): 741–752.

Hadaway, C. Kirk, Penny L. Marler, and Mark Chaves. "Overreporting Church Attendance in America: Evidence That Demands the Same Verdict." *American Sociological Review* 63 (1998): 122–130.

Mead, Sidney. *The Nation with the Soul of a Church*. 1975.

Princeton Religion Research Center. "Church Attendance Constant." *Emerging Trends* 14, no. 3 (1992): 4.

Roof, Wade Clark. *A Generation of Seekers*. 1993.

Roozen, David, and Jackson W. Carroll. "Recent Trends in Church Membership and Participation: An Introduction." In *Understanding Church Growth and Decline*, edited by Dean R. Hoge and David A. Roozen. 1979.

Penny Long Marler
C. Kirk Hadaway

Avatar

The Sanskrit word *avatara* ("that which crosses over" and thus a "descent" from heaven) refers to the incarnation of a deity or divine power in the world. Originally a concept held by a number of theistic Hindu traditions in classical India, the idea of an avatara has found a place in recent years in some religious American sensibilities that have been influenced by Indian thought.

Hindu texts from the third century B.C.E. to the twelfth century C.E. speak of such incarnations primarily in terms of divine salvation. Here, a divine being is said to take physical form as a way to save the universe as a whole from annihilation. But such an incarnation is also said to take place to give devout devotees a vision of divinity, rescue them from distress, or reward them for their service. In these instances, divine incarnation serves private or inward purposes rather than universal functions.

Some contemporary religious movements in America based on the disciple's reverential attitude toward a particular spiritual master use the word avatara (or avatar, as the word has entered the English lexicon) to represent the experience that the divine has taken form in the world in the person of the master himself or herself.

Although different deities are said in Hinduism to have taken embodied form in various ways, the term avatar is associated in classical texts most broadly with the incarnations of the god Vishnu, who throughout the centuries has been regarded as the divine power that protects the world against all debilitating and destructive forces. The number of Vishnu's incarnations varies from text to text, but most Hindu traditions recognize ten. Vishnu is said to have taken form as:

1. a fish, to save the righteous progenitor of the human race from a universal flood;
2. an immense boar who retrieved the goddess Earth from the bottom of the universal ocean, where she had been held by a cosmic demon;
3. a tortoise on whose back the gods placed Mount Mandara as a giant stick so they could churn the ocean to extract the elixir of immortality from it;
4. a half man, half lion to destroy a demon who could be defeated by neither human nor beast;
5. a dwarf who swelled to universal size to retrieve the world from a demonic king by winning all of the territory he could cover in three steps;
6. Rama the Ax-Wielder, who bravely corrected the warriors in their mistreatment of the priests whose rituals held the human community in contact with the sacred realm;
7. the heroic Lord Rama, who battled the evil Ravana, the latter of whose selfish acts threatened to destroy the world;
8. Lord Krishna, who took form as an adviser to Arjuna when that great warrior had lost courage in his fight against the forces of unrighteousness;
9. the Buddha, who deluded those whose views were already incorrect, thus making the way for their salvation;
10. Kalki, the avatar of the future who will return on a white horse at the end of time to destroy the evil world and usher in a new, golden age.

Understood theologically, Vishnu's incarnations mark his role as preserver of the world on whose being the entire universe is founded and who, in his great love for the world, sustains it and protects it against the powers of destruction.

Various traditions interpret some of these incarnations differently. For example, some regard the Buddha avatar not as one who deceives the ignorant, but rather as one who teaches nonviolence and compassion. The devotional tradition of Hinduism also includes a popular set of stories in which Krishna is described as a fun-loving, even mischievous child and as a supreme lover whose affection for his beloved Radha is an allegory of God's love for the human soul.

There are attestations in contemporary religious movements of the belief in an avatar in the form of a spiritual master independent of any reference to any particular classical deity, Vishnu or otherwise. In general, such traditional accounts are regarded as sacred narratives that reveal a deeper theological point, namely that an eternal truth or divine power can and does become incarnate in the world in the form of a particular spiritual master, and that this event is to the world's advantage.

See also DIVINITY; GURU; HINDUISM; SPIRITUALITY.

BIBLIOGRAPHY

Dimmitt, Cornelia, and J. A. B. van Buitenen. *Classical Hindu Mythology: A Reader in the Sanskrit Puranas.* 1978.

Parrinder, Geoffrey. *Avatar and Incarnation: The Divine in Human Form in the World's Religions.* 1997.

Purdom, C. B. *God-Man: The Life, Journeys and Work of Meher Baba with an Interpretation of His Silence and Spiritual Teaching.* 1971.

Murphet, Howard. *Sai Baba Avatar: A New Journey into Power and Glory.* 1977.

William K. Mahony

B

Baby Buster.

See Generation X.

Baha'is

The Baha'i religion has its origins in religious currents within Shi'i Islam in the first half of the nineteenth century. The religion was founded in the 1860s by the prophet Baha'u'llah (1817–1892) in the aftermath of the Iranian millenarian and heterodox movement Babism. Since Baha'is believe in a prophet after Muhammad, they are considered heretics by the Muslim *ulama* (doctors of Islamic religion and law), and the Baha'is of Iran have regularly been persecuted there.

The Baha'i religion is strictly monotheistic. According to Baha'i doctrine, the founders of all the great religions are human manifestations of an invisible and indescribable God. Baha'is believe that with Baha'u'llah's manifestation God had decided to unify all mankind into one religion and one world civilization. Around this central doctrine of unity, Baha'is claim a number of social and ethical principles that may be called liberal from a North American political perspective. For example, Baha'is condemn racial prejudice and praise ethnic and cultural pluralism. They insist on equal rights and opportunities for men and women, compulsory education, and elimination of the extremes of poverty and wealth. In their personal lives Baha'is are expected to work for

their profession and observe general moral codes of society.

Baha'i law forbids believers to drink alcohol and take drugs, and prescribes a yearly fasting period, but otherwise has retained none of the dietary prohibitions of Islam.

Through systematic missionary activity initiated by Baha'u'llah's son and successor, Abdu'l-Baha (1844–1921), Baha'i gradually expanded outside its Muslim environment. Baha'i missionaries came to the United States and Canada in the 1890s and to Europe in about 1900. The self-taught missionary and healer Ibrahim Kheiralla succeeded in converting several hundred Americans, mostly women of mainstream Protestant background but interested in alternative religious movements such as Theosophy, Swedenborgianism, and various Hinduistic traditions. Baha'i probably was accepted as part of these trends of the age. Kheiralla's teaching was, however, not consistent with Abdu'l-Baha's interpretation of Baha'i beliefs. In 1900 it came to a break between Kheiralla and the majority of the American Baha'is, and the resulting crisis took several years to overcome. In 1912 Abdu'l-Baha made a personal eight-month mission tour to North America to consolidate the religion there, and in subsequent years North American membership stabilized between one thousand and two thousand.

Later schisms among the Baha'is have led to insignificant and now largely defunct splinter groups.

Abdu'l-Baha's successor as head of the religion, Shoghi Effendi (1897–1957), reorganized the American Baha'i community and established elected administrative bodies on the local and national levels

The North American Baha'i Center in Wilmette, Illinois, is the main temple in the United States for the Baha'i faith. The temple has nine sides, symbolizing world unity, and a dome on top. (Credit: CORBIS/Joseph Sohm; Chromo-Sohm Inc.)

(the Baha'is have no priesthood). Shoghi Effendi assigned the organization a doctrinal significance as a blueprint for the future politico-religious world order, and the American Baha'i community served as a model for this so-called Administrative Order. Shoghi Effendi also launched several mission plans, in which the American Baha'is played a key role in spreading the religion to Europe after World War II.

Chicago was a stronghold of the early American Baha'i community, and in Wilmette, north of the city, the Baha'is began in the 1920s to build a temple on the shore of Lake Michigan. The spectacular, nine-sided building of mixed Oriental and Western architectural style was completed in 1953 and is open to the public.

During the 1940s, 1950s, and 1960s the American Baha'i community grew slowly, from a few thousand to about thirteen thousand. Then, in the wake of the youth rebellion, membership soared—partly through mass conversion—and reached a level of about one hundred thousand by the end of the 1970s. Membership has since then shown little or no growth, and the American Baha'i community seems to have developed from a liberal religious movement into a denominationlike organization with considerable direct and indirect influence on the international development of the religion.

The Baha'i International Community in New York was recognized by the United Nations as a nongovernmental organization with consultative status in 1970. The Baha'is have been active and visible at a number of U.N. events since the 1970s, including the series of world summits from 1990 to 1996. On November 23–26, 1992, the Baha'i World Congress was held in New York City, with about thirty thousand Baha'i delegates from 180 countries.

According to Baha'i sources the number of Baha'is worldwide is more than five million. Expatriate Iranian Baha'is make up a considerable percentage of most Western Baha'i communities. The supreme body of authority in the Baha'i religion is the nine-member Universal House of Justice, seated in the Baha'i World Center in Haifa, Israel. The members are elected for five-year periods by delegates from the national Baha'i communities.

See also ISLAM; MISSIONARY MOVEMENTS; RELIGIOUS COMMUNITIES.

BIBLIOGRAPHY

Smith, Peter. *The Babi and Baha'i Religions: From Messianic Shi'ism to a World Religion.* 1987.

Stockman, Robert H. *The Baha'i Faith in America.* Vol. 1, *Origins, 1892–1900.* Vol. 2, *Early Expansion, 1900–1912.* 1985, 1995.

Walbridge, John. *Sacred Acts, Sacred Space, Sacred Time.* 1996.

Margit Warburg

Baptism

Baptism and the Lord's Supper are the two most enduring rituals of the Christian Church. While they are symbols of the church's unity, they have also produced some of its most significant divisions. Jesus himself received baptism at the hands of John the Baptizer in the Jordan River (Matthew 3:13–16). The earliest Christians followed Jesus' example, receiving baptism as an outward and visible sign of their faith in Christ and their union with his body, the church. Adult immersion was generally the norm until the fourth and fifth centuries, when Augustine and others developed a theology that required the baptism of infants to cleanse them of the curse of original sin. During the Middle Ages, the Christianization of Europe created a link between infant baptism and citizenship. To be born into a Catholic state was to be baptized into the Christian Church. The Protestant reformers challenged Roman Catholic theological and political hegemony but retained the union of citizenship and in-

A Roman Catholic priest sprinkles holy water on a crying one-year-old girl, cradled in the arms of her father, during an infant baptismal ceremony at a Catholic church in Boston, in 1995.   (Credit: © David J. Sams/ Stock, Boston/PNI.)

fant baptism. The Wiedertaufer or Anabaptists of the sixteenth century rejected infant baptism, rebaptizing adults after their profession of faith in Christ. Their refusal to baptize infants meant that Protestants and Catholics often persecuted Anabaptists (Mennonites and others) as both heretics to the church and traitors to the state. In England, Anglicans and Puritans practiced infant baptism, the latter insisting that it was a "sign of the covenant," the Christian equivalent of Jewish circumcision, given to the elect "and their seed." These ideas were repudiated by the Baptists, a seventeenth-century sect who, like the Anabaptists, insisted on the baptism of adult believers. Their earliest method was affusion, pouring water on the head three times in the name of the Father, the Son, and the Holy Spirit. During the 1640s Baptists began to observe baptism by dipping, or immersion.

Infant baptism was the normative mode for those English settlers who came to America in the seventeenth century. Religious establishments in Puritan New England and Anglican Virginia fostered persecution against those groups such as Quakers, Men-

nonites, and Baptists that refused to baptize infants. With disestablishment and religious liberty, debates over baptism merely increased as new denominations competed with each other. During the nineteenth century, especially on the American frontier, baptism was a major topic of discussion and division. Presbyterians, Methodists, and other "pedobaptist" (infant baptism) traditions debated Baptists and Restorationists (the Stone-Campbell tradition) over the proper candidate and the proper mode of baptism. Questions concerned the marks of the true church, admission of the nonimmersed to communion and church membership, and the process of conversion requisite for a valid baptism. The relationship of faith and baptism was also an unending point of controversy. Was baptism necessary for salvation, or did it simply accompany it? Was it sacrament or symbol? Should persons who received baptism as infants be "rebaptized" in adulthood, particularly after joining an immersionist communion? Baptist Landmarkists, for example, believed that Baptist churches alone had maintained the true baptism since New Testament times. Restorationists suggested that they alone had reconstituted baptism after it had been lost to all other churchly groups. Pedobaptists maintained that their tradition of baptism and confirmation had been administered since the earliest Christian era.

These debates continued throughout the twentieth century, with varying theological emphases and assorted revisions. First, many Christian communions continue to baptize infants, welcoming them into the world with an outward sign of God's grace. Such a pledge of faith is then renewed at a time of confirmation, usually in late childhood or early adolescence. Confirmation is the time when baptized individuals make the faith their own, confirming for themselves the faith that was pledged for them in infancy. Some communions, such as Roman Catholics, have extended the confirmation age from early to later childhood, with the average age around ten to fifteen or so.

Second, those who practice immersion continued to revisit questions raised when persons baptized in infancy join their churches. Mobility, intermarriage, and changing religious preferences brought many persons with varying baptismal histories into immersionist churches. In such instances, some Baptist churches require all persons to receive Baptist immersion before they can be admitted to full church membership. Other congregations admit as members all who have received immersion in any Christian tradition. Still others accept all those who have received baptism, whatever the mode, with no rebaptism required. Baptist groups themselves divide over the practice of open or closed baptismal policies. Some immersionist congregations (especially among the Baptists) refuse the Lord's Supper to any who have not received Baptist immersion. Other traditions (e.g., the United Methodists) repudiate any efforts to perform "rebaptisms" of persons who have received the rite in infancy.

Third, the growth of nondenominational congregations, many of them large "megachurches," created a pluralism of baptismal practices in one church. Some of these congregations administer baptism in multiple forms, to infants, children, and adults, by sprinkling, pouring, or immersion. Many permit families or individuals to choose the particular method

Clergy members baptizing a group of African-American worshipers outdoors in a river near Newelton, Louisiana, ca. 1982.   (Credit: CORBIS/Philip Gould.)

of baptism that best reflects their own needs and traditions. In some contexts, an emphasis on personal religious experience has led certain congregations to minimize the role of baptism for the church and the individual.

Fourth, the mode of baptism remains diverse among many churches and denominations. In most communions that practice infant baptism, the mode of baptism involves sprinkling water on the head of the child. Churches of the Eastern Orthodox tradition continue their centuries-old practice of immersing naked infants three times in the name of the Trinity. While Roman Catholic churches retain infant baptism as normative for entrance into the church, many have added baptismal pools for use in total immersion of adults. Most immersionist churches construct indoor, heated baptisteries in their houses of worship. Some rural churches continue to perform baptisms outdoors in rivers, lakes, or creeks.

During the 1980s, a document produced by the World Council of Churches titled *Baptism, Eucharist, and Ministry* engaged many American churches in a discussion of the unifying elements of that most Christian rite. It facilitated ecumenical discussion regarding the classic biblical confession of "one Lord, one faith, one baptism" (Ephesians 4:5) for all the church.

See also BAPTISM IN THE HOLY SPIRIT; BAPTIST TRADITION; BELONGING, RELIGIOUS; CHURCH; PRACTICE; PURIFICATION; RELIGIOUS COMMUNITIES; RITES OF PASSAGE; RITUAL; SACRAMENTS.

BIBLIOGRAPHY

Beasley-Murray, G. R. *Baptism in the New Testament.* 1981.

Bridge, D., and D. Phypers. *The Water That Divides.* 1977.

Moody, Dale. *Baptism: Foundation for Christian Unity.* 1967.

World Council of Churches. *Baptism, Eucharist, and Ministry.* 1982.

Bill J. Leonard

Baptism in the Holy Spirit

Although this term has been used in various ways in American religious history, its contemporary association is usually with the Pentecostal and Charismatic movements. American Pentecostals are accustomed almost exclusively to baptism by immersion in water on profession of faith. They use the phrase "baptism in (or with or of) the Holy Spirit" to describe another distinct experience that they visualize as an immersion in the Holy Spirit.

Since this is a spiritual experience, they proclaim as its evidence the outward sign of speaking in tongues. They derive this doctrine from the New Testament book of Acts. In the account of the Pentecost in Acts 2, the writer records that those who received the Holy Spirit spoke in other languages. Acts records other instances in which reception of the Holy Spirit was evidenced by speaking in tongues. From the passages Pentecostals have constructed their theology of tongues speech as the "immediate uniform initial physical evidence" of baptism in the Holy Spirit. They make a distinction between baptism with the Holy Spirit (accompanied by evidential tongues) and the gifts of the Spirit cited in I Corinthians 12 (of which speaking in tongues is but one).

While Charismatic Christians often speak in tongues, they tend on the whole to be less dogmatic about tongues speech as the uniform evidence of baptism with the Holy Spirit. They are also likely to prefer the language of "filling" to that of baptism. While Pentecostals have a low-church ecclesiology and may accept rebaptism, charismatics have often been reluctant to diminish the significance of their water baptism by expecting another baptism of any sort. Such people may refer more readily to being "filled" with the Spirit, in reference to the biblical image of the Old Testament woman pouring oil into empty vessels. While Pentecostals also find this metaphor appealing, they use it more readily for fillings with the Spirit subsequent to their baptism in the Spirit.

For Pentecostals, baptism with the Holy Spirit is primarily an "enduement with power for service." They make a close association between this baptism and their effectiveness in evangelism and other forms of Christian service. In this, they adhere closely to the views of some late-nineteenth-century non-Pentecostal advocates of a distinct baptism or filling with the Holy Spirit. One of these non-Pentecostals, Moody Bible Institute Superintendent R. A. Torrey, argued that one needed this baptism before undertaking any form of Christian work. However, Torrey differed from Pentecostals on the evidence required. Whereas he took the experience by faith, Pentecostals affirmed the need for a particular sign. One danger in the Pentecostal view, Torrey and others after him insisted, was seeking the sign.

Pentecostals also teach that baptism with the Holy Spirit has a relationship to holiness. For some Pentecostals, Spirit baptism follows the second blessing—an experience of entire sanctification that prepares the believer to receive what Pentecostals call simply "the baptism." Those Pentecostals who view sanctification as progressive rather than instantaneous also urge adherents to pursue holiness. Among early Pentecostals, baptism with the Holy Spirit followed seasons of prayerful, repentant waiting, known as tarrying. At the end of the century, this practice has generally been replaced by teaching on how to receive baptism with the Holy Spirit. In Pentecostal denominations, this still includes speaking in tongues. In other settings, it may not.

While Pentecostal denominations continue to urge members to seek baptism in the Holy Spirit, surveys indicate that many members never receive it. Denominations' wording on evidence is more contested within these groups than ever, as newer Charismatic and other movements exercise spiritual gifts without insisting on any one as evidence or without referencing a doctrine of Holy Spirit baptism. Theologians have challenged the validity of theology constructed on historical narratives. The experience around which Pentecostals built their movement is less central in Pentecostal and Charismatic circles at the end of the century than it was at the beginning or in the middle. Superseded by other signs of spirit possession, especially being "slain in the spirit," "holy laughter," and prophetic utterances (often offered by people who attend "schools of the prophets"), the traditional Pentecostal teaching on baptism with the Holy Spirit, with its evidential tongues and connotations of empowerment and holiness, is associated more with the past than with the present. For increasing numbers who embrace this spirituality, any spiritual gift or numerous "manifestations" may attest the Holy Spirit's empowerment. Outside of Pentecostal denominations, the term "baptism in the Holy Spirit" is not necessarily at the core of Charismatic spirituality. In the new century, notions of "filling," "possessing," "receiving," and "yielding" may be more cogent than the older language of baptism.

See also CATHOLIC CHARISMATIC RENEWAL; CHARISMATIC MOVEMENT; GLOSSOLALIA; PENTECOSTAL AND CHARISMATIC CHRISTIANITY; SPIRIT POSSESSION.

BIBLIOGRAPHY

Bennett, Dennis, and Rita Bennett. *The Holy Spirit and You.* 1971.

Christenson, Larry. *The Charismatic Renewal Among Lutherans.* 1976.

Hamilton, Michael, ed. *The Charismatic Movement.* 1975.

Hayford, Jack. *The Beauty of Spiritual Language.* 1976.

Horton, Stanley. *What the Bible Has to Say About the Holy Spirit.* 1976.

McDonnell, Killian. *The Holy Spirit and Power: The Catholic Charismatic Renewal.* 1975.

Synan, Vinson. *The Holiness-Pentecostal Tradition: Charismatic Movements in the Twentieth Century.* 1997.

Edith L. Blumhofer

Baptist Tradition

Baptists trace their beginnings to the early seventeenth century and a group of English Separatist Puritans who administered believers' baptism to one another while in exile in Amsterdam. These General or Arminian Baptists returned to England and formed the first Baptist church there in 1612. Arminians in theology, they affirmed free will, general atonement, prevenient grace, and the possibility of "falling from grace." During the 1630s groups of Particular or Calvinist Baptists began in London, stressing total depravity, limited atonement, the unconditional election of some persons for salvation, and the perseverance of the redeemed. Both Baptist groups practiced baptism by affusion or pouring until the 1640s, when total immersion became the normative form. Their early confessions of faith stressed biblical authority, freedom of conscience, a believers' church, baptism by immersion, congregational polity, local church autonomy, associational cooperation, and religious liberty. Indeed, they were probably the first in England to call for complete religious liberty for heretic and atheist alike. All Baptists practice two "ordinances" or sacraments: baptism and the Lord's Supper. Some Baptist groups such as the Free Will or Primitive Baptists also practice foot washing as another ordinance.

The Puritan dissenter Roger Williams (1603–1683) founded the first Baptist church in America at Providence, Rhode Island, in about 1638–1639. The movement expanded throughout the colonies, not without significant persecution from religious establishments in New England and Virginia. Divisions developed over theology and practice, creating numerous subgroups including the Calvinistic Regular Baptists, the more revivalistic Separate Baptists, Seventh-Day Baptists, Six-Principle Baptists, and others. A national foreign missionary society—the Triennial Convention—began in 1814. A home missionary society was formed in 1832. In 1845 the Triennial Convention split over slavery, a division that produced the Northern Baptist Convention (now American Baptist Churches, U.S.A.), and the Southern Baptist Convention. African-American Baptist groups developed during the mid-nineteenth century, as did a Baptist presence among German, Swedish, Norwegian, and other ethnic groups. Disputes over election, predestination, and missionaries led to the formation of highly Calvinistic groups such as the Primitive and the Two-Seed-in-the-Spirit Predestinarian Baptists.

Controversy has been and remains a hallmark of Baptist life. Throughout the twentieth century, Baptists confronted numerous debates and divisions, many of which mirrored controversies in the broader American culture. In the North, Baptists contributed to the Social Gospel movement through the writings of Walter Rauschenbusch (1861–1918). Many Baptists worked to establish settlement houses and other responses to poverty. In the 1920s northern Baptists divided over fundamentalist/modernist debates about the nature of the Bible, the role of modern science, and the use of creeds. These theological tensions continued throughout the century. In the South, issues of race, segregation, and civil rights confronted Baptists, black and white, often creating tension and division. Martin Luther King, Jr. (1929–1968), and many of the other civil rights leaders were Baptist ministers. African-American Baptist churches such as Dexter Avenue Baptist Church, Montgomery, Alabama; and Ebenezer Baptist Church, Atlanta, Georgia, also served as centers for civil rights rallies and demonstrations. In August 1963 four little girls were killed in the bombing of Birmingham's Sixteenth Street Baptist Church, an act that became a defining moment for the civil rights movement in the South.

African-American denominations also experienced division, even schism. In 1961 the Progressive National Baptist Convention was formed from a split with the National Baptist Convention, Inc., in a battle over denominational governance. In 1999 Henry Lyons, Florida pastor and president of the National Baptist Convention, Inc., was found guilty of financial irregularities in his use of denominational funds, actions that divided the convention between his supporters and his critics. At century's end, African-American Baptist churches retained a significant role in their communities while confronting significant social problems such as the incarceration of large numbers of black men and the absence of males in many African-American families.

The Southern Baptist Convention, America's largest Protestant body, claiming some 17 million members, experienced significant divisions during the last twenty years of the century. In 1979 a coalition composed of fundamentalists instigated a process of electing a series of convention presidents who would use their appointive powers to move denominational boards more to the right. The fundamentalists asserted that the convention was moving toward liberalism in its schools, literature, and leadership, thus requiring a "course correction." They were particularly concerned that the doctrine of biblical inerrancy (a belief that the original manuscripts of the Bible are

The Ebenezer Baptist Church in Atlanta, Georgia, on April 6, 1968, shortly after the assassination of the Rev. Dr. Martin Luther King, Jr. (Credit: AP/Wide World Photos.)

without error in every matter they discuss) be established as the primary theory of biblical inspiration for churches, ministers, schools, and agencies. Moderates asserted their theological conservatism but resisted what they believed to be a "takeover" movement by the fundamentalists. The moderates affirmed belief in biblical inspiration but refused to make inerrancy theories normative for all churches and denominational employees. By 1990 fundamentalists gained control of the national convention, creating major changes in denominational personnel and programs. State and regional divisions extended the controversy, with state Baptist conventions in Virginia and Texas controlled by the moderates, while Georgia, Florida, and South Carolina were controlled by the fundamentalists. Fragmentation led to the formation of new moderate-based organizations such as the Alliance of Baptists (1986) and the Cooperative Baptist Fellowship (1991). Many Baptist colleges and universities redefined their relationship with the state Baptist conventions, eschewing denominational control and establishing self-perpetuating trustee boards. More than ten new theological institutions—seminaries, divinity schools, and Baptist houses—were founded during the 1990s. These included Baptist Theological Seminary, Richmond, Virginia; Truett Theological Seminary at Baylor University; and McAffee School of Theology at Mercer University. North Carolina schools included Campbell University Divinity School, Christopher White Divinity School at Gardner Webb University, and Wake Forest University Divinity School. Baptist houses were organized at Duke Divinity School, Candler School of Theology, and Texas Christian University.

Baptists in the Appalachian region from Virginia to Alabama represented one segment of "mountain religion," with their own unique traditions and rituals. Primitive Baptists, Old Regular Baptists, Union Baptists, Free Will Baptists, and other regional groups were small and less formally organized than other Baptist groups in the United States. Although these groups remain small in number, their practices, such as outdoor baptisms, memorial services, foot washing, and preaching style (manifested in the "holy whine"), have created a distinctive Baptist identity. They are also determined to retain these "primitive" (New Testament) practices in the face of modernity, mobility, and other encroachments. One of the smallest Appalachian Baptist subgroups, the "No Hellers," represented a form of Primitive Baptist Universalism, insisting that divine redemption would ultimately find all persons before they leave this world.

American Baptist Churches, U.S.A., experienced significant numerical decline during the latter twentieth century, confronting controversies over the ordination of gay and lesbian ministers, the authority of Scripture, and the governance of the denomination itself. Baptist denominations, churches, state conventions, and regional associations experienced significant divisions over issues of homosexuality, divorce, abortion, women in the ministry, and other hotly debated ethical and theological questions.

When the presidential election of 1976 brought southern Baptist Jimmy Carter to the White House, American media gave extensive attention to the nature of evangelical or "born-again" religion in politics and throughout the culture. As president, Carter continued his longtime tradition of teaching Sunday school, serving a class at First Baptist Church, Washington, D.C. During the 1990s the media gave extensive attention to the ideological diversity of many political leaders who claimed Baptist identity. These included Republicans such as House Speaker Newt Gingrich, Senate Majority Leader Trent Lott, and Senator Jesse Helms of North Carolina, as well as Democrats such as African-American leader Jesse Jackson, Vice President Al Gore, and President Bill Clinton. Clinton's impeachment trial and related moral issues in 1998–1999 created significant discussion within the Baptist community regarding sin, forgiveness, reconciliation, and politics.

In 1979 Jerry Falwell, an independent Baptist pastor from Lynchburg, Virginia, founded the Moral Majority, a conservative religious/political organization aimed at promoting social conservatism and spiritual renewal in American life. The movement claimed significant influence in bringing conservative evangelical Christians—Baptists and others—into the political square, and in advocating such issues as prayer in schools, tuition tax credits for parochial schools, pro-life agendas, and other conservative causes. By 1989 the movement had largely disbanded, acknowledging its frustration, because changes had not occurred as hoped. The Moral Majority created divisions among Baptists, some supporting its agendas and others opposing it.

Like other American denominations, Baptists divided over the ordination of women for Christian ministry. Many Baptist groups reject it entirely; others support it strongly; still others have a mixed reaction. American Baptist Churches, U.S.A., have generally given greater affirmation to women in pastoral ministry, a tradition of female ordination dating to the nineteenth century. Baptists in the South, black and white, have been substantially divided over the issue, with a probable majority opposing the practice. Nonetheless, the autonomy of local Baptist congregations means that many congregations have chosen to ordain women. In 1963 Addie Davis became the first woman ordained in a church affiliated with the Southern Baptist Convention. Many women, ordained and unordained, have served in a variety of ministerial capacities in Baptist churches, and as missionaries, professors, and denominational leaders. Placement of women as senior pastors in Baptist churches, however, generally remains the exception and not the rule.

During the latter decades of the twentieth century, many Baptist churches felt the impact of the "charismatic" movement with its emphasis on "baptism in the Holy Spirit," worship services characterized by contemporary Christian music and drama, and involvement in cross-denominational religious groups such as Promise Keepers. Many Baptist churches utilized television as a means of evangelization, syndicating worship services and other programs. "In Touch Ministries," developed by Charles Stanley, pastor of First Baptist Church, Atlanta, Georgia, was one of the most widely circulated religious television programs in the nation. While promissionary Baptists continued to support career missionaries around the world, a growing number of churches also sent out many of their own members—youth and adults—in short-term missionary service, evangelizing, building homes and churches, and providing various types of medical care.

Baptist denominations in America claim more than forty million adherents, with innumerable denominational subgroups. Contemporary Baptist bodies also reflect a variety of theological orientations—Calvinist and Arminian, liberal and fundamentalist, promission and antimission. By the end of the century some Baptists, North and South, promoted a resurgent Calvinism as the appropriate theological center of the tradition. Others sought links with broader evangelical movements, while still others advocated more liberal approaches to women's ordination, homosexual relationships, and biblical interpretation.

See also AFRICAN-AMERICAN RELIGIONS; APPALACHIA, RELIGIONS OF; BAPTISM; FUNDAMENTALIST CHRISTIANITY; KING, MARTIN LUTHER, JR.; MAINLINE PROTESTANTISM; MORAL MAJORITY; PROMISE KEEPERS; RELIGIOUS COMMUNITIES; RELIGIOUS RIGHT.

BIBLIOGRAPHY

Ammerman, Nancy T. *Baptist Battles.* 1990.
Brackney, William H. *The Baptists.* 1988.
Goodwin, Everett C. *Baptists in the Balance.* 1997.
Leonard, Bill J. "Independent Baptists: From Sectarian Minority to Moral Majority." *Church History* 56 (1987): 504–517.
McBeth, Leon. *The Baptist Heritage.* 1987.
Washington, James Melvin. *Frustrated Fellowship: The Black Baptist Quest for Social Order.* 1986.

Bill J. Leonard

Bar Mitzvah and Bat Mitzvah

Bar mitzvah and bat mitzvah are the rites recognizing the beginning of responsibility for carrying out the religious commandments of Judaism, ordinarily celebrated at puberty, age thirteen for boys, age twelve for girls. "Bar" (m.) and "bat" (f.) stand for "son" or "daughter" but, more broadly, "one who is subject to," and "mitzvah" means "commandment"—hence, one who is now obligated to carry out religious duties and is regarded as mature in the setting of the duties imposed by the Torah. The occasion is celebrated in synagogue worship by according to the young person for the first time a principal honor of the liturgy. Specifically, the bar/bat mitzvah is called to participate in the public declamation of the weekly passage of the Torah (here, Pentateuch) and given the honor of reciting the corresponding lection of the prophets. The practice of including both sexes in the rite began in the United States with the Reconstructionist movement and is virtually universal in non-Orthodox synagogues. Orthodox Judaism does not provide for calling women to participate in the declamation of the Torah except when women alone are present, but provision for a bat mitzvah observance is made in many integrationist Orthodox synagogues. In Orthodox synagogues the bat mitzvah has yet to reach a standard definition, whether solely in the home or partly in the synagogue. In the state of Israel the bat mitzvah is marked by calling the girl's father and brothers to the Torah.

Because Judaism lays heavy emphasis on genealogical continuity of the children of Abraham, Isaac, Jacob, and their wives, the bar/bat mitzvah rite bears deep meaning for parents and grandparents, who see in the community's recognition of the young-

A thirteen-year-old boy reads from the Torah, during a bar mitzvah ceremony. (Credit: CORBIS/Ted Spiegel.)

ster a mark of the continuity of the heritage of holy Israel. That explains why a family celebration is associated with the occasion, relatives coming from distant places to participate in the rite. In some places elaborate parties, comparable to weddings, with meals and dancing, are held as well. When the bar/bat mitzvah is called to the Torah, the parents and grandparents participate as well. When the father ascends, he recites the blessing "Blessed is He who has freed me from responsibility of this one." The parents commonly recite the blessing "Blessed are you, Lord our God, king of the universe, who has kept us in life and sustained us and brought us to this occasion." In the same spirit, many Reform and Conservative congregations have adopted the rite of calling all practicing members of the older generation of a family to the altar and there symbolically handing the Torah scroll from one generation to the next, and finally to the bar/bat mitzvah. In that way the place of the newcomer to responsibility in the chain of tradition is established. It is common for the family of the bar/bat mitzvah to provide a celebration meal at the end of the services.

From the youngster's advent at the age of responsibility, he or she is counted for a quorum (ten persons) for worship and is expected to participate regularly in worship, and those who have reached the age of carrying out the commandments also lead the community in worship. In the United States it is not uncommon for the bar/bat mitzvah to lead part of the services on the occasion of the rite itself. The bar/bat mitzvah also may give an address on the occasion and expound the passage of the Torah read that Sabbath. The address ordinarily includes thanks to parents for nurture and guests for participating in the rite. In the State of Israel some bar mitzvah celebrations take place at the Western Wall of the Temple in Jerusalem, and on occasion Diaspora families conduct the rite there as well.

Although forms of celebration have changed over time, the recognition of puberty as the advent of responsibility to keep the commandments is well attested from ancient times. In the Mishnah (M. Nedarim 5:6) the vows of a boy from thirteen and a day are binding. Abraham rejected his father's idols when he reached age thirteen, and Jacob and Esau parted company at that same age; from then on, the bar/bat mitzvah youngster is expected to fast on the Day of Atonement and to don phylacteries at morning worship.

Confirmation, a variation on the bar/bat mitzvah ceremony developed by Reform Judaism in nineteenth-century Germany and commonly practiced in the United States, sometimes substitutes for and often supplements the bar/bat mitzvah rite. The rite is carried on for groups of young people, not individuals, ordinarily at sixteen or seventeen, when they have reached a more mature age. It is generally observed on the festival of Weeks (Shavuot) and marks the graduation of an entire class of a religious school. The confirmands read from the Scriptures and declare their commitment to Judaism, receiving certificates that they are accepted into the Jewish community.

See also BELONGING, RELIGIOUS; JEWISH IDENTITY; JEWISH OBSERVANCE; JUDAISM; RELIGIOUS COMMUNITIES; RITES OF PASSAGE; RITUAL; SYNAGOGUE.

BIBLIOGRAPHY

Cardozo, Arlene Rossen. *Jewish Family Celebrations: Shabbat Festivals and Traditional Ceremonies.* 1982.

Maslin, Simeon J., ed. *Shaarei Mitzvah: Gates of Mitzvah.* 1979.

Neusner, Jacob. *The Enchantments of Judaism: Rites of Transformation from Birth Through Death.* 1987.

Trepp, Leo. *The Complete Book of Jewish Observance.* 1980.

Jacob Neusner

Base Communities

"Basic Christian communities" or "basic ecclesial communities" (BECs) are probably the most accurate translations of the names given in Portuguese and Spanish to a new form of church organization that appeared in Latin America in the 1960s. More common in English, however, are the terms "base communities" and "small Christian communities." "Basic" or "base" refers to the social location of the participants: people at the bottom of society, the exploited workers whose labor is the foundation of the wealth and power denied to them. "Ecclesial" indicates the explicit affiliation with the visible church (understood denominationally or ecumenically). "Community" points to the sharing and solidarity expected of members.

Originally, base communities were predominantly Brazilian, Roman Catholic phenomena: groups of five to thirty Christian laypersons from among the urban and rural poor, usually without a permanent local pastor, gathering once or twice a week in one of their homes, or in a makeshift chapel in their neighborhood, to pray, sing, read the Bible, interpret it in relation to their own lives, plan appropriate action to improve their lives, and evaluate the fruits of previous endeavors. The exact role of the clergy and religious personnel in the launching, continuance, and dissemination of BECs—important indeed—has been much debated among sociologists of Latin American Christianity.

BECs started as a church initiative in about 1963, when Pope John XXIII encouraged lay experimentation and autonomy. BECs responded, first, to the scarcity of clergy. Second, they seemed one of the few available ways to counter the challenge of both Protestantism and Marxism, while revitalizing the church. Finally, there was a crucial contributing factor through the 1970s and 1980s in Brazil and Central America: As U.S.-endorsed dictatorships made it increasingly dangerous for workers to gather, organize, and/or protest while their living conditions worsened, the sacred space of religious meetings often became the only environments left where workers could still somewhat safely convene, organize, share information, and plan protests; but also, perhaps more urgently, they increasingly became vital places to find healing, mutual support, and occasions for the cathartic release of the pains and frustrations of daily life.

BECs contributed much to the education of those unable to go to school regularly. They also constituted a privileged place to become biblically literate, to build self-worth and leadership abilities, to question racism and sexism, and to internalize a democratic spirit of equality, dialogue, and collective decision-making—thus providing an arena for both the empowerment of the laity and a "new reformation" of the church, as Richard Shaull has suggested.

BECs thus repeatedly became places where liberation theology was transmitted to "the masses," and where their leaders got much of their energy, inspiration, themes, approaches, and examples.

In many countries, such as Brazil, Guatemala, and El Salvador, BECs became not just religious phenomena in the narrow sense (regularly serving as a platform for ecumenical and interreligious dialogue and initiatives), but also mainsprings of protests against poverty, exploitation, and the violation of human rights; BECs became loci for the democratization of society as well.

The backlash—from both churches and states—was overwhelming. From approximately 1966 on, hundreds of thousands of defenseless BEC members were killed by state-sponsored, U.S.-trained military, paramilitary, and police forces in no less than ten Latin American countries. Where church leaders clearly took the side of the victims, these forces did not spare foreign missionaries (even from the United States), local pastors, religious sisters and brothers, or even a few bishops. In the late 1980s, when the few remaining U.S.-backed military dictators in Latin America were being replaced by elected civilians, the probable cradle of the first Latin American BEC (the

slum of San Miguelito, in Panama City) was wiped out by U.S. bombs.

At the height of the BECs' flourishing, in the mid-1980s, some sources estimated their number above a hundred thousand, and their membership at two million—most in Brazil, precisely at the moment in 1984 when the democratization of society, which they had fought for, finally started.

At the end of the twentieth century, BECs seem to be losing ground. Ironically, more than the bloody repression, the causes of this downturn seem to be twofold: (1) the further worsening of the poverty against which BECs emerged (a worsening so severe that it has crushed hopes of, and enthusiasm for, social change), and (2) the arrival of democratization for which the BECs had struggled, creating other venues beyond the churches and consuming much of the time and energies BECs used to attract.

See also BELONGING, RELIGIOUS; LIBERATION THEOLOGY; RELIGIOUS COMMUNITIES; RELIGIOUS PERSECUTION; ROMAN CATHOLICISM; ROMERO, OSCAR ARNULFO; SOCIOLOGY OF RELIGION.

BIBLIOGRAPHY

Adriance, Madeleine Cousineau. *Promised Land: Base Christian Communities and the Struggle for the Amazon.* 1995.

Boff, Leonardo. *Ecclesiogenesis: The Base Communities Reinvent the Church.* 1977.

Torres, Sergio, and John Eagleson, eds. *The Challenge of Basic Christian Communities.* 1982.

Otto Maduro

Bawa Muhaiyaddeen

(?–1986), spiritual teacher.

His Holiness Muhammad Raheem Bawa Muhaiyaddeen, a venerated spiritual teacher in Sri Lanka from the 1940s to his death in 1986, brought his teachings to the United States in 1971 and became a major figure in the development of Sufism in the West.

Sufism is the mystical dimension of Islam, whose expositors, such as Hasan al Basri (d. 728), Rabia al-Adawiya (d. 801), al-Hallaj (d. 922), Abd al-Qadir al-Jilani (d. 1166), Ibn Arabi (d. 1240), and Jalal al-Din Rumi (d. 1273), sought to inculcate deepened devotion, an understanding of the forces of illusion and forgetfulness that cause separation from God, and a means of acquiring the "qualities of God"—his love, justice, compassion, patience, and wisdom. Bawa Muhaiyaddeen was a contemporary teacher (shaykh) of these traditional Sufi themes. In his early career his audiences in Sri Lanka were local Hindus and Muslims. Bawa's disciples in the United States also came from a variety of religious and ethnic backgrounds. His earliest American members tended to define themselves as "sixties spiritual seekers," inspired by Bawa Muhaiyaddeen's charismatic, loving character; his abilities in teaching "wisdom" through such vehicles as stories (from Indian Puranas to the Islamic "Tales of the Prophets"), songs, metaphysical discourses, artwork, cooking, and farming (the latter two terms were used in both their literal and their metaphorical senses); and his view of Islam as an essential state of unity without divisions of race, class, or religion. Bawa instructed his Fellowship to buy land in Coatesville, Pennsylvania, to be used for farming; for burial of members; for family gatherings; and for his *mazar* (burial site), which is now a pilgrimage site for Muslims and other spiritual seekers from around the world. Bawa's universal message of peace and unity was not seen by most of his early American followers as being directly related to "Islamic" religious teachings; Bawa was often referred to as "Guru" Bawa, a term with Hindu associations. Bawa made a clearer connection with Islamic religion when he had the membership build a mosque (1982–1983); although persons of any religion were welcome to visit and pray in the mosque, he instructed that the five-times prayer and Friday congregational prayers were to be practiced in traditional Sunni Muslim form. The Fellowship increased its international and African-American Muslim membership with the building of the mosque; however, the Fellowship has an openness to the variety of ways in which members define their relationship to traditional Islam. Bawa instituted such Islamic religious and cultural practices as the Ramadan fast, the Id celebration, *maulids* (celebrations) in honor of the Prophet Muhammad, and maulids in honor of "the *qutb*," a term used in Sufism denoting the spiritual "pole" or axis of an era. In the "Maulid al-Qutb," Bawa's followers honor previous qutbs, primarily Abd al-Qadir Jilani, a twelfth-century medieval Sufi shaykh, as well as Bawa Muhaiyaddeen himself, who is revered as shaykh and qutb.

The Fellowship has about one thousand members, with branches in locations other than Coatesville; a vast library of audio- and videotapes of Bawa's discourses (still used at Fellowship meetings); a press that distributes his books internationally; and an outreach program that includes prisons.

See also GURU; ISLAM; MYSTICISM; PILGRIMAGE; SUFISM.

BIBLIOGRAPHY

Muhaiyaddeen, M. R. Bawa. *Golden Words of a Sufi Sheik.* 1982.

Muhaiyaddeen, M. R. Bawa. *Islam and World Peace: Explanations of a Sufi.* 1987.

Webb, Gisela. "Tradition and Innovation in Contemporary American Islamic Spirituality: The Bawa Muhaiyaddeen Fellowship." In *Muslim Communities in North America,* edited by Yvonne Haddad and Jane Smith. 1994.

Gisela Webb

Belonging, Religious

Belonging to a religion can have many aspects, including a sense of identity, confidence that one knows the truth about the supernatural, hostility toward people who do not belong, emotional attachment to the group, and fellowship with other members. All these factors vary across individuals and denominations. The nominal Christian, who decorates a Christmas tree and hides Easter eggs for the children but never attends church and is not listed as a member of any particular congregation, belongs only in a sentimental manner. In contrast, a sect member who attends several meetings a week, has few friends outside the group, and frequently goes door to door to spread the doctrines of his or her faith belongs in a far more profound sense. When pollsters ask Americans superficially what religion they belong to, many respond in terms of their nominal affiliation with a religious tradition, which may merely reflect a vague sense of cultural identity. More painstaking research methods are required to reveal the complex and often subtle ways in which a person may be religious.

In the early decades of the sociology of religion, scholars tended to conceptualize religious identity rather globally in terms of the three major western historical traditions: Jewish, Roman Catholic, and Protestant. Classic studies, such as *Suicide* (1897) by Émile Durkheim and *The Protestant Ethic and the Spirit of Capitalism* (1904–1905) by Max Weber, described people primarily as belonging to one of these three heritages. For example, Durkheim noted that Protestantism was split into a number of denominations and sects, but for him this meant that Protestants lacked the full benefits of belonging to a religious community enjoyed by Catholics, rather than that each separate Protestant group was a community of belonging.

In the following decades, American sociologists of religion tended to write about denominational differences as historical residues that should be outgrown, or as the expression of unfortunate social conflicts that should be resolved. Even as late as the 1950s, American sociologists of religion conceptualized "the religious factor" primarily in terms of these three gross categories, and many even argued that they were in the process of merging into a single nationwide sense of belonging to American religion without any consciousness of sectarian barriers.

During the 1960s, however, the rapid development of survey research revealed that American religion was a patchwork of a bewildering number and variety of faiths. Some denominations began to some extent as ethnic churches—for example, German Lutherans; English Episcopalians; and Irish, Italian, and Polish Roman Catholics. The decline of ethnic barriers, however, did not lead to a blending of the denominations, because social and theological cleavages sustained differences between existing groups and even created new dimensions of religious variation. America has proved to be an especially fertile ground for the emergence of new sects within existing traditions and for the irruption of largely new traditions, pejoratively called "cults" but more neutrally called "new religious movements." By the end of the twentieth century, scholars had written about more than a thousand separate American denominations, any one of which was capable of providing a distinctive sense of belonging.

Members of a particular group may believe that the only legitimate faith is their own, and all others are mistaken or even sacrilegious. This view is called particularism, and it can be found among some believers and groups in every religious tradition. Many Christians believe that a person can gain salvation only through faith in Jesus and that everyone who rejects Jesus is damned. Survey research studies tend to find low levels of particularism among very liberal Protestant denominations (e.g., Episcopalians, Methodists, United Church of Christ), moderate levels in a number of other large groups (e.g., Presbyterians, Disciples of Christ, Northern Baptists, and some Lutheran groups), and high levels at the sectarian end of the Protestant spectrum (e.g., Southern Baptists and sect members). Overall, Protestant-Catholic differences are insignificant. Some sects are so particularistic that members are encouraged to believe that only those who belong to their specific organization will be saved.

At the extreme, particularism can be associated with outright antagonism toward other groups. In their influential book *Christian Beliefs and Anti-Semitism* (1966), Charles Glock and Rodney Stark argued that Christian particularism is a major source of hostility toward and discrimination against Jews. However, this study has been faulted for using rather longs chains of inference from one statistical analysis to another and for using measures of anti-Semitism that emphasized the doctrinal differences between Christians and Jews rather than focusing on actual behavior directed against Jews. Even if the claim was true when the data were collected, it may no longer be true today. Many evangelical Protestant leaders have made highly publicized tours of Israel, which may have reinforced positive images of Israelis as the heirs of the ancient Hebrews, thus encouraging philo-Semitism among particularistic Protestants. Members of particularistic sects see the world as a moral theater where good battles against evil, but they are quite capable of scripting positive roles for nonmember allies in this drama. The diffuse but powerful evangelical movement testifies to the possibility of cooperation among people in different particularistic groups, as long as they have a sense of belonging to a shared crusade.

Fundamentally, religious belonging means membership in a particular social group, with strong attachments to other individual members. This is clear in the contemporary sociological literature on religious conversion, which emphasizes that an individual must develop strong social bonds to members before he or she becomes a committed member of the group, and that attachments to nonmembers can prevent conversion. Few people convert merely because they find a group's beliefs attractive, or because they undergo an intense emotional experience. Rather, belief and emotional attachment tend to grow gradually under the influence of friends or relatives who already belong.

Generally, to belong to one religious group means not to belong to another, so all religions are to some extent particularistic and socially separated. To attend religious services at one place and time, with one subset of one's neighbors, means to be cut off to some extent from the other neighbors. People turn to religion to solve the inescapable human problems of death, deprivation, and meaninglessness, and a religion must demand something particular of its adherents if its promises are to be at all credible. The decades-long hope of the ecumenical movement that all Christian denominations could come together seems as far from fulfillment as ever. People feel the need to belong to a particular religious group, even if it is not theologically particularistic, and belonging to American religion in general is tantamount to not belonging at all.

See also CHURCH; CONGREGATION; CONVERSION; CULT; DENOMINATION; ECUMENICAL MOVEMENT; NEW RELIGIOUS MOVEMENTS; PROSELYTIZING; RELIGIOUS COMMUNITIES; RELIGIOUS STUDIES; SECT; SOCIOLOGY OF RELIGION; SYNCRETISM.

BIBLIOGRAPHY
Herberg, Will. *Protestant, Catholic, Jew.* 1955.
Lenski, Gerhard. *The Religious Factor.* 1961.

Niebuhr, H. Richard. *The Social Sources of Denominationalism.* 1929.

Roof, Wade Clark, and Wilham McKinney. *American Mainline Religion: Its Changing Shape and Future.* 1987.

Smith, Christian. *American Evangelicalism.* 1998.

Stark, Rodney, and William Sims Bainbridge. *The Future of Religion.* 1985.

Stark, Rodney, and William Sims Bainbridge. *A Theory of Religion.* 1987.

Stark, Rodney, and Charles Y. Glock. *American Piety: The Nature of Religious Commitment.* 1968.

William Sims Bainbridge

Bhagavad Gītā

The Bhagavad Gītā (Sanskrit, "The Song of the Lord") is the single most popular and influential religious text of the Hindu tradition. The exact dating of its writing is difficult; the best estimates are between 400 B.C.E. and 400 C.E. (Indian scholars generally prefer earlier dates than those of their Western counterparts.) Though it is self-contained and reads as an independent work, its seven hundred Sanskrit verses (divided into three sections and eighteen chapters) are placed in the sixth major book (*Bhiṣmaparvan*) of the Indian national epic the *Mahābhārata,* attributed to the sage Vyasa. This epic, an enormous collection of Indian legends, romances, royal history, theology, and philosophy, tells the story of a great Indian civil war (ca. 1200 B.C.E.?) between two royal factions, the Pandus and the Kurus. The Gītā begins as the leader of the Pandus, Arjuna, and his four brothers mass their troops to confront the evil forces of their usurping cousins and reclaim the kingdom that is rightfully theirs. In the face of the impending mass slaughter of relatives and friends on both sides, Arjuna, confused as to his true duty (*dharma*), refuses to begin the bloody conflict. His charioteer, Lord Kṛṣṇa (Krishna) who happens to be the supreme God incarnate, resolves his perplexity in an ongoing dialogue that clarifies and summarizes not only Arjuna's duty but also the nature of life, God, and the three paths to spiritual liberation.

The Message

Kṛṣṇa urges Arjuna to uphold his caste duty as a warrior and fight. Arjuna's confusion reflects a transition in Indian society from a tribal level whose worldview, the *karma* or action path, is focused on caste duty and priestly rituals, to a more complex society focused on growing feudal kingdoms and their expanding commerce and warfare. This social revolution helped to engender new religious movements: on one side a retreat into introspective, impersonal (and often nontheistic) mysticism, the *jñāna Yoga* or knowledge path, and on the other the rise of personal devotion to a single chosen deity, the *bhakti* or devotional path. In advising Arjuna, Kṛṣṇa reinterprets the ancient *karma Yoga* path; while acknowledging the path of jñāna Yoga that threatens to divert Arjuna from his social duty. He steers Arjuna, and Indian society as a whole, toward an active engagement with life, fulfilling traditional social duties with heartfelt bhakti to the supreme personal God. Any action, according to Kṛṣṇa, not just sacrificial rituals, performed as duty and without attachment to the results, can be a path of spiritual discipline (Yoga) that brings salvation. "Your claim is to action alone, never to its fruits; don't let the fruits of action be your motive, nor attach yourself to inactivity" (II.47). The easiest path to attain this equanimity in action is the discipline of devotional surrender (bhakti Yoga) to the Lord. "With mind fixed on Me you shall pass over all problems through my grace. . . ." (XVIII.58). Although three main paths to liberation are put forward, it is the bhakti path, supplemented by action and knowledge, that Kṛṣṇa emphasizes. Certainly Kṛṣṇa's awesome revelation to Arjuna of his "universal form" in chapter XI is a vision of the divine unique in world religious literature in its sheer intensity. Even so, the Bhagavad Gītā's interpreters have never agreed on its fundamental message, either in India or in the West. The text is poetic, unsystematic, and filled with philosophical ambiguity and a variety of viewpoints drawn (sometimes verbatim) from the Upaniṣads (Upanishads), early Sāṃkhya philosophy, and the devotional Bhāgavata movement. The genius of the text is just this mix, which appeals to different inclinations and social strata, opening Hindu religion to all, whether in the village or the city, male or female, high caste or low. The ambiguity and variety of viewpoints bolster reconciliation and acceptance of diverse paths to salvation. Traditionally it is read by worshipers of Viṣṇu (Vishnu) as well as Śiva (Shiva), the two principal deities of Hinduism. Leaders of the chief Hindu philosophical schools have each written important commentaries interpreting the Gītā for their own support. Śankara (eighth century), whose commentary is the oldest, saw it as a bulwark of absolute nondualism emphasizing jñāna-Yoga; Ramānuja (eleventh century) read it as qualified nondualism, and Madhva (thirteenth century) as dualism, both emphasizing bhakti Yoga. Nationalists seized upon it as a karma Yoga path to inspire their struggle for independence from British rule. Indeed, only since 1880 and the Hindu "renaissance" has the Gītā achieved wide popularity beyond scholarly circles, often as a symbol of national unity and a prod toward political action. B. G. Tilak (1856–1920) used it to justify violence in the name of patriotic duty and defense of traditional caste structures, whereas Mohandas K. Gandhi (1869–1948) relied on it to inspire nonviolent resistance to foreign rule and abolition of caste untouchability. In Indian law courts today Hindus swear with their right hand on the Gītā.

The Bhagavad Gītā in the West

The Gītā has been translated more often than any book except the Bible. The first English translation was by Charles Wilkins in 1785. In the United States the Transcendentalists were the first to celebrate the romantic appeal of Eastern wisdom. Both Emerson and Thoreau praised the Gītā in glowing terms and found in it an apparent confirmation of their own viewpoints, valuing inner discipline and intuiting the divine spirit in nature.

With a famous speech of Swami Vivekananda in 1893 at the Chicago World's Parliament of Religions, Americans became aware of a newly invigorated Hinduism, relying on the Bhagavad Gītā as its central text. This Hindu missionary succeeded in planting several chapters of a Hindu religious organization, the Vedanta Society, in American cities. At about the same time Madame H. P. Blavatsky's Theosophical Society, founded in New York in 1875, began to emphasize Hindu themes and promote its own influential translations of the Gītā by William Q. Judge in the United States and by Annie Besant in Great Britain, both emphasizing the allegorical and occult dimensions of the text and little informed by the Indian context. Gandhi himself, according to Eric Sharp, first encountered the Gītā in England in this theosophical milieu and popularized an allegorical rather than a historical or critical interpretation.

Among other influential readings of the Gītā in the twentieth century is that of the poet T. S. Eliot, who found inspiration in the text's vision of time and in the selfless path of karma Yoga. However, by far the greatest surge of Western interest in the Gītā took place in the religious counterculture of the 1960s, which, dissatisfied with traditional religion and social norms, encouraged millions of young people to experiment with new forms of consciousness and new types of religious experience. In this efflorescence of religious experimentation, disciplines (Yogas) of the East became widespread and popular. The Bhagavad Gītā held pride of place—no important teacher of meditation, yoga postures, or devotional worship in the Hindu mode could ignore its authority or refrain from commenting on its interpretation. Maharishi Mahesh Yogi, the founder of the Transcendental Meditation movement, emphasized the *jñāna*-Yoga of the first third of the *Gīta* to millions of followers. Likewise, Swami Prabhupada, the founder of the Hare Krishna movement (International Society for Krishna Consciousness, or ISKCON), made his literal interpretation—*The Bhagavad Gītā, As It Is*—the center of his own worldwide bhakti Yoga teaching. Famous stars such as the Beatles echoed and amplified these Indian movements by mixing their religious themes with psychedelic music.

From the 1970s the religious counterculture continued to blend the Theosophy and New Thought from the beginning of the twentieth century with Christian, Buddhist, and Hindu themes. These movements understood themselves as heralds of an evolutionary "New Age" of human spiritual development. Such New Age movements often found the diverse yogic paths of the Gītā congenial to their eclectic approach, harmonizing Eastern and Christian elements.

At the same time, starting with a liberalization of U.S. immigration laws in 1965, an increasing number of Indians immigrated to the United States and soon made their own ethnic religious identities felt. More than a million strong by 1999, Hindu groups now have multiple temples, most with regular Gītā study classes, in all major American cities.

The growth of interest in Eastern philosophy and religion that burgeoned in the late 1960s also promoted the academic study of non-Western religions. Today more than four hundred institutions of higher learning feature religious studies programs, and the Bhagavad Gītā, because of its beauty and accessibility, continues to be one of the most widely read and studied of world scriptures.

See also DHARMA; HINDUISM; INTERNATIONAL SOCIETY FOR KRISHNA CONSCIOUSNESS; KARMA; NEW AGE SPIRITUALITY; NEW THOUGHT; PACIFISM; RAMAKRISHNA MOVEMENT; THEOSOPHICAL SOCIETY; TRANSCENDENTAL MEDITATION; UPANISHADS; VEDANTA SOCIETY; VEDAS; YOGA.

BIBLIOGRAPHY

Desai, Mahadev. *The Gospel of Selfless Action, or the Gita According to Gandhi.* 1948.

Deutsch, Eliot. *The Bhagavad Gītā.* 1968.

Edgerton, Franklin. *The Bhagavad Gītā.* 1944.

Larson, G. J. "The Song Celestial: Two Centuries of Bhagavad Gītā in English." *Philosophy East and West* 31 (October 1981): 513–541.

Sastri, Allādi Mahadeva. *The Bhagavad-Gītā with the Commentary of Srī Sankarachārya.* 1961.

Sharpe, Eric J. *The Universal Gītā.* 1985.

Zaehner, R. C. *The Bhagavad Gītā.* 1973.

Lloyd W. Pflueger

Bible

The Bible (Latin singular *Biblia,* from the Greek plural *ta Biblia,* "the Books") is a collection of documents representing various literary genres: epic, poetry, legal codes, historical accounts, prophetic oracles, wisdom sayings, letters, and gospels, the last a unique genre combining features of biography and foundational legend. The Bible is meaningful to many religions in the United States; in it, Muslims, Jews, Christians, and Mormons find the sacred stories concerning the founders of their religions. The Bible is authoritative, however, only in Judaism and Christianity.

Origin and Contents

There are many "bibles," for each biblical tradition has its own authoritative collection of books known as a "canon" (from the Greek *kanon,* "measuring stick"). The Jewish canon consists of twenty-four books known as the Hebrew Bible, although parts of Daniel and Ezra are in Aramaic, a Semitic language less ancient than Hebrew. This collection is called *Tanakh,* from the first letters of the three Hebrew words *Torah* ("instruction"), *Nevi'im* ("prophets"), and *Ketuvim* ("writings"). The first five books, known as the *Torah* or the *Pentateuch* (from the Greek, "five scrolls"), are the earliest and derive from oral narratives traditionally assigned to Moses (ca. 1200 B.C.E.). These narrate the creation; God's covenant with Abraham, the progenitor of the Jews; and the giving of the Torah (the "Law") to Moses. Literary evidence suggests that the oral traditions were put into writing during and after the exile (586–539 B.C.E.), when the nation of Israel was conquered and brought captive to Babylon. The Nevi'im also date from the exile, though most of the prophecies were spoken by figures from the eighth through sixth centuries B.C.E. They warn Israel of the coming judgment of God, realized in the exile, for their disobedience to the covenant. The Ketuvim contain the latest of the books, some from as late as the second century B.C.E.

The Hebrew Scriptures are also authoritative for Christians, who know them as the Old Testament, or Old Covenant. The Christian canon takes three different forms that have their basis in the history of the Jewish canon. The earliest collection of Jewish biblical writings dates to the third and second centuries B.C.E., when the various Hebrew writings were translated into Greek for the many Greek-speaking Jews outside Palestine. Together with some later works composed in Greek, this collection became the Septuagint (from the Latin for "seventy," referring to the seventy scribes who translated it). When the Jews in Palestine, who still could read Hebrew, compiled their canon in the second century C.E., they admitted only those works

A Bible is displayed with symbolic candles on its left and right during a student mass at St. Ignatius Church, on the campus of the University of San Francisco, ca. 1989. (Credit: CORBIS/Phil Schermeister.)

written in Hebrew. Some of the later works in the Septuagint were either originally written in Greek or had lost their Hebrew original and thus were excluded.

The early Christians, however, were predominantly Greek-speaking, and had always used the Septuagint. Saint Jerome, although he could read the Hebrew texts, used this larger Greek collection as the basis of his Latin translation of the Bible, the Vulgate (from the Latin for "common," completed in 405 C.E.). This translation achieved authoritative status, finally ratified at the Council of Trent (1545–1563), and was the first book produced by Gutenberg on the printing press (1456). The Roman Catholic church uses this canon and thus has an Old Testament with forty-six books. The Christian reformer Martin Luther (1483–1546 C.E.) followed the Hebrew canon as the basis of his German translation of the Bible (1534 C.E.), printing the remaining books of the Septuagint in a separate section, the "Apocrypha" ("hidden things"). The Protestant canon accordingly contains thirty-nine books, because it excludes the same works as does the Hebrew canon (the Protestant Old Testament has a higher number of books because it subdivides several of the Hebrew works). Most Russian Orthodox do not consider the Apocrypha authoritative. The Greek Orthodox do, and include five additional books not accepted by Roman Catholics, such as Psalm 151 and 3 Maccabees.

The twenty-seven Greek works about Jesus and his teachings are authoritative for all Christian denominations. These are designated the "New Testament" or "New Covenant," on the assumption that they supersede God's covenant with Israel in the "Old Testament." These date from the mid-first century C.E. into the second century and comprise a number of biographies of Jesus (gospels), a history of the early church, letters of instruction to churches by Paul and others, and a prophetic oracle. For Christians, the Hebrew Bible is read in light of the New Testament, which is regarded as more normative.

Liturgical Use in Community

In modern American religious communities the Bible is the prime source of normative ethical and moral instruction read and explicated during weekly ceremonies. Jewish communities read the entire Torah every year, in short passages in synagogue each Sabbath, completing the cycle at the festival of Shavuot ("Weeks"). Sermons each week offer commentary on the text. Among Christians, the Roman Catholics, Episcopalians, and Lutherans have three set readings each Sunday (the two Testaments and the Gospel) on a similar yearly schedule called the lectionary, followed by a brief sermon. In evangelical denominations, the service contains no lectionary but consists of a lengthy sermon interpreting Biblical passages. For both Christians and Jews, the house of worship is also the location for the study of the Bible during the week, either in consultation with the leaders of the congregation or in organized study groups.

Individual Piety

From the Torah, Jews derive the 613 commandments that form the basis of their covenant with God. The ability to read the Torah in the original Hebrew is taught to children in Orthodox and Reform Judaism, and the successful public demonstration of this ability, expected at the age of thirteen, is a rite of passage into adulthood celebrated by one of the main ceremonies of Jewish life. The child who can read the Torah is known henceforth as a *bar Mitzvah* or *bat Mitzvah* ("son" or "daughter" "of the commandment"), and is expected to follow the commandments as a responsible member of the community.

Most Christian denominations have similar rites of instruction. In the Roman Catholic church, confirmation, one of the seven sacraments, occurs upon completion of a course in doctrine (the catechism) around the age of eight or ten; this follows similar instruction around the first eucharist, at the age of five or six. The Bible has received greater emphasis in this instruction since the Second Vatican Council (1962–1965), which also encouraged accessible English translations. Although for Protestants confirmation is not a sacrament, most denominations offer a course of formal instruction that marks an impor-

tant stage in a young adult's life, and the emphasis is usually on the Bible rather than on doctrine.

For both Jews and Christians, formal instruction in the Bible is only the beginning of a lifelong vocation of reading, study, and memorization. The Bible is the source of moral guidance and the basis of ethical decisions throughout life, and the revelation of the will and character of God himself. Proper application of its commandments is the primary form of personal piety in Judaism. The constant presence of the Torah in daily life is symbolized in most Jewish houses by a mezuzah at the doorway, a small box containing a parchment with a passage from the Torah. Many Christians engage in daily devotional reading of the Bible along with their prayers. For them, the Bible is the source of a unitary message of God's forgiveness of sins through the self-sacrifice of Jesus. Reading the Bible gives encouragement in personal difficulties through its message of God's love and providence. Some Christian denominations encourage memorization through contests or public recitals by young people.

Formation of Religious Communities

Attitudes toward biblical interpretation have defined denominational movements within Christianity and Judaism. Luther's original grievance with the Roman Catholic church concerned its role in the mediation of God's forgiveness, but he defended his position by biblical interpretation, extending the biblicist positions of radical reformers John Wyclif (1328–1384) and Jan Hus (1373–1415): *sola scriptura*, "scripture alone," not church dogma, was the only source of authority. This emphasis on the Bible, the Protestant Reformation's "paper pope," led to its rapid translation from the Latin Vulgate into modern European languages, which, coupled with the recently invented printing press and concomitant spread of literacy, made of Protestant Europe a continent of Bible readers. Many of the most radical colonized the United States. Their predilection for democratic preaching direct from the Bible played an important role in nineteenth-century American Protestantism, and Evangelicalism in particular. The Fundamentalist movement (ca. 1910) championed the literal inerrancy of the Bible, forming further denominations in the conservative wing of American Evangelicalism.

The Enlightenment of the eighteenth century marked a watershed in attitudes toward the Bible in all traditions. It was henceforth studied not only as a sacred text, but also as any other historical document, resulting, for example, in the discovery that the Torah was not written by a single author, but revised several times by editors with varying theological perspectives (the documentary hypothesis). This undercut the notion of Mosaic authorship. Reform Jews, although accepting the authority of Torah, correspondingly do not believe that Moses wrote all of it, which the orthodox do believe. The debate between these two movements about proper ritual behavior, such as how to keep dietary laws, is ultimately a dispute over the interpretation of the Bible in the modern age.

Culture

Even before the age of widespread literacy, the Bible dominated Western Christian culture as the source of narratives for art, literature, and music. Cathedral windows illustrating biblical stories were the "Bibles of the poor," available even to the illiterate. Widespread literacy led to the Christian possession of what Jews had always retained: a deep verbal resonance with the text of the Bible. Bible narratives were the content of early American primary readers, imbuing everyday language with proverbs and metaphors, such as "the blind leading the blind" (Luke 6:39). Every page of Shakespeare and Milton is dotted with biblical language and allusions to biblical narratives, an influence also perceptible in American classics such as Herman Melville's *Moby Dick* and the novels of William Faulkner.

American political life also owes a large biblical debt; the form of government itself derives from the concept of covenant found in the Hebrew Bible, and orators have turned time and again to the Bible for powerful language. The speeches of Dr. Martin Luther King, Jr., demonstrate how effectively biblical turns of phrase can motivate Americans to positive civil action, for the Bible expresses a heritage shared not only by Christians and Jews, but also by Muslims and by American popular culture outside the three monotheist traditions.

See also BAR MITVAH AND BAT MITZVAH; BOOK OF MORMON; EVANGELICAL CHRISTIANITY; FUNDAMENTALIST CHRISTIANITY; JESUS SEMINAR; JUDAISM; LITURGY AND WORSHIP; MAINLINE PROTESTANTISM; QUR'AN; RELIGIOUS COMMUNITIES; ROMAN CATHOLICISM; SABBATH, JEWISH; SACRAMENTS; TORAH; VATICAN II.

BIBLIOGRAPHY

Ackroyd, P. R., and C. F. Evans, eds. *The Cambridge History of the Bible.* Vol. 1: *From the Beginnings to Jerome.* 1970.

Anderson, Bernhard W. *Understanding the Old Testament.* 1986.

Frerichs, Ernest S., ed. *The Bible and Bibles in America.* 1988.

Greenslade, S. L., ed. *The Cambridge History of the Bible.* Vol. 3: *The West from the Reformation to the Present Day.* 1963.

Kee, Howard Clark, ed. *American Bible Society Symposium Papers on the Bible in the Twenty-First Century.* 1993.

Koester, Helmut. *Introduction to the New Testament.* 1995.

Lampe, G. W. H., ed. *The Cambridge History of the Bible.* Vol. 2: *The West from the Fathers to the Reformation.* 1969.

Christine M. Thomas

Bible Tract Society.

See Jehovah's Witnesses.

Bioethics

Bioethics seeks to reflect on the moral dilemmas encountered as society explores new ways of understanding and controlling the biological and physical world. Bioethics is both an interdisciplinary field of academic inquiry and a larger field of social discourse. As it emerges, it is most particularly animated by the intensity of the confrontation between traditional issues of theology or moral philosophy and the dazzling potential of the biological sciences, which have transformed contemporary medicine. The field of bioethical inquiry emerges at the points of convergence among the tradition of moral standards in the medical profession, the normative thrust of health law, and the classic pursuits of theology and philosophy, drawing as well on the insights of sociology, philosophy, psychology, anthropology, and literature.

Bioethics looks at theoretical questions in the development and pursuit of new scientific research, and at practical clinical questions, such as how to resolve dilemmas of reproduction, end-of-life decisions, and the basic social contract between patient and health care provider. Bioethics also reflects on the nature, goal, meaning, and ideological construction of medicine and of medical and nursing education. Essential to the field's aims and history is participation in the making of health care policy, the just distribution of health care, and the protection of vulnerable populations.

This multidisciplinary discourse between the broad range of humanities policy and the sciences was brought into being by dramatic changes in medicine in the post–World War II era, which changed medicine from a profession that largely reacted to what were believed to be the inevitabilities of the human condition to a science intent on changing the essential perimeters of human existence, of birth, death, aging and disease. Suddenly it became possible for mechanical creations and pharmaceutical interventions to alter apparent truths of biology.

The scientific advances opened troubling questions both for the scientists involved in the work and for philosophers, theologians, lawyers, and other "outsiders" watching from the sidelines. Just at the points where religion had offered faith, communal support, or redemption, medical science could deliver satisfying solutions, changing the very boundaries of the human reach. But with the power to extend life and challenge mortality came haunting questions of fittingness and of distributive justice. As these questions deepened, physicians turned to the moral traditions (which had long claimed the metaphysical-ethical realm as their own) as they collectively tried to set new limits on the reach and range of scientific advance.

New technology changed birth, death, and the venue of care and permanently altered medical norms in areas that had been considered solely theological. Birth control and safe legal abortion meant that sexuality and procreativity could be separated, and *in vitro* fertilization and other advances in reproduction meant that the central drama of the matriarchal biblical life—infertility—could now be addressed medically.

Replacement of parts of the body by machines (respirators and kidney dialysis) and replacement of one set of organs by another, taken from another human or from an animal body, challenged ideas about the inviolability and discreteness of the embodied self. Heart, lungs, intestines, liver, kidney, cornea, blood, bone, and marrow all could be exchanged in increasingly routinized procedures. Machines could maintain respiration and hence heart rates long after consciousness had been destroyed, allowing the emergence of new forms of existence, such as permanent, twilight-state comas named "persistent vegetative state."

The modern emergency room, the intensive-care unit, and other specialty units replaced the home, the charity ward, and the church as centers of care. New technology demands far more money and far more social organization than was available in any one family. No longer could the locus of care be family, church, or a healing that was based on a relationship to the community. Further, visualization of the unknown inner body with sonogram, MRI, CAT scan, and genetic testing meant that much more could be known and seen for certain and thus altered vastly; this changed the sense of power over the human body and fate.

Finally, in the long war between microbes and humans, antibiotics and antiviral agents seemed to ensure a victory. One by one the traditional plagues of humanity, named as death itself in many traditional religious texts, were eliminated, allowing the human life span to increase dramatically; adults now live far longer than ever before in human history.

At the same time that these biological barriers were being broken, social movements challenged traditional constraints of ideology and morality. Traditional values, a hierarchy of virtues, and family and community standards were uncertain loci of moral consensus. Finally, and at the very moment when scientific expertise and authority were triumphant, serious questions were raised about the moral character and the justice of the leadership of the medical profession. These questions emerged in a variety of venues. The first was the research setting. Postwar revelations of Nazi medical experiments; disclosure of serious violations of human rights and dignity in the Tuskegee syphilis experiments; disclosure of the harmful side effects of DES, thalidomide, and experimental drugs; and the use of human subjects in radiation research led to calls for codes of ethics that would respect the autonomy and require the informed consent of subjects. Such discourse led to the codification, first articulated in the Belmont Report of the National Commission on Human Subjects and later by national and state commissions on bioethics, of essential principle of bioethics: beneficence, nonmaleficence, autonomy, and justice.

Others raised calls for caution about the effects of science on the environment, or about the accountability of corporate-sponsored scientists to the public welfare. The ferment of the civil rights, feminist, ecological, and consumer activist movements created a climate in which the appropriateness of scientific gains was questioned at the very moment when science was able to deliver its most breathtaking advances. These movements led to national debate about the meaning, purpose, and goals of human life, and attendant ideological discourse about autonomy and freedom and the dangers of unlimited power. As it became clear that scientists were able to have tremendous power over nature—both our "nature" and the natural world and its physical limits—the issue no longer became the probability of the accomplishments but their effects and consequences in a world created by such unlimited power.

The field advances by such challenges to the theoretical approaches of ethics, and challenges to the accepted parameters of medical knowledge. Bioethics gains authority as a field at this juncture, asking what is gained and what is lost by so profound a change, such a radical transformation of the human condition. There are ontological, epistemological, and normative responses to this question. Identity, the nature of knowledge, and the problem of the limits of our ability to alter our very capacity and identity are at the heart of the field.

Bioethics asks these questions: What is the right act, the good, human, moral gesture? What makes it so? What is the meaning of a good life? How is a good life made? How is justice best achieved among competing moral appeals? Who should I be? How should I treat others? What are the criteria for knowing such things? How can society use technology for good? What sort of goods will benefit society in the long run? How can we ensure that the power given to medicine will be moderated? By whom? In a society of deep inequality, how can the marginal, the vulnerable, and the disadvantaged be protected from abuse of this technological power? How will we create policy to regulate our new power? What sort of enforcement mechanisms will be needed?

Challenges to the field emerge not only because of new technological advances but also because of our increasing awareness of the frailty of consent. Bioethics, in evaluating the moral gestures that make up human activity, traditionally assumed that humans are rational actors, capable of pre- and postreflective accounts of their action, and that they can give coherent linguistic justifications for their actions, relying on sociability, accountability, conscience, and rationality. But such a set of assumptions has been under increasing scrutiny. First among the considerations is whether a single standard for goodness, rightness of action, or even evaluative criteria can be constructed in a world understood as profoundly diverse. Both our expanding understandings of religion and culture and our attention to feminist insights have been central to the development of the field.

As a recently defined field, albeit with deep roots in older tradition, bioethics has been deeply influenced by contemporary scholars of religion. Theologians and religious studies scholars whose writings shaped the field in its early years understood that what was at stake in medicine was how technological possibilities, miracles, and burdens changed the meaning of ultimate questions of nature, purpose, and destiny. In each contemporary religious tradition, scholars and laity reflected on what their particular tradition offered in response, as theorists seek to explore the meaning of Jewish, Christian, Islamic, or Buddhist bioethics.

Religion offers more than an interpretive frame, a set of common textual languages, a venue for a discourse on morality, and an ideological coherence for bioethics. It also offers a praxis model. Bioethics and pastoral care often share the role both of witness at the bedside of the dying, and of creating a meditative and reflective process for families and staff as they face, together, the choices offered by new technology. In clinical medicine, for example, hospital ethics committees meet to discuss difficult ethical choices and to offer recommendations to the staff and family, working closely with pastors in both a supportive and an advisory capacity in the creation of a moral community that supports the consequences of the decisions. Medicine, law, and religions that are based in classical texts all must make changes in interpretations as new issues arise that could not have been foreseen in canonical texts.

For contemporary American religions, the questions raised by the field are central to the problems that leadership and congregants face in applying religion to their daily life choices, to moments of personal crisis, and to the moment when Americans turn to face the stranger as public justice is forged. Bioethics is of value because it seeks to create a common moral language that is wrought of the common experience of suffering and succor, of mercy and obligation.

See also ABORTION; ALTERNATIVE MEDICINE; BIRTH; BIRTH CONTROL; BODY; CHURCH AND STATE; DEATH AND DYING; ETHICS; EUTHANASIA AND ASSISTED SUICIDE; RELIGIOUS STUDIES; SUFFERING.

BIBLIOGRAPHY

Arras, John, and Bonnie Steinbock. *Ethical Issues in Modern Medicine.* 1995.

Beauchamp, Thomas, and James Childress. *Principles of Biomedical Ethics.* 1998.

Callahan, Daniel. *What Kind of Life: The Limits of Medical Progress.* 1990.

Davis, Dena, and Laurie Zoloth, eds. *Notes from a Narrow Ridge: Religion and Bioethics.* 1999.

Jonson, Albert. *The Birth of Bioethics.* 1998.

Lammers, Steven, and Allen Verhay, eds. *On Moral Medicine.* 1998.

Montgomery, Kathryn. *Doctor's Stories: The Narrative Structure of Medical Knowledge.* 1991.

Moreno, Jonathan. *Undue Risk: Secret State Experiments with Humans from the Second World War to the Gulf War and Beyond.* 1999.

Shelp, Earl, ed. *Theology and Bioethics: Exploring the Foundations and Frontiers.* 1985.

Veatch, Robert M. *A Theory of Medical Ethics.* 1981.

Laurie Zoloth

Birth

By 1960, American women were challenging the dominant medical model of childbirth from several political and religious perspectives. Today many "rituals" of hospital birth have changed as a result, and a vocal minority of women avoid the hospital altogether by giving birth at home or in birthing centers. Already in the 1950s, some women questioned what had become the conventional anesthetized hospital birth during which they lay alone on their backs with shaved pubic hair, hands strapped to a table, and legs in stirrups. They were encouraged by British obstetrician Grantly Dick-Read's (1890–1959) model of "natural childbirth" described in *Childbirth without Fear* (1959), which asserted that childbirth could be "spiritually uplifting." Women also joined grassroots organizations such as the La Leche League, begun in 1957 by a group of midwestern, middle-class Catholic women as a mother-to-mother support group that questioned medical attitudes toward childbirth and breast-feeding. In *The Womanly Art of Breastfeeding* (1958), the La Leche League urged mothers to ignore their doctors' orders about formula feeding and to breast-feed their babies, and advocated unanesthetized birth as an important benefit to a mother learning to nurse her baby. Religion played an important role in the turn of many Christian women to natural childbirth. In a religious context that was spawning the Christian Family Movement and other groups focused on family ethics, childbirth activists such as Helen Wessel (1924–), author of *Natural Childbirth and the Christian Family* (1963), argued that childbirth could prompt profound religious experiences.

Countercultural reformers who called for a return of childbirth to the home soon joined these more mainstream critics of medicalized birth. For example, Ina May Gaskin (1940–), a member of "The Farm," a Christian- and Buddhist-influenced alternative community in Tennessee, became renowned in the 1970s for her abilities as a home birth midwife, as documented in *Spiritual Midwifery* (1975). Feminism and the women's health movement soon brought a new perspective to childbirth reform, one that was decidedly less Christian. Feminist critics insisted on women's right to control over their birthing bodies, though many still insisted that childbirth was ripe with "spiritual" possibilities. The revitalization of midwifery in the United States was important for the growth of feminist interpretations of the spirituality of childbirth. The two national professional midwifery associations—the Midwives' Alliance of North America (MANA), formed in 1982; and the more medically mainstream American College of Nurse Midwives (ACNM), formed in 1955—both contend that birth is spiritually important for a birthing woman and her family and community. The emphasis that post-1960s midwifery placed on birth as not only a physical but also a spiritual event challenged medicalized portray-

als of birth while drawing from deeply rooted midwifery traditions from various regions of the United States. Latina *parteras* in the Southwest, African-American grand-midwives in the South, and Amish midwives in Pennsylvania and the Midwest have all played important roles in sustaining alternatives to medical models of childbirth. Currently the legal status of midwifery and home birth varies throughout the United States. While certified nurse-midwives are legal throughout the country, most practice only in the hospital. Direct-entry (nonnurse) midwives, who constitute the majority of MANA and practice mostly in the home, are illegal in some states. Therefore, the religiously diverse home birth movement remains "underground" in many states.

With the exception of distinct religious communities such as the Amish and some New Age communal groups, religious traditions have rarely cared to articulate consensus about modes of birthing, despite the extensive network of religiously sponsored hospitals. However, women from a diversity of religions have seen childbirth as a religious act. For example, Jewish Reconstructionist rabbi Tikva Frymer-Kensky, author of *Motherprayer* (1995), and Lutheran pastor Margaret Hammer, author of *A Spiritual Guide through Pregnancy* (1997), have argued that with sufficient attention and preparation a woman can make her birth a religious experience, whether in the hospital or at home. Others—ranging from Marilyn Moran, a Catholic and author of *Birth and the Dialogue of Love* (1981); to Carol Balizet, Pentecostal author of *Born in Zion* (1996)—have insisted that childbirth be left in God's hands (with the husband as the chief earthly authority), to the point of advocating birth without medical or midwifery assistance. The meanings of childbirth are intimately tied to constructions of femininity and the maternal body, not all of which are shared by those working toward childbirth reform or those satisfied with medical models of birth. As a result, the religious meanings attributed to birth in America reflect all the diversity of American religion itself.

See also Alternative Medicine; Birth Control; Body; Feminist Spirituality; Matriarchy; New Age Spirituality; Religious Experience; Spirituality; Women's Studies.

Bibliography

American College of Nurse-Midwives (ACNM). "ACNM Philosophy." Website: http://acnm.org.

Davis-Floyd, Robbie E. *Birth as an American Rite of Passage*. 1992.

Fraser, Gertrude. "Modern Bodies, Modern Minds: Midwifery and Reproductive Change in an African American Community." In *Conceiving the New World*

Order: The Global Politics of Reproduction, edited by Faye D. Ginsburg and Rayna Rapp. 1995.

Klassen, Pamela E. *Blessed Events: Religion and Home Birth in America.* Forthcoming.

Leavitt, Judith Walzer. *Brought to Bed: Childbearing in America, 1750 to 1950.* 1986.

Midwives Alliance of North America (MANA). "MANA Core Competencies for Basis Midwifery Practice." Website: http://www.mana.org/manacore.html.

Rooks, Judith. *Midwifery and Childbirth in America.* 1997.

Wertz, Richard W., and Dorothy C. Wertz. *Lying-In: A History of Childbirth in America.* 1989.

Pamela E. Klassen

Birth Control

Birth control refers to the variety of ways in which human reproduction is kept in check. The common term "contraception" means literally the way in which the process of pregnancy is stopped. Religious people hold a range of views on the matter linked to their anthropology and ethics. Such views play a major role in legal, economic, and political options with regard to availability, access, and use of contraceptives.

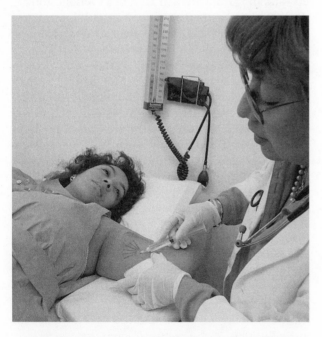

A nurse injects an anesthetic into a young woman's arm prior to the insertion of a Norplant birth control device in New York City, January 1993. (Credit: CORBIS/Robert Maass.)

Earliest forms of contraception thousands of years ago included crocodile dung used as a kind of diaphragm. There were also vaginal sponges and pessaries. Abstinence from heterosexual relations is the only 100 percent reliable form of birth control. But a range of other methods have emerged over time, including coitus interruptus (Genesis 38:8–10); rhythm (referred to as natural family planning); male condoms (especially important to protect against sexually transmitted diseases during the HIV/AIDS pandemic); intrauterine devices (IUDs); sophisticated varieties of diaphragms; female sterilization and vasectomies; oral contraceptives (commonly called the Pill); Norplant; injectable vaccines; female condoms; and, in some instances, abortions. The advent of RU486, a pharmacological procedure that acts to counter gestation, pushes the boundaries between contraception and abortion. Most of the methods are geared toward women's assuming major responsibility for birth control, including incurring health risks, even though a woman's right to make reproductive decisions is still limited in many instances.

Margaret Sanger (1879–1966), a nurse and midwife, was a pioneer in the birth control movement. While religious progressives have been identified with promoting birth control and religious conservatives with opposing it, important considerations of racist and eugenic motivations require nuanced discussion.

The breakthrough oral contraceptive, the Pill, became widely available for middle-class women in the United States and elsewhere in the 1960s. The so-called sexual revolution was in full swing. Models of family were changing, with the large number of children so common in rural areas giving way to a population-conscious two or three offspring and shifts in population to the cities. Women claimed that choosing whether and when to have children was a basic human right. In 1965 the U.S. Supreme Court declared access to contraceptives a right for married couples. In 1973 its famous decision *Roe* v. *Wade* gave women the right to obtain abortions.

Religious disagreements over birth control have been most virulent in the Roman Catholic Church, which continues to oppose birth control in any form except abstinence and rhythm. By the 1930s the Anglican Church had moved away from such a view, with most other Protestant churches following suit. Exceptions include the Mormon Church, favoring large families, and the Christian Coalition, opposing birth control information for young people. Jewish groups, while promoting family life and the growth of their community, tend to allow most forms of birth control. Islamic groups have been mixed on the question, with some form of birth control permitted virtually all the time. But Islamic traditionalists discourage contraception, since it might lead to promiscuity, or, if the birth control fails, to abortion, which they condemn.

The Catholic debate heated up in the 1960s, when the Second Vatican Council opened the way to church changes and the Papal Birth Control Commission recommended a more liberal policy. It culminated in the promulgation of an encyclical, *Humanae Vitae* (July 29, 1968), by Pope Paul VI, in which all "artificial means" of birth control were rejected. Widespread disagreement among Catholics followed. The religious issue was as much freedom of conscience as it was the actual use of contraceptives. Now a majority of U.S. Catholic women of childbearing age use some form of contraception prohibited by the Catholic Church. Ironically, total fertility rates in Spain and Italy, nominally Catholic countries, are among the lowest in the world.

The Catholic Church's position is predicated on the philosophical approach called "natural law," based on ideas of Thomas Aquinas (1225–1275) that certain behaviors and practices are "given" in the order of things and therefore ought to be normative. The "natural" end of heterosexual intercourse is seen as its openness to procreation. Opponents argue that contemporary contraceptive advances have made heterosexual intercourse without procreation just as "natural"—indeed, better—when personal choice and population considerations are taken into account.

In 1994, at the UN International Conference on Population and Development in Cairo, the Vatican and some fundamentalist Muslim groups joined forces to weaken language promoting reproductive rights. The debate has moved from birth control, about which there is widespread agreement to use it effectively despite the teaching, to abortion, over which many Catholics disagree.

See also ABORTION; CHRISTIAN COALITION; CHURCH OF JESUS CHRIST OF LATTER-DAY SAINTS; ENCYCLICAL; HUMANAE VITAE; MARRIAGE, CHRISTIAN; ROMAN CATHOLICISM; SEXUALITY; VATICAN II.

BIBLIOGRAPHY

Hartman, Betsy. *Reproductive Rights and Wrongs: The Global Politics of Population Control.* 1995.

McClory, Robert. *Turning Point: The Inside Story of the Papal Birth Control Commission, and How Humanae Vitae Changed the Life of Patty Crowely and the Future of the Church.*

Noonan, John T., Jr. *Contraception: A History of Its Treatment by the Catholic Theologians and Canonists.*

Mary E. Hunt

Black Elk

(1863–1950), Oglala Lakota spiritual leader and healer.

Nicholas Black Elk attracted international attention with the publication of *Black Elk Speaks* (1932), a narrative of his life and visions based on interviews by John G. Neihardt. Black Elk's "Great Vision," which came in a twelve-day coma when he was nine years old, revealed to him the roles of warrior, healer, and spiritual guide that would be his responsibility for the remainder of his life; the images also showed the coming devastation of his people, but ended with his seeing, from the top of Harney Peak in the Black Hills, a future when all peoples would live in respect and harmony. In 1882 he did his first healing, using a flowering herb he found that he had seen first in his Great Vision and later during a vision quest when he was eighteen; other power-giving visions guided him throughout his life. Black Elk's personal story often mirrors the dramatic transition in culture his people endured. He was a participant in or in the vicinity of significant events: the battle with Custer (1876); the killing of his cousin Crazy Horse (1877); and the Wounded Knee massacre by the U.S. cavalry (1890). Before the massacre, he had joined Buffalo Bill's Wild West show (1886–1889), hoping his travels would help him to understand the religion and power of the Wasi'chu, the white people; and after returning he had taken part in the Ghost Dance cultural revival initiated by the Paiute Wovoka. In 1904 he was baptized a Catholic, receiving the name Nicholas. He became a catechist for the church, often working with the Jesuits; appeared on the cover of *The Indian Sentinel* magazine of the Bureau of Catholic Missions in 1926; and was a representative to the Catholic Sioux Indian Congress in 1946. But he retained an affinity for traditional spiritual ways, and he wove them into his Christian faith; the two spiritual approaches had been integrated in his Ghost Dance vision of a man bathed in light, whom he later identified as the son of the Great Spirit. While earlier books focused exclusively (Neihardt 1932) or primarily (Brown 1953) on Black Elk's Lakota ways, recent works (DeMallie 1985, Steltenkamp 1993, Holler 1995) have rounded out his story with details and analysis of his life and work as a Catholic. Today Black Elk's legacy for many is his exposition of fundamental Lakota beliefs, ceremonies, and spiritual teachings; the ageless quality of this focus often obscures the Christian era of his life, when he internalized Lakota and Catholic spiritual dynamics as complementary expressions of sacred reality. Black Elk has become an inspiration to generations of Native American men and women seeking their historical and spiritual roots. Stories of his visions and teachings helped inspire the twentieth-century revival of Native American culture, and aided Native American indigenous peoples' human rights struggles initiated in the 1960s and continuing to the present. He is revered as a visionary, healer, and teacher among the Lakota, members of other indigenous cultures, and people of all faiths.

See also NATIVE AMERICAN RELIGIONS; ROMAN CATHOLICISM; SPIRITUALITY; VISIONARY; VISION QUEST.

BIBLIOGRAPHY

Brown, Joseph Epes, ed. *The Sacred Pipe: Black Elk's Account of the Seven Rites of the Oglala Sioux.* 1953.

DeMallie, Raymond J., ed. *The Sixth Grandfather: Black Elk's Teachings Given to John G. Neihardt.* 1985.

Holler, Clyde. *Black Elk's Religion: The Sun Dance and Lakota Catholicism.* 1995.

Neihardt, John G. *Black Elk Speaks: Being the Life Story of a Holy Man of the Oglala Sioux.* 1932.

Steltenkamp, Michael F. *Black Elk: Holy Man of the Oglala.* 1993.

John Hart

Black Muslims

"Black Muslims," a name coined by C. Eric Lincoln in 1960, refers to the members of one of the most militant and separatist black religious movements in America, the Nation of Islam. Although it uses the term "Islam" as part of its official name, the Nation is essentially a "proto-Islamic" movement; it utilizes some of the symbols and trappings of Islam, but its central message is black nationalism. Although it is not a part of orthodox Sunni Islam, the Nation can be considered as a stage in the development toward orthodoxy, which is a role it has played throughout its history.

In the midsummer of 1930, a friendly but mysterious peddler appeared among the poor rural southern migrants in a black ghetto of Detroit called "Paradise Valley," selling raincoats and silks and other sundries but also giving advice to the poor residents about their health and spiritual development. He told them about their "true religion"—not Christianity, but the "religion of the Black Men" of Asia and Africa. Using both the Bible and the Qur'an in his messages, he taught at first in the private homes of his followers, then later rented a hall that was called the Temple of Islam. This mysterious stranger often referred to himself as Mr. Farrad Mohammed, or sometimes as Wali Farrad,

W. D. Fard, or Professor Fard. Fard came to be recognized in 1931 as "the Great Mahdi," or "Savior," who had come to bring a special message to the suffering African Americans in the teeming ghettos of America.

Master Fard, as he was called, taught his followers about a period of temporary domination and persecution by white "blue-eyed devils," who had achieved their power by brutality, murder, and trickery. But as a prerequisite for black liberation, he stressed the importance of attaining "knowledge of self." He told his followers that they were not Americans and therefore owed no allegiance to the American flag. He wrote two manuals for the movement: *The Secret Ritual of the Nation of Islam,* which is transmitted orally to members; and *Teaching for the Lost-Found Nation of Islam in a Mathematical Way,* which is written in symbolic language and requires special interpretation. Within three years Fard had established several organizations: the temple, with its own worship style and rituals; the "University of Islam" to propagate his teachings; the "Muslim Girls Training" to teach female members home economics and how to be a proper Muslim woman; and the "Fruit of Islam," consisting of selected male members, to provide security for Muslim leaders and to enforce the disciplinary rules.

One of the earliest officers of the movement and Fard's most trusted lieutenant was Robert Elijah Poole (1897–1975), who was given the Muslim name Elijah Karriem Muhammad by Fard. As the son of a rural Baptist minister and sharecropper from Sandersville, Georgia, Poole had migrated with his family to Detroit in 1923, and he and several of his brothers joined the Nation of Islam in 1931. Although Elijah Muhammad had only a third-grade education, his shrewd native intelligence and hard work enabled him to rise through the ranks rapidly, and he was chosen by Fard as the chief minister of Islam to preside over the daily affairs of the organization.

Fard's mysterious disappearance in 1934 led to an internal struggle for the leadership of the Nation of Islam among several contending factions. As a result of this severe strife, Elijah Muhammad eventually moved his family and close followers several times before settling in 1936 on the South Side of Chicago, where they established Temple of Islam No. 2, which eventually became the national headquarters of the movement. Throughout the 1940s Elijah Muhammad reshaped the Nation and gave it his own imprimatur. He firmly established the doctrine that Master Fard was "Allah," or God is a black man, and that he, the "Honorable" Elijah Muhammad, knew Allah personally and was anointed the "Messenger" of Allah. Muhammad continued the teachings of Fard but also infused the lessons with a strong dose of black nationalism, which came from earlier movements: Marcus

Garvey's United Negro Improvement Association and Noble Drew Ali's Moorish Science Temple.

Under Muhammad's guidance the Nation developed a two-pronged attack on the problems of the black masses: a stress on the development of economic independence, and an emphasis on the recovery of an acceptable identity. "Do for self" became the rallying cry of the movement, which encouraged economic self-reliance for black individuals and the black community. The economic ethic of the Black Muslims was a kind of "Black Puritanism"—hard work, frugality and the avoidance of debt, self-improvement, and a conservative lifestyle. This formula soon made the Black Muslims conspicuously different from most of their fellows in the same socioeconomic class in the black ghetto. Their reputation for discipline and dependability helped many of them to obtain jobs or to start their own small businesses. During the forty-one-year period of his leadership, Muhammad and his followers established more than one hundred temples nationwide, innumerable grocery stores, restaurants, bakeries, and other small businesses. The Nation of Islam also became known for its famous bean pies and whiting (a kind of fish), which were peddled in black communities to improve the nutrition and physical health of African Americans. It strictly forbade alcohol, drugs, pork, and an unhealthy diet. Elijah Muhammad was prescient in his advice to his followers on nutrition: "You are what you eat," he wrote in one of his books, *How to Eat to Live.*

Muhammad's ministers of Islam found prisons and the streets of the ghetto fertile recruiting grounds. His message of self-reclamation and black manifest destiny struck a responsive chord in the thousands of black men and women whose hope and self-respect had been all but defeated by racial abuse and denigration and by addiction to alcohol and drugs. As a consequence of where they recruited and the militancy of their beliefs, the Black Muslim movement has attracted many more young black males than any of the other black movements or institutions, such as black churches.

In his book *Message to the Black Man in America,* Muhammad diagnosed the vulnerabilities of the black psyche as stemming from a confusion of identity and self-hatred caused by white racism; the cure he prescribed was radical surgery, through the formation of a separate black nation. Muhammad's 120 "degrees," or lessons, and the major doctrines and beliefs of the Nation of Islam elaborated on aspects of this central message. The white man is a "devil by nature," unable to respect anyone who is not white, and he is the historic and persistent source of harm and injury to black people. The central theological myth of the Nation tells of Yakub, a black mad scientist who rebelled

A black Muslim boy reads from the Koran during Traweeh Prayer in the holy month of Ramadan, when the entire Koran is read from cover to cover. (Credit: © Jeffry D. Scott/Impact Visuals/PNI.)

against Allah by creating the white race, a weak, hybrid people who were permitted temporary dominance of the world. But according to the apocalyptic beliefs of the Black Muslims, there will be a future clash between the forces of good (blacks) and the forces of evil (whites) in the not too distant future, a Battle of Armageddon from which black people will emerge victorious and re-create their original hegemony under Allah throughout the world.

All of these myths and doctrines have functioned as a theodicy for the Black Muslims, as an explanation of and rationalization for the pain and suffering inflicted on black people in America. For example, Malcolm Little (1925–1965) described the powerful, jarring impact that the revelation of religious truth had on him in the Norfolk state prison in Massachusetts after his brother Reginald told him, "The white man is the Devil." The doctrines of the Nation deeply affected his thinking; the chaos of the world behind prison bars became a cosmos, an ordered reality. Malcolm finally had an explanation for the extreme poverty and tragedies his family suffered and for all the years he spent hustling and pimping on the streets of Roxbury in Boston and Harlem as "Detroit Red." The conversion and total transformation of Malcolm Little into Malcolm X in prison in 1947 is a story of the effectiveness of Elijah Muhammad's message, which was repeated many thousands of times over during the forty-one-year history of the Nation of Islam under Muhammad's leadership. Dropping one's surname and taking on an X, standard practice in the movement, was an outward symbol of inward changes: It meant ex-Christian, ex-Negro, ex-slave.

The years between Malcolm's release from prison and his assassination, 1952 to 1965, mark the period of the greatest growth and influence of the Nation of Islam. After meeting Elijah Muhammad in 1952, he began organizing Muslim temples in New York, Philadelphia, and Boston in the Northeast; in the South; and on the West Coast as well. Malcolm founded the Nation's newspaper, *Muhammad Speaks,* in the basement of his home, and he initiated the practice of requiring every male Muslim to sell an assigned quota of newspapers on the street as a recruiting and fundraising device. He rose rapidly through the ranks to become minister of Boston Temple No. 11 and was later rewarded with the post of minister of Temple No. 7 in Harlem, the largest and most prestigious temple in the Nation of Islam after the Chicago headquarters. The Honorable Elijah Muhammad recognized his organizational talents and his enormous charismatic appeal and forensic abilities by naming Malcolm his National Representative of the Nation of Islam, second in rank to the Messenger himself. Under his lieutenancy the Nation of Islam achieved a membership estimated at half a million. But as in other movements of this kind, the numbers involved were quite fluid, and the influence of the Nation of Islam, refracted through the public charisma of Malcolm X, greatly exceeded its actual numbers.

Malcolm's keen intellect, incisive wit, and ardent radicalism made him a formidable critic of American society, including the civil rights movement. As a favorite media personality he challenged Dr. Martin Luther King, Jr.'s, central notions of "integration" and "nonviolence." Malcolm felt that what was at stake, at a deeper level than the civil right to sit in a restaurant or even to vote, was the integrity of black selfhood and its independence. His biting critique of the "so-called Negro" and his emphasis on the recovery of black self-identity and independence provided the intellectual foundations for the American "Black Power" and black consciousness movement of the late 1960s and 1970s. In contrast to King's nonviolence, Malcolm

urged his followers to defend themselves "by any means possible." He also articulated the pent-up anger, the frustration, the bitterness, and the rage felt by the dispossessed black masses, the "grass roots."

As a result of an internal dispute with Elijah Muhammad on political philosophy and morality, Malcolm left the Nation of Islam in March 1964 to form his own organizations, the Muslim Mosque, Inc., and the Organization for Afro-American Unity. He took the Muslim name "el-Hajj Malik el-Shabazz" after converting to orthodox Sunni Islam and participating in the hajj, the pilgrimage to Mecca. Malcolm was assassinated on February 21, 1965, while he was delivering a lecture at the Audubon Ballroom in Harlem.

From 1965 until Elijah Muhammad's death in February 1975, the Nation of Islam prospered economically, but its membership never surged again. Minister Louis X of Boston, also called Louis Abdul Haleem Farrakhan, replaced Malcolm as the National Representative and the head minister of Temple No. 7 in New York. During this period the Nation acquired an ultramodern printing press, cattle farms in Georgia and Alabama, and a bank in Chicago.

After a bout of illness, Muhammad died in Chicago, and one of his six sons, Wallace Deen Muhammad (later Imam Warith Deen Mohammed), was named Supreme Minister of the Nation of Islam. However, two months later Wallace shocked his Black Muslim followers and the world by declaring that whites were no longer viewed as devils and they could join the movement. He began to make radical changes in the doctrines and the structure of the Nation of Islam and moved it in the direction of orthodox Sunni Islam. Wallace dismantled the Nation and created the American Muslim Mission, which is now called the Muslim American Society, the largest movement of African-American Sunni Muslims.

The changes introduced by Imam Warith Deen Muhammad led to a splintering of the movement, especially among the hard-core black nationalist followers. In 1977 Minister Louis Farrakhan led a schismatic group that succeeded in resurrecting the old Nation of Islam. Farrakhan's Nation, which is also based in Chicago, retains the black nationalist and separatist beliefs and doctrines that were central to the teachings of Elijah Muhammad. Minister Farrakhan displays much of the charisma and forensic candor of Malcolm X, and his message of black nationalism is again directed to those mired in the underclass, as well as to disillusioned intellectuals, via the Nation's *Final Call* newspaper and popular musical rap groups such as Public Enemy. Besides rebuilding the Nation, Minister Farrakhan's greatest achievement was in mobilizing the Million Man March on October 19, 1995, in Washington, D.C., the largest event of its kind in American history.

For more than sixty years, the Nation of Islam in its various forms has become the longest-lasting and most enduring of the black militant and separatist movements that have occasionally appeared in the history of black people in the United States. Besides its crucial role in the development of the black consciousness movement, the Nation is important for having introduced Islam as a fourth major religious tradition in American society, alongside Protestantism, Catholicism, and Judaism.

See also AFRICAN-AMERICAN RELIGIONS; CIVIL RIGHTS MOVEMENT; FARD, W. D.; FARRAKHAN, LOUIS; ISLAM; KING, MARTIN LUTHER, JR.; MALCOLM X; MUHAMMAD, ELIJAH KARRIEM; MUHAMMAD, WARITH DEEN; MUSLIM BROTHERHOOD; NATION OF ISLAM; PRISON AND RELIGION; PROSELYTIZING; QUR'AN.

BIBLIOGRAPHY

Breitman, George, ed. *Malcolm X Speaks.* 1965.

Clegg, Andrew Claude, III. *An Original Man: The Life and Times of Elijah Muhammad.* 1997.

Essien-Udom, E. U. *Black Nationalism: A Search for Identity in America.* 1962.

Farrakhan, Louis. *A Torchlight for America.* 1990.

Gardell, Mattias. *In the Name of Elijah Muhammad: Louis Farrakhan and the Nation of Islam.* 1996.

Lincoln, C. Eric. *The Black Muslims in America.* 1960.

Mamiya, Lawrence H. "From Black Muslim to Bilalian: The Evolution of a Movement." *Journal for the Scientific Study of Religion* 21, 2 (1982):138–152.

Muhammad, Elijah. *Message to the Black Man in America.* 1965.

Muhammad, Warith Deen. *As the Light Shineth from the East.* 1980.

Waugh, Earle H., Baha Abu-Laban, and Regula B. Qureshi, eds. *The Muslim Community in North America.* 1983.

Lawrence H. Mamiya

Blasphemy

In the most general sense blasphemy is an offense, in word, symbol, or action, against the sacred. The sacred may be the deity, a person, an object, or a doctrine. Blasphemy is usually associated with monotheistic religions—religions that recognize and worship one god. The offense can also occur in polytheistic religions—religions with more than one god. It is often the case, however, that polytheistic religions would use "sacrilege" to connote similar concepts.

The concept of blasphemy in the Hebrew Bible is limited in scope. In the Mosaic law is the regulation "Do not blaspheme (or revile) God or curse the ruler of your people" (Exodus 22:28). The text, however, gives no further indication at this point of what it means. The most notable text on blasphemy in the Hebrew Bible is in Leviticus 24:10–23. In this story, a man whose mother was an Israelite and whose father was an Egyptian fought with another Israelite in the camp. During the fight the former "blasphemed the name of the Lord with a curse" (Leviticus 24:11). The Israelites kept the accused blasphemer in custody until God indicated what should be done. The word came through Moses that the man should be taken outside the camp and stoned to death.

This event in Leviticus indicates that the penalty for blaspheming the name of God was death. Further, interpreters generally agree that the offense against God consisted of pronouncing aloud his ineffable name. Talmudic teaching later expanded this tradition by declaring that in a trial of one having blasphemed by speaking God's name aloud, the exact words of the offender could be repeated only before the judges alone. All others present at the trial had to be dismissed from the room. And having heard the name, the judges stood and tore their clothes as a sign of their grief and mourning over this sinful act.

The New Testament accepted the Jewish teaching on what constituted blasphemy and added the offense of rejecting Jesus as the Christ and speaking evil of him or his actions. Jesus himself was accused of blasphemy on several occasions (e.g., Matthew 9:3, 26:65; John 10:33). But Christian interpreters of these and other verses take the meaning to be that it was Jesus' accusers who actually committed the blasphemy by reviling and not believing in Jesus.

Islam does not have any laws or prohibitions against blasphemy as such. The Qur'an does include teaching against infidelity and apostasy. Infidelity, the Islamic concept perhaps most closely related to blasphemy, is the intentional rejection of God and divine revelation. Islamic law further makes clear that any insult to God, to Muhammad, or to any part of divine revelation is a crime. Without actually using the term, Islam generally considers blasphemy to be any statement that is an indication of apostasy. This concept of blasphemy is more or less equivalent to heresy, which is any teaching at variance with orthodox Islamic teaching. Heresy not only is a crime against Islam but also can be understood as a crime against the state.

The Christian Church has at times made a similar identification between blasphemy and heresy. In the first four Christian centuries many competing forms of Christianity spread around the Mediterranean world. These forms variously claimed that Jesus was human and not divine, or divine and not human; that he had one nature and two wills; that he had two natures and two wills; and so on. Controversies raged over the concept of the Trinity, its nature, and the supposed relationship of the persons of the Trinity. The various advocates of the competing positions frequently leveled the accusation of blasphemy at their opponents. The early Christians used the accusations as a tool to try to win support for their differing positions. Through these early centuries, as an orthodox Christian consensus emerged and was codified at the Council of Nicea (325 C.E.), the emergent majority moved away from calling dissenting opinions blasphemy. "Heresy" was the term that emerged after the great councils of the church established an orthodox doctrine. For the church in the Middle Ages heresy was a more useful concept than blasphemy because it was not weighed down or confined by biblical teaching as to what it meant. Therefore, church leaders could bend or alter the term to fit a variety of situations.

During and after the Reformation in the sixteenth century the Roman Catholic Church leveled the charge of blasphemy against Protestants. Protestants, in turn, later charged Anabaptists, Quakers, Baptists, and others with blasphemy.

Through the centuries following the Reformation the churches used the threat of the allegation of blasphemy with decreasing frequency. However, there was a surge in the number of blasphemy trials in the United States and England in the late eighteenth and early nineteenth centuries. In the majority of the cases the issues had more to do with maintaining the peace of a community than with any supposed blasphemy. By the turn of the twentieth century the number of occurrences had again decreased.

In the United States there have been few blasphemy trials in the twentieth century. Even so, several states still have blasphemy laws on the books. However, the current interpretation of the First Amendment by the U.S. Supreme Court renders these laws essentially unenforceable.

From time to time various religious groups still raise the concept of blasphemy. Most recently two specific cases have drawn a good deal of attention, and both occurred in 1988. The first had to do with the release of the film *The Last Temptation of Christ*. In the film, based on a novel by Nikos Kazantzakis, Jesus is depicted as having the experience of coming down from the cross and living a full and happy life. He married, had children, and lived to his old age. This is his last temptation and one that he ultimately overcomes. Even so, conservative Christians in the United States were outraged by the idea at the heart of the film. Protests were mounted around the country. The film played in movie theaters for a short time before going to video.

The second occurrence was related neither to the Christian tradition nor to the United States specifically. It was the controversy surrounding the publication of *The Satanic Verses* by Salman Rushdie. The reason this case is mentioned here is that while Islam does not actually have a doctrine on blasphemy, the popular understanding of Rushdie's offense was that he had committed the crime. The Ayatollah Khomeini of Iran rendered a nonbinding decision, called a *fatwa*, that the book indicated Rushdie's apostasy and proclaimed that the author should die. Popular media interpreted the fatwa as a death sentence. Rushdie was forced to live in seclusion. Even now, after Khomeini's death, some consider the death proclamation still in effect, though it has been officially lifted.

Blasphemy has had different meanings at different times. The threat of punishment for this offense has been used by many majorities to silence dissenting voices and to maintain stability in both church and state.

See also ALLAH; CHURCH AND STATE; FREEDOM OF RELIGION; GOD; HERESY; RELIGIOUS PERSECUTION; SACRILEGE.

BIBLIOGRAPHY

Brichto, Herbert Chanan. "Blasphemy." In *Encyclopedia Judaica*. 1971.

Buckley, G. A. "Blasphemy." In *New Catholic Encyclopedia*. 1967.

De Vries, S. J. "Blasphemy." In *Interpreters' Dictionary of the Bible*. 1962.

Ernst, Carl W. "Blasphemy: Islamic Concept." In *Encyclopedia of Religion*. 1987.

Lawton, David. *Blasphemy*. 1993.

Levy, Leonard W. *Blasphemy: Verbal Offense Against the Sacred, from Moses to Salman Rushdie*. 1993.

Levy, Leonard W. *Treason Against God: A History of the Offense of Blasphemy*. 1981.

Tommy L. Faris

Body

In recent years, numerous scholars of religion have focused their studies on the human body, asking questions such as: How do different religions understand the human body? In what ways does one's individual body reflect social and cultural religious understandings? How is the body used in religious practices, such as during rituals? In what ways do religious feelings and experiences become embodied? Along with these more practical research questions come theoretical and philosophical debates about the relationship between mind and body, the subjectivity or objectivity of the body, the embodiment of knowledge, and the use of the body to reflect and resist social power relations. In her 1989 Presidential Address to the Society for the Scientific Study of Religion, Meredith B. McGuire asked her audience to consider how their work might change if they were to include their research subjects' physical bodies within their analytical scope. McGuire was referring to the historical tendency of religious study to concern itself more with religious institutions and ideas than with how people physically express and experience their religiosity. Thus scholars in many disciplines—sociology, anthropology, psychology, history, and theology—are now focusing on how human bodies act within and are shaped by their religiocultural social contexts.

One of the central problems in studying the human body is defining exactly what it is. Regardless of their seemingly obvious biological concreteness, bodies have no meaningful existence outside the social spheres within which they function; bodies are, in a sense, reflections or symbols of their cultures. The religious actor's body is a changeable site that is continuously being molded by one's religious community to reveal the group's beliefs and values about human existence. For example, according to anthropologist Mary Douglas, who was the first social scientist to pay close attention to ways in which the natural human body symbolizes the social body (*Natural Symbols,* 1973; *Purity and Danger,* 1966), religious communities that promote clearly defined social boundaries between themselves and the larger world tend to have strict regulations about individual members' bodily activities. Thus, among contemporary American Orthodox Jews, who live in close-knit communities to maintain social and religious purity, specific bodily practices—hair and clothing styles, food and sexual practices, and family and community religious rituals—define the group as separate from and different from the larger culture.

Human bodies are not only the objects of shaping or control by their religious cultures; they are also subjects embodying human agents who are empowered to reproduce and express the values of their religious social groups and to experience those values physically and emotionally in deeply meaningful ways. This distinction between the body as object or social construction and the body as subject or agent of religious expression, personal experience, and social change—a distinction often expressed in terms of power relations of domination and resistance—is a central issue in discussions about the human body.

The debate has been clearly defined by feminist scholars, who, beginning in the 1970s, were some of the earliest and most influential theorists to articulate the importance of attending to corporeal experience, especially that of women. Many scholars are working to find ways to view the embodied human being as simultaneously a social construction and an individual agent. For ritual studies theorist Catherine Bell (*Ritual Theory, Ritual Practice,* 1992), a religious ritual inscribes its particular schema on the body of a participant by regulating appropriate gestures, speech, or bodily adornment, and, in so doing, empowers the participants to act with mastery to experience and manipulate the ritual for their own purposes. What makes religious practices particularly powerful for these enactments of domination and resistance is that they affect the individual below the level of explicit social discourse; social schema are absorbed and reproduced in new ways by the body without necessarily reaching personal consciousness. During a Christian Pentecostal or charismatic worship service, for example, while participants understand their active physical expressions and intense emotional experiences as divinely inspired, their bodies have, in fact, through identification with the expectations of the particular religiocultural group, absorbed a corporeal knowledge about how to behave and feel in ways appropriate to that group. Some charismatic Christian women, having assumed personal mastery of these ritual activities, have empowered themselves to subvert traditional gender roles and act with authority both publicly within the social group and privately within their families.

The trend in academia is toward further analyses of the human body that locate specific bodies in particular, concrete social settings, to detail more clearly how religious cultures and human bodies interact and engender change in each other. Theoretically, scholars continue to struggle with how to define the human body and understand how human beings create religious meanings that are not merely conceptual but also grounded in immediate, embodied experiences and practices.

See also FEMINIST SPIRITUALITY; FEMINIST THEOLOGY; GENDER ROLES; PRACTICE; PSYCHOLOGY OF RELIGION; RELIGIOUS COMMUNITIES; RELIGIOUS STUDIES; RITUAL; SOCIOLOGY OF RELIGION.

BIBLIOGRAPHY

Coakley, Sarah, ed. *Religion and the Body.* 1997.
Hollywood, Amy. "Transcending Bodies." *Religious Studies Review* 25 (1999): 13–18.
LaFleur, William R. "Body." In *Critical Terms for Religious Studies,* edited by Mark C. Taylor. 1998.

McGuire, Meredith B. "Religion and the Body: Re-materializing the Human Body in the Social Sciences of Religion." *Journal for the Scientific Study of Religion* 29 (1990): 283–296.

Martha L. Finch-Jewell

Book of Changes.

See I Ching.

Book of Common Prayer

The Book of Common Prayer, understood as a unifying symbol of Anglican tradition and worship, represents a common core of worship services, patterns, and language that draws on the traditions of early Christianity and holds together diverse perspectives within the U.S. Episcopal Church.

The prayer book traces its history to England, following Henry VIII's break with the Roman Catholic Church in 1531. The first English-language version, published in 1549, contained the official prayer services, communion, and sacramental rites of the Church of England. Subsequent revisions reflected struggles among Puritan, Reform, and Catholic factions and the influences they sought to exert on the church, as well as political and religious interests of the throne.

With the U.S. Episcopal Church's emergence following the Revolutionary War, severed from its Church of England roots, an Americanized version of the Book of Common Prayer was adopted in 1789, although with a distinct Scottish influence that reflected the strong ties the new denomination had formed with the Episcopal Church of Scotland. The new prayer book also was influenced by Anglican clergyman John Wesley's revised services for American Methodists, and the revised liturgy adopted by the independent King's Chapel in Boston.

The U.S. Book of Common Prayer underwent revision in 1892 and 1928. Yet the mid-twentieth century's growing interest in ecumenism, liturgy, and early church practices, combined with a decreasing tolerance of archaic worship language rather than contemporary usage, resulted in the most radical revision of the Book of Common Prayer to date. A series of Prayer Book Studies was commissioned in 1949, culminating in final approval of a new prayer book thirty years later. The 1979 revision has been recognized for including both traditional and contemporary worship forms as well as a flexible rite for the worship needs of specific occasions or communities,

for placing Holy Communion as the central act of worship, for pastoral sensitivity, and for urging laity to participate actively in corporate worship and ministry. It also reflects diverse ecumenical perspectives, including both Catholic and evangelical influences.

A strong dissenting movement against the 1979 Book of Common Prayer came from the Prayer Book Society, claiming about ten thousand members, which decried both the loss of traditional language and the liberalizing theology underlying the revisions. Criticism also has been leveled by feminists for the prayer book's androcentric wording and imagery, with concern about its power to shape both sacred and secular relationships. Work on a new revision was authorized by the Episcopal Church General Convention in 1994, and reinforced in 1997 by the initiation of a process for authorizing additional worship forms that reflect multicultural, multiethnic, multilingual, and multigenerational realities in society.

The Book of Common Prayer has been studied by other religious traditions intrigued by its common liturgical core as well as its flexibility and diversity. Similarities to the United Methodist Book of Worship remain evident. Comparison of the compatibility of the Book of Common Prayer and the Lutheran Book of Worship has been central to the ongoing work of developing intercommunion between those denominations.

See also EPISCOPAL CHURCHES; JOURNALISM, RELIGIOUS; LITURGY AND WORSHIP; PRAYER; PUBLISHING, RELIGIOUS; RELIGIOUS STUDIES.

BIBLIOGRAPHY

Hatchett, Marion J. *Commentary on the American Prayer Book.* 1981.

Summer, David E. *The Episcopal Church's History 1945–1985.* 1987.

Paula D. Nesbitt

Book of Mormon

The Book of Mormon is a foundational sacred text for the Church of Jesus Christ of Latter-day Saints (whose members are commonly called "Mormons," after the book itself). Mormonism was organized as a religion after Joseph Smith, the movement's founder, published the Book of Mormon in upstate New York in 1830. Smith claimed to have been led by an angel to a cache of buried golden plates, which contained a record of the former inhabitants of the American continent. He was then given the ability and the tools

Mormon Church President Gordon B. Hinckly holds a copy of the first edition of the Book of Mormon *during a speech at the General Conference of the Church of Jesus Christ of Latter-day Saints in Salt Lake City, Utah, on April 4, 1998.* (Credit: AP/ Wide World Photos.)

to translate the record from its language, called Reformed Egyptian, into English. Today the Book of Mormon is one of four chief texts accepted as scripture by Latter-day Saints (LDS). The others are the Bible (both the Old and the New Testaments), the Doctrine and Covenants (revelations from God to Joseph Smith and other church leaders, mostly in the nineteenth century), and the Pearl of Great Price (a collection of other revelations to, and writings of, Joseph Smith).

Basic Plot

The Book of Mormon begins with the story of Lehi, an ancient prophet in Jerusalem who fled that city shortly before its destruction in the early sixth century B.C.E. Lehi followed God's directions to build a ship and take his family across the Atlantic Ocean to the Americas. Problems arose, however, when his sons Nephi and Laman took up arms against each other, beginning a blood feud that would last for centuries. Nephi's descendants (the Nephites) are generally depicted in the Book of Mormon as righteous and civi-

lized, while their opponents, the Lamanites (after Nephi's brother Laman), are often caricatured as savage heathens.

Much of the book describes warfare and cycles of destruction, but a significant portion preaches of the peace that will come when the Redeemer, Jesus Christ, visits America. The Book of Mormon claims that Christ visited America for the three days between his death and resurrection, and that he preached and taught among the Nephites. For two centuries after his visit, the Nephites and the Lamanites were able to live in harmony, but eventually they reinstituted their former battles. In about the year 421 C.E., a prophet named Moroni wrote that he was the last of the Nephites left to preserve the sacred record of their history. According to Mormon belief, Moroni sealed up the record, which we call the Book of Mormon, and buried it in the earth so it would be preserved from the Lamanites. This same Moroni was the angel who appeared to Joseph Smith in 1823 and instructed him about where to find the record.

Controversies over Authorship

Latter-day Saints believe that the Book of Mormon is a compilation of the writings of many ancient prophets over the span of nearly a thousand years. Yet many critics in the nineteenth century ridiculed Joseph Smith's claim to have found and translated a "golden Bible." Some claimed that Smith wrote it himself, while others tried to prove that he had plagiarized the book from existing sources. To counter such charges, Smith published the Book of Mormon with affidavits attesting to its miraculous origins; a total of eleven witnesses testified that they had seen the golden plates from which the book was translated. These testimonies still appear at the beginning of every printed copy of the Book of Mormon.

Theological Legacies

The Book of Mormon is more of a historical record than a theological work. Many of the core beliefs of contemporary Mormonism, such as eternal marriage and temple worship, are not mentioned in the book. Yet some of the historical legacies from the book have influenced Mormon theology and practice. For example, Mormons believe that contemporary Native Americans and indigenous peoples are the literal descendants of the Lamanites of the Book of Mormon. The first Mormon missionaries were sent by Joseph Smith to Missouri to try to convert some of these "lost" Lamanites and return them to the fold. More recently, Mormons have attempted to reclaim the Native Americans as Book of Mormon peoples. In the 1960s and 1970s, hundreds of Navajo children were bused away from their reservation and placed with LDS foster families during the school year, to assist in their education and to instruct them in the Mormon faith.

Current Emphases

The Book of Mormon is extremely important to contemporary Latter-day Saints, who consider it the most perfect book on earth. In the 1980s, LDS prophet and president Ezra Taft Benson initiated a sort of renaissance by encouraging church members to read the Book of Mormon daily. The book is used heavily in the church's extensive missionary outreach, with missionaries offering free copies and instruction to anyone investigating the church. This instantly recognizable dark blue missionary copy received a face-lift in the early 1980s with its new subtitle "Another Testament of Jesus Christ." The 1990s have seen a heightened emphasis on the book's Christ-centeredness and its message of Christ as the redeemer of humankind.

See also BIBLE; CHURCH OF JESUS CHRIST OF LATTER-DAY SAINTS; MORMON TEMPLE.

BIBLIOGRAPHY

Benson, Ezra Taft. *Beware of Pride: The Book of Mormon: Keystone of Our Religion.* 1998.

Bushman, Richard. *Joseph Smith and the Beginnings of Mormonism.* 1984.

Shipps, Jan. *Mormonism: The Story of a New Religious Tradition.* 1985.

Jana Kathryn Riess

Books, Religious.

See Publishing, Religious.

Born Again Christians

The term "born again" leaped into public discourse in America when Jimmy Carter was running for president in 1975 and 1976. The candidate and future president of the United States openly used the common evangelical phrase for a decisive conversion to Christ to describe his own spiritual experience and status. At about the same time, convicted Watergate conspirator and former Nixon aide Charles Colson titled his spiritual autobiography *Born Again*. These and other events brought the concept of "born again Christians" into common usage. It had previously been used primarily by evangelical Protestant Christian evangelists and theologians to distinguish be-

tween themselves and their followers and other types of Christians who do not believe that initiation into authentic Christian life involves a conscious commitment to Jesus Christ as lord and savior.

The phrase "born again" is derived from Jesus' statement to a potential follower named Nicodemus in the Gospel of John, chapter 3: "You must be born again." (Some scholars prefer the translation "born from above," but "born again" is the more common English translation of the Greek.) This and other references to a "new birth" or a "new creation" in the New Testament were often interpreted as referring to the gift of God's grace in water baptism throughout church history. During the Reformation of the sixteenth century, however, especially the "radical reformers" (primarily those called "Anabaptists") emphasized the necessity of a personal crisis of conversion involving conscious repentance and faith for authentic Christian existence. In the seventeenth century the German Pietists proclaimed the necessity of a *Busskampf*—"struggle of repentance"—for true Christian conversion. The revivalists of the Great Awakenings in Great Britain and the American colonies, including John Wesley, George Whitefield, and Jonathan Edwards, all focused their messages to the masses on the transforming experience of encounter with Jesus Christ through personal decisions of faith. The phrase "born again" became attached to the work of God in a person's life when he or she repented of sin and believed in Jesus Christ. Modern American revivalists such as Charles Finney, D. L. Moody, Billy Sunday, Aimee Semple McPherson, and Billy Graham all used this terminology and required such an experience as the entrance into authentic Christian life.

The best-known purveyor of a "born again experience" in the twentieth century is evangelist Billy Graham. Through numerous sermons (many broadcast on radio or television), columns, articles, and books, the Southern Baptist preacher and "pastor to the presidents" promoted the experience of personal conversion resulting in being "born again." Like evangelical revivalists before him, Graham interpreted this experience as a transforming work of God known as "regeneration" in which the Holy Spirit goes beyond forgiving the converted person's sins to imparting a new affection for things of God. That is, a person who is born again desires to please and serve God more than anything else. Graham and other evangelical Protestants believe that when a person is born again the Holy Spirit (third person of the Trinity) enters into his or her life in a special way and begins to eradicate original sin and establish love for God and others. Baptist theologian Augustus Hopkins Strong defined regeneration—being "born again"—as "the expulsive power of a new affection."

Throughout at least the first half of the twentieth century, being a "born again Christian" was something of an oddity. While most Americans belonged to Christian churches, they placed their hope for eternal salvation in the grace of God received through the sacraments—especially infant baptism and the eucharist (Lord's Supper). Many were influenced by the newer liberal theologies of preachers such as Harry Emerson Fosdick, who implied a universal salvation and emphasized Christian nurture and a social gospel more than or even in place of special grace received through sacraments or personal repentance and faith. Those who spoke of the need of a personal decision for Jesus Christ (conversion) and regenerative work of God (born again experience) were often considered fanatics by more mainstream Protestants.

The second half of the twentieth century has witnessed a rise of respectability of born again Christians. This is so much the case that many evangelical Christians (a term virtually synonymous with born again Christians) began to shy away from the term "born again" out of concern that it was being too widely used for too many vague religious experiences. Some polls taken in the 1980s placed the total of the adult American population who claimed to be "born again" at as high as 40 percent. What changed? The answer lies in several new religious movements that affected numerous people across a broad spectrum of Christian denominations.

During the 1950s and 1960s Billy Graham and a host of other tent and television evangelists moved around the North American continent preaching the message of the born again experience. Many of them did not identify with any specific denomination and urged those who surged forward to their altar calls (invitations to accept Christ) to join the church of their choice. No longer did one have to join a fringe church or denomination to be a born again Christian. To the dismay of many more traditional and liberal Protestant ministers, many of their parishioners brought the gospel of being born again into their congregations and lobbied there for church renewal, revival, and even charismatic experiences.

The 1960s saw the rise of the so-called Charismatic Movement of neo-Pentecostal Christians, who remained in their mainline Protestant and Catholic churches while speaking in tongues and exercising gifts of healing, prophecy, and other spiritual experiences once confined almost exclusively to what traditionalists and liberals had considered a lunatic fringe of Christianity. Almost all charismatics considered themselves born again. The 1970s witnessed the rise of the so-called Jesus People Movement of hippies and other countercultural young people who converted to Christ and spoke often and loudly of being "born again Jesus freaks." When many of them eventually put on three-piece suits and joined the mainstream of society, they continued to believe that their true Christian lives (as opposed to nominal Christian identities as members of churches) began with their born again experiences.

The 1980s were the decade of the "Reagan revolution" in politics and the rise of the so-called Religious Right in American society. Previously, most evangelical (born again) Christians had avoided direct political action based on their religious beliefs and values. Throughout the 1980s, however, many self-appointed spokesmen for conservative evangelical Christians formed Christian organizations to promote a generally conservative social, political, and economic agenda. Two notable ones were the Moral Majority, founded by fundamentalist minister Jerry Falwell; and the Christian Coalition, founded by televangelist and educator Pat Robertson. Many journalists and other social critics and observers assumed that these right-wing Christian political action groups represented all born again Christians. While many evangelicals did support conservative causes in a new way, many others chose to avoid labeling the entire evangelical movement as politically conservative. Tony Campolo and Jim Wallis rose to prominence as speakers and writers among more politically moderate and liberal evangelical Christians. Nevertheless, in the public mind, "born again Christian" came to be identified as virtually synonymous with the Religious Right.

By the early 1990s born again Christians had entered the religious and social mainstream of American society. The stigma often attached to being born again in the early part of the twentieth century largely dropped away as evangelical Christians exerted their voices and inserted their institutions firmly into the middle of American social, political, and religious life. Some observers believe that this mainstreaming process of evangelical, born again Christianity in the 1990s weakened its prophetic voice and that with respectability and acceptance came a certain vagueness about the message of being born again. At least three major challenges face the born again Christian community at the turn of the century and millennium: How will it avoid losing its cutting edge as a distinctive movement as it gains respectability and social acceptance? How will it be affected by the inevitable and impending death of leaders such as Billy Graham? The third challenge arises out of the politicizing of the community during the Clinton impeachment. Can the community reposture itself politically?

See also CHARISMATIC MOVEMENT; CHRISTIAN COALITION; COLSON, CHARLES; EVANGELICAL CHRISTIANITY; FALWELL, JERRY; GRAHAM, BILLY; MAINLINE

Protestantism; Moral Majority; Pentecostal and Charismatic Christianity; Religious Right; Robertson, Pat; Televangelism.

Bibliography

Balmer, Randall. *Mine Eyes Have Seen the Glory: A Journey into the Evangelical Subculture.* 1989.

Carpenter, Joel. *Revive Us Again: The Reawakening of American Fundamentalism.* 1997.

Colson, Charles, *Born Again.* 1976.

Graham, Billy. *Just As I Am: The Autobiography of Billy Graham.* 1997.

Roger E. Olson

Brainwashing

"Brainwashing" is a term with negative connotations, used to refer to the recruitment processes of disfavored religious and political groups. It represents one of the most effective social weapons adapted for use in efforts to exert social control over so-called New Religious Movements, sometimes referred to by the similarly negative term "cult."

The term was developed in the anti-Communist hysteria of the 1950s, first being used by Edward Hunter, a CIA operative paid to write propaganda about the Communist takeover in China. He developed the ideologically based term to describe the processes whereby ordinary Chinese citizens were allegedly converted to Communist beliefs. Others used the term to refer to methods used in Korean POW camps, especially after some POWs chose to remain in Korea rather than return home.

The ideological term became popularized and was a staple in the linguistic arsenal of the anti-Communists. Brainwashing then developed a life of its own, being used to refer to any questionable practices of recruitment and socialization. The term achieved fame and became a part of everyday lexicon when defenders of Patty Hearst attempted to use the brainwashing metaphor to explain why she had begun to cooperate with her captors in the Symbianese Liberation Front, going so far as to rob banks with them.

The term was ready-made when controversy erupted in the late 1960s and early 1970s over the development of many New Religious Movements in American society, such as the Unification Church and the Hare Krishna Movement. Those opposed to the groups, including many parents who were unsatisfied with the religious choices of their children, sought a simple explanation of why some of America's brightest and best would choose to abandon their normal career trajectories and families to follow a strange and new religion. Thus brainwashing became a popular explanation of such events: People were brainwashed and being held under mind control; they did not join of their own volition but were tricked into participating, according to the brainwashing perspective.

Such ideas rejected notions of free will or agency on the part of the joiner. The paternalism of designating decisions made by young people choosing to try out another ethic or belief system as resulting from brainwashing seems obvious, but it was often overshadowed by genuine concerns of parents for their children's well-being, even if those children were of age.

Thus many parents chose to intervene in their children's religious choices, giving rise to the new pseudoprofession of deprogramming. Deprogrammers kidnapped thousands of young people out of newer religions, subjecting them to considerable physical and psychological coercion in an effort to get them to leave their group of affiliation. This controversial process, which has been used less in recent years (mainly because of some adverse legal decisions), was based almost entirely on the idea that because of brainwashing the members had to be "rescued" by those wanting to "help them exercise their free will."

Originally the concept of brainwashing was based on the physical coercion allegedly used by the Chinese against Korean POWs and by the Communists in the 1950s who gained control of China. Supposedly the use of physical coercion not only could result in compliance, but could also, if skillfully done, turn the person into a robotlike entity programmed to follow orders at the exertion of certain stimuli. Films such as *The Manchurian Candidate* were based on this view of brainwashing. Such views have been soundly critiqued by scholars (e.g., Anthony 1990; Anthony and Robbins 1994; Barker, 1986; Richardson 1991, 1993).

This robot conception was not applicable in the circumstances of recruitment to new religions, since few examples of physical coercion could be found in such groups. However, enterprising legitimators of the anti-cult movement redefined brainwashing in a creative way. They developed the concept of "second-order brainwashing," which referred to the use of psychological coercion, including even positive emotion, in recruitment. This approach to recruitment, in which people were encouraged through positive emotion and affective ties to join a group, was deemed even more insidious and effective than the original physically coercive methods of the Communists. Thus the anti-cult movement attempted to redefine brainwashing, placing more emphasis on psychological coercion than on physical coercion.

Although brainwashing as an explanation for participation in new religions has fallen from favor in recent years among scholars and in the courts, the term is still quite popular in general parlance. A few scholars have made efforts to revive the term, but with little success among the scholarly community. Most scholars accept research results indicating that newer religions are actually very small (even if very well publicized) and have very high attrition rates. Both of these characteristics undercut any effort to support so-called brainwashing theories of recruitment.

See also ANTI-CULT MOVEMENT; CULT; CULT AWARENESS NETWORK; ELVIS CULTS; INTERNATIONAL SOCIETY FOR KRISHNA CONSCIOUSNESS; NEW RELIGIOUS MOVEMENTS; PROSELYTIZING; PSYCHOLOGY OF RELIGION; UNIFICATION CHURCH.

BIBLIOGRAPHY

Anthony, Dick. "Religious Movements and Brainwashing Litigation: Evaluating Key Testimony." In *In Gods We Trust,* 2nd ed., edited by Tom Robbins and Dick Anthony. 1990.

Anthony, Dick, and Thomas Robbins. "Brainwashing and Totalitarian Influence." In *Encyclopedia of Human Behavior,* edited by V. S. Ramachandran. 1994.

Anthony, Dick, and Thomas Robbins. "Negligence, Coercion, and the Protection of Religious Belief." *Journal of Church and State* 37 (1995): 509–536.

Barker, Eileen. *The Making of a Moonie: Choice or Brainwashing?* 1986.

Richardson, James T. "Cult/Brainwashing Cases and the Freedom of Religion." *Journal of Church and State* 33 (1991): 55–74.

Richardson, James T. "A Social Psychological Critique of Brainwashing Claims About Recruitment to New Religions." In *The Handbook of Cults and Sects in America,* edited by Jeffrey Hadden and David Bromley. 1993.

Richardson, James T., and Brock Kilbourne. "Classical and Contemporary Brainwashing Models: A Comparison and Critique." In *The Brainwashing/Deprogramming Controversy,* edited by David G. Bromley and James Richardson, pp. 29–45. 1983.

James T. Richardson

Branch Davidians

The Branch Davidians (Students of the Seven Seals) trace their history to the Seventh-Day Adventist Church, one of several successors to the nineteenth-century Millerite movement. The group was founded by Victor Houteff, a Bulgarian immigrant who converted to Adventism in 1919. Ten years later Houteff produced a manifesto, *The Shepherd's Rod,* accusing the church of blocking Christ's return by scriptural unfaithfulness and materialism. He announced himself a divinely appointed messenger to lead human purification and reveal end-time chronology by unlocking the secrets of the Seven Seals contained in the Book of Revelation. Houteff established the Mount Carmel Center near Waco, Texas, in 1935, and millennial expectations gradually receded. The group dissolved ties with the Adventists in 1942, but virtually all of the few dozen adult members were former Adventists. Houteff served as community leader until his death in 1955; he was succeeded by his wife, Florence, who built group membership to more than a thousand. Florence Houteff predicted apocalyptic events for 1959; following the failure of her prophecy and her admission of error, membership plummeted to a few dozen. Houteff then attempted to dissolve the group and sell the property. However, Davidian Benjamin Roden successfully reconstituted the group and assumed spiritual leadership. Upon his death in 1978, his wife, Lois, assumed leadership, but she became locked in a power struggle with her son George for group control. It was this polarized situation that Vernon Howell (David Koresh), who himself had been an Adventist, entered in 1981 at age twenty-two. He was initially employed as a handyman at Mount Carmel, quickly gained spiritual influence, and in 1983 was named Lois Roden's successor. This triggered another protracted power struggle, including one violent confrontation between George Roden and Koresh; ultimately Koresh prevailed in the late 1980s.

Throughout their history the Davidians retained many of the Adventist traditions (Saturday Sabbath, vegetarianism, millennial expectations). The group was organized as a network of patriarchal families ordered hierarchically. Koresh ascended to leadership at a moment when the group's financial and membership bases had collapsed. He responded by launching recruitment campaigns, initiating business enterprises (including weapons sales), refurbishing the community dwellings, and claiming prophetic status. Membership climbed again to several hundred. In 1990 Vernon Howell changed his name to David Koresh, thereby identifying himself as the spiritual descendent of King David and as a messianic figure carrying out a divinely commissioned errand. According to Koresh's New Light Doctrine, Christ died only for those living prior to his crucifixion. Koresh's mission would allow salvation for subsequent generations by revealing the end-time message in the Seven Seals and creating a new spiritual lineage through sexual unions with disciples. The children created through these unions would erect the House of David and ultimately rule the world.

The Branch Davidians' Mount Carmel Compound at Waco, Texas, in flames on April 19, 1993. The fire was ignited by cult members after federal agents had pumped tear gas into the compound and were about to storm it.   (Credit: REUTERS/Reed Schulman/Archive Photos.)

Implementation of the New Light Doctrine (which led to defections, child abuse allegations, and child custody disputes), along with the gun-related business, resulted in charges of both illegal possession and sale of weapons and child sexual abuse. On February 28, 1993, a firefight erupted between the Davidians and federal ATF agents serving a warrant, during which ten people died and twenty-four others were injured. The FBI then launched a fifty-one-day siege of the compound that ended on April 19, 1993, when an armed assault on the compound resulted in the death of seventy-four Davidians. Several Davidians who survived the conflagration were subsequently convicted on weapons and manslaughter charges. Only a few, small, competing factions of the Davidians now remain. The validity of the legal charges and the jurisdiction of the government agencies involved in the confrontation with the Davidians remain contested, and this episode has been linked to increased militancy among Christian militia groups and specifically to the bombing of the Oklahoma City Federal Building.

See also ADVENTISM; APOCALYPSE; KORESH, DAVID; MILLENNIALISM; PREMILLENNIALISM; SEVENTH-DAY ADVENTISM; VEGETARIANISM.

BIBLIOGRAPHY

Anthony, Dick, and Thomas Robbins. "Religious Totalism, Exemplary Dualism, and the Waco Tragedy." In *Millennium, Messiahs, and Mayhem,* edited by Thomas Robbins and Susan Palmer. 1997.

Tabor, James, and Eugene Gallagher. *Why Waco? Cults and the Battle for Religious Freedom in America.* 1995.

Wright, Stuart. *Armageddon in Waco: Critical Perspectives on the Branch Davidian Conflict.* 1995.

David G. Bromley

Bricolage

The French word *bricolage* can be translated as "patch-up" or "do it yourself" in English. This term has been used as a metaphor to designate the combining of a variety of religious practices and representations found in certain oral societies and, in a different form, in the most modern societies.

The French anthropologist Claude Lévi-Strauss, in *The Savage Mind* (1966), was the first to use the term bricolage. From a structuralist perspective, bricolage is understood as a metaphor for mythic thought. On the practical level, bricolage takes objects that have been used before and reorganizes them within a new perspective. For example, one would take spare parts from old automobiles to construct a new one. Similarly, on a theoretical level mythic thought takes bits and pieces that have perhaps already been elaborated in previous myths and puts them together to form a new narrative. Lévi-Strauss asserts that mythic images, like the materials of a *bricoleur* (a person who does bricolage), have a dual characteristic: They have already been used and they can be used again. According to structuralist theory, mythic bricolage is not arbitrary: By necessity it takes into account the heterogeneous nature of the preformed elements it uses. This is why the number of rearrangements of mythic elements is limited. Also, mythic bricolage is *not* the product of individual caprice; it is guided by general structures of the human mind of which individuals are not aware.

Cuban Santería and Haitian Vodun (Voodoo), which are found in the United States today due to Caribbean immigration, are good examples of this first type of bricolage found in oral societies. Slaves who had been taken to Cuba and Haiti associated West African divinities with Catholic saints. But the links among European and African belief systems were not formed randomly. An African god and a Catholic saint were identified with one another when they possessed a common characteristic. For example, in Santería, Ogun corresponds to St. Peter because the first is the African god of iron, while the second, who guards the gates of paradise in the Catholic tradition, always carries metallic keys in Catholic iconography. In Vodun, the same African divinity is often identified with St. James the Elder, a warrior spirit much like Ogun.

The term bricolage is used today to describe certain religious behaviors that are characteristic of the most modern societies. Just as in oral societies, in the modern West one can observe the phenomenon of the combination of preexistent religious elements that have been abstracted from the belief systems in which they were previously embedded. But contemporary religious bricolage is nevertheless very different from the mythic bricolage described by Claude Lévi-Strauss. First, contemporary religious bricolage rests on the free choice of individuals. In a context of a great diversity of religious beliefs and practices, individuals choose among these according to their personal inclinations. Religious bricoleurs no longer accept institutional dogmas. Furthermore, they do not submit to the demands of coherence that guided mythic thought according to structuralist theory. Individuals borrow elements from heterogeneous traditions without attempting a logical synthesis. Contemporary religious bricolage is an individual juxtaposition of religious elements that are not organized within a structure. Finally, bricoleurs neglect the religious stability of tradition. In constructing their own religion, they aim for personal achievement. Therefore they can at any moment abandon certain beliefs or practices in favor of others they consider more efficacious, and this without excluding the possibility of returning to their previous position if they feel the need. Therefore it is only with difficulty that modern religious bricoleurs tie into a historical continuity shared by a community of believers, because their beliefs have no institutional base and vary in the short term.

The New Age is a characteristic example of this second type of bricolage. New Agers patch together elements of Western and Eastern religious traditions such as Christianity, Hinduism, Buddhism, or Islamic Sufism, to which they add astrological or parapsychological beliefs as well as other elements that issue, notably, from Native American religions. New Agers seek neither to systematically organize this ensemble of beliefs, nor to maintain it over time, nor to organize collectively. Within the range of available religious resources, New Agers choose those elements that will best serve their corporal and psychic development. This ensemble of individual beliefs can evolve over time as a function of the needs of the person concerned. These asystematic and unstable individual religious combinations of New Agers thus typify the religious bricolage found in modern societies.

See also ANTHROPOLOGY OF RELIGION; MYTH; NEW AGE SPIRITUALITY; SANTERÍA; SYNCRETISM; VODUN.

BIBLIOGRAPHY

Hervieu-Léger, Danièle. *Religion and Memory.* 1999.

Lévi-Strauss, Claude. *The Savage Mind.* 1966.

McCarthy Brown, Karen. *Mama Lola: A Vodou Priestess in Brooklyn.* 1991.

York, Michael. "New Age and the Late Twentieth Century." *Journal of Contemporary Religion* 12, no. 3 (1997): 401–419.

Erwan Dianteill

British Israelism

British Israelism (BI) is primarily a cosmology combining ancient and more recent themes. Ancient themes are picked up in the story that after their capture by Assyria (721 B.C.), the ten northern tribes of Israel trekked over the Caucasus Mountains. First settling along streams tributary to the Danube (which, allegedly, is named after the tribe of Dan), they eventually migrated to Western Europe. Today, several countries are reputed to share the namesakes of their founders: Macedonia (from *Moeshi* [Moses] + *Dan* + *ia* [land of]); Iberia (Spain, land of the Hebrews); Hibernia (Ireland, also land of the Hebrews), etc. Britain was the destination point for the tribe of Ephraim, claims BI. This is why, in accordance with Jacob's blessings to his children, it is "a company of nations."

The second theme in BI relates how God granted the British the scepter of planetary rule. When the last Davidic king, Zedekiah, was overthrown and his sons were murdered by the Babylonians (587 B.C.E.), his eldest daughter, Tea Tephi, fled. Carrying with her the coronation stone from Solomon's Temple, she eventually landed in Ulster. There she was married to the local "Hebrew" (Hibernian) king, Eochiadh. It is from this union that all British monarchs are said to trace their lineage.

As for the stone, originally it had served as the pillow upon which Jacob rested his head the evening he was named Israel; later it was smote by Moses to provide saving water for the wandering Israelites; today it sits beneath the royal throne in Westminster Abbey.

Biblical prophecies are offered as proof of these tales, together with alleged connections between English and Hebrew (including the argument that "English" itself is a Hebrew word [from *an* (one) + *gael* (stammering) + *ish* (man)]. There are also numerologies, heraldry, and pyramidology. That the English inch and pyramid inch are identical "proves" that both measurement systems were carried by the same folk, the Israelites, and that the megaliths at Stonehenge and Avebury (Hebrew-town) were built by Hebrews.

BI is a cosmology, not a church. It is disseminated through interdenominational meetings, lectures, and books to a largely middle-class, Anglophilic audience. This explains its reluctance to include Germany (derided as Asshur, Assyria) as part of Israel.

Exported to America in the late nineteenth century, BI spread through the Midwest, where it was infused with Pentecostal and Methodist fervor. It arrived in southern California with the belongings of Dust Bowl migrants in the 1930s. There it assumed the pro-German, anti-Semitic, racist overtones characteristic of Identity Christianity.

While BI understands them as only one thirteenth of Israel, it considers the Jews bona fide blood brothers. Even if "fallen away" from the covenant, Jews are of the Chosen People and equal sharers in God's promises. Until the Jews sought independence from British guardianship after World War II, Jewish efforts to secure a home in Palestine were avidly supported by BI followers.

See also ANTI-SEMITISM; IDENTITY CHRISTIANITY; ZIONISM.

BIBLIOGRAPHY

Allen, J. H. *Judah's Sceptre and Joseph's Birthright.* 1902.

Bennett, W. H. *Symbols of Our Celto-Saxon Heritage.* 1976.

James A. Aho

Brownsville Revival

Since its inception during the Azusa Street Revival (1906–1909) in Los Angeles, the Pentecostal movement has regularly experienced similar revivals that have served as antidotes for the corrosive forces of religious routinization. Paranormal charismatic phenomena, including glossolalia, miraculous healing, prophecies, deliverance from demons, and miracles, as well as unexplained bodily manifestations, have become hallmarks of Pentecostalism and its more recent charismatic offshoots in mainline and independent churches. Despite the persistent attack of modernist thought on its distinctive worldview, the supernatural perspective espoused by Pentecostals has experienced ongoing revitalization through fresh outbursts of charismatic phenomena. The Latter Rain and Healing movements of the late 1940s and early 1950s, the neo-Pentecostal movement in the mainline American denominations during the 1960s and 1970s, the Third Wave of the 1980s, and now the renewal/revivals of the 1990s—each has given new vitality to the Pentecostalism of its era. The Brownsville Revival, originating at the Brownsville Assembly of God in Pensacola, Florida, on Father's Day 1995, with the charismatic "anointing" of evangelist Steve Hill and under the leadership of Pastor John Kilpatrick, is a major player in the larger revival movement sweeping the globe.

The Brownsville Revival was preceded and fueled by the Argentine Revival, which began in 1982 and which continues today throughout Argentina—a movement that has served as a catalyst for a number of the revival fires now dotting the North American landscape. Steve Hill, the evangelist who launched the Pensacola Revival in 1995, had been a missionary church planter in Argentina and was greatly influenced by the Argentine evangelist Carlos Annacondia. Some years later Hill experienced the so-called Toronto Blessing, another stream of this worldwide Pentecostal revival, which began at Toronto Airport Vineyard in Ontario, Canada, and was transported to Holy Trinity Brompton (HTB) Anglican Church in London. It was after Hill received prayer from Vicar Sandy Millar of HTB that Hill believed he had received the anointing he sought. It was the story of his transformation that Hill shared with the congregation of Brownsville Assembly of God on Father's Day in 1995 that marked the beginning of the revival that the *New York Times* called "apparently the largest and longest-running . . . revival in America in almost a century." People came from around the world, often standing in line for hours, before entering the 2,500-person sanctuary; Lindell Cooley would lead animated worship in song, Hill would preach a sermon calling for old-time repentance, and throngs would respond as fifteen-year-old Charity James sang out the haunting theme song "Mercy Seat." A reported 108,000 (of an estimated 1.7 million visitors) responded to altar calls within the first year of the revival, with many of them shaking violently and "falling out in the spirit," two phenomena not experienced at this Pentecostal church before the revival. Testimonies were given nightly by those who claimed to be set free from drug and alcohol addiction, who had been healed from emotional or physical ailments, or whose lives were otherwise changed through the revival.

Revival meetings continue at Brownsville Assembly of God from Wednesday through Saturday nights, supplemented by more than a dozen annual "Awake America" crusades led by the Brownsville Ministry Team in cities throughout the United States, and monthly special conferences held at the church in Pensacola for special groups (e.g., men's conference, youth, ministers). In January 1997 Dr. Michael Brown, a recognized authority on revival, founded the Brownsville Revival School of Ministry. The school has a faculty of fifteen and more than eleven hundred students enrolled in the two- to three-year program who are being immersed in the "fires of revival" and then being "sent forth." Although there is a wide denominational representation at the school, as there is among those who attend the revival, this stream of the larger renewal/revival movement is predominantly revitalizing (although not without some resistance) the Assemblies of God, the largest white Pentecostal denomination in the United States and one of the major Pentecostal denominations in the world.

See also CHARISMATIC MOVEMENT; HEALING; PENTECOSTAL AND CHARISMATIC CHRISTIANITY; RELIGIOUS EXPERIENCE; TELEVANGELISM; TORONTO BLESSING.

BIBLIOGRAPHY

Brown, Michael L. *From Holy Laughter to Holy Fire: America on the Edge of Revival.* 1996.

Hill, Stephen. *The Pursuit of Revival.* 1997.

Poloma, Margaret M. "The Spirit Movement in North America at the Millennium: From Azusa Street to Toronto, Pensacola and Beyond." *Journal of Pentecostal Theology* 12 (1998): 83–107.

Synan, Vinson. *The Holiness-Pentecostal Tradition: Charismatic Movements in the Twentieth Century.* 1997.

Wagner, C. Peter, and Pablo Deiros, eds. *The Rising Revival.* 1998.

Margaret M. Poloma

Bruderhof

In 1920 Eberhard Arnold; his wife, Emmy Arnold; and a few friends opened a small commune in a farmhouse in Sannerz, Hesse, Germany. Passionate Christian socialists, they were fascinated with the early Anabaptists and sought especially to emulate the Hutterites, Anabaptists who live communally and hold all goods and money in common. They called their community the Bruderhof.

The rise of the Nazis in Germany brought persecution of the Bruderhof, and the community moved to England and then Paraguay in an effort to maintain its communal way of life and avoid military conscription. In the early 1950s the group began to move to the United States, which soon became its headquarters and where in 1998 it had six colonies (two others were in England). The Bruderhof colonies have prospered, with membership reaching some twenty-five hundred in the 1990s, and it built a robust industry, Community Playthings, which produces sturdy children's toys for schools and day-care centers. In the 1970s formal links were established between the Bruderhof and some of the Hutterite colonies in the western United States and Canada. However, in the 1990s

Children and adult members of the pacifist Bruderhof sect march through Hopwood, Pennsylvania, on Monday, August 18, 1997, the first day of their three-day, thirty-mile Children's Crusade protesting against the death penalty. The march culminated on August 20 outside the Greene County State Prison.   (Credit: AP/ Wide World Photos.)

internal disputes among the Schmiedeleut, the branch of Hutterites that had the best relations with the Bruderhof, spilled over onto the Bruderhof, and the formal relationship between the two movements was acrimoniously broken. The Bruderhof also experienced problems with some of its overseas outposts. A colony planted in the homeland, Germany, in 1988 experienced local resistance to its presence and was dissolved six years later. A Nigerian colony, Palmgrove, became affiliated with the Bruderhof but soon foundered among heavy recriminations on both sides. The periodic expulsion of members and ongoing hostility from a network of former members, many of whom have family members still resident in the community, also roiled the otherwise calm life of the Bruderhof. Problems notwithstanding, however, new members joined and the movement continued to expand.

The theology of the Bruderhof resembles that of the other Anabaptists the movement has always emulated. Membership must follow a conversion experience, and upon joining one gives up all private ownership of goods and vows to live a life of obedience to authority, humility, and loving concern for other human beings. Worship, prayer, and singing are daily occurrences in community life. Bruderhof faith has a strong social activist bent; members were involved in the civil rights movement of the 1950s and 1960s, and since then have been vocal in supporting a variety of peace- and justice-oriented causes.

Eberhard Arnold died unexpectedly in 1935, and after a lengthy period in which no single individual formally led the movement, Arnold's son Heini assumed the office of elder in 1962. Heini was succeeded as elder, after his death in 1983, by his son Christoph, who remained in office in the late 1990s. Spiritual leadership and major secular leadership roles are filled exclusively by males, although women do play important roles in some parts of community life. Families live in apartments, take most meals together in common dining halls, and work in the community at duties assigned by the leadership. Children attend private Bruderhof elementary schools and then public high schools. Some go on to college and can return to community life only by applying for membership in the same manner as other newcomers.

See also AMISH; CIVIL RIGHTS MOVEMENT.

BIBLIOGRAPHY

Oved, Yaacov. *The Witness of the Brothers: A History of the Bruderhof.* 1996.
Zablocki, Benjamin David. *The Joyful Community.* 1971.

Timothy Miller

Buddha

With more than three million Buddhists now living in the United States, much attention is currently being paid to the development of American Buddhism. Literary periodicals regularly publish features on American Buddhism, many celebrities support Buddhist causes, and the Dalai Lama is a regular visitor to the United States. In the midst of this interest in American Buddhism, a consideration of the life of the founder of the Buddhist religion is a requisite for a clear understanding of the American mission of Buddhism.

The Legend and Life of the Buddha

Early Buddhist literature informs us that the Sanskrit word *buddha* means "to wake up" and is a title used to describe an individual who has awakened to "seeing the world as it really is." In so doing, Buddhas escape from the suffering that characterizes the mundane world, and teach others to do the same out of compassion for all sentient beings.

Early Buddhist records reveal very little information about the historical Buddha. Although many modern sources identify his life as having lasted eighty years—from about 563 to 483 B.C.E.—even those dates may not be accurate. Piecing together a biography of the founder is aided by the survival of many texts in Buddhism, with each adding some information or perspective.

Preliminary to his appearance in the world, the Buddha presumably underwent a long series of rebirths, each of which provided the occasion for the development of spiritual perfection. Eventually, it is said, he was born into the Śākya tribe of the Gautama clan, a warrior family ruled over by Śuddhodana and his queen, Māyā. The child was raised in luxury, protected from experiencing any of the vagaries of ordinary life. At the proper time for a youth of his background, he married Yaśodharā.

As restlessness drove him to experience some of the world outside his princely existence, the young man, named Siddhārtha Gautama, encountered an old man, a sick man, a corpse, and an ascetic on successive nights. Summarizing the first three cases, his charioteer explained that just as a man is born, he grows old; just as he grows old, he also grows sick; moreover, growing sick ultimately leads to death. The wise charioteer noted that the ascetic he observed on the last night had renounced the world in favor of seeking an end to old age, sickness, and death. The ascetic sought to end life's suffering, and with it, continued rebirth in an endless cycle known as *saṃsāra*. The young prince renounced the world at age twenty-nine, promising himself that, upon attaining his goal, he would teach the method of salvation to his family.

After six years of wandering, he eventually concluded that religious salvation, or enlightenment, cannot be found in the extremes of life he had experienced but can be found only in a middle path. He wandered on, and in a night of contemplation, eliminated the last of his imperfections, arising at dawn as the Buddha, having put an end to suffering and having attained enlightenment, *nirvāṇa*. Virtually all the Buddhist legends describe the remaining forty-five years of his life as a wandering ministry, establishing communities of monastics and lay disciples. While the specifics of the sectarian stories differ, the Buddha established a way of life based on what has come to be known as the "Three Jewels": Buddha, his teachings (called *dharma*), and his community (called *sangha*). Although he is reputed to have offered doctrinal statements on many issues, his quintessential doctrine was known as the "Four Noble Truths," namely that (1) all life is characterized by suffering and (2) caused by craving. In addition, (3) this suffering can cease by (4) practice of the "Eightfold Path" involving right view, intention, speech, action, livelihood, effort, mindfulness, and concentration. Continuing his ministry, continually proclaiming only his humanity and not any divinity, Buddha died at eighty.

The Ongoing History

Within a short period, the religious tradition of "Buddhism" began to divide internally. In about 200 B.C.E. a new, liberal movement called Mahāyāna or "Great Vehicle" emerged, branding the prior Buddhist schools Hīnayāna or "Lesser Vehicle." Later, a third major Buddhist division occurred, with the Vajrayāna or "Diamond Vehicle" combining the application of sophisticated Buddhist philosophical issues with new, esoteric Buddhist practices.

Over time, one of the major schools of the so-called Hīnayāna tradition—the Theravāda—was exported, initially through the missionary efforts of King Aśoka, to South and Southeast Asia. Mahāyāna also subdivided internally, and its many schools came to pervade East Asia. The Vajrayāna school became sectarian as well, and spread throughout Tibet and Inner Asia.

Buddha Comes West

In the twentieth century, Buddhism became a world religion. As the varieties of Buddhist sectarian groups found an eager audience, each Buddhist group brought its own unique understanding of Buddha to its members.

The Theravāda school, serving the largely ethnic communities of South and Southeast Asian immigrant

Five thousand onlookers, the Dalai Lama among them, stand before the world's second-largest indoor statue of the Buddha, at Chuang-Yeng Hall in Carmel, New York, on May 24, 1997. (Credit: AP/Wide World Photos.)

Buddhists, sees Buddha as the exemplar of religious realization, the *one* individual who attained Buddhahood and pointed the way to the spiritual realization of nirvāṇa for other beings. His attainment is unique; he is credited with having realized spiritual omniscience. Any followers of the Buddha who attain salvation experience nirvāṇa but not Buddhahood.

The Mahāyāna school, followed largely by the ethnic East Asian immigrant communities throughout the world, sees Buddha as a complete spiritual being, compassionate in all respects, but also as one of a plethora of "celestial" Buddhas who inhabit the universe and share their wisdom freely out of compassion for all suffering beings. It is the endeavor of Mahāyāna Buddhists to become Buddhas. They do this by first becoming *bodhisattvas*, or Buddhas-to-be, trying to realize their "Buddha nature," said to be inherent in all

beings. Various Mahāyāna schools—such as Zen—have become popular to many American convert Buddhists.

The Vajrayāna tradition has also become highly visible and immensely popular in the United States. Unlike the Theravāda and various Mahāyāna schools, which have a large number of ethnic Asian members, Vajrayāna has a minimal number of Tibetan refugees and immigrants from Inner and Central Asia. Instead, the followers of Vajrayāna in America are almost exclusively convert Buddhists. Vajrayāna adds a "fourth" jewel to the traditional three: the *guru*. Without undermining the Mahāyāna notion of celestial Buddhas, this school identifies the primary teacher or "root guru" of each practitioner with the Buddha. In a very real way the guru is the Buddha, and his or her behavior must be regarded as a manifestation of that status.

Conclusion

As the ancient beginnings of Buddhism fade into the distant past, so also do the earliest descriptions of the historical Buddha. Increasingly, American Buddhist groups are becoming profoundly democratic, emphasizing changing patterns of authority and also aggressively practicing what has come to be known as "socially engaged Buddhism." As a result, less emphasis is being placed on the specifics of the Buddha's life and practice, while more and more emphasis focuses on Buddha as a social reformer. Buddha's life is understood not as the archetypal model for bygone times, but rather as that of a pioneer who offered a resilient set of human values that could stand the rigors of changing times and cultures. Although many Asian immigrant Buddhists persist in seeing Buddha through the eyes of their ancestors, most American convert Buddhists have revisioned Buddha into an idealized picture of human wholeness, speaking to everyone's needs in modern society.

See also BUDDHISM; DALAI LAMA; DHARMA; GURU; NIRVĀṆA; REINCARNATION; TIBETAN BUDDHISM.

BIBLIOGRAPHY

Carrithers, Michael. *The Buddha.* 1983.

Collins, Steven. *Selfless Persons: Imagery and Thought in Theravāda Buddhism.* 1982.

Katz, Nathan. *Buddhist Images of Human Perfection: The Arahant of the Sutta Pitaka Compared with the Bodhisattva and the Mahasiddha.* 1982.

Thomas, Edward J. *The Life of the Buddha as Legend and History,* 3rd ed., rev. 1960.

Charles S. Prebish

Buddhism

Without doubt, the growth of American Buddhism has been enormously prolific in the past quarter century. In part as a result of a rather dramatic increase in the number of Asian immigrant Buddhists following the 1965 change in U.S. immigration laws and an ongoing expansion in the various American convert Buddhist communities, there are currently in excess of three million Buddhists residing in the United States.

It is now quite ordinary to find features on American Buddhism in popular and varied print media. In the fall of 1997, *Time* magazine did a comprehensive cover story of the American Buddhist movement, but much of the media interest in the current development of American Buddhism focuses on a variety of celebrity Buddhists. This focus on highly visible icons in the popular culture world, however, belies the fact that there have been Buddhists on this continent for more than a century and a half.

Historical Beginnings

The first Chinese, some of whom were Buddhists, arrived in California in 1849, shortly after the discovery of gold at Sutter's Mill, and by 1860 roughly 10 percent of Californians were Chinese. By 1870 there were more than sixty thousand Chinese in the United States.

Following the passage of the Chinese Immigration Exclusion Act of 1882, new Asian immigrant Buddhists began to appear in the United States, primarily from Japan. Following the World Parliament of Religions in Chicago in 1893, a number of the Rinzai Zen teachers began to take up residence in America. In addition, in 1899 two Pure Land missionaries settled in San Francisco as the first Buddhist clergy to become permanent American residents. Buddhism did not gain much support during the Victorian era because it appeared to be lacking two qualities especially attractive at the time: optimism and activism. Although Buddhism appealed to some aspects of the Victorian ethos, it was perceived as being largely pessimistic and passive.

Twentieth-Century Historical Developments

In the first decade of the twentieth century, U.S. census figures reveal that the Japanese population tripled (from 24,326 to 72,157). Rinzai Buddhist teachers continued to appear on the American scene, as did additional teachers in the Pure Land tradition, the latter group naming itself the Buddhist Mission of North America in 1914. Pure Land and Zen were not the only Japanese Buddhist groups to appear in America during this early period. In 1912 the Shingon sect established a temple in the "Little Tokyo" area of Los Angeles. The growth and development of all of these groups were severely truncated by the Japanese Immigration Exclusion Act of 1924.

The outbreak of World War II was a catastrophe for the development of Buddhism in the United States. By June 1942 more than a hundred thousand people of Japanese ancestry had been interned. During this period the Buddhist Mission of North America renamed itself the Buddhist Churches of America—a title that is preserved today.

While many of the Japanese returned to the West Coast following the war, others did not, relocating on the East Coast and in the Midwest, thus spreading the Buddhist tradition throughout America. In addition, the Sōtō lineage of Zen made its first sustained emergence in about 1950. A third form of Zen appeared—known as the Sanbo Kyodan—which employed both Rinzai and Sōtō practices.

Perhaps more important, new Buddhist groups, not only from the Japanese Buddhist tradition but also from other Asian Buddhist cultures, began to appear following a change in U.S. immigration laws. As a result, the Sōka Gakkai tradition from Japan appeared, as did additional Chinese, Korean, and Vietnamese Buddhist groups. Tibetan Buddhist groups from each of the major sectarian lineages appeared, as did a variety of Buddhist communities from the Theravādin tradition in Burma, Sri Lanka, Thailand, Cambodia, and Laos. By 1990 there were 500,000 to 750,000 Theravāda Buddhists living in the United States. At the close of the millennium, every Buddhist sectarian tradition, from every Asian Buddhist culture, was represented on American soil.

The Continued Growth and Popularity of American Buddhism

By the mid-1950s a variety of circumstances and events coalesced in American culture that provided the occasion for Buddhism to leap out of its appeal to primarily ethnic Asian immigrant groups and to attract substantial numbers of American converts largely, but not only, of European-American ancestry.

In the first place, America was witnessing an incipient secularization. Moreover, secularization ushered in a profoundly pluralistic situation in America's religious landscape, creating what one writer called a "market situation." Buddhism was able to capitalize on that market situation by capturing a substantial following among religiously disenchanted Americans. Influenced by both the attraction of the "Beats,"

Buddhist monks demonstrating their thousand-year-old system of medicine by carefully spreading colored sand across an elaborate mandala, at the Arthur M. Sackler Gallery in Washington, D.C., on August 7, 1998. The following day they ceremonially dumped the mandala into the Potomac River, to spread its healing qualities outward into the Chesapeake Bay and throughout the world. (Credit: AP/Wide World Photos.)

who championed Buddhism, and the "consciousness explosion" of the 1960s, many Americans began to turn East in their search, eventually settling into Buddhist practice with one Buddhist teacher, or "dharma-hopping" from one teacher or center to another. An added impetus to the general movement was the development of a plethora of university courses in Buddhism, providing inquirers with the potential to study Buddhism, sometimes with professors who were Buddhists themselves.

Many Asian Buddhist teachers who appeared on the American scene in the latter half of the twentieth century became popular figures as they spread their Buddhist teachings across the continent. However, as American Buddhism approaches the turn of the century, first- and second-generation Western dharma heirs of these teachers have come to dominate the picture in American Buddhism. Interestingly, a whole new literature has developed to investigate the tradition. Popular and scholarly books on American Buddhism have developed into a cottage industry, and an

impressive list of Buddhist periodicals and dharma products can be found in the marketplace.

Major Issues in American Buddhism

In their 1998 edited volume *The Faces of Buddhism in America*, Charles S. Prebish and Kenneth K. Tanaka outline five major multifaceted issues confronting American Buddhism today: ethnicity, practice, democratization, engagement, and adaptation. Preliminary to a consideration of these issues, however, American Buddhism faces a more critical concern: How does one decide just who actually is a Buddhist? Each of the Buddhist traditions currently present on American soil offers its own unique answer—and these answers differ significantly from one another. As Jan Nattier notes in *The Faces of Buddhism in America*, "Is it enough merely to call oneself a Buddhist, or are other features—certain beliefs, certain ritual practices (such as meditation or chanting), or perhaps even active membership in a specific organization—

required as well?" To date, the question remains unresolved.

Today the vast majority of Buddhists in the United States are Asian Americans. There has been much discussion about whether there are two Buddhisms in America (Asian American and European American Buddhism); three Buddhisms (elite Buddhism, evangelical Buddhism, and ethnic Buddhism); or some other designation. There seem to be as many theories as there are theorists. Perhaps the best solution is that of Paul D. Numrich, who simply divides American Buddhists into "Asian immigrants" and "American converts." This delineation has an added bonus. The category of American converts includes all Americans who might adopt the Buddhist tradition, including African Americans and Hispanic Americans, among others. Numrich also shows that the "Asian immigrants" and "American converts" are not as disparate as one might think, using to term "parallel congregations" to describe a growing movement in some Buddhist centers to include *both* groups in the overall community.

There seems little disagreement that Asian immigrant communities and American convert communities engage in significantly different Buddhist practices. The American community tends to gravitate toward the meditational traditions, while the Asian community generally maintains practices consistent with ritual activity or Pure Land observance. The single exception is Sōka Gakkai, a mostly convert tradition that engages in ritual chanting of a Buddhist text. Various aspects of Buddhist practice have also been utilized in psychotherapy, stress reduction, and similar enterprises.

Unfortunately, beginning in the 1980s some American Buddhist communities began to experience the fallout of a variety of scandalous behaviors by some of their Asian and Western Buddhist teachers. As a reaction against this, many American Buddhist communities—probably even the majority—have begun to undergo a process of democratization that encompasses changing patterns of authority, changing gender roles, and an acceptance of nontraditional lifestyles. This has included creative consideration of the largely nonmonastic preference of the American Buddhist community, its profoundly city-based membership, the decision-making process within communities, regulation of behavior within both monastic and lay communities, the equality of women in American Buddhism, and sanction for homosexual Buddhists.

Only a century after Buddhism in America was criticized as being socially passive and perhaps even world-rejecting, a form of profoundly active "socially engaged Buddhism" has developed on the American landscape. Utilizing Buddhist values and American forms of protest and active social involvement, socially engaged Buddhists have aggressively undertaken hospice work, ecological programs, prison reforms, and other techniques in an attempt to infuse sanity into our dialogue with the planet and with each other. While a large portion of this work has been coordinated by an organization known as the Buddhist Peace Fellowship, founded in Hawaii in 1978, a huge number of other communities, from virtually all the American Buddhist traditions, have taken up the cause.

Nearly all of the early researchers in American Buddhism focused much attention on the issue of adaptation—the degree to which Buddhist groups acculturated to the American religious environment. The question continues to occur in the literature. Almost uniformly, each writer suggests that Buddhism must develop some distinctive Americanization process to become an integral part of the fabric of America's religious heritage. Lately a few voices of dissent are beginning to appear. Victor Hori, a Canadian Rinzai priest and academic professor, suggested in *The Faces of Buddhism in America* that "The call for an Americanization process is unnecessary. . . . What Americans have been practicing for the last several decades is already Americanized Zen. Pouring wine into a new bottle immediately made it a different wine, although it is an ongoing process." In a chapter of the same book, Jan Nattier pointed out that American Buddhism may eventually remove some of the distinctly American elements in the developing American Buddhism.

If one of the bookends of the five issues facing American Buddhism is the question "Who is a Buddhist?" the other is the equally important question of whether American Buddhism will develop an ecumenical sense of itself. To date there have been few attempts. Although a few ecumenical organizations have formed, there seems little certainty that these have been successful efforts in assisting American Buddhists to talk across cultural, racial, ethical, doctrinal, and social lines.

Conclusion

It would not be incorrect to assert that virtually all of the earliest conclusions about the future of Buddhism on this continent have been mostly wrong. The first inkling of sane and accurate conclusions emerged from two small and often overlooked articles appearing near the end of the 1980s. The first, Rick Fields's "Future of American Buddhism," was published in a 1987 issue of the *Vajradhatu Sun*. The second, written by Jack Kornfield, was called "Is Buddhism Changing

North America?" and was published in Don Morreale's *Buddhist America: Centers, Retreats, Practices* (1988). Each focused on the issues discussed above, offering insightful perspectives on how to infuse a powerfully sane application of Buddhist ethics into all aspects of the concerns embraced by ethnicity, practice, democratization, engagement, and adaptation.

About a decade later, in a conference on Buddhism in America held in Boston, Lama Surya Das, a leading figure in American Buddhism, delivered the closing keynote address, titled "Emergent Trends in Western Dharma." He identified ten items that he believed would characterize the American Buddhism of the future: (1) dharma without dogma; (2) a lay-oriented *sangha;* (3) a meditation-based and experiential tradition; (4) gender equality; (5) a nonsectarian tradition; (6) an essentialized and simplified tradition; (7) an egalitarian, democratic, and nonhierarchical tradition; (8) a psychologically astute and rational tradition; (9) an experimental, innovating, inquiry-based tradition; and (10) a socially informed and engaged tradition. Although there are very many variables, both internal and external, it is quite likely that Surya Das's vision reflects an accurate picture of the American Buddhism that will develop in the next millennium.

See also BUDDHA; CHANTING; CHINESE-AMERICAN RELIGIONS; DALAI LAMA; DHARMA; GURU; JAPANESE-AMERICAN RELIGIONS; NIRVĀṆA; REINCARNATION; SOKA GAKKAI; TIBETAN BUDDHISM; ZEN.

BIBLIOGRAPHY

Batchelor, Stephen. *The Awakening of the West.* 1994.

Fields, Rick. *How the Swans Came to the Lake: A Narrative History of Buddhism in America,* 3rd ed., rev. 1992.

Morreale, Don, ed. *The Complete Guide to Buddhist America.* 1998.

Numrich, Paul D. *Old Wisdom in the New World: Americanization in Two Immigrant Theravāda Buddhist Temples.* 1996.

Prebish, Charles S. *Luminous Passage: The Practice and Study of Buddhism in America.* 1999.

Prebish, Charles S., and Kenneth K. Tanaka, eds. *The Faces of Buddhism in America.* 1998.

Tweed, Thomas. *The American Encounter with Buddhism, 1844–1912: Victorian Culture and the Limits of Dissent.* 1992.

Williams, Duncan Ryûken, and Christopher S. Queen, eds. *American Buddhism: Methods and Findings in Recent Scholarship.* 1998.

Charles S. Prebish

Buster, Baby.

See Generation X.

C

Calendars

Knowledge of seasons and the ability to measure the passage of time have long been associated with religious powers in human societies. This knowledge was essential for most types of economies: Seasons predicted success in hunting, fishing, and planting. Many religious calendars used today observe festivals of the seasons that derive from these ancient usages. The similarity of the lunar cycle to the female menstrual cycle gave a gender dimension to certain aspects of cosmology and was reverenced in ritual observances. A lunar calendar produces months of 25 to 28 days; the solar calendar measures a year of the earth's orbit around the sun. Although few calendars have been able to exactly mark the time of the earth's orbit, which is 365 days, 5 hours, 49 minutes, and 46 seconds, it was possible to measure the solar cycle by careful measurement of the position of the stars. Since the earth's orbit allowed for a different view of surrounding constellations at each phase, ancient star watchers could predict the position of the stars from one year to the next.

Calendars often provide for syncretism of religious systems. For instance, the birth of Christ is commonly celebrated by Christians on December 25, approximately coinciding with the pagan Roman feast of Saturnalia, which was dated with the winter solstice. By making virtually the same date the occasion for Christmas, Christianity appropriated elements of the Roman festival into the celebration of Christ's birth. Among Jews in the United States, the winter festival of Chanukah (or Hanukkah), whose original purpose was to celebrate the reconsecration of the Temple in Jerusalem, has acquired customs of gift-giving similar to those of the Christian feast of Christmas.

Although it is more easily discerned, the lunar calendar does not exactly coincide with the solar cycle. As a result, after a period of years the months of a lunar calendar occur in different seasons. The solar calendar has a similar problem in that the earth's orbit around the sun requires an uneven part of a day. Thus, without some device of adjustment, both calendars lose accuracy from one year to the next. Talmudic practice, for example, periodically adds a lunar month to the Jewish calendar. The most accurate calendar was kept by the ancient Mayans and later adopted by the native peoples of Mexico. The Mayans used both the lunar and the solar calendars in separate calculations that reflected the dualistic currents of their cosmology. Divided into four sets of thirteen years each, every fifty-two-year cycle harmonized the two calendars.

Contemporary practice adds a single day to the month of February, allowing for a "leap" year in years divisible by four, an innovation introduced in Catholicism by order of Pope Gregory XIII (1572–1585). The Gregorian calendar is more accurate than the Julian calendar established by Julius Caesar in 47 B.C. In fact, the implementation of the Gregorian calendar required the loss of ten days (October 5–14) in 1582 to correct the discrepancies of the Julian calendar, which had celebrated February 24 twice each four years. The Julian calendar is still used, however, for certain liturgical feasts in some Orthodox Christian churches.

Calendars often begin their count from religious events. The Jewish calendar is based on the conjectured first year of Abraham's faith, considered to date some four thousand years before Christ. The Christian calendar was created by a monk who used the supposed year of the birth of Jesus Christ as the center of all time. Although the monk's calculations are now considered to have been incorrect, Christians calculate events before Christ's birth as "B.C." (Before Christ), and the years after his birth as "A.D." (*Anno Domini*, "in the year of Our Lord"). Muslims use the flight of the Prophet Muhammad from Mecca to Medina, the *hegira*, as the central date of their calendar. To avoid favoring one religion over another, dates are sometimes listed with the Christian calendar dates but with the letters "B.C.E." (Before the Common Era) and "C.E." (Common Era).

Calendars today continue to exercise an important function in contemporary religious observances. There is concern, however, that the commercialization of popular religious feasts such as Christmas and Easter obscures their spiritual meaning. Secularization is considered to have occurred for St. Valentine's Day (February 14), a date that no longer enjoys a direct connection with the feast day of the Christian martyr. Nonetheless, contemporary religion generates new festivals such as Kwanza, begun in the 1960s among African Americans as a transdenominational feast. Old traditions are also regenerated, like the Day of the Dead, taken from Mexican traditions and now incorporated into popular U.S. culture. Many religious festivals are observed in the calendars of public schools as part of civic tolerance for religious heritage.

See also CHANUKAH; CHRISTMAS; DAY OF THE DEAD; PASSOVER; PATRON SAINTS AND PATRON-SAINT FEASTS.

BIBLIOGRAPHY

Eliade, Mircea. *The Myth of the Eternal Return, or Cosmos and History.* 1954.

León-Portilla, Miguel. *Time and Reality in the Thought of the Maya.* 1973. Beacon Press. (Translation of *Tiempo y Realidad en el Pensamiento Maya: Ensayo de Acercamiento.* 1968.)

Neusner, Jacob. *Between Time and Eternity: The Essentials of Judaism.* 1975.

Ana María Díaz-Stevens

Calvary Chapel

The first Calvary Chapel was founded in 1965 by Chuck Smith in Costa Mesa, California. Thirty years later, there were more than 600 Calvary Chapels in the United States, as well as nearly 100 mission churches in other countries. The largest concentration of Calvary Chapels (255 churches) is in California, but 42 other states also have Calvary Chapels, including Washington, Oregon, Arizona, and Florida, each of which in the mid-1990s had more than 25 churches. There were also Calvary Chapels in 35 different countries, including Russia, the Philippines, Hungary, India, and several European nations. In a survey of several hundred Calvary pastors done in the early 1990s, the median church had 138 people in weekly attendance, but the modest size of these congregations is due to the fact that a quarter of these churches were less than two years old, and three-quarters had been founded in the past twelve years. Within the Calvary Chapel movement there are a number of churches that average more than 5,000 people in weekly attendance, including 5 such churches within the Southern California area.

Calvary Chapels have several distinctive hallmarks. They typically meet in buildings that are highly utilitarian and lack religious symbolism (e.g., public auditoriums, former grocery stores and warehouses, rented school gymnasiums, and storefronts). Worship is contemporary, led by a team of people playing guitars, electronic keyboards, drums, and other assorted instruments, depending on local talent. The sermon is typically a verse-by-verse exposition of a chapter from the Bible. During the week there are home Bible study groups led by members of the church, and these informal gatherings often include time for personal sharing and prayer for each other's needs. Larger megachurches also have dozens of different interest groups that meet weekly.

When Chuck Smith started the church in the mid-1960s, it was in reaction to the organizational formalism of his own Foursquare denomination. His early ministry was to "hippies" and other people associated with the counterculture who were trying to get off drugs and live a productive life. In the early boom years of the church, it met in a circus tent before finally building in 1974 a permanent sanctuary that seats 2,300 people. In the first decade of the Calvary movement Christian concerts that featured the music of recent converts attracted many people who might never have stepped through the doors of a traditional church. Even today, worship services have a casual style, with members and clergy dressing informally. The constituency of the church is largely baby boomers and their children. In spite of the growth of Calvary Chapels, Chuck Smith claims that it is not a denomination but instead a network of independent churches. There is no central seminary where pastoral training occurs; instead, the conservative biblical theology of the movement is maintained through thousands of hours of tapes of Smith's sermons, which are now augmented by radio ministries and tapes by pastors of the many megachurches that have evolved over the years.

See also CHURCH; DENOMINATION; MEGACHURCH; NEW RELIGIOUS MOVEMENTS; POSTDENOMINATIONAL CHURCH.

BIBLIOGRAPHY

Balmer, Randal. *Mine Eyes Have Seen the Glory.* 1989.
Miller, Donald E. *Reinventing American Protestantism.* 1997.
Smith, Chuck, and Tal Brooke. *Harvest.* 1987.

Donald E. Miller

Campbell, Joseph

(1904–1987), writer, mythographer, teacher.

Joseph Campbell was the foremost American theorist of myth and evangelism for myth. Born in New York City and educated at Columbia University, he was professor of literature at Sarah Lawrence College. His first book on myth was the coauthored *Skeleton Key to Finnegans Wake.* While working on this book, he heard lectures by the German refugee Indologist Heinrich Zimmer and was mesmerized. Campbell devoted twelve years to turning the lecture notes of Zimmer, who died suddenly, into four tomes: *Myths and Symbols in Indian Art and Civilization; The King and the Corpse, Philosophies of India,* and *The Art of Indian Asia.* While formally only the editor, Campbell was in fact more like a coauthor. It was from Zimmer even more than from Jung, with whom Campbell is commonly linked, that Campbell took his comparative and symbolic approach to myth worldwide. From Zimmer, Campbell also took his interpretation of myth as mystical.

Even before undertaking the editing of Zimmer, Campbell had been writing the book that remains his best known: *The Hero with a Thousand Faces.* Here, in contrast to subsequent books, Campbell ties the meaning of myth to the plot, and claims to have deciphered the common plot of all hero myths. Whereas the plot of Otto Rank's *Freudian Myth of the Birth of the Hero* (1909) covers the hero's life from birth to young adulthood, the plot of Campbell's hero covers the hero's adult life. Whereas the heart of Rank's plot is the male hero's killing his father (thereby paving the way for sex with his mother), the heart of Campbell's plot is the male or female hero's journey to a strange, new, divine world. That plot is far more Jungian than Freudian: the encounter occurs in adulthood rather than childhood, is with gods rather than with parents,

Joseph Campbell in 1986, a year before his death. (Credit: © Joseph Campbell Foundation, www.jcf.org. Used with permission.)

and is loving rather than hostile. Understood psychologically, the journey symbolizes the rediscovery of the unconscious, from which an adult has lost contact in the process of growing up. *Hero with a Thousand Faces* became popular in the 1960s as a credo for "tripping." As Jungian as the meaning of the book is rightly taken to be, Campbell breaks with Jung in espousing a fusion of consciousness with unconsciousness, of humanity with divinity, for Campbell's human hero returns home to discover that divinity lay there all along, simply unrecognized. There is no opposition or even distinction between consciousness and unconsciousness; the two are identical. Campbell's interpretation reflects the influence of Zimmer, for whom consciousness must remain distinct from unconsciousness.

In addition to editing various books for the Jungian-oriented Bollingen Series, Campbell wrote a four-volume survey of world mythology called *The Masks of God.* Sometimes he remains a Jungian, but at other times he is more of a Freudian or even more of an ethologist, indebted to Niko Tinbergen and Konrad Lorenz. Sometimes Campbell roots myth in the unconscious; at other times, in conscious experience. Always obsessed with demonstrating the similarities among myths—the one hero with a thousand faces, the one god with many masks—he attributes the similarities sometimes to independent invention by each culture but at other times to diffusion from one culture around the world. Not only does his theory of myth fluctuate, so does his assessment of his four main branches of myth. Sometimes he favors the East over the West, primitives over moderns, planters over hunters. By the final volume, which is devoted to Western mythology from the mid-twelfth century on, he despises primitives, planters, and the East and now celebrates a self-reliant, heroic individualism epitomized by America. Gone is the advocacy, first expressed in *Hero,* of mystical oneness among all persons and all peoples. Now he advocates the triumph of individuals, and their triumph in the human, not the divine, world. To some critics, Campbell sounded like a cold warrior. Certainly his politics were unabashedly conservative. He was a staunch supporter of the Vietnam War and, ironically, an equally staunch opponent of the freedom-loving, consciousness-raising generations that took his *Hero* as their inspiration.

In his other main opus, the unfinished *Historical Atlas of World Mythology,* Campbell juxtaposes diffusion alongside independent invention as the sources of similarities among myths and elaborately traces the routes of diffusion. In the best-selling *The Power of Myth,* the book form of the eight-part 1988 TV interview with Campbell that Bill Moyers conducted for the Public Broadcasting System, Campbell sums up his lifelong advocacy of myth as necessary and virtually sufficient for a happy life. He returns to the theme "we are one," originally enunciated in *Hero.* Now he finds the unity not merely in the similarities among myths worldwide but also in the newest source of myths: space travel. Seen from outer space, the earth seems one.

See also DIVINITY; MYSTICISM; MYTH; PSYCHOLOGY OF RELIGION; PSYCHOTHERAPY; SPACE FLIGHT.

BIBLIOGRAPHY

Campbell, Joseph. *The Hero with a Thousand Faces.* 1949. 2nd ed., 1968.
Campbell, Joseph. *The Masks of God.* 4 vols. 1959–1968.
Campbell, Joseph. *The Mythic Image.* 1974.
Campbell, Joseph, with Bill Moyers. *The Power of Myth.* 1988.
Golden, Kenneth, ed. *Uses of Comparative Mythology.* 1992.
Larsen, Stephen, and Robin Larsen. *A Fire in the Mind.* 1991.
Noel, Daniel C., ed. *Paths to the Power of Myth.* 1990.
Segal, Robert A. *Joseph Campbell: An Introduction.* 1987. 2nd ed., 1990.
Zimmer, Heinrich. *The King and the Corpse,* edited by Joseph Campbell. 1948. 2nd ed., 1956.

Robert A. Segal

Campus Crusade for Christ

Campus Crusade for Christ is a conservative evangelical parachurch organization focusing on evangelism and discipleship. Founded on the campus of UCLA in 1951 by former candy salesman and Fuller Theological Seminary graduate William R. "Bill" Bright (1921–), Campus Crusade quickly became well known through a revival that claimed more than 250 converts, including many prominent campus leaders and athletes. The organization grew steadily during the 1950s, keyed by its leader's pragmatic evangelical ecumenism and emphasis on a simple, nondenominational "spiritual pitch," standardized in the late 1950s in Bright's tract *The Four Spiritual Laws.*

In 1962 Campus Crusade moved to an expansive new headquarters at Arrowhead Springs, a former resort near San Bernardino, California. At that time the organization created the Institute of Biblical Studies (later, the International School of Theology) to train workers for its expanding array of outreach programs. Among Campus Crusade's new initiatives in the 1960s were evangelistic training programs for laypeople and businessmen; work among military personnel both within the United States and overseas; and Athletes in Action, a venue for Christian athletes—most notably basketball players—to evangelize athletes and sports fans through exhibition games with college and professional teams.

The period from the late 1960s through the 1970s was one of meteoric growth and substantial visibility for Campus Crusade. From a full-time staff of fewer than 2,000 in 1969, the organization grew by nearly 500 percent during the 1970s. Part of this was tied to Bright's support for traditional American values, patriotism, and close identification with growing evangelical involvement in conservative politics. More important, however, was Campus Crusade's timely and innovative strategies that reemphasized traditional evangelical themes of conversion and repentance. Most successful during this period was its intensive evangelistic program "Here's Life America." Built around the ubiquitous catchphrase "I Found It!" the campaign targeted more than 250 metropolitan areas between 1973 and 1978, utilizing a combination of interchurch cooperation and savvy use of various media, from billboards and bumper stickers to telephone counseling and television specials.

During the 1980s and 1990s Campus Crusade continued to expand its scope of operation. In recognition of the growing multicultural realities of American society, it began new programs on campus aimed specifically at Hispanic, Asian, and African-American students. After the collapse of the Soviet Union, Campus Crusade played a central role in the cooperative North American evangelical CoMission and CoMission II efforts to promote Christian morals and evangelism in Russian schools. But, undoubtedly, the organization's most successful project was the film *Jesus*. A presentation of the Gospel of St. Luke originally distributed to American theaters in 1979, it was adapted as a nonthreatening tool for foreign evangelism, eventually being translated into more than five hundred languages. In the 1990s the free distribution of videocassettes of *Jesus* became the focal point for communitywide cooperative evangelistic efforts, particularly in North America. By the late 1990s Campus Crusade claimed that more than one billion people had seen the film worldwide.

Although detractors have criticized Bright's theology as simplistic, and his organization as too closely identified with middle-class American values, Campus Crusade's stature within the evangelical subculture was immense by the late 1990s. Its bimonthly magazine *Worldwide Challenge* had more than 250,000 subscribers, and an enormous expansion of its new (1991) Orlando, Florida, headquarters was well under way. With more than 13,000 full-time staff worldwide, and an operating budget of nearly $300 million a year, Campus Crusade for Christ stood second only to the Billy Graham Evangelistic Association in terms of size, influence, and historic importance among the evangelical parachurch organizations that emerged in the second half of the twentieth century.

See also CONVERSION; EVANGELICAL CHRISTIANITY; INTERVARSITY CHRISTIAN FELLOWSHIP; PROSELYTIZING; TELEVANGELISM.

BIBLIOGRAPHY

Bright, Bill. *Come Help Change the World.* 1970.
Bright, Bill. *A Movement of Miracles.* 1977.
Campus Crusade for Christ International Archives. Orlando, Florida.
Quebedeaux, Richard. *I Found It! The Story of Bill Bright and Campus Crusade for Christ.* 1979.
Sherer, Joel. "Bill Bright." In *Twentieth-Century Shapers of American Popular Religion,* edited by Charles H. Lippy. 1989.
Zoba, Wendy Murray. "Bill Bright's Wonderful Plan for the World." *Christianity Today* (July 14, 1997): 14–20, 22, 24, 26–27.

Larry Eskridge

Capital Punishment

The practice of punishing wrongdoers with death has been a common feature of many cultures throughout human history. Ancient law codes, such as those of Hammurabi and the ones found within the Hebrew scriptures, illustrate this graphically. During the first three centuries of Christianity, it was probably the memory of the execution of Jesus and the early martyrs that led Christians to oppose capital punishment, but after the alliance of the church with the Roman Empire under Constantine I (A.D. 313), churchmen largely set aside objections and accepted use of the death penalty by combining elements of the Christian Old Testament and earlier Roman law.

The execution of Priscillian of Avila in A.D. 385, although protested by prominent Christian leaders, nonetheless set an ominous precedent—Christians killing fellow Christians over doctrinal differences. When a spate of popular heresies arose in the eleventh and twelfth centuries, the bishop of Rome enlisted the state as the church's "secular arm" to carry out the execution of condemned heretics. The groups that were the prime candidates for conviction of heresy (e.g., the early Waldenses) were also understandably the ones who openly declared that capital punishment was contrary to the teachings of Jesus.

It was only in the eighteenth-century Enlightenment that nonreligious attention was focused on the death penalty and arguments against it were formulated on philosophical grounds. Cesare Beccaria (1764), reinforced by Voltaire (1766), assembled an influential series of criticisms on rational, utilitarian grounds. This brought a reaction from others, such as Immanuel Kant, who formulated retributive counterarguments, insisting that execution was necessary for the balance of justice to be restored (1797).

Dr. Benjamin Rush, a Philadelphia physician, was the first American to call publicly for abolition, combining both religious and secular arguments against what he dubbed "the absurd and un-Christian practice" of capital punishment (1787). It is thus not surprising that controversy and confusion have dogged the issue throughout U.S. history. Strong voices both for and against it have often been heard, with most nineteenth-century Christian clergy supporting it by appeal to the Bible, and most abolitionists opposing it on humanitarian grounds.

A candlelight procession organized by People of Faith Against the Death Penalty on its way to Central Prison in Raleigh, N.C., on January 28, 1998, to protest the execution of thirty-eight-year-old Ricky Lee Sanderson, a confessed rapist. (Credit: AP/Wide World Photos.)

The Death Penalty After World War II

Two extraordinary periods full of change, however, have in the past half century affected usage of the death penalty dramatically.

1948–1976: Unexpected Opposition and Decline of Use

The excesses of totalitarian regimes, using state power to kill vast numbers of their own citizens, raised daunting questions about the future of humankind. Part of the postwar response was the adoption of the Universal Declaration of Human Rights in 1948 and the total abolition of the death penalty in the constitution of the new West German government (Article 102) in 1949. These two signs of hope for a new dawn opened the most intense European debate ever held about the morality of capital punishment. New to the conversation was the frank recognition given to the fact that state power had been horrendously abused. Awareness was high that governments could not function without errors and abuses, and it would therefore be well not to entrust them with the power of putting their citizens to death. The European consensus grew that the death penalty should no longer be a part of ordinary law codes in a modern state. The importance of strong safeguards to foster and protect human life from potential state abuse won new appreciation, with leaders of many Protestant churches joining in.

In the United States it was especially the executions of Julius and Ethel Rosenberg in New York (1953) and of Caryl Chessman in California (1960) that served to generate the first major protests with conspicuous religious involvement. By 1968 the National Council of Churches of Christ actually reached unanimity in endorsing (103 to 0) a statement that provided member churches with ten different reasons why the death penalty no longer deserved church support. First on that list was the Christian belief in "the worth of human life and the dignity of human personality as gifts of God," and last on it was "our Christian commitment to seek the redemption and reconciliation of the wrongdoer." But sandwiched between these two religious arguments were all the usual secular objections, now reinforced from a religious perspective as well.

This development within major U.S. churches coincided with a nationwide decline in, and then an actual moratorium on, executions for ten years (1967–1977). The United States was moving in the same direction as most nations of the Western world. In *Furman* v. *Georgia* (1972), the U.S. Supreme Court, pointing to the "freakish" and "arbitrary" ways in which the death penalty was being carried out, declared that such use was "cruel and unusual punishment in violation of the Eighth and Fourteenth Amendments." The pendulum swing toward abolition seemed almost total.

1976–1999: Unexpected Reinstatement, and Opposition

But in 1976, the Court intervened again and brought the abolitionist trend against capital punishment to an abrupt halt when it ruled 7 to 2 in *Gregg* v. *Georgia* that "the punishment of death does not invariably violate the Constitution" and went on to indicate how new capital statutes could pass constitutional muster. This reversal rested essentially on the assumption that the admitted flaws in the system could be fixed if the states adopted laws with more "objective standards to guide, regularize, and make rationally reviewable the process for imposing death."

The confident optimism informing this grand act of faith in the system is one major difference that divides proponents and opponents of the death penalty. The former think the past shortcomings either are not relevant or can easily be remedied by revising the statutes, whereas the latter point to the escalating empirical evidence of wrongful convictions, prosecutorial misconduct, ineffective counsel, death-prone juries, racial bias, and discrimination against the poor and the mentally incompetent as a few of the flaws that make the system inherently unfixable.

Ironically, just as polls showed increasing support for the death penalty and as the execution of Gary Gilmore by Utah (1977) opened the new era with greater public support for the death penalty than ever, the National Conference of Catholic Bishops refused to go along. Their post–Vatican II transformation from being classical proponents to becoming staunch opponents of capital punishment first found full expression in their 1980 statement. Just as in the statements made earlier by many other U.S. religious groups, the bishops were careful to include the many secular reasons for opposing the death penalty, but these were secondary to the newly crystallized religious rationale that they pressed to the fore.

Since the Middle Ages Catholic theologians had defended as God-given the right of the state to execute wrongdoers. After World War II, however, the practical realization gradually imposed itself that this uncritical approval in theory was irrelevant, if not irresponsible, in light of the grim reality of modern killings by the state. Secular arguments might still persuade one to be theoretically either for or against the death penalty, but the new factor in the conversation was the change of priorities, starting with a religious appreciation of the special dignity of human beings as the handiwork of God. This cleared away the theoretical smoke screen. Capital punishment was exposed as a direct and deliberate act of destruction of human life, unnecessary (and therefore unjustified) in a modern society.

Many Catholic laypeople were initially slow to appreciate this historic shift. But as the challenge to embrace consistency in the religious evaluation of life was taken up vigorously by Pope John Paul II in the 1990s, and as its consequences were incorporated into the *New Catholic Catechism*, it soon became obvious that an important corner had been turned. Support for the death penalty was definitively relegated to the Catholic past. The burden of proof was radically shifted. The presumption was now in favor of the right of the human person to live. The modern state has no right to use the extreme penalty of death when its goals can be just as effectively achieved by remedies short of death.

While this "conversion" of Catholic leadership is clearly the most striking development on the U.S. religious scene regarding capital punishment, what it means for the future is not at all clear. The situation is extremely fluid. As polls confirm, many Americans still find the death penalty acceptable by an appeal to the Bible. Their defense of this position in the past was unshakable even when the system misfired. But how they and others may respond this time is an open question. With well over thirty-five hundred people waiting on death row, and with efforts being made by some politicians to further shorten the time between condemnation and execution, the prospect of the United States engaging in unparalleled destruction of its own citizens in the near future is disturbing to say the least.

One incident in early 1998 suggests that religious support for the death penalty may be softer than many assume. When the state of Texas carried out the execution of a converted murderer, Karla Faye Tucker, the evangelical weekly *Christianity Today*, after careful review of all the inhumane aspects, including the media circus, withdrew its former support step by step and concluded that "the death penalty has outlived its usefulness."

Conclusion

Capital punishment has undoubtedly occupied a surprisingly privileged pedestal in Christian ethics for most of the past millennium, but as the millennium ends, religious support for it is clearly diminishing. Currently in many U.S. religious circles it is viewed as strikingly parallel with that other "peculiar institution" in U.S. history—human slavery—which in its day was likewise sanctioned with biblical argument by many of its Christian practitioners. Both of these inhumane institutions lose any religious warrant when the biblical evaluation of the human person as made in the image and likeness of God is given greater prominence.

In the 1990s it became standard practice in death-penalty states for religious groups to hold vigils protesting every execution. In 1997 the American Friends Service Committee (Quakers) began a national project, "Religious Organizing Against the Death Penalty," aimed at raising consciousness and consciences. Sister Helen Prejean's book *Dead Man Walking*, and the film based on it, were used as tools for helping to introduce groups of church people to the stark reality of the system that is so easily ignored. A broad variety of Jews, Christians, Buddhists, Muslims, and others shared resources, illustrating that the use of the death penalty is basically incompatible with central religious insights and values of the major traditions.

The continued flaws plaguing the post-*Gregg* system just as they did the pre-*Furman* system led the American Bar Association in 1997 to call for another national moratorium on executions. Many religious groups have joined in, organizing signature-gathering campaigns to promote a "Moratorium 2000." Such initiatives are among the more visible ways in which many Americans are trying to bring their religious convictions to bear on the issue of the U.S. death penalty as the new millennium approaches.

See also BIBLE; CONSCIENTIOUS OBJECTION; DEATH AND DYING; MAINLINE PROTESTANTISM; PACIFISM; ROMAN CATHOLICISM.

BIBLIOGRAPHY

Bedau, Hugo Adam, ed. *The Death Penalty in America: Current Controversies.* 1997.

Bowers, William J. *Legal Homicide: Death as Punishment in America, 1864–1982.* 1984.

Costanzo, Mark. *Just Revenge: Costs and Consequences of the Death Penalty.* 1997.

Hanks, Gardner C. *Against the Death Penalty: Christian and Secular Arguments Against Capital Punishment.* 1997.

House, H. Wayne, and John Howard Yoder. *The Death Penalty Debate: Two Opposing Views of Capital Punishment.* 1991.

Mackey, Philip. *Voices Against Death: American Opposition to Capital Punishment, 1787–1975.* 1976.

Masur, Louis P. *Rites of Execution: Capital Punishment and the Transformation of American Culture, 1776–1865.* 1989.

Megivern, James J. *The Death Penalty: An Historical and Theological Survey.* 1997.

Melton, J. Gordon, ed. *The Churches Speak on Capital Punishment.* 1989.

Prejean, Sister Helen. *Dead Man Walking: An Eyewitness Account of the Death Penalty in the United States.* 1993.

Stassen, Glen H., ed. *Capital Punishment: A Reader.* 1998.

Steffen, Lloyd. *Executing Justice: The Moral Meaning of the Death Penalty.* 1998.

Amnesty International. *United States of America: The Death Penalty.* 1987.

James J. Megivern

Catholic Charismatic Renewal

Catholic Charismatic Renewal (CCR), the largest Catholic renewal movement in the United States, was founded in February 1967 at Duquesne University in Pittsburgh, Pennsylvania. On February 17, two Duquesne theology professors, William G. Storey and Ralph W. Keifer, experienced baptism with the Holy Spirit as evidenced by speaking in tongues. Their decision to embrace the Pentecostal experience was shaped by contacts with the Pentecostal movement and Presbyterian and Episcopalian charismatics, and by reading the New Testament Book of Acts, David Wilkerson's book *The Cross and the Switchblade* (1963), and John Sherrill's book *They Speak with Other Tongues* (1964). From Duquesne, CCR quickly spread to Catholic student organizations at Notre Dame University, Michigan State University, and the University of Michigan. After this, CCR spread into mainstream American Catholicism.

The first nationwide Catholic charismatic conference took place at Notre Dame University on April 7–9, 1967. In the early 1970s CCR had attracted the support of national and international Catholic leaders such as Father Kilian McDonald and Belgian cardinal Leon Joseph Suenens. The growing popularity of CCR was due to *New Covenant* magazine, which in 1975 had more than 60,000 subscribers in approximately 90 countries around the world. By the mid-1980s CCR claimed more than 6,000 prayer groups throughout the United States. In 1987 more than 35,000 participants attended the CCR national conference in New Orleans. From the United States CCR spread to Latin America (1969), Mexico (1970), Puerto Rico (1971), Korea (1971), Italy (1971), France (1972), Germany (1972), and Ireland (1972). The Catholic charismatic movement can now be found in more than 108 countries throughout the world. In 1973, leaders from CCR and eight Latin American countries met in Bogotá, Colombia, where they established the Carismatico Católico Latino-Americano (CCL-A). The renewal has since expanded to every country in Latin America. Today there are more than 1.9 million Catholic charismatics throughout Latin America. The Spanish-speaking Catholic charismatic movement in the United States does not trace its roots back to CCR but rather originated with the ministry of Glenn and Marilynn Kramar. These former Assemblies of God missionaries to Colombia converted to Roman Catholicism in 1972 and in that same year founded Charisma in Missions in East Los Angeles.

CCR was born at a significant moment in the history of Catholicism. The Cursillo movement, Vatican II, the ecumenical movement, the Jesus movement, and the counterculture movement of the 1960s all created an openness to experiential religions such as Pentecostalism. Vatican II declared: "These charismatic gifts, whether they be the most outstanding or the more simple and widely diffused, are to be received with thanksgiving and consolation, for they are exceedingly suitable and useful for the needs of the church." This statement contributed to the decision of thousands of Catholic leaders and laypeople to embrace CCR. In light of this comment, in 1969 the U.S. Catholic hierarchy recommended that CCR be allowed to develop. CCR grew rapidly because of the thousands of charismatic prayer groups, conferences, and retreats; *New Covenant* magazine; the Southern California Renewal Center (SCRC); and the support of more than 400 charismatic priests and half a dozen bishops. CCR was also spread through the writings of Ralph Martin, Kilian McDonald, Kevin Ranaghan, F. A. Sullivan, and Edward O'Connor. Today there are more than 3.3 million active Catholic charismatics in the United States and Puerto Rico.

In 1973 the growth of the Catholic charismatic movement attracted the attention of Pope Paul VI, who asked Cardinal Suenens to serve as his international liaison with the movement. In 1975 Pope Paul addressed 10,000 Catholic charismatics at St. Peter's Basilica in Rome, and in 1984 Pope John Paul II and Mother Teresa spoke to more than 7,000 charismatic priests from around the world at the International Catholic Charismatic Renewal conference in Rome. CCR is growing rapidly throughout Latin America, Africa, and Asia. Today there are 10 million active Catholic charismatics and 60 million postcharismatics (those no longer actively involved in charismatic gatherings) in more than 108 countries around the world.

Catholic Pentecostals began to call themselves Catholic charismatics after 1970 to distinguish themselves from the larger Protestant Pentecostal movement. Despite this change in name, CCR theology is very similar to that of classical Pentecostalism in its emphasis on baptism with the Holy Spirit, divine healing, spiritual renewal, a born-again experience with

Jesus Christ, and enthusiastic worship services. Pentecostal leaders such as David du Plessis (Assemblies of God) have had an important influence on the movement. Catholic charismatics differ from Protestant Pentecostals in their belief that speaking in tongues is not the initial evidence of baptism with the Holy Spirit. Furthermore, they also stress the importance of Catholic tradition, sacramental theology, hierarchy, the Eucharist, and the Virgin Mary. Today the University of Notre Dame, the University of Steubenville in Ohio, and the SCRC serve as the three centers of CCR in the United States. CCR has spread not only through conferences and prayer groups but also through the ministries of charismatic Catholics such as John Bertolucci and Mother Angelica. Although the high-water mark of CCR in the United States was in the 1980s, CCR is still one of the largest and most active spiritual renewal movements in the Catholic Church today.

See also CHARISMATIC MOVEMENT; GLOSSOLALIA; LITURGY AND WORSHIP; PENTECOSTAL AND CHARISMATIC CHRISTIANITY; ROMAN CATHOLICISM.

BIBLIOGRAPHY

O'Connor, E. D., C.S.C. *The Pentecostal Movement in the Catholic Church*. 1971.

Ranaghan, K., and D. Ranaghan. *Catholic Pentecostals*. 1969.

Sullivan, F. A. *Charisms and the Charismatic Renewal*. 1982.

Gastón Espinosa

Catholicism, Roman.

See Roman Catholicism.

Catholic Worker

The Catholic Worker is an eight-page tabloid newspaper published seven times a year by the Catholic Worker community, located on the Lower East Side of New York City. First distributed at New York's Union Square on May 1, 1933, *The Catholic Worker* announced Catholic social teaching to the unemployed and poor, but it soon came to represent the movement spawned by its readership. As that movement spread, Catholic Worker houses in other cities started their own newspapers, consistent with the style and content of the original paper. Conflicts have arisen within the movement—for example, during World War II over pacifism—but the New York paper has retained preeminence among other Catholic Worker papers.

The shaping vision of *The Catholic Worker* newspaper came from the movement's cofounders, Peter Maurin (1877–1949) and Dorothy Day (1897–1980). Maurin believed that the cure to modern social ills is to be found in a return to Christ and the social teachings of the church, which meant establishing houses of hospitality for the poor, roundtable discussions for the clarification of thought, and agronomic universities where people would learn to live on the land. Maurin expounded his three-pronged program of social regeneration in "easy essays"—clever, laconic commentaries on the church and world that appeared in most issues of the paper. Day revered Maurin but brought a more concrete view of social problems to the paper, much in the manner of the leftist publications for which she had written in her youth. Her editorials and columns contained detailed accounts of strikes, evictions, life on the streets, and the day-to-day hardships of the poor, along with stories of how Christians, past and present, have alleviated such hardships through works of mercy. The combined visions of Maurin and Day marked the paper with a unique blend of traditional doctrine and piety and revolutionary economics and politics now known as "Catholic radicalism."

Day was the chief editor of *The Catholic Worker,* but she always recruited community members to help, several of whom emerged as effective editors and writers, such as Michael Harrington, Tom Cornell, and Jim Forest. The paper has published an array of prominent authors, including Jacques Maritain, Martin Buber, Maria Montessori, Catherine de Hueck Doherty, Paul Hanly Furfey, Eileen Egan, Thomas Merton, and Daniel Berrigan. It has also regularly displayed the woodcuts of Fritz Eichenberg and Ade Bethune, whose images of gospel scenes and worker-saints vividly portray the ideals of the movement. It published articles and editorials decrying Nazi German anti-Semitism in the late thirties, condemning the atomic bomb one month after it was dropped, warning against U.S. involvement in Vietnam during the fifties, and supporting the civil rights movement early on and the United Farm Workers in 1973. The paper's editorial policy has remained consistent since Day's death, as can be seen in its condemnation of the Gulf War and its reports on the effects of the economic embargo against Iraq.

The paper's annual circulation increased dramatically in the early years: from 2,500 copies of the first issue to 20,000 copies in November 1933; 110,000 in May 1935, and 190,000 in May 1938. Circulation dropped sharply, but not below 50,000, during World War II, largely due to the paper's pacifist stance. Since 1950 it has fluctuated between 58,000 and 106,000, with the most recent records (December 1998) showing a subscription-copy production of 83,449 and a total run of 91,000. These figures are of limited usefulness because many copies are mailed in bulk to Catholic parishes and organizations, and the paper is often passed from one person to another. In any case, the numbers are a rough estimate, as is characteristic of such a far-flung, loosely organized movement. The price has been consistent from the start: a penny a copy, twenty-five cents per year. Originally set at a rate affordable to the poor, the price has also come to symbolize *The Catholic Worker*'s stance against the capitalist profit-making system.

See also JOURNALISM, RELIGIOUS; PACIFISM; PUBLISHING, RELIGIOUS.

BIBLIOGRAPHY

Cornell, Thomas C., Robert Ellsberg, and Jim Forest, eds. *A Penny a Copy: Readings from* The Catholic Worker. 1995.

Klejment, Anne, and Alice Klejment. *Dorothy Day and "The Catholic Worker."* 1986.

Roberts, Nancy L. *Dorothy Day and* The Catholic Worker. 1984.

Michael J. Baxter, C.S.C.

Celibacy

Celibacy is the practice of remaining unmarried for religious reasons. The term derives from the Latin *caelebs* and *caelibatus,* meaning "single" or "alone," and usually refers to the state of being unmarried. The practice of celibacy includes the intentional abstinence from sexual relations. While the word directly pertains to the state of being unmarried, a marriage may be described as "celibate" when a couple chooses to refrain from genital sexual activity.

Celibacy is adopted for various purposes, but most commonly for spiritual and ascetical reasons. Seeing it as a spiritual discipline that can enrich the life of prayer, religious traditions acknowledge that celibacy involves self-denial and renunciation. The practice of celibacy is found in various forms in Hinduism, Buddhism, and Christianity. Permanent celibacy is rare in Confucianism. In American Judaism, which places great emphasis on marriage and family, the practice is all but nonexistent. In Buddhism and Christianity, persons who choose celibacy often reside together in religious communities.

The practice of celibacy is generally not widespread within mainline Protestant communities in the United

States. However, one Protestant group known as the American Shakers did adopt strict observance of the practice. Beginning in the 1840s, this Christian group practiced celibacy as protection from what it saw as threats by the sensual, physical world. By the late twentieth century only a small number of American Shakers remained. Among U.S. Christian churches, the practice of celibacy is most often identified with the Roman Catholic Church, which requires a promise of celibacy for members of religious orders and for priests and bishops.

Origins and Historical Development

In Christianity, the practice of celibacy has a long and complex history. The earliest origins of the practice can be traced to religious cultic observance and to customs of sexual abstinence. Jewish Levitical laws of ritual purity and cleanliness influenced the liturgical practices of the first Christians. For centuries, Christianity has understood the celibate lifestyle to be a radical following of the example of Jesus Christ, who was unmarried. Christians believe that through the renunciation of the positive values of married life the celibate person embraces a deeply intimate spiritual relationship and union with Jesus Christ. Early believers were required to abstain from sexual activity in preparation for reception of the Eucharist, as priests were required to abstain from sexual relations for certain periods of time prior to offering sacrifice at the altar. At the end of the fourth century these customs led to sexual abstinence laws for then married priests. The monastic movements of the tenth and eleventh centuries also influenced the practice, as the celibate lives of monks gradually came to be seen as an ideal for all priests. Economic issues also played a role in clerical celibacy as churches dealt with questions related to the inheritance of church property by the children of priests. In the twelfth century, ritual laws of sexual abstinence for priests led to official church laws on celibacy. At the First Lateran Council, in 1123, the Roman Catholic Church formally required celibacy of all members of the clergy. During the Second Lateran Council, in 1139, canon law forbade the ordination of married men to the priesthood. Since the twelfth century in the West, celibacy has remained a universal requirement for ordination to the Roman Catholic priesthood. In the East, Christianity followed a different course, as many churches allowed the marriage of priests and deacons prior to ordination while forbidding marriage after ordination. Some Eastern churches continue to require a promise of celibacy by bishops.

Two major forms of the practice exist in present-day Christianity. First, celibacy is a monastic or ascetical practice whereby an individual makes a commitment to a religious way of life that precludes marriage. In this view, celibacy is seen as a symbolic manifestation of a Christian's status as a stranger or pilgrim in the world. Second, clerical celibacy is a practice whereby priests, bishops, and ministers remain unmarried as part of their service in the church. In this view, celibacy is seen as integral and necessary for clerical life in the church. The Christian practice of celibacy has often been described as a special gift "for the Kingdom of God" (Matthew 19:10–12; 1 Corinthians 7:7; 32–33) that enables ministers to be uniquely available for the service of others. Celibacy is seen as a gift and a special calling that is accepted by some Christians as a way to live their faith in the world.

Contemporary Questions

For centuries, Christians have both embraced and questioned the practice of celibacy. In recent years, the practice of mandatory clerical celibacy has become the subject of considerable debate in the U.S. Roman Catholic Church. Since the close of the Second Vatican Council in 1965, studies have predicted that a present shortage of priests will worsen due to retirements, fewer men entering seminaries, and departures from active priestly ministry. The requirement of priestly celibacy is frequently cited as one explanation for the decline in the numbers of U.S. Catholic priests. In 1975, approximately 57,500 priests served a Catholic population of about 48 million persons. In 1998, the Roman Catholic Church was the largest single U.S. religious denomination, with more than 61 million members. In that same year there were approximately 47,500 priests in active service. Since church law requires that a priest preside at the celebration of the Eucharist, theologians continue to study how these recent trends may affect this important Catholic ritual. In recent years, theologians have also begun to examine the relationship between celibacy and the nature of the priesthood itself. In 1965 the Second Vatican Council declared that celibacy "is not demanded of the priesthood by its nature," but the council strongly affirmed the suitability of the practice for priestly ministry. In the United States and elsewhere there have been calls for study of the feasibility of ordaining married men to the priesthood. Some bishops from Eastern Christian churches in North America—such as the Melkite Catholic Church—have recently ordained married male deacons to the priesthood.

Scholars continue to study how ecumenical dialogue between Eastern and Western Churches may be affected by these developments. Since 1965, the Roman Catholic Church has reaffirmed its teachings on mandatory priestly celibacy. Vatican II's decree on the priesthood, *Presbyterorum ordinis,* states that celibacy is "in harmony with the priesthood" and is "a feature of priestly life." In 1967, Pope Paul VI warmly praised priestly celibacy in the encyclical *Sacerdotalis caelibatus* and taught that the practice signified a love that "is open to all." Since 1978, Pope John Paul II has consistently endorsed and reaffirmed these earlier teachings. It is likely that discussion and debate about celibacy will continue in the U.S. Catholic Church for years to come.

See also CHASTITY; CLERGY; DEACON; ENCYCLICAL; PRACTICE; PRIESTHOOD; ROMAN CATHOLICISM; SEXUALITY; SPIRITUALITY; VATICAN II.

BIBLIOGRAPHY

Bassett, William, and Peter Huizing, eds. *Celibacy in the Church.* 1972.

Frazee, Charles A. "The Origins of Clerical Celibacy in the Western Church." *Church History* 57 (1988): 108–126.

Garrity, Robert M. "Spiritual and Canonical Values in Mandatory Priestly Celibacy." *Studia Canonica* 27 (1993): 217–260.

Pope Paul VI. *Sacerdotalis caelibatus* (The Celibacy of the Priest). 1967.

Schillebeeckx, Edward. *Celibacy,* translated by C. A. L. Jarrott. 1968.

Vatican Council II. *Presbyterorum ordinis* (Decree on the Ministry and Life of Priests). 1965.

Francis T. Hannafey, S.J.

Celtic Practices

Celtic practices are based on popular and historical conceptions of ancient Celtic culture, primarily of the British Isles and Ireland. Such practices and beliefs are today most commonly a matter of ideological preference rather than heritage, and more of a spiritual preference than an organized movement or religion. There is no evidence to suggest that the cultures we now refer to as Celtic thought of themselves as "Celts." Names such as "Celt," "Gaul," and "Gael" were bestowed by outsiders including Greek geographers, Roman historians, and various invading forces. The whole of the British Isles, Gaul (now France), and much of northern Europe were in the common language group that defined the Celtic culture. Those attempting a serious study of Celtic cultural history tend to draw from two broad categories: early Greco-Roman writings, which demonstrate clear biases against the Celts (the Romans would eventually con-

quer them), portraying them as barbarous and mysterious; and later Celtic sources, largely composed of Christianized Celts writing long after the systems of Celtic belief had vanished. Most works on ancient Celtic history insist that the cultures left no writings and transmitted all knowledge orally, though several sources report that St. Patrick ordered the burning of the books of the early Celts as part of a campaign of Christian missionization.

As no widely accepted historical record of the Celts yet exists, conceptions of Celtic history and contemporary Celtic spirituality are continuously reconstructed. Perhaps the most compelling figures to emerge from the mists of Celtic lore are the druids. Although druids were rumored to have practiced human sacrifice and other objectionable acts, most of these reports originated with classical writers. According to modern reconstructed Celtic cultural history, druids commonly appear as a wise priesthood, ecologically aware, holders of ancient wisdom, masters of natural power, and custodians of Celtic culture and religion. The druids, combination priest and magician, represent the spiritual side of the Celts, although they also are believed to have had an influence in governmental matters, serving as advisers to kings and chieftains. The role of Merlin in relation to King Arthur in literature is representative of this relationship.

Druidical figures are a constant in Celtic mythology, along with heroes such as Cuchulainn and Fionn MacCool. These heroes were master warriors, an idealized version of the actual feared Celtic warriors. Celtic mythology is full of stories of endless possibility, ancient wisdom, and magical creatures such as the fairy folk, the White Stag, and the Salmon of Wisdom.

Contemporary interest in all things Celtic is concurrent with the larger questioning of the values of the Western worldview. Broadly, Greco-Roman religious forms are considered to be temporal and transcendent in nature. Celtic religion posits in immanent divinity (creation infused with the divine, no separation of the creator and the created) assuming a multitude of forms, a sacred presence accessible through the landscape. Water and nature were considered portals from "normal" reality to a supernatural realm, sometimes referred to as the Otherworld. Wells, streams, woods, and caves were all places where magic was possible or likely.

Celtic, or immanent, considerations of nature address growing anxiety about the physical survival of humanity. There is a conviction among a growing number of people that we are spiritually out of tune with nature, ourselves, others, and the universe. Ancient wisdom is considered the key to regaining the harmonious, balanced, sacralized life of our ancestors. For many people, this ancient wisdom is best exemplified in Celtic practices.

Many New Agers and some Neopagans believe that ancient Celtic wisdom was passed to Celtic Christianity in an essentially smooth and harmonious transition from the old religion to the new. Celtic Christianity is considered more spiritual, more intuitive, and more in touch with nature than its Roman counterpart. Celtic Christian churches exist in the United States in growing numbers, in many cases combining Eastern Orthodoxy with various aspects of ancient Celtic mythology. One may consider modern Celtic Christianity in the United States to be an example of a revitalization movement. Legend to outsiders and historical fact to followers, the Celtic Christian Church is believed to have originated in Glastonbury, England, quite early in the first century C.E. Joseph of Arimathea, said to have been a tin merchant, came to Glastonbury with Mary after the death of Jesus, carrying two vessels containing the blood and sweat of Jesus on the cross. It is widely accepted that Christianity met almost no resistance upon its introduction to the British Isles and Ireland. Brigit, a highly venerated triple goddess, was Christianized as St. Brigid; some druids assumed roles as Christian priests; and the filidh, or poets of Celtic culture, became monks. The fluid syncretism of Celticism and Christianity is summed up in St. Columba's famous sentiment "Christ the son of God is my Druid." Other syncretic elements include the Celtic cross, a creative combination of ancient Celtic and Christian symbolism; and the Christian baptismal fountain, reminiscent of Celtic sacred wells and water holes. Commonly, Celtic Christianity emphasizes equal rights for women both within and outside the church, a reverence for nature, the importance of community, the worship of Celtic as well as Roman saints, and the primacy of the Celtic church.

Celtic practices are also a vital component of many Neopagan groups, especially those self-identified as Wiccan. Wicca, or Witchcraft, employs both ritual magic and a reverence for sacred nature. Many Wiccan groups worship figures derived from Celtic mythology, including a horned god (commonly Cernunnos) and a triple goddess (Maiden, Mother, and Crone). Wiccan groups usually celebrate the equinoxes, solstices, and Celtic holy days, especially Samhain (October 31) and Beltane (April 30), and including Lughnasadh (July 31) and Oimelc (January 31).

The term "Wicca," as well as many of the rituals used in Wiccan groups today, derives from the work of Gerald Gardner, who created rituals and philosophies based on his interpretation of pre-Christian Celtic worship emphasizing a central great Goddess. Various forms of Gardner's teachings appeared in the United States during the 1960s, fueling the advent of

American Neopaganism and the Celtic revival. Most people embrace things Celtic on an individual level and have been dubbed "Cardiac Celts," those who feel in their hearts that they are Celtic. Many subscribe to Celtic magazines, acquire Celtic "artifacts," or attend workshops and seminars on Celtic wisdom. Many books continue to be published on Celtic tradition, mythology, and spirituality, written largely from Neopagan or New Age perspectives. The commodification of the Celtic revival is evident in a wide variety of retail contexts, with the promise that possession of Celtic-flavored items, usually crafts or books (though also including a seemingly endless array of consumer goods), connects one with a Celtic past. One thus "acquires" Celtic identity through the collection of purchased "artifacts" and reconstructed wisdom.

Modern manifestations of Celtic religion, whether based in Neopaganism, Celtic Christianity, or an individualized spiritual practice, encompass values of ecological responsibility, gender equality, and spiritual growth. The "Celtic revival" is both a commercial and a spiritual venture, resembling in many aspects mainstream America's artificial construction of a generic Native American spirituality. Constructed Native American and Celtic philosophies are devoid of an accurate historical context, representing an idealization of a "noble savage" archetype that serves as a model for ecological awareness, and serving as motifs for a wide array of consumer "artifacts," self-awareness and self-improvement seminars, and popular music and literature. A common claim in New Age literature is the similarity between druidic practices of the Celts and the "shamanistic" practices of North American Indians. Unfortunately, no widely accepted evidence exists detailing the practices of early Celts, making such generalized claims difficult to substantiate. Interest in things Celtic remains largely a spiritualized version of an unclear history, representing for many people a magical and harmonious way of living in balance with the world.

See also Divinity; Ecospirituality; Goddess; Liturgy and Worship; Magic; Missionary Movements; Myth; Nature Religion; Neopaganism; New Age Spirituality; Practice; Roman Catholicism; Spirituality; Wicca.

Bibliography

Cahill, Thomas. *How the Irish Saved Civilization.* 1995.

Ellis, Peter Berresford. *The Druids.* 1994.

Ellwood, Robert S. *Many Peoples, Many Faiths.* 1982.

Ellwood, Robert S., and Harry B. Partin. *Religious and Spiritual Groups in Modern America.* 2nd ed. 1988.

Green, Miranda. *The Celtic World.* 1995.

Green, Miranda. *Dictionary of Celtic Myth and Legend.* 1992.

Hutton, Ronald. *The Pagan Religions of the Ancient British Isles.* 1991.

Lewis, James R. *Magical Religion and Modern Witchcraft.* 1996.

Miller, Timothy. *America's Alternative Religions.* 1995.

John Baumann

Centering Prayer

Centering prayer is a modern Christian form of what in the East would be known as meditation. Along with Christian meditation, a parallel practice developed by Dom John Main, it offers contemporary Christians the opportunity to engage in this ancient and universal spiritual discipline within a fully Christian context.

The practice was developed in the early 1970s by a group of Trappist monks at St. Joseph's Abbey, in Spencer, Massachusetts, partially for their own spiritual rejuvenation and partially in response to the increasing attraction of younger Christian seekers to Eastern meditational paths. Though the method itself was first formulated by Father William Meninger, its development and popularization have been largely the work of his two prominent colleagues, Father Basil Pennington and Father Thomas Keating.

In offering centering prayer as a contemporary spiritual practice, these monks insisted that they were merely recovering and presenting in an accessible, updated form the living core of their own contemplative heritage. Father Menninger claims to have developed the method of centering prayer directly from the fourteenth-century Christian spiritual classic of Juliana of Norwich, *The Cloud of Unknowing,* and Thomas Keating bases his own exposition of the method largely on the desert fathers (particularly John Cassian) and St. John of the Cross.

Like all forms of meditation, the goal of centering prayer is to move beyond the "faculties" (memory, imagination, reason, and affective emotion, which tend to reinforce the self-defining mechanisms of the ego) and to open to God at the most primordial level of the soul. This aspiration, well attested in Christian mystical tradition, is known as the as the *apophatic* path, or "via negativa." But centering prayer is innovative in its approach. Traditional meditation practice prescribes the use of a mantra, a word or a phrase repeated continuously throughout the period of meditation as a focal point for attention. In centering prayer the "sacred word" is used not continuously but only discretely, when one is aware of being attracted by a passing thought, emotion, or sensation. Like a piece of string tied around one's finger, it serves as a simple mnemonic device to remind one to let go of the thinking and to rest in the bare presence of God.

Because the mental band in which centering prayer operates has significant overlap with the dream state, there is a tendency for the unconscious to become significantly engaged, far more so than in more traditional forms of meditation. Thomas Keating noticed this tendency (which he identified as a "purification of the unconscious") and recognized its enormous implications for the integration of ancient spiritual practice and modern psychological insight. Upon this cornerstone he constructed his highly influential teachings on the idea of "the divine therapy."

While centering prayer has found broad acceptance within the Roman Catholic and Protestant mainstream, it is not without controversy. Like other forms of Christian meditational prayer, it has periodically come under attack from the Religious Right as a thinly disguised attempt to introduce "Eastern" spiritual practices into the Christian milieu. But it has raised concerns among some in the meditation camp as well, who look with alarm on centering prayer's instruction that it is acceptable to let go of the sacred word—a permissiveness, purists claim, that can lead to a state of fuzzy, diffuse spiritual perception known as "sinking mind." Centering prayer adherents counter that letting go of thoughts (and it is *thoughts* one lets go of, not the sacred word) is intended as a gesture of spiritual surrender. Theologically it resonates with Christ's prayer in the garden of Gethsemani, "Not my will but thine be done, O Lord." The goal is not a still or clear mind, but an attentive heart.

Despite its naysayers, centering prayer has gained ground steadily in thirty years. Now numbering tens of thousands of practitioners worldwide (well organized in a network called Contemplative Outreach, Ltd.), it has emerged as a significant force in the contemporary spiritual renewal.

See also DIVINITY; DREAMS; GOD; MAINLINE PROTESTANTISM; MANTRA; MEDITATION; MYSTICISM; ROMAN CATHOLICISM.

BIBLIOGRAPHY

Bourgeault, Cynthia. "From Woundedness to Union: The Psychology of Centering Prayer." *Review for Religious* 58, no. 2 (March 1999): 158–167.

Keating, Thomas. *Intimacy with God.* 1994.

Keating, Thomas. *Invitation to Love.* 1992.

Keating, Thomas. *Open Mind, Open Heart.* 1987.

Pennington, Basil. *Centering Prayer.* 1980.

Cynthia Bourgeault

Chakra

Literally meaning "wheel" but also figuratively referring to an unfolded lotus blossom, the word "chakra" (Sanskrit, *cakra*) comes from India. In the context of meditation and related spiritual practices, it has been used in relatively esoteric texts since roughly the fifteenth century C.E. (although similar ideas appear in texts as early as the fourth century B.C.E.) to refer to a number of energy centers in the subtle body along the spinal column and associated with various states of consciousness, colors, deities, geometrical shapes, and sounds. The idea of such energy centers appears also in various traditions in Asian cultures beyond India, and the term has now entered the vocabulary of American psychological, medical, and spiritual discourse influenced by traditional Asian thought.

The classical idea of the chakras is associated with the notion that the physical body is infused by a subtle but powerful inward energy said to be of the nature of divine consciousness. (Some contemporary therapeutic theories associate the chakras with various external auras, but these are not mentioned in traditional Indian texts.) This conscious energy is known in Indian languages by various terms, the most common being shakti (Sanskrit, *sakti,* "effective power") or kundalini (Sanskrit, *kundalini,* "coiled"), the latter because it is said to rest dormant at the bottom of the spine, like a sleeping snake. In Chinese this energy is known as *chi* (pinyin *qi,* "life force").

Through the practice of meditation and Yoga and, according to some classical traditions, the compassionate grace of God given through the guidance of a spiritual master, this dormant consciousness is said to become "awakened" and to move up the spine along a subtle channel known in Indian texts as the *susumna nadi* ("gracious stream"). As it does so, this energy opens the various chakras, which are sometimes described as beautiful lotuses that unfold their petals when nourished by the power of ascending consciousness.

The number and location of the chakras vary somewhat according to different texts, but most relevant traditions recognize at least six such centers of consciousness within the subtle body in addition to a seventh, said to exist above the head. According to the sixteenth-century *Sat Cakra Nirūpana* (Investigation into the Six Chakras), the six subtle body chakras reside at the base of the spine, the reproductive region, the navel area, the heart, and the throat, and between the eyebrows. These are known as the muladhara, svadhisthana, manipura, anahata, visuddha, and ajña chakras, respectively. Above the head unfolds the splendid sahasrara chakra, the "thousand-petaled lotus" of universal consciousness.

Thoughts and motivations centered in the region of the muladhara chakra are said to be driven by brute animal desires and framed by feelings of insecurity. When awakened by the shakti, however, this chakra stands as the source of creativity and change, without which there can be no transformation. Attitudes and motivations at the level of the svadhisthana chakra turn on sexual feelings and are associated with such qualities as pretense, suspicion, disdain, delusion, false understanding, and petty self-centeredness. When purified by the shakti, these attributes are said to be transformed into trust, concern, purity of intention, genuine understanding, and warm affection. Thoughts and emotions arising in the manipura chakra are based in competition, treachery, shame, jealousy, inertia, sadness, ignorance, and fear. However, the shakti transforms the preoccupation with shame into an emphasis on honor, deceit into authenticity and loyalty, sadness into joy, and so on.

Unawakened attitudes and motivations at the lower three chakras tend to be negative, self-centered, and finite. Entry into more expansive, even universal modes of consciousness takes place when the shakti ascends to the anahata chakra at the level of the heart. This is said to be to be the home of compassion and the place where awareness becomes immersed in the foundational love that supports the universe. The visuddha chakra, at the throat, is concerned with the ability to listen acutely, both to sacred teachings and to the voices of those who need help, and with the skill to express oneself in a way that brings understanding to others. Entering the ajña chakra, between the eyebrows, the shakti emerges into transcendental consciousness unbound by time and space. The sahasrara chakra, above the head, is depicted as a fully blossomed lotus flower from which drop golden streams of nectar and is said to be the realm of the infinite, divine consciousness in which all modes of awareness have their source and toward which all are pulled.

See also DIVINITY; HEALING; HINDUISM; MEDITATION; YOGA.

BIBLIOGRAPHY

Avalon, Arthur [Sir John Woodroffe], trans. *The Serpent Power.* 1974 (repr.).

Brennan, Barbara Ann. *Hands of Light: A Guide to Healing through the Human Energy Field.* 1988.

Judith, Anodea, and Selene Vega. *The Sevenfold Journey: Reclaiming Mind, Body and Spirit through the Chakras.* 1993.

Kripananda, Swami. *The Sacred Power: A Seeker's Guide to Kundalini.* 1995.

Myss, Caroline. *Anatomy of the Spirit: The Seven Stages of Power and Healing.* 1997.

Ravenwolf, Silver, and Anodea Judith. *Wheels of Life: A User's Guide to the Chakra System.* 1987.

William K. Mahony

Channeling

Channeling might be broadly defined as an individual receiving or transmitting information through a consciousness not his or her own. By this definition there are certain continuities between channeling and many other forms of religious revelation, including those of shamans, oracles, and prophets. Channeling's closest predecessor in American religion is perhaps spiritualism, a nineteenth-century movement concerned with contacting the spirits of the dead.

But if channeling is more narrowly defined as a person (the "channel" or "channeler") inviting an entity to speak through his or her body for a certain period of time, then channeling is best seen as a late-twentieth-century phenomenon. Noted scholar of the New Age J. Gordon Melton has argued in his *New Age Almanac* that the term itself dates to the UFO contact movement of the 1940s and 1950s, and the use of radio and television as metaphors, when contactees would claim to have received messages "channeled" from the flying saucers.

The era of modern channeling might be said to have begun in 1963, when Jane Roberts (1929–1984), a housewife from New York state, began channeling "Seth." Roberts's books, such as *The Nature of Personal Reality* and *Seth Speaks* (in which she writes as Seth), have sold in the millions.

Channeling became part of American popular culture when it played a part in Shirley MacLaine's series of New Age autobiographies and the TV movies based on them. The channeler Kevin Ryerson played himself in MacLaine's 1987 TV movie *Out on a Limb.*

The most successful channels currently active are J. Z. Knight and Jach Pursel, who channel the warrior from Atlantis Ramtha and the disembodied entity Lazaris, respectively. Their organizations gross millions of dollars annually. But for every high-end channel there are thousands of small-scale ones, who might channel for a few people at a time and work free or for donations.

A typical channeling session might begin with the channel closing his or her eyes, perhaps first making an invocation. Then the "entity" would speak from the body of the channeler, often using different mannerisms, vocabulary, and accents from the host. The "entity" might lecture on a specific topic, or take ques-

New Age channeling energy spot marked by two concentric rings of stone on the ground near Sedona, Arizona, ca. 1988. (Credit: © Tom Bean/All Stock/PNI.)

tions from the audience. The content of channeled information varies somewhat but actually is fairly consistent and might include alternative histories (Atlantis, etc.), individual psychic readings, predictions of upcoming events, and techniques for healing the mind and body.

Anthropologist Michael Brown has pointed out that channeling has spread across America and is "now a well-established form of religious exploration that is likely to be with us for a while." One 1987 estimate was that tens of thousands of people had consulted channels and millions more had read up on them (John Klimo, *Channeling*). "Do-it-yourself" channeling is increasingly popular as more and more classes and books are available for getting in touch with your own spirit guide.

See also Lazaris; New Age Spirituality; Occult, The; Psychic; Séance; Shamanism; Spirit Guides; Spirit Possession; Spiritualism; Trance; Unidentified Flying Objects.

BIBLIOGRAPHY

Brown, Michael F. *The Channeling Zone: American Spirituality in an Anxious Age.* 1997.

Klimo, John. *Channeling.* 1987.

Melton, J. Gordon. *The New Age Almanac.* 1991.

Elijah Siegler

Chanting

Clearly contemporary diversity in North American religion limits our ability to define sacred rhythmic speech and chant with any specificity. Both these forms are found in rituals, and this has led to speculation about the relationship of speech, chant, and ritual at the birth of language. Both will be treated here under the general rubric of chant.

The chant serves several important functions in the history of religions, and religious chanting is usually set apart from secular song by virtue of context, personnel, and intent. In general it has been a universal medium linking the human with the divine, examples of the earliest of which may be found in the Rig Veda. These chanted phrases, intoned by priests, were deemed to have power because the very sounds were said to be rooted in the tonal structure of the universe. Both Buddhist and Hindu groups in contemporary America continue to ascribe to this view, and they practice accordingly.

Concepts analogous to this are being studied in current musical research, such as studies on sound color. Chanting of myths apparently has the same assumption system, for the ritual is held for only carefully chosen initiates by North American aboriginal tribal specialists, and then is performed only at specific sacred times. Moreover, the chant has been a means of communicating between the religious specialist, such as the shaman, and the greater-than-human powers, for it is through this vehicle that such a person has the authority to beseech favors from the sacred source. Thus having moral and religious authority to speak sacred phrases is a central belief for many practitioners of such sacred acts, and the probable foundation of professional priesthood.

However, chant also imposes other kinds of restrictions, such as proper expression, and this limits who may participate in vocal expression. This is evident in the recitation of the Qur'an in Islam, where only those properly trained in classical Arabic diction and in the rules of Qur'anic vocalization may publicly intone the sacred text. Paradoxically, chant is based on the premise that the sacred is approachable, perhaps even deliverable through repetitive patterns of vocal articulation, and, as a consequence, one could say that the ritual moment is "mythicalized" by the chant. Such a notion is crucial because it enlarges the personnel involved in ritual acts to cantors, choirs, and choral accomplices, even to listeners—as one hears strikingly in Eastern Orthodox liturgies.

Furthermore, there is an intrinsic connection between proper, even aesthetic, performance and effective rituals. Hence it is important that one maintain the correct tonal comportment, since deviations can not only change the religious effectiveness but also imply different meanings; chant usually tolerates only a narrow range of modifications before the performance is regarded as deviating from the acceptable norm. This suggests a clearly demarcated text for chant, as well as guidelines for musical and choral phrasings—a boundary setting that we are familiar with, for example, in Judaic Torah readings. These "normative" musical expressions may even lead to larger cultural definitions of aesthetic beauty, as is the case with Gregorian chant. Yet it should be noted that both rhythmic speech and chant have an identifiable relationship with popular song and folk culture, since many of the tonal and/or song phrasings have those origins. It follows, then, that certain kinds of chant have passed out of popular use. For example, little medieval Christian chant is found in modern Catholic worship, and new church groups, such as the Pentecostals, utilize popular songs and tunes almost exclusively in their services; in these, repetitive song choruses constitute something like chant. Another dimension of the chant is present in the so-called Negro spiritual, where call-response has a repetitive cadence.

It is also important to note that chant has functioned as a means of educating the participants in the verities of religion, since there is often a pedagogical element present, as is evident, for example, in Sufi *dhikr* in North America. Finally, some scholars see slogan chanting, such as occurs at political rallies, conventions, and sports events, as an appropriation of the religious form for social cohesion in a secular environment.

See also LITURGY AND WORSHIP; MUSIC; PRAYER; RITUAL; SOCIOLOGY OF RELIGION.

BIBLIOGRAPHY

Apel, Willi. *Gregorian Chant.* 1970.
Hill, Jonathan D. *Keepers of the Sacred Chants.* 1993.
Nelson, Kristine. *The Art of Reciting the Qur'an.* 1985.
Spector, Johanna. "Chanting." In *The Encyclopedia of Religion,* edited by Mircea Eliade. 1987.
Slawson, Wayne. *Sound Color.* 1985.
Waugh, Earle H. *The Munshidin of Egypt: Their World and Their Song.* 1989.

Earle H. Waugh

Chanukah

This eight-day festival, also known as "Festival of Lights," begins on 25 Kislev (late November to December). One of the few Jewish holidays not ordained in the Hebrew Bible, Chanukah or Hanukkah ("Rededication") commemorates the 165 B.C.E. victory of Jewish traditionalists over a military/political alliance of Syrian Greeks and Jewish Hellenists trying to eliminate Judaism in the land of Israel. Under the leadership

A young Jewish girl lights the candle on a menorah during Chanukah, 1994. She is aided by her grandfather, who is wearing a yarmulke (kippah). (Credit: © Richard Hutchings/PhotoEdit/PNI.)

of Judah Maccabee and his four brothers, the Jerusalem Temple was cleansed of foreign idols and rededicated to divine service, and this new festival was proclaimed. These events are recorded in the Apocrypha (1 and 2 Maccabees). A Jewish legend from early rabbinic times (second to third centuries C.E.) associates a miracle with Chanukah: Pure oil used to rekindle the menorah (candelabrum) in the temple, apparently only sufficient for one day, lasted eight days. Also in this period the central holiday ritual, kindling lights on a Chanukah menorah (or *chanukiah*) for eight nights, beginning with one and moving up to eight, was instituted. Many modern Jews understand Chanukah as epitomizing human struggles for religious freedom.

Chanukah is a minor holiday, and its observance, primarily domestic, doesn't require absence from work or school. A joyous holiday for children, traditionally celebrated with games, small money gifts *(gelt)*, and oil-fried foods such as potato pancakes *(lat-*

kes), Chanukah has disproportionate prominence in North America because it occurs near Christmas. Although the two holidays have no connection, giving of presents, sending cards, and inclusion of Chanukah in public seasonal celebrations are features of this festival's contemporary commemoration.

See also BELONGING, RELIGIOUS; JEWISH IDENTITY; JEWISH OBSERVANCE; JUDAISM.

BIBLIOGRAPHY

Dosick, Wayne. *Living Judaism: The Complete Guide to Jewish Belief, Tradition and Practice.* 1995.
Ross, Lesli Koppelman. *Celebrate! The Complete Jewish Holidays Handbook.* 1994.

Judith R. Baskin

Charismatic Movement

The Charismatic Movement is a Christian movement focused on individuals and communities experiencing through the Holy Spirit the presence, power, and love of God. The movement celebrates the presence and power of the Holy Spirit in and among believers, and its affirmation of spiritual gifts appeals to participants in many Christian communions. The Charismatic Movement finds expression in denominationally sponsored institutions in white and African-American groups as well as in independent congregations and voluntary associations.

Although it has affinities with Pentecostalism, the Charismatic Movement emerged at midcentury among people whose affiliations and education stood in marked contrast to those of most Pentecostals. Early Pentecostals had spoken often of Protestant unity, insisting that their teaching represented nothing more than New Testament experience in the twentieth century. As purveyors of "old-time religion," they hoped to forge unity on a basis of restoration. Instead, mainline denominations dismissed Pentecostalism, challenging both theology and practice. Early Pentecostals regarded Roman Catholic and Orthodox Christians as objects of evangelization. Speaking in tongues and other spiritual gifts, they insisted, belonged only to those who had first been "born again." Despite their rhetoric of unity, Pentecostals had little contact with non-Pentecostal churches. (They called the latter "dead denominational churches.") Sixty years later, those who had once spurned tongues speakers found their denominations wrestling with forms of piety that resembled Pentecostal practices.

The Charismatic Movement had diffuse sources. With hindsight, it becomes evident that the groundwork was laid by specific events of the 1950s. In 1951, the Full Gospel Businessmen's Fellowship International (FGBMFI) organized in Los Angeles as an association of Pentecostal businessmen. Chapters opened across the country, and a monthly magazine, the *Full Gospel Business Men's Voice,* began publication in 1953. FGBMFI chapters hosted meetings for business professionals, featuring testimonies of members who had been baptized in the Holy Spirit. During the same years, David du Plessis, a South African immigrant who held Assemblies of God ministerial credentials, gained the friendship of leaders in the newly formed National Council of the Churches of Christ and the World Council of Churches. He discovered widespread curiosity about Pentecostals and attended ecumenical gatherings as an observer, making the acquaintance of many who would participate in the next decade in the Charismatic Movement. In Southern California in 1959, speaking in tongues occurred among a handful of Episcopalians. The most influential person to be drawn into this circle was Dennis Bennett, the successful rector of St. Mark's Episcopal Church in Van Nuys. Services at St. Mark's remained traditional, but religious enthusiasm ran high at charismatic prayer meetings. Amid rumors and dissension, Bennett resigned in the spring of 1960 and accepted a call to St. Luke's Episcopal Church in Seattle, a small mission church. A decade later, the church was thriving and Bennett had become the symbol of a large charismatic presence in his denomination. He noticed that charismatic experience tended to strengthen participants' commitment to their church and its endeavors. Whereas many early Pentecostals had been "come outers," midcentury tongues speakers were encouraged by mentors like David du Plessis on the outside and others within their denominations to remain in their churches.

Time and *Newsweek* stories about Bennett helped surface others in non-Pentecostal denominations who shared his experience. Within three years, the quarterly *Trinity* (the organ of the first charismatic renewal fellowship, the Blessed Trinity Society) reported that about 200 Episcopalians in greater Los Angeles spoke in tongues; several nearby American Lutheran Church congregations as well as the Bel Air Presbyterian and Hollywood First Presbyterian Church had tongues-speaking members. Through the 1960s, the Charismatic Movement grew in most mainline Protestant denominations. Participants believed they had rediscovered the Holy Spirit, and their manifestations of this rediscovery forced some denominations to issue statements about belief and practice with regard to the Holy Spirit. Denominations established renewal service agencies, and many charismatics stayed in their denominations. An important book

that gave the movement visibility and impetus appeared in 1965: John and Elizabeth Sherill's *They Speak With Other Tongues.*

In 1967, the Charismatic Movement (or "Renewal," as participants preferred to call it) broke out in Roman Catholicism. A result of the interest of several Catholic laymen faculty members at Duquesne University in Pittsburgh, this renewal had ties to Pentecostalism through a book by David Wilkerson, a Pentecostal pastor who established a ministry to drug addicts and gang members in Brooklyn. Wilkerson's book, *The Cross and the Switchblade,* recounted his adventures but also explained the Pentecostal experience of Spirit baptism that Wilkerson believed stood at the core of his work. The group also read the Sherills' book, and in January 1967, several members spoke in tongues. News spread quickly to the University of Notre Dame. In the summer of 1967, renewal came into focus during the regular Notre Dame summer school, and participants carried word to their campuses. Within a few months, charismatic prayer groups were scattered on Catholic university campuses as well as within Catholic groups at secular schools. A vigorous community at the University of Michigan issued a monthly known as *The New Covenant,* and soon a publishing house, Servant Publications, emerged in South Bend, Indiana. For the next decade, Notre Dame hosted ever-larger renewal conferences each summer. From fewer than 150 participants in 1968, the conferences grew to include some 45,000 by 1977. By then, fully half of the attendees came from other communions.

Charismatics (sometimes called Neo-Pentecostals) shared the conviction that Pentecostal experience belonged to all of them and that institutional unity was not a prerequisite for the exercising of spiritual gifts. By the 1970s, Pentecostal denominations were being forced to evaluate the renewal. International in scope, it differed from Pentecostalism in important ways. For Pentecostals, perhaps the two most important were theological and cultural. While some Charismatics emphasized speaking in tongues as the evidence of a baptism in the Holy Spirit, others did not. Charismatics expected to speak in tongues but celebrated other spiritual gifts as well and seemed less concerned about evidence than about experience. They also often neglected the rest of the Pentecostal theological package. They remained in churches Pentecostals considered coldly formal and theologically unorthodox. Yet they exercised spiritual gifts more readily than did second- and third-generation Pentecostals. Their theology was only part of the problem. Pentecostals looked on in dismay when Charismatics smoked, drank, danced, attended theaters, and engaged in other "worldly" pursuits. Pentecostal denominations reacted with caution, although some of their members and prominent pastors readily embraced the renewal.

The Charismatic Movement spawned countless new ministries, associations, and teachings. Some were short-lived. Others have endured. Those who became restless when denominational renewal agencies did not meet their expectations sometimes left historic denominations. They often found Pentecostals, whose impatience with their denominations' conservatism had prompted them to establish independent congregations and missions agencies. The growth of independent charismatic efforts is a phenomenon that is only beginning to be studied. The monthly magazine *Charisma* chronicles the events and teachings that sustain this movement.

In the 1990s, the focus shifted from baptism (or filling) with the Holy Spirit to other exercises that are understood to manifest the Holy Spirit's presence. Contemporary gatherings, stimulated by highly visible revivals in Toronto and Pensacola, may feature being "slain in the Spirit," dance, raucous laughter, prophecy and, as in 1999, mysterious appearances of gold dust. Charismatic Christians have embraced America's therapeutic culture. Their language and practice of spiritual warfare have influence far beyond their immediate circles. Their simple worship choruses have fueled fundamental changes in Christian church music.

Pentecostals have been deeply influenced by the Charismatic Movement. Distinctions among the constituencies have blurred considerably. Newer groups like the Vineyard Christian Fellowship and Calvary Chapel as well as networks of independent congregations focus some of the energies of this constituency. Television evangelists and teachers help sustain it, as do thriving nonaccredited Bible institutes scattered across the country. Boundaries seem less important than ever, as constituencies use one another's curricula and music, buy study tapes, or attend conventions featuring the year's most popular speakers. Charismatics sponsor prayer walks and Jesus Marches, but they blend easily with evangelicals at Promise Keepers rallies. The Charismatic Movement has made its mark on the forms and message of American Christianity.

See also BAPTISM IN THE HOLY SPIRIT; BORN AGAIN CHRISTIANS; BROWNSVILLE REVIVAL; CALVARY CHAPEL; CATHOLIC CHARISMATIC RENEWAL; GLOSSOLALIA; PENTECOSTAL AND CHARISMATIC CHRISTIANITY; PROMISE KEEPERS; TELEVANGELISM; TORONTO BLESSING; VINEYARD CHRISTIAN FELLOWSHIP.

BIBLIOGRAPHY
Blumhofer, Edith, Russell Spittler, and Grant Wacker, eds. *Pentecostal Currents in American Protestantism.* 1999.

Quebedeaux, Richard. *The New Charismatics II*. 1983.
Sherill, John, and Elizabeth Sherill. *They Speak With Other Tongues.* 1965.

Edith L. Blumhofer

Chastity

The term "chastity" refers to religiously authorized sexual contact. Thus, within a given religious tradition, someone who is "chaste" has sexual contact only in a religiously sanctioned manner, usually vaginal intercourse with a spouse of the opposite sex. The word "chaste" is etymologically related to the word "caste," which similarly is concerned with rules of interpersonal contact. Chastity is often confused with celibacy, which refers only to abstinence from sexual contact.

The value of chastity is emphasized most strongly in Christian traditions, and it is a key element in Roman Catholic teachings. According to the 1992 *Catechism of the Catholic Church,* chastity is one of the twelve Fruits of the Holy Spirit, derived from the cardinal virtue of temperance. The Roman Catholic Church defines chastity as "the successful integration of sexuality within the person" (*Catechism,* paragraph 2337) and links it inextricably with the notion of self-mastery over human passions. Chastity may be exercised through celibacy or through marriage; among the young it is preserved through virginity and continence (abstinence by a couple engaged to be married). "Offenses against chastity" include lust, masturbation, fornication (sexual relations between two unmarried partners), pornography, prostitution, and rape. Although homosexual practices are also considered offenses against chastity, Roman Catholic teachings explicitly state that homosexuals are "called to chastity" and may "approach Christian perfection" by refraining from sexual relations (*Catechism,* paragraph 2359).

Protestant denominations place tremendous value on chastity as well but sometimes emphasize interpersonal morality more than self-mastery. This has historical roots in the Protestant rejection of Roman Catholicism's traditional preference for celibacy over marriage. Contemporary campaigns for youth morality, such as the popular True Love Waits initiative, treat chastity as a lifelong value that encompasses both premarital abstinence and marital union. These campaigns encourage self-discipline and stress that love, purity, faithfulness, and even sexual pleasure are stronger and more permanent in a marriage where both partners have avoided premarital sex.

Chastity does not have a direct counterpart in Judaism. While some rules governing interpersonal contact are governed by notions of *tze'niut* (modesty), others are governed by concepts of *tumah* (taboo). To describe a "chaste" Jew one would speak of a *shomer ne'giyah,* who does not touch members of the opposite sex outside his or her immediate family; this is a question of modesty—propriety—as much as of sexual purity.

Certainly traditional Judaism frowns on sexual relations outside of marriage, but with the exception of adultery (defined as sexual intercourse involving a man and a married woman), the ideal to be upheld is not sexual purity but rather privacy and dignity. At issue is not sexual intercourse, but rather uncovering: One should not be naked before anyone other than one's spouse, nor should one "uncover the nakedness" of anyone other than one's spouse. Some ultra-orthodox groups restrict uncovering even between husband and wife.

The taboo rules—analogous to certain restrictions on intercaste contact in Hinduism—are a series of prohibitions against sexual intercourse during menstruation and on certain holy days, such as Yom Kippur, the Day of Atonement. A violation of the taboo places the transgressor in a state of ritual impurity that must be purged through immersion in the *mikvah* (ritual bath). Thus, in questions both of modesty and of ritual purity, Judaism's notions about chastity do not simply restrict extramarital sexual contact; they also concern relations between man and wife.

Although attempts to "update" Christian and Jewish teachings about chastity for the contemporary world have taken a variety of forms, many of them have centered on new notions of marriage and family. Retaining a basic framework that locates sexual expression inside clearly marked long-term relationships (often including same-sex unions), these proposals seek to encourage self-mastery, interpersonal morality, and human dignity and propriety in both traditional and nontraditional situations.

See also CELIBACY; JUDAISM; MAINLINE PROTESTANTISM; MARRIAGE, CHRISTIAN; MARRIAGE, JEWISH; PRACTICE; ROMAN CATHOLICISM; TEMPERANCE; TRUE LOVE WAITS.

BIBLIOGRAPHY

Breidenthal, Thomas. *Christian Households: The Sanctification of Nearness.* 1997.

Catechism of the Catholic Church. 1992.

Goldman, Alex J. *Judaism Confronts Contemporary Issues.* 1978.

Gordis, Robert. *Love and Sex: A Modern Jewish Perspective,* 2nd ed. 1988.

Lamm, Maurice. *The Jewish Way in Love and Marriage.* 1980.

McDowell, Josh, and Bob Hostetler. *Right from Wrong.* 1994.

Waskow, Arthur. *Down-to-Earth Judaism: Food, Money, Sex, and the Rest of Life.* 1995.

J. Shawn Landres

Child Abuse by Clergy

In the mid-1980s a scandal emerged in the United States and Canada that would have a profound impact on the trust people have in their clergy. Clergy who had been entrusted with the care of children in the course of church activities had abused that trust by engaging in sexual acts with those children. With each allegation and conviction, more cases emerged. Today many denominations have developed or are in the process of developing protocols designed to limit the possibility of sexual abuse of children by pastors and other church workers. Nonetheless, much damage has been done to individual children, their families, and to the credibility of the church.

Social Context

What was the context in which this crisis emerged? A number of factors contributed to the coming to light of this abuse of children. First, the late seventies and eighties were a time of growing recognition of the nature, extent, and impact of child sexual abuse. Mandatory reporting of abuse to social workers was one of the legal markers of this shift in attention to the problem of abuse of children (Burkett and Bruni 1993, p. 29). It was thus an issue that was highlighted in the public consciousness at the time that the church-related abuses began to come to light. Second, as a result of this growing awareness, police, social workers, and the justice system became increasingly receptive to and prepared to deal with allegations of child sexual abuse. Despite this growing receptivity, feelings of shame and guilt by the child victims and adults' trust in the clergy meant that there was some degree of obliviousness to the abuse and reluctance to report it. In addition, the controversial issue of repressed memory meant that some victims were coming forward twenty or thirty years after the abuse was said to have actually occurred.

Explanations for Clergy Abuse

The majority of the incidents of abuse that attracted attention in the 1980s involved Roman Catholic clergy. One of the "intuitive" responses offered to the question "Why?" has been the requirement of clerical celibacy within the Roman Catholic Church. The suppression of natural sexual urges, it is argued, results in a perversion of sexuality, which in turn results in abuse of children and other inappropriate sexual behavior. One weakness with this explanation lies in the fact that while the majority of abuse of children has been documented as happening in the Roman Catholic faith community, it is not under the exclusive purview of Catholic priests (Bottoms et al. 1995; Jenkins 1995). Estimates of the number of clergy who are abusive range from 2 to 6 percent for both Protestant and Catholic clergy (Jenkins 1996, p. 50; Burkett and Bruni 1993, p. 57).

Another explanation for this abuse of children is individual psychosis. Some people argue that clergy abuse children because of their own personal histories, which themselves may involve abuse. Such psychological explanations may have some validity, but they ignore the structural context in which abuse takes place. They pathologize abuse as a sickness, to be dealt with at the individual level. It is also critical to examine the sorts of social relations and structures that facilitate the abuse of children in sacred settings.

One of the accomplishments of the feminist movement has been to frame abuse of many types as an abuse of power. Thus rape is defined as being about power and control, not about sexual desire. So, too, can we see clerical abuse of children as an abuse of power, in which religious authorities are in fiduciary relationships with children. Both power and trust facilitate the possibility of abuse and the preservation of its secrecy when it does occur: "[T]o child (and adult) parishioners, clergy are inherently powerful, trustworthy, and free by definition of mortal vice in much the same way as is God" (Bottoms et al. 1995, p. 90).

Problems of Definition

Although defining child abuse by clergy might seem to be an easy task, a number of issues have emerged in the process of the definition of the problem. Described as "pedophilia," the problem has been limited by definition to one involving young children. Yet the diversity of circumstances challenges this simplistic description. Very young boys and girls have been abused, as have teenage males and females (Jenkins 1996, p. 79).

One of the most troubling definitional issues has arisen in the conflation of "homosexuality" with the abusive behavior of priests and other clergy against children. A proclivity to engage in sexual intercourse or other sexual acts with children of the same sex is not homosexuality and has nothing to do with gay or lesbian identity or orientation. Yet the crisis of abuse of children by the clergy has been used as a launchpad for antigay and antilesbian crusades.

The Response of the Church

Although the church has gradually acknowledged the need to respond to the crisis in its midst, it has been slow to do so. "The poor response of the Roman Catholic elite to the sexual abuse crisis made the process of dealing with the scandal even harder for Catholic believers" (Nason-Clark 1998). The response of the church elite in the case of the abuse of aboriginal children in residential schools in Canada has been especially problematic. Denial of both incidence and harm has resulted in the alienation of Native Americans from the Christian church, and further, in the inscription of "messages of pathology over the texts of Christian forbearance, sacrifice, and self-discipline (Fiske 1999). Debate continues to rage over whether the appropriate response to abusive priests is to ban them from ministry completely, or to limit their contact with children while allowing them to continue to perform their clerical functions.

The Impact on Faith

What impact has the abuse had? Capps (1992, 1995) discusses the possible negative effects of physical and emotional abuse of children in the context of the church. These effects include adult disassociation manifested by withdrawal of feeling and lack of confidence. We do not yet have a full picture of the effects of child abuse, however.

At the level of the church congregation, parishioners of abusive clergy have understandably felt hurt, betrayed, and angry. Parents have been devastated by the thought that a person they viewed as called by God, with whom they have trusted their children, is capable of such treachery. Nancy Nason-Clark and Anne Stapleton have explored the impact of the scandal of clerical abuse of children on Roman Catholic women in Newfoundland. Some women left the church completely, some left for a time, and others continued to participate in Mass and other church activities, arguing that it was individual clergy, rather than the church or God, who were to blame.

Clerics' abuse of children raises important issues about faith and authority. At a broader level it forces us to ask questions about social institutions and abuse of power. Abuse of children takes place within families, in schools, in sports, and in other recreational groups. However, it is viewed as especially heinous when it takes place in a religious context.

See also CELIBACY; CHASTITY; CLERGY; MAINLINE PROTESTANTISM; PRIESTHOOD; ROMAN CATHOLICISM.

BIBLIOGRAPHY

Bottoms, Bette L., Phillip Shaver, Gail S. Goodman, and Jianjian Qin. "In the Name of God: A Profile of Religion-Related Child Abuse." *Journal of Social Issues* 51, no. 2 (1995): 85–111.

Burkett, Elinor, and Frank Bruni. *A Gospel of Shame: Children, Sexual Abuse and the Catholic Church.* 1993.

Capps, Donald. *The Child's Song: The Religious Abuse of Children.* 1995.

Capps, Donald. "Religion and Child Abuse: Perfect Together." *Journal for the Scientific Study of Religion* 31, no. 1 (1992): 1–14.

Fiske, Jo-Anne. "Ordered Lives and Disordered Souls: Pathologizing Female Bodies of the Colonial Frontier." In *Perspectives on Deviance: The Construction of Deviance in Everyday Life.* 1999.

Jenkins, Philip. "Clergy Sexual Abuse: The Symbolic Politics of a Social Problem." In *Images of Issues: Typifying Contemporary Social Problems,* edited by Joel Best. 1995.

Jenkins, Philip. *Pedophiles and Priests: Anatomy of a Contemporary Crisis.* 1996.

Nason-Clark, Nancy. "The Impact of Abuses of Clergy Trust on Female Congregants' Faith and Practice." In *Wolves Within the Fold: Religious Leadership and Abuses of Power,* edited by Anson Shupe. 1998.

Shupe, Anson. *In the Name of All That's Holy: A Theory of Clergy Malfeasance.* 1995.

Lori Beaman

Children of God.

See Family, The.

Chinese-American Religions

The Chinese were the first Asian group to immigrate in large numbers to the United States. In the first hundred years from the mid–nineteenth century, almost all Chinese immigrants were laborers from rural areas of Guangdong (Canton). They suffered exclusion and discrimination and had to stay in ghettolike Chinatowns in major metropolises. After World War II, especially since 1965, Chinese immigrants have come in large numbers in several waves. The Chinese population doubled between 1970 and 1980, doubled again between 1980 and 1990, and reached 2.3 million in 1997. Many new Chinese immigrants came first as college or graduate students, then found professional jobs in nonethnic companies or in governmental agencies, and have settled in ethnically mixed suburbs. The overall image of the Chinese in America is as one of the "model minorities" of successful assimilation.

The contemporary Chinese-American population is tremendously diverse. The immigrants come from very different societies (e.g., the Republic of China, or Taiwan; the People's Republic of China; Hong Kong, the British colony until 1997; Indochina) and speak many dialects, including Taishanese, Cantonese, Mandarin, Taiwanese, and others, that are mutually unintelligible even though the written characters and grammar are the same. Some ethnic Chinese from Southeast Asia speak none of the Chinese dialects but rather Vietnamese, Tangalo, or English. Among the American-born Chinese, while many are the second generation of the new immigrants, some are third-, fourth-, or even fifth-generation descendants of the earlier immigrants.

Contemporary Chinese-American religions are also diverse. In the traditional Chinatown, formal religious institutions were almost absent. However, *huiguan* (same-district and clan associations) and *tang* (triads or secret societies) had some religious elements. Same-district associations often kept shrines to their tutelary deities. Clan associations always performed rituals of venerating common ancestors, real or imagined. Triads commonly held cultic practices. Since the 1950s new Chinese immigrants have brought or joined a variety of religions. Generally speaking, Christianity has become the most practiced institutional religion, with Buddhism the second; traditional Chinese folk religions have revived since the late 1970s, but various sectarian or cultic traditions, such as Mormonism and Jehovah's Witnesses, have attracted few Chinese followers.

Chinese Folk Religion

In the second half of the nineteenth century, Chinese immigrants brought along their gods and established many temples, which were commonly referred to as joss houses. The word *joss* is a corruption of the Portugese word *deos,* meaning "god." A joss house is thus a house of gods, which are often combinatively taken from Buddhism, Taoism, and local cultic deities. A joss house is primarily for individual rituals and devotions, not for adhering to a set of defined dogmas. The first two joss houses were believed to be the Kong Chow Temple and the T'ien Hou Temple, built in the early 1850s in San Francisco. The principal deity in the Kong Chow Temple was Guan Gong (Kuan Kung), and the T'ien Hou was the temple for the Queen of Heaven (Tian Hou, or T'ien Hou). In the second half of the nineteenth century, hundreds of

Sticks of incense are burned inside the Kong Chow Buddhist Temple in San Francisco's Chinatown, ca. 1989.   (Credit: CORBIS/Phil Schermeister.)

joss houses were built in America, but most were abandoned soon after (Wells 1962).

Since the late 1970s the traditional Chinese folk religion has been revived, mostly by ethnic Chinese who are refugees from Vietnam. From Los Angeles to New York, from Washington, D.C., to Houston, many temples have been built in Chinatowns or suburbs. In Houston, for example, Chinese from Indochina (Vietnam, Cambodia, and Laos) built three temples with magnificent Chinese-style architecture in the 1990s: Tien Hou, Teo Chew, and Guan Di. The Tien Hou Temple worships the Queen of Heaven along with Taoist deities and some other gods. Tian Hou (Heavenly Queen) is a popular goddess in the coastal provinces of China and among the Chinese diaspora in Southeast Asia. This sea goddess is believed to have the power to protect fishermen and sailors, to heal, and to answer all kinds of prayers. The Teo Chew Temple worships a major god named Bentougong, along with various Buddhist and Taoist deities. Bentougong is the tutelary god in Chao Zhou (Teo Chew) district of Guangdong Province. The newest Guan Di Temple is dedicated to worshiping Guan Di, a historical figure of the third century, who was praised as symbolizing loyalty and righteousness and deified as the god of wealth. A statue of Confucius stands among the gods as well.

Festival celebrations in these temples are based on the Chinese traditional calendar system, although adjustment to a weekend schedule is often made. Important gatherings include the Chinese New Year, the Qingming, and the birthdays of Tian Hou, Guan Di, Guan Yin (Kuan Yin), buddhas, and other gods. Buddhist sutras and Taoist scriptures sometimes can be found in these temples. They often have a weekend Chinese school in which children are taught the Chi-

nese language, values, cultural customs, and martial arts.

Besides these temples, some Chinese maintain tablets of ancestors and altars of gods at home, observe fengshui, consult fortune tellers, conduct divination, and practice qigong, most of which may be regarded as part of the traditional Chinese folk religion. Fengshui is a type of astrology using the concepts of yin, yang, five elements, eight *gua,* and stars to maximize harmony and minimize conflicts of a person with his or her surrounding environment. Practitioners consult fengshui masters in choosing the location of their houses and graveyards, decorating rooms, and selecting the best time for doing certain things, such as opening a store. In the past few decades, fengshui has spread among many non-Chinese people. Qigong is a type of still or moving meditation for the purpose of physical health, psychological peace, and spiritual enrichment. In the last two decades, hundreds of qigong schools have emerged throughout China, and a few qigong masters have adventured into North America. In the United States, two qigong schools have gained large numbers of practitioners, including some Caucasians. One is Yan Xin Qigong; the other is Falun Gong or Falun Dafa. It is interesting that the spread of fengshui, qigong, and other traditional Chinese folk religious practices has extensively involved the latest technology—the Internet.

Buddhism

Chinese Buddhism, in more organized and less combinative forms, appeared in America only along with the coming of post–World War II immigrants. In the 1950s some Chinese Buddhist immigrants organized to sponsor monks and nuns from Asia to lead them. The first to do so was the Chinese Buddhist Association of Hawaii, which was formed in 1953; it sponsored a monk from Hong Kong in 1956 and constructed the Hsu Yun Temple in 1965. In San Francisco, an important group was the Sino-American Buddhist Association, which was organized in 1959; it sponsored a monk from Hong Kong in 1962, built the Gold Mountain Temple in 1970, and since then has established several branch temples on the West Coast. In New York, the first Chinese Buddhist group was the Eastern States Buddhist Association, which was started in 1962 and completed the Mahayana Temple in 1971. This association has sponsored more than a dozen monks and nuns from Taiwan, Hong Kong, Burma, and mainland China; most of them then left to start up their own groups in New York or other places. Later more monks and nuns came to gather their own followers and establish their own temples. In the late 1970s Buddha Light Mountain Sect, under Hsing Yun, came and constructed the grandiose Hsi Lai Temple near Los Angeles, the largest and best-known Chinese temple in America (Lin 1996). In the mid-1980s, a Taiwanese immigrant, Lu Shengyan, came to Seattle, Washington, and founded his True Buddha Sect, which has established more than a dozen branch temples in several metropolises in North America.

By the end of the 1990s, there were about 120 to 150 Chinese Buddhist groups (temples, associations, and centers) in the United States. Most of them were concentrated in the largest metropolitan areas—New York, San Francisco, Los Angeles, and Houston. These Chinese Buddhist groups tend to be organizationally independent; practice a combination of Pure Land, Chan, Tian Tai, and other Chinese Buddhist traditions; and primarily serve Chinese immigrants. Some non-Chinese, especial Caucasians, have been drawn into a few well-established Chinese temples under renowned monks. Overall, most of the regular participants in temple activities are middle-aged and old immigrants, with a clear majority of women.

Christianity

The history of Chinese Christianity in America is almost as long as that of Chinese immigration. However, Christianity was not a traditional Chinese religion. Unlike European immigrants, who transplanted their Protestantism and Catholicism to the New World, earlier Chinese Christian churches were missions started by American denominations. The first such church was established in San Francisco in 1853 with the support of the Presbyterian Board of Foreign Missions. By 1892 eleven denominations established 10 Chinese churches (including three in Canada), 10 Chinese Christian associations, and 271 Chinese Sunday schools and missions in thirty-one states. Up to the 1950s the mission churches had only very limited success in converting the Chinese.

Since the 1950s the number of Chinese churches has rapidly increased, and it had reached eight hundred in the mid-1990s. Most of the new Chinese churches were founded by Chinese immigrants themselves, and many evolved from Bible study groups on university campuses. These Chinese-American churches have tended to be theologically conservative and organizationally independent. About half of Chinese churches have no denominational affiliation; the denominations most attractive to Chinese Christians are conservative in theology and less centralized in organization, such as the Southern Baptist Convention and the Christian and Missionary Alliance. In many Chinese churches, members are from widely divergent backgrounds, and a majority of immigrant members are adult converts from non-Christian family back-

grounds. Meanwhile, these churches also selectively preserve Chinese traditional values, rituals, and symbols. Many churches have a Chinese school to teach the Chinese language and traditional Chinese values that are perceived as compatible with their Christian beliefs, including respecting parents, thrift, and strict moral codes regarding smoking and sexuality.

In the last decade or so, some American-born Chinese have joined other Asian-American Christians to establish Asian-American churches in metropolitan areas, especially on the West Coast. These churches are monolingual (English), and consciously target descendants of various Asian immigrants, especially East Asians.

See also BUDDHISM; CONFUCIANISM; FENG SHUI; TAOISM.

BIBLIOGRAPHY

Chandler, Stuart. "Chinese Buddhism in America: Identity and Practice." In *The Faces of Buddhism in America,* edited by Charles S. Prebish and Kenneth K. Tanaka, pp. 13–30, 1998.

Lin, Irene. "Journey to the Far West: Chinese Buddhism in America." *Amerasia Journal* 22 (1996), no. 1: 107–132.

Pang, Wing Ning. "The Chinese American Ministry." In *Yearbook of American & Canadian Churches, 1995,* edited by Kenneth B. Bedell, pp. 10–18. 1995.

Wells, Mariann Kaye. "Chinese Temples in California." M.A. thesis, University of California, 1962.

Woo, Wesley. "Chinese Protestants in the San Francisco Bay Area." In *Entry Denied: Exclusion and the Chinese in America, 1882–1943,* edited by Sucheng Chan, pp. 213–245. 1991.

Yang, Fenggang. "ABC and XYZ: Religious, Ethnic and Racial Identities of the New Second Generation Chinese in Christian Churches." *Amerasia Journal* 25, no. 1 (1999): 1–26.

Yang, Fenggang. "Hsi Nan Chinese Buddhist Temple: Seeking to Americanize." In *The Religious Mosaic: The Diversity of Immigrant Congregations,* edited by Helen Rose Ebaugh and Janet S. Chafetz. 2000.

Yang, Fenggang. "Religious Diversity among the Chinese in America." In *Asian American Religions,* edited by Pyong Gap Min and Jung Ha Kim. 2000.

Yang, Fenggang. "Tenacious Unity in a Contentious Community: Cultural and Religious Dynamics in a Chinese Christian Church." In *Gatherings in Diaspora: Religious Communities and the New Immigration,* edited by R. Stephen Warner and Judith G. Wittner, pp. 333–361. 1998.

Fenggang Yang

Christian Church (Disciples of Christ).

See Mainline Protestantism.

Christian Coalition

In preparation for his campaign for the presidency in 1988, religious broadcaster Marion G. "Pat" Robertson created an effective grassroots organization known as Freedom Council in several states. Though defeated, Robertson made a surprisingly strong showing and determined to create a more permanent political organization that could help elect Christian candidates to public office and gain substantial power within the Republican Party. The result was Christian Coalition, launched in 1989 with the assistance of its first executive director, Ralph Reed. Under Reed's leadership the organization grew steadily until, in 1996, it claimed a membership of 1.9 million in two thousand chapters across the country, and a budget of $26.5 million. Critics questioned the membership figures, but no one doubted that the organization has had a significant influence and impact on American politics.

In founding Christian Coalition, Robertson asserted that atheistic and humanistic forces had transformed America from a Christian nation into an "anti-Christian pagan nation" and that he hoped the new organization could help reverse that change. Key causes have included opposition to gay rights, abortion, and pornography; a tax cut for middle-class families with children; vouchers that could be used to enable children to attend private religious schools; and efforts to protest anti-Christian bigotry and to defend the legal rights of Christians. In the service of its "pro-family" agenda, the organization seeks to inform Christians of timely issues and legislation; to represent them before local councils, state legislatures, and Congress; and to train them for effective political action.

In addition to providing detailed instruction as to how committed activists could seize control of local and state-level political organizations and mobilize voters on behalf of candidates and key issues, Christian Coalition has specialized in producing and distributing voter guides that, though ostensibly nonpartisan, draw sharp distinctions between candidates they favor and those they oppose. In the 1996 and 1998 general elections, the organization claimed to have distributed upward of forty million voter guides, often in the form of leaflets placed on the windshields of

The then director of the Christian Coalition, Ralph Reed, acknowledges applause during a speech at a Road to Victory Conference in Washington, D.C., on September 13, 1996. (Credit: AP/Wide World Photos.)

cars in the parking lots of evangelical churches. In 1994 and 1996 an estimated 40 percent of candidates backed by Christian Coalition were victorious. In 1998, however, Coalition-backed candidates fared much more poorly. More significant than individual elections, however, has been the organization's impact on the Republican Party. A 1995 survey conducted by *Campaigns & Elections* magazine found that Christian Right forces had "dominant strength" in the Republican Party in eighteen states and "substantial" influence in thirteen others. Christian Coalition was widely regarded as the political organization most responsible for this development, and its annual "Road to Victory" conference is considered an important opportunity for conservative politicians to establish or strengthen ties to evangelical supporters. The close ties between Christian Coalition, officially a nonpartisan organization, and the Republican Party led to a lawsuit by the Federal Election Commission and a review of the organization's tax-exempt status by the Internal Revenue Service, which revoked that status in 1999.

Christian Coalition's future was somewhat difficult to predict at the end of the 1990s. Contributions dropped from $26.5 million in 1996 to $17 million in 1997. Also in 1997, Ralph Reed resigned his position, turning the reins over to new executive director Randy Tate, a former Republican congressman from Washington state, and former Reagan cabinet member Don Hodel, who served as the organization's president. Hodel resigned in February 1999 and Pat Robertson reassumed the post of president. Under the recent leadership, ties with the Republican Party have been somewhat deemphasized in favor of a new strategy called Families 2000, in which the organization seeks to achieve its goals by working more closely with local churches. Other changes included discontinuing a minority outreach program known as the Samaritan Project and severing ties with the Catholic Alliance, a largely unsuccessful attempt to recruit like-minded Catholics into its ranks.

Ralph Reed's remarkable skills as a political organizer and his pragmatic willingness to accept partial victories and limited gains and to use a rhetoric less harsh and threatening than that of some of his colleagues contributed mightily to Christian Coalition's early success. However, it offended some who regarded him as too willing to compromise on issues they held dear. In adjusting its tactics and public image in the post-Reed era, the organization was faced not only with striking an acceptable balance between the demands of its constituency and the tolerance of the general public toward hard-line moral and political positions, but also with competition from other conservative organizations. The most notable of these were Focus on the Family, headed by influential radio broadcaster and author James Dobson, and the Family Research Council, led by Gary Bauer.

See also DOBSON, JAMES C.; EVANGELICAL CHRISTIANITY; FOCUS ON THE FAMILY; FUNDAMENTALIST CHRISTIANITY; RELIGIOUS RIGHT; ROBERTSON, PAT.

BIBLIOGRAPHY

Martin, William. *With God on Our Side: The Rise of the Religious Right in America.* 1996.
Reed, Ralph. *Contract with the American Family.* 1995.

William Martin

Christian Identity Movement.

See Identity Christianity.

Christian Right.

See Religious Right.

Christian Science

In 1875 Mary Baker Eddy, one of the most fascinating and controversial religious leaders in American history, finished her best-known work, *Science and Health.* Her followers are known as Christian Scientists, and she is the founder of what is called Christian Science. The Church of Christ (Scientist) was incorporated in 1879. Today Christian Science is known mainly for its famous newspaper (*The Christian Science Monitor*) and for the reluctance of members to follow traditional medical procedures.

Boston is the site of the Mother Church and the denomination's world headquarters. Christian Science has a worldwide following, though its popularity has declined since the death of Eddy in 1910. Born on July 16, 1821, in Bow, New Hampshire, Eddy (née Baker) joined the Congregational Church in her teenage years. Her religious outlook changed in the early 1860s through her contact with Phineas Parkhurst Quimby (1802–1866).

Quimby, a native of Maine, was shaped in his medical and religious outlook by the thought of Franz Mesmer (1734–1815), an Austrian physician known for his radical views on the power of trancelike states. Quimby became fascinated with Mesmerism, hypnotism, and other medical therapies that illustrated the profound impact of the mind on human health. Quimby's ideas were revolutionary to Mary Baker

Eddy and also had an impact on the founders of the New Thought movement (Warren Felt Evans, Annetta Seabury Dresser, and Julius Dresser), a religious cousin to Christian Science.

In Eddy's life and since her death, her relationship with Quimby has been the source of much debate. New Thought leaders have accused Eddy of plagiarism, suggesting that there is nothing original in her ideology. Christian Scientists have preferred to downplay Quimby's role in Eddy's development. However, it is evident that his impact on her was considerable, though the departures from Quimby on key theological and ecclesiastical issues and her own originality must be noted.

Christian Scientists point to Eddy's own healing story as the central biographical moment in the life of Christian Science. After she had a nasty fall on February 1, 1866, Eddy claimed that her miraculous healing came because of her prayers, her faith in God, and the recognition that mind has power over false beliefs about illness. This healing claim is expressed in Eddy's well-known (and complicated) view that matter is not real. Healing comes as one places trust in God (the author of Spirit) over the illusory power of false material claims.

As Eddy developed her own healing and religious ministry, her movement was hurt by internal division and by external critiques. Mark Twain wrote a biting exposé about her, accusing her of money grubbing, dictatorship, medical fraud, and outright delusion. Eddy weathered these storms, and she sheltered herself in later years in her home in Concord, New Hampshire.

Christian Science is a version of absolute idealism. Resistance to traditional medicine is rooted in an objection to emphasis on the physical realm. The focus away from the physical also explains why the church has no rite of water baptism and communion is understood as meditation only. Christian Scientists use traditional theological vocabulary, though the meaning of words is oriented to Eddy's symbolic and idealistic interpretations.

Conservative Christians have always attacked the Christian Science understanding of the Trinity, creation, the nature of Christ, the meaning of the death of Jesus, and views about heaven and hell. They have also targeted Christian Scientists for their elevation of Mary Baker Eddy, their reliance on her writings, and their understanding of divine healing.

Secular criticism of Christian Science has been directed to recent economic turmoil in the movement, and also to the church's controversial rejection of standard medical procedures, particularly in cases involving children. Internally, Christian Science has suffered from strong dissent over some disastrous financial moves by church leaders, the church-sponsored publication of a very controversial book about Mary Baker Eddy by Bliss Knapp, and allegations that the church is dictatorial in its mode of decision making.

Bliss Knapp (1877–1958) was the son of a prominent early follower of Eddy. The younger Knapp inherited his father's love for the Book of Revelation. Out of that study, Bliss Knapp speculated that Eddy had status equal to Jesus and that she was one of the central figures in the apostle's apocalyptic visions. Knapp's book *The Destiny of the Mother Church* (privately printed in 1947) was later refused publication by the Christian Science Publishing Society. In his will Knapp threatened that his family's wealth would not go to the church unless it published his book by 1993. The amount in question was over $90 million by 1990. The church met the deadline with official publication, but that move created enormous controversy.

The more vigorous external attack on the church's controversial healing methods has been met by the decades-long assertion of the freedom of Christian Scientists to practice their religion and of the right of Christian Science parents to raise their children in obedience to church belief and tradition. American courts have been reluctant to prosecute adults who choose to reject traditional medicine. Cases involving children have been much more complicated—emotionally, morally, and legally.

Caroline Fraser drew national attention to this issue in a major report in the April 1995 issue of *The Atlantic Monthly*. Under the title "Suffering Children and the Christian Science Church," Fraser, herself from a Christian Science background, documented the recent woes of Christian Science, focusing on dramatic cases of childhood deaths involving Christian Science faith healing. Church members replied to her article by citing alleged cases of positive healing, disputing the causal elements in the relevant cases she cited, and chiding her for not allowing freedom of religion.

Rita and Doug Swan, former Christian Scientists, started a national organization called CHILD (Children's Healthcare Is a Legal Duty) in 1983. Their work arose out of their lengthy legal battle with the church over the death of their son Matthew. He had meningitis, but they refused standard medical treatment for him out of belief that Christian Science healing traditions were correct. Caroline Fraser draws attention to this death, among others. She ends her article with bitterness: "As it is, if 7,000 children attend Christian Science Sunday schools in this country, then 7,000 children may have nothing standing between themselves and death but *Science and Health* and dumb luck."

One impact of the tragic cases Fraser cites is a growing moderation among some Christian Science faith healers. There have been arguments advanced that Eddy allowed a combination of faith and medicine in her own life (she is said to have taken morphine in her later years) and that common sense demands greater access to traditional medical procedures. These moderates also argue that Christian Scientists are allowed to go to dentists, wear glasses, and have broken bones fixed at the local hospital. Why not allow surgery for cancer or drugs for diabetes?

Christian Science leaders have responded aggressively in court to challenges about medical malpractice and have mounted effective public relations campaigns about the importance of religious liberty in American life. Ironically, some Christian Science dissidents (like Stephen Gottschalk) have accused the church of ignoring the liberty of its own members to ask hard questions about what constitutes true allegiance to Eddy's teachings. These questions will continue to dominate Christian Science as it continues into its second century as one of America's most controversial religious movements.

See also FREEDOM OF RELIGION; HEALING; NEW THOUGHT; TRANCE.

BIBLIOGRAPHY

Gardner, Martin. *The Healing Revelations of Mary Baker Eddy.* 1993.

Gill, Gillian. *Mary Baker Eddy.* 1998.

Gottschalk, Stephen. *The Emergence of Christian Science in American Religious Life.* 1973.

Peel, Robert. *Mary Baker Eddy.* 3 vols. 1966–1977.

Twain, Mark. *Christian Science.* 1907.

James A. Beverley

Christmas

Since time immemorial European cultures have pursued a great many different activities connected with the winter solstice, and that pervasive human instinct is the basic reason for observing Christmas in December. Pre-Christian festivals in the Mediterranean world included many variations on Saturnalia, a period of revelry scheduled at the end of each calendar year. Other celebrations stemmed from Syria and the Mithra cult and were associated specifically with the sun. By 274 C.E. the Roman emperor Aurelian designated December 25 as *natalis Solis Invicti*, birthday of the unconquerable sun, the point where cold and darkness yielded once more to warmth and light. In northern Europe there was similar notice of the winter solstice in festivals featuring gifts, food, greenery, and lights. Germanic peoples made the yule log conspicuous in such observances, and the Celts used mistletoe and holly as symbols of longevity and endurance.

It was only in the late fourth century that churches began to designate a special place for a Mass of Christ in the liturgical calendar, a feast called *Cristes-maesse* in Old English. There is no evidence that early churches attributed much importance to the physical birth of Jesus of Nazareth, and the date of the actual event is not known. But when a Christian holiday was named for it, church officials deliberately chose December 25 in an attempt to supplant the pagan rituals that were already in place. Once incorporated theologically as well as liturgically into the ecclesiastical calendar, Christmas provided a general focus for a cycle of related feasts that stretched from Advent to Epiphany (January 6). Songs about "The Twelve Days of Christmas" refer to those between Christmas and Epiphany. Western churches say that the Magi appeared to adore the newborn infant on Epiphany, whereas Eastern Orthodox churches designate that day to commemorate Christ's baptism.

Christmas celebrations have always exhibited a mixture of ecclesiastically sanctioned religious observances and remnants of pre-Christian practices that vary widely with local custom. Many sixteenth-century Protestants condemned Christmas festivals because of the pagan and frivolous qualities that persisted despite Christian overtones. Calvinists were particularly emphatic in this regard, and wherever Puritan influence was strong in the American colonies, Christmas festivities were outlawed. The holiday did not become legal in New England until 1856. Puritan repressions have largely disappeared from today's world, however, and celebrations surrounding Christmas are now quite varied and widespread.

In colonial times the Dutch introduced traditions related to St. Nicholas, especially the custom of giving gifts to children. In time the practice spread throughout America and expanded to include presents for adults as well. When people from different ethnic backgrounds tried to pronounce the saint's name, there were many versions, but the most widely accepted reference became "Santa Claus." Ideas about this Santa Claus were greatly influenced by the poem "A Visit from Saint Nicholas," first printed in 1823. Clement C. Moore, a seminary professor, wrote the poem as a present for his children, and when a New York newspaper published it, the narrative that begins "'Twas the night before Christmas . . ." became one of the most frequently recited verses of the season. Though St. Nicholas had previously been depicted as

A spruce tree from the Black Hills of South Dakota is decorated and lit on December 10, 1997, in front of the Capitol building in Washington, D.C. (Credit: AP/Wide World Photos.)

old and thin, Santa Claus became universally described as plump and jolly, clad in fur-trimmed red clothing. This visual image was due to Thomas Nast, a cartoonist who began drawing Santa Claus this way in 1863. Moore's poem and Nast's pictures established a pattern that has remained much the same through current times. No other figure dominates Christmas festivities in the United States as much as Santa Claus.

Nineteenth-century England also witnessed an expansion of Christmas observances, most of them Germanic in origin because of Prince Albert, Queen Victoria's husband. Christmas trees decorated with ornaments, and tinsel, holly wreaths, bells, carols, and exchanging Christmas cards all added to the general atmosphere of merrymaking. These influences quickly made their way across the Atlantic and have remained basic elements in U.S. popular culture for well over a century. Of all British influences that have shaped ideas about the season, probably the most important was *A Christmas Carol,* written by Charles Dickens in

1843. That story, which depicted the callousness and eventual repentance of Ebenezer Scrooge, together with humble faith and forgiveness in the Cratchit family, has become another perennial feature of the modern North American Christmas.

Public affirmation of and participation in Christmas have increased throughout the twentieth century. Religious observances of Christ's birth still give central purpose and meaning to the holiday for many people. But in contemporary times commercial interests have dominated public awareness of the season, forcing theological-liturgical considerations into a place of secondary importance. While many traditions still focus on children and family, others now include celebrations in the workplace, school plays, and municipal pageants. Exchanging gifts has become so widespread as to include friends and acquaintances at virtually every level of contact. It has made the Christmas season a boom time, one of the most important parts of the commercial year for selling consumer goods. The Macy's Thanksgiving Day parade in New York City (inaugurated in 1924 and widely emulated throughout the United States), featuring Santa Claus and many huge balloons, is often taken as the signal for Christmas shopping to begin. In more recent times people have begun seasonal shopping even earlier. Christmas creates many extra jobs as temporary sources of income, and in business corporations it is often the occasion for bonuses and promotions. Buying and spending for home decorations are quite widespread, as is consuming rich foods such as eggnog, roast turkey or goose, and mince pies. The choice of foods, types of presents, and party activities differ widely according to the many cultures that make up modern North American life, but all of them emphasize a time of celebration, indulgence, and sharing. Jewish Americans have made much of Hanukkah, or Chanukah, the Festival of Lights, as a way of sharing common elements of the holiday season while still emphasizing their own faith and cultural heritage. Many African Americans have begun observing Kwanza for similar reasons.

Music has always played a part in Christmas festivities, and that is still the case in contemporary usage. Classical performances often feature Handel's oratorio *The Messiah,* as well as many renditions of the aria "Ave Maria." Several hymns or carols such as "Silent Night" and "O Little Town or Bethlehem" remain perennial favorites, too. On a more popular level, perhaps the best-loved song of all is "White Christmas," written by Irving Berlin and first sung by Bing Crosby in 1942. Many other vocalists recorded versions of the standby thereafter, and additional songs enrich Christmas music, but none has superseded the original in popular esteem.

The movies and television have contributed heavily to the generalized sentimentalism that characterizes Christmas today. Hollywood has produced a bewildering variety of Christmas films, some of which are only loosely connected to holiday themes. Almost a dozen versions of Dickens's tale about Scrooge have appeared, and each year new films emerge that both reinforce and exploit popular sympathies. Two movies that receive much attention every year are *Holiday Inn* (1942) and *Miracle on 34th Street* (1947), whose plot turns on the Macy's parade, Santa Claus, and childlike trust in human goodness. Many television programs further these sentiments, too. Popular favorites each year feature animated versions of Rudolph the Red-Nosed Reindeer or Frosty the Snowman, plus many others, notably *Merry Christmas, Charlie Brown* and *How the Grinch Stole Christmas.*

For most of the twentieth century, Christmas observances have included a display of manger scenes on municipal properties, indicating how deeply ingrained the holiday had become in accepted American routines. But in recent decades several non-Christian groups have challenged activities that recognize the holiday of just one religion at the expense of all citizens. Lawsuits backed by the American Civil Liberties Union have been successful in several states, where courts have found it unconstitutional for governmental offices to aid or further any religious interest. Exhibiting crèches has been singled out as a particularly blatant abuse of this sort, and therefore such displays have disappeared from public squares in many parts of the country. Arguments over separation of church and state will continue in this area for some time to come. But no litigation will ever succeed in suppressing all the symbols connected with Christmas, private and public, sacred and secular, because their protean meanings have become so inextricably mixed with contemporary culture.

See also ADVENT; CELTIC PRACTICES; CHANUKAH; CHURCH; CHURCH AND STATE; EPIPHANY; FOOD; LITURGY AND WORSHIP; LIVED RELIGION; MUSIC; POSADA, LA; RITUAL; SECULARIZATION.

BIBLIOGRAPHY

Ickis, Marguerite. *The Book of Festival Holidays.* 1964.

Miles, Clement A. *Christmas in Ritual and Tradition: Christian and Pagan.* 1913.

Robbins, M., and J. Charlton. *A Christmas Comparison.* 1991.

Rulon, P. *Keeping Christmas: The Celebration of an American Holiday.* 1990.

Schmidt, Leigh E. *Consumer Rites: The Buying and Selling of American Holidays.* 1995.

Henry Warner Bowden

Church

The term "church" dates back to a Christian context in the third or fourth century after Christ to denote an "assembly of believers." Since then, the use of the word has spread worldwide to denote a variety of Christian as well as non-Christian groups. The label is also used to describe a variety of forms of religious organizations, including those sometimes referred to as "cults," "sects," or "denominations."

Within the social sciences, however, the concept of "church" has a long and complex history. The concept first became influential as part of an idealized typology of religious organizations (a.k.a. church-sect typology) constructed by Max Weber in his massive work *Economy and Society* and later elaborated by Ernst Troeltsch in *The Social Teaching of the Christian Churches.*

In his church-sect typology, Weber focuses on the relationship between a society's political contexts and its religious communities. He sees the church type and the sect type as opposing models of religious organization, distinguished primarily by their very different relationships to the society in which they exist. Whereas the church is defined largely in relationship to its alliance with secular political authority in pursuit of its goal of world domination, the sect is characterized by its withdrawal from society, the voluntary basis of its membership, the subjective acceptance of Christ into the lives of its members based on an individual conversion experience, and the small, democratic nature of its community.

Weber and Troeltsch draw heavily on the model of the European Catholic Church to illustrate the main characteristics of the church type, while drawing on the example of Christ's apostles and the monastic orders of the Catholic Church for their model of the sect type.

Weber's church model is distinguished by a number of historically related characteristics:

1. The goal of the church organization is world domination, and through universal conversion.
2. Church organizations typically enjoy the support and sponsorship of one or more political states.
3. This alliance with secular authority forces the church to accommodate itself to the values of the secular world.
4. Religious membership within a state-church regime is compulsory, a matter of birth or citizenship rather than choice.
5. In church organizations, salvation and grace tend to be both formal and objective, allowing them to be ritualistically administered by professional specialists independent of the conscious volition of participants, as in the case of

infant baptism, conversion by conquest, or membership by birth. These characteristics are elaborated more fully below.

To understand Weber's reasoning it is important to recognize that his concept of the church is modeled on a historical European context in which state-church alliances are normative. In this context, religion is a state-supported political institution. All citizens are automatically members of the state-established church and are required by law to pay taxes in support of that church. The church and the religious values it supports are a primary institution through which the state exercises social control and maintains its authority among the people. For this reason religious dissent can be viewed as a challenge to political authority. Religious dissenters were often treated harshly as political criminals and were often killed for refusing to accept the religious views of the state.

Weber saw world domination by a single faith as the primary goal of the church organization. Consequently, many of the characteristics he associates with the church function to further this end. The goal of world domination is mainly pursued through the strategy of universal conversion—that is, the conversion of the world's population to the faith of the true church. In Weber's observation, the alliance of church and state is instrumental to this goal insofar as churches have historically pursued the goal of universal conversion through the territorial and political expansion of state power. As nations conquer new territories, the church has followed. For Weber, religious conversion goes hand in hand with colonization both as a means of reinforcing the social and political control of conquered populations and by extending, through persuasion and coercion, the extent of the church's influence. This form of territorial conversion is made possible through the mechanism of compulsory membership. The citizens of nations that have been conquered through war or annexation thus become "converted" to the religious faith of the conquerors.

Another device that functions in the service of universal conversion is the "formalized means of acquiring grace and salvation." Weber argues that through a process of institutionalization, the charisma or mystery of a religion is eventually separated from a particular person or leader (such as Christ or the pope) and relocated to an institution or office. The transformation of charisma from a person to an institution is achieved through a lengthy organizational process marked by the development of a professional priesthood; the rationalization of dogma and rites; and claims of universal domination that transcend allegiances to family, household, ethnicity, or nation. An

important outcome of this transformation is the objectification of the church's authority and discipline, which allows one to obtain grace and salvation through formal as opposed to subjective means.

The objectification of salvation is important because it makes the mass conversion of politically conquered peoples possible. Through the objectification of salvation, entire nation-states can be converted to the "true faith" en masse, by observing formal rituals. Weber contrasts this with the case of sect membership, in which conversion to a faith must be voluntary and must be based on an individual conversion experience.

For Weber, the political strategies pursued by church organizations inevitably lead to compromises between religious values and worldly goals. Troeltsch's work elaborates the organizational problems that the pursuit of universal domination creates for the Christian churches. He shows that in seeking to dominate the world, the church is forced to accommodate itself to secular values. Thus a consequence of the church type is its tendency to adjust to, and form compromises with, existing society and its values and institutions. These compromises set up a dynamic tension with the church's religious values, and in turn lead to the formation of revolutionary sects within the church that seek to return the church to its religious priorities. Troeltsch sees the monastic orders of the Catholic Church as an illustration of these revolutionary sects. He sees them as a source both of tension and of potential renewal for the church.

Because of the centrality of the state in Weber's understanding of the church, Weber's understanding of the concept may be more useful for investigating the dynamics of religious institutions where state-church alliances still exist around the world. However, the guarantees of religious freedom that exist in the United States have posed problems for the translation of this concept to the American context.

The Church Concept in the American Context

Weber's writings on religious organization are both complex and historically conditioned by the European context. This has lead to many debates among American scholars concerning the utility of Weber's church type in the context of the United States. A chief obstacle to the conceptual translation of his work is the absence of the church-state relationships that Weber assumed were a foundation of church authority. In the United States there is a constitutional separation of church and state that gives rise to a diversity of competing religious beliefs. Whereas the European church-state model supports a monopoly of faith by a single church, the explicit separation of church and state in the United States supports a competitive marketplace of faiths and religious organizations. While there may be *de facto* compulsory membership in that children generally adopt the religious faith of their parents, legally all religious belief is voluntary, and indeed, over the life course, many people switch their religious allegiances.

A further complication is that many of the religious institutions in the United States today originated as European churches that were transplanted to American soil by European immigrant groups. The Catholic Church in America, for example, has many of the characteristics ascribed to Weber's church type but is also very different in many ways from its European counterpart. Scholars have argued that the American Catholic Church has more in common with its American Protestant neighbors than it has with the European Catholic Church because the American Catholic Church been forced to accommodate itself to the competitive marketplace that characterizes the American religious environment.

Contemporary Usage of the Church Concept

The United States is overwhelmingly Christian in character, and many religious groups call themselves a "church." However, the freedom of religion in the United States makes many of Weber's assumptions and defining characteristics moot. So-called churches in the United States are largely voluntary associations; they cannot pursue the goal of universal conversion through political domination, nor can they exercise a monopoly of religious authority. Instead they must achieve conversion through strategies of persuasion and evangelization while competing in a marketplace of religious ideas. This forces them to resemble in many respects what Weber called the "sect type" organization, in which religious membership is voluntary, salvation depends on the subjective choice of the member, and religious authority tends to be communal and democratic.

Attempts to reclaim the utility of the church-sect model by American scholars, however, have led to a number of other conceptualizations of "church." One of the more fruitful strategies has been to abandon the multiplicity of characteristics that Weber identified as being associated with the church type and select one theoretical dimension on which to classify a range of religious organizations. Thus Peter Berger proposed defining religious organizations as either "church" or "sect" based on where they were located on a dimension he called the "nearness of the religious spirit" (1954). Benton Johnson proposed classifying religious organizations based on their degree of acceptance or rejection of the social order in which

a religious body is located, or the degree to which they are in tension with society (1963). More recently Laurence Iannaccone (1994) has adopted a similar approach in seeking to define religious organizations in terms of the social "costs" or demands they place on members.

Another strategy for classifying religious organizations in the American context has been to create new "types" of religious organization, such as the "cult" (Becker 1932), the "denomination" (Niebuhr 1929), the "established sect" (Yinger 1946), and the "ecclesia" (Becker 1932), or to distinguish among various types of sects based on their worldviews (Wilson 1959). While these strategies reject the utility of the church-sect typology, they acknowledge the conceptual foundations of Weber's work.

Today the term "church" is rarely used to label a distinctive form of religious organization. It is used to denote a range of organizational types, from the universal Catholic Church to the local neighborhood congregation. The word "church" appears in the names of a variety of religious organizations, including those that are as theologically and organizationally diverse as the "Unification Church," the "Church of Jesus Christ of Latter-day Saints," the "United Methodist Church," and the the "First Presbyterian Church." Thus perhaps its original definition remains its most useful, a term used to denote an "assembly of believers."

In the United States, the term "denomination" seems to have replaced the term "church" as a generic descriptor for national religious membership organizations, particularly those from a Christian background. Some of the common characteristics associated with the term "denomination" include voluntary membership, a national orientation, and association with one of the traditional religious families in the United States.

See also Anthropology of Religion; Church and State; Church Growth Movement; Communes; Cult; Denomination; Names and Naming; Peace Churches; Practice; Religious Communities; Religious Studies; Sect; Sociology of Religion.

BIBLIOGRAPHY

Becker, Howard. *Systematic Sociology.* 1932.

Berger, Peter. "The Sociological Study of Sectarianism." *Social Research* 21 (Winter 1954).

Iannaccone, Laurence R. "Why Strict Churches Are Strong." *American Journal of Sociology* 99, no. 5 (1994): 1180–1211.

Johnson, Benton. "On Church and Sect." *American Sociological Review* 28 (1963): 539–549.

Niebuhr, H. Richard. *The Social Sources of Denominationalism.* 1929.

Troeltsch, Ernst. *The Social Teachings of the Christian Churches,* vols. 1 and 2, translated by Olive Wyon. 1981.

Weber, Max. *Economy and Society: An Outline of Interpretive Sociology,* vols. 1 and 2, edited by Guenther Roth and Claus Wittich. 1978.

Wilson, Bryan. "An Analysis of Sect Development." *American Sociological Review* 24 (1959): 3–22.

Yinger, J. Milton. *Religion in the Struggle for Power.* 1946.

Patricia Mei Yin Chang

Church and State

All enduring societies have arrangements for governing (a "state"), and all have arrangements for expressing ultimate things (a "church"). But both sets of arrangements are involved in the "good life"—the state in efforts to bring it about, the church in efforts to define and justify it. No political order will declare itself in search of what is bad, and no religious order leaves the good life unexamined; even the most ascetic, monastic religion, in ignoring this life to focus on the next, has consequences for the earthly world. As a result, all enduring societies have some arrangements for relating church and state.

For most of human history this relationship was not complicated, because in simple, small-scale societies the arrangements for governing and those for expressing ultimate things were identical. The political leader was also the religious leader, and society members probably did not differentiate their "politics" from their "religion." By the time large-scale societies came into existence, however, the two spheres were differentiated, and some conscious thought had to address the issue of the relationship between them.

One obvious solution, called caesaro-papism, was for the state to give one religion a monopoly, making all citizens be members of that church (or face persecution). The head of the church (the pope in medieval Europe, hence "papism") would legitimize the political leader (hence "caesaro") in exchange for the state's endorsement. This solution was imperfect, however, as evidenced by witch-hunts, heresy trials, and even disputes between kings and popes. It is no coincidence, therefore, that the time of the Protestant Reformation (sixteenth century) overlapped the time of emerging nation-states. While caesaro-papism did not disappear—even today in Europe, Great Britain and the Scandinavian countries maintain "established" churches—the presence of the ever more bureaucratized state and the ever more pluralistic religious population in every society have stimulated development of other ways to structure the relationship between church and state (Demerath, 1991).

When the United States of America was born, the founders and framers had no choice but to devise a church/state policy. Their solution, found in the First Amendment to the Constitution, reads, "Congress shall make no law respecting an establishment of religion, or prohibiting the free exercise thereof." While much scholarly debate occurs over the meaning of these words and over the "real" intention of those who wrote, adopted, and/or ratified them, for all practical purposes their meaning is found in the succession of judicial decisions based on these religion clauses. Our understanding, at least of the past, is aided by the clean "order" to be found in that succession of cases, following two paths, one having to do with the "establishment of religion," the other with its "free exercise" (Flowers, 1994). Before we take those paths, however, five background generalizations must be stated:

1. The first American citizens were religiously concerned, even though only a minority were formally church members.
2. They, and especially their political leaders, believed that the good society required morally upright citizens and that religion led to morality.
3. It was common in the colonies (and continued in some of the first thirteen states) to use tax money to support the teaching of religion and morality, generally by paying a clergyman of the most favored Protestant denomination in each town to be a teacher.
4. It makes sense to suppose, therefore, that the First Amendment prohibition on laws "respecting an establishment" meant not only that Congress could not set up a national church but also that it must leave alone whatever "establishments" of religion existed in the several states.
5. Though evidence exists that some religious persecution occurred in the colonies, by the time of the Constitution, most Americans were in favor of free exercise of religion, and even where religious prejudice was found, it took the form of denying rights (e.g., to hold office if Roman Catholic or atheist) rather than active punishment.

Over the next two hundred years, many of the conditions implied in these five generalizations have changed in the direction of greater separation between church and state (Handy, 1991). Two huge causal forces can be seen to have operated. One is the enormous waves of immigration that began in the nineteenth century and continue today, bringing infinitely greater religious pluralism and therefore pressures to redefine what can be "freely exercised." The second force is the enormous growth of the bureaucratic state, especially since World War II, which, by intruding more and more into once private matters, increasingly exposes unconstitutional "establishments" of religion. Each force generated a path of change in the interpretation of the two religion clauses. We begin first down the path of free exercise (Hammond, 1998).

The constitutional guarantee of free exercise of religion was never understood as a license to do anything in the name of one's faith. Of course, human sacrifice at an altar is illegal, but so is failure to pay taxes even if one believes that that is what God demands. In effect, while laws could not be enacted that targeted religion, laws that are religiously neutral were to be obeyed by everyone, including those whose religious practices were thereby inconvenienced or compromised.

In 1879 the U.S. Supreme Court ruled that the practice of polygamy was unconstitutional (*Reynolds* v. *United States*). Reynolds had claimed that his Mormon religion required him to have more than one wife, and the Court responded that while he was free to *believe* in polygamy, he was not free to *behave* in accord with his belief.

This belief-behavior distinction was the principle for deciding church-state cases for the next six decades. In 1940, however, a case came before the Supreme Court that altered the free-exercise path. It involved a Jehovah's Witness who was arrested for disturbing the peace when he played a phonograph recording castigating the Roman Catholic Church in a heavily Roman Catholic neighborhood. The Court overturned his conviction, and in so doing declared that persons who are *religiously motivated* in their behavior may have a right that other persons do not have (*Cantwell* v. *Connecticut*).

The *Cantwell* decision led inevitably to a recognition that some systematic method must be found for deciding between religious behaviors that had such protection and those that did not. The clearest expression of this method emerged in 1963 in *Sherbert* v. *Verner*. Mrs. Sherbert was a Seventh-Day Adventist whose employer wanted her to work a Saturday (her Sabbath) shift. When she refused she was fired and then applied for unemployment compensation, which was denied. Reading this case makes clear that the Supreme Court was addressing three questions that, together, came to be called the "Sherbert test." They are: (1) Does the regulation in question place a burden on the plaintiff, and if so, how heavy is it? (2) How important to the state is it to apply the regulation in every instance, and what would be the consequence

of not doing so? (3) Are there alternative means the state might take to achieve the regulation's purpose without burdening the religious plaintiff?

Many cases of free exercise after *Cantwell* and before *Sherbert* had been decided, but with the Sherbert test, subsequent cases followed a routine procedure, the most important element of which is the requirement that the state demonstrate a "compelling interest" served in burdening someone's religion.

Just as *Cantwell* led to the need for something like a Sherbert test for deciding *which* religious behaviors are protected, so, at about the same time (1944), did *United States* v. *Ballard* force the Court to answer another question: What *is* religion? Guy Ballard and his family were arrested for mail fraud because they used the U.S. Post Office to announce their capacity to heal—for a fee—ailments that medical doctors had been unable to cure. In a lower court hearing the case, the judge instructed the jury to ignore the question of whether Ballard's beliefs were *true* but decide only whether Ballard *sincerely* believed them. The jury decided Ballard was sincere, and, on appeal, the U.S. Supreme Court heard the case and agreed. In effect the Court said the state has no business judging the theological merits of anyone's religion, no matter how bizarre. Religion now was to be defined not by its contents but by how conscientiously it is held.

The implications of this ruling became fully explicit in 1965 in *United States* v. *Seeger*, when the agnostic Seeger sued for conscientious objector status and won a unanimous decision. The Court declared that, though Seeger was not religious in the usual sense of that word, the state could ask if his beliefs occupied the same place in his life that orthodox beliefs occupy in the lives of "religious" people. The answer in his case, the Court said, was yes.

It is not a great stretch to see that the Supreme Court was concluding that even if Seeger did not articulate his conscience in religious language, he nonetheless *had* a conscience, and the conscience, the Court was seeing, is what the Constitution says may be freely exercised. But then came a bump in the free-exercise path.

In 1990 the Court heard a case in which two members of the Native American Church had been denied unemployment money because they lost their jobs for admitting their use of peyote in their church's ritual. The Court upheld that decision (*Oregon Unemployment Division* v. *Smith*). Remarkably, however, in his majority decision Justice Scalia declared that since the state had not classified peyote an illegal drug in order to target Native Americans, it therefore did *not* have to find a compelling reason for burdening these members of the Native American Church. In other words, the majority voided the Sherbert test and returned, in effect, to the pre-Cantwell, 1879 Reynolds standard.

The *Smith* decision upset many Americans, including a few justices on the Supreme Court. A movement in response to *Smith* led to Congress's passing the Religious Freedom Restoration Act (RFRA) in 1993, which, though worded slightly differently, said that the government must follow the rules of the Sherbert test if any religion is burdened. Many observers hoped the Supreme Court would find a church-state case in which it could undo its *Smith* decision, but instead, in the first opportunity it had (*Boerne* v. *Flores*, 1997), it reaffirmed the *Smith* reasoning and announced that RFRA was unconstitutional because Congress was usurping the authority of the judicial branch. Though the justices were unanimous in the second of these statements, several wanted to revisit the *Smith* case and/or reinstate the Sherbert test. At this time, the free-exercise situation is ambiguous in the extreme. We must await further decisions before knowing where the path will go.

So is the situation surrounding the establishment clause ambiguous, though for different reasons.

As noted earlier, several of the first thirteen states of the new union had established religions of a sort. These were seen as accommodations by the government to enable communities to educate children in an acceptable manner. In retrospect it can be shown that the government permitted all manner of accommodation, much of which was later found to be unconstitutional, or was voted out of existence, or simply ceased to exist. Such practices as opening government meetings with prayer, using only the Protestant version of the Bible in schools, prohibiting many activities on Sunday, and arrests for blasphemy are examples where the state was preferring one kind of religion over others, or preferring religion over irreligion. Little by little, these things—at one time unquestioned—*were* questioned, and the state found itself more and more separated from religion.

Many accommodations of religion still exist, and some Americans would restore practices that now are outlawed, such as allowing public schools to sponsor prayers. (Anyone in public school is free to pray now, subject only to restrictions of time, place, and manner. The political football called "prayer in the schools" is a deception; what its supporters really want is government *endorsement* of prayer, something the establishment clause seems clearly to prohibit.)

Since its founding, then, the country has shifted from more accommodation to less, and from less separation to more. As particular issues have arisen, the Supreme Court—much as it did with the Sherbert test of free-exercise issues—eventually developed a method for deciding establishment cases. It is called the "Lemon test," because it was formalized in the 1971 court case of *Lemon* v. *Kurtzman*. At issue was whether a government can pay some of the costs—for example, pay the salaries of teachers of secular subjects, or provide secular textbooks—of religiously operated schools. In deciding that governments may not provide such aid, the Court declared that a publicly funded program, to be constitutional, must meet three criteria: (1) Its purpose must be neither to advance nor to inhibit religion, (2) its primary effect must be neither to advance nor to inhibit religion, and (3) it must be free of "entangling alliances" between religion and government (e.g., it cannot require constant monitoring by the state to ensure that religion is being neither advanced nor inhibited).

Like the Sherbert test, the Lemon test is not automatically applicable. Justices do not always agree on what constitutes an "advance" or an "inhibition," or how much entanglement is too much. Justice O'Connor in several opinions has argued that the purpose and effect criteria should be changed to the question of whether the government's program appears to "endorse," by intention or effect, a religion.

The fact is that considerable disagreement exists both in the American public and in the courts regarding how much religion should exist in public places *in a manner that connotes governmental approval* of religion. To some, outlawing prayer by a local clergyman before a Friday night football game in a town where no known non-Protestants exist is simply idiotic. Such people are unable even to see the matter as an establishment issue because they see it as curtailing their free exercise. To others, a Roman Catholic hospital that receives government support should not be allowed to display images of the Virgin Mary in the hallways or on the grounds, for that puts the state in the position of fostering Catholicism.

The Lemon test thus is controversial, not—like the Sherbert test—over fundamental jurisprudential principles, but over the confusing, even contradictory, decisions the test has led to. Just as with free exercise, then, the establishment path's direction is hard to predict. In the long run, the order found along each path will be followed, but as long as controversy envelops the U.S. Supreme Court's various rulings in church-state cases, disorder may appear more the order of the day.

See also CIVIL RELIGION; CONSCIENTIOUS OBJECTION; FREEDOM OF RELIGION; PRAYER IN SCHOOL; RELIGIOUS FREEDOM RESTORATION ACT; RELIGIOUS PERSECUTION.

BIBLIOGRAPHY

Demerath, N. J., III. "Religious Capital and Capital Religions: Cross-Cultural and Non-Legal Factors in the Separation of Church and State." *Daedalus* 120 (1991): 21–40.

Flowers, Ronald B. *That Godless Court.* 1994.

Hammond, Phillip E. *With Liberty for All.* 1998.

Handy, Robert T. *Undermined Establishment: Church State Relations in America, 1880–1920.* 1991.

Journal of Church and State Quarterly.

Miller, Robert T., and Ronald B. Flowers. *Toward Benevolent Neutrality: Church, State, and the Supreme Court.*

Phillip E. Hammond

Church Growth Movement

Donald A. McGavran (1897–1990) is considered the founder of the modern Church Growth Movement. McGavran, a third-generation missionary to India for the Disciples of Christ, felt a call to return to India as a missionary while studying law in the United States. Entering Yale Divinity School, he studied under Kenneth Scott Latourette, who documented the history of Christianity as the spread and growth of the church. In the early 1930s a Methodist missionary, J. Wascom Pickett, surveyed Christian mass movements in India. McGavran acknowledged that he "lit his fire at Pickett's candle" and subsequently invested his life in clarifying the most effective ways to reach large numbers of people with the Christian gospel.

The Church Growth Movement arrived in the United States in 1961, when McGavran established the Institute for Church Growth at Northwest Christian College in Eugene, Oregon. Four years later McGavran and his colleague Alan R. Tippett moved to Pasadena, California, where they launched the School of World Mission at Fuller Theological Seminary. Over the next fifteen years almost all of the current leaders in this movement were greatly influenced by the teachings and writings of McGavran and Tippett and the team of missiologists they gathered.

Distinctive aspects of the Church Growth Movement include: (1) an emphasis on making disciples over securing decisions; (2) the use of sociological research to analyze data, discern receptivity, set goals, and design strategies; (3) a recognition that context and culture—not ecclesiastical tradition—properly determine the methods employed; (4) an acceptance of the fact that people most naturally trust and converse with others like themselves (the homogeneous unit principle); (5) an appreciation of the indigenous church as God's instrument for evangelizing all peoples; and (6) an optimism based on case studies from around the world.

During the 1970s denominational leaders began to recognize the movement as a force to be reckoned with. Some saw it as a distortion of true Christianity—a theologically thin numbers game, a lopsided evangelical counter to the social gospel, blatant racism, or a dependence on human strategies rather than on the Spirit of God. Nevertheless, membership losses, especially in mainline denominations, caused a growing awareness that "business as usual" evangelism was no longer bearing fruit. By the end of the 1980s nearly every North American Protestant denomination was restructuring its evangelism, its new church development, and its leadership training efforts to reflect insights and strategies gleaned from the Church Growth Movement.

Additional emphases emerging from the movement include: (1) seeing North America as a mission field; (2) accepting cultural anthropology as a tool for Christian mission; (3) employing computer technology across denominational lines for reaching new groups of people; (4) assisting laity to discover and invest their spiritual gifts for ministry; (5) training people to use their existing social networks for lifestyle evangelism; (6) equipping leaders for the Church Growth Movement through ecumenical networks and teaching churches rather than relying solely on denominational staffs or seminary education; (7) exploring experiences of "power encounter" and "spiritual warfare" as challenges to twentieth-century Western understandings of reality; and (8) uniting the spiritual disciplines of fasting and prayer with strategic planning.

Among the most influential contributors to North American Church Growth Movement literature today are Lyle Schaller, Peter Wagner, Win and Charles Arn, George Hunter, James Engel, Elmer Towns, Flavil Yeakley, Tetsunao Yamamori, Harvey Conn, Dean Hoge, David Roozen, John Vaughn, Kent Hunter, Carl George, Herb Miller, Gary McIntosh, Kennon Callahan, Kirk Hadaway, Bob Logan, Loren Mead, Bill Easum, George Barna, Aubrey Malphurs, Bill Hybels, and Rick Warren.

See also ANTHROPOLOGY OF RELIGION; BELONGING, RELIGIOUS; ECUMENICAL MOVEMENT; FUTURE OF RELIGION; MAINLINE PROTESTANTISM; MISSIONARY MOVEMENTS; POPULAR RELIGION; RELIGIOUS COMMUNITIES; TELEVANGELISM.

BIBLIOGRAPHY

Hunter, George G. III. *To Spread the Power.* 1987.

McGavran, Donald A. *Understanding Church Growth,* rev. 3rd ed. 1990.

Warren, Rick. *The Purpose Driven Church.* 1995.

Ronald K. Crandall

Church of Christ, United.

See Mainline Protestantism.

Church of Jesus Christ of Latter-day Saints

The Church of Jesus Christ of Latter-day Saints (hereafter referred to as the "LDS Church" or the "Mormon Church") is the largest of the churches in the Restorationist tradition, with more than ten million members in 1999.

Early History

Mormonism began in western New York state in the 1820s, during a period of great religious excitement. A young farm boy, Joseph Smith, Jr., found himself so confused by the competing claims of various Christian sects that he prayed to God to instruct him about which church to join. According to Smith, God appeared to him in a pillar of light and told him that all of the churches were corrupt; he was to join none of them. Several years later, Smith claimed to have had another vision, this one a visitation by the angel Moroni. Moroni informed him that "plates of gold" were buried in a nearby hill, and contained an important ancient record. Smith was eventually led to find and translate the plates from hieroglyphics with the help of two "seer stones."

Smith published the translation as the Book of Mormon in March 1830, stating that the book recorded God's dealings with the former residents of North and Central America, and went back many centuries before the time of Christ. The book became the foundation of a new religious movement. On April 6, 1830, soon after the publication of the Book of Mormon, Smith organized the fledgling Church of Jesus Christ with six members—it later became known as the Church of Jesus Christ of Latter-day Saints.

In the early 1830s Smith settled his growing church in Kirtland, Ohio, experimenting with communitarian principles. He immediately sent missionaries to Jackson County, Missouri, which he later proclaimed to be the "center place" of Zion. He encouraged the Mormons to gather in Jackson County, where he joined them several years later. But angry neighbors forced the Mormons out of Missouri in 1838. They fled across the Mississippi to Nauvoo, Illinois, where the governor offered them a liberal charter and promised religious asylum. In the early 1840s Nauvoo flourished, becoming the largest town in Illinois as Mormon converts gathered there from England, Scandinavia, and the eastern part of the United States. Nauvoo's neighbors became less tolerant when the Mormons organized a militia and destroyed an anti-Mormon printing press in the city. Rumors also circulated that the Mormons had revived the Old Testament practice of polygamy and that Smith and other leaders had taken multiple wives. In June 1844 Joseph Smith was arrested and imprisoned in nearby Carthage, Illinois. While in prison, he was assassinated by a mob.

The Mormons were shaken by the sudden loss of their prophet, especially since he had never designated a successor. For more than two years, various leaders attempted to gain control of the movement, and several factions splintered off from the main body. Most Mormons chose to follow Brigham Young, a charismatic leader and vigorous organizer, when he proposed that they establish a haven for themselves far west in the Rocky Mountains.

In February 1846 the first Mormons fled Nauvoo and began their long trek across the plains. Some rode in covered wagons, carting everything they owned and provisions for the harsh journey. Others had to walk, pulling handcarts for more than a thousand miles. Many Latter-day Saints died on the trail, especially during that first harsh winter. More would have surely perished if not for Brigham Young's remarkable planning ability. Young organized the Mormons into camps and instructed the first travelers to plant crops on the trail to benefit later groups.

After arriving in the Salt Lake Valley on July 24, 1847, the Mormons endeavored to tame the desert and build a prosperous colony. Young designated lands for farming, and the Mormons planted vegetables and grains, though they experienced difficulties with insects, the weather, and the primitive conditions. Young encouraged self-sufficiency and restricted commerce with the "Gentile" (non-Mormon) population so the Mormons would never have to depend on outsiders for survival.

In 1852 Young publicly acknowledged that the Mormons were practicing polygamy, which they called "celestial marriage." Mormons believed that taking additional wives would add to a man's exalted status in the Celestial Kingdom, the highest level of the Mormon afterlife. Of those who practiced polygamy, few men had more than two or three wives, though the non-Mormon public often perceived Utah as a "harem" where women were mistreated and enslaved. Non-Mormons abhorred the practice, and the next forty years saw the U.S. government employ various means to abolish polygamy, including military force. In 1890 the LDS prophet and president Wilford Woodruff finally bowed to the tremendous public pressure, promising that the Mormons would no longer take plural wives. This "manifesto" paved the way for Utah to be admitted as a state in 1896.

Statue of Mormon pioneer leader Brigham Young in front of the Church of Jesus Christ of Latter-day Saints Temple in Salt Lake City, Utah, on April 1, 1998.   (Credit: AP/Wide World Photos.)

Theology

Latter-day Saints believe that theirs is the "restored church of Jesus Christ," the only true church now on earth. Mormons share with other Christians a deep belief in the atonement of Jesus Christ. They differ, however, as to Christ's role in the godhead: Whereas Protestants and Catholics proclaim Christ to be simultaneously God's son and God incarnate, Mormons believe only that Christ is God's son. For Latter-day Saints, God the Father, Jesus Christ, and the Holy Ghost are three distinct personages, not a unified Holy Trinity.

Mormons believe that human beings chose to be born into this world to acquire a mortal body, as Jesus did, and become more like their Heavenly Father. All humans are the spiritual children of Heavenly Parents who possess physical bodies of flesh and bone (an-

other prominent divergence from traditional Christianity). Mormons believe that they can progress spiritually throughout eternity. Past statements by LDS leaders have indicated that human males can aspire to godhood themselves, just as their Heavenly Father progressed from a mortal state to godhood. In recent years, however, Church authorities have deemphasized this doctrine, choosing instead to accentuate beliefs held in common with other Christians, such as the atonement.

Like other Christians, Mormons uphold the Old and the New Testaments as sacred texts, but they also regard the Book of Mormon, Doctrine and Covenants, and Pearl of Great Price as scripture. Unlike other Christians, however, Mormons believe that God has yet to reveal many important doctrines pertaining to humanity's salvation. The canon of scripture is not closed, and continuing revelation remains a foundational premise of Mormon theology.

Since World War II, LDS theology has particularly emphasized the importance of the nuclear family. Worthy Latter-day Saints may be sealed to their spouses and children for all eternity in any of nearly one hundred sacred temples around the globe. In 1995 the Church issued the statement "The Family: A Proclamation to the World," which, though still noncanonical, is quickly becoming accepted as doctrine. Among other things, the proclamation declares gender to be an eternal human characteristic, restricts sexual expression to heterosexual marriage, and affirms that "mothers are primarily responsible for the nurture of their children."

Behavioral Principles

Mormonism is a lifestyle as well as a belief system, and Latter-day Saints are recognized as often for their strict behavioral code as for their theology. Most prominent among these principles is the Word of Wisdom, a revelation of 1883 that enjoined the Saints to abstain from alcohol, tobacco, and "hot drinks" (understood as coffee and tea). The revelation also encourages the use of grains, herbs, and fruits in season, and meat only sparingly. Orthodox Mormons also tithe 10 percent of their income to the Church, contribute additional monthly fast offerings for the poor, and support missionary work. Many college-age men and women devote up to two years as unpaid volunteers in the Church's missionary force, currently more than fifty thousand strong.

The LDS Church encourages the cultivation of strong families. On Mondays many Mormons hold "Family Home Evening," a time intentionally set aside for family togetherness and a spiritual message. In the United States Mormons have traditionally reared more children than the national average, though this trend is slowing as Mormon families begin to demographically resemble non-Mormon families.

Church Polity

The basic unit of institutional Mormonism is the ward, a local congregation with several hundred members. Mormons are assigned to wards geographically, and boundaries change frequently as the Church grows. Each ward is supervised by a bishop, an adult Mormon male who typically serves for up to five years in that position. Mormons have no paid clergy. As with most "callings" in the Mormon Church, bishops volunteer their services above and beyond their responsibilities at work and at home and receive no special theological training.

Several churchwide auxiliary programs enhance the Mormon experience. The Relief Society, commissioned in 1842 by Joseph Smith, involves all adult Mormon women and provides charitable relief and fellowship to church members. Other auxiliaries include the Primary (a children's organization), and complementary programs for adolescent girls and boys. At the ward level, most Mormons fulfill a calling as a teacher or leader in one of these organizations, service that often consumes many hours a week.

Leaders in Salt Lake City, called General Authorities, oversee the Church's expansion into new regions of the world and communicate doctrine to members. Twice a year the LDS Church holds a General Conference, which is televised via satellite to members all over the world. The president of the Church, whom Mormons revere as a Prophet, Seer, and Revelator, usually addresses the faithful at Conference. Members do not nominate or elect the Church president; generally, church tradition holds that the most senior member of the Quorum of the Twelve Apostles will succeed as the next prophet/president and serve for life.

Globalization and Growth

In the past few decades Mormonism has evolved from a regional American religion to a new world faith. In 1947 Church membership passed the one million mark; exactly half a century later, that number had increased tenfold. One prominent sociologist predicted in 1984 that there would be 265 million Mormons by the year 2080. Thus far growth has exceeded his estimations.

Most of this growth has sprung from the Church's extensive missionary activity in more than 150 nations, with conversion rates especially high in Latin America and Africa. Today there are nearly three times as many convert baptisms as baptisms of members' children.

In 1996 the Church passed another institutional milestone: More members now live outside the United States than within its borders. (As recently as the 1960s, 90 percent of Mormons had lived within the United States.)

Rapid international expansion has brought new challenges of language barriers, socioeconomic disparity, and occasional doctrinal misunderstandings. Since the 1960s the Church streamlined all of its activities under a massive program called Correlation. Sunday school lessons, instructional handbooks, and Church policies have all been centralized by officials in Salt Lake City. Auxiliary organizations such as the Primary and Relief Society, which had previously controlled their own finances and leadership decisions, now operate under the authority of the priesthood. Correlation seeks to ensure that LDS doctrine and practice will be uniform in every culture where the Church has a presence.

Internal Challenges

Not all Mormons are happy with Correlation, the Church's emphasis on numerical growth, or its increasingly conservative outlook. The 1970s witnessed some internal dissent because priesthood ordination was denied to male members of African ancestry; President Spencer Kimball reversed this policy by revelation in June 1978. Since the 1970s as well there has been an emerging feminist voice within the LDS Church. Many women are disturbed by the Church's refusal to grant them priesthood authority. LDS leaders have not hesitated to discipline those who question its policies, especially concerning gender roles. Of the six Mormons who were excommunicated or disfellowshiped in the well-publicized "purge" of September 1993, five had written about women and the priesthood.

See also BOOK OF MORMON; MISSIONARY MOVEMENTS; MORMON TEMPLE; PROSELYTIZING.

BIBLIOGRAPHY

Arrington, Leonard. *Brigham Young: American Moses.* 1985.

Arrington, Leonard, and Davis Bitton. *The Mormon Experience: A History of the Latter-day Saints.* 1979.

Hinckley, Gordon B. *Truth Restored: A Short History of the Church of Jesus Christ of Latter-day Saints.* 1979.

Shipps, Jan. *Mormonism: The Story of a New Religious Tradition.* 1985.

Stark, Rodney. "Modernization and Mormon Growth: The Secularization Thesis Revisited." In *Contemporary Mormonism: Social Science Perspectives,* edited by Marie Cornwall, Tim B. Heaton, and Lawrence A. Young. 1994.

Taber, Susan Buhler. *Mormon Lives: A Year in the Elkton Ward.* 1993.

Jana Kathryn Riess

Church of Satan.

See LaVey, Anton; Satanic Bible; Satanists.

Church Universal and Triumphant

Church Universal and Triumphant (CUT) is a New Age religion that has its roots in alternative reality traditions such as Theosophy, New Thought, and the "I Am" Activity. The church gained attention during the late 1980s when it built a sophisticated network of fallout shelters on its property near the border of Yellowstone National Park in southern Montana. The shelters were deemed necessary after the church's leader, Elizabeth Clare Prophet, predicted a heightened probability of nuclear war between 1989 and 1991. Following this period of intense apocalyptic expectation, the church lost one-third of its membership and began selling parcels of its Montana property to raise operating funds. Since 1996, Gilbert Cleirbault, a Belgian corporate executive, has reorganized the church's operations and refocused its activities on the publication of Prophet's writings and international outreach. Prophet announced that she was suffering from Alzheimer's disease in November 1998 and stepped down as the church's leader in 1999.

CUT is a study in religious syncretism, apocalypticism, American neognosticism, and entrepreneurism. It began its life as Summit Lighthouse in 1958 in Washington, D.C., with a mission to disseminate the teachings of highly evolved spiritual guides called "ascended masters." Founder Mark L. Prophet (1918–1973) claimed to receive the masters' teachings as dictations and distributed them as *Pearls of Wisdom,* still CUT's most important publication.

Mark Prophet married Elizabeth Clare Wulf (b. 1939), a student, in 1963, and soon the couple claimed to be the sole messengers of the ascended masters in the dawning Aquarian Age. Following a move to Colorado Springs in mid-1966, the movement began to attract large numbers of counterculture young people. When Mark Prophet died in 1973, Elizabeth Prophet renamed the group "Church Universal and Triumphant" and relocated to Southern California. There she founded Summit University, a "New Age mystery school," in Malibu. The move to Montana, which occurred in 1986, was related to a costly lawsuit in California, the suit's attendant negative publicity, and local zoning problems.

CUT sees itself as the true church of Jesus Christ and teaches the "lost arts" of Christian healing, the science of the spoken word, karma and reincarnation, and an amalgam of esoteric religious techniques. Its primary spiritual practice is decreeing, a form of vocal affirmation that occurs in both private and group settings. Members believe that this practice can neutralize negative personal and group karma, heal the sick, protect the church from enemies, and speed up spiritual evolution. The church teaches that the purpose of life is to attain personal ascension, a process whereby the soul balances its karma and merges with the Christ consciousness and divine self within. Once ascension has taken place, the soul is believed to become a permanent atom in the body of God. Church members come from diverse racial, national, and socioeconomic backgrounds.

Prior to the onset of her disability, Prophet claimed to be the sole messenger for the ascended masters in the new age. She took care to distinguish between her dictations and the "channeling" and "spiritualism" of the New Age movement, which the church disparages. Despite recent challenges to its survival from the Internal Revenue Service and from hostile neighbors in Montana, the group has managed to emerge with its core leadership, finances, and teachings intact. CUT's long-term survival, however, depends on its successful transfer of leadership in the wake of Ms. Prophet's disability and its movement beyond apocalypticism.

See also CULT; MILLENNIALISM; NEW AGE SPIRITUALITY; NEW THOUGHT; THEOSOPHICAL SOCIETY.

BIBLIOGRAPHY

Lewis, James R., and J. Gordon Melton. *Church Universal and Triumphant: In Scholarly Perspective.* 1994.
Prophet, Mark, and Elizabeth Clare Prophet. *The Lost Teachings of Jesus.* 1988.

Phillip Charles Lucas

Circumcision

The following words of God to Abraham are the biblical origin of the practice of circumcision among Jews:

> Throughout the generations, every male among you shall be circumcised at the age of eight days. . . . Thus shall My covenant be marked in your flesh as an ever-lasting pact. And if any male who is uncircumcised fails to circumcise the flesh of his foreskin, that person shall

be cut off from his kin; he has broken My covenant. (Genesis 17:12, 14)

Ever since, circumcision has been an important mark of the Jewish covenant with God. Recognizing this, Antiochus Epiphanes forbade Jews to circumcise their sons (I Maccabees 1:48) and punished those who did (II Maccabees 6:10) precisely as a way of suppressing Jewish identity and faith. Despite the powerful religious and national meaning of circumcision for Jews, any boy born of a Jewish mother is Jewish, whether circumcised or not.

The primary party responsible for circumcising a Jewish infant male is his father. He may do it himself but most often appoints an expert in the operation and the ritual (a *mohel*) to do so. If the father fails to fulfill his responsibility, the duty falls to the rabbinic court acting on behalf of the community. If the court neglects to do so, the man himself has the duty to have himself circumcised once he reaches adulthood (age thirteen or above).

In accordance with the biblical command in Genesis and in Leviticus 12:3, the rabbis determined that circumcision must occur on the eighth day of a boy's life, even if that happens to fall on the Sabbath or a fast day. Preparations for the operation must be made before the Sabbath, but the acts involved in the operation itself, some of which are otherwise prohibited, are permitted so that circumcision can take place on the eighth day (Talmud, *Shabbat* 130b; Mishneh Torah, *Laws of Circumcision* 2:6). The joy of bringing a new child into the covenant supersedes the solemnity and fasting of minor fast days, and on major fast days (the Day of Atonement and Tisha B'Ab) the wine used in the ceremony is given to a minor to drink. The circumcision is postponed only if the baby's health status makes it unsafe to circumcise him on the eighth day. Usually doctors require that the baby weigh more than five pounds and have no medical problems to ensure the safety of circumcision. The rabbis interpreted the Torah's requirement of performing the circumcision on the eighth day to require that it be done during daylight hours.

The Torah does not specify any ceremony to accompany the circumcision or any particulars about the operation itself, but later Jewish law filled in both gaps. The *mohel* may be any male or female Jew, but preferably one loyal to the tenets and practices of Judaism. He or she is trained in the specific requirements of how the surgery is to be performed and the liturgy that is to be recited (although a rabbi or any other Jew may be given the honor of reciting the liturgy). The blessings recited announce that the circumcision is in fulfillment of God's command and that it is intended as a sign of the Jewish covenant with God. Thus the Hebrew term for the ceremony is *brit milah*, "the covenant of circumcision" (or, in Yiddish, *bris*, "covenant"). The boy is given his Hebrew name as part of the liturgy. A male convert to Judaism who was circumcised at birth undergoes a symbolic Jewish circumcision by extracting a drop of blood from the head of the penis (*hatafat dam brit*, "the spilling of the blood of the covenant").

Some Jews during Hellenistic times (second century B.C.E.) and in the nineteenth and twentieth centuries who have wanted to assimilate into the general culture more fully have objected to circumcision because it identifies the boy too noticeably as a Jew (see Jubilees 15:33–34). Others have objected to circumcision as being medically unnecessary. There has been some controversy among American physicians over the strictly medical advisability of circumcision, but from the mid-twentieth century on, most American boys have been circumcised in the hospital (unless the parents objected) as a way of avoiding infections and penile cancer in themselves and cervical cancer in their sexual partner or partners. In any case, circumcision has been almost universally practiced by Jews of all forms of belief and practice, not so much for its medical benefits as for its religious meaning.

The religious meanings of circumcision include the following:

1. The covenant of God is sealed in the infant's flesh, thus symbolizing and guaranteeing its permanence in his own life. (Consider the parallel way in which we seal important documents by changing the surface of the paper on which they are written.)
2. The circumcision is performed on the boy's generative organ, symbolizing the continuity of the covenant in future generations.
3. The tradition associates circumcision with Elijah, the prophet who restored the practice of circumcision after Queen Jezebel expunged it (I Kings 19:14). In later Jewish literature, Elijah became the herald of the Messianic age, and so at every *brit milah* there is a "chair of Elijah" on which the baby is briefly placed, indicating hope for the messianic future—and even that this boy will be the Messiah.
4. When asked by a Roman official why God had not made Jewish men circumcised if that is how He wanted them, Rabbi Oshaya replied that it was in order to give man an opportunity to perfect himself and the world in fulfillment of the divine command (Genesis Rabbah 11:6). Thus circumcision symbolizes the Jewish mission to improve the world.

5. Finally, even though circumcision apparently predated Abraham in some ancient Near Eastern cultures, and even though approximately a sixth of the modern world circumcises its sons, circumcision remains a powerful symbol of Jewish identity, linking Jews through the generations to the commandment of God to circumcise Isaac and all his descendants.

See also JEWISH IDENTITY; JUDAISM.

BIBLIOGRAPHY

Kunin, Samuel A. *Circumcision: Its Place in Judaism, Past and Present.* 1998.

Snowman, Leonard V. "Circumcision." *Encyclopedia Judaica* 5: 567–576.

Elliot N. Dorff

Civil Religion

In 1967 Robert Bellah published an essay titled "Civil Religion in America." There followed a flurry of articles and books about civil religion, most of which, instead of analytically appraising the concept, debated whether such a thing exists. Considerable ambiguity surrounded the topic, therefore, and after a decade or so, scholarly interest in civil religion waned. It lingers, however, not just in America but in other countries as well. The result, unfortunately, is not a codified set of findings about civil religion, surrounded by a systematic theory explaining those findings.

This regrettable situation stems from the overemphasis on debating whether civil religion exists. One does not ask if, in a society, an economy exists, or a polity, or a religion. Instead, one investigates how elaborate or encompassing those institutions are. One looks at how many people are involved and what they are doing. One looks at how those institutions are stratified and how authority is distributed and maintained. And one inquires into the beliefs and practices of those involved in the economy, the polity, and the religion. Despite enormous variation in these institutions through time and space, we have no difficulty identifying them sufficiently to study them without wondering if they exist.

Why, then, is the analysis of civil religion different? It is because so many analysts are not prepared for the amorphous character of this particular institution. They fail to see that the term "civil religion" is a construct, not an objective thing. Moreover, it is a construct consisting of many elements that *are* objective, but they have been investigated piecemeal, and de-

tractors can claim that a particular objective element is not itself a civil religion. Of course it is not, but that does not mean a civil religion does not exist. Bellah's analysis, for example, borrowed much from presidential inaugural addresses, which had the effect of highlighting civil religion's ritualistic element. Others have explored the religio-political thought of the major figures giving shape to American society. Fourth of July and Memorial Day celebrations—celebrations that affirm the goodness of America—have been the focus of some, while still others see in the rhetoric of the civil rights and anti–Vietnam War campaigns how American civil religion can judge and condemn the nation. In each case an objection can be raised that ritual alone, or the founders' philosophy alone, or patriotic holidays alone, do not indicate civil religion.

What, then, *is* a civil religion? The phrase originated with the French philosopher Jean-Jacques Rousseau (1712–1778) in his book *The Social Contract*. He offered it as a solution to the dilemma of church-state relations in religiously plural societies. In his civil religion, what Rousseau called "positive dogmas" are simple and few in number: "The existence of a powerful, wise, and benevolent Divinity, who foresees and provides the life to come, the happiness of the just, the punishment of the wicked, the sanctity of the social contract and the laws." The only "negative dogma," he said, is "intolerance."

However attractive such a solution might seem, it is unrealistic because for a religion—any religion, including a civil religion—to be religious, it must be thought to be not a human but a supernatural creation. In the American case, the founders, while recognizing that they, as human beings, were *expressing* truths about the meaning of America, believed that the truths they expressed were not of *their* making but were truths reflecting *the natural order of things*. Moreover, as Bellah says,

> Though much [of what the founders said and did] is selectively derived from Christianity, this religion is clearly not itself Christianity. . . . [Rather, it] exists alongside of and . . . [is] clearly differentiated from the churches.

The result was a *civil* religion, which can be defined as any set of beliefs and rituals related to the past, present, and/or future of a people ("nation") that is understood to have not only political but also supernatural meaning.

By this definition, *any* group of people has the potential to evolve a civil religion. The chances that this will happen increase under certain conditions: if a group believes that it has a political history, if it traces that history to real or mythical founders, if it experienced a dramatic founding and/or suffered challenges to its unity, etc. The list could go on, but the point is clear: Whether a civil religion does emerge depends on many factors. And something else is just as clear: The visibility of civil religion increases and decreases with events. An inaugural address, or the assassination of a president, or an Olympic gold medal, or a Ku Klux Klan parade reminds us that we are fellow citizens of a group where political events can take on transcendent meaning.

It is not surprising, then, to find that in modern societies, the groups most likely to experience emergent civil religions are nation-states, and books have been written about not just the civil religion of America, but also that of Israel, South Africa, and others. Ethnic groups likewise may have civil religions, since so often their origins are found in a mythic past with sacred meaning.

This does not mean that because civil religions exist, all elements of them are everywhere and always in the minds of citizens. Nor does it mean that citizens cease to practice the religious tradition in which they were raised. Religions whose origins are found in one of the world's major traditions are thoroughly institutionalized, with buildings, bureaucratic administrations, budgets, membership rolls, and so forth. For the most part, these features are missing in civil religions, though temporary arrangements might exist to organize a July Fourth celebration, for example, or a civil rights rally.

There is one major exception to this claim that civil religions have little in the way of institutionalized facilities. In America at least, civil religion historically has been maintained and transmitted by a system of public schools that, among other things, rather self-consciously taught "civics" or "Americanism." Two forces in the twentieth century served to mute this effort, however. One is the increased awareness of religious pluralism in the United States. As long as nearly everyone was at least vaguely Christian or Jewish, an ethic—a civil religion—could be articulated that was believed to be a secular reflection of "Judeo-Christianity." Will Herberg, in his 1955 *Protestant-Catholic-Jew,* argued that this advocacy was occurring, and he also excoriated its inauthenticity and departure from the three "real" religions. The public and their schools are very mindful of how many religions get left out by this strategy, however, and, where it passes constitutional muster, how tepid it is.

The second force is similar in form, but instead of a plurality of religions it is the plurality of ethnicities that makes difficult using public schools as conduits of the doctrines and rituals of supernaturally understood unity.

Such barriers to the socialization of young Americans into their civil religion do not mean that the civil religion does not exist or is dying out. It may mean that younger generations are less knowledgeable about, less observant of, and less fervent toward their civil religion. But something of the same charge can be leveled at Methodists, for example, or Catholics, and nobody suggests that those two religions are on their way to oblivion. Civil religions, like all religions, are group properties, as Émile Durkheim showed. Their constituent elements are, therefore, always potentially present in a group. Whether they emerge and whether they cohere and form an identifiable civil religion depends on many things. Most analysts of the subject have not appreciated this amorphous quality of civil religion. They ask if it is there—whether it *exists*—which leaves only yes and no as possible answers. As should now be clear, however, such an approach to the topic is not very productive.

See also CHURCH AND STATE; CIVIL RIGHTS MOVEMENT; JUDEO-CHRISTIAN TRADITION; RELIGIOUS COMMUNITIES; RELIGIOUS PERSECUTION; SOCIOLOGY OF RELIGION; WORK.

BIBLIOGRAPHY

Albanese, Catherine L. *Sons of the Fathers.* 1976.
Bellah, Robert. "Civil Religion in America." *Daedalus* 96 (1967): 96–121.
Bellah, Robert, and Phillip E. Hammond. *Varieties of Civil Religion.* 1980.
Durkheim, Émile. *The Elementary Forms of Religious Life,* translated by Joseph Swain. 1915; repr., 1926.
Gehrig, Gail. *American Civil Religion: An Assessment.* 1979.
Hammond, Phillip E. "The Sociology of American Civil Religion: A Bibliographic Essay." *Sociological Analysis* 37 (1976): 169–182.
Herberg, Will. *Protestant-Catholic-Jew.* 1955.
Liebman, Charles, and E. Don-Yehiya. *The Civil Religion of Israel.* 1985.
Moodie, T. Dunbar. *The Rise of Afrikanerdom.* 1975.
Rousseau, Jean-Jacques. *The Social Contract,* translated by G. D. H. Cole. 1893; repr., 1913.
Wilson, John F. *Public Religion in American Culture.* 1979.

Phillip E. Hammond

Civil Rights Movement

One of the distinguishing features of the civil rights movement of the mid-twentieth century in America was that it was both a grassroots and a religiously based phenomenon whose aim was to protest against and demand the dismantling of the apartheidlike system

(From left to right) Bishop Julian Smith, Dr. Martin Luther King, Jr., and Rev. Ralph Abernathy in a civil rights march in Memphis, Tennessee, on March 28, 1968.   (Credit: AP/Wide World Photos.)

of racial segregation, so-called Jim Crow, that defined the politics of white supremacy, especially in the southern states.

From the days of slavery, blacks had suffered the indignity of racial discrimination in which they were thought inferior to whites and denied the most basic of rights. They could not ordinarily vote, attend the same schools and colleges as whites, eat in the same restaurants, share the same seats on buses, or use the same public amenities. In addition, blacks were routinely subject to acts of physical violence, most typical being the practice of lynching prevalent in the South.

It was in this context that the modern civil rights movement arose. To be sure, blacks had always resisted both slavery and Jim Crow legislation. Men and women such as Nat Turner, Sojourner Truth, and Harriet Tubman had built a strong tradition of protest

and resistance, much of which had been surreptitious and largely uncoordinated. Indeed, throughout the 1930s and 1940s, churchmen such as A. D. Williams, Martin Luther King, Sr., and others were beginning to tap into that tradition by using it to organize acts of public resistance. But it was not until the mid-1950s that black protest became a mass movement of opposition to white supremacy. Historically, it was the bus boycotts of the 1950s that formally marked the beginnings of the movement. Throughout the South public buses had been segregated into racial sections. Blacks were required by law to sit in the back of the bus, leaving the front seats vacant for whites. The arrest of Rosa Parks in December 1955 for contravening such a law by refusing to yield her seat to a white man catalyzed the movement. This was not the first time blacks had defied bus laws in the South. In June 1953 blacks in Baton Rouge, Louisiana, boycotted segregated buses, as did their counterparts three years later in Tallahassee, Florida. Rosa Parks herself had refused to yield a bus seat to a white man earlier, in the 1940s. The bus boycotts typified a general spirit of civil disobedience that went far beyond concern with bus laws. The boycott itself, together with the sit-ins, the long marches, and, later on, the riots in the ghettos of northern cities, was a popular method of protest that blacks used effectively against white businesses, public institutions, and local governments. But there were also other methods, such as contesting the constitutional legality of racism in southern courts as well as in the Supreme Court of the United States. It was through this approach that one of the most important victories of the movement was achieved, when the Supreme Court ruled in 1955 that public school segregation in the South was illegal.

It was not, however, the use of legal action as a strategy for which the civil rights movement became famous; it was for its use of civil disobedience. Resorting to civil disobedience was not the result of acquiescing in white power but a carefully worked out strategy that was part of the nonviolent philosophy of the whole movement. The aim of this approach was to cause as much social disruption through what was called "nonviolent direct action" as was consistent with dismantling racist structures. Three important points must be made about what made this approach effective. The first is that it was the result of a highly organized effort and was not spontaneous; second, the organizers had at their disposal a significant pool of human and financial resources; and third, the church provided a broad mass of people which the civil rights movement was able to mobilize.

Regarding the first point, the movement consisted of an extensive network of civic and religious organizations such as the Southern Christian Leadership Conference (SCLC) and the Montgomery Improvement Association (MIA), both under the leadership of Rev. Dr. Martin Luther King, Jr.; the Inter Civic Council (ICC) in Tallahassee, under Rev. C. K. Steel; the Alabama Christian Movement for Human Rights (ACMHR), directed by Rev. Fred Shuttlesworth; the many local chapters of the National Association for the Advancement of Colored People (NAACP); and churches and denominational and interdenominational ministerial alliances, to name but a few. What is interesting about these organizations is that almost all of them (the exception being the church and the SCLC) represented other, smaller organizations in their geographical regions. Interestingly, they were either all-Christian or all under the leadership of churchmen. The SCLC became the central organization to which all the others were affiliated.

Although it has become customary to think of the center of this movement as Montgomery, Alabama, and to associate it with the historic figure of Martin Luther King, Jr., it is clear that it was widely dispersed. Of course, the leaders of the movement often met to discuss tactics and strategies, but the implementation of the latter was always constrained by local circumstances, a fact that sometimes led to tensions in the movement. But it was the charismatic figure of King that served as a point of reference for diffusing these tensions. What is important, however, is that together the elements of the movement represented a formidable challenge to the white power structure.

In addition to its strong organizational base, the civil rights movement could count on the financial contributions of its members. Churches and civic organizations as well as individuals gave whatever they could. It has been said that the MIA, for example, had huge bank accounts in nine states in the South. Much of the money came from poor blacks who saw clearly that social and political change was possible only through their active participation in the movement. There were also varied degrees of financial and other support by mostly northern whites sympathetic to the movement. The involvement of ordinary women, youth, and men and the diverse leadership that was represented by the numerous organizations of the movement were themselves other important resources. It was here that the church played a decisive role in giving shape and content to the development of a civil rights culture in the black community.

The black church has always been the only institution truly owned and run by blacks; the only one to serve as a significant gathering point, a structure around which a communal sense of self developed and individual identities took shape. In the southern states there were not many blacks who were not affected by it. Popular participation was indeed one of the hallmarks of the black church, which it bequeathed to the civil rights movement. It was the church's predominance together with the fact that the minister was a highly regarded person in the community that enabled the civil rights movement to be so effective in its mobilization of blacks and in the impact of its resistance on official racism.

But apart from the financial and human resources of the movement, there was also its theology or doctrine, which taught that freedom from slavery and racism was demanded by the gospel of Christ. Thus Christian teaching, especially that prophetic aspect of it concerned with justice, inspired the message and ideology of the modern civil rights movement. Christian prophetic teaching was in fact rooted in a long tradition of religious protest within the black church, a tradition that it had compromised at various times in its history but that it was now recovering with spectacular results. There can be little doubt that one of the contributions of the civil rights movement to modern thought was the development of black theology first formally articulated in the documents of the National Conference of Black Churchmen (NCBC) in the late 1960s and in the writings of James Cone. Black theology sees itself as a people's theology with a long history of religious protest inspired by the experience of the struggles against both slavery and racism.

See also AFRICAN-AMERICAN RELIGIONS; JACKSON, JESSE; KING, MARTIN LUTHER, JR.; LIBERATION THEOLOGY; SOUTHERN CHRISTIAN LEADERSHIP CONFERENCE.

BIBLIOGRAPHY

Hampton, Henry, and Steve Fayer, with Sarah Flynn. *Voices of Freedom: An Oral History of the Civil Rights Movement from the 1950s through the 1980s.* 1991.

Harding, Vincent, Robin D. G. Kelly, and Earl Lewis. *We Changed the World: African Americans, 1945–1970.* 1997.

Morris, Aldon. *The Origins of the Civil Rights Movement: Black Communities Organizing for Change.* 1984.

Weisbrot, Robert. *Freedom Bound: A History of America's Civil Rights Movement.* 1990.

Williams, Juan. *Eyes on the Prize: America's Civil Rights Years, 1954–1965.* 1988.

Edward P. Antonio

Clergy

In the Bible, the book of Acts, chapter 6, tells the story of the twelve disciples calling for a division of labor between those required to serve community needs and those responsible for preaching and teaching. They argued, "It is not right that we should neglect the word of God in order to wait on tables." As a consequence, the community chose seven leaders of good standing for special service, and they stood before the apostles, "who prayed and laid hands on them."

This biblical story is the beginning of a process in Christian history whereby the churches have "ordered" their ministries, creating two categories of believers: clergy and laity. From the very beginning, however, the argument has been that clergy are no better Christians than any other faithful Christian believer. God calls the whole people (the laos) into ministry, yet the people (led by the Spirit) have found it helpful to designate certain people for various forms of service to and for the church. The apostle Paul wrote about the church as the "body of Christ" filled with members pursuing a variety of callings. "The gifts [God] gave were that some would be apostles, some prophets, some evangelists, some pastors and teachers, to equip the saints for the work of ministry, for building up the body of Christ. . . ." (Ephesians 4:11–13). This diversity of roles, Christians came to believe, was not only efficient but also part of God's plan.

Yet designating some persons to be special religious leaders (clergy) is not exclusive to Christianity. In pre-Christian history the ancient Greeks held to a concept of service wherein a few leaders were recognized and charged to support and enable others. In Asia the Chinese philosopher Confucius taught that for the good of society certain leaders were needed to provide civil service—a high calling. In ancient Israel the priests, the prophets, and even the Pharisees were all valued as people whom God called to serve the wider community.

In the history of Western civilization Christian and Jewish communities have formalized religious leadership through a ritual ceremony known as "ordination," whereby clergy are formally authorized to preach and teach. Christians have further defined the clergy as persons linked directly to the life and ministry of Jesus through "apostolic succession." Apostolic succession connotes the idea that the clergy are "set apart" through prayer and the laying on of hands of Christian leaders who have themselves been ordained in a similar manner. The authority of Jesus Christ is channeled to each new generation of clergy through a succession of ordained leaders, or through the continuity of the Christian community as a whole. Once ordained, the clergy carry an "indelible mark" of sacramental privilege and identity. And even when the clergy cease to function in priestly roles, they are forever ordained—vested for life with a divine authority to serve the needs of the church and to spread the gospel message.

Threefold Ordering of Clergy

Christian practice has defined three orders of clergy: deacons, elders, and bishops. Building on the practices of Hellenistic Judaism, the early church designated certain leaders as elders, or *presbyteroi*. Such persons were charged with religious leadership on behalf of the whole Christian community, exercising ministries of word and sacrament in local congregations and shaping the teaching and outreach of the early church. This basic clerical office (priest or minister) was entrusted primarily with ministries of word and sacrament.

In the history of the church, however, two other orders of clergy developed. On the one hand there were the bishops, or *episkopoi*—priests with wider church responsibilities over especially large Christian communities, or over several congregations. The role of the bishop was patterned after the head of the Roman household and served to protect individual Christian groups from heretical ideas and practices. In time bishops came to exercise political power as well as provide theological guidance. And in Western Europe the bishop of Rome, the pope, became chief ecclesiastical and political overseer over all clergy and laity. The early church specified certain qualifications for bishops and maintained its right and responsibility to make judgments about the suitability of those chosen to oversee the Christian ecclesiastical household, as set forth in the biblical letters of Timothy and Titus.

Finally, as ministries of word and sacrament and ministries of oversight were defined and limited to priests and bishops, a third order of clergy took form. Although this third order was less formal, certain persons, called deacons or *diakonai*, were consecrated as servants to work within and for the churches and embody the caring mandate of the gospel. Deacons supported the work of the other clergy—elders and bishops. Deacons emphasized the servant calling of the whole Christian community and embodied the servant ministry of the servant community.

At one level the Christian church rejected all hierarchical value judgments made about its members and leaders. Christianity turned the world's standards upside down, stating that the first shall be last. Such radical theology argued against the need for having any clergy at all. In practice, however, the threefold ordering of clergy leadership became deeply embedded in Christian history. Bishops, priests, and deacons came to control incredible and sometimes destructive spiritual and material power. The Protestant Reformation in Western Europe tried to correct some of the problems in the sixteenth century by going back to first-century practices. Reformers rejected bishops and made deacons into a "lay" order. They defined the clergy almost exclusively in terms of word and sacrament.

Protestantism dramatically changed the relationship between clergy and laity. Although most Protestant churches continued to have clergy, Protestant theology emphasized the "priesthood of all believers." Clergy were not considered any better than laity but were simply viewed as persons blessed with needed talents and empowered to function religiously with, and on behalf of, the whole community. Protestants considered ordination a special or "holy" calling, but its holiness was connected with the actions of the whole people of God (the priesthood of all believers), rather than with the life of a particular individual. Apostolic succession, for many Protestants, was the collective legacy of the Christian community keeping faith through the ages, rather than a sequence of ceremonies (or hands) linking one ordained person to the next one.

Although Roman Catholicism continued to affirm the important role of the clergy, especially as sacramental leaders, in the Second Vatican Council in the 1960s, Catholics reaffirmed the importance of the ministry of the whole people of God. Progressive reforms were instituted to honor the diversity of ministries within the Christian community.

In North America all religious life and all practice were shaped by the democratic ideology of the United States. Critical of all privilege and status, some Christians rejected the importance of formal education for clergy and became followers of revivalists and preachers filled with the Holy Spirit. On the American frontier and in rapidly industrializing cities, the clergy reached out to serve the needs of society through social action ministries. In the United States the clergy became change agents committed to correcting injustices—taking leadership in movements for peace, for the abolition of slavery, for labor, for civil rights, and for the correction of numerous social problems. Although the clergy lost their stature in public life as an elite class of civic leaders, they became more directly involved in the lives of people.

The twentieth century has seen a renewed appreciation for the threefold ordering of ministry. Not only have Christians developed constructive ecumenical conversations about bishops, priests, and deacons, but also clergy in the United States have moved beyond traditional parish responsibilities to become preachers on the revival circuit, chaplains in hospitals and on campuses, missionaries to cities or distant lands, or leaders of developing ministries in totally new settings of need. Regardless of the arena of service, however, all clergy have been chosen by a religious community and authorized to provide religious support and guidance for the faithful.

Qualifications for Clergy

The question of qualifications for the clergy has been debated throughout Christian and Jewish history from the first century to the present. Do they need to be circumcised or uncircumcised? Youthful or mature? Well educated or especially pious? Charismatic preachers or skilled healers? Born-again believers or learned scholars? Married or celibate? Divorced or married only once? Polygamous or monogamous? Male or female? Heterosexual, homosexual, or bisexual? Persons with disabilities, or persons who have no obvious physical or mental limitations? In some settings there are additional questions generated by the cultural context within which the church exists. In the United States, the clergy are found to be all of these types of people, depending on the denomination. Although some of these qualifications are considered irrelevant in modern times, others continue to generate heated debate and painful choices. Controversies about who can be clergy often touch the most precious and sacred values of local congregations and wider church traditions.

Generally speaking, most religious communities look to the various practices and prohibitions outlined in the Bible to decide who is qualified to be clergy. Some (e.g., the Quakers) reject the idea of any clergy. Others believe that only men can be clergy. Still others insist that clergy should be celibate. Most traditions require some special education and training for clergy. Overall, people tend to believe that clergy are essential to the well-being of the religious community. They understand clergy to be "called" by God, as well as by the church or synagogue or mosque or temple, and they hold clergy to "holy" or "priestly" responsibilities—preaching and officiating at the sacramental rites of the traditions (ministries of word and sacrament). Within Judaism, Christianity, Islam, Buddhism, and so on rabbis, priests/ministers, imams, and monks teach and lead prayers for the whole community, keeping alive the traditions they represent. In all cases the clergy exercise a sacred trust for the well-being of all adherents of a particular religious tradition.

See also CHURCH; CLOTHING, RELIGIOUS; JUDAISM; JUDEO-CHRISTIAN TRADITION; LITURGY AND WORSHIP; MAINLINE PROTESTANTISM; MINISTRY; ORDINATION; ORDINATION OF WOMEN; PARISH; PRACTICE; PRAYER; PREACHING; PRIESTESS; PRIESTHOOD; RELIGIOUS COMMUNITIES; RITUAL; ROMAN CATHOLICISM; SACRAMENTS; SEMINARIES.

BIBLIOGRAPHY

Schillebeeckx, Edward. *The Church with a Human Face: A New and Expanded Theology of Ministry.* 1985.
World Council of Churches. *Baptism, Eucharist and Ministry.* 1982.

Barbara Brown Zikmund

Clothing, Religious

Distinctive clothing, a common and easily recognized feature of most religious practice, has five functions:

1. Clothing may serve to differentiate a religious group from the dominant culture in which it is found. The clothing worn by certain Amish communities or by Hasidic Jews serves this function. Often the clothing chosen by the group is

An orthodox Jewish rabbi wearing a tallith (prayer shawl) prays at a service in Philadelphia, Pennsylvania. (Credit: CORBIS/David H. Wells.)

self-consciously archaic or old-fashioned to distinguish it from current secular fashion.

2. Certain items of clothing identify individuals as members of a particular religious community. A distinctive head covering, such as the yarmulke worn by observant Jews as they go about in the world outside their own religious community, is an example.

3. Within a religious community, clothing often distinguishes those members who lead the community from those who are ordinary members. These articles of clothing function like the uniform of a secular official, such as the black robe of a judge. The use of clerical dress (such as the clerical, or Roman, collar) by Christian clergy apart from the assembly for worship exemplifies this use. The distinctive habit worn by members

of religious orders of nuns and monks or friars is another example.

4. Some items of religious clothing are associated specifically with devotional practice rather than office or position in the religious community. The prayer shawl (tallith) used by some Jews is an example of this use.

5. Items of clothing that are associated specifically with the assembly gathered for worship and that identify its leaders are generally called vestments. Identifying officially designated leaders is emphasized and the particular identity of the individuals is minimized.

Secular Origins

Using clothing as a way of distinguishing one group from another and individuals within a particular group is not limited to religions. Throughout history the color purple has been used to distinguish aristocratic or royal individuals from common persons. The distinctive clothing associated with particular occupations is another way of communicating the authority of the wearer, such as the uniform of a police officer.

Within the Jewish and Christian traditions distinctive clothing came to be associated with the exercise of leadership in assemblies that gathered for the worship of God. These traditions can be traced to Exodus, chapters 25 and 28. Particular dress was prescribed for particular classes of persons as they exercised their functions associated with worship (examples: Levites and priests and high priests). In the case of Judaism, this use was closely associated with the tabernacle and the succession of temples in Jerusalem.

Contemporary Jewish Use

American Jewish practice today reflects little of the vestments described for use in tabernacle and temple. The clothing associated with teaching and the handing on of the tradition now shapes Jewish usage. The gown of the scholar distinguishes the rabbi from the congregation of the faithful, not the ephod and breastplate of Exodus. This dress marks the rabbi's role as teacher. Some items of religious clothing that are not designated only for rabbis include the yarmulke (skullcap) and the tallith (prayer shawl).

Contemporary Christian Use

Contemporary Christian vestment draws from two distinguishable sources: first from ancient Roman secular garb and later from the clothing of the academy—especially the medibeval university. The church's use of vestments to distinguish the ministers of the Eucharist is traceable to the Romans. The bishop or priest presiding at the Eucharist was distinguished from the peo-

ple of the assembly by the conservative or even anachronistic use of a long white Roman tunic, the alb (from the Latin, *alba*). (The alb is an ankle-length long-sleeved white garment worn with the amice, a rectangle of fabric matching the alb, around the neck; the amice is secured with cloth tapes crossed over the chest and tied at the waist—but it is now seldom used. Other items of ceremonial attire include the cincture, a band of fabric or cord that secured the alb at the waist; a stole, a long narrow band of fabric worn over the alb or surplice; the maniple, a narrow band of fabric worn over the left forearm (its use was abandoned by the Roman church after the Second Vatican Council); and a chasuble, a sleeveless poncholike garment worn over the alb and stole by the minister presiding at the Eucharist. These garments designated the person wearing them as the leader of the assembly. They also functioned to identify the wearer as having authority to lead the community in this matter.

The vestments of the Orthodox Christian churches and Eastern Rite Catholic churches vary from those of the Roman Catholic church because of their differing point of origin—the Byzantine court dress influenced the Eastern church—and because subsequent patterns of development were careful to distinguish between East and West.

The second major source from which Christian vesture developed was the late medieval universities in the West. The mark of authority in this context was the robe worn by the professor, which marked the formal convocation of scholars and teachers. By the sixteenth century many Christian reformers made a decision to break with the Roman church's pattern of Eucharistic, or mass, vestments in favor of the professor's robe and the hood worn over it to indicate the degree held by the wearer. This was consistent with their emphasis on preaching and teaching.

Contemporary American Christian practice draws upon both of these traditions. The Roman Catholic practice today continues to honor the ancient tradition of Eucharistic vesture for the priest presiding at the mass and related vestments for those assisting. This practice is also common among Episcopal churches and in Lutheran churches. A recent trend is for presiding ministers to wear only the alb and stole in some settings (omitting the chasuble). For assemblies of worship that do not center on the Eucharist, these churches use the cassock and surplice, sometimes with added stole for ordained persons. This pattern of dress (without the stole) is used by choirs and lay servers as well as by the clergy in some congregations. Protestant churches drawing on the reformed tradition tend to prefer the academic gown of the doctor either with the academic hood (which now indicates the degree earned and the school granting the

Two elderly nuns (who happen to be twin sisters) stand under a tree in a grassy field, wearing their black-and-white habits. (Credit: © Mark Lyon/ Nonstock/PNI.)

degree) or with a stole indicating authorized religious leadership. The use of the alb and stole is also gaining among American Protestants.

Clothing and Office

Distinctive vesture also pertains to some forms or offices of ministry within the Roman, Episcopal, and Lutheran communities. A stole worn over the left shoulder and fixed at the right waist is a mark of ordained deacons. The dalmatic can also be a sign of diaconal office. The alb worn without other additions distinguishes baptized lay assistants and servers. Bishops also have clothing indicative of their office. A pectoral cross, a bishop's ring, a shepherd's staff (crozier), and a miter are used in Roman and Episcopal churches in America. Episcopal bishops also use the cassock, rochet, and chimere as clothing that distinguishes them in the exercise of their office in settings other than the Eucharist. The cope (a form of cape),

though not strictly limited even to ordained persons, is often associated with bishops in these churches. In America Lutheran bishops are identified primarily by the pectoral cross, though the use of the crozier is growing more common.

Eastern Orthodox and Eastern Rite Catholic vestments reflect the same basic patterns as those used by Catholics in the West, though the actual look of the vestments is quite distinct from the Roman. The head covering worn by bishops and priests apart from the liturgy (kamilaukion—worn by monks with a veil called the klobuk) is one distinctive feature.

Some American Protestant churches have abandoned the use of both these traditional forms of vestments in favor of clothing that mirrors secular use. Examples of this can be seen in individual congregations of many Protestant denominations. Such garments are also commonplace in distinctively American religions such as the various free church traditions and the Church of Jesus Christ of Latter-day Saints.

As a multicultural recovery and renaissance take place in American Christian churches, black robes trimmed with African cloth and other distinctive cultural features of Christian churches from around the globe can be expected to enrich American religious tradition.

See also Kippah; Ministry; Priesthood; Rabbinate; Religious Communities.

Bibliography

Philippart, David, ed. *Clothed in Glory.* 1997.

Paul R. Nelson

Colson, Charles W.

(1931–), presidential aide and religious activist.

Charles Colson was an aide to President Richard M. Nixon, is the founder and chairman of Prison Fellowship Ministries (PFM), and is an influential celebrity among evangelical Christians. Colson received an undergraduate degree from Brown University in 1953, served in the Marines from 1953 to 1956, and earned a law degree from George Washington University in 1959. In 1956 Colson officially began his career in politics as chief assistant to Massachusetts senator Leverett Saltonstall. In 1961, shortly after Saltonstall's reelection, Colson established a law firm in Washington, D.C., yet remained active in politics. From 1969 to 1973 he served as special counsel to President Nixon, and he was implicated in the Watergate scandal. Col-

Charles Colson, holding a Bible in his hands during a visit to the Powhatan Correctional Center in central Virginia. (Credit: © David Burnett/Contact Press Images/PNI.)

son pleaded guilty to obstruction of justice in 1974 and served seven months in federal prison. He became a born-again Christian in August 1973, and in 1976 he founded PFM.

PFM is an interdenominational organization that conducts Christian evangelism and Bible studies and provides practical assistance to prisoners, former prisoners, and their families. The organization also works to reform the penal system and to protect the rights of crime victims. Since its inception in 1976, PFM has grown tremendously, and in 1999 it had 350 employees and more than 50,000 volunteers working in all of the state and federal prisons in the United States. It also has prison ministries in more than 80 countries worldwide. PFM is essentially an umbrella organization for a number of other organizations and ministries. For example, PFM distributes *Inside Journal,* a bimonthly Christian newspaper for prisoners, to every state and federal correctional facility in the United States. Formed in 1983, Justice Fellowship is another affiliated ministry that promotes biblical standards of justice through legislative lobbying and public education. Other ministries include Prison Fellowship International, Angel Tree, Neighbors Who Care, and Mail Call.

In the evangelical Christian world, Colson is a celebrated speaker, author of numerous books and tapes, and columnist for the popular magazine *Christianity Today.* Many of his books, such as *Born Again* (1976)

and *Loving God* (1983), have become inspirational best-sellers. His evangelical radio broadcast, *Break-Point,* can be heard on 425 radio stations and reaches an audience of 5 million. His popularity in the evangelical community stems not only from his status as a former presidential aide and his work with PFM but also from his contribution as a specialist in the area of religion and politics. One of Colson's best-selling books, *Kingdoms in Conflict* (1987), examines the tense relationship between the Christian faith and politics. Further, he is often asked to offer a Christian perspective on a variety of social and political problems.

Colson's most recent honors include serving as a distinguished senior fellow of the Christian Coalition of Colleges and Universities. Also, in 1993 he won the prestigious $1 million John M. Templeton Prize for Progress in Religion, honoring his work with PFM. (Previous winners include Mother Teresa and Billy Graham.) Proceeds from his speaking fees, book sales, and the Templeton Prize benefit PFM.

See also BORN AGAIN CHRISTIANS; EVANGELICAL CHRISTIANITY; JOURNALISM, RELIGIOUS; PRISON AND RELIGION; PUBLISHING, RELIGIOUS; TELEVANGELISM.

BIBLIOGRAPHY

Colson, Charles W. *Born Again.* 1976.
Colson, Charles W. *Life Sentence.* 1979.

Jonathan F. Cordero

Communes

The explosion of communes in the 1960s seemed to many a fresh and unique flowering of the countercultural revolution that spread over America during that decade, but to more astute observers it was part of an older and continuing American tradition. That tradition had its roots in the Puritan and utopian notion of establishing a "city on a hill" where the covenanted saints might live in peace and harmony, in a socialist tradition that emphasized the need for "cooperative commonwealths" that could cultivate land for the common good rather than capitalist gain, and in a "seeker" tradition that emphasized the values of inner peace and tranquillity within the sheltered walls of a community.

Veterans who returned from World War II seeking a contemplative alternative to war and materialism found it within the walls of Trappist and Cistercian monasteries, and by rejecting the *vita activa* for the *vita contemplativa*, these veterans foreshadowed the 1960s' rejection of materialism and its embrace of communal values, both secular and religious.

The sharpest departure from prior patterns was the emergence of a significant number of Eastern-oriented communes that represented a rejection of Western religious alternatives and an embrace of mystical or transcendental teachings. The Ananda Cooperative Village, founded in 1967 in Nevada City, California, is emblematic of this tendency. The community was founded by Swami Kriyananda and followed the outlines established by an earlier swami, Paramahansa Yogananda, author of *Autobiography of a Yogi*, who asserted that "self-realization" colonies would form the basis for a better, more humane world. From 1948 onward Kriyananda was a disciple of Yogananda and lived in ashrams in India and the United States. In 1962 Kriyananda was dismissed as vice president of the Self-Realization Fellowship for urging reforms, and in 1967 he bought a twenty-four-acre site in Nevada City that attracted the attention of the poets Gary Snyder and Allen Ginsberg. Between 1968 and 1970 Kriyananda purchased additional parcels of land and established a meditation retreat. Members were required to pay an initial membership fee, and businesses were established on the site (an incense factory and a print shop). The seventy-two-acre retreat welcomed visitors, but had at its core believers who were expected to lead celibate lives, to cultivate their spiritual awareness by meditation and Yoga, and to follow the precepts of an ascetic life laid down by Swami Kriyananda. Numerous other "retreat" communes were established, such as the Lama Foundation near Taos, New Mexico, and the elaborate West Virginia home of the Society for Krishna Consciousness, better known as the "Hare Krishnas."

Several groups started as churches, then moved into intense communal phases. The Church Universal and Triumphant drew on the "I Am" movement, theosophy, and the esoteric tradition of past masters to emerge as a New Age religion under the guidance of Elizabeth Prophet, who engineered a series of moves that brought the group in 1981 to Montana, where they established a retreat on a twenty-four-thousand-acre site. The Children of God began as part of the Jesus Movement of the 1960s and blossomed under the leadership of David "Mo" Berg, who introduced free love as an element in the evangelical Christian mix and established communes across the world. In 1977 they became known as the Children of God. Often in trouble with the law because of their practices, the group abandoned free love in 1994 after Berg's death, began to emphasize a social agenda, and returned to a more traditional evangelical lifestyle.

One form of commune that emerged in the 1960s combined the charismatic, the apocalyptic, and the political. A notorious example was the Peoples' Temple, which grew out of a Christian Assembly of God Church in Indianapolis in 1957. Its leader was James Jones, an ordained Disciples of Christ minister, who announced to his congregation in 1966 that a nuclear holocaust would take place in 1967 and that the People's Temple should relocate to northern California. In 1970 Jones purchased churches in San Francisco and Los Angeles and his ministry became increasingly social and militant. He gained a following among inner-city blacks and radical whites and had an estimated five thousand followers in several locations. In 1977 nine hundred members of the church moved to Guyana to establish an interracial colony, Jonestown, on twenty-seven thousand acres leased from the Guyanese government. The members lived in primitive dwellings and tried to eke out a living as Jones became increasingly paranoid and sadistic. An investigation by an American congressman, Leo Ryan, triggered not only Ryan's murder but also the mass suicide of more than nine hundred members, including Jones. The colony was an outgrowth of Jones's messianic pretensions and a radical social agenda that sought to overthrow "racism, sexism, and ageism" and that mirrored certain assumptions prevalent in the 1960s about a radical transformation of society. Jonestown was a highly regimented "top-down" commune that was in sharp contrast to several anarchist colonies and decentralized groups, such as Sunrise Hill (1966) in Massachusetts, modeled along the lines suggested by decentralist critic Ralph Borsodi, though certain features, such as free love and group meditation, would hardly have met with Borsodi's approval. Drop City was an artists' commune founded in 1965 in Trinidad, Colorado, by Kansas and Colorado artists who saw themselves as harbingers of a new artistic age based on psychedelic drugs, Eastern mysticism, and avant-garde art. They traveled around the country promoting light shows and "Droppings" (their name for a "total environment media mix"), and in 1967 sponsored the "Drop City Joy Festival," which brought thousands of hippies onto their six-acre site. In 1973 the property was sold and the residents were evicted from their geodesic domes.

Just as Jonestown was an extreme example of a mixture of radical politics and religion, an offshoot of Seventh-Day Adventists, the Branch Davidians, represented the tendency of Protestant bodies to splinter and for communelike organizations to grow under the leadership of young, inspired leaders. Led by David Koresh and located at Waco, Texas, the Branch Davidians were one wing of a splinter group that emerged in the 1950s and for the next thirty years engaged in ideological sniping with the mainstream Adventists and other millennialist groups. In 1981 a young Adventist, Vernon Howell, emerged as a leader of the Branch Davidians and wrested control from Ben Roden. In 1987, after an armed confrontation with Roden's followers, Howell took control of the Davidian headquarters at Waco and began his reign as the leader under the name David Koresh, the Persian name for Cyrus the king. Koresh began an aggressive campaign to evangelize among Adventists, emphasized an "end of time" theology, and shifted the sect toward a more communal lifestyle that emphasized Koresh's prophetic leadership, the establishment of a core of dedicated followers, and the creation of "a new lineage of God's children from his own seed," according to two scholars. Bible study sessions led by Koresh strengthened his authority to interpret Adventists texts. As the result of a dispute with a local child protection agency the Branch Davidians barricaded themselves in their compound and engaged in combat with the U.S. Bureau of Alcohol, Tobacco, and Firearms (BATF). During the initial confrontation four BATF agents and six Branch Davidians were killed, and a protracted standoff between federal authorities and the Branch Davidians ensued. In April 1993, agents stormed the compound, there was a resulting fire, and seventy-four Branch Davidians died. Federal agents believed that the fire had been started by Koresh, but Davidian supporters argued that the cause lay with the federal officers. The deaths of David Koresh, James Jones, and their followers highlighted the volatile nature of religious and charismatic communes in this period and tended to overshadow the development of settled groups, such as the Christian group Reba Place in Evanston, Illinois; the interracial Koinona Farm in Georgia; and the Shiloh House in Oregon, dedicated to an evangelical community and the continuation of the monastic tradition of Trappist orders.

See also ANTI-CULT MOVEMENT; BELONGING, RELIGIOUS; BRANCH DAVIDIANS; CELIBACY; CHURCH UNIVERSAL AND TRIUMPHANT; CULT; CULT AWARENESS NETWORK; JESUS MOVEMENT; JONES, JIM; KORESH, DAVID; MEDITATION; NEW AGE SPIRITUALITY; NEW RELIGIOUS MOVEMENTS; PEOPLE'S TEMPLE; RELIGIOUS COMMUNITIES; YOGA.

BIBLIOGRAPHY

Bloesch, Donald. *Wellsprings of Renewal.* 1974.

Gardner, Hugh. *The Children of Prosperity.* 1978.

Glock, Charles, and Robert Bellah, eds. *The New Religious Conciousness.* 1976.

Rochford, E. Burke. *Hare Krishna in America.* 1985.

Veysey, Laurence. *The Communal Experience.* 1973.

Wagner, Jon. *Sex Roles in Contemporary American Communes.* 1982.

Wilson, Bryan. *The Social Dimensions of Sectarianism.* 1990.

Wright, Stuart. *Armageddon at Waco.* 1995.

Robert Fogarty

Communion

Communion, also known as Holy Communion, the Eucharist, Mass, or the Lord's Supper, is the liturgical act celebrated by Christians commemorating the death of Christ. Through the elements of bread and wine (or grape juice), Christians reenact Jesus' last meal with his disciples, recall his sacrificial death, anticipate their reunion with him in heaven, and reaffirm their unity with other believers. Communion is the central act of worship in nearly every Christian church. Only baptism is practiced as universally.

For all its centrality and emphasis on unity, however, communion has often been a source of division among Christians. In the United States, with almost two thousand different Christian denominations, Eucharistic practice and theology vary according to tradition. The major division in American Christianity is between those who understand the elements to convey God's grace and those who do not.

Sacramental traditions, such as those of Roman Catholics, Eastern Orthodox, Episcopalians, and Lutherans, teach that communion carries grace necessary for salvation and Christian living. Because the bread and wine are in some way revered, priests, ministers, or specially trained laypersons must be ordained or licensed to serve communion in these churches.

Roman Catholicism teaches transubstantiation, the belief that the bread and wine are changed into the actual body and blood of Christ through the act of consecration in the Mass. Mass is celebrated every Sunday and on major holy days (and is available daily in some parishes). Minimally, a Catholic must receive communion once a year to remain in good standing. Only baptized Catholics admitted to Mass may receive communion in Roman Catholic churches.

Roman Catholic and Eastern Orthodox Christians insist that communion is one of seven sacraments. The Orthodox refer to sacraments as "mysteries" and avoid the difficulties of philosophical ideas such as transubstantiation. Instead, Orthodox churches simply teach that the bread and wine become Christ's body and blood and that participation in the mystery is central to Christian holiness. All baptized members receive, and non-Orthodox Christians are welcomed into Eucharistic fellowship by partaking of nonconsecrated bread instead of the consecrated host.

Episcopalianism and Lutheranism, both Protestant sacramental traditions, generally reject transubstantiation. Instead, like the Orthodox, they affirm "real presence" in the Eucharist: Christ is actually present in some mysterious fashion that resists final definition. Lutherans (but not Episcopalians) refer to this as consubstantiation—Christ is present "with, in, and under" the elements. Episcopalians celebrate weekly communion and admit all baptized persons (including infants) into fellowship. Most Lutherans prefer monthly celebration and do not admit infants to communion.

Eucharistic sacramentalism, however, has not been the dominant tradition in American Christianity. In the United States, communion historically has been defined according to prevailing low church practices borrowed or modified from reformed theology.

Reformed thought is split on the issue of communion. Some in the reformed tradition (usually Presbyterians, Congregationalists, and reformed churches) follow the teachings of John Calvin (1509–1564) on communion. Calvin rejected the above views in favor of a doctrine of spiritual presence. He believed that Christ's body remained in heaven during communion while his spirit was manifested in the meal to those who received in faith. Although this is not sacramental in the strictest sense, Calvinism treats communion with the utmost seriousness and believes that the act shapes Christian piety. Because of the serious nature of communion, Calvinism insists that communion should be served by ordained ministers or trained laity. In the Calvinist tradition, communion often precedes personal or communal spiritual renewal.

A Hispanic Roman Catholic priest blesses the Host before commencing a communion ceremony during a mass in 1998. (Credit: © José Carillo/PhotoEdit/ PNI.)

The most influential reformed thinker on American communion practice, however, was the Swiss theologian Ulrich Zwingli (1484–1531), who argued for memorialism and held that Christ was in no way present in the bread and wine. Instead, the meal commemorated Christ's death and served to remind the faithful of God's love for them. According to Zwingli, the elements were only symbolic and the meal was a form of fellowship. His reforms democratized the Mass, shifting the emphasis away from priestly liturgical practitioners toward communion with other faithful believers. As American Christianity developed, Zwingli's views matched the ethos of democratic denominations such as Methodists, Baptists, Disciples of Christ, and Churches of Christ. Memorialism, with its attendant emphasis on the laity, came to define American communion practice and often put the more sacramental traditions on the theological defensive. Sacramentalism was often attacked as "medieval," "superstitious," "papist," or "foreign," all nineteenth-century code words for undemocratic and anti-American ideas. In some denominations, such as the Episcopal Church, arguments over communion became entangled in political and social conflict over issues of nativism, prohibition, women's rights, and slavery.

Although style (such as the Victorian preference for sacerdotal architecture) sometimes dictated its practice, communion in the United States has steadily become more lay-oriented, even in the most sacramental churches. Throughout the twentieth century, the liturgical renewal movement transformed American churchgoing. Begun by European Catholics, contemporary liturgical reform emphasized lay participation in Christian worship. For Catholics this renewal culminated with the Second Vatican Council and its "Constitution on the Sacred Liturgy" (1963), which legislated the vernacular in worship and the reform of the Mass. These changes had a profound impact on American Catholicism, as they encouraged the implicit cultural ideal of lay authority to (once again) challenge the church's hierarchy. Thus the new Mass served as a rallying point for women seeking ordination and those questioning Catholic teachings on divorce and remarriage. At the same time, movements to reinstate the Latin Mass are linked to Catholic traditionalism regarding women and sexuality.

Protestant liturgical reform renewed the priesthood of all believers, reconsidered Zwinglian memorialism, and has produced some historical ironies. Sacramental Protestants, such as Episcopalians, have affirmed lay ministry, introduced liturgies and hymnals, renovated liturgical space, and attempted to mitigate clericalism. Nonsacramental churches, such as some Baptists and Methodists, have adopted weekly communion and written new liturgies. Since World War II, mainline Protestants have moved closer to each other in communion theology and practice in both formal and informal ways. The theology expressed in the ecumenical movement and documents such as *Baptism, Eucharist and Ministry* (1982) helped restore the sacramental nature of communion. Interdenominational experiments, such as ecumenical social service agencies and the charismatic movement, gave Protestants firsthand experience in sharing worship and communion. Even prominent evangelicals such as theologian Robert Webber at Wheaton College in Illinois have argued for weekly communion and liturgical renewal. In contemporary America, communion is both more lay-oriented in its practice and more sacramental in its theology than at any time in the nation's history.

See also Eastern Orthodoxy; Liturgy and Worship; Mainline Protestantism; Roman Catholicism.

BIBLIOGRAPHY

Baptism, Eucharist and Ministry. 1982.

Butler, Diana Hochstedt. *Standing Against the Whirlwind: Evangelical Episcopalians in Nineteenth-Century America.* 1995.

Jones, Cheslyn, Geoffrey Wainwright, and Edward Yarnold, S.J., eds. *The Study of Liturgy.* 1978.

Macy, Gary. *The Banquet's Wisdom: A Short History of the Theologies of the Lord's Supper.* 1992.

White, James F. "Liturgy and Worship." In *Encyclopedia of the American Religious Experience,* edited by Charles H. Lippy and Peter W. Williams. 1988.

Diana Hochstedt Butler Bass

Communities, Religious.

See Religious Communities.

Confucianism

There is as great a debate about the religious dimension of Confucianism as there is about when Confucians first arrived in America. Many modern Confucians accept Confucianism as a religion, and others simply state that Confucianism is a philosophy and not a religion. The reason for this debate is that both sides are correct. Confucianism combines what Western intellectuals categorize as both philosophic and religious interests. Confucianism is most certainly a way of life for those who follow the teachings of the ancient sages.

The great contemporary New Confucian, Mou Zongsan (1909–1995), declared that if we demand that Confucianism resemble either the Christian churches or post-Enlightenment Western philosophy as a prototype, then we will find neither religion or philosophy in the Confucian tradition. However, if we define philosophy and religion as the perennial human quest for the ultimate significance of life, then Confucianism is both profoundly philosophic and religious. Confucianism cultivates the self in order to obtain the Way as the manifestation of the Mandate of Heaven and to serve others by creating a just, peaceful, and harmonious society. Following Paul Tillich's famous definition of religion, Confucianism represents a form of ultimate concern that has endured historically in East Asia and now in North America for over two thousand five hundred years.

Confucianism is a modern Western term used to describe an ancient Chinese "way" or practice. The name is a Latin version of Kong Fuzi (551–479 B.C.E.), the founder of the tradition. Confucius would have thought the founding of a new religion or philosophy odd if not unfilial. He lived at a time in classical China when the old Zhou dynasty was in a perilous state of decline. He believed that what was needed was a restoration of classical culture through the proper teaching of the way of the ancient sages. In short, Confucius wanted to inculcate in the young scholars of his day the teachings of the former worthies so that they could restore the world to harmony. His teachings included both the study of texts, later known as the Confucian classics, and the cultivation of virtue. Although Confucius was frustrated in achieving his hope for the reformation of China, he was venerated as the Teacher of the Ten Thousand Generations.

It is also important to recognize that Confucianism is an international movement. It rapidly spread from China to Korea, Vietnam, and Japan. It has now crossed the Pacific and Atlantic oceans and is finding new homes in Europe and North America.

There have been three major eras in the development of the Confucian Way. The first is that of Confucius, followed by Mencius (371–289 B.C.E.) and Xunzi (fl. 298–210 B.C.E.). This is the classical period. The second great age came with the revival of the tradition in the Northern and Southern Song dynasties (960–1279 C.E.) and its later flowering in the Ming (1279–1644) and Qing (1644–1911). This is the Neo-Confucian era, so called in order to distinguish it from the classical period.

The third era overlaps with the second and begins with the arrival of the Western imperial powers in East Asia in the middle of the nineteenth century. It is a period of both great decline and rebirth. By 1911, when the last dynasty fell in China, Confucianism was no longer the basis for Chinese, Korean, Japanese, or Vietnamese culture. Some people thought that Confucianism would disappear as the people of East Asia modernized their countries through contact with the Western powers. However, by the 1920s, a small group of committed public intellectuals had begun the reformation of the Confucian Way; this group became known as the New Confucians.

Mou Zongsan, acknowledged as the premier philosopher among the New Confucians, accepted and defined the religious dimension of Confucianism as a profound way of life based on the insights recorded in the classical texts. It is a tradition of study and practice and therefore has always been associated with the scholarly elites of East Asia. As the modern New Confucian Du Weiming states, commitment to the Confucian Way means engaging in the lifelong task of becoming human by means of an inclusive humanism that accepts the religious or spiritual dimension of the Confucian Way.

Mou Zongsan stipulates that any religious tradition must accomplish at least two fundamental movements of the human spirit. First, it must establish a vertical link between a human being and the divine reality, defined as ceaseless creativity. Second, it cultivates forms of ethical virtues and action between and among people. It must develop habits of the heart sufficient to sustain civilized human life and culture. According to Mou, what makes Confucius the great founder of the classical Confucian tradition is that Confucius was able to accomplish these two tasks through his reflections on the virtue of *ren*, or humaneness. Only a person who could abide in *ren* was on the true path of virtue. All the other virtues of civilized human life flowed from the cultivation of true humaneness. If a person could actually embody humaneness, she or he would become what Du, in a more modern idiom, calls a profound person.

The entire Confucian project of becoming human revolves around the cultivation of five prime virtues. Furthermore, each virtue is then symbolically correlated to a specific primordial social relationship:

- *Ren:* humanity or humaneness—father and son.
- *Yi:* righteousness or justice—ruler and minister.
- *Li:* ritual or civility (distinctions)—husband and wife.
- *Zhi:* wisdom or discernment—older and younger brother.
- *Hsin:* faithfulness—friend and friend.

Modern New Confucians have recognized that these basic relationships must be recast into less hierarchical and patriarchal modes. For instance, the father-son relationship now becomes parent-child, justice becomes the relationship of government and citizens, husband and wife remain but without the subordination of the distinct roles of women to men, older and younger brothers become siblings, and friend to friend no longer depends on deference based on age but resides in mutual respect and deference.

How does one move towards an inclusive humanism? To begin, one must study in order to become a humane person. However, true Confucian study is more than merely academic excellence. Memory or even wit is not enough. As the later Neo-Confucians taught, you have to taste the real teachings of the sages so that they become part of your living person. True learning then becomes the most profound form of self-cultivation. As the most religious of the Confucian classics, *The Doctrine of the Mean*, teaches, a person who is able to cultivate the mind-heart can become a cocreator of the world along with Heaven and Earth.

Americans first became aware of Confucianism in the early nineteenth century through the writings of scholarly Christian missionaries. The first major contact began with Chinese immigration into California during the gold rush of 1849. However, there was soon a reaction against any continuing immigration from Asia as well as concerted attacks on anything Chinese. Although knowledge of Confucianism grew during the next century, the decisive turning point came with the new Immigration Act of 1965, which finally did away with the race-based restrictions on entry of East and South Asians into the United States.

The growth of Confucianism in North America can be divided into two parts. The first derives from the dramatic influx of East Asian immigrants after 1965. They imported their culture of strong family ties along with their modern education and skills. The second part arose from growing scholarly interest in Confucianism in East Asia and in North America. Many younger Chinese intellectuals are reprising the ancient tradition, winnowing it for material to contribute to the ecumenical new world order. The future of Confucianism depends on how the tradition is presented to the larger world beyond the academy by the New Confucians. While the future is not yet known, it is clear that Confucianism will have a future.

One of the most interesting questions is whether or not Confucianism will flourish outside of East Asia. Although Confucianism is an international tradition that includes Chinese, Koreans, Japanese, and Vietnamese, it has yet to be truly transferred beyond the world of East Asia. Some scholars wonder if you can really be a Confucian without having recourse to the classical Chinese canon. However, there is a broad recognition that the tradition is moving out of East Asia via the Asian diaspora into Europe and North America. There is now a great deal of interaction between scholars of Confucianism in the West and in Asia. Confucianism is beginning to play a major role in Western cultural circles for the first time since people of the Enlightenment became fascinated with all things Chinese.

In Hong Kong in 1957 a group of Chinese intellectuals published a manifesto defending Chinese culture and Confucianism as worthy of study by all interested scholars. The New Confucians argued that Confucianism was not dead and that it had a major contribution to make to the emerging new global world culture. It was also at this time that North Americans began the intense study of all aspects of the Confucian tradition.

Because Confucianism had always respected the role of the scholar, it is not surprising that the renewed interest in Confucianism in North America was patronized by academicians. There was been a renaissance of Confucian studies in America over the last fifty years. Along with a fresh look at Confucianism as a living philosophic and spiritual movement, the Asian economic miracle focused new attention on the social dimensions of Confucianism. Du Weiming has made the point that even if many modern Chinese, Koreans, Vietnamese, and Japanese do not know a great deal about the history of their Confucian culture, Confucianism functions as deep form of cultural DNA within modern Asian societies and their diasporas.

Confucianism now plays a diffuse role in North America. It has become an object of study not only by students of Chinese culture but also by professionals in government, business, technology, and medicine concerned with understanding classical China in order to better engage modern China. Many Chinese at home and overseas are also pondering the fate of the tradition. To repeat, no one knows what the future will bring, though there is a growing consensus that Confucianism will reform and renew itself as it has done over and over again for more two thousand five hundred years.

See also CHINESE-AMERICAN RELIGIONS; FENG SHUI; I CHING.

BIBLIOGRAPHY

Berthrong, John H. *All Under Heaven: Transforming Paradigms in Confucian-Christian Dialogue.* 1994.

Berthrong, John H. *Transformations of the Confucian Way.* 1998.

Chan, Wing-tsit. *A Source Book in Chinese Philosophy.* 1963.

Ching, Julia. *Chinese Religions.* 1993.

De Bary, William Theodore. *East Asian Civilizations: A Dialogue in Five Stages.* 1988.

Jensen, Lionel M. *Manufacturing Confucianism: Chinese Traditions and Universal Civilization.* 1997.

Reid, T. R. *Confucius Lives Next Door: What Living in the East Teaches Us About Living in the West.* 1999.

Schirokauer, Conrad. *A Brief History of Chinese Civilization.* 2nd ed. 1991.

Spence, Jonathan D. *The Chan's Great Continent: China in Western Minds.* 1998.

Taylor, Rodney L. *The Religious Dimensions of Confucianism.* 1990.

Tu, Wei-ming. *Centrality and Commonality: Essays on Confucian Religiousness.* 1989.

Tweed, Thomas A., and Stephen Prothero. 1999. *Asian Religions in America: A Documentary History.*

John Berthrong

Congregation

"Congregation" is the word widely used in the United States to designate a voluntary local religious gather-

The minister and congregation of a church in Sandwich, New Hampshire, celebrate a service in July 1979. (Credit: CORBIS/Farrell Grehan.)

ing that has a publicly recognized name and identity (such as "First Presbyterian Church") and a public space in which regular meetings are held (whether a rented storefront space or a magnificent temple or cathedral). While a growing number of "house churches" and other home-based religious gatherings are present in the United States, they are not usually included when the term "congregation" is used.

There are no reliable comprehensive lists of congregations, but the best estimates place the number of active groups in the United States at approximately three hundred thousand. Many New England congregations are among the oldest organizations of European Americans, dating back to the early seventeenth-century Puritans. Many other congregations are brand-new. Every year many congregations go out of existence and many new ones are begun.

The term "congregation" comes from Protestant traditions but is also used in Judaism; Roman Catholics are more likely to use the term "parish," reserving "congregation" for religious orders. Muslims gather in this country in mosques (masjids); many Hindus and Buddhists construct temples. But despite differing nomenclature, local religious gatherings in the United States are very likely to assume congregational form, a point made by R. Stephen Warner in his essay "The Place of the Congregation in the Contemporary American Religious Configuration."

The congregational form normally includes a regular membership and a regular schedule of meetings, as well as a recognized professional leader. In addition, congregations are composed of voluntary members. Even religious traditions that assign members geographically recognize that members in this country are likely to attend a congregation other than the one to which they are assigned.

The regular schedule of congregational meetings almost always includes a worship service, in most cases held at least weekly. Those services usually include prayers and some sort of sermon or inspirational talk. Most religious traditions also include sacred music or singing, often by the congregation itself. In some traditions, the songs, prayers, and other rituals are very formalized, sometimes being recited in the same form at each gathering. In other traditions, the members themselves select and create, more or less spontaneously, the various elements of their worship.

Congregations are also the primary teachers of most religious traditions in this country. Some establish full-fledged day schools to teach their children, while most simply create weekly religious classes (often called Sunday schools)—almost always for children, but often for adults as well.

The religious traditions with which congregations are associated are often called "denominations." About three-quarters of Christian congregations are officially linked to one of several hundred denominations in the United States. The remaining congregations are independent, having been founded by a particular local group. Those with denominational ties may identify with groups as large and diverse as the Baptists or with relatively small but historic bodies, such as Unitarians. Many denominations—such as Ukrainian Catholics or the African Methodist Episcopal Church—also embody an ethnic heritage.

Congregations, then, often represent gatherings of people who identify both with a religious tradition and with a particular language or ethnic group. Congregations may be, in fact, among the first organizations formed by new immigrant groups as they seek ways to survive and thrive in a new country. Because congregations, whether immigrant or native, are voluntary gatherings, their memberships are usually relatively homogeneous (although some take the building of a diverse membership as a primary goal). They may draw most of their members from a single neighborhood or town, but they may also be magnets, drawing people from a wide region who are especially interested in certain forms of worship or ministry. Both the religious values and rituals of the congregation and the particular people who gather there constitute a significant point of identification and social support for many in the United States.

In addition to their significance as places where a sense of community and identity is created, congregations are also important contributors to the delivery of social services. They provide emergency food, clothing, and shelter; programs of education and recreation; and spaces for community meetings and cultural events, as well as pools of volunteers and activists to fight discrimination or violence or behavior deemed immoral. Not all congregations take such public activity as their mission, and many do their work primarily through cooperative arrangements with coalitions of other congregations and/or community agencies. Nevertheless, congregations are among the country's most important organizational vehicles for volunteering and charitable contributions.

Located in every community, representing virtually every conceivable social grouping, and expressing a vast diversity of religious tradition and ritual, congregations are the primary organizational form for religion in the United States.

See also ATTENDANCE; BELONGING, RELIGIOUS; CHURCH; MUSIC; PRACTICE; PRAYER; RELIGIOUS COMMUNITIES; SOCIOLOGY OF RELIGION; SYNAGOGUE; TEMPLE.

BIBLIOGRAPHY

Ammerman, Nancy Tatom. *Congregation and Community.* 1997.

Warner, R. Stephen. "The Place of the Congregation in the Contemporary American Religious Configuration." In *American Congregations: New Perspectives in the Study of Congregations,* edited by James Wind and James Lewis. 1994.

Warner, R. Stephen, and Judith G. Wittner, eds. *Gatherings in Diaspora: Religious Communities and the New Immigration.* 1998.

Wind, James P., and James W. Lewis, eds. *American Congregations,* 2 vols. 1994.

Wuthnow, Robert. *Producing the Sacred.* 1994.

Nancy T. Ammerman

Conscientious Objection

All religions must decide how "worldly" they will be, including the stance they will take toward the state. Within this larger issue is the issue of the religion's participation in war when the state undertakes military action. The Roman Catholic Church, for example, has long entertained the notion of "just" versus "unjust" war, the implication being that faithful Catholics should not fight in "unjust" wars. In Protestantism, objection to war became a central tenet of that branch most suspicious of worldly, secular authority, which gave rise to such denominations as the Amish, the Mennonites, the Brethren, and the Quakers.

In America, the Continental Congress in 1775, noting the presence in the colonies of conscientious objectors to war, passed a resolution that read: "As there are some people who, from religious principles, cannot bear arms in any case, this Congress intends no violence to their consciences, but earnestly recommends it to them, to contribute liberally in this time of universal calamity, to the relief of their distressed brethren in the several colonies.... (*Journals of the Continental Congress, 1774–1789,* vol. 2, p. 169).

The U.S. Constitution makes no reference to conscientious objection, its authors having decided to leave the matter to the individual states. Because there was no military draft in either the War of 1812 or the Mexican War, the fate of conscientious objectors depended on local opinion and whatever laws had been passed by state legislatures. In the Civil War, however, compulsory military service existed in both North and South, which made conscientious objections an unavoidable legal issue. Both sides adopted a policy recognizing that any person belonging to a recognized "peace" church had the choice of paying another person to substitute for him or else accept noncombatant duties.

World War I saw a similar resolution. Ordained ministers were exempt from the draft, and members of recognized "peace" churches were exempt from "combatant duty." This policy was challenged on the ground that it unconstitutionally "established" religion by failing to exempt persons of like belief who were not members of a recognized pacifist church. The U.S. Supreme Court rejected that argument, however.

Several legal battles took place after World War I, most involving pacifists applying for citizenship in the United States. However, with the knowledge that another world war was looming, Congress expanded its definition of eligibility for exemption from the draft. In 1940 the legislation that brought the Selective Service into existence exempted from combatant service any person "who, by reason of religious training and belief, is conscientiously opposed to participation in war in any form." During World War II, draft boards had difficulty interpreting those words when claims were made in the name not of "religious training" but of ethical, philosophical, or political belief.

In 1948, therefore, Congress amended the law by declaring that "religious training and belief" means "an individual's belief in a relation to a Supreme Being involving duties superior to those arising from any human relation, but [excluding] essentially political, sociological, or philosophical views or a merely personal moral code."

In 1965, in a case known as *United States* v. *Seeger* (380 U.S. 163), but in reality a combination of three similar cases, this 1948 language was challenged. All three defendants claimed to have no traditional concept of God or necessarily of a Supreme Being. Seeger, for example, stated his "belief in and devotion to goodness and virtue for their own sake, and a religious faith in a purely ethical creed." In a unanimous decision, the Court responded affirmatively, saying that the question is "whether a given belief that is sincere and meaningful occupies a place in the life of its possessor parallel to that filled by the orthodox belief in God with one who clearly qualifies for the exemption." In this remarkable decision, the U.S. Supreme Court declared that conscientious objector eligibility rests on the validity of conscience, not on the particular language used to express it.

Five years later, in *Welsh v. United States* (398 U.S. 333), a divided (5–4) Court reaffirmed this view that the key element was conscientious conviction, not the method by which such conviction comes about or is expressed. *Welsh*, more than *Seeger*, upheld conscientious objection based on beliefs that were wholly and unambiguously nonreligious.

One further case deserves mention. In 1971 the Court decided *Gillette v. United States* (401 U.S. 437), in which the plaintiff, a devout Roman Catholic, invoked his church's "just war" doctrine—that is, he was prepared to be drafted into some wars but not into the war against Vietnam because it was not a just war. By a vote of eight to one the Court said that such "selective" conscientious objection was not constitutionally protected.

Without a Selective Service Act, when the U.S. government has only a voluntary military, conscientious objection tends to fade away as an issue. Should the draft be reinstated, however, the nation would once again face the issue. If so, perhaps it might take yet another step away from its earliest positions on conscientious objection, when only members of pacifist churches qualified.

See also AMISH; CHURCH AND STATE; CIVIL RELIGION; FREEDOM OF RELIGION; MENNONITES; PACIFISM; PEACE CHURCHES.

BIBLIOGRAPHY

Moskos, Charles C., and J. W. Chambers II, eds. *The New Conscientious Objection: From Sacred to Secular Resistance.* 1993.

O'Gorman, J., ed. *The Universal Bends Toward Justice: A Reader of Christian Nonviolence in the U.S.* 1990.

Schlaback, Theron F., and R. T. Hughes, eds. *Proclaim Peace.* 1997.

Phillip Hammond

Conservative Christians.

See Fundamentalist Christianity; Religious Right.

Conservative Judaism.

See Judaism.

Conversion

In the simplest terms, religious conversion is changing from one religion to another or from no religion to any religion. Conversion away from a religion is usually termed "apostasy" by adherents of that religion. In practice, however, conversion is an intricate process that is difficult to comprehend and to define.

Judaism uses the word "proselyte" to refer to converts. In some periods of history, such as the Second Temple period, large numbers of individuals have converted to Judaism. But in the main, Judaism has not placed much emphasis on conversion. This is due in part to the unique status of Judaism as not only a religion but also a national identity.

Becoming a proselyte is a process that entails a period of study. The proselyte learns about Jewish ceremony and ritual as well as Jewish history. Some branches of Judaism will actively discourage proselytes in an attempt to determine their sincerity. During the period of study, proselytes must answer questions about their reasons for becoming Jews. Converts could gain admittance into the community for any number of reasons—to enter into marriage with a Jew, for example—but the preferred reason for converting has always been religious or spiritual conviction. In addition to study, proselytes must undergo a ceremonial baptism by immersion. Men must also be circumcised. If the man is already circumcised, there is a ritual drawing of the "blood of circumcision." Proselytes during the Temple period had to make a sacrifice, but this requirement was dropped when the Romans destroyed the Temple in Jerusalem and sacrifices became impossible.

During the Middle Ages, the Roman Catholic Church in Europe forced Jews to attend an annual sermon designed to encourage them to convert to Christianity. Frequently, social and economic benefits would accompany the conversion of Jews living in a Christian society. In some countries of Europe, especially Spain in the fourteenth and fifteenth centuries, Jews had to convert under threat of death. Some of these Jews hoped to be able to return to their faith and continued to adhere to their Jewish traditions in secret.

Conversion in Christianity has as many variations as Christianity has individual expressions. The churches that practice pedobaptism place comparatively little emphasis on conversion. The primary means of growth in these churches is through family growth. This is not to say that the churches make no allowance for conversion or that they do not actively recruit new members, but merely to say that in general they place less emphasis on conversion than churches that do not baptize infants.

It is among the evangelical churches in the United States that conversion receives the greatest emphasis. Evangelical and fundamentalist churches make conversion a high priority in their ministries. They spend a good deal of time and money in an ongoing attempt to "win lost souls to Jesus Christ." Usually some evidence of a changed life must accompany conversion. Converts often must make some public statement, called "giving one's testimony," that demonstrates the changes that "a relationship with Jesus Christ" has wrought in the life of the convert.

The emphasis on conversion is typical of the Arminian theology that has been a hallmark of evangelicalism since early in the nineteenth century, although Arminianism itself is much older. In Arminian theology the individual has a high degree of choice. One can choose to enter a relationship with God. Evangelicals do not believe that individuals are able to "save" themselves, but they do believe that individuals are able, on some level, to initiate the salvific process. This is in contrast to Calvinism, which had dominated religion in America. Calvinists believed that salvation is God's choice alone, that individuals have nothing to do with effecting their own salvation. Arminianism brought a tremendous change in the ways that churches spread the message of salvation.

The development of Arminianism brought mass revivals, camp meetings, and new measures. The evangelists who worked during the first third of the nineteenth century, such as the Methodist circuit riders and, most notably, the Presbyterian preacher Charles Grandison Finney, preached that conversion was necessary to salvation and that people had a hand in their own conversion.

In the twentieth century, evangelical emphasis on conversion has become even more important. Revivalists have crisscrossed the country spreading the evangelical gospel. Evangelists such as Billy Graham have preached to millions of potential converts, always with the intent of leading their audiences toward conversion.

Conversion has even played a role in politics. In part, Jimmy Carter was able to win the 1976 presidential election because of his willingness to state publicly that he had been "born again." This is a reference to the language used by Jesus in the third chapter of the gospel of John in the New Testament. Evangelicals adopted the phrase to refer to the conversion experience. Since that election—which saw the emergence of evangelicalism after a half century of self-imposed exile from politics—religious conversion, or at least the language of religious conversion, has played a role in many national, state, and local elections.

Conversion in Islam is essentially a matter of sincerely repeating and meaning the *shahadah,* which states, "There is only one God (Allah), and Muhammad is his Prophet." This is the first "pillar" of Islam. The remaining pillars are *salat,* which is praying five times daily; *zakat,* or almsgiving; *sawm,* which is daily fasting during the pilgrimage month of Ramadan; and *hajj,* or pilgrimage to Mecca, a pilgrimage that all Muslims are to make at least once in their lives if it is possible. Once Muslims have made the shahadah, they live in submission to the teachings of Allah, as given through the words of the Qur'an. In the first centuries of Islam, Muslims believed that only Arabs could become Muslim. There was therefore little emphasis on conversion. Muslims allowed conquered nations to carry on their own religious traditions as long as the conquered peoples had some form of written scriptures. As time passed, however, more people wanted to become Muslim, often for political, social, and economic reasons as well as for religious reasons.

In the twentieth century, Islam has spread far beyond the Middle East and Southeast Asia. It is growing at a rapid pace in the United States today. Islam, which has developed a more aggressive stance in attempting to convert non-Muslims, has found an especially receptive audience among African Americans.

See also CHURCH; EVANGELICAL CHRISTIANITY; FUNDAMENTALIST CHRISTIANITY; ISLAM; MISSIONARY MOVEMENTS; PREACHING; PROSELYTIZING; TELEVANGELISM.

BIBLIOGRAPHY

Altemeyer, Bob, and Bruce Hunsberger. *Amazing Conversions: Why Some Turn to Faith and Others Abandon Religion.* 1997.

James, William. *The Varieties of Religious Experience.* 1902, 1936.

O'Rourke, David K. *A Process Called Conversion.* 1985.

Rambo, Lewis R. *Understanding Religious Conversion.* 1993.

Tommy L. Faris

Coptic Orthodox Church

According to tradition, the Coptic Orthodox Church was established in Alexandria between 55 and 68 C.E.

by St. Mark the Apostle. Coptic means "Egyptian" and "orthodox" means "original/straight faith." The doctrine of the church follows New Testament teachings, as does Coptic Christology. Copts were the first Christians to establish monasticism in both its solitary and its communal forms, following the example of St. Antony of Egypt (251?–356). Another Copt, St. Pachomius (290–346), wrote the first rule for Christian monks, which influenced such later monastic leaders as St. Basil in the East and John Cassian and St. Benedict in the West.

The Coptic Orthodox Church practices the seven sacraments observed by other Eastern churches as well as by Roman Catholicism. Copts venerate the saints, especially the Virgin Mary. The Coptic Church believes that the Holy Trinity is of Father, Son, and Holy Spirit, One. Both faith and works are required for salvation, along with the sacraments. Copts believe in the resurection of the dead and a final judgment. The Old Testament, the Apocrypha, and the New Testament, as well as traditions of the Disciples, Apostles, and Fathers of the Church are followed. The church believes in divine intercession, recognizes Sunday as its holy Sabbath, and observes the feasts of Christmas, baptism, and Easter; the memorials of the martyrs and the saints; and the appearance of the angels. Copts practice fasting, prayers, and offering incense during worship, both in churches and in private homes. Hymns and other music are used in worship.

The Coptic Church has seven Holy Orders: bishop, hegumenos (archpriest or abbot of a monastery), priest, archdeacon, deacon, subdeacon, and reader. The patriarchs or popes of the church had their seat in Alexandria, but in the eleventh century the pope moved his seat to Damru in the Nile delta. Ultimately the patriarchate was settled in Cairo, although the popes retained their title "Our Most Holy and Most Blessed Father, Pope . . . Patriarch of the great city of Alexandria and of all the Land of Egypt, of the City of our God, Jerusalem, or the Pentapolis, of Libya, Nubia, Ethiopia, and Africa."

The Coptic Church of Egypt started during the Roman Empire and continued under the Byzantine Empire, and thereafter under Islamic rule until modern times. From Egypt, the motherland of the faith, the Coptic Church was established in other countries, such as Ethiopia, where it has continued to the present. The Copts endured ten persecutions during the church's first three centuries. Indeed, Coptic Christianity is defined in important ways by its twin legacies of monasticism and martyrdom. And, in the Coptic communion's long history, the monastic establishment and the laity have been in a close, mutually supportive relationship; monks regularly return to society to serve parishes, and laypeople observe retreats in monasteries and convents.

The popes of Alexandria and the Coptic societies that were established in the late nineteenth and early twentieth centuries have worked together in modern times for the benefit of their community worldwide. Some of the societies work with youth and the new generations, supplying them with libraries, teaching them doctrine, preaching, interpreting the Bible, and giving public lectures. Some of these societies, as well as many individual Coptic parishes, have Sunday schools. Adjoining such local churches are day care centers for children and sports clubs for youth. From time to time other churches arrange bazaars or organize trips to visit archaeological sites, monasteries, and old churches in Egypt. Coptic congregations sometimes also travel to the Holy Land of Israel to visit the historic Jewish and Christian sites.

His Holiness Pope Shenouda III, the current spiritual leader of all Copts, oversees churches and communities in Africa, Europe, Asia, North America, Central America, South America, and Australia. The pope and bishops visit churches in those global regions occasionally and ordain priests and bishops to serve the churches worldwide.

The Coptic pope works with the heads of other Christian churches, seeking Christian unity and encouraging Copts in each nation to build churches and monasteries. American Copts are building or have built a cathedral in nearly every state, and some states have more than one Coptic parish church. The Coptic Church of Egypt is involved at home in building and rebuilding churches, monasteries, chapels, altars, and houses of retreat, as well as sending missions of priests, monks, and bishops worldwide. The church has established a theological seminary, the Higher Institute of Coptic Studies, the Didymus School, the Coptic Museum and Library, papal libraries, Sunday schools, the University Families, and nurseries, and has encouraged scholars to establish *La Société de l'Archéologie Copte*. The church is offering its services not only for the Copts or other Christians of Egypt but also for non-Christians as well as international visitors, especially in locations where monasteries and convents exist. These institutions have built schools for both children and adults and have opened the churches of monasteries and convents to visitors. The villages and their Christian and non-Christian families that are near these monasteries and convents have benefited in many ways, including financial support.

Coptic societies, in Egypt and elsewhere, have established factories, hospitals, and dispensaries as well as girls' schools and boys' schools open to the general public. Other societies publish newspapers, bulletins, books, monographs, newsletters, and special reports about the Coptic legacy. Copts also are involved in excavating archaeological sites in Upper and Lower Egypt. Many other Coptic societies are supporting the poor, orphans, handicapped people, and the elderly. Moreover, the Coptic Church and its societies provide employment opportunities, nursing homes, day care for children, investment in economic projects, participation in the construction of apartment buildings, assistance to newlyweds in setting up households, stipends for those temporarily unemployed, and free medicine for those in need. American and other Coptic communities contribute millions of dollars annually in support of the patriarchate, the bishoprics, and Coptic societies. There are approximately twelve million Copts in the world, with about five hundred thousand in the United States. Sizable Coptic populations exist in New York, Michigan, and southern California.

See also EASTERN ORTHODOXY; LITURGY AND WORSHIP; PRACTICE.

BIBLIOGRAPHY

Atiya, Aziz S. *A History of Eastern Christianity.* 1968.
The Coptic Encyclopedia, edited by Aziz S. Atiya. 8 vols. 1991.
Elmasry, Iris Habib. *Introduction to the Coptic Church.* 1977.
Elmasry, Iris Habib. *Survey of the Coptic Church.* 1961.
Kamil, Murad. *Coptic Egypt.* 1968.

Boulos Ayad Ayad

Cortese, Aimee García

(1929–), evangelist.

Aimee García Cortese was born to Puerto Rican parents in New York City on May 26, 1929. Named after the famous Pentecostal evangelist Aimee Semple McPherson, Cortese decided to go into the ministry at age fifteen. After discussing the desire with one minister, she was told, *"Las mujeres no predican"* (Women do not preach). Despite this discouragement, her father (who was a Pentecostal minister) encouraged her to go into the ministry. She attended the Hispanic American Bible School in New York City and then Central Bible College (CBC) of the Assemblies of God in 1951. Licensed to preach in 1951, she was later ordained by the Wesleyan Methodist Church (1964) and the Assemblies of God (1974). Aimee García married Rafael Cortese and raised four children. She served as an evangelist and then the director of education and associate minister at Thessalonica Christian Church in the Bronx, New York. Because of the

legalism she saw in the Assemblies of God, she joined the Wesleyan Methodist Church (1962–1964) in San Juan, Puerto Rico, before returning to the Assemblies of God in 1965. Cortese was a delegate to the First World Congress on Evangelism in West Berlin, Germany, in 1966. She later served as the legislative aide (1969–1972) to her brother, New York State senator Robert García. Cortese became the first female chaplain (1973–1983) in the history of the New York State Department of Corrections. In 1983 she founded Crossroads Tabernacle Church of the Assemblies of God in the South Bronx. It has grown from a few dozen people in 1983 to fifteen hundred members in the 1990s. Her church is one of the largest multicultural churches in New York City. Cortese is a highly sought-after speaker and has preached throughout the United States, Puerto Rico, Cuba, Mexico, Venezuela, Guatemala, Colombia, and Bolivia. She was chosen to be a member of the New York State Governor's Task Force on Domestic Violence and New York mayor Edward Koch's Commission on Hispanic Affairs and Commission on Bias Affairs. She has also been invited to attend and/or address the National Convention of the Assemblies of God, the Black and Hispanic Caucus Group of New York State, the New York State Senate, the U.S. House of Representatives, U.S. Hispanic Caucus in Washington, D.C., the National Hispanic Bar Association, and the Federation of Hispanic Women in America. She is considered one of the most respected Hispanic Protestant women ministers in the United States and has served as a role model for dozens of women in the ministry.

See also EVANGELICAL CHRISTIANITY; FEMINIST SPIRITUALITY; LATINO TRADITIONS; MINISTRY; ORDINATION OF WOMEN.

BIBLIOGRAPHY

Espinosa, Gastón. "'Your Daughters Shall Prophesy' ": A History of Women's Roles in the Latino Pentecostal Movement in the United States. In *Women and Twentieth-Century Protestantism,* edited by Virginia Brereton and Margaret Bendroth. 2000.
Korrol, Virginia Sánchez. "In Search of Unconventional Women: Histories of Puerto Rican Women in Religious Vocations Before Midcentury." In Denis Lynn Daly Heyck, ed. *Barrios and Borderlands.* 1994.

Gastón Espinosa

Counseling, Pastoral.

See Pastoral Counseling.

Creationism

Creationism affirms that God directly created the first humans. Creationism is, therefore, a particular interpretation of a broader notion of creation, widely shared among world religions, that attributes the ultimate origins and ongoing ordering of the cosmos to a being that transcends it. Although Judaism and Islam share the same basic creation account with Christianity, creationism is a uniquely Christian notion that cuts across denominational boundaries. To varying degrees, all Christian creationists share opposition to a biological evolutionism that accounts for the uniqueness of the human species exclusively through adaptive processes that began on Earth more than 3.5 billion years ago.

The two major models of Christian creationism are found in Roman Catholicism and among North American Protestants who regard the inerrancy of the Bible to be a "fundamental" tenet of Christian faith. The roots of Roman Catholic creationism can be traced to the fourth century and the position of Hilary of Poitiers (ca. 315–367) that though human flesh is always born of flesh, the human soul can be "from nowhere else than from God." (*On the Trinity,* Book 10, no. 22). This form of creationism is rooted in a metaphysical notion of the human borrowed from the classical Greek philosophy that held that the human is composed of body and soul. This metaphysical anthropology is evident in the positions of Roman Catholic popes in the second half of the twentieth century. Although Pius XII (the encyclical *Humanae Generis,* 1950) and John Paul II (the address "Evolution and the Living God," 1996) do not explicitly use the term "creationism," both argue that God immediately creates the spiritual soul of the human, while the body depends on its origins from cells provided by the parents. John Paul II, although cautious about scientific reductionism, explicitly accepts evolutionism (a.k.a. "generationism") as the origin of the human body, while retaining creationism as the origin of the spiritual soul. Since the teachings of Pius XII and John Paul II on human origins have the authority of "non-infallibility," they are not necessarily the final word and are subject to revision. What is likely not to be revised is the position that the capacity of human persons for relationship with God cannot be accounted for on scientific grounds.

The Protestant model of creationism is different from that of Roman Catholicism, because Protestant creationists reject metaphysical anthropology of soul and body in favor of a biblical one that envisions the human person as a unity. The goal of Protestant creationists is to end the hegemony of the theory of Darwinian evolution by proposing an alternative theory that they call "scientific creationism" or "creation science."

The roots of creation science can be traced in the United States to the 1920s and the antievolution articles published in the *Princeton Theological Review,* as well as to the antievolution movement promoted by William Jennings Bryan (1860–1925), a prohibitionist and three-time presidential candidate. Creationists gained notoriety in the well-publicized trial of John T. Scopes in 1925. Earlier that year, the Tennessee state legislature passed a bill banning public school teachers from instructing their students about any theory that denies the divine creation of humanity as taught in the Bible. Scopes broke that law by teaching evolution. At the trial Bryan represented the school board of Dayton, Tennessee. Clarence Darrow, a lawyer associated with the American Civil Liberties Union, represented Scopes. The decision of the "Scopes Monkey Trial" went against Scopes but was reversed on a technicality. Shortly after the trial, many southern states passed antievolution legislation.

In 1967 an antievolution law passed in Arkansas in 1928 was tested by Susan Epperson, a first-year biology teacher who chose a textbook that included evolution. The case went all the way to the U.S. Supreme Court, which in 1968 declared the Arkansas law unconstitutional on the grounds that it violated the establishment of religion clause of the First Amendment of the U.S. Constitution. In the wake of this decision, creationists had reason to believe that any legislation that forbade evolution to be taught in public schools would meet the same fate.

In 1969 the California Board of Education agreed to have the Genesis account of creation taught in public schools as an alternative to the evolutionary account. In 1970 Henry Morris, a hydraulic engineer, founded the Christian Heritage College at San Diego, as an educational center explicitly committed to creation science and the defeat of evolutionism. In 1974 California reversed its decision, but in 1981 "balanced treatment" legislation was passed in Arkansas (no. 590) and Louisiana (no. 685), requiring public schools teaching Darwinian evolution to give equal attention to creation science. Among the tenets of creation science included in these statutes are positions that reflect a literal interpretation of Genesis 1–11:

1. The sudden (special) creation of the universe, energy, and life from nothing.
2. The insufficiency of mutation and natural selection to explain all living kinds of organisms.
3. The separate ancestry for humans and apes.
4. Explanation of the earth's geology by catastrophism, including the occurrence of a worldwide flood.

5. The relatively recent inception of the earth and life (six thousand to ten thousand years ago). [Arkansas Act no. 590, *Science, Technology and Human Values* 7 (1982): 11–13.]

The "balanced treatment" acts of Arkansas and Louisiana were struck down in U.S. District Court in Arkansas (January 5, 1982) and in the U.S. Supreme Court (June 19, 1987) because they contravened the First Amendment of the federal Constitution and promoted the advancement of religious doctrine.

Creation science not only has political significance for the relations between church and state in the United States but also has cultural significance for how the relations of religion and science are conceived. For people who interpret the scriptures literally, the Bible, as the inerrant word of God, presents a higher truth than fallible human reason, including science, can know. Biblically based religion and evolutionary science, therefore, necessarily conflict.

Not all North American Christians agree with the creationists. Other Christians interpret the Bible symbolically rather than literally. Some simply see creation doctrine and biological evolution as independent and contrasting conceptions of reality, while others believe that society can benefit from dialogue between Christians and scientists. Many in the latter group perceive meaningful analogies between cosmic evolutionary processes and God's continuous creative activity.

See also BIBLE; CHURCH AND STATE; FUNDAMENTALIST CHRISTIANITY; GOD; PRAYER IN SCHOOL; ROMAN CATHOLICISM; SECULARIZATION.

BIBLIOGRAPHY

Barbour, Ian. *Religion and Science.* 1997.

Colin, Norman. "Supreme Court Strikes Down 'Creation Science' Law as Promotion of Religion." *Science* 236 (1987): 1620.

Gilkey, Langdon. *Creationism on Trial: Evolution and God at Little Rock.* 1985.

Larson, Edward. *Trial and Error: The American Controversy Over Creation and Evolution.* 1985.

Morris, Henry. *Scientific Creationism.* 1974.

Pope John Paul II. "Evolution and the Living God." In *Science and Theology. The New Comsonance,* edited by Ted Peters. 1998.

Anne M. Clifford

Creation Spirituality

Creation Spirituality (CS) is a theological movement that gained recognition and momentum in the 1980s and 1990s. Associated most widely with the work of former Dominican priest Matthew Fox, CS seeks to shift the emphasis of Christian life, belief, and practice from a focus on redemption to a focus on creation. In *The Coming of the Cosmic Christ* (1989) and *Creation Spirituality* (1990), Fox posits CS as a synthesis of wisdom drawn from indigenous cultures, mystical traditions of the West, world religions, scientific cosmological explanations of the universe, and the artist's creative ethos. CS also draws inspiration from movements in social justice, feminism, environmentalism, and process thought.

Often called a spirituality of earth and cosmos, CS views creation as primary revelation that is perpetually emerging. Fox asserts that this creation-centered consciousness can be sought and found in the oldest traditions of the Hebrew Bible and especially in the reflections of medieval Christian mystics such as Meister Eckhart (c. 1260–1327), Hildegard of Bingen (1098–1179), Julian of Norwich (1342–c. 1415), and Mechtild of Magdeburg (1210–1280).

CS is also associated with the work of Passionist priest and cultural historian Thomas Berry. In both *The Dream of the Earth* (1988) and *The Universe Story* (1992), the latter work written with cosmological physicist Brian Swimme, Thomas Berry identifies contemporary environmental destruction as symptomatic of a culture that has ceased to have a "functional cosmology." A disciple of French Jesuit paleontologist and theologian Pierre Teilhard de Chardin, Berry contends that the Western philosophical split between (1) religion, (2) science and humanity, and (3) creation must be mended by recognizing the profound spiritual dimension of the fifteen-billion-year epic of cosmic evolution, or the "universe story." The Genesis story of Jewish and Christian traditions, argues Berry, has failed to provide modern humanity with a sense of communion and kinship with a universe that is alive, intrinsically sacred, intelligent, and still in the process of creation. On the other hand, he finds that Western science's evolutionary narrative, when told in a context detached from spirituality, fails to capture the intrinsic "mystery" and sacredness of the cosmic evolutionary process. Berry speaks of the need for a common creation story that understands the human not only as an intimate part of a sacred, evolving universe, but also as the being in whom the universe has become conscious of itself.

CS has inspired several outlets for spiritual practice and community that celebrate creation both in specialized ceremony and in everyday life. New York City's Cathedral of St. John the Divine, also called the "Green Cathedral," has made creation-centered liturgies and worship a priority in its programming. In 1985 Dean James Parks Morton commissioned Grammy Award–

winning "earth musician" Paul Winter to perform his first *Earth Mass* or *Missa Gaia* at the cathedral. Featuring a unique blend of musical styles including the voices of tundra wolves, whales, eagles, and harp seals, Winter's hymns include "For the Beauty of the Earth" and "Return to Gaia." The cathedral's St. Francis Day Animal Blessing, ecological meditation trail, and living "earth shrine" also honor and celebrate creation.

In 1996 Matthew Fox founded the University of Creation Spirituality in Oakland, California, where students pursuing their doctorates of ministry can use a ritual laboratory equipped with Internet and CD-ROM capabilities to produce "techno-masses" aimed at using technology in sacred ways that further bridge the rift between religion and science. CS publications include *Creation Spirituality* magazine and the *Original Blessing Newsletter*, both offshoots of Fox's Creation Spirituality Network (CSN). CSN also provides nationwide networking for those who wish to form discussion groups or promote the celebration of creation spirituality within local communities.

The Epic of Evolution Society, formed in 1997, similarly provides networking and support for discussion of Thomas Berry and Brian Swimme's work and its translation into ritual expressions and everyday practice. One of Berry's primary disciples has been "earth activist" Dominican sister Miriam Therese MacGillis, who founded Genesis Farm, an organic farm and retreat center devoted to "living the universe story." MacGillis was the first to develop the practice of "Walking the Cosmic Path," a ritual in which individuals mystically go back in time to the "flaring forth" of the universe by walking through a spiral marked with major cosmic evolutionary events. Centers such as Genesis Farm, which actively integrate Berry's principles into spiritual life, proliferated in the late twentieth century and include Spiritearth in New York's Hudson River Valley, Crystal Spring in Massachusetts, Michaela Farm in Indiana, and a variety of ecological learning centers across the United State that are sponsored by Catholic nuns.

See also ECOFEMINISM; ECOSPIRITUALITY; FEMINIST THEOLOGY; PROCESS THEOLOGY.

BIBLIOGRAPHY

Bard, Sharon. "The New Story: An Interview with Miriam MacGillis." *Creation Spirituality* (Autumn 1994): 15–23.

Berry, Thomas. *Befriending the Earth: A Theology of Reconciliation Between Humans and the Earth*. 1991.

Berry, Thomas. Riverdale Papers, Riverdale Center for Religious Research, Riverdale, N.Y. 1974–1983.

Conlon, James. *Earth Story, Sacred Story*. 1994.

Fox, Matthew. *Original Blessing*. 1981.

Fox, Matthew. *Wrestling with the Prophets: Essays on Creation Spirituality and Everyday Life*. 1995.

Leciejewski, Mary Ellen. "Common Ground: Women Religious Healing the Earth" (video recording). 1995.

Swimme, Brian. *The Universe Is a Green Dragon: A Cosmic Creation Story*. 1985.

Sarah McFarland Taylor

Creeds

A creed (in the Eastern churches called the "symbol" of faith) was originally a short confession of belief that was taught in antiquity to Christian baptismal candidates and repeated by them as their profession of faith. At first a brief statement, varying among local churches, the creed became standardized more and more in the fourth century, when the liturgical forms of early Christianity were becoming internationalized under episcopal and synodical direction.

The creeds at first were threefold in structure, shadowing the seminal text of Matthew 28:19, which itself is one of the earliest baptismal confessions. Originally the recitation of the creed repeated the great cycle of salvation events that make up the Christian faith (analogous to the use of Psalms 105–106 in the liturgy of the Jerusalem Temple), and to that extent the use of the creed in liturgy was a natural development, even though the regular (eucharistic) confession of a creed is not attested until after the fifth century in Syria and Constantinople. The practice appeared in Spain in the sixth century but was adopted by Rome only as late as the eleventh century.

In the second-century Gnostic crisis, the credal articles on belief in the Fatherhood of God were expanded greatly to oppose Gnostic conceptions of a God who was not primarily involved in the creation of the material world. In all the classical early creeds the opening section of the text still bears this primary anti-Gnostic character. In the later fourth century, again in times of theological controversy, the credal articles on Jesus were expanded from their original focus on the biblical accounts of his life, death, and resurrection to function as doctrinal synopses of correct belief (orthodoxy). The symbol of Nicea is a prime example of the creed now serving as a dogmatic digest. The confessional elements relating to Jesus were amplified by parallel statements inserted into the text (in the case of the Nicene Creed, teaching the consubstantiality of the divine Logos in terms drawn from contemporary Greek philosophy). The articles on the Holy Spirit were the least developed. Up to the late fourth century the creeds simply stated a belief "in the Holy Spirit," but the work of the Cappadocian Fathers expanded this to include four doctrinal statements: that the Spirit was Lord and Life-Giver, proceeding from the Father, worshiped with the same veneration as the Father and the Son, and the divine source of the inspiration of the prophets. The so-called creed of Chalcedon in 451, a precisely shaped Christological definition, is the apex of this kind of credal development, but it never achieved a liturgical usage, and it explicitly claims to recognize no other "creed" than that of Nicea.

This was the last great theological development to occur in antiquity through the medium of the creed; henceforward theological development was to be based mainly on rhetorical and apologetical discourse, something that applied more or less up to the time of the Reformation, which reopened an active period of creedmaking and confessionalism.

In Catholicism and the Orthodox family of churches the Nicene-Constantinopolitan creed still serves as a liturgical confession. It is a congregational prayer that serves to introduce the Anaphora or central element of the Eucharistic prayer. Catholicism gives preeminence to three historical creeds: the Nicene-Constantinopolitan, the Athanasian Creed, and the Apostles' Creed. The last is commonly recited as part of the rosary. Orthodoxy uses only the Nicene-Constantinopolitan in its original form. Both communions, however, have continued to issue confessional statements, often from a synodical basis, into modern times. The documents of the Second Vatican Council are one large example of this. But these documents and texts do not carry the status of the historical creeds in any comparable way, nor have they entered the liturgy.

The Reformed churches often took the Apostles' Creed as the basis of their confessional statement. Sometimes a more directly focused statement was originated, based on the catechisms operative in various groups, as for example the Heidelberg Catechism, or Luther's Small Catechism. Historical confessions in the early Reformation period also served as a new basis for what the creeds did in ancient times, as can be seen, for example, in the Augsburg Confession.

In the longer term, in the Reformed family of churches, the creeds often did not retain their importance in a liturgical role and thus were not reinforced through recitation at weekly worship so as to become the central articulators of the belief system of the various churches. They took on more of the role of historic formulations of belief, and they were supplemented by a range of contemporary theological "confessions" regularly renewed in light of the perceived needs and controversies of the times. The central Protestant belief in the sole regulatory force of the scriptures afforded to ecclesial creeds merely an auxiliary and directional role that stood subject to constant review and amendment. Modern American church movements, such as the Universalist Unitarians, who hold more lightly than most to any formal credal system, nevertheless continued to express their fundamental orientations of belief in confessional statements of varying binding force. The National Conference of Unitarian Churches meeting in 1865 made it clear that the creeds of this communion had simply the authority of a statement reflecting the mind-set of the majority of the time "and are dependent wholly for their effect upon the consent they command on their own merits from the churches here represented." (Schaff 1877, vol. 3, p. 935). All in all, in the wider topography of American Christianity, the old ambivalence over creeds as fixed foundational constitutions of ecclesial identity, or as temporary guidelines for the contemporary redefinition and reconstruction of ecclesial or sectarian identities, remains an enduring aspect of indigenous forms of Christianity.

See also CHURCH; DOGMATISM; GNOSTICISM.

BIBLIOGRAPHY

Kelly, J. N. D. *Early Christian Creeds,* 3rd ed. 1972.
Leith, J. H. *Creeds of the Churches.* 1982.
Schaff, P. *The Creeds of Christendom,* 3 vols. 1877.

John Anthony McGuckin

Cremation

Cremation, the incineration of a corpse by heat or fire, emerged as an alternative to burial in the United States in the 1870s, when social reformers began to argue for the practice on sanitary grounds. A series of epidemics had devastated U.S. cities, and many physicians placed the blame on corpses decaying in crowded urban graveyards. In 1876, cremation advocates, led by Theosophical Society president Henry Steel Olcott, conducted the first indoor cremation in America (many Native American tribes had previously cremated in the open air) at a private crematory built on the estate of Dr. Julius Le Moyne in Washington, Pennsylvania. Opposition was widespread. Many viewed cremation as an affront to the Jewish and Christian doctrine of bodily resurrection, and in 1886 the Catholic Church banned it. But the practice of cremation grew quickly nonetheless. By 1900, twenty-four crematories were operating in fifteen states and more than ten thousand Americans had cremated deceased relatives.

Growth moderated in the first half of the twentieth century. Between World War II and the early 1960s, the cremation movement stagnated, hurt by associations with Nazi concentration camp crematoriums. The cremation rate (the ratio or cremations to deaths) hovered for nearly two decades at just under 4 percent. Beginning in the sixties, however, cremation rapidly gained ground. By 1998, roughly one in every four deceased Americans was cremated (24 percent). Although cremation has remained out of favor in some Bible Belt states and among African Americans, Jews, and Muslims, it has become more common than burial in Hawaii and in many western states.

A number of factors contributed to cremation's ascent. In 1963 the Catholic Church lifted its ban. In the same year, Jessica Mitford's best-seller *The American Way of Death* focused public attention on funeral costs and promoted cremation as an inexpensive alternative to burial. Cremation received another boost in the seventies when businesses such as the Telophase Society (established in 1971) began offering cut-rate "direct cremation" services. No longer driven by sanitary concerns, cremation had hitched its star to the consumer movement.

In the 1990s, the Cremation Association of North America (CANA), a trade association originally organized in 1913 as the Cremation Association of America (CAA), cited many factors for cremation's popularity, including environmentalism and Asian immigration. But theological shifts were also at work. In the nineteenth century, U.S. Christians and Jews typically held a psychosomatic view of the person as a body/soul mix, and many hoped for a resurrection of that whole person. For such believers, cremation was a pagan horror. But by the 1990s, popular theologizing had changed dramatically. Many had come to view the self as spirit (or body) only. Belief in heaven and hell had declined. And while the vast majority still affirmed an afterlife, belief in a bodily resurrection had yielded ground to belief in the soul's immortality. All these trends were conducive to the growth of cremation, which has typically been practiced in civilizations (such as ancient Greece) that viewed the self as spirit or mind only.

Cremation got another boost at the end of the twentieth century from baby boomers, who saw the practice as more friendly than burial to mass customization and more in tune with generational values such as simplicity, informality, and spontaneity. In the 1990s, Americans tailored cremation rites to fit the unique personalities of the deceased. Manufacturers advertised golf bag urns for golfing enthusiasts and pink triangle urns for gay men. Families, rather than yielding to the authority of funeral directors or clerics, crafted customized death rites at both crematories and scattering sites. Some critics continued to associate cremation with offbeat personalities (such as LSD guru Timothy Leary, whose cremated remains were rocketed into orbit in 1997), but the practice was clearly going mainstream. Now a consumer option rather than an urgent social reform, cremation had become by the end of the millennium a death rite of choice not only for U.S. Buddhists and Hindus but also for many Christians and some Reform Jews.

See also AFTERLIFE; BODY; DEATH AND DYING; HEALTH; PRACTICE; RELIGIOUS COMMUNITIES; RITES OF PASSAGE; SPIRIT; THEOSOPHICAL SOCIETY.

BIBLIOGRAPHY

Habenstein, Robert W., and William M. Lamers. *The History of American Funeral Directing*, 3rd rev. ed., edited and revised by Howard C. Raether. 1995.

Prothero, Stephen. "Lived Religion and the Dead: The Cremation Movement in Gilded Age America." In *Lived Religion in America: Toward a History of Practice*, edited by David D. Hall. 1997.

Stephen Prothero

Crowley, Aleister

(1875–1947), occultist.

A prolific poet, essayist, artist, mountaineer, world traveler, and *bon vivant*, Aleister Crowley—born Edward Alexander Crowley—was the most influential occultist of the twentieth century. Echoes of his work on magical theory and practice are ubiquitous throughout modern paganism. Since 1923, when a newspaper article branded him "the wickedest man in the world," Crowley—who variously styled himself "Baphomet," "the Beast 666," and "To Mega Therion" (the Great Beast)—has served as a public icon of transgressive power, celebrated by counterculturalists, and maligned by conservatives.

Crowley's parents were wealthy and devoted members of the Plymouth Brethren (Exclusive), an independent evangelical sect noted for its biblical literalism, strict moralism, and millennialism. His father's death in 1887 left Crowley financially independent. After his last term at Trinity College, Cambridge, he was inducted in 1898 into the Order of the Golden Dawn, a society devoted to hermetic lore whose members included W. B. Yeats and Florence Farr. A series of schisms fragmented the order after 1900, and Crowley redirected his energies to learning a form of

Yoga meditation. Combining Western esotericism and Egyptian cosmology with Eastern technologies of transcendence, Crowley developed his own religious system of "scientific illuminism," which he called Thelema, a transliteration of the Greek term for "will."

The scriptural heart of Thelema is *The Book of the Law* (also cited as *Liber AL*), a prophetic text dictated to Crowley in 1904 by what he believed to be "a praeterhuman intelligence." At its most basic level, Thelema may be understood as a method of self-understanding and self-actualization. Its aim is to help the practitioner discover his or her purpose in life, or True Will, and empower him or her to take the necessary steps to accomplish it. The Thelemic motto, "Do what thou wilt shall be the whole of the Law," is not an antinomian creed but rather an injunction to know oneself. The processes through which one realizes one's True Will may include textual study, meditation, divination, and ritual practice. These techniques are grouped under the larger rubric of Magick, which Crowley defined as "the Science and Art of causing Change to occur in conformity with Will." The process of attaining spiritual perfection—"the union of the individual as a microcosm with the divine macrocosm"—is termed the Great Work.

The advanced operations of Magick involve sexual acts consecrated to a higher (though not necessarily nobler) purpose. Crowley was evasive in his public writings on these matters. A notorious chapter in his most popular text, *Magick in Theory and Practice* (1929–1930), appears to advocate the ritual sacrifice of "a male child of perfect innocence and high intelligence," but this is an allusion to the expenditure of semen. Thelema's ethical code demands that one respect the rights of others—in the words of *Liber AL*, "every man and every woman is a star."

Crowley propagated Thelema through two organizations, the A∴ A∴, which he founded in 1907–1908; and the Ordo Templi Orientis (O.T.O.), a Masonic offshoot that he joined in 1912 and led after 1923. A fixture of the international bohemian subculture that flourished before World War II, Crowley led a commune in Cefalú, Sicily, between 1920 and 1923. After his death, the O.T.O. languished for several decades until it was revitalized in the 1970s by Grady McMurtry. In addition to the A∴ A∴ and the O.T.O., there exist a number of other organizations in the United States and abroad devoted in greater or lesser degree to Crowley's work. However, Crowley's readership—and his cultural influence—extend far beyond the limited membership of these institutions.

See also MAGIC; NEOPAGANISM; OCCULT, THE; PARANORMAL; PSYCHIC; TRANSCENDENCE.

Aleister Crowley and his ominous silhouette, ca. 1945, about two years before his death. (Credit: CORBIS/Hulton-Deutsch Collection.)

BIBLIOGRAPHY

Crowley, Aleister. *The Confessions of Aleister Crowley: An Autohaigiography,* edited by John Symonds and Kenneth Grant. 1970.

Crowley, Aleister. *The Law Is for All: The Authorized Popular Commentary to Liber Al Vel Legis Sub Figura CCXX, the Book of the Law,* edited by Louis Umfreville Wilkinson and Hymenaeus Beta. 1996.

Crowley, Aleister. *Magick: Liber ABA,* Book 4, Parts 1 to 4, 2nd rev. ed., edited by Hymenaeus Beta. 1997.

Crowley, Aleister, Mary Desti, and Leila Waddell, eds. *The Equinox: The Official Organ of the A∴ A∴: The Review of Scientific Illuminism,* 10 issues. 1909–1913, 1998.

Symonds, John. *The Beast 666: The Life of Aleister Crowley.* 1997.

Bradford Verter

Crypto-Judaism

As a contemporary phenomenon in American culture, crypto-Judaism has its roots in medieval Spain. In response to the hostility, persecution, and forced conversion of the Spanish Jews (*Sephardim*) in the fourteenth and fifteenth centuries, a segment of the Jewish converts (*conversos*) publicly accepted Christianity while secretly retaining Jewish beliefs and practices. This form of religious resistance came to be known as crypto-Judaism. In the fifteenth and sixteenth centuries, crypto-Judaism expanded into Portugal and the colonized territories of the Americas as crypto-Jews (also known as *marranos*) fled to escape prosecution for heresy during the Spanish Inquisition. Crypto-Jewish populations settled in regions of Latin America and Mexico, as well as into areas of North America that now comprise Arizona, Colorado, New Mexico, and Texas.

As fear of exposure continued to sustain the secrecy that surrounded Jewish-based rituals in Latino Catholic and Protestant families, this crypto-Jewish diaspora led to the creation of a hidden religious culture that has survived into the twentieth century. Although over time, Jewish practices became fragmented and their meanings obscured, contemporary scholars have found evidence of crypto-Jewish rituals in Latin America, Mexico, and the southwestern United States. Among the traditions that have survived are those relating to the observance of the Sabbath, dietary laws, family purity rites, and the celebrations of Chanukah (Hanukkah), Passover, and Purim.

With regard to the Jewish holidays, a syncretic form of ritual practice has developed through the blending of Jewish and Christian religious customs. In the twentieth century, this aspect of syncretism was found in rituals that appear to merge Passover with Easter and Purim with devotions to St. Esther. In comparison, the observance of the Sabbath among crypto-Jews tended to be less syncretic in nature. In accordance with Jewish tradition, candles or oil lamps were typically lit on Friday nights, although this custom was frequently performed in areas of the home that were shielded from public view.

A significant component of both historical and twentieth-century crypto-Judaism is the role that gender plays in cultural persistence. As medieval persecution led to the privatization (i.e., concealment) of Jewish religious practice, women assumed a significant function in the crypto-Jewish household through the practice of secret rituals and the transmission of religious culture. This pattern of gender and cultural survival has been found among modern descendants whose mothers, grandmothers, and aunts have been identified as those members of the family who hold the knowledge of Jewish ancestry and who sustain some of the Jewish customs that were observed by their forebears.

Over the last two decades, a current generation of crypto-Jewish descendants have been engaged in the recovery of their Spanish Jewish roots, sometimes joined by those whose ancestors were later-era *conversos* (i.e., those who had converted to crypto-Judaism in the Americas). Through the study of family genealogy, the identification of Jewish-based rituals in the home, and the disclosure of Jewish ancestry among surviving family members, individuals throughout the Americas are openly acknowledging their family's Jewish past. Furthermore, many of those who have established their Sephardic ancestry are also seeking to return to a Jewish faith perspective. This religious trend among modern descendants has contributed to the debate within Jewish law concerning who is a Jew and what defines Jewish practice and religiosity among a population of individuals who were raised as non-Jews but whose ancestry is Jewish in origin. In particular, the question of conversion has become a site of tension as both the descendants and the rabbinic authorities explore the contested terrain of crypto-Jewish heritage and its meaning for modern Jewish identity.

See also JEWISH IDENTITY; JUDAISM; LATINO TRADITIONS; RELIGIOUS PERSECUTION; SYNCRETISM.

BIBLIOGRAPHY

Gitlitz, David. *Secrecy and Deceit: The Religion of the Crypto-Jews.* 1996.

Hernandez, Frances. "The Secret Jews of the Southwest." In *Sephardim in the Americas,* edited by Martin A. Cohen and Abraham J. Peck. 1993.

Hordes, Stanley. "The Inquisition and the Crypto-Jewish Community in Colonial Spain and New Mexico." *In Cultural Encounters: The Impact of the Inquisition in Spain and the New World,* edited by Mary Elizabeth Perry and Anne J. Cruz. 1991.

Roth, C. *A History of the Marranos.* 1932.

Janet L. Jacobs

Cuban Religions.

See Afro-Cuban Religions.

Cult

The meanings of the term "cult" in American society underwent a radical transformation during the latter half of the twentieth century. Until the 1960s, cult was generally used to denote a system of religious beliefs and ritual that sometimes included the system's body of adherents. With the growth in religious experimentation that accompanied the counterculture of the 1960s, cult came to be used in a much more pejorative sense. Due in large degree to the efforts of the anticult movement, cult has popularly come to mean a kind of deviant or spurious religious organization characterized by a naive and exploited body of members, unsavory charismatic leaders, and practices of "brainwashing," or systematic psychological indoctrination. This negative characterization of unconventional religions has been used to justify the forcible abduction of members by deprogrammers, who have been employed by worried parents to rescue family members from these religious communities. The 1978 mass suicides and murders at Jonestown, Guyana, greatly accelerated the demonization of unconventional religions in the American news media and led to the current state of affairs in which the term "cult" is popularly used to smear any religion with whose doctrines or practices a person does not personally agree.

Throughout the past thirty years, academic researchers of new religions have developed a large body of empirical data and interpretive insights that have helped to balance the one-sided characterizations of "cults" disseminated by the anti-cult movement and the mass media. Many researchers have challenged the very use of the term "cult" because of its overwhelmingly negative connotations. In its place, terms such as "new religions," "emergent religions," "alternative religions," and "new religious movements" have been substituted in scholarly writing and, increasingly, in media coverage.

Researchers such as Rodney Stark and William Sims Bainbridge have attempted to salvage the term "cult" by using it to distinguish certain religious organizations from others. "Denominations," in their typology, are established Christian churches in America that have their roots in one of the historic European confessions. They tend to be inclusive in their membership, to have professionally trained leaders, and to be positively aligned with the dominant social structure. Examples include Episcopalians, Presbyterians, Methodists, Lutherans, and Roman Catholics.

"Sect movements" are voluntary organizations that begin as offshoots from a denomination. Typically, a small group of members become convinced that their denomination has veered away from its original doctrines and become hopelessly compromised by worldly values. These members break away (and sometimes are expelled) and set about to re-create their former church in its original purity. Sect movements tend to be homogeneous and exclusive in their membership, to espouse strict codes of ethics, to have an egalitarian organizational structure, and to hire leaders distinguished more by personal charisma than by education and training. Examples include Carl McIntire's Bible Presbyterian Church, a sectarian offshoot of the Pres-

byterian Church, USA; and the Branch Davidians, a sectarian offshoot of the Seventh-Day Adventists.

A "cult movement," according to Stark and Bainbridge, is a religious community that begins independently of any established denomination or sect movement. In other words, it is an original creation—usually by a charismatic leader and his or her early followers—that has no ties to established churches. This does not mean that cult movements do not adopt beliefs and practices from existing traditions, only that they do so in a piecemeal fashion so that the end result does not resemble any established sect or denomination. Both cult movements and sect movements are usually small and have a tightly knit membership. They also exist in some degree of tension with the surrounding culture, since they often consider conventional society to be corrupt.

Stark and Bainbridge also distinguish among "audience cults," "client cults," and "cult movements." Audience cults are loosely organized groups whose primary mode of expression includes lectures, conferences, and meetings through which a variety of esoteric and unconventional teachings are communicated. This form of cultic activity tends to be ephemeral, and its attendees generally remain mere consumers of the audience cults' books, pamphlets, and products. Prominent examples of audience cults include much of what passes for "New Age" religion and various UFO-related groups.

"Client cults" have a higher degree of organization than audience cults, and the relationship between members and leaders resembles the relationship between therapists and clients. Some client cults attract a large number of adherents, but these adherents remain individual consumers of a technique or practice and rarely are organized into a social movement. Indeed, adherents of client cults regularly maintain active commitments to other religious organizations. Prominent examples of client cults are est (Erhard Seminars Training) and its offshoots Lifespring and Actualizations.

"Cult movements," in this limited sense, are comprehensive organizations that try to satisfy all the religious needs of members. Typically, they demand a high level of commitment and personal sacrifice and see themselves as instrumental in bringing about needed changes in society. The longer a member remains in this form of cultic organization, the more difficult it becomes to leave its ranks. Cult movements usually place a high priority on missionary outreach and on the recruitment of new members. Aggressive recruitment practices have been a major focus of societal unease with these movements. The International Society for Krishna Consciousness, the Family,

The front page of the Heaven's Gate cult's website as seen on March 27, 1997, shortly after the group's mass suicide.   (Credit: AP/Wide World Photos.)

and the Church Universal and Triumphant are prominent examples of cult movements.

Researchers have observed that both sect and cult movements tend to change over time, most often in the direction of increasing accommodation to the norms and values of the larger culture. As one example of such change, the Church of Jesus Christ of Latter-day Saints (commonly referred to as Mormons), a cult movement founded in the 1830s, dropped its practice of polygamy and its proscription of black men in its priesthood in response to societal pressures. The Holy Order of MANS, an independent New Age community founded in 1968, slowly accommodated itself to mainstream Christian norms and joined the Eastern Orthodox Church in 1988.

As recent history has proved, some cult movements can become dangerous both to their own members and to society at large. Aum Shinrikyo, a Japanese movement, released poisonous Sarin gas into the Tokyo subway system in 1995, killing and injuring more than one thousand people. Heaven's Gate, a UFO religion founded during the 1970s, committed mass suicide in 1997 to rendezvous with a spacecraft said to be trailing the Hale-Bopp comet. For people who find themselves involved in such groups, anti-cult organizations such as the American Family Foundation rec-

ommend extensive psychotherapy to facilitate disengagement and subsequent reentry into society. The goals of this therapy are: (1) to help ex-members recognize and come to terms with the abuse and manipulation they may have experienced in a cult movement; (2) to help ex-members manage the psychological disorientation and crises of self-esteem that often occur once they have left their former community; and (3) to facilitate the ex-member's reconnection to family, old friends, and personal goals. Some ex-members find a new sense of purpose in their lives by speaking out publicly about their "cult" experience and by warning society of the dangers of unconventional religions.

During the past thirty years, anti-cultists and academic researchers have often found themselves at odds over the putative dangers posed by cult movements to American society. As a result of the anti-cult movement's skillful use of the news media, a great deal of misinformation has been fed to the general public. The common misconceptions concerning cult movements include:

1. Cult movements have many members and are growing rapidly. In fact, the proportion of the general population who belong to cults at any

one time is fairly small. The best evidence available—based on meticulous counting—indicates that there are about 200 viable cult movements at the present time, and their aggregate membership is 150,000 to 200,000 members. Most cults have 200 to 2,000 members, peak in membership within their first 10 to 20 years of existence, and then rapidly decline. The exceptions often go on to become established denominations, such as the Mormons, Jehovah's Witnesses, and Seventh-day Adventists.

2. Cult movements are led by abusive, greedy criminals who exploit their followers for their own personal gain. Certainly, there have been instances in which a group's leader became progressively more abusive and self-serving, but this is not the norm. Most movement leaders sincerely believe in their religious vision, are law-abiding, and are committed to serving humanity along with their followers. No institution in modern life is free of persons with criminal inclinations, but this does not mean that the institution itself is a criminal operation.

3. The only reliable account of what a cult movement is like comes from ex-members. Although former members can often provide useful insights about the inner workings of a group, their accounts cannot be taken at face value. Often, people in the midst of leaving a relationship of any kind tend to display a selective memory about their past partners and are inclined to amplify negative aspects of a person or group. Moreover, there have been instances in which therapists and anti-cult counselors coached former members to accept a prefabricated "script" concerning their involvement.

4. Brainwashing has been proved to exist in cult movements. On the contrary, the vast majority of scholars have concluded, from their research in the field, that nothing that resembles the "brainwashing" techniques employed by North Koreans against American POWs exists in cult movements. Rather, they have discovered that people who join cults do so of their own free choice as part of a search for a meaningful way of life. Researchers have also found that most members leave when they want to, in spite of group pressures to have them remain.

Cult movements have long been part of American religious culture. Their growth during the late twentieth century, however, may be one indicator of an increasingly pluralistic religious environment and the continuing breakdown of the Protestant hegemony that began during the early twentieth century.

See also ANTI-CULT MOVEMENT; BELONGING, RELIGIOUS; BRAINWASHING; CHURCH UNIVERSAL AND TRIUMPHANT; CULT AWARENESS NETWORK; ELVIS CULTS; FAMILY, THE; FREEDOM OF RELIGION; INTERNATIONAL SOCIETY FOR KRISHNA CONSCIOUSNESS; NAMES AND NAMING; NEW AGE SPIRITUALITY; NEW RELIGIOUS MOVEMENTS; PROSELYTIZING; PSYCHOLOGY OF RELIGION; PSYCHOTHERAPY; RELIGIOUS COMMUNITIES; SECT.

BIBLIOGRAPHY

Beckford, James. *Cult Controversies: The Societal Response to the New Religious Movements.* 1985.

Bromley, David G., and Jeffrey K. Hadden, eds. *Religion and the Social Order.* Vol. 3, *The Handbook on Cults and Sects in America,* Parts A and B. 1993.

Dawson, Lorne. *Comprehending Cults: The Sociology of New Religious Movements.* 1998.

Jacobs, Janet Liebman. *Divine Disenchantment: Deconverting from New Religions.* 1989.

Langone, Michael D., ed. *Recovery from Cults: Help for Victims of Psychological and Spiritual Abuse.* 1993.

Lucas, Phillip Charles. *The Odyssey of a New Religion: The Holy Order of MANS from New Age to Orthodoxy.* 1995.

Stark, Rodney, and William Sims Bainbridge. *The Future of Religion: Secularization, Revival and Cult Formation.* 1985.

Phillip Charles Lucas

Cult Awareness Network

During the cultural upheavals of the 1960s and 1970s, a significant number of American teens and young adults broke away from conventional religious communities and began a search for spiritual fulfillment. At the same time, numerous new religious movements (NRMs)—both Christian and non-Christian in orientation—emerged claiming to offer salvation and mystical enlightenment. College students appeared especially open to religious experimentation during this period, and many joined these alternative spiritual communities. Not surprisingly, the parents of these students were upset upon learning that their sons and daughters had dropped out of school or left jobs to join high-demand communities that engaged in strange ritual practices and were critical of normative societal institutions. Oftentimes, membership in an NRM also coincided with a sudden break in family relations. Out of these family problems were born local groups of parents, such as Free the Children of God (FREECOG), whose mission was to warn society of the dangers of "cultic" groups and to rescue young people—by force if necessary—from their grasp.

Eventually these local groups saw the need for a national organization and formed the Citizens' Freedom Foundation. This group had fifteen hundred members by 1975. Between 1976 and November 1978 the "anticult movement" began to decline due to infighting and tax problems. What survived were local groups of parents who were concerned with cult activity in their city. The groups typically published a newsletter, sponsored programs to inform local citizens about the dangers of alternative religions, and helped anxious parents get in touch with "deprogrammers."

In November 1978 the Jonestown community in Guyana engaged in collective suicide, and the resulting public outcry gave the anti-cult movement, and the Citizens' Freedom Foundation, a new lease on life. Throughout the 1980s the foundation, which was renamed the Cult Awareness Network (CAN), spearheaded the anti-cult movement on the national level. It had a paid staff of four and a national network of volunteers. CAN's literature described itself as "a national, tax-exempt nonprofit educational organization, dedicated to promoting public awareness of the harmful effects of mind control." The organization sold anti-cult books and videos and collected information about alternative religious communities. It also organized a support group for former cult members called Focus. CAN spokespersons such as Cynthia Kisser regularly appeared on national news programs to warn of the growing danger of new religions.

In the 1990s CAN was forced into bankruptcy when it lost a lawsuit brought by a young man in a Pentecostal church in Washington State. The plaintiff, Jason Scott, had chosen to stay with the church when his mother left after a disagreement with church leaders. Scott's mother contacted Shirley Landa, a volunteer for CAN in Seattle, Washington. She helped the mother get in contact with professional "deprogrammer" Rick Ross. Ross kidnapped Scott and held him for five days against his will in an attempt to get the youth to change his beliefs. The deprogramming was unsuccessful, and Scott subsequently won a historic $1.8 million judgment against CAN. This judgment—which has been upheld on appeal—coupled with lawsuits brought against CAN by the Church of Scientology led to the network's demise on June 21, 1996.

In an ironic denouement, lawyer Steven L. Hayes, a member of the Church of Scientology, purchased CAN's name, logo, P.O. box, and toll-free phone number in bankruptcy court. To its credit, the new CAN has made every attempt to connect anxious parents with NRM scholars who have researched particular groups and can thus provide an informed perspective on their beliefs and practices.

See also ANTI-CULT MOVEMENT; BELONGING, RELIGIOUS; BRAINWASHING; CULT; FREEDOM OF RELIGION; NEW RELIGIOUS MOVEMENTS; PROSELYTIZING; PSYCHOLOGY OF RELIGION; RELIGIOUS COMMUNITIES; SCIENTOLOGY, CHURCH OF.

BIBLIOGRAPHY

Bromley, David G., and Anson Shupe. *Strange Gods: The Great American Cult Scare.* 1981.

Shupe, Anson, and David G. Bromley. *The Anti-Cult Movements in Cross-Cultural Perspective.* 1994.

Phillip Charles Lucas

Culture Wars

Contemporary politics in the United States is often described as involving a "culture war." The central claim of those describing a culture war is that the major political cleavage in contemporary American politics is no longer economic class, race, gender, geographical region, or any of the many "social structural" differences that divide our population. Rather, the idea is that a major realignment of sensibilities and controversial issues has occurred since the 1960s, and now the body politic is rent by a cultural conflict in which values, moral codes, and lifestyles are the primary objects of contention. Issues such as abortion, homosexuality, pornography, and drug use are the typical points of culture wars contention; others have used the phrase to discuss issues of multiculturalism, diversity, and school curricula. Religious commitments, symbols, and groups have been strongly connected to culture wars politics.

The "culture war" idea has been promoted by journalists, academics, campaigning politicians, and social movement activists. The most developed and systematic academic version of the thesis appeared in sociologist James Davison Hunter's 1991 book *Culture Wars: The Struggle to Define America.*

The Genesis of the Culture War Idea

In *The Restructuring of American Religion* (1988), Robert Wuthnow argued that since World War II, changes in American culture and institutions—in particular the rise of mass access to higher education, and the divisive politics of the civil rights struggle and the Vietnam War—had produced a new cleavage in American religion: The older divisions of Protestant, Catholic, and Jew have been crosscut by a liberal-conservative divide running through all three groups. Where religious and denominational identity, largely articulated in terms of doctrine, theology, and religious practices, had once been the focus of conflict, now issues of ideology and culture crosscut identity divisions. As a result, conservative Protestants, for example, now have more in common with conservative Catholics and Jews than they do with liberal Protestants.

Martin Marty (1970) articulated another restructuring when he noted the "public-private" dichotomy in American religion. Marty distinguished public from private denominations by their attitudes and strategy toward the church and society. Public groups articulated a plan of social reconstruction through institutional change, and they entered the public arena through political and social activism. In the 1950s and 1960s these were the liberal, mainline denominations. Private groups understood change as occurring through a "hearts and minds" strategy of individual conversion, generally eschewing public politics. Evangelical Protestant denominations represented this orientation. The rise of the Christian Right in the late 1970s, among other changes, has led scholars to question this particular distinction.

Hunter's *Culture Wars* expanded the scope of Wuthnow's claims even as it narrowed the source of, and explanation for, the conflict. Hunter divided Americans into two opposing camps, the "orthodox" and the "progressives," based on a single dimension, where they locate the source of moral and social authority. The orthodox believe that authority emanates only from transcendent sources—that is, authority is external to society. Progressives, on the other hand, find authority within society, in human-generated knowledge, moral codes, and culture. This division is intractable, in Hunter's view, and has an internal logic that leads inevitably to escalating conflict. While the origins of these worldviews clearly relate to religious outlooks, culture war proponents claim that the division between the sides has expanded beyond religion, into secular politics. Hunter's book had a tone of urgency and sweeping analyses that painted a gloomy portrait of our political present and future; similarly, most other academic and journalistic accounts of the culture war find the conflict to be uncompromising and growing. Indeed, Hunter maintains that even recognizing the potential authenticity of the rival worldview can be a threat to the authority and coherence of one's own. This leads away from moderation.

Testing the Culture Wars Idea

A number of scholars have begun to test these assertions with a variety of empirical evidence. In general, whether one studies individual attitudes, subcultural values, political party dynamics, or culturewide ideological currents, the culture wars ideological divide is found to be overly simplistic. Careful analysis of American public opinion finds it more diverse and complex than the culture wars idea will admit. Further, it is clear that "cultural warriors" such as politician Pat Buchanan are more successful in generating media attention than in winning elections.

Nonetheless, if it is articulated broadly enough, there is something in the culture wars idea. Certainly the rhetoric resonates with portions of the electorate, and because it does, it can be a successful mobilizing metaphor for certain kinds of politicians and issue activists. Also, several of the most contentious and passionate issues in current politics revolve around what can be called "cultural" issues. The culture wars idea calls attention to the extent to which politics is more than just a matter of dividing the economic pie. The symbolic aspects of our collective life are great sources of both conflict and solidarity. People do act in the public arena on the basis of assumptions about what the "good society" is, what we must do to achieve it, and what constitutes a "moral" life. Sometimes these assumptions about the public moral order are indeed incompatible with rival assumptions; and when moral worldviews align with social structural differences, political conflict can turn from civil politics to cultural war. In sum, a broad reading of "culture wars" has much to recommend it and has great relevance to American politics, where religion has often been and continues to be a potent force.

However, the narrower version of the culture wars idea ignores a crucial paradox in American politics. That paradox is built on the tendency of American political institutions to produce centrist solutions, while social movement–style politics tends to inflate rhetorical and ideological differences into cultural "war." Institutional pressures force political parties and interest group organizations into behaving more and more similarly. But social movement activists need dire and dramatic symbols to motivate people to action. Thus organizational pressures are centripetal even as ideological tendencies are centrifugal. Institutions aggregate differences, force compromise, and facilitate crosscutting cooperation. Social movements polarize political identities and tend toward uncompromising, moral absolutist rhetoric. Too many culture wars proponents mistake the latter for the central feature of American politics, when in fact it is but one dimension. And this leads to the clear implication that the culture wars idea is both simultaneously true and mistaken.

See also ABORTION; CHURCH AND STATE; DRUGS; EVANGELICAL CHRISTIANITY; LIBERATION THEOLOGY; MAINLINE PROTESTANTISM; RELIGIOUS RIGHT.

BIBLIOGRAPHY

Gitlin, Todd. *The Twilight of Common Dreams: Why America Is Wracked by Culture Wars.* 1995.

Green, John C., James L. Guth, Corwin E. Smidt, and Lyman A. Kellstedt. *Religion and the Culture Wars: Dispatches from the Front.* 1996.

Hunter, James Davison. *Before the Shooting Begins: Search for Democracy in America's Culture War.* 1994.

Hunter, James Davison. *Culture Wars: The Struggle to Define America.* 1991.

Marty, Martin E. *Righteous Empire.* 1970.

Nolan, James, ed. *The American Culture Wars: Current Contests and Future Prospects.* 1996.

Williams, Rhys H. "Is America in a Culture War? Yes—No—Sort of." *The Christian Century* (November 12, 1997): 1038–1043.

Williams, Rhys H., ed. *Cultural Wars in American Politics: Critical Reviews of a Popular Myth.* 1997.

Wuthnow, Robert. *The Restructuring of American Religion: Society and Faith Since World War II.* 1988.

Rhys H. Williams

Cursillo Movement

Roughly translated as "short course" in English, Cursillo refers to an intensive weekend retreat experience and includes both opportunities for individual spiritual renewal and the ensuing evangelical activities of small groups formed from the weekend retreat participants.

Originating in Spain during the 1940s and drawing its initiative from a major pilgrimage to the shrine of St. James of Compostela, Cursillo owes its genesis to the restless response to a lukewarm spirituality that characterized post–civil war Spain. As pilgrimage has long been a method for experiencing this kind of spiritual restlessness, the Cursillo has maintained and built upon this pilgrim spirit. The weekend retreatants are handpicked for their leadership skills as well as for the presence of this pilgrim spirit, seen as an asset for returning to the community and aiding in a larger spiritual renewal within the parish. To this end, the Cursillo members return to the parish willing to aid in sacramental and educational events designed to enliven the parish and prompt the congregation to a deeper relationship with Christ.

According to a World Wide Web page maintained by Andrew Lang, the first Cursillo in the United States was held in Waco, Texas, in 1957 and was organized by a Roman Catholic priest and two Spanish airmen who were training in Texas with the U.S. Air Force. After being transferred to a new base in Mission, Texas, the two airmen soon established another Cursillo weekend, and the tradition began to take off from there.

The basic elements, with surprisingly little regional (or even denominational) variation, are the pre-Cursillo, in which the prospective participants are identified and invited; the weekend experience itself; and the "Fourth Day," a term comprising the ongoing involvement in the Cursillo community.

During the pre-Cursillo, veterans of Cursillo weekends who are participating in their own "Fourth Day" are assembled to offer sponsorship for participants, to serve as planning and implementation teams for the weekend experience, and to commit to the enduring community encouraged by the Cursillo format. The Cursillo weekend itself follows a specific format designed to gradually draw the participants into a comfortable sharing atmosphere, with increasingly evocative activities culminating in a deeply prayerful experience on Saturday evening of the weekend. The "Fourth Day" refers to a lifelong commitment to one's spiritual promises made during the weekend retreat. These include community with participants from one's own weekend in the form of weekly "reunions"; the "Ultreya," a monthly meeting of several cadres of "Fourth Day" participants; and spiritual direction, a person to be sought by each individual in either the clergy or the laity with whom the participant can share his or her spiritual walk in a mentor relationship.

This format and the spiritual principles undergirding the movement have found their way into Protestant congregations as well, mostly in the Episcopalian and Anglican communities. In addition, the Cursillo Movement has been adopted as a model by other subgroups within church communities such as Marriage Encounter, Search youth retreats, and addiction recovery programs.

See also PILGRIMAGE; RETREAT.

BIBLIOGRAPHY

http://www.westtexasonline.org/cursillo.htm
http://www.natl-cursillo.org/index.html
Marcoux, Marcene. *Cursillo: Anatomy of a Movement: The Experience of Spiritual Renewal.* 1982.

Dennis Kelley

Cyber Religion

ENIAC, the first modern computer, was a room-sized machine. Built in the 1940s by IBM, it required specially conditioned air to function and could perform only simple mathematical calculations. By the late 1990s, computers with capacities far exceeding those of ENIAC had no special environmental requirements, could easily fit on a desktop, and had portable counterparts that fit inside a briefcase.

One of the most fascinating uses to which the rapidly evolving computer was put was communicating with other computers via a protocol across telephone lines through a modem. Begun as a strategic defense initiative by the U.S. Department of Defense, the first computer network, ARPANET (Advanced Research Projects Agency Network), was established in 1969 to provide an assault-proof communications network for key strategic defense installations. As of the early 1980s, computer communication networks had spread to institutions of higher education and business corporations, and from there to the general populace. A major criticism of this expansion was that the general populace who had access these networks was not truly general, but geographically clustered in first world, industrial, and postindustrial nation-states that possessed sufficient infrastructure and economic excess to support their development.

The Internet is the term used for this conglomeration of interconnected computer networks, with a similar stand-alone network called the Intranet. The initial uses of the Internet included electronic mail (or e-mail), transferring files (via ftp protocols), bulletin boards and newsgroups (Usenet), and obtaining remote computer access (via Telnet). In 1989, two graduate students—Tim Burners-Lee and Mark Andreeson—independently devised the idea of the World Wide Web (WWW), a globally interconnected set of web pages readable from any computer in the world that is hooked into the Internet, and a software program to access them known as a browser. Within two years the WWW became the most active aspect of computer-mediated communications.

Introduced by science fiction author William Gibson in his 1984 novel *Neuromancer,* the term "cyberspace" refers to the part-imaginative/part-concrete experience of place people have when they are engaged in computer-facilitated electronic communications. At its most basic, cyber religion refers to the presence of religious organizations and religious activities in this semi-imaginative place.

Traditional and alternative religious groups have almost unanimously concurred that cyberspace is a place where they will be active; consequently there are thousands of religious Usenet groups and electronic mail discussion lists, a host of religious Intranets, and official web sites on the WWW for almost every major world religion along with web sites detailing the doctrines of countless new religious groups. In a typical religious organization's web site, web surfers (as people who explore the WWW came to be commonly called) can find an introduction to the religion that describes its official history, its major beliefs and rituals, and its sacred texts, and a directory for local groups.

One significant effect of the move into cyberspace by an incredibly diverse collection of religious groups is the appearance of new instances of convergence and cooperation among them. It is not at all rare for the web site of a Christian group espousing strong millennial beliefs to be linked to a Jewish Zionist web site, for example. Cyberspace also has become a place where a significant amount of popular religious expression takes place. By the late 1990s it was common for people who had novel religious experiences at large parachurch events to congregate afterward in cyberspace to confirm the experiences and to support each other. It also became commonplace for religious groups experiencing considerable tension with society to use the WWW to communicate their stance on issues to the wider world. One of the more infamous such uses of the web by a religious group occurred with the alternative religious community Heaven's Gate. Shortly after thirty-nine members of the group were found dead on March 25, 1997, it was discovered that Heaven's Gate had posted a farewell statement to the world on its web site. Another significant consequence of cyber religion has been the gradual emergence of new, electronically inspired religious practices and ideas. As religious groups grew accustomed to maintaining a presence in cyberspace, they developed innovative uses of computer-mediated communications for spiritual practices. These included online global prayer chains, e-prayer wheels, and even online multiuser religious rituals. In a more mundane vein, they also included a plethora of online religious instruction and cyberspace-linked social justice activism.

Among the more provocative developments to arise from the intersection of cyberspace and religion were repeated attempts by some to launch pure cyber religions—that is, religions whose sole existence was in cyberspace. To many, these attempts raised problematic questions regarding the value of face-to-face human contact. Equally innovative and no less controversial was the onset of various hybrids, as people associated with traditional religions attempted to relate their faith to and through the new medium. One early innovator was Jacque Gaillot, a Roman Catholic bishop. Finding himself reassigned from the French diocese of Évreux to the diocese of Partenia, an obscure, largely nonexistent site located somewhere in the Sahara, after criticizing on French television orthodox Roman Catholic positions on subjects such as priestly marriage, Gaillot declared himself bishop of cyberspace and ministered to those who contacted him via a Partenia web page.

With cyberspace still in its infancy, many important questions about the character and import of cyber religion remain unanswered. It is unclear whether cyber religions attract new people to religion or religious practice or merely provide a new means of communicating with or supporting those already involved. It is also uncertain whether the phenomenon of cyber religion intrinsically contains the potential to alter the character of the religious traditions that have rushed to embrace it—akin to the dramatic manner in which the printing press made possible serious challenges to the traditional authority structure of Christianity in the Latin West.

See also HEAVEN'S GATE; JOURNALISM, RELIGIOUS; NEW RELIGIOUS MOVEMENTS; PUBLISHING, RELIGIOUS; TELEVANGELISM.

BIBLIOGRAPHY

Brasher, Brenda E. *Give Me That Online Religion.* 2000.

Cobb, Jennifer. *Cybergrace: The Search for God in the Digital World.* 1998.

Zaleski, Jeff. *The Soul of Cyberspace: How New Technology Is Changing Our Lives.* 1997.

Brenda E. Brasher

D

Dalai Lama

(1935–), spiritual leader, head of state.

Born Lhamo Dhondrub on July 6, 1935, in the small Tibetan village of Taktser, Tenzin Gyatso (as he was later renamed) was formally enthroned as the Fourteenth Dalai Lama in Lhasa, Tibet's capital, on February 22, 1940. In the ensuing years, His Holiness the Dalai Lama has clearly emerged as the world's foremost Buddhist, both within and without the traditionally Buddhist world. He has traveled to all the continents except Antarctica and has spoken to millions of people in numerous cultures. He has authored several dozen books—nearly a hundred, if one includes edited transcripts of his talks and teachings, which have been translated into over thirty languages, with bestsellers on record in Germany, France, Italy, England, and recently the United States. He is present in published audio and video tapes and has appeared on television in most countries of North and South America, Australia, Southern and Southeast Asia, and Europe, including Russia, Japan, Taiwan, and even mainland China.

He received the Nobel Prize for Peace in 1989, in recognition of his tireless application of the spiritual principles of nonviolence and reasoned dialogue to the tragic situation the Tibetan people have suffered since 1949 under China's genocidal invasion, occupation, and colonization of Tibet. He has been more and more universally recognized as the living successor to Gandhi and Martin Luther King Jr. in spiritually directed, nonviolent, political activism. In an increasingly complex postcolonial, postindustrial, postmodern world of economic injustice, environmental degradation, and ethnic violence, he is the main Buddhist spokesperson holding out hope for a positive future for all humanity, for the restoration of a healthy environment, and for the reconciliation of conflicts, both ancient and modern.

In the United States, the Dalai Lama has very few detractors, other than Maoist sympathizers, who wrongly consider the old Tibet to have been a "medieval, feudal, theocratic" society of horrors that deserved the Maoist destruction, or corporate or political advocates of "engagement" with China, who consider it any industrial power's right to do whatever it wants with its own "indigenous minorities" and thus regard the Dalai Lama as an irritating embarrassment.

In religious circles, the Dalai Lama has a special aura, due to his resolute refusal to proselytize or convert anyone to Buddhism. When approached by enthusiastic followers, his constant refrain is that it is better for people to retain the religion with which they grow up and, if they so desire, intensify their practice with philosophical, meditational, or ethical methods borrowed from other religions or from secular humanist psychologies. Of course, he applauds the freedom of a modern, pluralistic society that allows people to choose their own religious path (he often jokes that he approves of the usually derogatory concept of a "spiritual supermarket"). He does not hide the fact that he likes the Tibetan Buddhism with which he was raised, and he makes himself available to American Buddhists to give whatever teachings they request, provided he can fit them into his busy

The Dalai Lama smiles as he observes the large crowd that has come to hear his outdoor lecture at the Tibetan Buddhist Learning Center in Washington, New Jersey, May 7, 1998. (Credit: AP/Wide World Photos.)

schedule. His priority when traveling is always clearly his representation of the plight of the Tibetan people, seeking help from politicians and diplomats in getting the Chinese to moderate their hard-line policies and overtly destructive practices.

Among American Buddhists, the Dalai Lama is consistent in applying his pluralistic principles: He makes a point of not criticizing the practices of Theravada, Zen, Pure Land, Nichiren, or any other national forms of Buddhism, and within the various schools of Tibetan Buddhism he does not uphold the Gelukpa order in which he was primarily educated as if its teachings were superior to those of the other orders. In the 1970s before he was able to visit the United States (he was officially blocked until 1979 by the Kissinger policy of alliance with the Communist Chinese against the Soviet Union), there was a strong strain of sectarian competition between the various forms of Buddhism in America, especially between the various orders of Tibetan Buddhism. He calmed these waters enormously during his early teaching tours in 1979 and 1981, when he visited all the new centers and demonstrated his in-depth knowledge of all the traditions and his appreciation of their various strengths and advantages. Further, in line with his basic policy of discouraging hasty conversion to Buddhism, he was always clear that those who felt they had to convert should realize this to be their per-

sonal choice, not to criticize their original religion as having been defective in general, and to respect family and friends who are better able to find satisfaction within their original faiths. In these ways, the Dalai Lama has had an immensely positive impact on Buddhism and on interreligious relations in the United States.

See also BUDDHA; BUDDHISM; ECUMENICAL MOVEMENT; TIBETAN BUDDHISM.

BIBLIOGRAPHY

Dalai Lama. *Freedom in Exile: The Autobiography of the Dalai Lama.* 1991.

Piburn, Sidney, and Claiborne Pell, eds. *The Dalai Lama, A Policy of Kindness: An Anthology of Writings by and About the Dalai Lama.* 1999.

Robert A. F. Thurman

Damnation.

See Hell.

Dance

Dance and religion began together; dance was an early expression of man's relationship to the earth, to the establishment of community, and to the cosmos. In the Jewish and Christian traditions, however, dance and the body became separated from the soul and the spirit. In contemporary postmodern cultures, many people who have been feeling a sense of alienation and unease from this separation are searching to bring back embodied practices to religion and spirituality. As this shift takes place, dance therapy, as a practice that brings back the body into expressions of the sacred, has an important role to play to restore the balance between mind and body, harmonizing the connections among the individual, the community, and the cycles and forces of nature.

Sacred Dance

Dance, expressing the human relationship to creation and to the gods, had sacred roots. By imitating the motions of the celestial order, primitive humans understood patterns of the divine. The body, its movement, food, drink, breath, and sexuality were all understood as sacred channels through which power could enter.

The mysteries of creation were celebrated through the patterns of the dance. The earliest religious experiences were experienced physically, as the deity was felt to enter and transform participants. The early Greek writer Lucien noted in his book *On Dances* that all mystery inductions were associated with dance, and that Orpheus's prescription for those being introduced to the mysteries was to receive them with dancing.

The floor plan of ancient churches reflected the movements of procession around an altar, while the repetition of pillar and arch induce an altered state of consciousness. Plato was reported to have said that the circle connected the human to cosmic patterns.

Basic to all mystery celebrations in the Mediterranean was the ring dance. The celebration of the Eleusian mysteries "was combined with a ring dance which appears to have begun when the spirit emerged from its symbolic underworld journey and reached the splendid fields of the blessed" (Backman 1972, p. 3).

A group of itinerant healers in fifth-century B.C. Greece known as the *orpheotelestae* danced around the sick, usually in the form of a ring. In the Middle Ages, ring dances were used to protect newborn children against evil spirits. Midsummer festivals, still performed in Scandinavia, originated with pagan dances in which dancers would go to the streams, dance in a circle around a fire, heap flowers, and leap through the flames, purging themselves with smoke and fire.

Line dances also had sacred origins. In the first century B.C., a Jewish sect called the Therapeutae would eat a sacred meal, have a night watch, then perform a dance in which one line of males and one line of females would stand facing each other. Alternating singing and stillness, moving forward and backward, they would imitate and celebrate Moses' crossing of the Red Sea.

Dance as an Altered State

Dance induced a form of knowing that was ecstatic, intuitive, and revelatory, and that involved cyclical time.

As a heightened form of life that had its origins in its original relation to the gods, its connection to the sacred through form, patterns, and transformative consciousness, dance was the original form of devotion:

> The dance is the mother of the arts. Music and poetry exist in time; painting and architecture in space. But the dance lives at once in time and space. The creator and the thing created, the artist and the work are still one and the same thing [Sacks, p. 5].

Religion and the Body

As the matriarchial earth-based religions were replaced by patriarchial conceptual systems, the body and bodily arts were lost. Some attribute the shift particularly to the fourth-century saint Augustine of Hippo, who "... placed virginity, celibacy and continence as the highest good in Christian life" (E. G. Cowan unpublished manuscript, p. 41). Hierarchies of intermediaries between the individual and God and dogma replaced direct revelatory knowing. Although sacred dance survived, it existed as performance rather than as communal participation.

Religious practices have changed dramatically during the past forty years, however. Affected by the social and political revolutions of the 1960s, the women's movement, Vatican II, and AIDS, individuals have been searching for new forms of practice. Gays and lesbians have challenged ordination practices, and women have challenged the church's ban on abortion and contraception. Single parents and interfaith couples have challenged traditional religion, while the abstraction and rigidity of some religions have sent members to seek a more direct and participatory experience with the divine. Buddhism, with its emphasis on direct experience and contemplative practices, has attracted many disaffected seekers. Neopagan rituals and Goddess celebrations have become popular for some, while others search for their roots in the wilderness or in born-again fundamentalism. Many take up Yoga or t'ai chi, going to Eastern religions to bring back embodied practices. The result has been an enormous American melting pot, or spiritual smor-

Justin Nesahkluah, a Kiowa Apache from Anadarko, Oklahoma, performing a traditional Native American dance during an intertribal Pow Wow at the W. H. Sommer Park in Peoria, Illinois. Performing such dances, as he has since he was a boy, is a spiritually uplifting experience for Nesahkluah. (Credit: AP/ Wide World Photos.)

gasbord. The advantages of this movement include the freedom to explore a spirituality tailored to one's own lifestyle; the disadvantages include too much individualism, gullibility, and the potential for the rise of cult messianic figures. For many who attempt to cobble together an eclectic mix of practices in a postmodern society, difficult decisions about how to raise children and combine practices remain.

Symptoms of the dark or "shadow" sides of religious practices today include not only such phenomena as clergy sexual abuse scandals and massacres like that at Jonestown but also the institutional churches' reactions to attempted innovations. For example, in his "Letter to the Bishops of the Catholic Church on Some Aspects of Christian Meditation," Joseph Cardinal Ratzinger's Congregation for the Doctrine of the Faith (formerly the Office of the Holy Inquisition) warned that meditation could become a "cult of the body" and could "lead to psychic disturbance and, at times, to moral deviations" (*San Francisco Chronicle,* December 16, 1989).

Dance Therapy: Bridge Between Spirit and Body

Dance therapy was founded in 1966, as ". . . the psychotherapeutic use of movement as a process which furthers the emotional and physical integration of the individual" (American Dance Therapy Association 1973–1974). Dance therapists use movement for diagnosis and treatment; movement reflects patterns of coping, defenses, memories, inner states, and relational patterns that are concretized as qualities in relation to space, time, weight, and flow. Dance therapy in a group setting has powerful precedents as a healing art, particularly during times of social breakdown. For example, after World War II, community dance or *Bewegungschor* (movement choirs) became popular across Europe. Started by the Hungarian architect and dancer Rudolf von Laban, these movement choirs were performed by young and old alike and, like other Utopian movements, expressed hope for an ideal and better society: "It is at this point where the healing force of the arts and particularly dance are seen as vital. Increasingly I feel that part of the struggle for ordering our lives in thought, feeling, and action can be facilitated through the crystallization of such movements of revelation and discovery into group ritual dance" (Bartenieff 1974, p. 122).

Dance therapy sessions often show elements of ancient sacred dance practices. For example, group members often spontaneously repeat archetypal motions of scattering and gathering, of rising and falling, of stomping and clapping, in a process of psychological and physical regeneration. The circle and its center, essential to sacred dance, are still used in dance therapy to start sessions and to provide a sense of boundary, inclusion, and closure. In many modes of dance therapy, particularly those derived from the Chace method, reintegrating the patient back into the group circle through the use of rituals is central to healing. Dance therapists often involve the whole group, or the whole clinic center staff and patients, choreographing rituals to celebrate new members, old members leaving, changes in community, and in season. Finally, the predominance of women dance therapists echoes the prominence of women as early religious and ritual leaders.

See also BODY; DIVINITY; LIVED RELIGION; MUSIC; PRACTICE; PSYCHOTHERAPY; RELIGIOUS EXPERIENCE; RITUAL; SUN DANCE.

BIBLIOGRAPHY

American Dance Therapy Association. *ADTA: Writings on Body Movement and Communication. 1973–1974.*

Backman, L. *Religious Dances.* 1972.

Bartenieff, I. "Exploring Interaction Through Ritual Structure. Therapeutic Process: Movement as Integration." In *Proceedings of the Ninth Annual Conference, American Dance Therapy Association,* pp. 118–123.

Batchelor, S. *The Awakening of the West: The Encounter of Buddhism and Western Culture.* 1994.

Chaiklin, S. "Dance Therapy." In *American Dance Therapy Association Proceedings. Fourth Annual Conference,* pp. 25–32.

Geller, J. "The Body, Expressive Movement and Physical Contact in Psychotherapy." In *The Power of Human Imagination: New Methods in Psychotherapy,* edited by J. Singer and K. Pope. 1978.

Needleman, J. *The New Religions: The Meaning of the Spiritual Revolution and the Teachings of the East. 1974.*

Sachs, C. *World History of the Dance.* 1937.

Serlin, I. "A Psycho-Spiritual Body Approach to a Residential Treatment of Catholic Religious." *Journal of Transpersonal Psychology* 21, no. 2 (1989): 177–191.

Serlin, I. "Body as Text: A Psychological and Cultural Reading." *The Arts in Psychotherapy* 23, no. 2 (1996): 141–148.

Serlin, I. "To Buddhism and Back." *Lilith* 1, no. 2 (Fall 1988).

Singer, J., and K. Pope, eds. *The Power of Human Imagination: New Methods in Psychotherapy.* 1978.

Tucker, M. *Dreaming with Open Eyes: The Shamanic Spirit in Twentieth Century Art and Culture.* 1992.

Ilene Ava Serlin

Da'wa

The Muslim word *da'wa* can be translated, approximately, as "bearing witness." It is an invitation to the Way of Allah. The Qur'an (16:125) says, "Invite [all] to the Way of your Lord with wisdom and beautiful preaching and argue with them in ways that are best and most gracious." Muslims, in the United States and elsewhere, believe that the message of God given to the Prophet Muhammad is the same as that given to other prophets, including Abraham, Moses, and Jesus. Whenever Muhammad's name is mentioned, Muslims always declare, "Salla Allahu Alayhi wa Salam." ("Peace and blessing be upon him.") The Qur'an (37:37) says that Muhammad has "come with the [very] Truth and he confirms [the message] of apostles before him." Muslims also believe that it is incumbent on them to invite others to the worship and service of the one true God.

Abul A'la Mawdudi, a major modern-day Muslim revivalist, points out that bearing witness by means of da'wa is the most important duty entrusted to Muslims by God. The Qur'an repeatedly reminds Muslims of this duty toward God and their fellow beings (e.g., at 2:143, 3:110, and 5:8), and declares at 2:140, "And who is a greater wrongdoer than he who suppresses a witness entrusted to him by God?"

Despite the weight of this obligation, a Muslim's responsibility has parameters spelled out in the Qur'an (16:125), to "invite [all] to the Way of your Lord with wisdom and beautiful preaching and argue with them in ways that are best and most gracious. . . ." The limits of responsibility are demarcated where the Qur'an says, at 46.9, that Muhammad was not saying anything of his own but is only "a warner open and clear." Muslims are also aware of the etiquette of offering the invitation. The Qur'an says that Moses, who was sent to Pharaoh, was advised by Allah to "speak to him mildly . . . perchance he may take warning or fear."

The practical example of this attitude toward the followers of other faiths is apparent in the confessional makeup of Muslim countries and even of Muslim societies of the past. Muslims, upon entering Jerusalem under the leadership of the second caliph Omar, were welcomed by the Christian clergy. Despite this, the caliph did not pray in the church, signaling that religious places were inviolable. Muslim Spain had thriving Jewish and Christian populations; India, after more than a thousand years of Muslim rule, had only a Muslim minority; and Jews who were expelled from Christian-conquered Spain were offered asylum in Ottoman Turkey.

Da'wa's Pivotal Role

The centrality of da'wa in Islam is evident from the fact that even within the *Zakaat*—the obligatory alms giving for the needy from one's earnings—system there is a provision whereby a portion can be paid to a non-Muslim to mellow his or her heart toward Islam and Muslims. Muhammad Hamidullah has written that the two interrelated aspects of the Prophet Muhammad's life were the propagation of Islam and his treatment of non-Muslims. In undertaking da'wa, the Muslim can commit it through words or action. Soon after receiving the Revelation and being instructed on the mode of prayer, the Prophet—as his biographical accounts mention—occasionally prayed publicly with his wife Khadijah in front of the Ka'bah at a time when the people of Mecca had never seen such a mode of prayer.

In the postcolonial period, da'wa has increasingly moved from its traditional sense of inviting others and has expanded to include calling on Muslims themselves to return to Islam, to more fully and self-consciously reappropriate their Islamic identity and be observant in the practice of their faith—both reform and renewal. Muslims are increasingly striving to put the Islamic system into practice, with efforts such as establishing Islamic schools and financial institutions. Such efforts, they feel, will entice others to look into the merits of the tradition of Islam.

Mawdudi (1986) advises Muslims to let their "lives speak the truth, and let the world hear it [not] merely from our lips but also from our deeds; let mankind witness all the blessings that Divine guidance brings to human life."

Etiquette of Da'wa

Da'wa is but an invitation, and the *da'i* (inviter) should observe appropriate etiquette toward the invitee and not cause annoyance in any sense to the listener of the message. The da'i should not expect that his addressee will conform to his ideas but should fully recognize the freedom of the addressee to accept or reject his ideas. Yahiya Emerick, himself a revert to Islam, advises the da'i to talk *with* the listener and not *at* him. He should accept the rejection of his ideas with utmost tolerance and respect, since the Muslim is told by God in the Qur'an (2:143), "We have made you a moderate community that you may be a witness to humanity even as the Messenger is a witness to you."

An essential etiquette of da'wa that is advised by the Prophet and all Muslim scholars is to illustrate the message by living it. One such example from the Prophet's life is the incident when a mother asked him to admonish her child for eating too much sugar. Instead of advising the child immediately, he asked her to bring her son the next day. When she brought him as asked, the Prophet not only dispensed his guidance but also informed the mother that yesterday he himself was enjoying a piece of hard sugar and thus was not morally in a position to advise the child.

See also CONVERSION; ISLAM; MISSIONARY MOVEMENTS; PRACTICE; PROSELYTIZING; PSYCHOLOGY OF RELIGION; QUR'AN.

BIBLIOGRAPHY
Emerick, Yahiya. *How to Tell Others About Islam.* 1996.
Hamidullah, Muhammad. *The Emergence of Islam,* edited and translated by Afzal Iqbal. 1993, 1995.
Manual of Da'wah for Islamic Workers. 1989.
Mawdudi, Sayyid Abul A'la. *Our Message.* 1992.
Mawdudi, Sayyid Abul A'la. *Witness unto Mankind: The Purpose and Duty of the Muslim Ummah,* edited and translated by Khurram Murad. 1986.

Omer Bin Abdullah

Day of the Dead

Rituals of honoring the dead rank among the most important spiritual traditions for Chicanos and Mexicanos on both sides of the United States/Mexico border. Rooted in Mesoamerican indigenous practices of welcoming, nourishing, and communicating with the dead on a cyclical basis, the tradition reinforces cosmologies that understand death to be complementary to life—an aspect of life not to be feared, but to be honored. Through communing with the dead, the living are nourished and life continues.

In Mexico, evidence of rituals for the dead exist from 1500 B.C.E. Among the Mexica, the ninth and tenth months of their eighteen-month calendar year were devoted to rituals for the deceased children followed by rituals for the deceased adults. Special altars offering flowers, foods, drinks, incense, and wood-carved images of the dead enhanced the public cere-

A Latino woman, her face painted in a festively ghoulish manner, celebrates the Day of the Dead in Los Angeles, ca. 1997. (Credit: CORBIS/Richard Cummins.)

monies and sacred dances. Following the introduction of Spanish Christianity in the sixteenth century, the Catholic feasts of honoring the dead on November 1 and 2 merged with the indigenous traditions as structural and ideological similarities between the practices facilitated a fusion. In both religious traditions, the dead were regarded as protectors of the household and were entitled to particular rites. During the Christian vigil, the souls in heaven returned in spirit to bless the households where they had died. For the Mexica, during the last three days of the tenth month, the dead came back to interact symbolically with their families. The dead in both theologies did not hold power in their own right, but functioned as intermediaries and intercessors before the respective deities. A complex integration of the traditions occurred rather than a simple syncretism.

The celebration of the dead today varies in many parts of Latin America and the United States, depending on several variables, including religious and ethnic identity, acculturation, and class. In 1972, Chicana/Chicano artists and cultural workers in California reintroduced the tradition to Chicano urban populations. Self-Help Graphics, a community art center in East Los Angeles, held its first Day of the Dead celebration as a form of healing for a community devastated by police brutality during Vietnam War protests. By the early 1990s, schools, colleges, community centers, and galleries throughout the United States held their own Day of the Dead celebrations.

Ofrendas (offerings) placed on family and/or public altars are the mainstays of the ritual observance, in addition to cemetery visits and graveside offerings. The style and elaborateness of the offerings vary, depending on aesthetics, income, and the influence of Catholic and/or indigenous ways. Symbols from both religious traditions can easily coexist on an *ofrenda* (offering) representing a *mestiza* or *mestizo* spirituality. The *cempasúchil* (marigold flower), with its bright color and strong scent, leads the dead to the altars. Candles, incense, photographs, food, and drink that the dead enjoyed while living enhance the offering. Sugar skulls colorfully decorated represent "the icon of our dual existence" and are playful reminders of human mortality. Pottery, memorabilia, embroidered cloths, and toys for the children present only the best of material possessions for the dead. Ofrendas reflect the aesthetics of the living as much as those of the dead.

Catholic observances traditionally focus on the Eucharistic celebrations of November 1 and 2 to honor the dead. As the centrality of the ofrenda receives wider recognition by pastoral agents, some church communities are constructing Day of the Dead altars inside their sanctuaries.

Public celebrations on both sides of the border reflect a very festive mood as the living joyously remember their loved ones. In many parts of southern Mexico, overnight visits with food, music, and drink at the cemetery unite a family as they accompany their dead. Processions, plays, and musical entertainment characterize many of the celebrations in the United States. The festivities also provide a time to present Chicana or Chicano art and poetry reflecting themes of bringing death and life to Latino communities. While these public celebrations might appear to be very secularized, the underlying spiritual orientation of communing with the dead shapes all the activities. This tradition holds political as well as cultural and spiritual significance as marginalized ethnic communities in the United States claim public space to annually honor the dead in a society that generally limits "death" to the few days preceding and following a funeral. Many non-Latinos appear to be attracted to the tradition, as it facilitates an ongoing relationship with deceased loved ones.

See also BELONGING, RELIGIOUS; DEATH AND DYING; LATINO TRADITIONS; MESTIZO WORSHIP; POPULAR RELIGION; RELIGIOUS COMMUNITIES; RELIGIOUS EXPERIENCE; RITUAL; SOCIOLOGY OF RELIGION; SPIRIT.

BIBLIOGRAPHY

Garciagodoy, Juanita. *Digging the Days of the Dead.* 1998.

Hoyt-Goldsmith, Diane. *Day of the Dead: A Mexican-American Celebration.* 1994.

Lara Medina

Deacon

The office of deacon has a long history in the Christian church. In the New Testament, deacons were included in the list of church leaders along with bishops or presbyters. Deacons were charged with caring for the poor, collecting offerings, and serving the church. The Greek word *diaconos* means "servant" and is used to describe a church leader (Phil 1:1). As church offices evolved, the diaconate came to be both a lifetime office for some and an early stage on the way to full ordination to the priesthood. Deacons were charged with gathering and distributing alms to the poor and needy. In the Middle Ages the office of archdeacon represented the chief among deacons, a post often identifying an assistant to the bishop.

Among Roman Catholics, Vatican II returned the twofold nature of the deacon's office, permitting life tenure for deacons, even allowing them to be married if the marriage is prior to ordination. These lay members assist the clergy in caring for the needs of parishioners. While they cannot consecrate the sacraments, they can distribute the Eucharist in churches, homes, and hospitals where no priest is available. The office of deacon also remains an early stage on the way to full ordination as a priest.

Protestants have made wide use of the deacon's office. For many communions—Episcopal, Lutheran, and Methodist, for example—the deacon's office is usually an early step on the way to ordination as a priest or pastor. In those traditions it also may be a permanent office. In Roman Catholic, Anglican, Swedish Lutheran, and Orthodox communions the deacon is ordained in the presence of a bishop and with the laying on of hands. Presbyterians number deacons among their four offices along with pastors, teachers, and elders. Among Baptists, deacons and pastors are the two ordained officers of the church. The diaconate is a lay office, serving in some churches as a type of governing board and in others as a group of spiritual caregivers. During the 1980s and 1990s many Baptist leaders urged churches to emphasize the servant role of deacons. Some congregations developed "deacon family ministry" plans by which individual deacons had specific spiritual care for specific segments of the membership. Some Baptist churches formally ordain deacons with the laying on of hands, a ceremony also used in the ordination of official clergy. Others simply elect deacons without a service of ordination.

In some Baptist churches the question of the ordination of women as deacons remains controversial. The local autonomy of congregations means that some Baptist churches choose to ordain women deacons while others reject the practice. Opponents insist that there is no biblical precedent for the practice, citing certain texts that call for the silence of women in church, and their subordinate role in church leadership. Those who ordain women deacons note various roles for women in the New Testament church, including that of servant, or *diaconos*. They also note that some of the earliest Baptist churches utilized women's services as deacons or deaconesses in the seventeenth century.

See also CHURCH; CLERGY; MAINLINE PROTESTANTISM; MINISTRY; ORDINATION; ORDINATION OF WOMEN; PARISH; PASTORAL COUNSELING; PRIESTHOOD; ROMAN CATHOLICISM.

BIBLIOGRAPHY
Abbott, Walter M., ed. *Documents of Vatican II.* 1966.
Deweese, C. W. *The Emerging Role of Deacons.* 1979.

Bill J. Leonard

Death and Dying

Death is an event that demands explanation. Every human society has recognized the importance of orienting its members to the phenomenon of death, the process of dying, and death's aftermath. So powerful is the event of death, with its demand for interpretation, that it may well have been one of the first causes of religion and philosophy in primitive people.

Ancient Views on Death and Dying

The Hindu religion views life as connected not with concrete personal, historical existence as such, but rather with the concept of being, which is contrasted with both life and death. Life and death are a form of existence, which is not real in the sense that being is real. Therefore, death is not the loss of being as such, but merely the end of the illusion of life as existence in time.

For the Buddhist, the self exists as a sheer moment of becoming in history. Life and death as a process of time and history are fictions that prod the self to discover the liberation of the self from reflection and feeling alike. Death is not an enemy in Buddhist theology; instead it is a goal, which produces a liberation from the cravings and sensations of life.

In ancient Greek philosophy we see a quite different answer to the question of death. Here there is a concern for immortality as a specific object of philosophical reality. Whereas Jews find continuity in the purpose of history as a dialogue with God, Hindus in the Atman as the reality of being, and Buddhists in the contentless moment of not knowing, Greek philosophers seek continuity in knowledge as the eternal reality. Death has been dissolved of its power to destroy the self; because all of life itself in its bodily form is only of passing significance, death, too, is viewed only as a passing away of that which is unnecessary to the true personality of the soul. "True philosophers," Socrates suggested, "make dying their profession."

A common assumption among the Hindu, Buddhist, and Greek concepts of death is a fundamental dualism with regard to the reality of the "otherworldly" and the unreality of this present temporal existence. The individual dying in such a culture, whether an ancient, preindustrial one or a contemporary one, is thus equipped with a religious or philosophical system that transcends death and that can offer experiential training in altered states of consciousness, including symbolic confrontations with death. The approach to death may even be accompanied by the nourishing context of extended family, clan, or tribe, and may even include specific guidance through the successive stages of dying.

A Judeo-Christian theology of death stands in stark contrast to the dualism of the Greek, Hindu, and Bud-

Cardinal John J. O'Connor officiates at the Mass of Christian Burial at New York City's St. Patrick's Cathedral on Thursday, August 1, 1996, for a mother and daughter who died in the crash of TWA Flight 800. Behind O'Connor is New York Mayor Rudolph Giuliani, and in the front pew on the left are members of the deceaseds' immediate family.   (Credit: AP/Wide World Photos.)

dhist theology of life and death. A theology of death within Judaism builds on foundations that are unique to the beginnings of Israel as a historical community, set within the temporal bounds of a created world. For Hebrews, death comes from the hand of God and has no power of its own. Death does not have an arbitrary power to break the continuity of life, because life is related to the continuity of God's purpose in history. The Hebrew understanding of the meaning of death lies with the affirmation that death marks an absolute end of personal existence on earth. Continuity consists, therefore, not in a theory of personal immortality that extends the individual's life beyond death, but instead in the assurance of a future in which there is continuing conversation and relation between God and his people.

There is no concept of an immortal soul in Hebrew anthropology as presented in the Old Testament. The critical issue in the doctrine of the immortality of the soul is the continuity of the self through the dissolution of the body in death. In the biblical view, this continuity resides in the continued power of God, who created the human person in his own image and likeness and who upholds that person in a relation that guarantees life, even in the face of being mortal by nature. In the Christian tradition, continuity of life beyond death in terms of the essential unity of body and soul is strongly supported by the biblical teaching on the nature of the resurrection of the body as well as the soul to eternal life.

There is a close affinity between the Christian and the Jewish perspectives on death. There also remains, however, a fundamental difference. The Christian tradition, building on the foundations of ancient Israel's belief in God as the creator and sustainer of life, answers the question of death through its testimony to the death and resurrection of Jesus Christ.

Contemporary Views on Death and Dying

The typical Western view of death has become more pragmatic and dissociated from religious or philosophical worldviews. Aging and dying are seen not as integral parts of the life process but as reminders of our limited ability to control nature, despite technological and scientific achievements in this regard. The educated Westerner tends to regard belief in consciousness after death as a manifestation of primitive fears and relics of religion. Nietzsche even went so far as to say that fear of death is a "European disease," and attributed it largely to the influence of Christianity. Ernest Becker, in his classic work *The Denial of Death* (1974), argued that an attempt to deny human mortality leads to neurotic patterns of behavior, while accepting the reality of our mortality through faith in a transcendent source leads to faith and mental health.

Death is becoming more difficult to define. Advances in medical science in the last half of the twentieth century have made the moment of death more ambiguous. The empirical sciences explain death in terms of mechanistic and organic processes, with loss of brain function taken as a sign of clinical death. To provide the dying with the maximum benefits of scientific medical research and technology, they are usually institutionalized under the assumption that the vital processes of life are essentially organic and physical. In our contemporary Western society, while the costs of dying and burying the dead have increased dramatically, there is also a denial of the reality of death and a tendency to separate the moment of death from life.

Having compartmentalized death so that we no longer live in continuity with the dead, our contemporary culture is nonetheless preoccupied with an awareness of death such as never before (Bregman 1992). Anecdotal accounts of "near death" experiences give many reason to believe in the possibility of life after death. Persons lying unconscious in wrecked cars or on operating tables awaken and report seeing and hearing events from a perspective that suggests an "out of body" experience. Some report moving through a tunnel toward a bright light, which includes appearances of figures representing persons who have died or supernatural beings. While these experiences are sometimes said to defy scientific explanation, they also fall short of providing evidence for the existence of life beyond death, for they are not "after death" accounts but "near death" experiences.

An encouraging sign of the development of a human ecology of death and dying is the modern hospice movement. The hospice movement, with a focus on caring for dying persons, had its beginning in the founding of St. Christopher's Hospice in London. Dr. Cicely Saunders, founder and director, traces the antecedents of the modern hospice back to medieval hospices, but more recently to Mother Mary Aiden-

head, who used the concept of the hospice when she founded the Irish Sisters of Charity in the middle of the nineteenth century. Dr. Saunders's work at St. Christopher's began in 1967, and since that time the hospice movement has developed in England and has spread to the United States. At the center of the hospice community is the concept of a body coexisting with a belief. The body is the dying patient, and the belief is that the patient is something more than a body. The hospice community embraces patient, family, and close friends, not only during the final days and weeks of the patient's life but also long after death, offering consolation and support during the time of bereavement.

The universality of the human experience of death is finally an individual experience that has not changed from the beginning of human history. Philosophers seek to comprehend it with wisdom, poets inspire us to face it with courage, priests clothe it with sacred ritual, psychologists offer inner healing, and religion weaves the fabric from which we shape our shroud. In the Bible, the tormented Job cries out in his agony, "If mortals die, will they live again?" (Job 14:14). Jesus, the crucified messiah, promises, "I am the resurrection and the life. . . . I am the first and the last, and the living one. I was dead, and see, I am alive forever and ever. . . ." (John 11:25; Revelation 1:18).

See also AFTERLIFE; BODY; DEATH OF GOD; ETHICS; NEAR DEATH EXPERIENCES; RITES OF PASSAGE; SPIRIT.

BIBLIOGRAPHY

Anderson, Ray S. *On Being Human: Essays in Theological Anthropology.* 1982.

Anderson, Ray S. "On Being Human: The Spiritual Saga of a Creaturely Soul." In *Whatever Happened to the Soul? Scientific and Theological Portraits of Human Nature,* edited by Warren S. Brown, Nancy Murphy, and H. Newton Malony. 1998.

Anderson, Ray S. *Theology, Death and Dying.* 1986.

Becker, Ernest. *The Denial of Death.* 1974.

Bregman, Lucy. *Death in the Midst of Life: Perspectives on Death from Christianity and Depth Psychology.* 1992.

Carse, James P. *Death and Existence: A Conceptual History of Human Mortality.* 1970.

Choron, Jacques. *Death and Western Thought.* 1963.

Corr, Charles A., Clyde M. Nabe, and Donna M. Corr, eds. *Death and Dying, Life and Living,* 2nd ed. 1997.

Dumont, Richard G., and Dennis C. Foss. *The American Way of Death: Acceptance or Denial?* 1972.

Foos-Graber, Anya. *Deathing: An Intelligent Alternative for the Final Moments of Life.* 1984.

Grof, Stanislav, and Christina Grof. *Beyond Death: The Gates of Consciousness.* 1980.

Kübler-Ross, Elisabeth. *On Death and Dying.* 1969.

Mills, Listen O., ed. *Perspectives on Death.* 1979.

Mitford, Jessica. *The American Way of Death.* 1963.

Moody, Raymond. *Life After Death.* 1975.

Shneidman, Edwin, ed. *Death: Current Perspectives.* 1976.

Stoddard, Sandol. *The Hospice Movement: A Better Way of Caring for the Dying.* 1978.

Thielicke, Helmut. *Living with Death.* 1983.

Wass, Hannelore, Felix M. Berardo, and Robert A. Neimeyer, ed. *Dying: Facing the Facts,* 3rd ed. 1995.

Wolf, Richard. *The Last Enemy.* 1974.

Ray S. Anderson

Death of God

"Is God dead?" asked *Time* magazine's cover story on April 6, 1966. The article referred to the nineteenth-century German philosopher Friedrich Nietzsche, whose answer had definitely been yes. Nietzsche, however, was not the primary reason for the story. Nor was American atheism. To the contrary, *Time* noted mid-1960s opinion polls, indicating that 97 percent of the American people believed in God and 44 percent attended religious services weekly. A post–World War II religious revival had peaked, but church membership still grew percentage-wise at a rate faster than that of the U.S. population.

Nevertheless, *Time* detected that the twentieth century made traditional religious faith problematic. World War II questioned God's providence, especially as awareness about the Holocaust, Nazi Germany's annihilation of Europe's Jews, began to emerge in full force. At the same time, scientific accomplishments, bolstered by emphasis on human responsibility for the world's future, energized optimism that found little use for a God whose reality was difficult to verify in a secular age. Thus, even if nearly all mid-sixties Americans claimed to believe in God, *Time* reported that fewer than 30 percent identified themselves as deeply religious.

The context for *Time*'s 1966 story included four American theologians who stressed the death of God. Among them was the Jewish theologian Richard Rubenstein. His influential book, *After Auschwitz: Radical Theology and Contemporary Judaism* (1966), was the first by any American to probe systematically the Holocaust's religious implications. After Auschwitz, Rubenstein contended, belief in a redeeming God—one who is active in history—was no longer credible.

The stir caused by *After Auschwitz* linked Rubenstein to three young American Protestant thinkers—Thomas Altizer, William Hamilton, and Paul van Buren—who were dubbed "death of God theolo-gians." Neither the labeling nor the clustering was entirely apt. None of the four was atheistic in any simple sense of the word. Nor were their perspectives, methods, and moods identical. What they loosely shared was the feeling that talk about God could not mean what it had meant in the past. In that respect, the term "radical theology" described their work better than the more sensational phrase "death of God."

Hamilton's essays in *Radical Theology and the Death of God* (1966) emphasized the optimistic mood of secular consciousness. Announcing the end of pessimism, Hamilton saw the late 1960s as a time for celebration and hope. He thought that despair-creating conditions—for example, poverty and racial discrimination—could be overcome by human ingenuity. Such views left little room for the God proclaimed by the Protestant Christian establishment. Van Buren also emphasized the secularity of postwar consciousness, but his book *The Secular Meaning of the Gospel* (1963) concentrated on the issues of verifiability and falsifiability concerning religious language. Given the linguistic criteria that he held at the time, the problem was that declarative propositions about God could not be uttered meaningfully. *The Gospel of Christian Atheism* (1966) displayed Altizer's speculative boldness. Advancing radical concepts of incarnation, it celebrated a rebirth of freedom and set forth a view of history in which all things were being made new. Unlike the three American Protestants, who hailed the death of God enthusiastically, Rubenstein was saddened to conclude that the idea of a God of history lacked credibility after the Holocaust. At least for him, history had shattered a system of religious meaning that had sustained people, especially Jews and Christians, for millennia. To live in the time of the death of God, he cautioned, was scarcely a cause for celebration.

These four diverse thinkers developed overlapping ways of thinking, sometimes independently and sometimes in relation to one another, that drove home the awareness that gods die when the visions they support disintegrate. Their work did not "prove" God's non-existence; it showed little interest in that sort of philosophical argument. Instead the radical theologians' approaches, like Nietzsche's before them, emphasized analysis of current culture and experience. They sensed the onset of a fundamental spiritual change, one that put God's significance into eclipse.

The radical theologians' judgments were less than completely vindicated. Hamilton was too optimistic. Van Buren abandoned his linguistic criteria and returned to theological pursuits, especially those involving Jewish-Christian dialogue. Altizer's work did not sustain the interest it generated in the 1960s and 1970s. Only Rubenstein's post-Holocaust reflection got ongoing attention. Nevertheless, as a group these theologians made important, if unintended, contributions. Far from discouraging talk about God and religion, their questions, protests, criticisms, and alternative visions helped to guarantee an increasing diversity of religious life in the United States.

See also ATHEISM; GOD; HOLOCAUST; HUMANISM.

BIBLIOGRAPHY

Haynes, Stephen R., and John K. Roth, eds. *The Death of God Movement and the Holocaust: Radical Theology Encounters the Shoah.* 1999.

Ice, Jackson L., and John J. Carey, eds. *The Death of God Debate.* 1967.

Ogletree, Thomas W. *The Death of God Controversy.* 1966.

John K. Roth

Death Penalty.

See Capital Punishment.

Deep Ecology

Deep ecology is a new religious movement that believes Western civilization's anthropocentric (human-centered) religion and philosophy is the root cause of a currently unfolding ecological catastrophe. Deep ecologists believe that for humans to live harmoniously with nature they must reject anthropocentric worldviews and resacralize their perceptions of nature as sacred, thus recognizing that nature has intrinsic value (value apart from its usefulness to humans). In the late twentieth century, pagans accurately viewed deep ecology as a kindred form of nature religion.

Deep ecology has greatly influenced grassroots environmentalism, especially in Europe, North America, and Australia. Interest in the movement has spread through road shows and ritual enactments led by touring movement advocates, through the writings of its architects (often reaching college students in environmental studies courses), and perhaps especially through the dramatic activism of the vanguard radical environmental movement Earth First! Participants in this movement probably number in the low tens of thousands.

Arne Naess, a Norwegian philosopher and mountain climber, coined the term *deep ecology* during a 1972 conference in Bucharest, Hungary, and soon afterward in print. He argued that nature has intrinsic

value and criticized "shallow" nature philosophies that only value nature instrumentally.

Naess insisted that there are plural paths to a deep ecological perspective. Indeed, a wide range of religious perspectives, especially indigenous religions (i.e., Native American religions), Buddhism, Taoism, and neopaganism, have influenced those drawn to deep ecology. It is, however, the personal experiences of a spiritual connection with nature and related perceptions of nature's sacredness that ground deep ecological commitments; a secular rationale is almost wholly absent.

Naess's own path to deep ecology began with a mountain-oriented nature mysticism that convinced him of the sacred interrelatedness of all life. He subsequently found in Baruch Spinoza's pantheism and Mahatma Gandhi's notion of self-realization the key ideas upon which he would build his environmental philosophy.

Although Naess coined the umbrella term now used for most nonanthropocentric environmental ethics, many other individuals were contemporaneously criticizing anthropocentrism and developing the new movement's ideas. One crucial event early in deep ecology's evolution was the 1974 Rights of Non-Human Nature conference held at a college in Claremont, California. Inspired by Christopher Stone's influential 1972 law article (and 1974 book), "Should Trees Have Standing: Toward Legal Rights for Natural Objects," the conference attracted many of those who would become the intellectual architects of deep ecology. These included George Sessions, who, like Naess, drew on Spinoza's pantheism and who later coauthored *Deep Ecology* with Bill Devall (1985); the poet Gary Snyder, who in 1969 published *Turtle Island*, asserting the value of place-based spiritualities, indigenous cultures, and animistic perceptions, ideas that would become central to bioregional deep ecology; and Paul Shephard, who argued that people in the world's remnant foraging societies were ecologically superior and emotionally healthier than those living in agricultural societies. Shephard thereby provided radical greens with a cosmogony that explained humanity's fall from a pristine nature paradise.

By the early 1970s, these early architects of deep ecology and the thinkers they drew upon had put in place the central ideas of the deep ecological worldview. Soon additional works, some penned by early participants in Earth First!, such as the movement's cofounder Dave Foreman, Bill Devall, and Christopher Manes were added to the mix. Later works expanded and reinforced the cultural critiques and spirituality of deep ecology. Especially influential were those by Dolores LaChapelle, John Seed, Joanna

Macy, Arne Naess, Warwick Fox, George Sessions, David Abram, and Freeman House.

Since the mid 1980s, deep ecology increasingly has shared ideas, myths, rituals, and personnel with pagan and bioregional groups. (Bioregionalism shares a spiritual affinity with paganism and deep ecology, but its emphasis on developing sustainable lifestyles and redrawing political boundaries to reflect the contours of differing ecosystem types gives it a distinctive name and identity.) The connections among these groups have deepened the pagan and countercultural character of the deep ecology movement. Despite its environmental apocalypticism, deep ecology entered a period of institutionalization, establishing a variety of institutes and organizations to promote its objectives. Indeed, it is its expectation of a biological meltdown that gave the movement its urgent passion to promote Earth's spirituality, a sustainable society, and environmental activism.

See also ECOFEMINISM; ECOSPIRITUALITY; NATURE RELIGION; NEOPAGANISM; NEW AGE SPIRITUALITY; PANTHEISM; RELIGIOUS EXPERIENCE.

BIBLIOGRAPHY

Devall, B. *Simple in Means, Rich in Ends: Practicing Deep Ecology.* 1988.

Devall, B., and G. Sessions. *Deep Ecology: Living As If Nature Mattered.* 1985.

Drengson, A., and Y. Inoue, editors. *The Deep Ecology Movement: An Introductory Anthology.* 1995.

LaChapelle, D. *Earth Wisdom.* 1978.

Macy, J. *World as Lover, World As Self.* 1991.

Manes, C. *Green Rage: Radical Environmentalism and the Unmaking of Civilization.* 1990.

Seed, J., J. Macy, P. Fleming, and A. Naess. *Thinking Like a Mountain: Towards a Council of All Beings.* 1988.

Sessions, G., ed. *Deep Ecology for the Twenty-first Century.* 1995.

Shepard, P. *Nature and Madness.* 1982.

Shephard, P. *Coming Home to the Pleistocene.* 1998.

Snyder, G. *Turtle Island.* 1969.

Stone, C. D. *Should Trees Have Standing—Toward Legal Rights for Natural Objects.* 1974.

Bron Taylor

Denomination

"Denomination" is a term that is often used when describing the variety of Christian religious groups in American life. In the contemporary United States "denomination" is a relatively neutral term, denoting a large, nationally oriented, religious organization based on voluntary membership.

The Denomination as a Sociological Concept

Sociological approaches have attempted to classify the denomination as an intermediate type of religious organization on the church-sect continuum defined by Max Weber and Ernst Troeltsch. This typology poses the church and the sect as two polar organizational types on a conceptual continuum. The church is characterized by its alliance with secular political authority and its goal of worldwide conversion. The pursuit of this goal forces it to compromise its religious ideals with worldly values. The sect is characterized as a small, voluntary band of believers who separate themselves from society to follow a disciplined and ascetic lifestyle consistent with their conception of pure religious values untainted by secular priorities. While these two types are polar opposites of one another, Troeltsch saw them coexisting in a dynamic tension. Because of the conflict between secular and religious values, Troeltsch saw the existence of the church as a continual impetus for the formation of revolutionary sects. He also saw that successful sects would inevitably be drawn toward the worldly values characteristic of the church.

There is a tendency among some scholars to view the denomination as an advanced or mature form of the sect (Niebuhr 1929). It is argued that the sect-type organization is inherently difficult to sustain over time for two reasons. First, the religious fervor of the original members is seen as diminishing with succeeding generations of followers. Second, the disciplined ascetic lifestyle practiced by sect members is likely to lead to worldly success that will consequently make separation from the secular world more difficult for successive generations. H. Richard Niebuhr (1929) predicted that as the sect develops, the institutionalization of its original charisma inevitably results in an increasing pressure to make compromises with secular values, resulting in the "denomination." However, J. Milton Yinger (1946) noticed that the process of accommodation was not inevitable. In some cases, sects were able to maintain their separation from society over succeeding generations, resulting in what he called "established sects," among which he classified such groups as the Quakers, Amish, and Mennonites.

D. A. Martin (1962) also disagrees with the argument that denominations are a mature form of the sect. He argues that sects generally succeed in maintaining their sectarian character over time, and that denominations such as the Baptists, Methodists, and Congregationalists have tended to possess a denominational character—that is, a pragmatic relationship with society—from the very beginning. He sees the denomination as neither universal in the churchly sense nor sectarian, but as defined by a unity of experience. Organizationally he sees the denomination as pragmatic and instrumental. Sacramentally, he sees the denomination as being defined by subjective individualism. Martin feels that the denomination is in part a reflection of the social environments found in Britain and the United States, specifically as they are characterized by liberalism, individualism, pragmatism, and consensual pluralism.

The Denomination as a Theological Concept

Although the term tends to be used in a rather neutral and generic fashion by many scholars, Niebuhr (1929) and his followers have argued that in a theological sense, denominationalism represents a failure of the universal Christian church. In his book *The Social Sources of Denominationalism* (1929), Niebuhr views denominationalism as the unfortunate fragmentation of the Christian churches into various religious bodies organized along class, caste, ethnic, regional, and national cleavages. Niebuhr sees denominationalism as a sign of the moral failure of the values of love, unity, and brotherhood—universal values of the Christian churches—to overcome the divisions of secular society. In this sense, "denominationalism" signifies a condition of failure rather than a neutral description. It is often equated with the term "sectarianism," implying competing and exclusive claims to the authority of Christ.

An alternative view of denominationalism is that put forward by the historian Winthrop Hudson (1955), who sees the original meaning of the term "denominationalism" in a more positive light. His argument is that the true church is not identified with any exclusive type of ecclesiastical institution. No denomination, he argues, can claim to represent the whole church of Christ; rather, "the outward forms of organization and worship are at best but differing attempts to give visible expression to the life of the church in the life of the world." Using historical sources, Hudson argues that as originally used in the United States, "denominalationism" is an inclusive term conveying mutual respect and recognition. He associates the term with the principles of religious toleration and freedom that prevailed in the early part of the nineteenth century and sees it as a response to the problems created by competing Christian bodies that shared a common faith but were divided by differences in church government and worship. In this sense denominationalism is viewed positively, as a flowering of the plural expressions of Christian faith.

Stages of Denominational Development in America

In addition to approaches that have studied the denomination as a theological concept and as part of the church-sect typology, there have been numerous studies of specific denominational histories, and smaller areas of study that have treated the denomination as a voluntary association, as an organization, and as an ethnic group. However, it may be more useful to see these different approaches as being consistent with different stages in the development of the denomination within the context of American history.

Russell Richey (1994) proposes that one can discern five American denominational styles or stages within the historical development of this institutional form. The first stage is located in colonial America and is characterized by what he calls "ethnic or provincial voluntarism." In this stage, religious bodies in America tended to be defined by their ethnic community, and organizationally still viewed themselves as under the authority of the European churches from which they had emigrated. While the First Great Awakening provided some of the dynamics by which these separate groups began to see themselves as theologically part of a wider religious community, their primary identity was still largely ethnocentric.

The second stage is what Richey calls "purposive missionary association" and emerged in the early national period after the American Revolution. In this period, denominations began to see themselves as American institutions rather than as European missionary outposts, and these denominations elaborated a public theology oriented around the construction of a morally ordered civil society. To this end, a number of highly entrepreneurial voluntary societies were launched, devoted to various aims such as proselytization, the formation of Sunday schools, the distribution of Bibles and religious tracts, temperance, and the funding of international missions. Eventually many of these independent agencies were incorporated into the associations of local churches, creating a new form of missionary-oriented denominationalism.

In response to this missionary or purposive denominationalism, Richey identifies the development of a third stage of denominationalism, which he calls "churchly denominationalism." He argues that purposive denominationalism resulted in an identity crisis among traditional elements of the denomination that led to a reemphasis on the traditional markers of ecclesial identity, including the churchly, sacramental, and catechetical traditions. At the same time, the organizational divisions resulting from such explosive issues as the abolition of slavery exposed weaknesses in the theological foundations and organizational authority animating the narrowly instrumental purposes of these denominational movements, and further reinforced the grounding of denominational identity along theological and ecclesiological principles.

In the late nineteenth and early twentieth centuries, denominations entered a fourth stage of development, the "corporate denomination," again propelled by an instrumental approach to missionary outreach. In this stage, denominational leaders adopted lessons from the revolution in organizational management and began to redesign their internal structures into "corporate organizations." Denominational agencies were reorganized, functions were specialized, volunteer staffs were replaced by professionals, and decision-making processes became increasingly dependent on expert, as opposed to ecclesiastical, authority.

The current stage is what Richey calls "postdenominational confessionalism" and is characterized by the loss of a distinct identity to attract and retain members. He argues that the mainline denominations have lost their claim to the larger purpose that previously shaped them: the building of a Christian society. This agenda has instead been captured by evangelical denominations and transdenominational conservative organizations that have transformed "Christian America" into a series of issue-oriented moral campaigns involving abortion, school prayer, family values, and homosexuality. Meanwhile, most denominations are increasingly divided by a liberal-conservative split that results in internal battles over the identity of the denomination and the distribution of denominational resources. All of this has resulted in a collapse of denominational purpose as well as confusion over why denominations should remain together as a unified collective. Richey ends his essay by raising the possibility that denominationalism may have outlived its usefulness.

While the analytical utility and social meaning of the denomination as a concept and as a historical entity may be contested, more than half of the population of the United States claims membership in something called a "denomination," and its empirical reality therefore suggests that it will not fade easily.

See also CHURCH; CHURCH AND STATE; CREEDS; CULT; ECUMENICAL MOVEMENT; HERESY; MEGACHURCH; MISSIONARY MOVEMENTS; NAMES AND NAMING; NEW RELIGIOUS MOVEMENTS; POPULAR RELIGION; POSTDENOMINATIONAL CHURCH; PROSELYTIZING; SECT; WORLD COUNCIL OF CHURCHES.

BIBLIOGRAPHY

Hudson, Winthrop. "Denominationalism as a Basis for Ecumenicity: A Seventeenth-Century Conception." *Church History* 24 (1955): 32–50.

Martin, D. A. "The Denomination." *British Journal of Sociology* 13 (March 1962): 1–14.

Niebuhr, H. Richard. *The Social Sources of Denominationalism.* 1929.

Richey, Russell E. "Denominations and Denominationalism: An American Morphology." In *Reimagining Denominationalism,* edited by Robert Bruce Mullin and Russell E. Richey. 1994.

Troeltsch, Ernst. *The Social Teaching of the Christian Churches,* vols. 1 and 2, translated by Olive Wyon. 1981.

Weber, Max. *Economy and Society: An Outline of Interpretive Sociology,* vols. 1 and 2, edited by Guenther Roth and Claus Wittich. 1978.

Yinger, J. Milton. *Religion in the Struggle for Power.* 1946.

Patricia Mei Yin Chang

Devils, Demons, and Spirits

No formal lines of distinction exist among demons, devils, and spirits, supernatural beings possessed of extrahuman powers and capable of impinging on human affairs. "Spirit" is the most inclusive term, referring to any entity inhabiting an intermediary plane of existence between the mundane and the divine realms. "Devil" is the narrowest term, always referring to malevolent spirits, the evil analogues to angels. "Demon," however, is subject to a wider range of interpretation. The term is from the Greek word *daimon,* which in its earliest usage connoted a divine spirit. When Socrates spoke of his daimon, he was referring to what might now be termed a guardian angel. The early monotheistic sects tended to regard such spirits in a negative light. In the Greek versions of the Hebrew Bible and the New Testament, the term "daimon" is used as a synonym for "devil," and in subsequent Jewish and Christian traditions demons serve as minions of Satan.

In other traditions, however, the moral character of demons and spirits is much more complex. Hinduism, Buddhism, and Shinto feature both compassionate and malicious demons. There are some evil Native American spirits—monstrous entities such as the Windigo among the Algonquins or the Uktena among the Cherokee. But these are less common than such numinous powers as the Algonquin *manitou,* which can either plague or protect. Similarly, Islamic *jinn* are inherently neither good nor bad, and African diasporic religions such as Vodun (Voodoo) and Santería are centered on mercurial, morally ambiguous spirits who mete loving protection and stern justice in equal measure. A number of traditions, including Neopaganism, revere *genii loci,* the indwelling spirits of trees, mountains, crossroads, and other sacred places.

The Spiritual Landscape

Because so many different religions have taken root in American soil, the spiritual landscape of the United States is extraordinarily rich and variegated. Haitian *mambos* and *houngans,* Cuban *santeros* and *babalawos;* Puerto Rican *espiritistas,* Mexican *curanderas,* Chinese *wu,* Korean *mudang* and *manshin,* Taiwanese *dangki,* Native American dream doctors, evangelical faith healers, New Age channelers, and other ritual specialists in all fifty states traffic in legions of benign and baneful spirits every day.

Many spirits, particularly evils ones such as the *peey* of Hinduism, appear as undifferentiated specters, horrific or nebulous in appearance. Others, such as the *kami* of Shinto or the *lwa* of Vodun, are distinctive components of complex pantheons and are represented through detailed iconographic traditions. (Though the lwa live in compassionate reciprocal relationships with their human followers, there are other Vodun spirits, unambiguously evil entities known as *baka* or *kombinayson,* whom the faithful diligently avoid.) Some demons are the spirits of animals. Yet others are members of the family—ghosts of ancestors who have remained to aid or to vex their descendants.

Immigrant spirits may undergo processes of acculturation. Although Jews once boasted a rich demonological tradition, this was lost during the movement during the nineteenth century to rationalize Jewish belief. Devilish spirits *(shedim)* inhabit the pages of Isaac Bashevis Singer's fictional depictions of East European *shtetl* life, but in contemporary America even Orthodox Jewish communities have abandoned these Old World folkways. Recently, however, *klipot*—"shells" or evil powers—have made a comeback in the context of the popular revival of Kabbalah.

Another example of demonic adaptation may be found in the recharacterization of jinn among African-American Muslims. Although there are incarnations of evil and mischief in Islam in the form of Shaitan or Iblis, many Muslims regard jinn as morally neutral, though their manifestation on the mortal plane always invites concern. Individuals who display extraordinary abilities may be suspected of being jinn who have taken on human form. However, among members of the Nation of Islam, one of the largest African-American Muslim sects in the United States, jinn have been recast as exclusively malevolent and as responsible for the system of racial oppression. It is in this sense that Elijah Muhammad, the major herald of the Nation of Islam, famously referred to white people as "devils."

Conversion may transform one's spiritual perceptions. For example, Haitian converts to evangelical Protestantism typically maintain their belief in the power of the lwa, the tutelary spirits of Vodun. But whereas the lwa appear to most Haitians as deities worthy of love and reverence, they appear to proselytes as devils requiring extirpation. Charismatic Christians also identify as demonic the spirits and energies cherished by New Age practitioners.

Although benevolent spirits make cameo appearances in popular novels and films, evil powers typically get the starring roles. Following the success of *The Exorcist* (1976), Hollywood has produced a great many movies chronicling the sanguinary exploits of hellish spirits, including a series of films about Chucky, a doll infested by a homicidal devil. Millions of readers consume stories of demonic conflict by novelists like Stephen King and Frank E. Peretti. Horrific kami are stock characters in Japanese cartoons *(anime)* and comic books *(manga),* which have found a wide audience in America. Popular fantasy role-playing games such as Dungeons & Dragons, Magic, and Diablo feature spirits from various religious traditions.

Spiritual Warfare

Devils and other malefic spirits represent, for many Americans, abysmal sources of illness and woe. In popular conception, Satan and his subordinates are directly responsible for a range of maladies—medical (epilepsy, cancer, the flu), material (a flat tire, a car crash), psychological (alcoholism, depression, delinquency), interrelational (spousal infidelity, filial insubordination, parental abuse), and social (abortion, pornography, drug abuse, unemployment, crime). Devils accomplish their work by adopting human forms, by infesting mortal bodies, by sowing evil ideas in impressionable minds, and by manipulating the natural and material worlds. Charismatic Christians liken their struggle against such infernal machinations to "spiritual warfare."

Although the term is new, the idea of spiritual warfare is not. Battling and exorcising demons has been a prominent feature of popular Christianity in America since the Colonial period. In the 1950s, Pentecostal evangelists such as A. A. Allen (1911–1970) and Oral Roberts (1918–) built popular ministries on "deliverance"—spiritual healing through the repulsion of evil forces. In the 1960s and 1970s, Neopentecostals such as Derek Prince (1915–) and Don Basham (1926–1989) introduced deliverance to a wider audience, including priestly and lay members of the Charismatic Renewal Movement within the Roman Catholic Church.

Charismatic Christians fend off demons through personal and group prayer, healing ceremonies, and rituals of exorcism. The therapeutic process differs for Americans of faith who consult mambos, mudang, curanderas, and other shamans. New Age practitioners have also adapted and developed many techniques for repelling destructive spirits.

Exorcism is not always an appropriate response to supernatural affliction. Sometimes the source of ill fortune is an ancestral spirit seeking to rebuke misconduct by the living. In such cases, relief will be found only by divining and redressing the concerns of the deceased, a process that may involve a shaman becoming possessed by a spirit. Protective measures are also common. Charms, amulets, prayer cloths, oils, incense, crystals, and other articles are sold as guards against evil forces and as channels for benign energies.

See also ANGELS; CATHOLIC CHARISMATIC RENEWAL; EVANGELICAL CHRISTIANITY; EXORCISM; MAGIC; PENTAGRAM; PENTECOSTAL AND CHARISMATIC CHRISTIANITY; SANTERÍA; SATANISTS; SPIRIT GUIDES; SPIRITUALISM; VODUN.

BIBLIOGRAPHY

Andrews, Ted. *Enchantment of the Faerie Realm: Communicate with Nature Spirits and Elementals.* 1993.

Basham, Don. *Deliver Us from Evil.* 1995.

Berg, Philip S. *To the Power of One.* 1991.

Brown, Karen McCarthy. *Mama Lola: A Vodou Priestess in Brooklyn.* 1991.

Cervantes, Fernando. *The Devil in the New World: The Impact of Diabolism in New Spain.* 1994.

Csordas, Thomas J. *The Sacred Self: A Cultural Phenomenology of Charismatic Healing.* 1994.

"Demons and Spirits." In *Encyclopedia of Religion and Ethics,* edited by James Hastings. 1911.

Godbeer, Richard. *The Devil's Dominion: Magic and Religion in Early New England.* 1992.

Goodman, Felicitas D. *How About Demons? Possession and Exorcism in the Modern World.* 1988.

Grim, John A. *The Shaman: Patterns of Religious Healing Among the Ojibway Indians.* 1988.

Hammond, Frank, and Ida Mae Hammond. *Pigs in the Parlor: A Practical Guide to Deliverance.* 1973.

Kendall, Laurel. *The Life and Hard Times of a Korean Shaman: Of Tales and Telling Tales.* 1988.

Linn, Matthew, and Dennis Linn, S.J. *Deliverance Prayer: Experiential, Psychological and Theological Approaches.* 1981.

Martin, Malachi. *Hostage to the Devil: The Possession and Exorcism of Five Living Americans.* 1976.

Mickaharic, Draja. *Spiritual Cleansing: A Handbook of Psychic Protection.* 1989.

Peretti, Frank E. *This Present Darkness.* 1986.

Richardson, James T., Joel Best, and David Bromley, eds. *The Satanism Scare.* 1991.

Sherrer, Quin, and Ruthanne Garlock. *A Woman's Guide to Spiritual Warfare: A Woman's Guide for Battle.* 1991.

Bradford Verter

Dharma

"Dharma" is a key term in religious traditions that originate in India—Hindu, Buddhist, and Jain—but one with several different meanings. Its root in Sanskrit has the sense of "that which supports or holds together," while its variant form of *dhamma* in Pali refers to one of the smallest and most temporary of the several kinds of constituent units that make up the world as it appears to us. Dharma is used in Jainism to refer to the noncreated medium within which all movement takes place. In Buddhism, whether in its Pali or its Sanskrit form, the meaning of constituent unit in

The Wheel of the Law and Deer, a sculpture that symbolically represents the Buddhist concept of dharma, the natural order and the fundamental principles or truths of existence. (Credit: CORBIS/ Luca I. Tettoni.)

the changing world of appearances is complemented by the quite different meaning of the doctrine or teaching of the Buddha that offers an understanding of things that can make it possible to pass beyond the world of appearances. In this latter sense, the teaching (*dharma*) is honored as one of the three gems of Buddhism, along with the teacher (Buddha) and the monastic community (*sangha*). In English any reference to the dharma in the singular almost certainly means the teaching or truth as transmitted by the Buddha.

In Hindu tradition, one of the influential senses of dharma is as the structural power that holds things together and arranges them into a meaningful cosmos. Dharma in this sense is manifested in the order of nature, in the patterns of traditional society, and in the integrity of anyone who appropriately embodies their traditionally prescribed roles and responsibilities. Dharma as a principle of order, along with the dynamic principle of karma (the acts and consequences that generate patterns over time), is one of the most central Hindu ideas and sometimes serves as a synonym for Hinduism itself.

In Hindu thought, dharma organizes by differentiating. The dharma of various people differs in correlation with their birth into a particular genetic (gender, family, kin, and caste) endowment, their marital status, and their current age. A repeated theme in the popular Hindu text the *Bhagavad Gītā* is that it is better to enact your own dharma poorly than another's, however well. The *Gītā* opens with a crisis in which its central character is unable to act consistently with his dharma, and its teachings along with divine intervention allow him to perform it properly. The range of meanings, history, and prestige of the term may give deep seriousness to any situation in which a Hindu speaks of his or her duty, which is a typical way of referring to dharma in relation to present circumstances. How does a Hindu know how dharma applies to him or her and to particular circumstances? This is not a matter left to individual conscience alone, but is supported by an array of traditional authorities, both oral and written, that includes religious specialists attached to temples, study and pilgrimage centers, and families over the generations. As the twenty-first century begins, the modern emphasis on universal rights and responsibilities makes traditional notions of dharma implausible for some people, but reformers such as Mahatma Gandhi have renewed the power of the idea and have brought out its inherently ethical as well as social component.

See also BHAGAVAD GĪTĀ; BUDDHISM; HINDUISM; JAINISM; KARMA.

BIBLIOGRAPHY

Boucher, Sandy, ed. *Turning the Wheel: American Women Creating the New Buddhism.* 1993.

Doniger, Wendy, and Brian K. Smith, trans. and eds., *The Laws of Manu.* 1991.

Ellwood, Robert S., ed. *Eastern Spirituality in America: Selected Writings.* 1987.

Fields, Rick. *How the Swans Came to the Lake: A Narrative History of Buddhism in America.* 1992.

Juergensmeyer, Mark. *The New Cold War? Religious Nationalism Confronts the Secular State.* 1993.

Miller, Timothy, ed. *America's Alternative Religions.* 1995.

Neusner, Jacob, ed. *World Religions in America: An Introduction.* 1994.

Prebish, Charles S., and Kenneth K. Tanaka, eds. *The Faces of Buddhism in America.* 1998.

Smith, Wilfred Cantwell. *The Meaning and End of Religion.* 1964.

Tweed, Thomas A., and Stephen Prothero, eds. *Asian Religions in America: A Documentary History.* 1999.

Williams, Raymond Brady. *Religions of Immigrants from India and Pakistan: New Threads in the American Tapestry.* 1988.

Gene R. Thursby

Dianetics.

See Scientology, Church of.

Disciples of Christ.

See Mainline Protestantism.

Dispensationalism

Dispensationalism is a system of biblical interpretation popular with Protestant evangelicals and fundamentalists. Dispensationalists divide biblical history into different periods, called dispensations, in which God covenanted with humanity in particular ways. Although not all conservative Protestants hold dispensational views, as both a scheme of interpreting the Bible and a popular religious movement, dispensationalism is influential in the United States, where it helped define modern American evangelicalism.

Dispensationalism did not originate in the United States. Historically, Christians identified two dispensations of God's work: the Old Covenant and the New. In each testament, God unfolded a plan of salvation—through Moses or Jesus—effective for a given time. In the 1830s John Nelson Darby (1800–1882), a Church of England minister who founded the Plymouth Brethren, elaborated upon this notion to further decipher biblical history and prophecy. Instead of just two covenants, Darby identified numerous dispensations in the Bible.

Every dispensation follows the same pattern: God issues a command that tests human obedience, human beings fail the test, and God judges their failure. In the Adamic dispensation, for example, God forbade humans to eat from the tree of the knowledge of good and evil. But Adam and Eve disobeyed and ate. Thus, God condemned humans to suffer and die and expelled them from Eden's bliss. Throughout Israel's history, this pattern of testing and judgment continues.

These failures should have prepared Israel to recognize Jesus as the Messiah. However, the Jews again disobeyed God by rejecting Jesus. Accordingly, God might have punished humanity with final destruction. Instead, God postponed judgment until the Jews repent and accept Jesus Christ. Hence, a great "pause" occurred in the biblical timeline. For an undetermined time, the church, God's New Israel, replaces ethnic Israel as the center of biblical history. When the church successfully completes its mission to evangelize the Gentiles, a seven-year tribulation will engulf the world, the Antichrist will deceive humanity, many Jews will finally believe in Jesus, the battle of Armageddon will occur, Christ will return and defeat Satan, and God will establish the kingdom on earth. Unique to dispensationalism is the doctrine of the "secret rapture," the belief that Christians will be snatched from earth by Jesus, who will "catch them up in the clouds" (1 Thessalonians 4:15–17). Although the majority of dispensationalists place the rapture before the tribulation, some locate it halfway through or at the end of the tribulation.

In the United States, influential ministers in the late nineteenth century advocated dispensationalism through revival meetings, Bible and prophetic conferences, and Bible institutes. Many American Protestants became convinced that dispensationalism was the key to unlock biblical prophecy. Even mainline denominations—including the Presbyterians and Episcopalians—had dispensational factions. In 1909 the new Scofield Reference Bible made dispensational theology widely accessible, and the book became a best-seller (expanded in 1917; revised in 1967). In 1924 dispensationalists founded the Dallas Theological Seminary to train pastors for their burgeoning movement.

Although dispensationalism experienced continued popularity with conservatives, it seemed to decline at midcentury with negative public perceptions of fundamentalism. In 1970 Hal Lindsey, a Dallas Seminary graduate, published *The Late Great Planet Earth* as an up-to-date explanation of dispensational teachings. By 1974 Lindsey's book had gone through forty editions and sold four million copies. His rendering of prophecy shaped the political views of the nascent Religious Right, despite dispensationalist pessimism regarding human institutions. Part of Ronald Reagan's appeal to the Religious Right came from his ability to synthesize prophetic concerns into Republican politics and foreign policy. Influential dispensationalists, such as Jerry Falwell and Pat Robertson, retained elements of the theology while adapting it to the politics of the 1980s and 1990s. As of 1999, *The Late Great Planet Earth* remained in print. However, as the century ended, it had been somewhat supplanted by Tim LaHaye and Jerry Jenkins's fictional *Left Behind* series, which repackaged dispensationalism in the guise of political-religious thrillers.

See also EVANGELICAL CHRISTIANITY; FALWELL, JERRY; FUNDAMENTALIST CHRISTIANITY; RAPTURE; RELIGIOUS RIGHT; ROBERTSON, PAT.

BIBLIOGRAPHY

Carpenter, Joel A. *Revive Us Again: The Reawakening of American Fundamentalism.* 1997. Lindsey, Hal. *The Late Great Planet Earth.* 1970.

Marsden, George M. *Fundamentalism and American Culture: The Shaping of Twentieth-Century Evangelicalism, 1870–1925.* 1980.

Sandeen, Ernest R. *The Roots of Fundamentalism: British and American Millenarianism, 1800–1930.* 1970.

Smith, Christian. *American Evangelicalism: Embattled and Thriving.* 1998.

Weber, Timothy P. *Living in the Shadow of the Second Coming: American Premillennialism, 1875–1982.* 1983.

Diana Hochstedt Butler Bass

Divine Light Mission

The Divine Light Mission (DLM) was one of the more controversial and colorful Indian-based new religions that flourished in the United States during the 1970s. The mission had its roots in the Sant Mat tradition of northern India. This Sikh-based religion emphasizes a cosmic sound current that sustains all life and teaches meditation techniques that allow initiates to experience this inner current and thereby gain spiritual liberation. Shri Hans Ji Maharaj, an initiate of both the Advait Mat and Radhasoami branches of Sant Mat, established the Divine Light Mission in about 1960 in India. The movement gained a growing Indian membership during the 1960s, and after Shri Hans's death in 1966 continued under the leadership of his wife, Mata Ji, and their four sons, Bal Bhagwan

Ji, Bhole Ji, Raja Ji, and Maharaji. Maharaji (b. December 10, 1959), the youngest son, soon gained recognition as Shri Hans's successor. In late 1969 Maharaji sent a representative to London to found the mission's first Western ashram. The mission grew slowly until 1971, when the "boy guru" traveled to England, Canada, and the United States. In his many appearances, Maharaji taught a simple message of universal love, peace, and devotion to himself as "Satguru" (literally, teacher of truth), this era's divine incarnation. Maharaji's siblings and mother were also accorded exalted spiritual status and called "the divine family."

Maharaji offered his devotees (called "premies") four secret meditation techniques, collectively called "knowledge." The devotee, after pledging never to reveal the techniques to nonmembers, received initiation in a "knowledge session" from one of the guru's specially trained teachers, or "mahatmas." The techniques consisted, generally speaking, of traditional yogic practices, including: (1) focusing one's closed eyes toward a point in the middle of the eyebrows and meditating on the divine light; (2) closing one's ears with both hands and listening to the divine sound of creation—often using a beragon, or small support stool; (3) a simple meditation on one's breath, sometimes using a mantra; and (4) tasting the divine nectar by rolling one's tongue backward into the cavity of the cranium.

During the early and mid-1970s, thousands of Westerners received "knowledge" and set up ashrams—intentional spiritual communities—in major cities. DLM was incorporated in the United States in Denver in 1972 and soon was holding festivals in both the United States and India that regularly attracted thousands of seekers. The former student radical Rennie Davis became a prominent spokesperson for the mission. Premies took vows of obedience, poverty, and celibacy, practiced meditation, and sang devotional songs to a large image of Maharaji each morning and evening.

The mission underwent major upheavals during the 1970s, mostly related to Maharaji's marriage in 1974 to a California airline stewardess. The marriage prompted his mother to reject him and to attempt to install Bal Bhagwan Ji as the head of the DLM in India. Meanwhile, Maharaji built up a small financial empire and lived in luxurious homes in Malibu and Miami Beach. After closing the DLM's ashrams in 1983, Maharaji changed his movement's name to Elan Vital and became the sole transmitter of "knowledge." Elan Vital organizes Maharaji's teaching tours around the world and distributes videos, audiotapes, and publications under its Visions International subsidiary.

See also ASHRAM; GURU; SIKHISM; YOGA.

BIBLIOGRAPHY

Juergensmeyer, Mark. *Radhasoami Reality.* 1991.
Messer, Jeanne. "Guru Maharaji and the Divine Light Mission." In *The New Religious Consciousness,* edited by Robert Bellah and Charles Glock. 1976.

Phillip Charles Lucas

Divine Principle

Divine Principle is the name given to translations of the basic teachings of the Reverend Sun Myung Moon (1920–), the founder of the Unification Church. These consist of Moon's interpretation of the Old and New Testaments and of history from the time of Jesus up to the period following the Korean War, and are arguably one of the most comprehensive of the theological systems to be found among the present wave of new religious movements. They contain a cosmology, theodicy, soteriology, Christology, historical interpretation, and eschatology with messianic and millennarian features. Scholars have pointed to the influence of Eastern (Confucian and Taoist) thought.

According to the *Divine Principle,* God created Adam and Eve so he could enjoy a loving relationship with them. The plan was that, once they had reached the stage of perfection (having first achieved a level of responsibility), they would be blessed in marriage, with their offspring eventually populating the world. This would enable the "Three Blessings" to be fulfilled: First, the individual would perfect himself or herself. Second, the ideal or true "God-centered" family, as the basic unit for a true society, would be created. Finally, humanity's dominion of love over the whole of creation would be the realization of God's Third Blessing to man. However, the Archangel Lucifer, whom God had given the task of looking after Adam and Eve until they reached sufficient maturity to marry, was jealous of God's love for them and entered into a spiritual sexual relationship with Eve, who then persuaded Adam to have a premature physical relationship with her. The result was that their liaison was not God-centered, and their children and subsequent generations were born with original sin and a "fallen nature." Thus the Fall is seen as the misuse of the most powerful of all forces: love. History is understood as the struggle of certain key persons and nations to restore the kingdom of heaven on earth and to establish the ideal, God-centered family and thus end the suffering that God has been experiencing since the Fall.

Jesus was, the *Divine Principle* teaches, a perfect man who was meant to marry and establish such a family. However, due partly to John the Baptist not unambiguously proclaiming him to be the messiah, Jesus was murdered before he could get married. Subsequent history is seen as a series of parallels between the period between Abraham and Jesus and the past two thousand years. Calculations based on the *Divine Principle*'s numerology reveal that the Lord of the Second Advent would have been born in Korea between 1917 and 1930. Members of the Unification movement have long believed Moon to be this Messiah, but it was not until August 1992 that he made a public announcement that he had achieved this status and that he and his wife were the "True Parents."

A number of scholars have translated, interpreted, and/or developed the *Divine Principle*. It has been expounded and placed within a wider context of both Eastern and Western ideas by some academic Unificationists (e.g., Dr. Sang Hun Lee's *Unification Thought* [1973] and Dr. Young Oon Kim's *Unification Theology and Christian Thought* [1975]). It has also been presented in response to non-Christian perspectives (e.g., *Introduction to The Principle: An Islamic Perspective* [1980] cites passages not only from the Bible, but also from the Qur'an, and *Introduction to the CAUSA Worldview* [1985] poses "Godism"—the Divine Principle—as an alternative to communism). The movement has, furthermore, published a score or so volumes in which non-Unificationist scholars discuss the teachings, either between themselves or with students from the Unification Theological Seminary.

The *Divine Principle* does not, however, encompass all of Moon's teachings. Important developments of Unification theology have been Moon's less widely publicized but ongoing revelations that center around him and his immediate family, explaining the crucial role they have been playing in the restoration process, one of the earliest and most important events being the 1960 marriage of Moon and his present wife. These teachings also include explanations of the significance of rituals such as the Holy Wine Ceremony, which takes place before the marriage blessing, ensuring that the new generation of "blessed Children" will, like Adam and Eve, be born without original sin. Since the mid-1990s, the possibility of having one's marriage blessed has been extended not only to millions of living non-Unificationists (who may be unaware of the Unification understanding of the phenomenon), but also to many more who have passed into the spirit world—a blessing that, we are told, has embraced both saints (such as Confucius, Jesus, and Muhammad) and sinners (such as Hitler, Stalin, and Kim Il Sung). In the implementation of such significant events, Moon's mission is, according to the teachings, now being extended within the spirit world by his son Heung Jin, who died in 1984, and by Mrs. Moon's mother, Dae Mo Nim.

Transcribed versions of Moon's recorded speeches have appeared in more than 230 volumes, and many of these are now available on the Internet (www.unification.net/teachings.html). Edited selections have been published as the *Gathering for Teaching and Learning (Hoon Dok Hae) Series* (15 volumes, 1996–1998), from which members are enjoined to study for about an hour each morning.

See also BELONGING, RELIGIOUS; BIBLE; CHURCH; KOREAN-AMERICAN RELIGIONS; NEW RELIGIOUS MOVEMENTS; PRACTICE; RELIGIOUS COMMUNITIES; RELIGIOUS STUDIES; RITUAL.

BIBLIOGRAPHY

Beverley, James A. "The Religious Teaching of Sun Myung Moon in the English Version of His Sermons and Related Esoteric Unification Documents (1965–1993)." Ph.D. thesis, University of Toronto. 1994.

Kim, Young Oon. *Unification Theology.* 1980.

Moon, Sun Myung. *Exposition of the Divine Principle.* 1996.

Eileen Barker

Divinity

When people refer to something as divine, they employ one of the most basic concepts found in any religion. This generalized idea points to a person or a power that is recognized as superhuman, supernatural, godlike, or supremely good. Every religion around the world contains such references. Most of them in daily use are personifications of the supernatural, portrayed in terms that the local population can understand. Even abstract notions about the divine, such as the "ground of being" or "uncaused cause," still emphasize the importance of divine influence in the world, a presence noticed in events that range from private experiences to cosmic phenomena.

Religions in several parts of the world revere a great many separate divine beings, represented in human and animal forms, male and female. But in contemporary Europe and the Americas the predominant orientation is monotheistic. The oldest such tradition is Judaism, whose exclusivist worship of Yahweh or Jehovah dates back to at least the fifth century B.C.E. Forms of Christianity that evolved from Judaism claim this monotheistic focus, too, holding the three persons of Father, Son, and Holy Spirit as expressions of a single divine being. Islam, the third important faith to emerge in Western culture, professes belief in only one true God, Allah, who is known primarily through revelations made to the prophet Muhammad. Variations and secondary materials related to these monotheistic figures abound, but the primary written sources for information about Jehovah, the Trinity, and Allah are the Hebrew Scriptures (Old Testament and Apocrypha), the Greek New Testament, and the Arabic Qur'an.

Religious expressions are products of the cultures in which they are formed. Interestingly enough, such expressions often continue long after their nurturing cultural context has changed. The Judeo-Christian tradition still perpetuates references to God as royalty—for instance, using words such as "king," "lord," and "majesty"—even though democracies have replaced most monarchies in modern times. This is perhaps proof that concepts of divinity convey the notion of transcendence or distance from the mundane to maintain dignity and to command respect. Sometimes language about God tends to emphasize power and other fearful aspects associated with divinity. These references are accompanied by stress on human sinfulness and the need for repentance. At other times the central features emphasized about divinity are gentleness and warmth. These positive characteristics usually elicit such human responses as love and thanksgiving.

Cultural change has greatly affected references to divinity that are tied to gender language. Traditionally, the three major Western religions have referred to God as a male, describing divinity usually as an elderly, bearded patriarch. This divine person is naturally described as having the physical appearance that is to be found in the varying ethnic cultures around the globe. In contemporary America, however, this male dominance has been challenged. Some theologians argue that any gender references at all are too restricting, but the majority of critics, affected by the women's liberation movement, have called for simple parity. If the divine can be called "Father" and considered almighty in masculine terms, then divinity should also be called "Mother," they argue, and revered as well in nurturing, feminine terms. Those who seek reform in this area also suggest that biblical terminology should either avoid gender specifics completely or use both male and female forms of language when describing divine activity. This contemporary expansion of references to divinity is not debasing the concept but rather highlighting additional characteristics that can enhance human devotion.

On a more philosophical or abstract level, some people maintain that references to divinity should have no connection with gender or human personality at all. Anything that traps God within categories of this world is, they argue, too demeaning to honor the true nature of divinity. So instead of confining the divine to human form, they suggest it is better to think of God as the fundamental cause of all existence, the creative process that is at work in nature, the ultimate law of cause and effect at work in all of physics and morality. Process philosophers continue such reasoning today as a means of keeping discussions of divinity above mundane trivialities. Many others in contemporary America find this approach agreeable because it allows them to infuse religious commitment into their ecological concerns. Seeking the divine in nature as a sublime ideal, they can move beyond the standard Western religious traditions and yet serve high ideals while working to improve the natural environment around them.

American culture today has also produced a number of groups whose adherents seek divinity in ways that are openly antagonistic to the ways mentioned in Judaism, Christianity, and Islam. On occasion people of this sort deliberately call themselves witches, meet in covens, and pursue contact with divine beings known variously as Kore, Gaia, Mother Goddess, and Horned God to worship them. Others lay claim to reviving Neolithic sorcery cults. Feminine references predominate in these forms of worship, but male forms are mentioned, too. As multiple expressions of divinity abound, one finds a range of ideas stretching from polytheism to pantheism. Membership in these modern, expressly "neo-pagan" groups is small, their teachings are variable, and their leadership is more dependent on personal charisma than organizational strength. But the presence of such associations as Feraferia, the Church of All Worlds, and scattered clusters of Wiccans is evidence that modern life displays a great many ways in which people refer to divinity. While most contemporary Americans remain content with traditional references to divinity as described in the Bible and the Qur'an there are those who seek religious affirmation in other philosophical concepts, alternative altars, and speculative lifestyles.

See also ALLAH; GOD; GODDESS; INCLUSIVE LANGUAGE; THEISM; WICCA.

BIBLIOGRAPHY

Farley, Edward. *Divine Empathy: A Theology of God.* 1996.

Johnson, Paul G. *God and World Religions: Basic Beliefs and Themes.* 1997.

Schaefer, Lothar. *In Search of Divine Reality: Science as a Source of Inspiration.* 1997.

Summerell, Orrin F., ed. *The Otherness of God.* 1998.

Henry Warner Bowden

Divorce, Christian

Marriage is understood to be one of the cornerstones of support of the social institution of the family. Interestingly, its genesis and forms remain the subject of controversy, which challenges any conceptualization of it as fixed and stable. For example, marriage has not always been monogamous, and certainly the high divorce rate today illustrates that the "ideal" of a lifelong commitment is countered by the reality of relationships of a much shorter duration. Further, same-sex marriage has been much debated in the past two decades, and as Boswell (1994) illustrates, it may have a longer history than is popularly believed. Despite all this, Christian marriage is most commonly seen as the union of two people of opposite sex before God in a vow to remain faithful to each other for life. Divorce is regarded as the unfortunate termination of that union.

Until relatively recently the solemnization of marriage was under the exclusive purview of the church. While there has been a shift of this function to civil authorities, the majority of people still turn to the church to administer their marriage rites or sacraments. Divorce is discouraged by all churches, although the stigma that attaches to it varies, as do the circumstances in which it will be granted. For example, Roman Catholics must still seek papal approval of their divorces in order to remarry, in essence meaning that they must seek both a civil and an ecclesiastical divorce if they wish to remarry in the Church.

Religion, Culture, and Divorce

The secularization debate adds another dimension to this discussion of divorce. Some scholars argue that religious values that previously discouraged divorce have less and less impact in our society. There is evidence suggesting that religious commitment increases marital satisfaction, thus decreasing the likelihood of divorce (Guttman 1993). However, the increasing divorce rate may have less to do with the influence of the church than with the shift from a model of marriage that emphasized economic union to one based on romantic love. Some churches have attempted to stop the flood of divorce by imposing mandatory premarital counseling. A lower Roman Catholic divorce rate (combined with the more restrictive Catholic approach to divorce) may be evidence of the success of this strategy.

We also need to consider the impact of religion on culture. Religiously rooted traditional beliefs about marriage and its intended lifelong commitment infiltrate civil notions of how families should look and who can be married. State policies protect and valorize the "traditional" family, and legal decisions are imbued with notions of how such families should look. The impact of the Religious Right in its promotion of "family values" on the process of state conceptualization of marriage and family life should not be underestimated (Shriver 1989).

The relationship between civil law and ecclesiastical "law" is also complicated. In the 1970s and 1980s divorce law underwent a radical transformation. Grounds for divorce in North America have greatly expanded, and in some states divorce is routinely considered "no-fault." Waiting periods between filing and finalization of the divorce have been decreased sharply in most states. There is a varying degree of acceptance of civil authority in relation to marriage and divorce. For example, while Protestants accept the authority of the state to marry and divorce, the Roman Catholic church retains jurisdiction over both marriage and divorce.

Women and Divorce

Feminist scholarship in the area of Christian marriage and divorce in the past three decades has focused on the presence of equality within marital relationships, and on the pressure on women to hold a marriage together at great cost to themselves. There is concern that, particularly among evangelical groups, teachings such as the submission of wives and headship of husbands have a detrimental effect on women in that they become "doormats" for their husbands. Yet research indicates that even in the face of such doctrine, women often negotiate their relationships with their husbands as partners, and not as subservient members of the family (Stacey and Gerard 1990; Stacey 1990; Pevey, Williams, and Ellison 1996).

Another concern is that because divorce is strongly discouraged, women remain in abusive relationships in an effort to adhere to church teachings. There is a fear that the emphasis on marriage as a lifetime commitment means downplaying the devastating effects of abuse. It is unclear whether this is in fact the case, as both Christian and non-Christian women who live in abusive relationships are reluctant to give up on them. Religious teachings may facilitate the self-conceptualization of the abused woman as the "suffering servant" who is living her life according to God's will by remaining in an abusive relationship (Beaman, 1999).

Religious Diversity

As we have already seen, to talk about divorce is a bit misleading in that there is not a monolithic approach to this issue among religious groups. For example, the

Church of Jesus Christ of Latter-day Saints views marriage as forever, for our earthly life as well as for all eternity. Tim B. Heaton identifies a number of distinguishing aspects of the Mormon approach to marriage, including their more conservative sexual behavior before marriage, a promarriage attitude, larger family size, and the fact that "Mormons believe in male authority and in a more traditional division of labor between husbands and wives" (1994, pp. 88–89). Divorce rates are lower among Mormon couples, perhaps reflecting the fact that the institution of "family" is central to Mormon theology and religious practice. Family is the basis of social order and development within Mormon culture (Foster 1991, p. 205): "For Latter-day Saints, marriage and family are more than a matter of social convention or individual need fulfillment; they are fundamental to personal salvation" (Holman and Harding 1996, p. 52). Mormon theology sees marriage and the family as being central to human salvation: "only those who have a marriage performed in a Mormon temple are candidates for the greatest rewards in the hereafter" (Heaton, Goodman, and Holman 1994).

Approaches to divorce vary widely among Christian religious groups (Airhart and Bendroth 1996), and it is therefore important to explore the teachings of each church and the social context in which each exists in order to fully understand the significance of divorce within a particular group.

See also CHURCH OF JESUS CHRIST OF LATTER-DAY SAINTS; DIVORCE, JEWISH; EVANGELICAL CHRISTIANITY; FEMINIST THEOLOGY; MARRIAGE, CHRISTIAN; MARRIAGE, JEWISH; RELIGIOUS RIGHT; SECULARIZATION; WOMEN'S STUDIES.

BIBLIOGRAPHY

Airhart, Phyllis D., and Margaret Lamberts Bendroth. *Faith Traditions and the Family.* 1996.

Beaman, Lori G. *Submissive Servants or Purposeful Agents?: An Exploration of the Lives of Evangelical Women.* 1999.

Boswell, John. *Same-Sex Unions in Pre-Modern Europe.* 1994.

Foster, Lawrence. *Women, Family and Utopia: Communal Experiments of the Shakers, the Oneida Community, and the Mormons.* 1991.

Guttman, Joseph. *Divorce in Psychosocial Perspective: Theory and Research.* 1993.

Heaton, Tim B., Kristen L. Goodman, and Thomas B. Holman. "In Search of a Peculiar People: Are Mormon Families Really Different?" In *Contemporary Mormonism: Social Science Perspectives,* edited by Marie Cornwall, Tim B. Heaton, and Lawrence A. Young. 1994.

Holman, Thomas B., and John R. Harding. "The Teaching of Nonmarital Sexual Abstinence and Members' Sexual Attitudes and Behaviors: The Case of Latter-day Saints." *Review of Religious Research* 38, no. 1 (1996): 51.

Pevey, Carolyn F., Christine Williams, and Christopher Ellison. "Male God Imagery and Female Submission: Lessons from a Southern Baptist Ladies' Bible Study." *Qualitative Sociology* 19, no. 2 (1996): 173.

Shriver, Peggy L. "The Religious Right: A Program of Intolerance and Coercion." In *The Religious Right,* edited by Gary E. McCuen. 1989.

Stacey, Judith. *Brave New Families: Stories of Domestic Upheaval in Late Twentieth Century America.* 1990.

Stacey, Judith, and Susan Elizabeth Gerard. " 'We Are Not Doormats': The Influence of Feminism on Contemporary Evangelicals in the United States," in *Uncertain Terms: Negotiating Gender in American Culture,* edited by Faye Ginsburg. 1990.

Lori Beaman

Divorce, Jewish

Divorce, while always regarded as sad, has been permitted in Judaism since the days of the Bible. Even though Genesis 2:24 describes marriage as becoming "one flesh," the Jewish tradition never understood that ontologically—that is, never understood that the husband and wife become one being, impossible to separate—but rather metaphorically, for their unity in sexual intercourse. Moreover, Deuteronomy 24:1–4, in the process of forbidding a man to remarry his original wife after taking another woman in marriage and divorcing her, specifically describes the approved grounds and method of divorce: "She fails to please him because he finds something obnoxious about her, and he writes her a bill of divorce, hands it to her, and sends her away from his house."

The method of divorce prescribed by the Torah is clearly a writ handed to the woman by the man. No court has the power to dissolve the relationship without the husband's act. While this protects the parties from public interference, it leaves the wife in a disadvantageous position. The rabbis of the Mishnah (ca. 200 C.E.) and Talmud (ca. 500 C.E.) tried to mitigate that by spelling out the duties of the husband toward his wife in marriage—duties that required him to provide her with food, clothing, housing, sex, medical care, and redemption from captivity—so that if a husband fails to furnish one or more of these things, the rabbinic court would exert social and ultimately punitive pressure on him either to fulfill his marital duties or to divorce her. In the end, though, in classical Jewish law only the husband can initiate a divorce, and several modern feminists are seeking to change that outright or to mitigate its sexism.

Because American law asserts authority over marital status, a divorcing American Jewish couple must first satisfy the state's requirements. Jewish law, though, also asserts authority over marital status, and it does not recognize the power of any court to substitute for the husband's initiative. To be remarried by an Orthodox or a Conservative rabbi, the couple must also obtain a Jewish writ of divorce (a *get*).

In a small number of cases, one or the other spouse refuses to carry through the procedure of Jewish divorce. If the woman refuses, the court will accept the husband's writ on her behalf and permit him to remarry. On the other hand, if the man refuses to authorize a writ of divorce, the court cannot act in his stead. If the man refuses for good reason—for example, as a means to pressure his former wife to adhere to the civil court's decree granting him visitation rights with his children—then the rabbinic court will not exert any pressure on him to authorize the writ until she complies with the terms of the divorce. If, though, he is simply trying to vex her or even to bribe her, the court will try to convince him to change his behavior, using social pressure if necessary. If that fails, the Conservative rabbinate will annul the original marriage so that she can remarry. The Orthodox rabbinate will not do that, and so a number of Orthodox women are "chained" (*agunot*) to their first husbands, unable to remarry in accordance with Jewish law. To avoid this problem, many Conservative rabbis and a few Orthodox ones use a special marriage contract (*ketubbah*) or write a special prenuptial agreement (*t'nai b'kiddushin*), indicating that the couple agrees that their marriage will be retroactively dissolved if they are divorced in civil law but fail to be divorced in Jewish law.

The Reform movement accepts the civil decree as the substitute for the Jewish writ of divorce. This, of course, simplifies the procedure and ensures a more egalitarian treatment of the individuals involved, but it poses the possibility that some Jews will be ineligible to marry others. Specifically, if a woman does not obtain a *get* before remarrying, her sexual relationship with her second husband is adultery, and her children by her second marriage are illegitimate (*mamzerim*)—disqualified from marrying another Jew for ten generations (Deuteronomy 23:3)!

The ambiguous language in Deuteronomy 24:1 led to a dispute in the first and second centuries regarding the grounds for divorce:

> The School of Shammai says: A man may not divorce his wife unless he has found something improper in her [that is, she violates Jewish law], as it is written, "because

he find something obnoxious in her." But the School of Hillel says, Even if she spoiled his food, as it is written, "because he finds something obnoxious in her." Rabbi Akiba says, Even if he found another more beautiful than she is, as it is written, "She fail to please him." (Mishnah, *Gittin* 9:10)

The law followed the School of Hillel, and so the couple need not show any grounds to justify their divorce; incompatible differences are enough. This is starkly different from the position taken by most forms of Christianity and most American states until the 1970s, where the couple had to show adultery or insanity to justify a divorce.

Even though Judaism does not consider divorce a sin, and even though divorce in some circumstances may be the best thing for all concerned, nevertheless Judaism recognizes that divorce is always sad. It represents, after all, the broken dreams and hopes of the couple, and it inevitably makes life more difficult for any children involved. The Talmud (*Gittin* 90b) declares that the altar in God's Temple sheds tears over divorce.

Thus the Jewish community historically has made every effort to keep marriages intact. Moreover, in Jewish tradition people should get married not so much for love, but rather to fulfill the divine plan for both men and women in enjoying sexual relations, having children, raising them, and caring for each other throughout life. For these reasons, the Jewish divorce rate before the last third of the twentieth century was less than 5 percent. The fact that the Jewish divorce rate in the United States is currently more or less the same as the rate among non-Jews—approximately 50 percent of all marriages—indicates that Jews have adopted America's individualism and its understanding of marriage as primarily a vehicle for romance. Rabbis are increasingly requiring couples to enroll in courses preparing them for marriage to diminish the instance of divorce.

See also DIVORCE, CHRISTIAN; FEMINIST THEOLOGY; JUDAISM; MARRIAGE, CHRISTIAN; MARRIAGE, JEWISH; SEXUALITY.

BIBLIOGRAPHY

Adler, Rachel. *Engendering Judaism: An Inclusive Theology and Ethics,* esp. pp. 198–207. 1998.

Dorff, Elliot N., and Arthur Rosett. *A Living Tree: The Roots and Growth of Jewish Law,* pp. 445–448, 515–563. 1988.

Klein, Isaac. *A Guide to Jewish Religious Practice,* pp. 449–508. 1979.

Orenstein, Debra. *Lifecycles: Jewish Women on Life Passages and Personal Milestones.* Vol. 1, pp. 185–210. 1994.

Elliot N. Dorff

Dobson, James C., Jr.

(1936–), evangelical leader.

James C. Dobson, Jr., is both founder and president of Focus on the Family (FOTF)—an evangelical organization "dedicated to the care and preservation of the home"—and an influential leader of America's Religious Right. Dobson earned a Ph.D. in child psychology from the University of Southern California in 1967. Until 1980 he worked as professor of pediatrics at USC's School of Medicine and remained an attending psychologist at Children's Hospital of Los Angeles until 1983. But it was Dobson's publication of *Dare to Discipline,* which sold 2 million copies in 1970, that established his reputation as the evangelical Dr. Spock and reset his career trajectory toward radio broadcasting. His show, *Focus on the Family, with Dr. James Dobson,* began broadcasting in 1977 over forty-two radio stations. Today Dobson leads FOTF, which has expanded into a multiservice evangelical agency with more than thirteen hundred employees and with an annual budget of more than one hundred million dollars. He also plays a central role in the Family Research Council (FRC), a political action organization

James C. Dobson, president of Focus on the Family, holding a Bible as he addresses attendees at the 1998 Southern Baptist Convention in Salt Lake City, Utah, on June 11, 1998. (Credit: AP/Wide World Photos.)

he launched in 1982 to promote a conservative "family values" agenda at all levels of government.

The key to Dobson's success at FOTF lay in his popularizing combination of contemporary psychology with evangelical faith, a destined-to-succeed combination given the ardent individualism of American evangelicals and psychology's focus on the individual. Moreover, Dobson's world is a simple one—there are those who are on God's side and those who are not, those who recognize sin as the cause of all destructive human behavior and those who do not. Dobson says permissive parenting has failed because it "spares the rod and spoils the child." Children need discipline, including spanking—though Dobson restricts parents with a history of abuse or violent tempers from striking their children and limits spanking to children 1.5 to 8 years old. Likewise, Dobson's sensationalistic, videotaped interview with serial murderer Ted Bundy in 1989—who attributed his actions to the influence of pornography (a claim disputed by experts on violent behavior)—distills tragic and deeply complex behavior down to a single simple cause. Dobson is, to be sure, an unyielding conservative idealist, and his many supporters enjoy the legitimation they find in calling him "*Dr.* Dobson."

This unyielding idealism also undergirds Dobson's political activism. Originally Dobson sought to keep himself and FOTF out of the political spotlight through founding the FRC and locating it in Washington, D.C. (The FRC, along with its thirty-five state Family Council affiliates, are legally separate organizations from FOTF, but pursue an agenda that mirrors Dobson's.) But in 1998, Dobson's frustration with the Republican Party's failure to act on his moral agenda moved him to publicly chastise Republican leaders, threatening to abandon them and form a third party that would not compromise on abortion, homosexuality, or other "traditional family values" issues. While subsequently mollified by Republican leaders, and now within the Republican fold so that he can aid his FRC president Gary Bauer's run for the U.S. presidency, Dobson may still make good on his threat to form a new political party. If so, his legacy may be less his books on parenting and marriage and more how he reoriented the Religious Right and possibly reconfigured the Congress of the United States.

See also EVANGELICAL CHRISTIANITY; FOCUS ON THE FAMILY; JOURNALISM, RELIGIOUS; PSYCHOLOGY OF RELIGION; PUBLISHING, RELIGIOUS; RELIGIOUS RIGHT; TELEVANGELISM.

BIBLIOGRAPHY

Gerson, Michael J. "A Righteous Indignation." *U.S. News & World Report* (May 4, 1998): 20–25.

Novosad, Nancy. "The Right's New Messiah." *Progressive* 60, no. 12 (1996): 20 ff.

Zettersten, Rolf. *Dr. Dobson: Turning Hearts Toward Home.* 1989.

Timothy C. Clydesdale

Dogmatism

Dogmatism is a theory of cognition and personality associated primarily with the work of Milton Rokeach summarized in *The Open and Closed Mind* (1960). Its focus is upon the organization and structure of both belief and disbelief systems rather than upon their content. The widely used Dogmatism Scale allows assessment of Rokeach's major theoretical construct, dogmatism, along a continuum. High dogmatism (closed-mindedness) is characterized by a relatively closed cognitive system of beliefs organized around a core set of assumptions about authority conceived to be absolute. Low dogmatism (open-mindedness) is characterized by a more open cognitive system of beliefs organized around the assumption that authorities are relative rather than absolute.

Associated with the theory of dogmatism is the assumption that certain kinds of primitive beliefs make one especially prone to develop dogmatism. Especially important are the primitive beliefs that individuals are alone and helpless in a hostile and threatening world. This is assumed to give rise to a closed-minded system linking the more cognitive dimension of the theory to personality dimensions associated with psychodynamic theories. High dogmatism is assumed to be essentially the totality of a person's defensive reactions in the face of a threatening world.

The ability to measure dogmatism has made it a useful tool in a wide variety of empirical research. Dogmatism theory is intimately linked with the psychology of religion, as it proposes that religious beliefs can be characterized to the extent that they are held in a relatively open- or closed-minded manner. This is proposed as an advance over earlier research heavily influenced by the authoritarian personality tradition in which certain religious beliefs, particularly fundamentalism, were found to be linked to authoritarianism, a construct initially quite similar to dogmatism. However, while authoritarianism was confounded with belief content, particularly orthodox and conservative beliefs, dogmatism was proposed as focusing on the process of belief rather than its content. Authoritarianism was conceptually linked to conservative beliefs, while dogmatism, at least theoretically, was not. Hence, whether or not religious beliefs were held

dogmatically was essentially conceived as an empirical issue. However, the persistent pattern of empirical research has tended to link dogmatism to more conservative and orthodox religious beliefs, particularly fundamentalism, just as earlier research linked authoritarianism to such beliefs. Dogmatism has seldom been found to be linked to liberal or heterodox religious beliefs.

Associated with dogmatism is the conditional acceptance and rejection of others based on belief content. Not surprisingly, dogmatism has been found to be related to a prejudice toward a variety of groups, particularly blacks and homosexuals. Dogmatism is also linked with antifeminist sentiments. Dogmatic beliefs, based on absolute authority, may only appear as prejudiced in that others who believe or behave in ways at odds with the absolute authority must be rejected. Thus empirical research linking dogmatism and prejudice must distinguish prejudice based on content of belief from prejudice based on process of belief. It is not *what* you believe that characterizes dogmatism as much as *how* you believe. This holds for the rejection of others as well. Rejection may occur for dogmatic or nondogmatic reasons.

Lee Kirkpatrick, Ralph Hood, and Gary Hartz (1991) tried to clarify the content vs. process aspects of dogmatism as it applies to religious beliefs and prejudice. They proposed that while dogmatism can theoretically be conceived independently of particular belief content, when the content of beliefs dictates a belief structure similar to dogmatism, there will be intercorrelations between religious beliefs such as fundamentalism and dogmatism for structural (process) reasons. This is particularly the case in the persistent empirical finding that certain conservative religious beliefs are associated with prejudice. However, when absolute authority is perceived to condemn others for the *content* of their beliefs or practices, *processes* operating within the dogmatic mind-set assure obedience, accounting for correlations between measures of prejudice and fundamentalism only when content is relevant to fundamentalist beliefs.

The fact that belief content and structure overlap in religious fundamentalism in a manner congruent with Rokeach's dogmatism theory suggests that from a postmodern perspective, fundamentalism simply is in a paradigm clash with those who would value more open cognitive systems based on relative and tentative acceptance of a variety of authorities. Fundamentalism's insistence that authority is absolute simply indicates a dogmatic structure that characterizes this one form of conservative Protestantism and is neither conceptually nor empirically true of the wide varieties of other forms of conservative religious beliefs that are neither empirically nor conceptually associated with dogmatism (Hood, 1983; Woodberry and Smith, 1998).

See also FUNDAMENTALIST CHRISTIANITY; PROCESS THEOLOGY; PSYCHOLOGY OF RELIGION.

BIBLIOGRAPHY

Hood, Ralph W., Jr. "Social Psychology and Religious Fundamentalism." In *Rural Psychology,* edited by Allen W. Childs and Gary B. Melton. 1983.

Kirkpatrick, Lee A., Ralph W. Hood, Jr., and Gary Hartz. "Fundamentalist Religion Conceptualized in Terms of Rokeach's Theory of the Open and Closed Mind: New Perspectives on Some Old Ideas." *Research in the Social Scientific Study of Religion* 3 (1991): 157–179.

Rokeach, Milton. *The Open and Closed Mind.* 1960.

Woodberry, Robert D., and Christian S. Smith. "Fundamentalism et al.: Conservative Protestants in America." *American Sociological Review* 24 (1998): 25–56.

Ralph W. Hood, Jr.

Dowsing

Dowsing is a centuries-old type of divination that involves finding water, minerals, and lost objects, and even diagnosing illnesses. Dowsing (also called "water witching," "doodlebugging," and other names) is practiced with the aid of a forked branch, an L-shaped piece of metal held out in front of the dowser, a pendulum, or occasionally the dowser's bare hands.

Contemporary dowsing has its origins in sixteenth-century German mining communities and probably came to New England during the colonial period. Dowsers were commonly used in the nineteenth century to find minerals, before the rise of geology as a science. Even when geologists were available, some companies continued to employ dowsers because they believed dowsing was more effective. In the twentieth century, dowsing was widely practiced throughout the United States, especially in rural areas and in the West. For most of its history dowsing has been local and loosely organized, but in 1961 the American Society of Dowsers was founded in Vermont.

Before this time dowsing was an uninstitutionalized, rurally based oral tradition. Men and women usually learned to dowse from neighbors and relatives and practiced their art in local communities. In the twentieth century, books, how-to guides, and Internet sites have made the practice more accessible to those who want to learn, though some argue that dowsers are born, not made. In *Water Witches,* Chris Bohjalian's 1995 novel about Vermont dowsers, dowsing runs in the family. These dowsers find water for their neighbor's farm as well as for a ski resort, and one of them

A man holds a dowsing rod with both hands as he searches for water in rural Massachusetts, in 1998.   (Credit: © Vincent DeWitt/Stock, Boston Inc./ PNI.)

locates a pilot who was lost in an airplane crash. Contemporary dowsers have located water for orchards and golf courses, found archaeological artifacts, and pinpointed underground tunnels and mines during the Vietnam War. Dowsers are also hired to locate objects from a distance using maps and pendulums.

Dowsing does not require belief in any particular doctrine or deity. Believers in dowsing find meaning in a range of explanations, both natural and supernatural. Some dowsers are Christian, while others might be called New Agers, whose interest in dowsing overlaps with other beliefs in phenomena such as ley lines (lines of magnetic force believed to run through the Earth at specific sites) and psychic healing. Some dowsing advocates say that dowsers intuitively know where water flows, while others suggest that they are influenced by electromagnetic or spiritual forces, both positive and negative. Dowsing, according to another explanation, is possible because the world around us is permeated with an undefined "energy," which humans can make use of if they focus their mind on some particular goal, such as finding water.

Twentieth-century critics of dowsing tended to be scientists, but its earliest opposition came from Christianity, beginning with Martin Luther's proclamation against the "divining rod" in 1518. Branded as Witchcraft from Luther's time on, dowsing has often been associated with alternative and marginal religions—most recently the New Age movement—and folk practices. Skeptics of dowsing abound, such as James Randi (the "Amazing Randi"), a stage magician who offers money to anyone who can pass his dowsing tests. Geologists point out that in areas where water is geologically possible, it will appear anywhere a well is drilled. But contemporary dowsers remain unmoved by attacks on their craft. Their evidence for the success of dowsing is based on different criteria—personal experience and their faith that, for whatever reason, dowsing works.

See also NEW AGE SPIRITUALITY.

BIBLIOGRAPHY

Bohjalian, Chris. *Water Witches*. 1995.
Vogt, Evon Z., and Ray Hyman. *Water Witching U.S.A.* 1959.

Sarah M. Pike

Dreams

The connection of dreams to religion might be best summarized by the widespread notion that "the gods speak through dreams." Dreams are relevant to the experiential dimension of religion, which encompasses many phenomena involving "altered states of consciousness." The 1969 work of the same name edited by Charles Tart covers dreams, meditation, hypnosis, and mystical experience. All of these rarefied states have been cultivated through history by adepts seeking religious visions. Interest in such ethereal states of mind has grown enormously in the United States since the 1960s by seekers and scholars alike.

A few prominent dreams have been recorded in the Hebrew Bible, notably Jacob's dream (at Genesis 28:12) of the ladder reaching to heaven with angelic beings ascending and descending on it, a nice representation of the notion of the accessibility of the divine through dreams. As the history of Judaism continues and Christianity is born, we see fewer references to dreams. In the New Testament, Jesus prefers the language of parables to dreams.

There are some references to dreams in ancient cultures, attested by an Egyptian papyrus on dream interpretation, held by the British Museum (Beatty Papyrus 3) and the *Oneirocritica* (Art of Judging Dreams), a dream handbook in Greek by the second-century physician Artemidorus. There is also the curious practice evidenced on many steles at temples of Asclepios, of sleeping in open porticoes of the temples of the god of healing. Patients would ask the god for a cure for specific medical problems, and these would be communicated through dreams, showing nicely the therapeutic value of dreams.

Probably the greatest emphasis on dreams is found in shamanic traditions of indigenous peoples across the world. Shamans have perennially utilized dreams and other altered states to facilitate "celestial journeying" on various missions. In Australian aboriginal culture, "dream time" is considered just as real if not more so than waking consciousness. The importance of dreams is witnessed also in the extreme attention given to the dream of a child, acted out by the entire tribe, as recounted by Sioux shaman Black Elk.

The steady rise of science and rationalism in Western history seemed nearly to eclipse interest in dreams, which are so manifestly illogical. But toward the end of the nineteenth century scientists eventually began investigating dreams when French archivist Louis Maury (1817–1892) conducted several experiments, such as having his assistant hold a hot iron near his face while he slept, or perfume under his nose, and so on. Each time he noted specific dream imagery correlating well with the experimental actions, such as his dream of wandering through a Middle Eastern marketplace full of pungent smells when the perfume was held under his nose. These data led Maury to the conclusion that dreams are caused by somatic stimuli. His theory, a product of nineteenth-century scientific positivism, led to the notion that "dreaming is caused by indigestion."

A veritable revolution in dream analysis was introduced by Sigmund Freud (1856–1939) in his landmark work of 1900, *The Interpretation of Dreams*. Freud suggested that such causal agents as Maury identified still cannot account for the elaborate imagery of the dream content. Why had Maury's dream placed him in a Middle Eastern bazaar and not in some other exotic environment, for example? Freud called dreams the "royal road to the unconscious" and thought they were produced by emotional factors. They function as a harmless release of built-up emotional tension. Dreams "protect sleep" by allowing an outlet for this turmoil. The dreamer's aggressive and sexual drives can be expressed harmlessly, since he or she is sound asleep and will not pose any danger to society.

The key mechanism at work in dreams, Freud thought, is wish fulfillment, and the dream is properly analyzed when one can identify the wish in question. He theorized that dreams bear a kinship with jokes and slips of the tongue, in that the same forbidden impulse that is hostile to society is allowed some measure of release. The joke, slip, or dream is a "compromise structure" in that only some degree of the full impulse is allowed expression. The dream is a "substitute" for the real desire, since the person only dreams about fulfilling it in place of actually doing so. The bizarre symbolism of dreams functions as a "disguise" to fool the conscious mind into thinking it has not really allowed a shameful impulse to come to expression. The apparent or "manifest content" of the dream disguises the real or "latent content," which carries the underlying wish.

Later studies have demonstrated the importance of dreaming to the psychic system. "Dream deprivation" experiments, carried out in the 1950s and 1960s by University of Chicago researcher William Dement, showed that in virtually 100 percent of test subjects, being deprived of dreaming (though still being allowed to sleep as long as they wanted) led to serious, even psychotic symptoms. These studies clearly show that dreams are tremendously important to maintaining psychological and physical health.

Possibly the greatest interest in dreams in contemporary research is shown by Jungian scholars. Swiss psychologist C. G. Jung (1875–1961) developed a complex theory in which dreams play a prominent role. His interest in dreams originated when he worked with psychotic patients early in his career. The grandiose visions and strange language these patients exhibited struck Jung as similar to the atmosphere of dreams. Surprised to find that the actual dreams of these psychotics were remarkably rational and un-

eventful, Jung developed his key theory of complementarity—that whatever is expressed on the outside, the opposite will be found on the inside. Rational people produce wildly illogical dreams, while the dreams of psychotic people appear to be rational. Psychotics are effectively in the dream state while awake.

Jung thought that psychoses and dreams appear to speak in the same "language": symbolism, the "native language" of the unconscious. Jung felt that symbols are multivalent—that is, carry many meanings—and that they are produced spontaneously by the unconscious to express profound realities that are ultimately ineffable—beyond description. Specific symbolic elements will appear commonly in dreams, such as the anima or animus, the complementary opposites to an individual's ego consciousness. A woman whose face is often obscured, appearing in a man's dream will represent his "anima," or female side. She will act as a psychopomp, or "soul guide," leading the dreamer into the vast treasure-house of the unconscious; and the reverse is true for the female dreamer. A dark or "savage" figure might represent the "shadow," the primal animal self within, as in a woman's dream of a boy she met at the edge of an Indian reservation. The boy invited her to come visit him whenever she wanted. As he ran off he turned into a wolf and slipped into the woods. This wolf-boy symbolizes the dreamer's animus, or masculine side, fused with her shadow, or healthy animal self—healthy because it appears as a natural animal at home in the wild place and who invites her interaction.

This shadow figure is in great contrast to that of a dream in which a dark man with a machine gun, who is as tall as the tallest buildings of the city, walks through town shooting at people randomly. The shadow figure of this dream exhibits Jung's concept of "inflation." Any repressed contents in the psychic system will gain great energy, inflate and distort, and act in a very menacing manner, as the savage "Mr. Hyde" does emerging from the meek "Dr. Jekyll." This indicates a terribly unhealthy "inflated" shadow, active in the whole collective consciousness in this dream, since the dark figure was threatening the whole city.

These are the sorts of markers Jungians look for in dreams. Jung posits two levels at work, the personal and collective, or "transpersonal." His signature theory of the "collective unconscious" was actually developed as an outgrowth of a dream in which he started on the top floor of a two-story house and continued down successive stairways deeper and deeper into the substructure. Any action of descending in dreams, Jung felt, symbolizes journeying into the unconscious, as does entering into bodies of water, or any dark place. Ascending would indicate moving toward higher consciousness. In Jung's dream, each successive layer of the house got older as he descended. He thought the dream represented a kind of structural diagram of the psyche, an ego consciousness at the top, undergirded by successively older layers containing the entire history and evolution of collective consciousness.

Certain "big" dreams, Jung thought, reveal mythic elements of profound transpersonal significance, as did one of his own earliest dreams. At age three he dreamed of an "underground god," an erect phallus on a golden throne, which, even at that age, he labeled the "underground Christ." This dream functioned in a "compensatory" way, representing the repressed sexual element denied Jesus and labeled "sinful" by church tradition. The dream "compensated" for these repressed contents, expressing the inflated "underground counterpart" to the church's Jesus, enthroned in a position of exaltation, representing sexuality itself in a sacred mode.

Dreams like this with powerful contents contain religious and mythic material. Alice's dream of falling down a hole into "Wonderland" (entering the unconscious) and Dorothy's dream of traveling to "Oz" represent the "hero's journey," the path of "individuation." Each element of Dorothy's dream bears important symbolic significance, from the Scarecrow, Tin Man, and Lion, her animus figures, whom she encounters and incorporates; to Toto, her shadow/trickster spirit; to the Wicked Witch, the distorted collective shadow; and to the Wizard, the wise old man archetype, an image of the great or "realized" Self. A dream like this represents the concept of soul transformation, the journey toward psychic integration or wholeness, as at the end the Wizard chants "*E pluribus unum,*" "the many brought into one." Like the journey to the Emerald City in the land of Oz, dreams, for Jung, altogether represent spontaneous products of the psychic system that function to make available to the dreamer the vast wealth held within the unconscious.

Jung drew a primary distinction between "big" dreams like Dorothy's and more ordinary or "little" dreams. Other researchers have added to this list. Some fourteen different types of dreams might be distinguished: (1) assimilation of daily experience dreams; (2) learning new tasks; (3) sensory stimulus; (4) wish fulfillment; (5) personal coping dreams; (6) anxiety dreams; (7) night terrors; (8) compensatory dreams; (9) repeating dreams; (10) prescient dreams, in which some specific dream content later happens in waking life; (11) lucid dreams, in which the dreamer is aware that he or she is dreaming; (12) archetypal or "big" dreams, often carrying collective contents; (13) karmic memory dreams; and (14) shamanic journeying.

See also ARCHETYPE; BLACK ELK; JOURNEYS AND JOURNEYING; MEDITATION; MYSTICISM; MYTH; PSYCHOLOGY OF RELIGION; PSYCHOTHERAPY; RELIGIOUS EXPERIENCE; SHAMANISM; TRANCE.

BIBLIOGRAPHY

Dement, William. "The Effect of Dream Deprivation." *Science* 131 (1960):1705–1707.

Dement, William. "Experimental Dream Studies." In *Science and Psychoanalysis,* edited by J. Masserman. 1964.

Diamond, Edwin. *The Science of Dreams.* 1963.

Eliade, Mircea. *Shamanism: Archaic Techniques of Ecstasy.* 1972.

Freud, Sigmund. *The Interpretation of Dreams.* 1900.

Jung, Carl G. *Dreams.* 1974.

Jung, Carl G. *Man and His Symbols.* 1964.

Jung, Carl G. *Memories, Dreams, Reflections.* 1961.

Luck, Georg. *Arcana Mundi: Magic and the Occult in the Greek and Roman Worlds.* 1985.

Neihardt, John G. *Black Elk Speaks: Being the Life Story of a Holy Man of the Oglala Sioux.* 1959.

Tart, Charles, ed. *Altered States of Consciousness.* 1969.

White, R. J. *The Interpretation of Dreams, the Oneirocritica by Artemidorus.* 1975.

Sharon L. Coggan

Drugs

Since 8000 B.C.E. and the Aztecs' ceremonial use of peyote, drugs have played an integral role in the religious history of the Americas. However, hallucinogenic drugs assumed a more visible role in the United States after World War II. Drugs penetrated mainstream society in the 1960s as the psychedelic revolution, led by such proselytizers as Timothy Leary and Ken Kesey, became part of the large-scale restructuring of American religion. The political and cultural radicalism of this decade led to the questioning of institutional authority at all levels of society, including that of the mainline churches. As demand increased for alternative spiritualities and experiential insights, drugs provided many with a readily available shortcut to mystical enlightenment.

When consumed under the proper conditions, marijuana, mescaline, magic mushrooms (psilocybin), and their synthetic counterpart, lysergic acid diethylamide (LSD), catalyze emotional states of a deeply religious character; mediating feelings of unity with the universe, deep community with peers, synesthesia, transcendence of time and space, and insight into the social construction of reality. As hallucinogens became more readily available in the 1960s, they provided an outlet and a vehicle for various forms of religious, social, and political protest against a status quo, perceived by many at the time as inhibiting individualism and limiting personal freedom.

The religious character of the psychedelic movement may be gleaned from William James's study of mysticism in his *The Varieties of Religious Experience* (1902). James, a psychologist and philosopher, experimented with nitrous oxide and peyote in exploring alternative states of consciousness. His dabblings reflected his preference for religion that was an "acute fever" rather than a "dull habit." James's statement on the matter would later be held up by proponents of chemical mysticism: that "rational consciousness as we call it, is but one special type of consciousness, whilst all about it, parted from by the filmiest of screens, there lie potential forms of consciousness entirely different" (p. 388).

The assault on this screen began well before the 1960s, among musicians and writers outside the institutionalized religious sphere. Their experiments with various drugs were the historical precursors to the psychedelic movement. By the early 1920s, marijuana was already a popular drug among jazz musicians. In the 1940s, Beat writers Jack Kerouac, Allen Ginsberg, and William S. Burroughs were experimenting with marijuana and Benzedrine. In 1953 the English essayist and novelist Aldous Huxley ingested four-tenths of a gram of mescaline at his home in Hollywood, California. He believed the experience to be confirmation of the insights he had written about in his 1945 study of world mysticism, *The Perennial Philosophy*. He quickly published *The Doors of Perception* (1954), a description of his newfound spirituality and visions of "naked existence."

Only a month before Huxley's revelation, the U.S. government authorized Operation MK-ULTRA. The CIA's drug and mind control program was complemented by a large increase in scientific studies of the therapeutic use of hallucinogens in treating alcoholism, narcotics addiction, and juvenile delinquency. It was during this period of curiosity that clinical psychologist and Harvard lecturer Timothy Leary began his research into the religious dimensions of psychedelics. In 1962 Walter Pahnke, a graduate student in religion and society at Harvard and advisee of Leary, conducted his famous "Good Friday experiment." During a religious service at Marsh Chapel of Boston University, Pahnke assembled twenty divinity students and administered psilocybin to half of them while the other half received a placebo. Nine of ten of those who had taken psilocybin reported having an intense

religious experience, while only one from the control group felt similar effects. Pahnke's results led Leary to conduct further experiments. After his expulsion from Harvard in 1963, Leary quickly set up a grassroots, nonprofit group called the International Federation for Internal Freedom (IFIF) and began to preach the gospel of psychedelics from a New York estate called Millbrook.

Psychedelic seeds of religious change were also being sowed on the West Coast. In 1960 Ken Kesey, a graduate student in Stanford University's creative writing program, tried LSD as part of a federally funded research program. Enamored by his experience, Kesey soon published his first novel, *One Flew over the Cuckoo's Nest,* and used the royalties to gather a group of "Merry Pranksters" at his residence in La Honda, California. In 1964 they bought a 1939 International Harvester bus. They renamed it FURTHUR, painted it with Day-Glo colors, pasted a sign to the rear end that read "Caution: Weird Load," and then drove cross-country to New York. Their hijinks did more than anything else to popularize LSD among the youth of America. In 1965 Kesey and his followers began their series of "acid tests" in the San Francisco area, all-night LSD parties that included strobe lights, costumes, and music by the Grateful Dead.

The momentum of psychedelic culture laid the religious groundwork for the emergence of the counterculture in the late 1960s in and around the Haight-Ashbury district in San Francisco. Media coverage and the relatively new medium of FM radio gave voice to the psychedelic gospel. As social protest became fashionable, drugs became even more accessible and more inviting to thousands of youths, who thought their domestic situation in need of a spiritual boost. However, psychedelics soon became a form of recreation for the "Woodstock nation" rather than a means to religious enlightenment.

While the contemporary meaning of the psychedelic revolution remains a point of contention among scholars, there is no doubt that it marked a dramatic shift in American religious history. Despite the founding of various psychedelic churches such as the Church of the Awakening and the Neo-American Church, the legacy of psychedelica lies not in its institutionalization but in its legitimization of personal discovery and resistance. The experimental attitude of the counterculture affected the entire religious landscape of the United States and wrenched open an alternative space for religious belief and practice: increased interest in Eastern mysticism and literature; the growth of small religious groups and practices in the 1970s, including Hare Krishna and transcendental meditation; and the decreased liturgical hegemony of mainline churches. Most importantly, however, the widespread use of hallucinogens in the 1960s complemented the growing emphasis on individual experience in the religious life of Americans. Whether or not they had used drugs, Americans of all stripes began to re-emphasize individual experience in their religiosity. This trend would continue through the rest of the century.

See also NATIVE AMERICAN CHURCH; NEW AGE SPIRITUALITY; NEW RELIGIOUS MOVEMENTS; PEYOTE; PROSELYTIZING; PSYCHOLOGY OF RELIGION; RELIGIOUS EXPERIENCE.

BIBLIOGRAPHY

Braden, William. *The Private Sea: LSD and the Search for God.* 1967.

Ellwood, Robert S. *The Sixties Spiritual Awakening: American Religion Moving from Modern to Postmodern.* 1994.

Farrell, James J. *The Spirit of The Sixties: The Making of Postwar Radicalism.* 1997.

Huxley, Aldous. *The Doors of Perception.* 1954.

James, William. *The Varieties of Religious Experience.* 1902.

Leary, Timothy. *High Priest.* 1968.

Lee, Martin A., and Bruce Shlain. *Acid Dreams: The Complete Social History of LSD: The CIA, the Sixties, and Beyond.* 1985.

Solomon, David, ed. *LSD: The Consciousness-Expanding Drug.* 1964.

Wolfe, Tom. *The Electric Kool-Aid Acid Test.* 1969.

John Lardas

Drumming

Percussive instruments are divided into two classes: idiophones, which produce vibrations as sounds (examples include bells, cymbals, castanets, and so on), and membranaphones, which produce sound through the vibration of a stretched membrane over a hollow interior (examples include snare drums, bass drums, and timpani). These descriptive definitions may be adequate for the meaning of the percussive instruments within the structure of formal musical ensembles such as orchestras or bands. These definitions, however, fall short of those sounds and meanings, which are designated as drums and drumming in the cultures of the world.

Drumming refers to the specific beating or striking of anything that is able to produce a rhythmic sound. The drum, in this sense, comes into being with the drummer and the drumming, and could be anything that is struck or beat in the production of this rhythmic sound. All sounds produced from striking or beating are not necessarily synonymous with drumming; drumming presupposes a cultural code within which the rhythmic beat and sound are understood and given specific meaning.

From this perspective, drums and drumming constitute a widespread phenomenon in the cultures of the world. Though some form of percussion is present in all cultures, it achieves prominence as a means of communicating in the traditional cultures and societies of Asia, Africa, and South America, and in the Native American cultures of Mesoamerica and North America.

The widespread pervasiveness of the percussive has led to various theories regarding the nature and meaning of percussive sound as a human universal. This point of view is clearly articulated in an article by Rodney Needham published in the journal *Man* in 1967. In this article, Needham stated, "All over the world . . . percussion . . . permits or accompanies communication with the other world." If this is true, what is the relationship between the percussive mode and the religious or spiritual reality? Needham's statements remind one of the meaning of the shaman's drum in shamanistic healing and of the inducement of trance states in the religions of West Africa and African-American religions in the western hemisphere. Needham's article raises the problem of the explicit relationship between percussive sound and ritual acts and actions. While percussiveness has a distinctive meaning in the ceremonial and religious life of several cultures, its meaning is not limited to this realm. Drums and drumming also define and fit into the structure of mundane and ordinary existence in many cultures.

Drums and drumming took on a new and different meaning in the lives of Africans enslaved in the Americas. In some cases—for example, in the Caribbean and in South America—Africans were able to bring over and retain significant aspects of their respective African cultures, drumming was *reintroduced* within the structures of an enslaved society. On the other hand, in North America, Africans *rediscovered* the meaning and nature of drums and drumming as a mode of creatively understanding and coping with their survival under slavery.

Drumming within the African diaspora was thus related simultaneously to what Needham referred to as "communication with the other world," and at the same time to survival in this world; as a matter of fact, the two meanings were the same. Slaves must perforce live within at least two worlds: the world of the slave owners and the world of the slave community. Often communication within the slave world had to be subversive and secret. Slaves thus resorted to encoding meanings by using drumming and song to convey these messages. In so doing they were recalling older traditions of communication through drums that were prominent in West Africa. In some instances, slave owners, surmising that drumming was a language, prohibited drumming among the Africans. Africans then had recourse to other means of percussive expression through the slapping of their bodies during dancing or the rhythmic tapping of their feet. The mundane otherness of the percussive may also be seen in the slave owners' identification of the percussive with savagery, licentiousness, uncivilized behavior, and the like. This meant that the meaning of a certain important aspect of the slave's life was understood negatively by the legitimizing structures of the prevailing "slavocracy."

Drums and drumming, or more precisely the percussive mode of musical expression, has entered American culture in general and African-American culture in particular as a specific and concrete source of meaning, value, knowledge, and thinking. In African-American culture in the United States, drumming—the beat—is synonymous with the notion of an other, alternative source of meaning, value, and sustenance. From this perspective, percussiveness has entered into the stylistics of speech, music, drama, and storytelling among African Americans. It points to other, alternate ways of healing and understanding the problematic dilemmas of American society and can be noted in all aspects and movements of African-American life. Likewise, just as sports and sporting events have brought new alliances and orientations among different ethnic groups, drumming has joined

members of various oppressed groups—as, for example, Native Americans—into a common mode of expression. It has also moved beyond the oppressed to become a badge or sign of a new late-twentieth-century spirituality, expressed, for instance, in the New Age Movement.

See also AFRICAN-AMERICAN RELIGIONS; DANCE; ECSTASY; HEALING; MUSIC; NATIVE AMERICAN RELIGION; NEW AGE SPIRITUALISM; RITUAL; SHAMANISM; SPIRIT POSSESSION.

BIBLIOGRAPHY

Blacking, John. *How Musical Is Man?* 1973.

Eliade, Mircea. *Shamanism: Archaic Techniques of Ecstasy.* 1964.

Elingson, Ter. "Drums." In *Encyclopedia of Religion,* edited by Mircea Eliade. Vol. 4, pp. 494–503. 1987.

Lévi-Strauss, Claude. "The Efficacy of Symbols." In Claude Lévi-Strauss, *Structural Anthropology.* Vol. 1. 1963.

Needham, Rodney, "Percussion and Transition." *Man* 2 (1967): 606–614.

Rouget, Gilbert. *Music and Trance: A Theory of the Relations Between Music and Possession.* 1985.

Southern, Eileen. *The Music of Black Americans: A History.* 1971.

Tirro, Frank. *Jazz, A History.* 1977.

Walker, Sheila. *Spirit Possession in Africa and Afro-America.* 1972.

Charles H. Long

E

Easter

Traditionally regarded as the most important Christian festival, Easter marks the end of Lenten penitence with the celebration of Jesus Christ's resurrection after his death by crucifixion. Though observance varied in early times, by the ninth century almost all Europeans accepted the designation of Easter as the first Sunday after the first full moon that follows March 21, the vernal equinox, or first day of spring in the Northern Hemisphere. Many Eastern Orthodox churches observe Easter somewhat later, according to differing timetables. It is also linked with the Jewish observance of Pesach, the Passover seder, which falls within these dates as well. The word itself, *Easter*, is of uncertain origin. Conventional wisdom holds that Eostre, the Anglo-Saxon goddess of spring, lies at the root of current usage, but linguists argue that *eostrum*, an Old German word for "dawn," is the more likely origin.

From the earliest days of Christianity, the biblical event that Easter commemorates has been affirmed as a crucial aspect of salvation. Just as Passover commemorated Israel's deliverance from Egyptian slavery, so Christ's resurrection from the tomb was thought to demonstrate a deliverance from sin and evil, a triumph over death itself. In addition to recalling what is affirmed as a historical event, Easter observances also include an anticipation of future resurrection for all believers. Many people choose to be baptized at Easter, thus demonstrating their faith in a resurrected Christ who rescues sinful human nature and raises it to a higher level of existence. Viewed as relevant to past event, present faith, and heavenly promise, Easter

vitalizes Christianity as a festival of redemption, with the prospect of eternal life with Christ.

Easter observance remained a basic feature throughout early and medieval Christian thought and practice. It continued to receive strong emphasis during the sixteenth-century Reformation period, but Puritans later disparaged its importance in England and early colonial America. Still, the pageantry as well as the theological significance of Easter continues as a highly visible feature of contemporary American religion. Palm Sunday inaugurates a series of events that come to pass during what is known as Holy Week. Four days later, Maundy (or Holy) Thursday commemorates the New Testament account of Jesus washing the disciples' feet and his observance of Passover (often called "the Last Supper") before arrest and imprisonment. Good Friday commemorates the crucifixion in poignant and painful detail, but the culminating event is Easter Sunday, which marks for Christendom the end of darkness and despair, the emergence of new hope, and the promise of life without end.

The specifically Christian aspects of Easter are still paramount in American churches today. But it is also worth noting that the season has been marked by many pre-Christian folk ceremonies as well. Almost all of these popular customs are related to the beginnings of new life in springtime. Lambs, rabbits, chicks, and ducklings point to another growth cycle. New clothing, feasting, and the exchanging of decorated eggs convey similar meaning. Many also celebrate the season by giving children baskets of sweets, referring to "the Easter bunny" as a benign donor. An egg-rolling contest on the White House lawn for local chil-

Priests at the Cathedral Basilica of Saints Peter and Paul hand out palm leaves following a Palm Sunday Mass in Philadelphia on Sunday, March 28, 1999. (Credit: AP/Wide World Photos.)

dren in Washington, D.C., lends governmental sanction to these ancillary but still widely enjoyed aspects of a contemporary American religious event.

See also Jewish High Holy Days; Lent.

Bibliography
Linam, G. *Celebrate Easter.* 1985.
Spong, J. S. *The Easter Moment.* 1998.

Henry Warner Bowden

Eastern Orthodoxy

Eastern Orthodox Christianity arrived in North America in the late 1700s by way of Russian Orthodox missionaries from the Valaam monastery who evangelized among Alaskan natives. Within two years the Russian missionaries had performed eleven thousand baptisms, consecrated two thousand marriages, and put up a church and two portable chapels. The Valaam monks translated the Bible and sacred texts into native languages, with a view toward reflecting local spiritual ideas and practices in their mission and to creating self-sufficient Orthodox churches led by local priests. The missionaries followed the practice of working in native languages and representing local customs in Orthodox worship established by Byzantine missionaries who spread Orthodoxy in the Balkans, Russia, and the Middle East.

Eastern Orthodox Christianity expanded in the United States throughout the 1900s with the influx of Russian, Balkan, Greek, and Middle Eastern settlers seeking refuge from economic hardship, political oppression, and war that prevailed in their homelands. Within the framework of religious freedom and tolerance in the United States, Orthodox Christians established parishes in which they worshiped according to their spiritual vision and were governed by their understanding of episcopal polity. Orthodox settlers in North America in the early 1900s adhered to nationalism and ethnic divisions fostered in Orthodox regions that were under Ottoman rule in Europe and the Middle East. Divisions along ethnic and national lines in the Orthodox Church were further entrenched in a climate of ethnic and racial hostility structuring American settlements and social institutions before the civil rights movement of the 1960s. While ethnicity persists in Orthodox churches, congregations are gradually becoming ethnically diverse as a result of interethnic marriages among first- and second-generation Orthodox Christians and a growing number of converts drawn by the ethos of Orthodox worship.

The Eastern Orthodox Church in North America today consists of about twenty communions with approximately 6 million adherents. Some of these bodies are variously under the jurisdiction of the patriarchs of Alexandria, Antioch, Constantinople, Jerusalem, Russia, Serbia, Romania, and Albania; these churches rely on their patriarch to appoint archbishops and bishops but are otherwise independent and self-reliant. A smaller number of Orthodox denominations are largely autonomous; they are not under the jurisdiction of a patriarch, they independently appoint the head of their church, and they govern their affairs and are self-sufficient. Since the late 1870s lay groups have established Orthodox parishes in North America. Orthodox parishes rely on volunteers to raise funds to support the clergy, maintain the church building, and sponsor church programs. In North America Orthodox churches elect a parish council from their members to direct church administrative affairs. By the mid-1960s the local parish had become a significant spiritual and social institution among Orthodox Christian minorities in North America. Within the framework of the church they determined their identity based on their articulation of Orthodox tenets and practices.

While Orthodox church buildings in North America vary, their structures adhere to the requirements for Orthodox worship. The church is conceived as heaven on Earth, a place were Orthodox Christians experience God on Earth. In the eyes of believers the structure is the embodiment of the work of the Holy Spirit. The building structure and interior narrate an Orthodox worldview. Icons are placed throughout the sanctuary in positions that are prescribed by Orthodox cosmology and practice. Icons are essential elements in Orthodox worship, and they are used to impart church teachings. Most Orthodox sanctuaries in North America include pews, organs, choir lofts, and fellowship halls. The fellowship halls are used for church organizational meetings, fund-raisers, socials, Bible study, and Sunday school. In the early 1900s some Orthodox churches also established primary schools that taught children their native language and culture as a way of continuing the ethnic identity and character of the group. Since the 1960s the curricula in Orthodox Church–based schools offer a bilingual and bicultural program.

Beliefs and Practices

While the Eastern Orthodox Church in North America is composed of autonomous and largely autonomous bodies, its members are united by shared beliefs and practices. Orthodox Christians believe that they bear the unbroken apostolic legacy; they see themselves as embodying the true and comprehensive faith. Orthodox Christians agree that the foundations of Orthodox spiritual beliefs and practices were established in seven ecumenical councils: Nicea I (325), Constantinople I (381), Ephesus (431), Chalcedon (451), Constantinople II (553), Constantinople III (680), and Nicea II (787). Orthodox Christians rely on the teachings and writings of the holy church fathers. They also believe in scriptural authority revealed to humanity through the church. They agree that the church should be governed by episcopal authority. The Orthodox Church is also united by

His Holiness Ecumenical Patriarch Bartholemew I, the leader of the Eastern Orthodox Church, leads a congregation in prayer near the site of San Francisco's old Annunciation Cathedral on November 6, 1997. The Annunciation Cathedral was destroyed in the 1989 earthquake. (Credit: AP/Wide World Photos.)

shared liturgical structure, sacraments, and church feasts. The liturgy of St. John Chrysostom has been used since the fifth century and is enacted on most Sundays in Orthodox churches. The liturgy of St. Basil, written in the fourth century, is a longer version of the text prepared by St. John Chrysostom and is sung ten times a year. The liturgy of the presanctified gifts, written by St. Gregory in the sixth century, is sung on Wednesdays and Fridays of Great Lent and on the first three days of Holy Week. There are seven sacraments enacted in the Orthodox Church: baptism, chrismation, Holy Eucharist, repentance, ordination, marriage, and holy unction. Each sacrament imparts a particular grace. The sacraments are the means by which Orthodox Christians are transformed into divine likenesses.

Orthodox Christians believe in a triune God—the Father, the Son, and the Holy Spirit. God the Father is creator of all things in the universe. God is Christ, the son of God who came to Earth as man and returned to God the Father in heaven. God is the Holy Spirit, who dispenses God's grace to humanity and the universe. Humanity experiences God the Father, who is transcendent and mysterious through God's energies. God is personal. God is reached by personal prayer and devotion conducted in the church and in private, everyday life. Orthodox Christians maintain a small iconostasis—a partition or screen—in their homes, where a small candle or lamp illuminates the family icons. The iconostasis is the site of private devotion and prayer in the home. Private devotion includes observing fasts that accord with Orthodox beliefs, taking part in the celebration of church feasts, and observing the sacraments.

There are twelve great feasts in the Orthodox calendar, excluding Easter. The celebration of Easter is the most significant church feast in Orthodoxy. Christ's resurrection is a central theme and a major structuring element in Orthodox worship; Christ's life, Passion, and resurrection figure prominently in the liturgies and icons represented in church interiors. Orthodox Christians venerate Mary, the mother of God; four church feasts are in Mary's honor. Commemorations of the church fathers and saints are represented throughout Orthodox thought and practice.

Ideological Conflicts

Second- and third-generation Orthodox Christians sustain the Orthodox Church in North America. Since the 1960s, ethnic divisiveness and separation have been waning in American society. New generations of Orthodox Christians who have been reared on American soil and have achieved upward mobility

Russian Orthodox church steeples in Sitka, Alaska. (Credit: CORBIS/The Purcell Team.)

in American society are not defensive about their ethnic and religious identity. For this generation, the homelands of their ancestors are points of honor and pride but not places where they seek to resettle. Thus Orthodox parishes in North America are no longer defensive and inward-looking. The expansion of Eastern Orthodox Christianity in a plural and open American society is creating the foundation for ecumenical and interfaith dialogue. Much of this dialogue is taking place at the local level as a result of the increasing pluralism in American society and the growing number of interfaith marriages and conversions. While some Orthodox Christians have left Orthodoxy since the 1960s, the signs of Orthodox renewal and revival abound. The first and second generations are restoring Orthodox churches, embracing the symbols and meanings embodied in Orthodox worship, and taking part in expanding church programs that include opportunities to discuss Orthodox sacred texts to give order and meaning to their lives. Orthodox parents are baptizing their children in the faith and fostering the Orthodox identity of their children.

Christian unity and ecumenical dialogue are major concerns among Orthodox Christians. The Orthodox Church takes part in the World Council of Churches (WCC). Within the framework of the WCC the Orthodox have an opportunity to address doctrinal differences that separate them from Protestant and Roman Catholic Christianity. However, within the WCC the Orthodox see themselves treated as a marginal minority whose concerns are disparaged by the Protestant majority. The Orthodox believe that the WCC should focus less on what Orthodox consider ephemeral concerns of inclusive language and the ordination of women and more on theological themes such as the veneration of Mary, the significance of icons in worship, and the foundations for unity in faith.

On the global scene there are several initiatives unfolding to provide opportunities for dialogue on the divisive issues of the authority of the pope, the veneration of icons, secularism, the primacy of theological claims based on the authority of rational discourse in Western Christianity, and the privileged authority of science in Western society. Orthodox Christians look to their sources—scripture, the teachings of the church fathers, the teachings of Jesus, Mary, and the saints, iconography, the apostolic legacy—to address these concerns. In North America, Orthodox Christians are faced with questions about the ordination of women, abortion, homosexuality, violence, poverty, and the environment. The second and third generations must reconcile the tenets of Orthodox faith that stress humility, self-sacrifice, and stewardship with the secular practices of unencumbered individualism and competition. Orthodox Christians must reconcile the utilitarian ethic defining everyday transactions in American society with the Orthodox ethic of love outlined in Orthodox discourse and practice. Orthodox Christians in North America are increasingly in a position to endow institutions in which they can retrieve their past in order to contemplate and act in the future. Less encumbered by the exigencies of ethnic discrimination and limited economic resources, they are in a position to shed their parochial legacy and reach for the cosmopolitan outlook and practice embodied in North American history during the initial landing of Orthodoxy in Alaska.

See also BELONGING, RELIGIOUS; BIBLE; CHURCH; GOD; ICONS; MISSIONARY MOVEMENTS; PRACTICE; RELIGIOUS COMMUNITIES; WORLD COUNCIL OF CHURCHES.

BIBLIOGRAPHY

Bulgakov, Sergius. *The Orthodox Church.* 1988.
Clendenin, Daniel. *Eastern Orthodox Christianity: A Western Perspective.* 1994.
Clendenin, Daniel, ed. *Eastern Orthodox Theology.* 1995.
Meyendorff, John. *Vision of Unity.* 1987.
Ouspensky, Leonid. *Theology of the Icon.* 1992.
Ware, Timothy. *The Orthodox Church.* 1997.

Frances Kostarelos

Eckankar

Also known as "The Ancient Science of Soul Travel" and "The Religion of the Light and Sound of God," the religion known officially as Eckankar was founded in 1965 by Paul Twitchell (d. 1971). Twitchell was a religious seeker and dabbler in various new religious movements, including Scientology and The Self-Revelation Church of Absolute Monism. He seems to have been influenced significantly by the Sikh-related philosophy and spirituality of the Radhasoami tradition of India. Students and critics of Twitchell's movement have pointed out striking parallels between its cosmology and that of Kirpal Singh, who brought the Radhasoami to America via a movement known as the Ruhani Satsang.

Twitchell first established Eckankar—a word seemingly derived from a Punjabi term for God—in San Diego, California. Soon after that he moved its headquarters to Las Vegas, Nevada. The members were primarily people who had attended Twitchell's lectures or read his spiritual autobiography *The Tiger's Fang.* Twitchell was also made famous by Brad Steiger's biography *In My Soul I Am Free.* Twitchell claimed to be the "971st Living Eck Master"—the most recent in an unbroken succession of oracles of God sent to Earth by the "Vairagi Masters," who oversee the spiritual unfoldment of the planet. In 1969 Twitchell's publishing house Illuminated Way Press published what has become Eckankar's standard introductory volume, *Eckankar: The Key to Secret Worlds.* Twitchell instructed his followers, known as "chelas" and "Eckists," in spiritual exercises such as "soul travel" (also known as "bilocation") and hearing the "light and sound of God" in meditation. He also taught Eckists to chant the mantra "Hu," which he declared an especially holy word for God. Chanting Hu is believed to burn off karmic debt and bring Eckists into higher consciousness and union with Sugmad—another term for the God of Eckankar.

Twitchell died suddenly and unexpectedly in 1971. His successor as the Living Eck Master and spiritual leader of Eckankar was Darwin Gross, who moved the headquarters of the religion to Menlo Park, California. Gross's tenure as the 972nd Living Eck Master ended in 1983, when he was ousted by the board of

Eckankar and replaced by his own appointed successor and "co-Mahanta" Harold Klemp (b. 1942). Guided by a "spiritual vision," Klemp and his lieutenant and president of Eckankar Peter Skelskey moved the headquarters of Eckankar from California to Chanhassen, a suburb of Minneapolis, Minnesota, in the mid-1980s. In spite of opposition from many citizens of Chanhassen, Eckankar built there an $8.5 million international worship center known as The Temple of Eck. The temple, with its golden step-pyramid "dome," rises conspicuously out of the surrounding prairie and suburban housing tracts.

Under Klemp, who is also known as the 973rd Living Eck Master, "the Dream Master," and "Wah Z" (his spiritual name on the "inner plane"), Eckankar has flourished and become a permanent part of the new religious landscape of North America and the world. Eckankar groups exist in many countries, and Eckankar is especially strong in Nigeria. Membership statistics are not published or revealed, but Eckankar president Skelskey claims that the religion has "tens of thousands" of followers worldwide.

Eckankar's appeal is primarily to religious seekers on the fringes of the amorphous New Age movement. The religion offers a spiritual home and community as well as structure to believers in reincarnation, paranormal experiences, and Eastern religious concepts who do not want to leave normal life to join a commune or obvious "cult." The religion claims to unlock the mystery and meaning of the "dream state," and that is another attraction for many Eckists.

See also CHANTING; KARMA; NEW AGE SPIRITUALITY; PARANORMAL; SCIENTOLOGY, CHURCH OF; SIKHISM.

BIBLIOGRAPHY

Klemp, Harold. *The Secret Teachings.* 1989.

Lane, David Christopher. *The Making of a Spiritual Movement.* 1993.

Olson, Roger E. "Eckankar: From Ancient Science of Soul Travel to New Age Religion." In *America's Alternative Religions,* edited by Timothy Miller. 1995.

Twitchell, Paul. *Eckankar: The Key to Secret Worlds.* 1969; reprint, 1987.

Roger E. Olson

Ecofeminism

Ecological feminism (ecofeminism) emerged in the 1970s predominantly in North America, although the term was coined by Françoise d'Eaubonne in *Le Féminisme ou la Mort* (1974). In 1975 feminist theologian Rosemary Radford Ruether suggested that there can be no liberation for women and no solution to the ecological crisis within a society whose fundamental model of relationships is one of domination (race, class, gender, sexual orientation, etc.). Ruether describes ecofeminism as the symbolic and social connection between the oppression of women and the domination of nature, grounded in a union between the radical ecology movement and feminism. Specifically she suggests that the women's movement must unite with the ecological movement to envision a radical reshaping of the basic socioeconomic relations and the underlying values of society.

The foundational perception is that connections exist between the oppression and domination of women and the oppression and domination of the Earth—or nature. In particular the mistrust or hatred of women (misogyny) and a fear of dependency on the natural world are the interlocking forces that ecofeminism is exposing and challenging. Ecofeminism expanded rapidly between the 1970s and the 1990s from numerous origins such as social and ecological activists and academics and from such diverse fields as feminism, social ecology, antiracism, and ecology. Ecofeminism is a convergence of the ecological and feminist analyses and movements. Like ecology and feminism, it is heterogeneous and has distinguishable components and orientations.

As Euro-Western societies developed, the combined influences of the rise of science, the dualisms of the Christian worldview, the philosophy of modernity, and the industrialization of the economy became the cultural forces that entrenched the feminizing of nature, the naturalizing of women, and their mutual entanglements in theoretical, historical, and cultural webs. The influence of what are called hierarchical dualisms is central to the development of the Western worldview and to ecofeminist critiques. Examples of such dualisms are men/women; heaven/earth; spirit/matter; mind/body; thought/emotion; culture/nature; order/chaos; rational/irrational; light/dark; and divine/demonic. These are hierarchical because the first receives a priority value over the second. They are dualistic because they are understood as opposites. However, there are also connections among the corresponding halves of the dualisms, such as among women, earth, matter, body, emotion, nature, chaos, irrational, dark, and demonic. Carolyn Merchant's study of the development of Western ideas and beliefs about the world has shown that these dualisms were, and continue to be, foundational to Western thought, values, and attitudes. They remain most often unconscious, yet they are fundamental to the Western worldview and belief systems, and they operate in every discipline and course of action. Ecofeminism challenges this hierarchical and dualistic worldview and holds that the domination of the Earth is enmeshed with the oppression of women. Ecofeminists claim that all oppressions, such as those based on class, race, gender, orientation, ableism, and the natural world, are interconnected within a logic of domination.

Ecofeminism is a third wave of feminism, meaning a convergence of ecology and feminism into a new social theory and political movement that addresses gender relations, social and economic systems, the use of science, the formation of cultural values, and human self-understanding in relation to the natural world. As feminism evolves into different branches, ecofeminism has embraced distinct feminist positions. Feminist theorists originating from liberal, cultural, social, socialist, radical, and postmodern critiques reflect distinctively on the relationship between women and the natural world and between misogyny and the ecological crisis. In addition, ecofeminist positions embrace distinct ecological paradigms, including resource-based environmentalism, social ecology, deep ecology, and/or cosmology. Many ecofeminists, such as Vandana Shiva, place a priority on action rather than theory. As ecofeminist philosopher Karen Warren remarks, the varieties of ecofeminism reflect not only the differences in the analysis of the woman/ nature connection, but also differences on such fundamental matters as the nature of and the solutions to women's oppression, the theory of human nature, and the conceptions of freedom, equality, and epistemology on which various feminist theories depend.

What makes ecological feminism feminist is the commitment to the recognition and elimination of male-gender bias and the development of practices, policies, and theories that do not reflect this bias. What makes it ecological is an understanding of and commitment to the valuing and preserving of ecosystems, broadly understood. Far from being reductionist or simplistic, ecofeminism is a textured field of theoretical and experiential insights encompassing different forms of knowledge and embodied in the concrete. It is an interdisciplinary discourse within academia, a critique and a vision, spawning myriad books, articles, workshops, conferences, retreats, rituals, art, activism, and politics. There are publications covering ecofeminist philosophy, spirituality and religion, science, psychology, sociology, political thought and activism, economics and animal rights. Some specific problems addressed have included the history of the ideologies of women and nature, ecological degradation, ecological stress and human health, biodiversity, population, militarism, globalization, and exposing the players in ecological disasters. Ecofeminism is international in scope and connects women from around the world. It is analysis, critique, vision, and action.

Ecofeminism and Religion

Ecofeminist perspectives have had an impact on all aspects of religious understanding. The accumulation of work bringing ecofeminist analyses to bear on religious histories, systematic theologies, scriptural interpretations, spiritualities, and ethics is creating both unique viewpoints and substantial challenges. Religions are very influential in the formation of worldviews, and some promote positions that are antiwomen, antinature, or both. This may be evident in the teachings or is a consequence of how religions have engaged with cultures.

The ecofeminist challenge to religion is profound and permeates all layers of religious reflection and praxis. Ecofeminist religious perspectives are developing within classical religions such as Judaism, Buddhism, Christianity, Islam, within new movements such as Wicca, Goddess, or New Age, and in some indigenous traditions. Some ecofeminists are examining their religions for insights, redeeming what could be helpful and negating detrimental aspects. Others are reclaiming ancient or obscured traditions or creating new ones. The issues are different in each case. The extent of the ecofeminist challenge to and confrontation with classical religions is in the initial states of articulation, most evident in the works of Rosemary Radford Ruether, an American Christian ecofeminist theologian.

As Ruether points out, the cultural-symbolic level of the relationship between sexism and ecological exploitation is the ideological superstructure that reflects and sanctions the social, economic, political, and religious order. Ecofeminist religious perspectives hold in tension the relationships between religion and culture, ethics of nature and history, and theory and praxis. One goal is to become conscious of the cultural effects of religious traditions and systems.

Current work involves the reinterpretation, expansion, or creation of particular doctrines, symbols, and metaphors that include and honor women and the natural world. Challenging foundational presuppositions and reshaping the infrastructure of religion remain the substantive and more difficult work. Although there are both continuities and discontinuities with classical religions, there are cherished notions in some traditions that need to be rejected, such as the inferiority of or the need to control women. Religious ecofeminists are also claiming that the Earth is sacred, and this is neither explicit nor accepted in some traditions. Yet a sense of the sacredness of the Earth and of all life has been central to spiritual awareness from time immemorial.

Given that ecofeminism embodies diversity and is evolving continuously, the implications of any ecofeminist theory or praxis are impossible to delineate.

There are lively debates within ecofeminism concerning essentialism, romantic or utopic dreams of a harmonious past or future, apolitical spiritualities, and the relationship between theory and social transformation. Yet ecofeminists desire to heal the wounds caused by the splits between nature and culture, mind and body, women and men, reason and emotion, spirit and matter, theory and action, and ultimately between humans and the Earth.

See also DEEP ECOLOGY; FEMINIST SPIRITUALITY; FEMINIST THEOLOGY; GENDER ROLES; MASCULINE SPIRITUALITY; MATRIARCHAL CORE; MATRIARCHY; NATURE RELIGION; ORDINATION OF WOMEN; PATRIARCHY; PRIESTESS; WOMANIST THEOLOGY; WOMEN'S STUDIES.

BIBLIOGRAPHY

Adams, Carol, ed. *Ecofeminism and the Sacred.* 1993.

Diamond, Irene, and Gloria Orenstein, eds. *Reweaving the World: The Emergence of Ecofeminism.* 1990.

Gaard, Greta. *Ecological Politics: Feminism and the Greens.* 1998.

Merchant, Carolyn. *The Death of Nature: Women, Ecology, and the Scientific Revolution.* 1980.

Plant, Judith, ed. *Healing the Wounds: The Promise of Ecofeminism.* 1989.

Plumwood, Val. *Feminism and the Mastery of Nature.* 1993.

Primavesi, Anne. *From Apocalypse to Genesis: Ecology, Feminism and Christianity.* 1991.

Ruether, Rosemary Radford. *Gaia and God: An Ecofeminist Theology of Earth Healing.* 1993.

Salleh, Ariel. *Ecofeminism as Politics.* 1997.

Shiva, Vandana, and Marie Mies. *Ecofeminism.* 1993.

Sturgeon, Noel. *Ecofeminist Natures: Race, Gender, Feminist Theory, and Political Action.* 1997.

Warren, Karen, ed. *Ecofeminism: Women, Culture, Nature.* 1997.

Heather Eaton

Ecospirituality

Ecospirituality expresses the joining of spirituality with ecological perspectives. There are numerous types, traditions, expressions, and understandings of ecospirituality. It does not refer to any one set of beliefs, but to a range of ethical or moral, religious, spiritual, or agnostic beliefs, tendencies, or actions that relate to ecological concerns. Ecospirituality has evolved since the 1960s and is currently part of popular culture in North America. The connection between spirituality and the Earth has deep and historical roots in many religious traditions and in particular with those that have remained in tune with the rhythms and lim-

its of the Earth, such as some indigenous traditions around the world.

Ecospirituality has many meanings, the first referring to a thirst for connection between spirituality and the Earth, given the extent of and the general lack of religious responses to the ecological crisis. There is a recognition that the ecological crisis threatens all life on Earth, and it is fundamentally a moral, spiritual, and religious problem.

Since the early 1970s there has been a global, public, and political consciousness of the need for ethics and religions to be consistent with ecological and social liberation, noting, as does Steven Rockefeller (1992), that there are many diverse cultural paths joining in this awareness. Discussions have been increasingly cross-cultural and interreligious. Organizations such as the United Nations, the World Wildlife Fund, World Conservation Strategy, and numerous religious groups have been involved in interdisciplinary work aimed at developing religious and spiritual responses to the ecological crisis that are connected to political decision-making. From the initiatives of Mary Evelyn Tucker and John Grim, the Harvard Center for the Study of World Religions hosted a Religion and Ecology Project involving ten conferences since 1996, bringing together scholars and environmentalists from Buddhism, Confucianism, Taoism, Shinto, Jainism, Hinduism, indigenous traditions, Judaism, Christianity, and Islam. This work is entering a phase of discussions with the United Nations.

The foundation of this collaboration among religions, academics, and activists is an awareness of a commitment to a new ecological worldview that reflects alternative values, ethics, and actions about and toward life on Earth. There is an understanding that religion not only broadens the conversation beyond discussing environmental issues in terms of economics, political legislation, or scientific analysis, but also that at the heart of spirituality is an encounter with the sacred: an intuition of the wondrous mystery in the power of life and being. Ecospirituality is a manner of speaking about this kind of religious experience that is awakening, slowly and unevenly, within the human community. As Rockefeller suggests, an appreciation of the miracle of life and of the beauty and mystery in the being of animals, plants, and the Earth as a whole becomes so intense as to generate a keen sense of the natural world's sacredness. This awareness of the inner mystery of life is at the heart of most religions.

Ecospirituality is not connected to any one tradition. As well as pertaining to established religious traditions, ecospirituality can refer to a myriad of Goddess, Wiccan, deep ecology, ecofeminist, or any mixture of Eastern, indigenous, and New Age beliefs and practices. Ecospirituality can refer to those who do not want any religious affiliation. It can have roots within the Gaia hypothesis, originating as a scientific theory in the 1970s from James Lovelock and which revives the name of a female Greek goddess of Earth. Lovelock proposed that the best way to understand the Earth is as a living planet on which all life functions as a systemic, interconnected whole—alive in the sense that the Earth is self-organizing and self-regulating. This theory has been debated intensely, and there is a slow acceptance of its validity. The relationship between ecospirituality and Gaia does not originate with Lovelock but with those who share his sense that the Earth is alive and humans are an integral member of a larger community of life.

Ecospirituality is also a term that can be applied to the work in cosmology and particularly that of Thomas Berry, a cultural historian of religions. Berry's work in scientific and religious cosmologies—stories about the origin of the world that provide orientation, guidance, and meaning to life—has done much to revive a sense of the sacredness of life, the Earth, and all the processes of the universe. He offers a comprehensive context for rethinking our current situation and for understanding ourselves as part of a larger evolutionary whole that is both spiritual and material.

There are several elements within ecospirituality, and priorities are divergent. One challenges the belief that humans are the center of life, or anthropocentrism. Some propose a biocentric approach wherein the intrinsic value of animals, plants, rivers, and mountains has a priority over their instrumental value as resources for humans. The ecospirituality insights emerging from deep ecology, ecofeminism, and cosmology are in this vein. Others would attend to the ethical dimensions, such as environmental ethics, ecofeminism and issues of domination, and social ecology wherein the relationships among ethics, social issues, and ecological issues are the central pieces of their ecospirituality. Others would put a priority on public policy and activism, seeking to change institutions, economic agendas, and legislation. Still others work to change the ideas, values, and beliefs at universities, colleges, workshops, and conferences. Finally, there is a plethora of ecospirituality rituals.

See also BIOETHICS; CREATION SPIRITUALITY; DEEP ECOLOGY; NATURE RELIGION; NEW AGE SPIRITUALITY; SPIRITUALITY; WICCA.

BIBLIOGRAPHY

Berry, Thomas. *Dream of the Earth.* 1988.
Gottlieb, Roger, ed. *This Sacred Earth: Religion, Nature, Environment.* 1996.
Griffin, David Ray. *Spirituality and Society.* 1988.
Hull, Fritz, ed. *Earth and Spirit: The Spiritual Dimension of the Environmental Crisis.* 1993.
Kinsley, David. *Ecology and Religion: Ecological Spirituality in Cross-Cultural Perspective.* 1995.
Lovelock, James. *The Ages of Gaia.* 1988.
Rockefeller, Steven, and John Elder, eds. *Spirit and Nature: Why the Environment Is a Religious Issue.* 1992.
Tucker, Mary Evelyn, and John Grim, eds. *Worldviews and Ecology.* 1993.

Heather Eaton

Ecstasy

In the 1830s Alexis de Tocqueville, the French observer of American nationalism, noted the propensity of some Americans toward forms of what he called "enthusiastic spirituality." As he saw it, residual Puritanism, citizenship, and capitalism tied antebellum Americans together firmly in bonds of material accumulation and spatial expansion. "Although the desire to acquire the good things of this world is the dominant passion among Americans," argued Tocqueville, "there are momentary respites when their souls seem suddenly to break the restraining bonds of matter and rush impetuously heavenward" (*Democracy in America,* 1840). Tocqueville spoke here especially of the Second Great Awakening (c. 1801–1830), an intense evangelical revival wherein the borders between spiritual "enthusiasm" and ecstasy were unstable, fluid, and shifting.

The term *ecstasy* comes to us from the Greek *ekstasis,* which means literally "to be placed outside." According to anthropological studies of religion, the cultivation of ecstasy in human experience is precipitated by the possession of an individual by a deity, a spirit, or both. That is, ecstasy occurs when a human's body is captured and controlled by an external, spiritual entity; ecstatic religious experience eventuates when a person loses—or perhaps better, relinquishes—control of the body/mind/soul to undergo a period of spiritual/psychological/physical transcendence at the behest of a supernatural being. This ecstatic episode is typically marked by the loss of bodily motor skills, fainting, (sometimes) unrecognizable speech and utterances, and strained bodily contortions that can mimic the gestures of certain animals, such as snakes. The accessory phenomena associated with ecstasy are distinctive markers of shamanism as well: "speaking in tongues, prophesying, clairvoyance, and transmission of messages from the dead" (Lewis, p. 15). Religious enthusiasts report the sensation of euphoria while in ecstasy and also the feeling of electricity surging through the body.

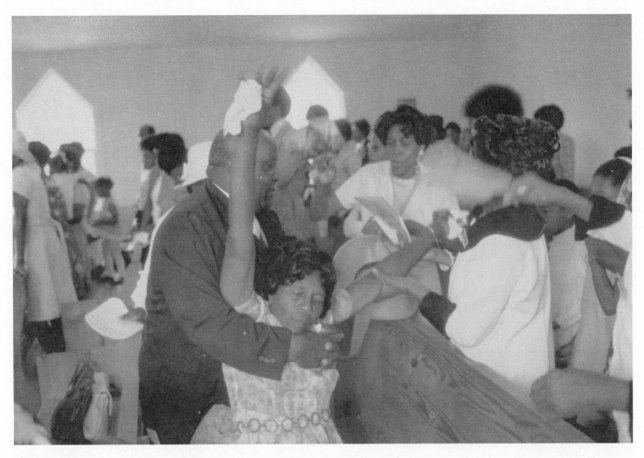

A man reaches over to catch a woman caught up in a religious ecstasy that causes her to speak in tongues, shake, and faint. Other churchgoers at the Mount Moriah Baptist Church in Beulah, Mississippi, look on in amazement and awe at the apparent revelation.   (Credit: © Nathan Benn/Stock, Boston/PNI.)

I. M. Lewis, an anthropologist and the author of the seminal work on ecstasy, suggests that ecstatic religious experience is only rendered intelligible when located within its social and cultural frame of reference. Within the variegated American frame, the literal definition of ecstasy—to be placed outside—best serves a hermeneutics of ecstatic religious practice. Lewis argued that spirit possession and its attendant ecstatic performance confer religious authority—a form of symbolic capital—on the marginal members of a given social order: the poor, the oppressed, children, and especially women. To speak with the voice of the divine, or to speak and act after having been publicly chosen as the receptacle of the divine, is to give voice and power to the formerly mute and weak. Ecstasy provides the religious engine that can mobilize social agents to advantageously navigate cultural terrain. Or as studies have shown, it can at once exacerbate social inequities and quiet potential protest, deepen pain, intensify fear, and perpetuate the status quo by mystifying injustice through the dissolution of material discomfort into moments of spiritual utopia.

In postmodern America, ecstasy is most fruitfully understood more broadly, not as the exclusive domain of those who are perennially on the outside, but as a spiritual realm entered into by those who seek escape from—to be placed outside of—the spiritual void that is the legacy of the Enlightenment. Tocqueville's keen observation on the proclivity of some Americans for spiritual enthusiasm as an antidote to the pathologies of capitalist citizenry in one sense prefigures Max Weber's later theory on American work ethics. Weber declared that capitalism developed from the Puritan mandate to demonstrate and confirm divine election through material accumulation—"blessings" functioned as a sign of election. As Puritan theology receded into the twentieth century, America implicitly retained the notion of amassing wealth as a sort of salvific ritual. Sadly, however, the obsessive drive for material benefit left little time for the enjoyment of wealth: Americans, according to Weber, had theologized themselves into an "iron cage." Ironically, the quest for comfort temporally precluded its actualization. Yet at the brink of the twenty-first century,

Americans are striving to emphasize rituals that attend to their collective soul. Theologian Harvey Cox claims that current practitioners of religious enthusiasm are responding to America's "ecstasy deficit." The development of modernity has left few choices for the gratification of the American spirit, which is configured largely by modalities of fundamentalism, rationalism, and liberalism. That is, given the conditions of possibility for making religious choices—the increasingly complex (dis)configuration of postmodern America—the capacity to create certainty, meaning, and physical gratification vis-à-vis mandated discipline is anguished and diminished. The explosion of ecstatic worship in contemporary America, according to Cox, is "a sure signal that the available religious idiom has become inadequate" (p. 315).

Thus, Christianity, like most major religious traditions, has unfolded emotional, pietistic (i.e., pertaining to religion of the heart), enthusiastic, and ecstatic expressions through time and the body. Some Catholics and mainline Protestants alike now enjoy charismatic worship where Holy Ghost–imbued emotional states are cultivated. Open weeping, unrestrained physical gyrations, somatic healing, and speech in tongues (glossolalia) sometimes mark such performances. This last, glossolalia, is the definitive characteristic of Pentecostalism, the fastest growing form of Christianity worldwide.

Beyond Pentecostals, evangelicals, and other charismatic Christians, there are many paths to ecstasy on the contemporary American religious map: Hasidic Jews "cling" to God in ecstatic worship known as *devekut*. Similarly, Islamic Sufism focuses on "mystical union with God," creating ecstatic experience. Phenomenologically, in both ecstatic devotions the Hasidim and the Sufis dramatically overcome the separation between humanity and the sacred.

Along the same lines, American spiritualists have performed spirit possession, ecstasy, and its attendant shamanic manifestations since at least 1848. Well before that (owing to the African diaspora) and continuing into the twenty-first century, devotees of Santería and vodou trafficked with the dead and produced ecstasy in the Americas. Early in the twentieth century the American philosopher William James noted that mystical experience can be engendered by mind-altering drugs (even alcohol), echoing the widely held belief that some religious truths can only be fathomed through mystical, ecstatic experience—that is, by way of sensation rather than rational thought. Small wonder, then, that in 1999 the prevailing "designer" drug of choice on the popular American scene was called "ecstasy," or "x." It is reported to produce euphoria, abandon, and heightened sexual pleasure. In late modernity ecstatic drugs have left an in-delible impression on American youth, especially since the rise of LSD in the 1960s.

When placed within the predicament of American cultural modernism, the sociology of ecstasy recalls Tocqueville's observation that if America's "social condition, circumstances, and laws did not so closely confine the American mind to the search for physical comfort, it may well be that when they came to consider immaterial things they would show more experience and reserve and be able to keep themselves in check without difficulty. But they feel imprisoned within limits from which they are apparently not allowed to escape." Religious enthusiasm provides Americans with the choice to be placed outside, provides an escape, an ecstatic space existing outside normative material and symbolic structural parameters. Cox sees the possibilities as follows: "The contest between the fundamentalist and the experientialist impulses has barely begun. The question of which one will eventually supersede the spent and weary forces of scientific modernity and conventional religion as the principal source of coherence and value in tomorrow's world is still undecided" (p. 308).

See also ANTHROPOLOGY OF RELIGION; CHARISMATIC MOVEMENT; DRUGS; GLOSSOLALIA; HASIDIM; PENTECOSTAL AND CHARISMATIC CHRISTIANITY; RELIGIOUS EXPERIENCE; SANTERÍA; SHAMANISM; SNAKE HANDLING; SPIRIT POSSESSION; SPIRITUALISM; SPIRITUALITY; SUFISM.

BIBLIOGRAPHY

Cox, Harvey. *Fire from Heaven: The Rise of Pentecostal Spirituality and the Reshaping of Religion in the Twenty-first Century.* 1995.

James, William. *The Varieties of Religious Experience.* 1902; reprint, 1982.

Lewis, I. M. *Ecstatic Religion: A Study of Shamanism and Spirit Possession.* 2nd ed. 1989.

Luis D. León

Ecumenical Movement

The emergence of a global ecumenical movement ranks among the more remarkable religious developments of the twentieth century. Christians have been sharply divided by doctrines, geography, and various institutional factors. Likewise boundaries usually have been quite rigid between persons of different world religions. But the last century, particularly since the 1960s, has witnessed an unprecedented degree of activity focused on enhancing religious understanding, cooperation, and unity.

Ecumenism Defined

The Greek word *oikonomos* has a broad meaning, sometimes referring to "ecumenics," "economics," or the management of a "household." When used as an adjective, the word *ecumenical* means "universal" or "global."

Christians historically have reserved its usage exclusively for conversations among its own communions and denominations. Increasingly, however, ecumenism is being understood to be a more relational and inclusive concept that extends beyond Christians and churches to the entire human community within the whole of God's creation. Thus interreligious relationships and dialogue are integral to the ecumenical movement of the twenty-first century.

The Quest for Christian Unity

Inspired especially by John R. Mott's vision at the turn of the twentieth century for "the evangelization of the world in this generation," the modern ecumenical movement began among Protestants (Reformation and Free). The 1910 International Missionary Conference in Edinburgh, Scotland, often is cited as the beginning of the modern ecumenical movement. Orthodox Christians, after World War I, became more involved, especially when the Ecumenical Patriarchate proposed a "league of churches." Founded in 1948 by merging several Protestant streams of ecumenical activity, the World Council of Churches since 1961 has included both Protestants and Orthodox in a global ecumenical organization.

A transforming breakthrough in contemporary ecumenism dawned when Pope John XXIII convened the Second Vatican Council (1962–1965). Roman Catholicism not only joined other Christians but began providing leadership in the quest for Christian unity. Past patterns of Christian insularity and exclusivity started to erode, and new modes of community and service began to emerge.

Not all Christians have been supportive or involved in ecumenical efforts toward dialogue and/or greater unity. Pentecostals generally have not participated and evangelicals often have registered suspicion or protested certain ecumenical developments and statements.

Varieties of Ecumenical Organizations

The ecumenical movement is represented in, but not contained within, any single organization. A variety of structures exist that facilitate ecumenical life and work. These exist not only on a global scale but also in regional and local settings. Increasingly, local councils of churches in the United States include persons of other religious faiths.

Roman Catholic ecumenical activity since 1960 has been centered in the Vatican's Secretariat for Promoting Christian Unity, while the World Council of Churches (WCC) membership incorporates roughly 500 million Protestant and Orthodox Christians in 120 countries. Many evangelical Protestants have globally organized through the World Evangelical Fellowship. In the United States, the National Council of Churches (NCC), founded in 1950, has represented thirty-four mainline Protestant, Orthodox, and Anglican church bodies, while evangelical Protestants have formed the National Association of Evangelicals.

Ecumenical organizations have not only been concerned with matters of theology, fellowship, and church organization. Direct services such as disaster relief, care for refugees, and food for the hungry have characterized Church World Service and other ecumenical organizations. Matters of public policy and justice, both nationally and internationally, have been addressed in resolutions, forums, and direct-action programs. Illustrative are the WCC's effort to eradicate apartheid in South Africa and the NCC's involvement in the 1960s civil rights struggles and the crisis of black churches being burned in the 1990s. Contemporary attention is being given to issues of justice, peace, and the integrity of creation.

Dialogians of the Faith

Christians are moving beyond monologue, and dialogue is replacing diatribe. They are becoming dialogians, not simply theologians, of the faith. The ecumenical movement has inspired a wide range of conversations, consultations, negotiations, and organizations.

Bilateral dialogues are interconfessional conversations in which two religious groups seek to determine the degree of consensus existing in their doctrinal teaching, liturgical worship, and church order. Generally bilateral dialogues do not lead to organic union between the two bodies, but rather they serve to eliminate misunderstandings and help define how far mutual recognition of ministries is possible. Illustrative are official church bilateral dialogues such as those between Roman Catholics and Anglicans, or between Methodists and Orthodox, or between Lutheran and Reformed.

Multilateral dialogues involving more than two religious bodies tend to focus on central themes of Christian faith. Sometimes they lead to organic union, such as the creation of the Church of South India in 1947 and the Church of North India in 1970. In the United

States the Consultation on Church Union (COCU) was begun in 1962 as an effort to create a "truly catholic, truly evangelical, and truly reformed" church. COCU has involved nine denominations (including three predominately African-American churches). Now known as the Church of Christ Uniting (with the same initials, COCU), it has moved away from its original emphasis on organic union toward a more covenanting, conciliar fellowship mutually recognizing one another's baptism, ministry, and so on. Special attention has been given to addressing racism and sexism in American church life.

Intrafaith dialogues focus on exploring unity and disunity within a confession or a denomination. Thus groups like the Lutheran World Federation or the World Methodist Council facilitate relationships within a particular religious heritage or "family." Increasing tensions and divisions within denominations have prompted internal dialogues between more "liberal" and more "evangelical" members. Other combinations have included dialogues such as the Wesleyan-Holiness consultation among persons from the United Methodist Church, Wesleyan Church, Salvation Army, Church of the Nazarene, Korean Holiness Church, and others.

Interfaith dialogues explore differences and similarities among world religions and movements, along with finding ways for mutual cooperation and service. Especially since the Holocaust of World War II, Christians and Jews have sought to build bridges of understanding and oppose anti-Semitism. Broad bilateral discussions between Christians and Buddhists, Jews and Muslims, and various other combinations also are occurring around the world. A loosely defined World Parliament of Religions met in 1893 and again in 1993. Particularly dramatic was when representatives of twelve major religions gathered in 1986, at the invitation of Pope John Paul II, in Assisi, Italy, to pray for world peace.

An Ecumenical Challenge for the Future

Just prior to his assassination, Martin Luther King, Jr., envisioned a "world house" in which persons of various races, nationalities, and religions had to learn to live together in peace, lest they "perish as fools." This ecumenical challenge poses both the great new problem and the great new opportunity for humanity in the twenty-first century.

See also ANTI-SEMITISM; CIVIL RIGHTS MOVEMENT; GLOBALIZATION; HOLOCAUST; NATIONAL COUNCIL OF THE CHURCHES OF CHRIST IN THE U.S.A.; VATICAN II; WORLD COUNCIL OF CHURCHES.

BIBLIOGRAPHY

Abbott, Walter M., S.J., ed. *The Documents of Vatican II.* 1966.

Cracknell, Kenneth. *Towards a New Relationship: Christians and People of Other Faith.* 1986.

Kinnamon, Michael, and Brian E. Cope, eds. *The Ecumenical Movement; an Anthology of Key Texts and Voices.* 1997.

Lossky, Nicolas, José Miguez Bonino, John Pobee, Tom Stransky, Geoffrey Wainwright, and Pauline Webb, eds. *Dictionary of the Ecumenical Movement.* 1991.

Donald E. Messer

Egyptian Church.

See Coptic Orthodox Church.

Elan Vital.

See Divine Light Mission.

Eliade, Mircea

(1907–1986), scholar of world religions.

Eliade was born in Bucharest, Romania, where he developed into a precocious writer, publishing his first article at age fourteen. From the beginning, he published both critical and creative works: studies in alchemy, the history of religions, Asian religions, and literary criticism, as well as stories, travelogues, and autobiographical writings.

In 1925 Eliade matriculated in the literature and philosophy department of the University of Bucharest. A gifted student of language, as a youth he learned Italian, English, Hebrew, and Persian; later he would come to know Sanskrit, Bengali, and French as well. In 1928 in Rome he completed a thesis on Italian philosophy. From there he went to India, where he worked for three years with Surendranath Dasgupta at the University of Calcutta; he also spent an additional six months studying yoga with Swami Shivananda in the latter's ashram at Rishikesh. Eliade's doctoral dissertation, entitled "A Comparative History of Yoga Techniques," is based on his studies in India.

After completing military service in Romania, Eliade served as an assistant to Naë Ionesco, professor of logic and metaphysics at the University of Bucharest. Early courses that Eliade taught include studies of Indian and Buddhist religious thought, Aristotle's *Metaphysics,* and religious symbolism. With the outbreak of World War II Eliade and his wife, Nina Mares, moved to London, where he served as cultural attaché to the Romanian royal delegation. He continued in the same capacity in Lisbon from 1941 to 1945. His wife died in 1944.

After the war Eliade and his stepdaughter, Adalgiza, moved to Paris, where he spent numerous productive years lecturing at the École des Hautes Études and publishing many of his major works. In 1956 he gave the Haskell Lectures, "Patterns of Initiation," at the University of Chicago. The next year he accepted a post as professor and chairman of the history of religions department and as professor in the Committee on Social Thought at the University of Chicago, where he lived for the rest of his life together with his second wife, Christinel.

It is certainly because of his work in Chicago that Eliade came to influence the study of religion in the United States. His thought became accessible to scholars and students, with lasting effect. Major publications include studies of yoga, shamanism, ritual, and myth, as well as encyclopedic works such as *The Encyclopedia of Religion* and three volumes of the series *A History of Religious Ideas.*

Eliade approached the study of religious phenomena as a historian of religions, along the lines of Raffaele Pettazzoni (1883–1959) and Joachim Wach (1898–1955). Eliade regarded the discipline as having three dimensions: history, properly speaking, together with the comparative study of religious morphology and phenomenology (Eliade 1962, n. 1). The goal of the history of religions, in his view, is hermeneutical—i.e., "making the meanings of religious documents intelligible to the mind of modern man" (Eliade 1962, p. 2).

Eliade's approach opens up three avenues for exploring religion. Above all, he provides a neutral language for talking about religious phenomena. For example, the term *hierophany,* which means "the appearance of the sacred," can be used to denote any subjective experience of what is felt to be ultimately real, regardless of the cultural context. The term suggests equally the revelation of a monotheistic God, the revelations of gods and goddesses in a polytheistic tradition, and nontheistic epiphanies. Likewise, *the sacred,* as Eliade uses it, is a neutral term. It points to an evaluative feeling, not to the cause of the feeling; that he leaves to other disciplines, such as metaphysics or psychology.

A second aspect of Eliade's scholarship that continues to influence the study of religion is his understanding of the symbolic nature of religion. Although the hierophany occurs on the subjective level of experience, its expression gives rise to objective phenomena: rituals, myths, sacred art, and ultimately the complex religious traditions that develop over time. Religion, in this sense, is man-made, the human re-sponse to the experience of the sacred. And the nature of religion is symbolic. Humans draw on objects from their everyday lives to express the subjective and ineffable nature of the hierophany. This understanding of the symbolic nature of religion leads to a recognition of the symbolic quality of specific worldviews, such as the historical worldview found in the West in contrast to certain cyclical, ahistorical notions found elsewhere.

Thirdly, this does not lead to a rejection of the historical method, but it does allow for a positive appreciation of nonhistorical ways of living in the world. Archaic cultures and peoples are seen to live richly and rationally within symbolic worlds that have integrity and value. Eliade described himself as a humanist, and the history of religions as a new humanism. His life and his work enrich our appreciation of the human being as always and everywhere creatively religious.

See also MYTH; RELIGIOUS STUDIES; RITUAL; SHAMANISM; YOGA.

BIBLIOGRAPHY

Allen, Douglas. *Structure and Creativity in Religion: Hermeneutics in Mircea Eliade's Phenomenology and New Directions.* 1978.

Allen, Douglas, and Dennis Doeing. *Mircea Eliade: An Annotated Bibliography.* 1980.

Culianu, Ioan Petro. *Mircea Eliade.* 1977.

Dudley, Guilford. *Religion on Trial: Mircea Eliade and His Critics.* 1977.

Eliade, Mircea. "History of Religions and a New Humanism." *History of Religions* 1(1) (1962):1–8.

Eliade, Mircea. *Ordeal by Labyrinth: Conversations with Claude-Henri Rocquet,* translated from the French by Derek Coltman. 1982.

Rennie, Bryan S. *Reconstructing Eliade: Making Sense of Religion.* 1996.

Ricketts, Mac Linscott. *Mircea Eliade: The Romanian Roots,* 2 vols. 1988.

Beverly Moon

Elvis Cults

It has been said that Elvis Aron Presley (1935–1977) is amazingly ubiquitous for a dead man. Mysteries abound—so, therefore, some Elvis devotees point to the hermetic truth that "l-i-v-e-s" is an anagram for "e-l-v-i-s." Similar sentiments have been expressed about other famous figures throughout world history—the most religiously and culturally compelling accounts involving the Jewish reformer known as Jesus

On the left is the Rev. Mort Farndu, cofounder of the First Presleyterian Church of Elvis the Divine, who raises a model of a pink Cadillac during a worship ceremony for Elvis Presley at Packer Memorial Church on the campus of Lehigh University in Bethlehem, Pennsylvania. On the right is the church's cofounder Karl Edwards. (Credit: AP/Wide World Photos.)

of Nazareth. And therein lies the provocative and (for some) disturbing rub when attempting to assess the popular manifestations of the quasi-religious personality cult that has emerged since the ignominious death of Elvis in his Graceland bathroom in Memphis, Tennessee, on August 16, 1977. The diffuse cultural complex that can be designated as the "Elvis cult" has its roots in Elvis's checkered career as a rock 'n' roll musician and celebrity, but it only assumed obvious and compelling religious characteristics in the mid- to late 1980s, at about the time of the tenth anniversary of his death. It was then that multiple "resurrection" and "miracle" accounts were added to the evolving "sacred biographies" and devotional activities associated with him.

An analysis of the current manifestations of the Elvis cult both in America and throughout the world reveals several specific religious traits and themes. An important initial qualification concerns the evident sociological and cognitive differences that define two often antagonistic groups of Elvis followers, somewhat

along the lines of "conservative" and "liberal" Protestants—that is, (1) the "true" fans or believers who constitute a loosely organized populist group of mostly "fundamentalist," "evangelical," or "literalist" devotees who seek a kind of "born again" experiential identification with Elvis, and (2) the "symbolist" devotees who passionately find ironic, satiric, or cultural truths revealed through the multivalent iconic power of Elvis. The first group is primarily made up of working-class people from the United States and other countries who contend most directly and tragically with the material and spiritual "hurt" of contemporary consumer culture. Many are older white women who have some specific memory of the historical "living" Elvis, but a younger generation composed of an ethnically diverse mix of women and men has emerged that knows only the presence of the "dead Elvis." While they are often members of conventional Christian churches, these devotees express their special Elvis religiosity both individually and within small voluntary "fan" associations. Their devotion tends to take the form of nostalgic remembrance via material icons, sacramental devotions, and ritualized pilgrimage to Graceland (especially during "death week" in August). Most distinctive is this group's patronage of multiple impersonators of the King (primarily in the guise of the jumpsuited Las Vegas Elvis), an incredible contemporary *imitatio dei* phenomenon that often has deeply religious trappings and emotions.

The other, more culturally eclectic group consists of various elite and "knowing" factions sharing an interest in "Elvis" as a symbolic metacommentary on various serious and absurd aspects of contemporary culture. This kind of devotion is seen in assorted artistic, playful, and humorous manifestations—especially via the Internet and in all sorts of other literary, cinematic, and televised forms (including semifictive tabloid media such as the *Weekly World News,* which regularly runs "stories" of Elvis sightings). There are also some partially organized mock ecclesiastical movements, some of which, such as the First Presleyterian Church of Elvis the Divine, have written scriptures ("the NIT or the New and Improved Testament"), a set of doctrines or "thirty-one Commandments," certain recommended rituals (facing Las Vegas daily; pork rind and Pepsi communion services), and various cyberspace activities. Finally, there are some interesting New Age appropriations of the Elvis cult that affirm both Elvis's real spiritual power and the esoteric and syncretistic symbolic nature of the movement. Much of this stems from the writings of Elvis's former hairdresser and confidant, Larry Geller, but it has recently given rise to the "spiritualist" speculations of the "near death" theorist Raymond Moody and the channeling experiences of the Canadian housewife Paula Farmer.

The complicated reality of the cult phenomena associated with Elvis Presley has taken many bizarre and often ludicrous turns during its ongoing life in American and world culture. But a recognition of the seriously playful and sometimes absurd nature of the Elvis cult during its recent efflorescence may constitute a realization that has some important bearing on the cultural dynamics associated with any emergent religious cult centered on the continuing mythological and ritual "presence" of a particular charismatic personality. The "founding" of a new religious movement (as well as the "charisma" and ongoing "life after death" of the "founder") is always a complex dialectical practice involving a deceased cult figure, the entrepreneurial "media," and various audiences (both hegemonic and marginal). In the final analysis and despite all the silliness, there is something quite significant going on—something that suggests important lessons about the redemptive role of "religion,"

"celebrity," and "humor" in a world making a confused passage to a new millennial age.

See also CULT; NEW AGE SPIRITUALITY; NEW RELIGIOUS MOVEMENTS; RELIGIOUS EXPERIENCE; SOCIOLOGY OF RELIGION.

BIBLIOGRAPHY

Chadwick, Vernon, ed. *In Search of Elvis: Music, Race, Art, Religion.* 1997.

Farmer, Paula. *Elvis Aron Presley: His Growth and Development as a Soul Spirit within the Universe.* 1996.

Farndu, Mort [Martin Rush]. *The New Improved Testament: The Guide Book of the First Presleyterian Church of Elvis the Divine.* 1997.

Harrison, Ted. *Elvis People.* 1992.

Henderson, William McCranor. *I, Elvis: Confessions of a Counterfeit King.* 1997.

Marcus, Greil. *Dead Elvis: A Chronicle of a Cultural Obsession.* 1991.

Moody, Raymond. *Elvis After Life.* 1987.

Rosenbaum, Ron. "Among the Believers." *New York Times Magazine* (September 24, 1995): 50 ff.

Strausbaugh, John E. *Reflections on the Birth of the Elvis Faith.* 1995.

Vikan, Gary. "Graceland as Locus Sanctus." In *Elvis + Marilyn 2 × Immortal,* edited by Geri DePaoli. 1994.

Norman J. Girardot

Encyclical

An encyclical is the most authoritative of official Catholic Church documents. Encyclicals provide the pope with an opportunity to comment on critical issues in the contemporary church and society (e.g., materialism) and/or to reassess official church teaching on a particular question (e.g., women's equality). Since the Catholic Church sees itself explicating a "universal" morality that transcends the doctrinal beliefs of any specific faith tradition, papal encyclicals are often used as a way to engage public debate on the morality of particular institutional practices. The outlines of Catholic social teaching on economic justice and the rights of workers, for example, were first elaborated in an encyclical issued in the late nineteenth century (Pope Leo XIII, *Rerum Novarum* [*On the Condition of Labor*], 1891), and subsequently elaborated by Pope Pius XI in his encyclical *Quadragesimo Anno* (*On Reconstruction of the Social Order*), 1931. In more recent times, similar themes have been expounded by Pope John Paul II (e.g., *Laborem Exercens* [*Engaged in Work*], 1981), who, like many of his predecessors, criticizes the inequalities associated with global capitalism and who, in reacting to the fall of the Soviet Union, has repeatedly cautioned newly developing capitalist societies against excessive materialism.

The Vatican has issued encyclicals on many diverse topics, but perhaps the most publicly known encyclical is Paul VI's 1968 *Humanae Vitae (On the Regulation of Births)*, which reaffirmed the church's opposition to artificial birth control, abortion, and sterilization. This encyclical caused public controversy at the time among theologians, priests, and laypeople in America and Europe, who argued against the unreasonableness and impracticality of the church's position on artificial contraception. After Vatican II's affirmation of religious freedom, lay competence, and the importance of conscience, these critics saw *Humanae Vitae* as an intrusive and authoritarian document.

The papacy of John Paul II (1978–) is renowned both for the extensive number of encyclicals issued and the didacticism of their tone. A common thread throughout many of these encyclicals is the Vatican's broadly encompassing concern with moral relativism, secularism, a self-indulgent consumer culture, and what John Paul sees as the break between faith and morality that allows individual and self-oriented reasoning to displace the relevance of moral conscience and "divine wisdom" (see especially *Veritatis Splendor,* 1983; *Evangelium Vitae* [*The Gospel of Life*], 1995; and *Fides et Ratio* [*Faith and Reason*], 1998). In *Evangelium Vitae,* for example, John Paul sees contemporary society as a "veritable culture of death" in which there is a "conspiracy against life" as exemplified by the prevalence of abortion, euthanasia, and capital punishment. John Paul calls for a profoundly consistent ethic of life that "cannot tolerate bias and discrimination" of any form and at any life stage, and he challenges people in both their personal and their professional lives to work for a more morally and economically just society (22, 30, 155ff). Although it is well documented that a majority of Catholics (and non-Catholics) do not necessarily follow papal exhortations on specific issues, papal encyclicals nonetheless remain a unique and important source of public theology in today's world and can orient political and intrachurch debate in ways that have the potential to build a more inclusive and just society.

See also BIRTH CONTROL; DOGMATISM; HERESY; HUMANAE VITAE; PAPACY; RELIGIOUS STUDIES; ROMAN CATHOLICISM; VATICAN; VATICAN II.

BIBLIOGRAPHY

Carlen, Claudia, ed. *The Papal Encyclicals, 1740–1981.* 1981.

John Paul II. *The Gospel of Life* (*Evangelium Vitae*). 1995.

Michele Dillon

Enlightenment

The term *enlightenment* is commonly used to refer to illumined states of consciousness in which one realizes the true nature of reality. Notions of enlightenment gained currency in the United States in the 1960s and 1970s as a result of the influx of Asian teachers who established movements throughout the United States during this period.

Among the first exponents of enlightenment during this period was Maharishi Mahesh Yogi, who came to the United States from India at the end of the 1950s and introduced the Transcendental Meditation and TM-Sidhi programs as practical techniques to develop higher states of consciousness. Other Indian teachers who established movements in the United States during this period include Swami Satchidananda, who founded the Integral Yoga Institute in 1966; A. C. Bhaktivedanta Swami Prabhupāda, who established the International Society for Krishna Consciousness in 1966; and Swami Muktananda, whose followers established the Siddha Yoga Dham Associates Foundation in 1974. A number of Zen Buddhist teachers, such as the Japanese master Shunryu Suzuki, founded Zen centers and monasteries in the United States in the 1960s and 1970s, building on the momentum generated by Zen popularizers D. T. Suzuki and Alan Watts. Tibetan Buddhist teachers also established centers and lectured throughout the United States, including Chogyam Trungpa Rinpoche, who founded the Naropa Institute in 1974, and the Fourteenth Dalai Lama, who is currently the most influential Buddhist leader in the world. Theravāda Buddhist traditions were transplanted in the United States as well through the establishment of Vipassanā meditation centers.

Contemporary American notions of enlightenment represent an appropriation and reinterpretation of a variety of conceptions, such as *mokṣa, kaivalya, nirvāṇa,* and *bodhi,* derived from Hindu and Buddhist traditions.

Enlightenment in Hindu Traditions

Indian conceptions of enlightenment generally take as their starting point the Upaniṣadic notion that the supreme goal of human existence is *mokṣa,* liberation from *saṃsāra,* the cycle of birth and death. Hindu traditions provide a range of contending interpretations concerning the nature of, and means to, liberation.

Conceptions of liberation in classical Sāṃkhya, as expounded in the *Sāṃkhya-Kārikā* of Īśvarakṛṣṇa (ca. 350–450 C.E.), are based on a dualistic ontology that posits two fundamental principles: Puruṣa, pure consciousness, and Prakṛti, primordial matter. Puruṣa is eternal, nonchanging, self-luminous consciousness, which is the silent, uninvolved witness of the ever-changing transformations of Prakṛti. Bondage and suffering (*duḥkha*) are caused by ignorance (*avidyā*) of Puruṣa as distinct from Prakṛti. Ignorant persons mistakenly identify with the activities of the intellect, ego, and mind, which are subtle forms of materiality, and thereby are subject to the binding influence of Prakṛti and its continuum of pleasure and pain that is perpetuated through the cycle of birth and death. Liberation from bondage and suffering is attained through the discriminative knowledge (*jñāna*) that distinguishes between Puruṣa and Prakṛti. The enlightened sage, having realized the luminous reality of Puruṣa, the nonchanging Self, attains *kaivalya*, a state of absolute isolation and freedom in which identification with the dance of Prakṛti ceases.

The classical Yoga system, first articulated in the Yoga-Sūtra of Patañjali (ca. 400–500 C.E.), builds upon the ontology and epistemology of Sāṃkhya in its discussions of liberation. However, in contrast to Sāṃkhya's emphasis on discriminative knowledge, classical Yoga gives primary emphasis to practical methods of purification and meditation as means to liberation. It outlines an eight-limbed program of Yoga (*aṣṭāṅga-yoga*), which includes physical and mental disciplines aimed at purifying the psychophysiology and attenuating the residual karmic impressions (*saṃskāras*) that perpetuate the cycle of rebirth. The program centers on a meditative practice that culminates in *samādhi*, an enstatic experience of absorption in the Self, pure consciousness. Through the experience of progressively refined states of *samādhi*, the *yogin* ceases to identify with the fluctuations of ordinary empirical awareness (*citta*) and realizes the true nature of the Self, Puruṣa, as separate from the realm of Prakṛti. The liberated *yogin* enjoys eternal freedom in *kaivalya* and manifests psychophysical powers (*siddhis*) as an expression of his enlightened state.

Conceptions of enlightenment in classical Advaita Vedānta, as expounded by Śaṃkara (ca. eighth century C.E.), are based on a monistic ontology in which the duality of Puruṣa and Prakṛti is subsumed within the totality of Brahman, the universal wholeness of existence, which alone is declared to be real. In its essential nature as *nirguṇa* ("without attributes"), Brahman is pure being (*sat*), consciousness (*cit*), and bliss (*ānanda*) and is completely formless, distinctionless, nonchanging, and unbounded. As *saguṇa* ("with attributes"), Brahman assumes the form of Īśvara, the Lord, who manifests the phenomenal world as an illusory appearance (*māyā*). Deluded by ignorance (*avidyā*), the individual self (*jīva*) becomes enchanted by the cosmic play and mistakenly identifies with the body-mind complex, becoming bound in *saṃsāra*, the cycle of rebirth. Liberation, *mokṣa*, is realized through knowledge (*jñāna*, *vidyā*) alone, for when knowledge dawns the individual self awakens to its true nature as Ātman, the universal Self, which is identical with Brahman. In this state of embodied liberation, *jīvanmukti*, the enlightened sage enjoys a unitary vision of the all-pervasive effulgence of Brahman in which he sees the Self in all beings and all beings in the Self.

Devotional (*bhakti*) schools provide alternative interpretations of enlightenment based on their respective theistic ontologies, recasting the *summum bonum* in terms of union with a personal God. Tantric traditions reconfigure enlightenment in terms of distinctively Tantric categories, including notions of a subtle physiology constituted by energy centers (*cakras*) and the serpentine power of the *kuṇḍalinī*.

Enlightenment in Buddhist Traditions

Among the diverse array of Buddhist traditions, we can distinguish three major complexes—Theravāda, Mahāyāna, and Vajrayāna—each of which presents itself as a distinct path to enlightenment.

Theravāda Buddhist traditions, which are prevalent today in Sri Lanka and Southeast Asia, invoke as their paradigm of enlightenment the Buddha Śākyamuni (ca. 566–486 B.C.E.), the historical founder of the Buddhist community, who is held to have attained *nirvāṇa* under the Bodhi Tree in Bodh Gaya, India, at the age of thirty-five. The Theravāda ideal is embodied more specifically in the *arhat*, the sage who has attained *nirvāṇa* by following the Eightfold Path and the Vinaya, rules of monastic discipline, prescribed by the Buddha. *Nirvāṇa* is described as awakening (*bodhi*) to a state of wisdom, *prajñā*, in which the sage attains direct insight into the nature of reality and realizes that all conditioned things are characterized by suffering (*duḥkha*), impermanence (*anitya*), and lack of a permanent self (*an-ātman*). By means of this wisdom the insatiable craving that is the cause of suffering is rooted out, and the sage crosses over the vast ocean of *saṃsāra* to the farther shore of *nirvāṇa*, attaining liberation from the cycle of birth and death.

The Mahāyāna, which emerged as a reform movement in India during the first century B.C.E., claims to provide a universal path to enlightenment, open to laypersons as well as to monks: the path of the *bodhisattva*, which culminates in the unsurpassable enlightenment of a perfect Buddha (*samyak-sambuddha*). From the Mahāyāna perspective the ideal of the *arhat*, who focuses on the self-centered cultivation of wisdom for the purpose of personal liberation, is inferior to the ideal of the *bodhisattva*, who embodies wisdom, *prajñā*, conjoined with compassion, *karuṇā*, and postpones final liberation until all beings are liberated.

The two major Indian branches of Mahāyāna philosophy, Mādhyamika and Yogācāra, each developed distinctive understandings of the nature of enlightenment. In the Mādhyamika school, founded by Nāgārjuna (ca. 150–250 C.E.), enlightenment is understood as the perfected state of wisdom, *prajñā*, which involves direct realization of the nature of reality as *śūnyatā*, emptiness. In this state of nondiscursive insight, free of conceptual and linguistic constructs, the enlightened sage realizes that all things, whether conditioned or unconditioned, are empty of essential nature. The sage awakens to the ultimate truth that *saṃsāra* is empty and *nirvāṇa* is empty and hence that there is no difference between *saṃsāra* and *nirvāṇa*.

Like the Mādhyamika school, the Yogācāra school maintains that the phenomenal world has no intrinsic reality, but the Yogācāras diverge from the Mādhyamikas by accepting the reality of consciousness (*vijñāna*). The Yogācāras posit that *ālaya-vijñāna*, "storehouse-consciousness," is the repository of all the seeds (*bīja*s) or impressions of past experiences from which the phenomenal world is manifested as an illusory projection of consciousness. Certain Yogācāra *sūtras* identify the *ālaya-vijñāna* with the Buddha-nature, *tathāgata-garbha* ("Buddha womb"), for when storehouse consciousness is purified, it becomes the womb of Buddhahood. In ignorant beings the Buddha-nature, which is inherently pure, is covered by defilements. Enlightenment dawns when the mind, purified through a system of yogic practice, awakens to its pure, luminous Buddha-nature.

Mahāyāna traditions have assumed diverse forms in China, Japan, Korea, Tibet, and Vietnam, including a variety of Zen, Pure Land, and Tibetan Buddhist schools. Each school has developed distinctive conceptions of enlightenment, appropriating and reformulating Indian Mahāyāna notions.

The Vajrayāna is the Tantric form of Buddhism that flourished in India from the eighth through twelfth centuries C.E. and is prevalent today in Tibetan Buddhism and the Shingon school of Japanese Buddhism. The Vajrayāna path to enlightenment shares with the Mahāyāna the *bodhisattva* ideal, the ontology of emptiness, and the goal of Buddhahood, while at the same time it diverges from the Mahāyāna in significant ways. Whereas the Mahāyāna *bodhisattva* path requires eons of spiritual preparation before Buddhahood is attained, the Vajrayāna insists that it is possible to attain Buddhahood in and through this very body, in this very lifetime. Moreover, the Vajrayāna reinterprets the ideal of enlightenment in terms of the figure of the *mahāsiddha*, an unconventional Tantric adept, often depicted as a wandering *yogin*, who embodies the wisdom and compassion of Buddhahood and displays psychophysical powers (*siddhi*s) as a sign of his illumined consciousness. The Vajrayāna path also involves a distinctive system of meditative and ritual practices (*sādhana*) aimed at transforming the psychophysiology and catalyzing the full awakening of Buddhahood.

See also BUDDHISM; DALAI LAMA; HINDUISM; INTERNATIONAL SOCIETY FOR KRISHNA CONSCIOUSNESS; MEDITATION; NIRVĀṆA; TANTRA; TRANSCENDENTAL MEDITATION; YOGA.

BIBLIOGRAPHY

Collins, Steven. *Nirvana and Other Buddhist Felicities: Utopias of the Pali Imaginaire.* 1998.

Eliade, Mircea. *Yoga: Immortality and Freedom.* 2nd ed. 1969.

Fort, Andrew O. *Jīvanmukti in Transformation: Embodied Liberation in Advaita and Neo-Vedanta.* 1998.

Fort, Andrew O., and Patricia Y. Mumme, eds. *Living Liberation in Hindu Thought.* 1996.

Kasulis, T. P. *Zen Action/Zen Person.* 1981.

Klein, Anne C. *Knowledge and Liberation: Tibetan Buddhist Epistemology in Support of Transformative Religious Experience.* 1998.

O'Flaherty, Wendy Doniger, ed. *Karma and Rebirth in Classical Indian Traditions.* 1980.

Streng, Frederick J. *Emptiness: A Study in Religious Meaning.* 1967.

Tweed, Thomas A., and Stephen Prothero, eds. *Asian Religions in America: A Documentary History.* 1999.

Welbon, Guy Richard. *The Buddhist Nirvāṇa and Its Western Interpreters.* 1968.

Barbara A. Holdrege

Epiphany

The feast of the Epiphany (a word meaning "manifestation" and particularly used in antiquity to connote the public manifestation of a deity) is an ancient Christian festival, observed in all the major traditions on January 6. The early Eastern Christian festival (also called the Feast of Lights or Theophany) correlated Jesus' Nativity with the concept of his divine "appearance" and "announcement" among humankind: Angels proclaimed his Epiphany to the shepherds and the Magi, and the voice of God from Heaven declared his Epiphany at his baptism, thus inaugurating his public ministry of salvation (Matthew 3:17). The connection of Nativity and baptism was thus very ancient. In the fourth-century East, the feast was a major occasion for the solemn administering of the sacrament of baptism to catechumens.

A Russian Orthodox priest blesses the waters of the Gastineau Channel in Juneau, Alaska, on Sunday, January 7, 1996. This annual Epiphany ceremony commemorates the baptism of Jesus Christ.   (Credit: AP/Wide World Photos.)

In the Western church, by the third century C.E. the celebration of the Nativity on December 25 had already been established, but by the end of the following century we begin to see a crossing over of liturgical influences, with the mutual observance of two feasts: the East adopting December 25 as well, and the West adopting Epiphany. In the Western approach to Epiphany, however, elements relating to the Nativity were minimally represented, as the major focus was on three principal occasions of Jesus' Epiphany to the wider world: his baptism in the Jordan River; his revelation to the Gentiles (for so the Magi were transmuted into foreign "kings"); and his manifestation to the disciples at the wedding feast of Cana (when they "saw" his glory).

The current forms of the Christian liturgy of Epiphany still reflect this diverse historical background. In modern America the currents of both traditions have been brought together in a creative mix, not the least from the large influx of Eastern European and Slav Christians, whose popular ceremonies mingled with those of Italian and other western Mediterranean forms of Catholicity. Eastern Orthodox

practice now marks Christ's baptism on January 6 with elaborate ceremonies of the "Blessing of the Water." The entrance into the Jordan by Christ symbolizes the purification of all material elements by the physical advent of the Savior. Orthodox Christians drink blessed water on that day, and it is taken home in large amounts for future use. Houses are also blessed by the priests in the week following the feast. In Greece there are large festivals: Boats and nets are blessed; even the sea itself. The village priest throws a blessing cross into the waves, and young men dive to retrieve it. In Greek-American parishes, usually with a dearth of skilled sponge-divers, the clergy take the wise precaution of attaching a line to the cross with which to retrieve it after it has been thrown into local sea or lake waters.

Eastern Christian practice was to associate this day with the giving of gifts to celebrate the Nativity. This was also a feature of many Mediterranean forms of Catholicism. In America and elsewhere, the economic and secular pressures attendant on December 25 are clearly pushing this custom aside. In Catholic custom, the crib often found in houses as well as churches during the Christmas season is "completed" on Epiphany day with the arrival into it of the wise men or kings. In some places (this is especially true for northern Italians) processions of the Magi are elaborately staged in the streets. It is often mistakenly thought that Russians celebrate Christmas on January 6. This is not so, but rather a reflection of the fact that many Russian Orthodox in America still observe the older Julian calendar, which is thirteen days behind the Gregorian calendar. The Armenian Church, however, does retain the feast of January 6 as its primary liturgical celebration of Christ's Nativity. The West has also marked the feast as its "Twelfth Night" on which Christmas festivities would be terminated and decorations removed from houses.

See also Baptism; Eastern Orthodoxy; Roman Catholicism; Salvation.

Bibliography

Bainton, R. H. "The Origins of the Epiphany." In *Collected Papers in Church History,* vol. 1. 1962.

Botte, B. *Les Origines de la Noël et de l'Epiphanie.* 1932.

Cobb, P. G. "The History of the Christian Year." In *The Study of Liturgy,* edited by E. C. Jones and G. Wainwright. 1978.

John Anthony McGuckin

Episcopal Churches

Although episcopal churches have diverse beliefs and practices, they are commonly rooted in the Anglican tradition. The Episcopal Church in the USA (ECUSA), with more than 2.3 million members, is affiliated with the worldwide Anglican Communion, a consortium of churches recognizing one another as legitimate representatives of Anglicanism in their respective countries.

As descendents of the Anglican tradition, episcopal churches have a direct lineage with the Church of England. King Henry VIII in 1531 declared the English church separate from the papal authority of the Roman Catholic Church, culminating a wider English dissatisfaction over matters of authority, discipline, and practice. Elizabeth I set forth the notion of *via media* for the church, meaning "middle road" between Roman Catholic and Protestant influence. Subsequent Puritan and Anglo-Catholic movements produced a turbulent history for Anglicanism.

The first permanent Anglican congregation in America was founded in 1607 at Jamestown, Virginia. By the time of the Revolutionary War, Anglicanism was the established religion in five colonies (North Carolina, South Carolina, Georgia, Maryland, and Virginia). Although bishops, many priests, and loyalists fled to Canada or England, most congregations supported the Revolution. Following the war, representatives gathered as a general convention in 1785 to develop an independent church. Since Anglicanism has a Catholic understanding of Apostolic succession, whereby apostles and subsequently bishops continuously have laid hands on one another since the time of Jesus Christ, the absence of bishops created a crisis. Samuel Seabury, elected bishop in Connecticut, traveled to England to seek consecration. He would not take an oath to the Crown, a required part of the rite; however, the Episcopal Church of Scotland (1784), which imposed no such obligation, consecrated him. This act provided the episcopal authority to initiate what would become the U.S. Episcopal Church (the term "episcopal" comes from the Greek *episkopos,* meaning "bishop").

Other Episcopal churches took a different direction. Church of England clergyman John Wesley had

The new bishop of the Episcopal Diocese of New York, Rev. Mark Sean Sisk, after his consecration ceremony at the Episcopal Cathedral of St. John the Divine in New York City, Saturday, April 25, 1998. (Credit: AP/Wide World Photos.)

founded the Methodist movement, emphasizing spiritual discipline and an evangelical emphasis on experience. Carried to the United States, the Methodist movement grew rapidly in the latter half of the eighteenth century. Partly reflecting the growing tension between Methodism and Anglicanism, the Methodist Episcopal Church in America organized as a separate denomination in 1784. The church, split over slavery in 1844, was reunified in a merger along with other Methodist groups in 1939, forming the Methodist Church. Racial discrimination also resulted in the breakaway and emergence of the African Methodist Episcopal Church (1816) and the African Methodist Episcopal Zion Church (1820), as well as other independent Episcopal churches. Over time, new episcopal churches have emerged with strong evangelical, reformed, Anglo-Catholic, orthodox, or charismatic influences, many catalyzed by protest over changes within the ECUSA since the 1960s.

The ordained hierarchical structure of the Episcopal Church consists of bishops, priests, and deacons, who, along with elected lay leaders, set doctrine and other matters of policy. Dioceses function as the chief administrative units, serving congregations within their geographic boundaries. Governance of the national church occurs primarily through a triennial General Convention, consisting of a House of Bishops and House of Deputies, the latter having equal numbers of clergy and laity elected by their respective dioceses. A presiding bishop, the chief representative of the denomination, is elected every twelve years.

Doctrinally, the Episcopal Church recognizes Anglicanism's three sources of religious authority: scripture, church tradition, and reason. Since church teachings are intended as guidance rather than as binding policy, a diversity of religious interpretation has emerged over time. Consequently, the church tenuously holds together evangelical, low-church Protestant, high-church Anglo-Catholic, charismatic, theologically conservative, liberal, and feminist strains. Partly because of this doctrinal flexibility and Anglicanism's traditional respect for personal conscience on matters of belief and practice, the Book of Common Prayer represents an important symbol of Anglicanism by binding together the diversity of beliefs and practices into a basic liturgical format. Another core symbol, with new prominence since the 1960s, is the centrality of Holy Communion in worship. Overall, Episcopal churches place a greater emphasis on sacramental rites as part of the core worship structure than do churches in more Protestant traditions. The seven sacraments—baptism, confirmation, communion, penance, ordination, matrimony, and laying

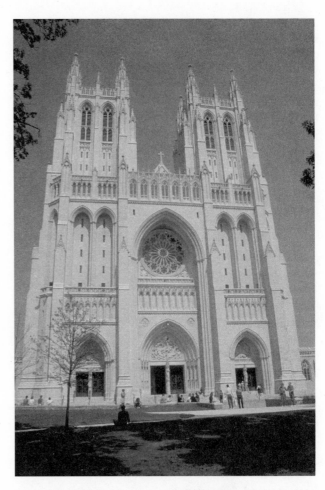

The National Cathedral in Washington, D.C., an Episcopal church in Romanesque style. (Credit: © Ann Purcell; Carl Purcell/Words & Pictures/PNI.)

hands upon the sick—symbolize the church's ties to Catholic tradition.

Contemporary Conflicts: Tradition vs. Transformation

The Episcopal Church has undergone more change and experienced more internal turbulence in the last half of the twentieth century than at any other time in its history. The most pressing issues have involved civil rights activism, conscientious objection to the Vietnam War, revision of the Book of Common Prayer to incorporate contemporary language and worship, women's ordination, and sexual orientation. Additionally, during the 1960s a charismatic movement evolved within the church, reminiscent of Pentecostal tradition and proliferating through the 1970s and 1980s through a variety of renewal movements. The outgrowth has been a growing tension between personal piety and social activism, resulting in a growing parochialism that includes loss of contributions to the national church, which has limited programs and ministries.

After experiencing nearly 20 percent growth in the 1950s and 1960s, peaking in 1966 with 3.6 million members, the Episcopal Church saw a sizable membership erosion in the 1970s as well as several schisms that resulted primarily from women's ordination and prayer book revision. Losses plateaued during the 1980s, with overall numbers of communicants at the end of the century up about 2 percent from 1950.

Some attribute a strong civil rights advocacy by many clergy and laity to expanding rights for women within the church. In 1950 women could neither be ordained nor hold elected lay governing positions in the church. Twenty years later, women were seated as delegates to the General Convention, and women's ordination to the diaconate was approved. Resistance to women's ordination to the priesthood effectively was blocked at the 1973 General Convention. Frustrated, three retired bishops ordained eleven female deacons to the priesthood on July 29, 1974, in a controversial irregular ceremony. Many credit these ordinations with regaining the progressive momentum that led to the 1976 General Convention's granting of priesthood to women. Another crisis arose surrounding the 1988 election of Barbara Clementine Harris as suffragan bishop in the Diocese of Massachusetts, the first female bishop in the Anglican Communion. Her consecration led to the formation of an irregular, nongeographic synod and more schism within the church. Today the church requires that women from any diocese have access to ordination on the same basis as men. Expectedly, the percentage of women clergy has grown, changing the overall demographic composition as men retire. By 1999 about 18 percent of the seventeen thousand clergy were female. Concerns have been raised about the feminization of the priesthood, although men continue to be more likely to attain leadership positions. So far, eight women have been elected bishops.

Issues surrounding sexual orientation also have created tension within the Episcopal Church. While homosexuality itself is not a barrier to ordination, sexual relationships outside of marriage have been affirmed as contrary to church teaching. Progressive movements have sought to liberalize this norm as well as develop a liturgical service for homosexual couples committing themselves to permanent partnership. Traditionalist factions have fought bitterly against such change. In 1996 they brought retired bishop Walter Righter to a church trial for heresy, for having ordained an active homosexual. Righter was acquitted, the verdict being that he violated church teachings but not canons.

Ecumenism has been a major interest of the Episcopal Church since 1960. Currently it is developing an intercommunion relationship with the Evangelical Lutheran Church in America. If approved, the Episcopal Church will retain its distinctive governance and tradition.

See also BOOK OF COMMON PRAYER; CHURCH; LITURGY AND WORSHIP; METHODISM; MINISTRY; ORDINATION OF WOMEN; RELIGIOUS COMMUNITIES.

BIBLIOGRAPHY

Booty, John. *The Episcopal Church in Crisis.* 1988.

Darling, Pamela W. *New Wine: The Story of Women Transforming Leadership and Power in the Episcopal Church.* 1994.

Hood, Robert E. *Social Teachings in the Episcopal Church: A Source Book.* 1990.

Nesbitt, Paula D. *Feminization of the Clergy in America: Occupational and Organizational Perspectives.* 1997.

Prichard, Robert W. *A History of the Episcopal Church.* 1994.

Sumner, David E. *The Episcopal Church's History 1945– 1985.* 1987.

Paula D. Nesbitt

Eschatology

Ideas about a possible end of time have inspired hope in some historic situations and fear in others. Handel's *Messiah* proclaims in majestic tones, "The kingdom of this world is become the kingdom of our Lord and of his Christ" (Revelation 11:15). Yet in works of art from many centuries, faces show terror before a final judgment. What array of ideas could lead to such widely divergent responses?

Eschatology is about end times or last things. Therefore it concerns the future, but it almost always also has a connection with the present. In many forms, its social-psychological meaning is in the longing for a transformation of present conditions of life and the social order. It is one way by which people of religious faith have come to terms with the experience and the theological problem of suffering. An eschatological vision of reality, especially seen as the destiny or goal of humanity, affects the way people view and live their lives in the present. Beliefs about history's end in the kingdom of God have fueled movements of social reform, while some apocalyptic groups who expect destruction to come have sometimes brought it about.

The overall category of beliefs labeled "eschatology" includes many variations. Most scholars agree that ideas about the kingdom of God are an integral part of any eschatology. Millennialism claims that the end will mean a thousand-year reign of Christ within history and is especially prevalent among American Evangelical Christians. Apocalyptic beliefs involve an extreme crisis or catastrophic end. Whether the end refers to human history, to the planet Earth, or to the universe is not usually specified.

Ideas about an end of time pertain especially to Western monotheistic religions and accompany a linear view of history. Eschatology is highly significant in American Christian thought and is also central to many religions that have begun in America, such as Mormonism, Jehovah's Witnesses, and many other movements.

Historically, some aspects of eschatological belief are derived from the ancient religion Zoroastrianism. Its founder, Zarathustra, taught that ethical behavior is connected to judgment at the end of the world. The dominant way that the idea of a radical historical change came to influence Western religious thought was through the Hebrew prophets. Isaiah wrote of a time when there would be no more suffering, when the lion would lie down with the lamb. Other prophets, such as Amos, wrote of the Day of the Lord, a time of judgment and punishment for unjust or merciless acts. Prophetic thought influenced later Judaism, Christianity, and Islam in differing ways. The prophets warned that unless the poor and the oppressed were treated with justice, destruction would follow. They also promised that suffering would cease someday. It is with the later prophet Daniel that visions of apocalyptic events come to the fore.

It is likely that apocalyptic Jewish beliefs prevalent at about the time of Jesus influenced his teaching as well as that of early Christianity. The idea that Israel had God as its ruler is the other major source of the idea of the kingdom of God in Jesus' teaching, where it is key. Scripture scholars have debated the meaning of the kingdom or reign, especially in the past several centuries. With Jesus' promise to return, many Christians in the early movement trusted that the event would take place in their own generation. Ever since, there have been speculations about "the day and the hour," though in the gospels Jesus warns against this. In some New Testament passages it appears that the kingdom of God is fulfilled in Jesus' life and ministry. Others indicate that it is within each person, while others suggest that it is still to come and will arrive like a thief in the night.

Varying interpretations have been given differing emphases depending on the time and place. St. Augustine developed the idea of two cities, the city of God and the city of humanity. More than a millennium later, the reformer Martin Luther (1483–1546) wrote of the two kingdoms. Christian thinkers of all times have tried to understand the relationship between the kingdom of God and the political realm in which they lived. Always the debate has included consideration of ethics: How are we to live? How are we to relate to the society around us? How do our acts relate to our destiny?

In modern times, especially with the influence of Immanuel Kant (1724–1804) and the Enlightenment, the kingdom of God came to be seen as an ethical kingdom and was sometimes associated with the culture of the day. Emphasizing a truly historical and future-oriented ("consistent") eschatology, thinkers such as Albert Schweitzer (1875–1965) and Johannes Weiss (1863–1914) brought a crisis to the biblical theology of their day. For if Jesus believed that God would bring about an imminent apocalypse, he was wrong and, according to the thought of the day, this called all of his teaching into question. It was not long before scholars began to write of a "realized eschatology," suggesting that the kingdom was fully present and realized in Jesus' life and ministry. Though the varying interpretations of the kingdom of God have been debated, most major theologians of the twentieth century agree on the importance of eschatology for Christian thought, many emphasizing some combination of the above interpretations.

In American religious thought, ideas about the coming kingdom of God have played a highly significant role and have influenced American social and political history. From the landing of the Puritans on the North Atlantic shore, religious and political leaders inspired the English-speaking settlers with the idea that it was their mission to build the new kingdom of God in America. They used biblical images such as "city on a hill" and phrases such as "witness into the wilderness." Belief that America was the new Israel in a promised land contributed to ideas about the manifest destiny of the United States.

The Social Gospel movement, led by Walter Rauschenbusch (1861–1918), carried forward the American religious ideal of transforming human society into the kingdom of God and called on the churches to fight the forces of evil in society. In 1937 H. Richard Niebuhr (1894–1962) published the book *The Kingdom of God in America*. In this book he outlined the history of the idea and its importance in relation to American social and political life.

In the latter half of the century, eschatology and the kingdom of God played a role in the social justice and peace movements of the 1960s and 1970s and in the various liberation theologies and came to the fore in the theology of hope. The civil rights movement, which began long before the 1960s, had at least some roots in eschatological hope, a hope that was not just for the far-distant future. Martin Luther King, Jr., emphasized the idea of the kingdom of God and drew upon the writings of Rauschenbusch. King developed the idea of the "beloved community," the ultimate goal of the Christian church. The primary aim was to seek reconciliation and the formation of a community based on love. King's speeches were filled with eschatological imagery, which is one of the features that gave them such power: "I have seen the promised land." Other justice movements combined religious and secularized versions of "bringing in the kingdom" with general religious and secular motivations for justice and equity.

Beginning in the late 1960s, various versions of the theology of hope became popular in American churches and seminaries. Jürgen Moltmann, Wolfhart Pannenberg, and Johannes Metz were three of the German theologians associated with this eschatological theology, and many of their books were quickly translated into English. The philosopher Ernst Bloch and his major work, *The Principle of Hope*, influenced both Moltmann and Pannenberg. Metz's eschatological-political emphasis influenced the development of liberation theologies, especially Latin American theology.

Pannenberg drew upon the eschatological emphasis in New Testament scholarship to call attention to the coming reign of God as a future event that influences the present. For Pannenberg, meaning in history comes only with the whole of history, including its ending. So the end of time, seen in the gospels as the promise of God's reign of love, is that which not only ends history but also brings it to fulfillment and completion. The promised coming of Christ is related to the belief in Jesus' resurrection, as the "inbreaking" of the kingdom of God in history. The end of time is thus related proleptically to the resurrection and to the community of believers. The future of God draws the present world toward itself in love and anticipation. Moltmann's widely read *Theology of Hope* placed similar emphasis on the future and God's reign of love.

In the environmental movement, the contemporary wave of which began in the 1960s, apocalyptic images have been used to motivate people to change their behavior in regard to environmental issues. In fact, at the end of the century, the fear of environmental catastrophe rivals the fear that a nuclear holocaust will end the world. At the same time, the belief of millennialists and apocalypticists that the world will end by God's plan anyway has been blamed for careless and irresponsible attitudes and behaviors regarding the world ecosystems. Along with others, several theologians such as Rosemary Radford Ruether and Catherine Keller have raised questions about apocalypticized eschatology, and instead emphasize human relatedness to all of creation and the need to nurture and care for all of life, so that we will not hasten its demise.

Finally, an important development since the 1960s in American religious thought (associated with an international movement) that is pertinent to eschatological beliefs is the growing dialogue between religion and science. For many theologians who also believe that it is important to understand the natural scientific descriptions of the world, scientific cosmology offers a challenge to teachings about the end of the world or of the universe. Theologian-scientists such as Robert Russell and others consider what scientific cosmology and theological cosmology have to offer one another.

For popular culture, the end of the world may mean the latest box-office thriller. But there are also many Americans whose lives are given meaning and purpose through the belief that the end and goal of history are in God's love and promise.

See also APOCALYPSE; BIBLE; FUTURE OF RELIGION; MILLENNIALISM; SECOND COMING.

BIBLIOGRAPHY

Keller, Catherine. "Women Against Wasting the World: Notes on Eschatology and Ecology." In *Reweaving the World: the Emergence of Ecofeminism*, edited by Irene Diamond and Gloria Feman Orenstein. 1990.

Moltmann, Jürgen. *The Coming of God: Christian Eschatology*, translated by Margaret Kohl. 1996.

Niebuhr, H. Richard. *The Kingdom of God in America*. 1937; reprint, 1988.

Pannenberg, Wolfhart. "Theology and the Kingdom of God." In *Theology and the Kingdom of God*, edited by Richard John Neuhaus. 1969.

Russell, Robert John. "Cosmology from Alpha to Omega." *Zygon* 29 (1994): 557–577.

Stone, Jon R. *A Guide to the End of the World: Popular Eschatology in America*. 1993.

Lou Ann G. Trost

est (Erhard Seminar Training)

Erhard Seminar Training (est) is a quasi-religious therapy developed by Werner Erhard that blends a variety of religious, philosophical, and therapeutic traditions. Norman Vincent Peale's positive thinking, hypnosis, Sigmund Freud's theory of personality, Alan Watts's philosophy, Gestalt psychology, Zen Buddhism, Scientology, Mind Dynamics, Silva Mind Control, Swami Muktananda's Yoga system, and Subud are frequently cited as important influences. Beginning in the early 1970s, est became an enormously popular self-help movement and has graduated more than one million trainees to date. Although est and its successors have undergone several restructurings since 1970 that have reoriented its operation and mission, the "technology" developed by Werner Erhard remains the core of the training. The vast majority of participants are young, middle-class adults employed in managerial occupations.

Werner Erhard was born John Paul Rosenberg in Philadelphia in 1935. After completing high school, Erhard married and worked in sales for several years before abandoning his family, moving West, changing his name, and remarrying in 1960. Over the next decade he worked as a manager in a firm selling *Encyclopaedia Britannica* editions while he explored the various traditions that he synthesized as est. He founded est in 1971 and led the organization for two decades before selling his technology to a consortium of employees and withdrawing from public view. He is most often reported to be residing in the Caribbean.

The organization has undergone several restructurings through its history. In 1984 est was transformed into The Forum, and in 1991 it became Landmark Education Corporation. The training in successor organizations to est is shorter, not as highly structured, and less confrontational. Landmark Education currently claims forty-two offices, primarily in eleven Western nations. Erhard also founded Transformational Technologies, Inc., which franchises management training programs based on Erhard's technology. The core insight that informs est and all its successors derives from a transformative moment in Erhard's life when he had what he describes as a direct experience of himself and discovered that "what is, is, and what isn't, isn't." This revelation led him to develop est, which has as its transformative insight "getting it."

According to est, beings begin as pure space or context and manifest themselves through content. Every being is coextensive with all existence and therefore has created everything else. This means that individuals are the creators of their own universes and that everything that exists arises from the self. Est also asserts that individuals ultimately choose the conditions of their existence and therefore are responsible for them. However, individuals have lost touch with true reality, which is experiential, and mistakenly accept ordinary reality, which is illusory and involves concepts (e.g., beliefs, values, attitudes, and rules). This occurs because the ego (the mind identified with the being) operates through concepts and develops an investment in them, treating concepts as true reality. As a result, individuals routinely fail to assume

responsibility for their own choices, and life does not work because they fail to keep their agreements.

Since individuals are pure beings and have chosen their own existence, the appropriate course of action is to accept one's responsibility for the world as it is and for one's self. Replacing concepts with experience also supplants traditional moral assessment of good or bad, right or wrong with a new standard for assessing the appropriateness of specific acts. This criterion is aliveness, which is defined in terms of such individual qualities as spontaneity, naturalness, centeredness, wholeness, awareness, and fulfillment.

The seminar training in its original form is an intensive two-weekend, sixty-hour marathon experience. In the first portion of the seminar, trainers harshly confront trainees. Trainers seek to undermine trainees' connection to ordinary reality, which is based on concepts, and put trainees in touch with their own direct experience. The processes that constitute this part of the training make trainees aware of their own space and of their ability to eliminate troublesome conditions by completely experiencing them. In later portions of the seminar, trainees confront more profoundly troubling conditions and experience them out. The trainer then describes in great detail how the mind works as a mechanism of survival and links with the being to create ego, which treats concepts as actual reality and defends them at all costs. The recognition that they are programmed into a reality of concepts by the mind but that they also possess the capacity to experience directly is a breakthrough moment for trainees. This transformative moment in which trainees recognize that they are ensnared in their own beliefs, that this self-constructed trap is the source of their demoralization, and that they are free to create their own experience is referred to in est as "getting it."

See also PSYCHOLOGY OF RELIGION; PSYCHOTHERAPY; SCIENTOLOGY, CHURCH OF; SILVA MIND CONTROL; YOGA; ZEN.

BIBLIOGRAPHY

Bry, Adelaide. *est—60 Hours That Will Transform Your Life.* 1976.

Rhinehart, Luke. *The Book of est.* 1976.

Tipton, Steven. *Getting Saved from the Sixties.* 1982.

David G. Bromley
Theresa Eddins

Establishment of Religion.

See Freedom of Religion.

Ethical Culture

Ethical Culture is a religious and philosophical movement founded by Felix Adler in 1876 in New York City. Adler was born in Alzey, Germany, in 1851. He immigrated to the United States with his family in 1857 when his father, Samuel Adler, was called to serve as rabbi of Temple Emanu-el in New York.

The younger Adler returned to Germany in 1870 to study for the Reform rabbinate while pursuing a doctorate in Semitics at the Universities of Heidelberg and Berlin. Adler became influenced by the idealistic philosophy of Immanuel Kant while studying with the foremost exponent of neo-Kantian thought at that time, Hermann Cohen.

Adler returned from Europe convinced that belief in a monotheistic, supernatural God was no longer possible in the modern world. He abandoned his plans to become a rabbi, but he continued to value religion in its power to sanction ethical absolutes, especially the worth of the person. He founded Ethical Culture as a new religious movement dedicated to making ethics primary in all relations of life. Reflecting the influence of Ralph Waldo Emerson, Adler began Ethical Culture as a "free religion," open to all, and without creedal test for affiliation.

Adler developed his own metaphysical system, broadly based on Kant's transcendental philosophy. In place of the traditional God, he developed his own idealistic formulation of the Godhead, which he termed the "infinite ethical manifold." It was an organic, spiritual notion of human unity in which individual identity would, nevertheless, be preserved.

In its early decades, Ethical Culture took on the evils spawned by the Industrial Revolution. Alone, or in partnership with other groups and individuals, Ethical Culture founded numerous organizations that continue to play important roles in promoting social justice in America. Among these are the Visiting Nurse Service, the Child Study Association, the American Civil Liberties Union, the Legal Aid Society, and the National Association for the Advancement of Colored People.

Ethical Culture was prominent in the settlement house movement, together with such pioneers as Lillian Wald in New York and Jane Addams in Chicago. Madison House, University Settlement, and the Hudson Guild remain important New York institutions providing educational and cultural activities for immigrants and the poor.

Adler lent his vision and energy to education as a vehicle for positive social change. He formulated the Fieldston Plan as an educational approach in which ethical and social values would be expressed through vocational training. Though the plan was never fully realized through the Ethical Culture schools he created, it found expression in the development of vocational high schools, now referred to as "magnet" schools in the New York public school system.

Adler considered support for the labor movement his most important social contribution. Finding both free-market capitalism and socialism too committed to material ends, Adler developed his own theory of "vocationalism." It required both workers and owners to more greatly appreciate the ethical component in the production of goods and services. He worked energetically with Samuel Gompers in the support of unionism, and with the assistance of his brother-in-law Louis Brandeis, Adler successfully negotiated a settlement of the 1910 strike in the garment industry, involving more than seventy-five thousand workers.

Adler trained generations of leaders of the Ethical Culture movement who became his associates in Philadelphia, Boston, Chicago, and St. Louis, among other cities. He also initiated an international Ethical Culture movement, with societies in England, Germany, Austria, and Switzerland.

After Adler's death in 1933, the naturalistic humanism of John Dewey replaced Adler's idealism as the implicit philosophical foundation of Ethical Culture. Adler's social commitments were carried on by his successors. John Lovejoy Elliott, renowned for his social work on the Lower West Side of Manhattan, succeeded Adler as leader of the New York Society of Ethical Culture. Henry Neumann, a liberal socialist, was for many years the leader of Ethical Culture in Brooklyn, New York. David Sayville Muzzey, a noted Columbia University historian, was professionally associated with the New York branch. Algernon D. Black, a fiery orator and progressive activist, introduced thousands of New Yorkers to Ethical Culture from the 1930s through the 1970s with his inspiring radio broadcasts.

In the decades since World War II, Black, with the assistance of Eleanor Roosevelt and suffragist Alice Politzer, founded the Encampment for Citizenship. The encampment, a multiracial, residential leadership program, trained youth from around the world in the values of progressive democracy. Participation in the civil rights movement and achieving conscientious objector status for nontheistic inductees during the Vietnam War were among Ethical Culture's initiatives in the 1960s.

Today Ethical Culture societies pursue their work in moral education for children and adults, for human rights, in combating homelessness, and in promoting mutual understanding among peoples in an increasingly diverse society. Ethical Culture also provides wedding and memorial services within a humanistic context.

There are twenty-five Ethical Culture societies in the United States, with centers in New York, Washington, D.C., and St. Louis. The American Ethical Union, based in New York, is the national federated organization of Ethical Culture societies. The American Ethical Union, in 1952, was a founder of the International Humanist and Ethical Union, which unites kindred groups in more than ninety countries worldwide.

See also CIVIL RELIGION; ETHICS; HUMANISM; HUMAN RIGHTS.

BIBLIOGRAPHY
Friess, Horace. *Felix Adler and Ethical Culture.* 1981.
Radest, Howard. *Toward Common Ground.* 1969.

Joseph Chuman

Ethics

The root of the term *ethics* is the Greek word *ethos,* which means the "character, spirit, customs, and guiding beliefs of a people." This is a good way to approach the discipline of ethics. Ethics is primarily the activity of reflecting upon the underlying assumptions, customs, stories, institutions, and accumulated experiences of a culture that guide its moral understandings and expectations. We receive our clues about what is right and wrong, good and evil, worthy and unworthy from this ethos. For example, in the North American ethos, the following are found: Aesop's fable of the boy who cried "wolf"; Walt Disney's tale of Pinocchio; a string of broken treaties with Native Americans; the ninth commandment given to Moses at Mount Sinai, "You shall not bear false witness against your neighbor"; the philosopher Immanuel Kant's terse warning, "By a lie a man annihilates his dignity as a man"; and the Fifth Amendment of the U.S. Constitution, which protects one from being a witness against oneself. This is a sampling of the raw material of our North American cultural ethos, the mixture of stories, key historical experiences, sacred and legal codes, and moral principles that we find ourselves inwardly answerable to whenever we contemplate, as this string of material illustrates, whether or not to tell a lie. A culture's ethos is this great mass of reference points that guide its behavior. Ethics, then, is thoughtful reflection on a culture's ethos, a kind of science of ethos. Ethics sorts through an ethos, inventorying it, bringing to the surface its inconsistencies, and determining its deepest patterns and commitments.

The material that is contained in an ethos will differ from culture to culture. To a Yanomamo Indian in Brazil, mention of Pinocchio will not trigger thoughts of the ugly consequences of lying, nor will a commandment coming from Mount Sinai necessarily have any compelling authority in parts of Asia. That this is so raises the question: If moral reference points are so culturally dependent, is there anything universally true about ethics? Is there any sort of action that is wrong regardless of the culture in which it occurs?

Ethics and the Will-to-Power

Some thinkers have concluded that there is nothing universal about ethics. Social theorists who have been influenced by the nineteenth-century philosopher Friedrich Nietzsche, particularly French deconstructionists (among them, Michel Foucault, Jacques Derrida, and Jean-François Lyotard) and American neopragmatists (such as Richard Rorty), have followed Nietzsche in reducing ethics to the most inventive way in which humans have masked their will-to-power, their fundamental instinct to discharge their own strength and have power over others. Ethical systems, in this view, are designed by the powerful to subdue the masses or by the masses to overthrow the powerful. Ethics, according to this view, is a matter of power contesting with power and has nothing to do with absolute or transcendent goods or rights—because there are no absolutes, nor is there a transcendent reality (God, moral law, or values such as beauty, goodness, or honesty that come to us from some truer dimension of reality) against which to measure human activity.

Natural Law Theories

Other thinkers, however, have retained some belief in the notion of natural law, an idea with deep religious roots in Western thought. Natural law refers to the idea that there is some higher law or moral order that runs through the cosmos, a law that persists in the background of all specific laws and legal codes and which all laws that govern human societies dimly reflect. It originated as a theory among ancient Greek philosophers, particularly the Stoics, and was picked up by Christian theologians, who attributed the validity of natural law to God. God, it was claimed, created the cosmos and ordered it according to certain fundamental principles, the primary of which is that all things are created to seek their own good and that the common good of the whole is found when all of its parts strive for and attain the purpose assigned to them by God. St. Augustine (fourth century C.E.) put his imprint on the idea of natural law in his claim that the human heart is restless until it finds rest in God.

Augustine offered Western thought one of its most enduring conceptions of the moral life—the idea that installed deep within each person is a homing device, as it were, that seeks God through a morally good life and that is agitated and ultimately disappointed when it seeks anything else. This became the preeminent way of understanding the work of the conscience in the West.

In another noteworthy development of this cluster of ideas, St. Thomas Aquinas (thirteenth century C.E.) suggested that the natural law consists in this simple fact: All human beings feel inclined to do what is good and to avoid what is evil. That simple fact, he insisted, is universal. The implication of this is that while different societies may disagree on which intentions and actions are good and which are evil, every society distinguishes between good and evil, and every person, by virtue of being human, senses an inward inclination that favors the good and is repelled by the evil. In spite of the differing moral systems found around the planet, this simple fact of conscience is virtually universal.

Natural Rights and Human Rights

The emergence of the concept of human rights is an important result of this doctrine of natural law and one in which the United States has played an important role. It was the sixteenth-century Dutch Protestant thinker Hugo Grotius who recast the discussion of natural law into the new concept of natural rights. While natural law theory had acquired too much confidence about the knowability of the moral order of the cosmos in Grotius's judgment, he was nevertheless unwilling to surrender a humbler confidence that we can know enough about human nature to base legal theory—the way governments are organized and run—upon it. This represents an interiorization of the doctrine of natural law. Given the renewed emphasis by Protestants on the deleterious effects of original sin on the human capacity to perceive reality clearly, Grotius insisted that we cannot trust our knowledge of the grand moral order of the universe, but we can know something true about our own internal moral order through introspection. What we thus learn is that certain features of human beings, the conscience in particular, ought not to be violated and that any person, institution, or government that attempts to do so is violating our natural rights. We have a right, Protestant thought increasingly insisted, to our deepest aspirations and convictions, and no religious or civil authority may be allowed to intrude upon that.

This appreciation for the sacredness of the conscience became a major catalyst for the Enlighten-

ment, and the United States emerged as an earnest experiment in building a society and its laws out of a recognition of this feature of the individual person. Philosophical reflection on natural rights was concretized into the U.S. Declaration of Independence and the Bill of Rights.

In the twentieth century, and as a direct reaction to the Holocaust and other atrocities surrounding World War II, a further development of the idea of natural rights occurred. In 1948 the newly founded United Nations issued the Universal Declaration of Human Rights, a document that elaborated in thirty-one articles the basic human rights that all nations and their governments must respect in order to satisfy the scrutiny of the international community. One thing that is extremely important but easy to miss in this is the success it represents of the basic natural law doctrine that humanly formulated laws ought to reflect some larger and ideal order of things. A second thing worth noting is the evolution in terminology here from natural rights to human rights, in a sense extending Grotius's religiously based suspicion of our capacity to know the cosmic order; the shift in language from "natural" to "human" is a shift in understanding what it is that grounds the rights that are being recognized. Natural rights were understood to be grounded in the order of nature, which was believed to be inherently moral. Nature bore within itself a moral design that Enlightenment science was confident it could discern. Human rights, on the other hand, are understood to be grounded in the obvious dignity of human beings. In earlier Jewish and Christian understandings, belief in human dignity was derived from biblical stories about humans being the "very good" and culminating act of God's creative work in Genesis, subsequently worthy of God entering covenantal agreements with them and of Jesus sacrificing his life in order to redeem them. In modern human rights thought, because it seeks to appeal to every society, the central idea of human dignity necessarily remains ambivalent toward specific traditional religious accounts for the source of this dignity. Human dignity, in other words, is simply asserted and not backed up with the authority of sacred scriptures or traditions. That humans possess an inherent dignity is presumed to be obvious. The evolution of this can be seen by comparing the opening statements of the U.S. Declaration of Independence (1776):

We hold these truths to be self-evident, that all men are created equal, that they are endowed by their Creator with certain unalienable Rights, that among these are Life, Liberty and the pursuit of Happiness.

with the U.N. Declaration of Human Rights (1948):

Whereas recognition of the inherent dignity and of the equal and inalienable rights of all members of the human family is the foundation of freedom, justice and peace in the world. . . . The General Assembly proclaims this Universal Declaration of Human Rights as a common standard of achievement for all peoples and all nations . . .

In the first, rights are understood to be derived from the divine Creator; in the second, rights are derived from human dignity itself.

Human rights thinking has come to prominence in the United States since 1960. The civil rights movement, seeking equal treatment under the law for people of all races, drew strength from the standard set by the U.N. declaration. Legal arguments are now often couched in the language of rights—the rights to privacy, to bear arms, to life, to free speech. Former president Jimmy Carter attempted to make human rights the centerpiece of his foreign policy. The Catholic Church, under the impetus of Pope John XXIII (in office 1958–1963) and Vatican II (a council occurring in a series of meetings, 1962–1965), offered an explicitly theological argument for understanding the recognition of human dignity and the observance of human rights as the foundation for world peace. In effect, in the 1960s Catholicism offered a theological undercarriage for a doctrine of human rights that returned it to its natural law roots, thus allowing the concept of rights to come full circle.

Toward a Global Ethic

In Chicago in 1993, there was a large gathering called the Parliament of the World's Religions. This was the second time this parliament had convened. The first time was also in Chicago, one hundred years earlier in 1893. The 1893 parliament was the first time that representatives from the world's major religions had met together in one place simply to hear one another out. In anticipation of the 1993 gathering, the Catholic theologian Hans Küng recruited leaders of the major religious traditions (Buddhism, Christianity, Hinduism, Islam, Judaism, Taoism, and so on) to draft the Declaration towards a Global Ethic, a document that isolates four irrevocable directives, upon which the religions are in agreement. The four grow out of the prohibitions found in virtually all religious traditions against killing, theft, lying, and sexual immorality. The declaration recasts these negative prohibitions into a positive framework for supporting human rights. The prohibition against theft, for instance, supports the rights to work, a fair wage, and certain basic forms of welfare. The prohibition against lying supports the right to institutions that provide education and ethical formation—forms of human development that make people less susceptible to lies.

To reach a consensus among the religions on even four ethical principles is an enormous achievement. It shows that the ethos of each has enough in common that agreement across cultural and religious boundaries is possible, at least to some extent. It is by means of the discipline of ethics that such patterns of agreement are discerned and sorted out.

See also BIOETHICS; CIVIL RIGHTS MOVEMENT; HUMAN RIGHTS; VATICAN II.

BIBLIOGRAPHY

Augustine. *Confessions.* Translated by R.S. Pine-Coffin. 1961.

Grotius, Hugo. *The Rights of War and Peace: Including the Law of Nature and of Nations.* 1814.

Human Rights Watch website: http://www.hrw.org.

John XXIII. *Pacem in Terris.* 1963.

Küng, Hans, and Karl-Josef Kuschel, eds. *A Global Ethic: The Declaration of the Parliament of the World's Religions.* 1993.

Mahoney, John. *The Making of Moral Theology: A Study of the Roman Catholic Tradition.* 1987.

Niebuhr, H. Richard. *Radical Monotheism and Western Culture.* 1960.

Perry, Michael J. *The Idea of Human Rights: Four Inquiries.* 1998.

Rauschenbusch, Walter. *Christianizing the Social Order.* 1912.

Traer, Robert. *Faith in Human Rights.* 1991.

Universal Declaration of Human Rights website: http://www.udhr50.org.

Kelton Cobb

Euthanasia and Assisted Suicide

Religious communities have vigorously participated in the extensive debate in the United States, particularly in the latter part of the twentieth century, about assisted suicide, especially physician-assisted suicide, and active euthanasia and about whether legal rules and professional norms should be altered to accommodate those actions. Suicide, the act of self-killing, is generally no longer illegal in the United States, although persons attempting to commit suicide may still be involuntarily hospitalized for their own protection. However, both assisted suicide and active euthanasia are illegal in virtually all jurisdictions in the United States. One notable exception is the experiment in legalized physician-assisted suicide that was inaugurated in Oregon in 1998. In general, American religious communities have continued to support legal and professional prohibitions of both assisted suicide and active euthanasia, often for specifically religious reasons but also because of fears about the negative societal effects.

Although the term *euthanasia,* with its roots in the Greek "eu" (good) and "thanatos" (death), broadly refers to a "good death," it has come to have a more definite meaning in many debates, denoting how the death is brought about as well as the goal that is sought. Thus, active euthanasia is often equivalent to mercy killing. The distinction between active euthanasia and assisted suicide hinges on who performs the final act—the individual whose death is brought about or someone else, such as a physician or a family member. In assisted suicide others may provide considerable assistance to the person wanting to end his or her life, but that person performs the final act. In active euthanasia, however, someone other than the person who dies performs the final act.

In voluntary active euthanasia, the person who dies chooses to be killed by someone else. If suicide, assisted suicide, and voluntary active euthanasia cannot be justified within a particular religious tradition, that tradition will almost certainly oppose nonvoluntary (without that person's will) euthanasia or involuntary (against that person's will) euthanasia.

The term *passive euthanasia* usually refers to letting patients die, in contrast to actively killing them. Even though most religious traditions eschew the language of passive euthanasia, in order to avoid confusion, they do hold that it is acceptable under some circumstances to withhold or withdraw medical procedures that could prolong life so that death can occur.

Within both Judaism and Christianity (Roman Catholicism, Eastern Orthodoxy, and Protestantism), the wrongness of assisted suicide and voluntary active euthanasia stems from the wrongness of suicide itself. If suicide itself is not justifiable, then assisted suicide and voluntary active euthanasia are not justifiable. Suicide is considered wrong in these traditions because it contravenes important moral laws set by God, who created human beings in his own image and who gives them life (Genesis 1:26ff).

Metaphors and analogies are central to theistic arguments against suicide. They involve, as Margaret Pabst Battin notes in *Ethical Issues in Suicide* (2nd ed., 1995), property relationships (for example, life is God's "image," "temple," or "handiwork," or is a "loan" or "trust" from God) and personal and/or role relationships (for example, human beings are God's "children," "sentinels," "servants," or "trustees"). Construing life as a gift invokes both types of metaphors and analogies. Hence, the obligation to protect human life, including one's own, grows out of God's gracious gift of life. According to *Evangelium Vitae* (*The Gospel of Life*), a 1995 papal encyclical, "Man's life comes from God; it is his gift, his image and imprint, a sharing in his breath of life. God therefore is the sole Lord of this life: Man cannot do with it as he wills. . . . the sacredness of life has its foundation in God and in his creative activity: 'For God made man in his own image'."

Debates about assisted suicide and euthanasia often probe these metaphors and analogies: Are there limits on what a recipient may do with a gift? If the gift is faulty—for example, an individual may have serious genetic defects—may it be returned or destroyed? Is the gift, which may cause considerable suffering on the recipient's part, then viewed as a way for God to test or educate the recipient? Centrally important in such debates are the evaluation of human suffering—whether it is valued, merely tolerated, or always opposed—and the implications of the quality of life for responses to God's gift of life.

Despite the general widespread affirmation of sanctity of life, human life does not have an absolute value in mainstream Judaism and Christianity. These traditions, for example, permit and even encourage martyrdom in some contexts, usually accept killing in war and in self-defense, often admit capital punishment, and under some circumstances authorize letting terminally ill patients die.

The Roman Catholic moral tradition has strongly opposed suicide, assisted suicide, and active euthanasia, while formulating several distinctions that allow patients to refuse and family members and health care professionals to withhold or withdraw life-prolonging treatment under some circumstances. It specifies the commandment against killing in the Decalogue (Ten Commandments) to prohibit directly killing an innocent human being. The distinction between direct killing and indirect killing is crucial in distinguishing unacceptable acts of suicide, assisted suicide, and active euthanasia, on the one hand, from acceptable acts of forgoing life-prolonging treatment and of using medications that may hasten death, on the other. It is wrong directly to kill a suffering patient even at his or her request, but it may be permissible to relieve that patient's suffering through medications that will probably, but indirectly, hasten his or her death.

Roman Catholic moral theology further distinguishes ordinary from extraordinary or proportionate from disproportionate treatments. If patients forgo ordinary or proportionate treatments, their actions constitute suicide, or if families and clinicians withhold or withdraw such treatments, their actions constitute homicide. However, if patients forgo or families and clinicians withhold or withdraw extraordinary or disproportionate treatments, which are sometimes called "heroic" or "aggressive," their actions do not constitute suicide or homicide. And they may be morally justifiable. In general, treatments with no reasonable chance of benefit or with burdens to the patient and others that outweigh their benefits may be considered extraordinary or disproportionate and thus may be forgone, withheld, or withdrawn without incurring a moral judgment of suicide or euthanasia.

Despite the great variety of Protestant denominations, there is widespread, but by no means universal, opposition to assisted suicide and voluntary, active euthanasia among denominational statements and theological writings. Some Protestants contend that suicide is wrong because it violates biblical rules against killing, while others hold that it is wrong because it displays a lack of gratitude toward, trust in, and faithfulness toward God as creator, preserver, and redeemer.

Much Protestant reflection on the subject has emerged from individual theologians. Two prolific and influential writers in biomedical ethics—Paul Ramsey and Joseph Fletcher—represent the two ends of the spectrum of Protestant positions on the weight or strength of the rules against suicide, assisted suicide, and active euthanasia. In general Ramsey viewed the rules as absolute, while Fletcher viewed them as mere guidelines. A proponent of "situation ethics," Fletcher defended suicide and active euthanasia in some situations, in part because of the value of personal choice and because of neighbor-love, which he identified with the principle of utility (the greatest good for the greatest number). By contrast, Ramsey in *The Patient as Person* (1970) rejected both suicide and active euthanasia because these acts contradict the meaning of neighbor-love and transgress important moral limits.

Other recent Protestant opponents of assisted suicide and voluntary, active euthanasia include Arthur Dyck, Stanley Hauerwas, William May, Gilbert Meilaender, and Allen Verhey, while defenders include James Gustafson and Lonnie Kliever. In volume two of *Ethics from a Theocentric Perspective* (1984), Gustafson contends that "[s]uicide is always a tragic moral choice; it is sometimes a misguided choice. But it can be, I believe, a conscientious choice. . . . Life is a gift, and is to be received with gratitude, but if life becomes an unbearable burden there is reason for enmity toward God."

Like Christianity, Judaism is not monolithic; there are variations among Orthodox, Conservative, and Reform branches of Judaism. In general, the Jewish tradition rules out both suicide and active euthanasia because of its conviction that human life is created in the image of God. It holds that the duty to protect human life takes priority except where murder, sexual immorality (i.e., incest or adultery), or idolatry would

be required in order to discharge that duty. Traditionally, it has required that nothing be done to the dying person that might cause or hasten death—for example, closing the patient's eyes or removing a feather pillow from under the patient's head. However, the tradition distinguishes actively hastening death, which is prohibited, from removing impediments or hindrances to death, which is permitted, but only for a person who is in his or her death throes.

Much of the discussion hinges on the conception of the dying person whose death is considered imminent (within three days, according to some authorities). Only a patient whose death is imminent and irreversible may be allowed to die under carefully drawn circumstances. Debates center on what kinds of impediments to death may be removed as well as the circumstances under which they may be removed.

In general, Islam's opposition to assisted suicide and voluntary, active euthanasia is similar to dominant positions in Judaism and Christianity, while both Hinduism and Buddhism have more ambiguous positions—for example, Hinduism and Buddhism have historically accepted some acts of suicide, such as those of holy men, but there is vigorous debate about whether such precedents can extend to assisted suicide and voluntary, active euthanasia as they are currently conceived and practiced.

Much of the debate in the United States in the late twentieth century has focused on whether laws should permit or regulate assisted suicide and voluntary, active euthanasia rather than continuing to prohibit them. While there is a rough correlation between moral judgments about such acts and moral judgments about laws regarding them, the latter judgments are more complex. According to sociologist Andrew Greely, opinion polls suggest that in recent decades there has been a substantial increase in support among religious believers for legalization of physician assistance in ending life.

Not all arguments by religious thinkers or communities for or against legal prohibition are themselves religious arguments. Proponents of legal prohibition frequently appeal to the probable negative consequences of permissive laws, including the difficulty of drawing and maintaining defensible lines, the dangers of abuse, especially because American society often devalues the elderly and fails to provide universal access to health care, and the risks of creating or extending what the Vatican calls a "culture of death." By contrast, opponents of prohibition generally believe that these dangers are exaggerated and/or that strong regulation could reduce their threat.

See also BIOETHICS; DEATH AND DYING; ETHICS.

BIBLIOGRAPHY

Campbell, Courtney S. "Religious Ethics and Active Euthanasia in a Pluralistic Society." *Kennedy Institute of Ethics Journal* 2 (September 1992): 253–277.

Childress, James F. "Religious Viewpoints." In *Regulating How We Die: The Ethical, Medical, and Legal Issues Surrounding Physician-Assisted Suicide,* ed. Linda L. Emanuel. 1998.

Dorff, Elliot N., and Louis E. Newman, eds. *Contemporary Jewish Ethics and Morality: A Reader.* 1995.

Greely, Andrew. "Live and Let Die: Changing Attitudes." *Christian Century* 108 (1991): 1124–1125.

Hamel, Ronald P., and Edwin R. Dubose, eds. *Must We Suffer Our Way to Death? Cultural and Theological Perspectives on Death by Choice.* 1996.

Kilner, John F., Arlene B. Miller, and Edmund D. Pellegrino, eds. *Dignity and Dying: A Christian Appraisal.* 1996.

Reich, Warren T., ed. *Encyclopedia of Bioethics.* 2nd ed., 1995.

James F. Childress

Evangelical Christianity

The word "evangelical" has several legitimate senses all related to the etymological meaning of "good news." For Christians of many types throughout history the word has been used to describe God's redemption of sinners by the work of Christ. In the Reformation of the sixteenth century it became a rough synonym for "Protestant." That history explains why many Lutherans still employ the term (e.g., the Evangelical Lutheran Church in America). The most common use of the word today stems from renewal movements among English and American Protestants in the eighteenth century and from practitioners of revival in the nineteenth and twentieth centuries. The early movements were led by larger-than-life figures such as John and Charles Wesley, founders of Methodism; George Whitefield, the most effective preacher of his day; and Jonathan Edwards, a Massachusetts clergyman known for his profound intellect and his passionate defense of Calvinism. The later revival movements have been represented by a noteworthy series of public preachers, including Charles Grandison Finney (1792–1875), D. L. Moody (1837–1899), and Billy Graham (1918–).

In one of the most useful definitions, the British historian David Bebbington has identified the key ingredients of evangelicalism as conversionism (an emphasis on the "new birth" as a life-changing experience of God), biblicism (a reliance on the Bible as ultimate religious authority), activism (a concern for sharing the faith), and crucicentrism (a focus on Christ's redeeming work on the cross, usually pictured as the only way of salvation). These evangelical traits have never by themselves yielded cohesive, institutionally compact, or clearly demarcated groups of Christians. But they do serve to identify a large family of churches and religious enterprises.

The prominence of the Bible and focus on Christ as the means of salvation link evangelical traditions with earlier Protestant movements such as English and American Puritanism. But where the Puritans worked for purified state-church establishments, most modern evangelicals have been independent-minded people delighted with the separation of church and state. In addition, where Puritanism retained an exalted role for the clergy and great respect for formal learning, modern evangelicalism, powered by lay initiatives, has been wary of formal academic credentials.

The relationship of African-American churches to evangelical traditions is complex. Blacks in America only began to accept Christianity in the mid-eighteenth century, when the Christian message was presented to them by evangelicals such as Whitefield or the Virginia Presbyterian Samuel Davies. To this day, most African-American denominations and independent congregations share many evangelical characteristics, including belief in the "new birth," trust in the Scriptures, and commitment to traditional morality. Some white evangelicals, such as the theologian Samuel Hopkins and the founder of American Methodism, Francis Asbury, were also early leaders in the fight against slavery. Yet other evangelicals, North as well as South, either tolerated or defended slavery. Throughout the nineteenth century almost all white evangelicals also frowned on elements of African ritual retained in the worship of black Christians. The fact that in the twentieth century white evangelicals have mostly supported the social and political status quo means that ties between black Protestants and white evangelicals are not as close as their shared religious beliefs might lead an observer to expect.

For much of the nineteenth century white evangelical Protestants constituted the largest and most influential body of religious adherents in the United States (as also in Britain and Canada). Methodists, Baptists, Presbyterians, Congregationalists, and many Episcopalians shared broadly evangelical convictions—though they could battle each other aggressively on the details of those convictions. Evangelical elements were prominent among Lutherans, German and Dutch Reformed, and the Restorationist churches (Churches of Christ, Disciples of Christ) as well.

Division in the Protestant tradition—especially the fundamentalist-modernist battles of the first quarter of the twentieth century—greatly weakened the public presence of evangelicalism. At about the same time, large-scale immigration of non-Protestants, the growth of cities as multicultural sites, and the secularization of higher learning also eroded evangelical cultural influence. The passing of evangelical cultural dominance, however, was also accompanied by significant new developments. The most important of these was the emergence of Pentecostalism, which began early in the twentieth century as an outgrowth of emphases on Christian "holiness" in several Protestant bodies. With its emphasis on the direct work of the Holy Spirit, Pentecostalism has become a major worldwide force in the twentieth century. Its influence is seen in denominations such as the mostly white Assemblies of God and the mostly African-American Church of God in Christ, but also in a wide variety of other denominations and traditions, especially through the charismatic movement after World War II.

In the period of the Great Depression and World War II, evangelicalism was less visible than it has ever been, before or since, in American life. The fundamentalist strand of evangelicalism promoted "separation" from the world and the construction of a self-contained network of churches, publishers, Bible schools, colleges, and radio broadcasting (in which fundamentalists were the pioneers for religious purposes). Out of sight of media elites and against the trend of the older Protestant groups, several evangelical denominations—including the Southern Baptist Convention, Assemblies of God, and the Christian and Missionary Alliance—grew rapidly in the 1930s and 1940s. In roughly the same period fundamentalists and evangelicals established new connections with a number of immigrant traditions, such as the Dutch-American Christian Reformed Church and several Mennonite denominations, which would later play a large role in post–World War II evangelical enterprises. It was often traveling ministers or radio broadcasts—such as those emanating from the Moody Bible Institute in Chicago—that made these connections.

The three decades from the end of World War II to the mid-1970s marked a distinct era in American evangelical history. The prominent public activity of the evangelist Billy Graham inspired many fundamentalists and evangelicals, especially in the North, even as it recruited new adherents for evangelical causes and created coalitions beyond previous evangelical boundaries. Postwar "neoevangelicalism," a phrase popular in the 1950s and 1960s to describe former fundamentalists who sought a positive public image, was, however, considerably more than Billy Graham. When Graham downplayed issues central to earlier

An evangelical minister leads congregants in a revival service in Tulsa, Oklahoma, in 1982.
(Credit: CORBIS/Annie Griffiths Belt.)

fundamentalist-modernist strife and set aside some fundamentalist shibboleths (such as avoidance of the cinema), many were eager to follow. In New England, the Philadelphia area, the upper Midwest, and California a small but vocal generation of articulate post-fundamentalists came of age as Graham's willing colleagues. During the war itself, these leaders founded the National Association of Evangelicals in 1942 to handle relations with the government and promote transdenominational cooperation. Soon the combined efforts of institutional leaders such as Harold John Ockenga, intellectuals such as Carl F. H. Henry, wealthy laymen such as Herbert J. Taylor of Club Aluminum and J. Howard Pew of Sun Oil, along with a host of missionary-minded young people, led to the creation or expansion of many ventures. These included Fuller (Pasadena, California), Gordon-Conwell (north of Boston), and Trinity (suburban Chicago) seminaries, which, along with Southern Baptist institutions, became by the 1980s the largest centers of pastoral training in the United States. They also included *Christianity Today* and several other periodicals, a number of active youth ministries such as Youth for Christ, InterVarsity Christian Fellowship, Young Life, and Campus Crusade for Christ. As part of this same surge, self-identified evangelicals soon made up the largest component of missionaries sent from the United States to other parts of the world.

The circle of individuals and agencies associated with Billy Graham was the most visible evangelical presence in these years, but many other evangelical groups were also at work. These included rapidly expanding Pentecostal denominations (whose leaders reached out to the Graham network), the strengthening of many evangelical churches in the South (which has always functioned as something of a self-contained religious domain), and the expansion of "holiness" denominations such as the Church of the Nazarene.

In marked contrast to the vigorous political activism of the nineteenth century, most evangelicals from 1928 (when the presence of a Catholic candidate for president on the Democratic ticket energized evangelical support for Republican Herbert Hoover) into the early 1970s remained largely quiet politically. Southern evangelicals were Democrats, like most of their region. Northern evangelicals leaned Republican but were not particularly active.

Since the early 1970s the diversity that always existed within American evangelicalism has become much more obvious. In addition, America's major social convulsions, such as racial conflict, the women's movement, and sexual permissiveness, have inspired a political reaction among many sectors of evangelicalism. Religious developments, including the charismatic movement, the decline of denominations, and the growth of parachurch networks have also shaped recent evangelical history.

Rulings by the U.S. Supreme Court in the 1960s that eliminated prayer in the public schools and in 1973 that legalized abortion on demand contributed to evangelical politicization. For many, these decisions, along with controversies over what should or should not be taught in the public schools and the growth of the federal government, were perceived as a decline in national moral values. Evangelicals of the Billy Graham sort remained relatively quiet in the face of these new political challenges. But other leaders, such as Baptist ministers Jerry Falwell and Timothy LaHaye, television broadcaster Pat Robertson, and lay psychologist and radio host James Dobson, entered politics with a vengeance during the 1970s and 1980s. These leaders, rather than the neoevangelical stalwarts of the previous generation, created the "New Christian Right" and made white conservative evangelical support an anchor in the presidential campaigns of Ronald Reagan and for much of Republican politics since Reagan.

Recent decades have also witnessed a repositioning of old antagonisms. While American evangelicals still keep their distance from institutional Roman Catholicism, a wide array of social, political, academic, and reforming efforts now link some evangelicals with some Catholics. Evangelicals have helped once-sectarian groups such as the Seventh-Day Adventists and the Worldwide Church of God in their move toward more traditional Christian affirmations. At the end of the century there were even a few signs of improved relations between some evangelicals and Mormons, whom most evangelicals had long considered far beyond the pale.

With the decreasing influence of the older, mainline Protestant churches, evangelicals now worry less about theological liberalism and more about multiculturalism, postmodernism, and the general secularization of public life. Evangelicals also now expend considerable energy in debating styles of worship, with much support in many churches for innovative contemporary styles (e.g., as on display at the seventeen-thousand-member Willow Creek Community Church in suburban Chicago), while others promote traditional patterns of worship, and many vacillate in between.

Charting the size of the American evangelical constituency at the close of the century depends on criteria for definition. A 1996 poll of three thousand Americans by the Angus Reid group included four questions related specifically to traditional evangelical concerns: Was the Bible the inspired Word of God? Are you a converted Christian? Does God provide forgiveness of sins through the "life, death, and resurrection of Jesus Christ"? Is it important to urge non-Christians to become Christians? Nearly a third of the U.S. sample answered affirmatively to all four questions, and another 20 percent affirmed three of the four. (Proportions of those answering positively were much higher than national population distribution in the South and considerably lower in the West and Northeast. In addition, about 35 percent of American Catholics answered positively to three or four of these questions.) Alternatively, a team of political scientists (John C. Green, James L. Guth, Corwin Smidt, and Lyman A. Kellstedt) has recently published a series of perceptive works on the political behavior of American religious groups. They find that about one-fourth of the American populace is associated with historically evangelical churches and denominations. Of that number they find about 60 percent quite active in their participation. As a third way of measuring the size of the evangelical constituency, a research team headed by sociologist Christian Smith has recently published important books and articles based on those who use the term "evangelical" to describe themselves, their churches, and their wider connections. These sociologists find about 7 percent of the population using that term of self-designation and participating actively in self-described "evangelical" enterprises.

Because of the imprecision of the term, more care is required than is often exercised in speaking of America's evangelical Christians. Yet however defined, it is clear that evangelical Christian traditions remain an important force in contemporary religious life—for social and political, but supremely for religious reasons.

See also AFRICAN-AMERICAN RELIGIONS; CAMPUS CRUSADE FOR CHRIST; CHARISMATIC MOVEMENT; FALWELL, JERRY; FUNDAMENTALIST CHRISTIANITY; GRAHAM, BILLY; INTERVARSITY CHRISTIAN FELLOWSHIP; MAINLINE PROTESTANTISM; PENTECOSTAL AND CHARISMATIC CHRISTIANITY; RELIGIOUS RIGHT; ROBERTSON, PAT; TELEVANGELISM; YOUNG LIFE; YOUTH FOR CHRIST.

BIBLIOGRAPHY

Balmer, Randall. *Mine Eyes Have Seen the Glory: A Journey into the Evangelical Subculture in America.* 1989.

Bebbington, David W. *Evangelicalism in Modern Britain: A History from the 1730s to the 1980s.* 1989.

Blumhofer, Edith L. *Restoring the Faith: The Assemblies of God, Pentecostalism, and American Culture.* 1993.

Carpenter, Joel A. *Revive Us Again: The Reawakening of American Fundamentalism.* 1997.

Dayton, Donald W., and Robert K. Johnston, eds. *The Variety of American Evangelicalism.* 1991.

Green, John C., James L. Guth, Corwin Smidt, and Lyman A. Kellstedt. *Religion and the Culture Wars: Dispatches from the Front.* 1996.

Marsden, George M. *Fundamentalism and American Culture: The Shaping of Twentieth-Century Evangelicalism, 1870–1925.* 1980.

Smith, Christian. *American Evangelicalism: Embattled and Thriving.* 1998.

Mark A. Noll

Evil

Evil is an umbrella concept that includes both a moral aspect (sin) and a natural, nonmoral aspect (suffering). Most religions address both moral evil and natural evil.

In the two largest religions in America, Judaism and Christianity, interest in the nature of evil is a secondary interest; the primary interest is in salvation from evil. Still, both of these religions, and many others, teach certain things about evil. Some religions approve of evil. For example, in Satanism it is taught that evil should be embraced. This is a rare view; most religions teach that moral evil is to be avoided rather than embraced. Some religions deny or minimize the importance of evil. For example, in the Church of Christ, Scientist, goodness has been understood to be more real than evil. This also is a rare view; most religions acknowledge the reality of evil.

In the early part of the twentieth century some liberal and modernist forms of Judaism and Christianity seemed to lack a serious view of moral evil; they were characterized by confidence in human progress by means of education and goodwill. Across several decades, optimism concerning the manageability of evil has diminished and is now regarded by many Americans as naive. The realistic attitude that Judaism and Christianity have traditionally taken toward evil is one of the factors that renders these faiths plausible to many thoughtful people in America. Embracing, denying, and minimizing the seriousness of evil are not characteristic of very much religion in America.

Moral Evil (Sin)

Moral evil is an important concept in the religious thought and action of the majority of Americans. Within the Jewish and Christian traditions, moral evil is presented as having two faces. Just as crimes have perpetrators and victims, so moral evil has perpetrators and victims. Perpetrators of moral evil are persons who know the difference between right and wrong, who have the power to choose either right or wrong, and who choose to do wrong. An example is a person who betrays and thereby needlessly hurts a friend. Victims of moral evil are persons who are in the grasp or power of forces beyond their control, so that they do not have the power to do what is right. Examples of victims are persons who, because of their addiction to drugs, diminish their own lives and harm the lives of those they love.

Most religions recognize the distinction between perpetrators and victims. Nevertheless, within the religions there are intense discussions about the distinction. One such discussion within Christianity and Judaism concerns the nature of the moral evil that victimizes people. For example, what is it that causes people to become addicts? There are both Jews and Christians who think that the question is not a proper one. They insist that every human being has the freedom to choose between good and evil, that some have freely chosen evil, that addicts are simply people doing what they have chosen to do, and that there is nothing else to be said about the matter. In other words, addicts are actually perpetrators, not victims, or at least they began as perpetrators and then developed a habit or taste for drugs. Those who take this position point out that it offers a high view of human beings because it holds human beings responsible for everything that is wrong in their lives. To do this, to hold people responsible, is to affirm their freedom and therefore their dignity.

Few if any Jews or Christians would retreat entirely from the concept that human beings are responsible for some of their conduct, but many have come to doubt that human beings are responsible for all of their conduct. They are convinced that there is more to evil than discrete choices made by free, rational individuals. One of the things that has called attention to the fact that there is more than this to evil is the history of the twentieth century. To speak of individual choices just does not seem to do justice to the immensity of the evils of the century. Something more seems needed to account for what Adolf Hitler did to millions of Jews, Gypsies, homosexuals, and others in the Third Reich, for what Joseph Stalin did to millions of his countrymen, and for what Pol Pot did to many of his countrymen.

But what is this "more"? One traditional set of candidates is the devil and the demons. In Europe and North America the view that there are actually personal demons that oppress people has been losing ground for centuries. It does not help the case for demons that they are widely believed in throughout the industrially undeveloped world, for that leads naturally to the conclusion that belief in demons is one of the superstitions that should be sloughed off once scientific enlightenment is available.

Some traditional Christians and Jews have always retained a belief in demons because there are references to demons in the Bible. This belief got support from one movement that arose within Christianity in the twentieth century: Pentecostalism. But most Christians who reflected carefully on the power of evil tended to turn in other directions. One of those directions is psychology. Throughout the century there has been widespread interest in psychology, and the principal forms of psychology have acknowledged that darkness exists deep within the self of human beings. Various explanations have been offered for this evil. For example, human beings have something like a memory of early childhood experiences of powerlessness that generate fear and rage, and these emotions propel human beings to do evil.

Others have sought an explanation for evil in evolution. Human beings, it is said, have evolved from lower forms of life whose survival depended on their being violent; the tendency to violence has remained in human beings as they have evolved, and their violence leads them to do evil things. Ironically, human beings, unlike lower animals, kill even when killing is not necessary for their survival. Others have looked for an explanation for evil in the social character of human beings, a view that owes much to the French philosopher Jean-Jacques Rousseau. In isolation human beings tend to be good, but in the collective they become capable of evil they would never dream of perpetrating on their own—for example, the evils of racism. Moral human beings create immoral societies. Still others have looked for an explanation for evil in the institutions of society. Organizations, bureaucracies, and especially governments diminish and dehumanize human beings and thereby launch them into conduct that is contrary to their otherwise good tendencies.

These explanations seem plausible to many Jews and Christians. There is much less naive optimism about people at the end of the murderous twentieth century than there was at its beginning. In the industrially developed world belief in personal demons still stretches the credulity of most people, but recognition that there is more to evil than the choices of individuals is widely accepted. Additionally, it is now widely acknowledged by Christians and Jews that there is a mystery to evil. Evil is not something that human beings happen not to understand; evil is something that will always defy human understanding. This is not surprising, because to understand is to grasp the rationality of things, and what is characteristic of evil is that it is not rational at all but rather irrational.

Natural Evil (Suffering)

In the Jewish and Christian faiths, there is a close connection between sin and suffering. Suffering, it is said, is a consequence of sin. The story of Adam and Eve in the Garden of Eden, told in the first book of the Bible, Genesis, displays that connection. Until Adam and Eve had sinned, they lived a life free of suffering; as a consequence of their sin—indeed, as a punishment for it—they were driven from Eden and began to experience suffering.

Formed by this teaching of Scripture, American Jews and Christians tend to acknowledge that moral evil can lead to suffering. They accept the link between sin and suffering that is taught in the Bible, but they also are aware that a great deal of suffering is not attributable to any moral failure. For example, some babies are born with birth defects that cannot be attributed to any conduct of either their parents or any other human beings. In the Bible the Book of Job is addressed to the question of undeserved suffering, so there has been an awareness of the problem for centuries.

Many Christians, Jews, and Muslims do not make any attempt to understand the problem. They see it as an act of loyalty to God to refuse to ask why bad things happen to good people. They regard uncomplaining submission to whatever happens to them as part of their obedience to God. Many others, however, do attempt to understand the problem of undeserved suffering. Their attempts are exercises in theodicy, a defense of the power and goodness of God in the face of undeserved suffering.

Suffering is a universal human problem, but it is a problem in a special sense for Jews, Christians, and Muslims. This is because these religions have an understanding of God that says that the one and only God is all-good and all-powerful. But, the argument goes, if God is all-good, then God must want to prevent undeserved suffering; and if God is all-powerful, then God must be able to prevent undeserved suffering; but since undeserved suffering happens, it follows either that God is not all-good or that God is not all-powerful. This is the most powerful and influential argument ever made against faith in God, so it is not surprising that some people have been led by this argument to surrender their faith in God altogether.

Others have been led to surrender some aspect of their faith in God. For example, in his book *When Bad Things Happen to Good People,* Rabbi Harold Kushner says that he believes that God is all-good but not all-powerful; God is very powerful but not powerful enough to prevent all of the suffering that occurs in the world. On the other hand, Christian theologian Frederick Sontag has affirmed that God is all-powerful but not all-good; he even speaks of a demonic side to God.

These are ideas that are held principally by intellectual minorities in Judaism, Christianity, and Islam. The majority of the faithful of these religions have retained the traditional belief in a God who is all-good and all-powerful. They recognize that there is a mystery about suffering that they cannot explain, but they also welcome such relief as the various explanations may provide. They look forward to a time when all undeserved suffering will be ended, and they expect that it is only then that human beings will have a full understanding of undeserved suffering.

Both moral evil (sin) and natural evil (suffering) continue to occupy an important place in American religions today, just as they have in most religions since ancient times, and there is no sign that their importance will be diminished in American religion in the near future. It is rare for anyone in an American religion to claim to have a comprehensive explanation for the nature of sin and suffering; it is much more common for people in American religions to acknowledge the mystery of these great human problems. It is even more common in religions in America for the claim to be made that God provides salvation from evil. In that claim lies the good news that is most characteristic of each of the religions.

See also Devils, Demons, and Spirits; God; Hell; Psychology of Religion; Psychotherapy; Satanic Bible; Satanists; Sociology of Religion; Suffering; Theodicy.

BIBLIOGRAPHY

Davis, Stephen T., ed. *Encountering Evil.* 1981.
Duffy, Stephen J. "Our Hearts of Darkness: Original Sin Revisited." *Theological Studies* 49 (1988): 597–622.
Hick, John. *Evil and the God of Love.* 1966.
Kushner, Harold S. *When Bad Things Happen to Good People.* 1981.
Niebuhr, H. Richard. *The Kingdom of God in America.* 1937.
Niebuhr, Reinhold. *Moral Man and Immoral Society.* 1960.
Niebuhr, Reinhold. *The Nature and Destiny of Man.* 1941, 1943.
Ricoeur, Paul. *The Symbolism of Evil.* 1967.
Tilley, Terrence W. *The Evils of Theodicy.* 1991.

Fisher Humphreys

Existentialism

Existentialism defies definition. Its most prominent representatives would rather say "I am I" than "I am an existentialist," because they see categorization as a betrayal of reality. Yet existentialism is a recognizable force in the modern world. A prominent philosophy, it has been an equally powerful movement in fiction, the theater, the visual arts, and music.

Existentialism explores human existence in its hopes and fears, its fragility, its conflicts and insecurities. Its vocabulary emphasizes freedom, angst (anxiety, anguish, dread), and absurdity. It sees reliance on pleasure, contentment, economic success, and security as a shallow, inauthentic existence.

The great personality at its source was the Danish Søren Kierkegaard (1813–1855). He cherished Socrates, the "gadfly" of Athens, and the Bible, especially the story of Abraham and Isaac, the Psalms, and the record of Jesus. His younger contemporaries Friedrich Nietzsche (1844–1900) and Fyodor Dostoyevsky

(1821–1881), although they did not know of Kierkegaard, were major movers in existentialism.

Kierkegaard, a witty man-about-town, enjoyed café life and the theater but believed that the aesthetic and even the ethical levels of life were inadequate. For true existence he urged a "leap of faith," a venturing far out on seventy thousand fathoms of water, trusting for security not the nearness of shore but the buoyancy of the sea.

That led to the great divide in existentialism: between believers and atheists. Nietzsche declared the death of God, killed by human beings in an act that led Nietzsche both to shudder and to exult. Martin Heidegger (1889–1976) was not quite an atheist; he described himself as "waiting" for God. Jean-Paul Sartre, Simone de Beauvoir, and Albert Camus, prominent French existentialists, were atheists. There were many other divisions among existentialists. If Kierkegaard was an individualist, the Jewish Martin Buber and the Roman Catholic Gabriel Marcel emphasized the social nature of selfhood. Some existentialists have been metaphysical skeptics; others have been concerned with the nature of "Being." Some, in their concentration on selfhood, have been apolitical; others have made deep commitments, wise or foolish, in political struggles. Existentialism does not represent consensus; it rebels against anything that obscures the absurdities of life and the radical commitments of authentic existence.

Kierkegaard declared that "truth is subjectivity." This was no quarrel with the objectivity of the multiplication tables or the findings of science. His point was that abstract truth is no answer to the fears and longings of the human person. Only when truth evokes loyalty and commitment does it rescue persons from triviality and frustration.

Existentialism arrived late in America. Kierkegaard was not published in English until the rush of translations beginning in 1936. He had already won some influence through the German theologian Karl Barth. Barth later turned away from existentialism toward a neo-Calvinism, but Rudolf Bultmann then became an influential existentialist voice in theology.

Following World War II, which blasted many of the assurances of Americans, existentialism made a powerful impact in the United States. The Niebuhr brothers (Reinhold and H. Richard) and Paul Tillich appropriated existentialist themes and gave them original interpretations. Many colleges and little theaters produced Sartre's one-act play *No Exit,* and his fiction and other dramas aroused wide interest. Camus's essays and fiction earned acclaim. (Both Sartre and Camus won Nobel prizes in literature, although Sartre, with characteristic contempt for established authority, rejected his.) Existential psychology earned considerable interest; Kierkegaard had anticipated, in some ways, Freud's exploration of the unconscious and the human id, although existentialist psychologists emphasized human freedom as against Freud's near-determinism. The "theater of the absurd" expressed existentialist themes, except when it portrayed persons as victims rather than as free agents.

Existentialist music and art are impossible to define, but unmistakable. Beethoven's late quartets have been described as existentialist. Tillich, in an essay "Existentialist Aspects of Modern Art," hailed Picasso's *Guernica* as "the best Protestant religious picture" because "it shows the human situation without any cover." This is not to say that Beethoven or Picasso discovered existentialism and applied it to art; it is to say that the cultural forces that led to verbal expressions of existentialism also produced great art.

The faddist stage of existentialism has faded, but many of its insights have entered the mainstream of theology and culture: its insistence that authoritative doctrine is no substitute for commitment; its attacks on cults of peace of mind, positive thinking, and self-esteem; its warning against religion that supports the idols of culture. There is wide belief that existentialism, whatever its excesses, recognizes insights of biblical faith that must be reappropriated perennially in the histories of Judaism and Christianity.

See also AGNOSTICISM; ATHEISM; DEATH OF GOD; GOD; HUMANISM; NIEBUHR, REINHOLD; TILLICH, PAUL.

BIBLIOGRAPHY

Barrett, William. *Irrational Man: A Study in Existential Philosophy.* 1958.

Kaufmann, Walter. *Existentialism from Dostoyevsky to Sartre.* 1956.

Macquarrie, John. *Existentialism.* 1973.

Roger Lincoln Shinn

Exorcism

In the United States today, a surprising number of groups and individuals believe not only that demons, or evil spirits, exist but that they routinely cause trouble in the lives of ordinary women and men. Many of these groups and individuals attempt to counteract demonization through exorcism, a religious rite aimed at expelling evil spirits or, at the very least, restraining their influence. During the last quarter of the twentieth century, exorcism was more widely practiced in the United States than perhaps ever before. Its popularity, especially in certain Christian circles, may be attributed to a curious conjunction of religious conviction, the influence of the broader therapeutic culture, and the enormous suggestive powers of the entertainment industry.

As recently as the late 1960s, Roman Catholic exorcism was all but dead and forgotten in the United States—a fading ghost long past its prime. It was rarely spoken of and even more rarely assumed to possess any practical significance. By the mid-1970s, however, the ghost had sprung miraculously back to life. Suddenly, thousands of people were convinced that they themselves, or perhaps a loved one, were suffering from demonic affliction. Exorcism was in hot demand. What brought this about? A number of factors, but none more important, arguably, than the release of William Peter Blatty's *The Exorcist* and the publication of Malachi Martin's *Hostage to the Devil*. The dramatic (and seductively grotesque) arrival of demons on the screen and the best-selling page helped create an unprecedented popular demand for Catholic exorcisms. The chances of anyone actually procuring an exorcism through official Catholic channels during the seventies and eighties, however, were exceedingly slim. Relatively few bishops believed in the possibility of diabolic possession, and no more than two or three Catholic dioceses in the United States at any given time over this period had bona fide priest-exorcists at their disposal. There was, however, a considerably greater chance of obtaining a Catholic exorcism through unofficial channels. Beginning in the mid-1970s, a small (but significant) number of maverick priests, most of whom inhabited the right-wing fringes of American Catholicism, attempted to respond to the burgeoning market for Catholic exorcisms by going into business on their own. For the most part, the exorcisms performed by these priests were clandestine, underground affairs, undertaken without the approval of the institutional Catholic Church and without the rigorous psychological screening that the church (at least in theory) required. In subsequent years the institutional Catholic Church took more aggressive action on the demon-expulsion front. Since the mid-1990s approximately a dozen priests have been appointed to the office of exorcist in American Catholicism; and in January 1999 the Vatican published a revised version of the Roman Catholic rite of exorcism, which superseded an earlier rite that had stood virtually unchanged since its publication by Pope Paul V in 1614.

For all its Hollywood-dusted glamour, Roman Catholic exorcism has been just a small part of the total picture. During the mid- to late 1960s, a number of prominent charismatic Christians (including Don Basham, Erwin Prange, and Francis MacNutt) began practicing a modified form of exorcism, which they referred to as deliverance. (Deliverance had been widely practiced by classical Pentecostals earlier in the century, but by the early 1950s it had fallen into a state of relative dormancy.) Most charismatic deliverance ministers made a distinction between demonic possession and affliction. While it was highly unlikely that true spirit-baptized Christians could actually become possessed, which meant falling completely under the sway of Satan, they argued, there was no reason to think that they could not be tormented or afflicted in some area of their lives by demonic powers. Deliverance eventually gained broad (if not universal) acceptance within the charismatic-renewal movement, and by the mid-1970s thousands of middle-class charismatics from virtually all of the nation's mainstream Christian churches were having their personal demons expelled. While charismatic deliverance was undoubtedly motivated by genuine religious conviction, it was also more in tune with the times than most of its practitioners would have cared to admit. Despite being cloaked in the time-orphaned language of demons and supernatural evil, the ritual was very much at home in the brightly lit, fulfillment-on-demand culture of post-1960s America. It could be engaged in as often as anyone wanted and for virtually any reason under the sun. If an individual charismatic complained of being afflicted by demons of cigarette-smoking or demons of marital infidelity or demons of anything in between, the solution was close at hand.

Exorcism experienced a major growth burst during the eighties and early nineties, this time in connection with mounting concerns on the part of many Americans that a satanic conspiracy was stalking the land. Indeed, one could describe, with a measure of sarcasm, the ten-year stretch from 1983 to 1993 as Satan's decade in America. From California to New York, alarm bells rang out: Satanists seemed to be lurking everywhere, torturing helpless toddlers in day-care centers, brainwashing adolescents through the sinister lyrics of heavy-metal music, sowing destruction through the drug trade, and savaging their own children in Black Mass orgies. These satanic scares were exploited by the popular media, which found them an irresistible (and highly profitable) source of entertainment, and once again, thousands of people, believing that they themselves or someone they knew had fallen victim to demonic influence, sent out calls for emergency assistance. This time, however, the demon-expulsion front got some unexpected reinforcements. Partly because of the heightened satanism scares of the day and partly for more complex theological reasons, exorcism had succeeded during the 1980s in gaining favor within certain sectors of evangelical Protestantism, and by the early 1990s several hundred evangelical-based exorcism (or deliverance) ministries had sprung up across the country. Some evangelical deliverance ministers, especially so-called "third-wavers" such as C. Peter Wagner and Charles Kraft, have been influenced by Pentecostalism and the charismatic renewal movement in their practice of exorcism, but most are strict theological conservatives who believe that the time has arrived for all Christians in America to commit themselves to a full-fledged campaign of spiritual warfare against the satanic realm.

Charismatic and evangelical exorcism is usually performed in private, following the norms of a typical client-practitioner relationship. Occasionally, however, entire auditoriums of people may be relieved of their demons all at once in what are referred to as public or mass exorcisms. Public exorcisms are usually accompanied by dramatic and visceral manifestations: vomiting, thrashing, wailing, and so forth. The majority of exorcism ministers (in both private and public settings) are men; the majority of subjects on the receiving end of exorcism are women. During the 1990s Christian exorcism in general underwent a kind of professionalization; it was incorporated by many Christian psychotherapists into their regular practice. Given the dearth of long-term, follow-up studies, the actual therapeutic benefits of exorcism (quite apart from the putative purpose of casting out demons) is very much an open question.

Although exorcism in the United States has experienced its greatest growth of late in specifically Christian circles, the ritual is also practiced in diverse forms in various other communities of faith. In many American urban centers today, one may find a wide variety of Afro-Caribbean exorcisms, Afro-Latin exorcisms, Asiatic folk exorcisms, and even New Age exorcisms. Exorcism (broadly conceived) is embroidered in the ceremonial complexes of Santería, vodou, syncretistic pentecostalism, Puerto Rican spiritualism, and more than a dozen other faiths. The driving away or the subduing of demons is accomplished through the use of cathartics or emetics, the recitation of spells, bodily massage or manipulation, shamanic sucking, and incantatory chanting. In some ritual contexts, demon expulsion is a deadly earnest enterprise, and demons themselves are regarded as literally real spiritual entities, with their own personalities and appetites and sometimes even their own telltale odors. In other contexts, it is rather more playful and metaphoric, with the boundaries between the natural and supernatural realms fluid and negotiable. In virtually all contexts, exorcism is a culturally scripted performance, with a carefully calibrated choreography of roles, behaviors, and expectations.

See also DEVILS, DEMONS, AND SPIRITS; PENTECOSTAL AND CHARISMATIC CHRISTIANITY; SATANISTS; SPIRIT POSSESSION.

BIBLIOGRAPHY

Anderson, Neil T. *The Bondage Breaker.* 1990.

Arnold, Clinton E. *Three Crucial Questions About Spiritual Warfare.* 1997.

Basham, Don. *Can a Christian Have a Demon?* 1971.

Brown, Karen McCarthy. *Mama Lola: A Vodou Priestess in Brooklyn.* 1991.

Canizares, Raul. *Cuban Santería.* 1999.

Csordas, Thomas J. *The Sacred Self.* 1994.

MacNutt, Francis. *Deliverance from Evil.* 1995.

Martin, Malachi. *Hostage to the Devil: The Possession and Exorcism of Five Living Americans.* 1976.

Murphy, Joseph M. *Santería: African Spirits in America.* 1993.

Nicola, John J. *Diabolical Possession and Exorcism.* 1974.

Peck, M. Scott. *People of the Lie.* 1983.

Pérez y Mena, A. I. *Speaking with the Dead: Development of Afro-Latin Religion among Puerto Ricans in the United States.* 1991.

Powlison, David. *Power Encounters.* 1995.

Richardson, James T., Joel Best, and David G. Bromley, eds. *The Satanism Scare.* 1991.

Wagner, C. Peter, and F. Douglas Pennoyer, eds. *Wrestling with Dark Angels.* 1990.

Michael W. Cuneo

Extraterrestrial Cults.

See Unidentified Flying Objects.

Extraterrestrial Guides

Contemporary interest in flying saucers or unidentified flying objects (UFOs) began when a pilot named Kenneth Arnold reported seeing a series of nine bright disks move across the sky near Mount Rainier, Washington State, on June 24, 1947. Reports of similar sightings followed, and it was widely assumed by the general public that the mysterious objects were vessels of extraterrestrial origin. Soon accounts of contacts with occupants of the vehicles appeared. In the 1950s, these visitors from other worlds were generally presented as wise, beautiful, almost godlike beings, come to warn humanity of its folly—especially in light of the recent development of atomic weapons—and help it in its much-needed spiritual evolution. They were, in the expression of C. G. Jung, "technological angels," space-age equivalents of the descending gods and saviors of old. The movements that grew up around "contactees," humans who claimed to have received messages from the visitors, were definitely religious in character, though these movements were, for the most part, small and ephemeral.

The first widely known contactee was George Adamski, who in his book *Flying Saucers Have Landed* (written with Desmond Leslie; 1953) reported meeting a man from Venus on November 20, 1952, on the Mojave Desert in California. Adamski was followed by others. Details varied considerably, but the overall messages were similar: The other worlds from which the visitors come are paradisal; to enter into fellowship with them, earthlings must acquire a cosmic perspective and develop a spirit of brotherhood and love. Information is often also given on the origin and occult history of humanity, frequently involving longstanding extraterrestrial relationships. Continuing messages are commonly given by the contactees through mediumship or channeling.

Groups based on extraterrestrial guides that seem to have acquired institutional stability include the Aetherius Society, founded by George King in London in 1954 on the basis of messages from the Master Aetherius of Venus; headquarters were later moved to Los Angeles. This movement has thrived on an almost apocalyptic stress on the repeated near-destruction of Earth by malign cosmic entities and its salvation by extraterrestrial masters, Aetherius and others, through the agency of King and the movement. The Raelian Movement, centered in France and Québec but with a U.S. center in Florida, was founded on contacts and messages received by Claude Vorilhon (Rael), then the publisher of a French racing-car magazine. Raelianism teaches the origins of life and humanity in the scientific experiments of aliens and inculcates the need to evolve beyond law and guilt; the movement has attracted some attention for its emphasis on the importance of sensual experience. Unarius was established in 1954 by Ernest and Ruth Norman; its central emphasis is on channeled information from extraterrestrial beings, especially about reincarnation, and the spiritual entry of Earth into the Galactic Federation, which occurred on September 14, 1973. The 1997 mass suicide of thirty-nine members of the Heaven's Gate group, apparently under extraterrestrial guidance and in conjunction with the arrival of the comet Hale-Bopp, showed the sinister potential of such direction.

See also CHANNELING; HEAVEN'S GATE; JOURNEYS AND JOURNEYING; NEW RELIGIOUS MOVEMENTS; STAR TREK; UNIDENTIFIED FLYING OBJECTS.

BIBLIOGRAPHY

Jacobs, David Michael. *The UFO Controversy in America.* 1975.

Lewis, James R., ed. *The Gods Have Landed.* 1995.

Robert Ellwood

F

Faith

In the United States, "faith" generally connotes two things: (1) a religious tradition, such as the "Christian faith" or the "Jewish faith," and (2) belief in or devotion to a particular religion, tradition, or ideology.

According to the first sense, there is no single American faith. In contemporary America, it is more appropriate to speak of "faiths" rather than of "faith." All major world religions—Christianity, Judaism, Islam, Buddhism, and Hinduism—can claim significant numbers of adherents in the United States. In addition to these classical traditions of both East and West, American religion includes a wide variety of new religions and homegrown faiths, from the tribal religions of Native Americans to Mormonism to the Nation of Islam. The 1993 edition of *The Encyclopedia of American Religions* lists 1,730 different religious organizations grouped into 19 families; 10 are Christian, 9 are not. While the United States has always been a religiously diverse nation, the scope of that diversity has broadened since the end of World War II. Faith in contemporary America may take a remarkable number of forms.

In the second sense, adherents of various religions are understood to "have faith" in the distinct doctrines, beliefs, and practices of their tradition. Faith is a quality of commitment or belief. Thus Jews have faith in the Hebrew God as expressed through Jewish tradition, kinship, and righteous living. Buddhists, who may or may not believe in a God or gods, have faith in a body of wisdom and practices that provide spiritual well-being and compassion. Muslims have faith in God as revealed in the Qur'an through the Prophet Muhammad. In the United States this definition of faith is nearly universal and malleable. Even those who hold no organizational affiliation may consider themselves people of faith. Outside of religious traditions, some might profess "faith in humanity," "faith in nature," or "faith in America." Indeed, having faith has sometimes been identified with the American character. As President Dwight D. Eisenhower was said to have commented, "Our government makes no sense unless it is founded in a deeply felt religious faith—and I don't care what it is." Because of such diversity and its porous nature, faith may be expressed in terms of family or ethnic tradition, personal conversion, intellectual assent, institutional membership, existential experience, social service, worship, ritual, or sacramental practice.

For all its generality in contemporary culture, however, Protestant theology and ideology still color the word "faith." In spite of national religious diversity, Americans have been overwhelmingly Protestant. Although the percentage is lower than in the past, roughly two-thirds of all Americans still profess Protestantism. Their theological and cultural understandings of "faith" have shaped much of the nation's religious ethos.

For Christians, faith means believing in a triune God embodied in Jesus Christ and known through biblical revelation. Faith has tended to mean assent to certain doctrines, particularly those beliefs surrounding the person and mission of Jesus. But understandings of faith throughout church history have not been static. The word "faith" has meant many things; most are interpretations of the simple New Testament definition, "Now faith is the assurance of things hoped for, the conviction of things not seen" (Hebrews 11:1). Differing definitions of faith have often led to internal Christian conflict.

Two major arguments about the nature of faith have shaped American religious history. The first argument sparked the Protestant Reformation in the sixteenth century. Late medieval Roman Catholics believed that faith involved human and divine cooperation. God offered the grace of faith to humankind primarily through the vehicle of the church's sacraments. People, in turn, could accept God's gracious gift or reject it. If they cooperated with God's grace in the Mass, baptism, and other sacraments, they would grow in faith and might one day merit a heavenly reward. Those who rejected or fell from the grace offered by the church were faithless and could expect to be damned.

The German reformer Martin Luther (1483–1546) argued that faith was solely and completely God's work. Faith was not a result of any human action. It was a disposition given to sinful humans as a gift from God. A person with faith could recognize that God was his or her savior, God having justified (made right) the sinner to enjoy a holy life and eternal bliss. Early Protestants understood that faith resulted in trust and gratitude—attributes both given by and directed toward God. Luther argued that the Catholic view, that justification followed a faithful life, was incorrect. Rather, he believed that God first justified men and women, and a faithful life of gratitude and Christian service followed. The repercussions of Luther's reformation of faith included a greater emphasis on the laity, the elevation of the Bible over tradition, and the diminishment of priestly authority.

Luther's insights brought into focus much of the religious and social discontent of his day. In the following 150 years, various forms of Protestantism took hold in most of northern Europe, and these early Protestants founded the colonies that would become the United States. Only small numbers of Catholics settled in the eastern seaboard colonies; Protestant pluralism dominated the embryonic nation's religious culture. As in Europe, the issue of the nature of faith divided Protestants and Catholics—along with a host of related concerns about the church and religious authority. In early America, however, historic Protestant ideals—such as the belief that faith should be discerned by the individual rather than mediated through the church—won the day. Elements of this broadly Protestant worldview still influence American culture.

A second argument over the nature of faith also affects contemporary religion. In the eighteenth cen-

tury, an intra-Protestant debate caused deep divisions within traditional Protestant communions. Many of the early reformers stressed the personal experience of faith. First-generation Protestants often recorded dramatic spiritual transformation along with their intellectual conversion to Protestant doctrine. Such fervor, however, was difficult to maintain. Succeeding generations of Protestants tended to locate faith in the mind. Thus faith was assent to certain dogma such as justification by faith alone and the rejection of papal authority. Serious and sober Protestant piety emphasized catechesis (doctrinal instruction), holy living, and good deeds. By 1700, most Protestants understood faith in scholastic and moralistic terms.

Some radical Protestant groups rejected these views in favor of a more experiential style of faith. This impulse, known variously as Pietism, Puritanism, or evangelicalism, castigated traditional Protestantism as "dead orthodoxy" and sought to "reform the Reformation." Although differing in particulars, these movements shared a concern for "heartfelt religion" and emphasized the human ability to know God through the senses. They envisioned churches full of "lively piety," places where all believers would lead devoted and earnest spiritual lives. The heart, not the head, was the seat of faith.

In Europe, traditional Protestant churches often persecuted these minority groups by charging their leaders with heresy, limiting their ability to preach, and jailing the overly zealous. Many advocates of Pietism fled to the colonies. From Puritans and Separatist Baptists to Moravians and Methodists, America proved fertile ground for the new style of purified Protestantism. Throughout American history, traditional, churchly Protestantism clashed with pietistic Protestantism, but rarely with more flair than during the ministry of George Whitefield (1714–1770). In the eighteenth century, Whitefield's dramatic, consumer-oriented revivalism spread the message of heartfelt faith across the colonies and spurred other evangelists to do the same. In midcentury, the conflict between the two styles fueled much religious conflict and caused a number of denominational splits. Partisans of the "Old Light" (the traditionalists) and the "New Light" (the evangelicals) vied for authority and popular support. Although the victory was neither easy nor complete, those on the side of heartfelt faith came to dominate American religion for the next century and a half.

Protestant conflicts over faith have had profound effects on American religious life. Arguments over faith have led to near-continuous denominational schisms and internal questions regarding the appropriate practice of piety. Some denominations, such as the Episcopalians and the Lutherans, struggled with the issue of how much they should adapt to the prevailing pietism. In the case of the nineteenth-century Episcopal Church, two church parties—the High Church and Evangelical parties—created their identities around the question of adaptation. High Church Episcopalians sought to retain Anglican sacramentalism; evangelical Episcopalians saw themselves as dignified revivalists. The first understood faith as tradition and liturgical devotion; the second understood it as conversion and personal piety.

The question of adaptation also affected non-Protestant religions. In the nineteenth century, Roman Catholics borrowed from evangelical Protestant styles and created parish missions intended to kindle personal devotion to the Sacred Heart of Jesus, the Virgin Mary, and the saints. Reform Jews adopted ideals of Protestant church organization and social concern. Muslims argued that their faith promoted the greatest social equality and liberty of the individual conscience. Religions that had little or no missionary concern in their native setting became more zealously evangelistic in the United States. American Protestant converts to other religions often—and successfully—used Protestant categories and practices to "Americanize" seemingly "foreign" religions. Thus, for many religious groups, the practice of faith—or even adopting the language or category of faith—took on Protestant overtones. While some of the impulses for reform within these religions were rooted internally, American Protestantism shaped these changes as they became enculturated.

Although American understandings of faith grew from theological conceptions, the term has broader civic connotations as well. Faith often refers to hope for or optimism regarding the future—especially the future of the nation and the potential of the American people. Political institutions carry religious or semi-religious national aspirations. Americans speak of "faith in democracy" or "faith in the president." This broad definition is rooted in generalized, and often romanticized, Protestant culture. For much of American history, faith formed an intrinsic part of the nation's creed and mission as God's new Israel. Protestant Christianity—and eventually a wider range of religions—allowed Americans to place themselves in cosmic history and participate in God's biblical plan. So while individual Americans were expected to have personal faith in God and a particular religion, generalized faith grounded civil piety and nationalism.

However important as a theological and a civic ideal, faith fell out of favor in some circles in the twentieth century. After the Civil War, secular philosophies and the natural and social sciences offered explanations for human history and the nature of the universe that were alternatives to those of traditional biblical accounts. Contrary to previous American expectations, faith and learning were in tension with one another. Some faith traditions, such as liberal Protestantism and Reform Judaism, adapted to the new learning. Others, however, resisted. Faith became equated with dogmatism, fundamentalism, and ignorance. The conflict between biblical traditionalism and secularism led to a diminishment of public expressions of personal faith in certain social classes and elite cultural institutions such as universities. Although most Americans no doubt continued to have faith, particularized faiths—especially pietistic faiths—were perceived as threatening to the common good.

In 1957, Harvard theologian Paul Tillich (1886–1965) redefined faith as "ultimate concern." Anything—nationalism, materialism, sexuality—that offered "the fulfillment of one's being" was faith. Tillich pointed out that everyone, even those cultural elites who scorned traditional religion, had faith. Whether faith is rightly placed in the God of justice or misplaced in human selfishness, Tillich believed faith to be the dynamic of human history. Tillich's definition of faith as ultimate concern influenced academics and church leaders. It widened the circle of what counted as faith, giving scholars and believers access to the category once again without the associated dogmatism.

When the twentieth century began, many scholars believed that religion would wither in the face of the secular onslaught. By Tillich's time, however, it had become obvious that this analysis was incorrect. Since World War II, the United States has experienced a dramatic series of religious renewals—from the upsurge of mainline religion in the 1950s and 1960s to the evangelical revivals of the 1970s and 1980s and the spirituality boom of the 1990s. Although not without eliciting some controversy, sociologists Roger Finke and Rodney Stark have argued that the United States is more religious now than in the past.

In the instance of contemporary movements, however, most (but certainly not all) believers have been careful not to define faith too narrowly. Mainstream Protestants, Catholics, and Jews tempered dogmatism with liberal learning and social activism. Evangelicals, often wrongly construed as rigid fundamentalists, abandoned many of the moral taboos of earlier generations and engaged broad political and social issues. The language of spirituality and spiritual journey, a kind of neomysticism, has given many people a faith without the baggage of institutional religion or doctrine. Thus, while the number of faiths was multiplying and the United States was becoming more obviously diverse, American citizens were less reluctant than their grandparents to "have faith" in something and to express it in the public arena. From the faith of the Puritans to the millennial pluralism of faiths, redefined by and constantly defining the culture, Americans see faith as part of their national birthright.

See also BELONGING, RELIGIOUS; CIVIL RELIGION; CREEDS; EVANGELICAL CHRISTIANITY; MAINLINE PROTESTANTISM; RELIGIOUS COMMUNITIES; RELIGIOUS STUDIES; SECULARIZATION; TILLICH, PAUL.

BIBLIOGRAPHY

Albanese, Catherine. *America: Religions and Religion*, 3rd ed. 1999.

Campbell, Ted A. *The Religion of the Heart: A Study of European Religious Life in the 17th and 18th Centuries.* 1991.

Corbett, Julia. *Religion in America*, 3rd ed. 1997.

Finke, Roger, and Rodney Stark. *The Churching of America: Winners and Losers in Our Religious Economy, 1776–1990.* 1992.

Marsden, George. *Religion and American Culture.* 1990.

Melton, Gordon. *Encyclopedia of American Religions.* 1993.

Roof, Wade Clark. *A Generation of Seekers: The Spiritual Journeys of the Baby Boom Generation.* 1993.

Tillich, Paul. *The Dynamics of Faith.* 1957.

Wuthnow, Robert. *After Heaven: Spirituality in America Since the 1950s.* 1998.

Diane Hochstedt Butler Bass

The Rev. Jerry Falwell, the leader of the Moral Majority, addresses a patriotic "I Love America" rally in front of the statehouse at Trenton, New Jersey, on November 11, 1980.   (Credit: CORBIS/Bettmann.)

Falwell, Jerry

(1933–), evangelist and political activist.

Jerry Falwell is pastor of Thomas Road Baptist Church in Lynchburg, Virginia; founder and chancellor of Liberty University; primary evangelist on the nationwide television program *The Old-Time Gospel Hour;* and founder of Moral Majority, the flagship organization of the Religious Right during the early 1980s. A native of Lynchburg, Falwell attended Lynchburg College for two years before transferring to Baptist Bible College in Springfield, Missouri, where he trained for the ministry. Shortly after graduation in 1956, he accepted an invitation to become pastor of a new church, which grew from a cluster of twenty-five families into one of the largest Protestant churches in America, with a membership of approximately twenty-two thousand people.

During the late 1950s and for most of the 1960s, Falwell supported racial segregation. In a notorious 1965 sermon titled "Ministers and Marches," he openly criticized Dr. Martin Luther King, Jr., and other clergymen who participated in the civil rights movement, charging them with insincerity and with being manipulated by Communists, if, indeed, they were not Communists themselves. "Preachers," he said, "are not called to be politicians, but to be soul winners." A little more than a decade later, Falwell repudiated this sermon, even calling it "false prophecy." Such a recanting was necessary, since by 1980 the American minister best known for his involvement in politics was none other than Jerry Falwell.

In 1967 Falwell founded Lynchburg Christian Academy, which subsequently grew into Lynchburg Baptist College, then Liberty Bible College, then Liberty University, all designed to provide fundamentalist Christian young people with an education untainted by secular humanism, an ideology fundamentalists feared was destroying the moral and spiritual foundations of the nation. As part of his campaign to combat secular humanism, Falwell invited prominent evangelical intellectual Francis Schaeffer to speak at the university. Schaeffer urged Falwell to use his television program, by then seen on more than 330 stations each week, to address social issues such as abortion and homosexuality. After his first such efforts began to draw attention, conservative political operatives approached Falwell, urging him to begin a grassroots political organization. The result, chartered in 1979, was Moral Majority.

During the 1980 election campaign, Moral Majority became the best-known component of the new movement that came to be called the Christian New Right or, more commonly, the Religious Right, and Falwell became the movement's ubiquitous spokesman. Moral Majority, though popular among fundamentalists, never developed highly effective political techniques or organization. Faced with failure to achieve major legislative victories for the organization's "promoral, profamily" agenda and with chronic financial problems at Liberty University, Falwell disbanded Moral Majority in 1989. Leadership of the movement shifted to other groups and organizations, most notably Pat Robertson and the Christian Coalition. Falwell retained a role as one of the movement's significant elder statesmen but turned most of his attention to Thomas Road Baptist Church, his television ministry, and Liberty University.

See also CHRISTIAN COALITION; FUNDAMENTALIST CHRISTIANITY; KING, MARTIN LUTHER, JR.; MORAL MAJORITY; RELIGIOUS RIGHT; ROBERTSON, PAT; TELEVANGELISM.

BIBLIOGRAPHY

D'Souza, Dinesh. *Falwell, Before the Millennium.* 1984.
Falwell, Jerry. *Listen, America!* 1980.
Martin, William. *With God on Our Side: The Rise of the Religious Right in America.* 1996.

William Martin

Family, The

It was during the late 1960s, an era marked by rapid social change and countercultural rebellion, that David Brandt Berg (1919–1994) founded a controversial worldwide religious organization, the Children of God (COG), known today as The Family. Berg began the group in 1968 in Huntington Beach, California, as a ministry to hippies, dropouts, and ex-junkies. At the time Berg was emerging from a largely unsuccessful career as an itinerant evangelist and minister. His radical antichurch, antiestablishment message was one of many voices in a much larger youth-oriented revival known as the Jesus Movement. He called his followers "revolutionaries for Jesus" and they referred to him, their prophet, as "Moses David" or simply "Mo."

Because of problems with the police emanating from the group's angry demonstrations and protests, Berg's followers left California in 1969 and established colonies throughout America. A few years later, prompted by Berg's prediction that comet Kohoutek would destroy America, the Children of God closed down most of their communes and moved to Europe. Within a short time, COG colonies were scattered throughout the world, with their leader's whereabouts shrouded in mystery and secrecy, a pattern he maintained for the rest of his life. Only a few trusted disciples and members of his immediate family were apprised of his residence location at any given time. He communicated with his followers through hundreds of "Mo Letters," which came to represent the sacred scriptures of the organization. During the 1990s the Children of God returned to the United States with a new name, "The Family." They also launched a public relations campaign in an attempt to sanitize their controversial image.

Almost from its inception, the Children of God generated attention and controversy because of its unconventional teaching and practices regarding sexual behavior. Allegations regularly surfaced concerning the group's teachings condoning sexual promiscuity, sex between children and adults, and incest. Perhaps the most controversial of the COG's sex-oriented doctrines was the practice of "flirty fishing," which encouraged female members to develop sexual relationships with men outside the organization as a means of evangelism, to "convert" strangers by demonstrating Jesus' love. David Berg referred to these women as "hookers for Jesus." The sect's literature became controversial because of its graphic depiction and discussion of sexual activity, all of which was linked to Berg's unorthodox interpretation of the Bible. Some observers have noted that The Family's obsession with sex is a reflection of Berg's own sexual fixations, which are said to stem from early sexual trauma that he experienced within a sexually repressive, fundamentalist family environment.

The group's version of religious prostitution, flirty fishing, was practiced until 1987, when it was discontinued, according to official explanations, due to the organization's need to expend more time in other forms of evangelism. Others feel that the AIDS epidemic played a major role in the decision.

Since Berg's death in 1994, The Family has distanced itself from some of its earlier practices, although critics doubt that there will ever be a total repudiation of the sensuous theology proclaimed by "God's End-Time Prophet."

See also COMMUNES; JESUS MOVEMENT.

BIBLIOGRAPHY

Davis, Deborah. *The Children of God.* 1984.

Enroth, Ronald M., Edward E. Ericson, and C. Breckinridge Peters. *The Jesus People.* 1972.

Kent, Stephen. "Lustful Prophet: A Psychosexual Historical Study of the Children of God's Leader, David Berg." *Cultic Studies Journal* 11 (1994): 135–188.

Van Zandt, David E. *Living in the Children of God.* 1991.

Ronald Enroth

Fard, W. D.

(c. 1877–1934), religious and political leader.

Master W. D. Fard founded the Nation of Islam, or the "Black Muslim" movement, in a Detroit ghetto called Paradise Valley in July 1930. His original name was Wallace D. Fard, but he was also known by other aliases, such as Farad Muhammad, F. Muhammad Ali, Wali Farrad, and Professor Fard. Much of what is known about him is shrouded in mystery, and it is difficult to separate fact from mythological stories. Fard appeared as a peddler "from the East," selling silks and other sundries and dispensing advice about health and spiritual development to his customers. Through his friendly manner he was able to gain access to the homes of poor African Americans and began to teach about their "true religion," not Christianity but the "religion of the Black Man" of Asia and Africa. Using both the Bible and the Qur'an, he began with meetings in houses until he had enough members to rent a storefront, which he called Temple of Islam No. 1. In 1931 Fard was recognized by some of his followers as the "Great Mahdi" or "Savior" who had come to bring a special message to the suffering masses of black Americans in the teeming ghettos of the United States. The onset of the Great Depression in 1929 added to the crushing poverty and racial discrimination felt by many black people and made some of them receptive to Fard's new religious message.

Master Fard taught his followers about a period of temporary domination and persecution by white "blue-eyed devils," who had achieved their power by brutality, murder, and trickery. But as a prerequisite for black liberation, he stressed the importance of attaining "knowledge of self." He told his followers that they were not Americans and therefore owed no allegiance to the American flag and could refuse to serve in its military. He wrote two books for the movement, *The Secret Ritual of the Nation of Islam,* which is transmitted orally to members; and *Teaching for the Lost-Found Nation of Islam in a Mathematical Way,* which is written in symbolic language and requires special interpretation. Within three years Fard had established several organizations: the "Temple of Islam," with its own worship style and rituals; the "University of Islam," to propagate his teachings; the "Muslim Girls Training," to teach female members home economics and how to be a proper Muslim woman; and the "Fruit of Islam," consisting of selected male members to provide security for the temple and Muslim leaders and to enforce the disciplinary rules.

Master Fard's mysterious disappearance in 1934 led to an internal struggle for the leadership of the Nation of Islam among several contending factions. His most trusted lieutenant and chief minister of Islam, Elijah Karriem Muhammad, the former Robert Elijah Poole of Sandersville, Georgia, eventually won control and reestablished the Nation of Islam in Chicago, with Temple No. 2 as its headquarters. Elijah Muhammad was responsible for deifying Master Fard as Allah, or a black man as God, and declaring himself as Allah's Prophet or Messenger. Both of these tenets are contrary to the creed of orthodox or Sunni Islam.

There is no consensus about Master Fard's identity. Members of the Nation of Islam believe that he was a light-skinned black man or mulatto who knew both the white and the black world and who was born on February 26, 1877. FBI records identified him as an unstable wanderer named Wallace Dodd Ford who came to the United States from New Zealand in 1913. Two sons of Elijah Muhammad have variously identified him either as an Aḥmadiyyah missionary from Pakistan, a position supported by Imam Warith Deen Muhammad, or as an Arab of "Turko-Persian" origins, a view offered by Akbar Muhammad. Master Fard's identity, origins, appearance, and disappearance remain mysterious and controversial.

See also AFRICAN-AMERICAN RELIGIONS; BLACK MUSLIMS; ISLAM; MALCOLM X; MUHAMMAD, ELIJAH KARRIEM; MUHAMMAD, WARITH DEEN; NATION OF ISLAM; QUR'AN.

BIBLIOGRAPHY

Essien-Udom, E. U. *Black Nationalism: A Search for Identity in America.* 1962.

Lincoln, C. Eric. *The Black Muslims in America.* 1960.

Muhammad, Akbar. "Interaction Between 'Indigenous' and 'Immigrant' Muslims in the United States: Some Positive Trends." *Hijrah Magazine* (March–April 1985).

Muhammad, Elijah. *Message to the Black Man in America.* 1963.

Turner, Richard Brent. *Islam in the African American Experience.* 1997.

Lawrence H. Mamiya

Farrakhan, Louis

(1933–), religious and political leader.

On November 8, 1977, Minister Louis Abdul Haleem Farrakhan, the former Louis Eugene Walcott, rebuilt the Nation of Islam, a militant and millenarian religious sect that preached black nationalism. He succeeded Master W. D. Fard, the Honorable Elijah Muhammad, and Wallace Muhammad as the key leader of the Black Muslim movement. Born on May 17, 1933, in the Bronx, New York, Louis was raised in Boston by his West Indian mother. He was an Episcopalian altar boy in the Roxbury section of Boston and graduated with honors from the prestigious Boston English High School, where he also was on the track team and played the violin in the school orchestra. After attending Winston-Salem Teachers College from 1951 to 1953, he dropped out to pursue his favorite avocation, music, intending to make it his career. An accomplished musician, Walcott performed professionally on the Boston nightclub circuit as a singer of calypso and country songs. He was known as the "Charmer." In 1955, at age twenty-two, Louis Walcott was recruited by Minister Malcolm X of the Nation of Islam. Following the custom of the Nation, he dropped his surname and took an "X," which meant "undetermined," ex-slave, ex-Christian, ex-smoker, ex-drinker, ex-mainstream American. After Louis X proved himself for a number of years, the Honorable Elijah Muhammad, the supreme leader of the Nation of Islam, gave him his Muslim name, "Abdul Haleem Farrakhan." He was appointed to be the head minister of Boston Temple No. 11. As a rising star within the Nation, Minister Farrakhan also wrote the only song, "A White Man's Heaven Is a Black Man's Hell," and his only play, *Orgena* ("A Negro" spelled backward), allowed by Elijah Muhammad.

After Malcolm X's assassination on February 23, 1965, Minister Farrakhan replaced Malcolm as the head minister of Harlem's Temple No. 7 and as the national representative of the Nation, the second in command. Like his predecessor, Louis Farrakhan was a dynamic, charismatic leader and a powerful speaker with the ability to appeal to the masses of black people.

When the Honorable Elijah Muhammad died on February 25, 1975, the Nation of Islam experienced several large schisms. Wallace Muhammad, the fifth of Elijah's six sons, was surprisingly chosen as the Supreme Minister by the leadership hierarchy. Disappointed that he was not chosen as Elijah's successor, Minister Louis Farrakhan led a breakaway group and began rebuilding his own Nation. Farrakhan disagreed with Wallace Muhammad's attempts to move

Nation of Islam leader Louis Farrakhan gazes pensively skyward on March 2, 1994, in New York City.   (Credit: AP/Wide World Photos.)

the Nation to orthodox Sunni Islam by getting rid of Elijah Muhammad's separatist teachings and radical black nationalism. Wallace eventually replaced the Nation with the American Muslim Mission and called himself Imam Warith Deen Muhammad.

Farrakhan's Nation of Islam has been successful in getting rid of drug dealers in a number of public housing projects and private apartment buildings. It has established a clinic for the treatment of AIDS patients in Washington, D.C. A cosmetics company, Clean and Fresh, has marketed its products in the black community. The group's weekly newspaper is *The Final Call*. Farrakhan has allowed his members to participate in electoral politics and appointed five women ministers, both of which were forbidden under Elijah Muhammad. Farrakhan came to national attention in 1984 through a series of allegedly anti-Semitic comments that triggered protests by Jewish groups.

On October 16, 1995, the Honorable Louis Farrakhan's Million Man March was held in Washington, D.C., drawing a crowd largely of black men, estimated from 800,000 to more than 1 million. It was the largest black gathering in history, surpassing the 250,000 people at the March on Washington rally led by Dr. Martin Luther King, Jr., in August 1963. Although the core of Farrakhan's Nation of Islam is estimated to be 50,000 to 100,000 members, his influence is much greater. His speeches across the country have attracted crowds of more than 40,000 in large cities. His group is the fastest-growing of the various Muslim movements, helped by the influence of rap groups such as Public Enemy and Prince Akeem. International branches of the Nation of Islam have been formed in Ghana, London, Paris, South Africa, and Caribbean islands.

Minister Louis Farrakhan and his wife, Khadijah, have eleven children, several of whom serve in the Nation of Islam's hierarchy.

See also Anti-Semitism; Black Muslims; Fard, W. D.; Islam; Malcolm X; Muhammad, Elijah Karriem; Muhammad, Warith Deen; Nation of Islam.

Bibliography

Farrakhan, Louis. *Seven Speeches by Minister Louis Farrakhan.* 1974.

Farrakhan, Louis. *A Torchlight for America.* 1990.

Gardell, Mattias. *In the Name of Elijah Muhammad: Louis Farrakhan and the Nation of Islam.* 1996.

Lincoln, C. Eric. *The Black Muslims in America.* 1960.

Mamiya, Lawrence H. "From Black Muslim to Bilalian: The Evolution of a Movement." *Journal for the Scientific Study of Religion.* 21, no. 2 (1982): 138–151.

Mamiya, Lawrence H. "Minister Louis Farrakhan." In *Contemporary Black Leaders,* edited by David DeLeon. 1994.

Lawrence H. Mamiya

Fasting

Fasting practices in the United States are as diverse as American religion itself. Not only have various immigrant traditions brought an assortment of fasting rituals with them to the United States, but also many original American religions have developed their own fasting practices. Motivations for fasting in American life include, but are not limited to, supplication, penitence, and the desire to draw closer to a divine power or being. Fasting involves refraining from eating or drinking for a prescribed amount of time, abstaining from particular foods or drink for set periods of time, or simply eating or drinking less than desired.

Supplicatory fasting, or fasting to make a request of a higher power, colors the tapestry of American religion. Many Hindu women in America, for example, continue to take a vow to fast weekly, monthly, or yearly to protect the lives of their husbands and sons. Some Native American tribes view fasting as a means to receive guidance from divine spirits. These are two examples of fasting practices utilized by Americans to make a request of a higher power.

Americans also fast to purify themselves before offering penance and asking for forgiveness, or to prepare themselves for an encounter with a divine power. For example, American Jews annually abstain from all food and drink on the day of Yom Kippur while praying to God for forgiveness for their transgressions. Muslims and Christians in the United States also fast to expiate past sins or to purify their bodies to prepare themselves for closeness to God. Mormons ritually fast, as well. They have established the first Sunday of each month as a fast day on which they abstain from food for twenty-four hours to prepare for testimonials of their faith.

Connection with a divine power is a common motivation for fasting in American religion. While American Catholics have obligatory days of fasting, such as Ash Wednesday and in Lent, American Protestants fast at their own discretion when they desire to draw nearer to God. For example, the Campus Crusade for Christ has organized a Fasting and Prayer event annually since 1994. In contrast, the Muslim-American community fasts during the month of Ramadan. From sunup to sundown each day of Ramadan, Muslims refrain from food and drink to develop their spiritual connection to God.

The practice of fasting in the United States, however, is not limited to the rituals of these organized religious traditions. In fact, many Americans chose fasting as a means to protest involvement in the Vietnam War in the 1960s and 1970s. There have also been connections drawn between anorexia and traditional religious practices of fasting, although there is debate concerning the legitimacy of this connection. The pursuit of health has become a popular motivation to fast in the contemporary United States. While these practices do not derive wholly from specific religious traditions, they appropriate the religious custom of fasting to achieve a larger goal, thus adding to the diversity of fasting practices in the United States.

See also Food; Practice; Vegetarianism.

Bibliography

Denny, Frederick. *Islam and the Muslim Community.* 1987.

Fenton, John Y. *Transplanting Religious Traditions: Asian Indians in America.* 1988.

Macculloch, J. A., and A. J. Maclean. "Fasting." In *Encyclopedia of Religion and Ethics*. 1912.

Rader, Rosemary. "Fasting." In *The Encyclopedia of Religion*. 1987.

Stamberg, Susan. *Talk: NPR's Susan Stamberg Considers All Things*. 1993.

Vandereycken, Walter, and Ron van Deth. *From Fasting Saints to Anorexic Girls: The History of Self Starvation*. 1994.

Williams, Peter W. *America's Religions: Traditions and Cultures*. 1998.

Sara E. Karesh

Father Divine

(1879–1965), ministers, activist, cult leader.

Father Divine, a Harlem-based minister, was worshiped as God on earth by members of his "Peace Mission" movement. Although widely derided as a cult "racketeer," Divine fed, sheltered, and helped find work for thousands of poor people during the Depression. He exemplified the tendency among black religious leaders toward greater social activism, declaring, "I would not give five cents for a God who could not help me here on the Earth."

Born George Baker to a black Baptist family in Rockville, Maryland, he encountered in 1906 a black preacher named Samuel Morris, who interpreted literally a phrase from 1 Corinthians (3:16), "Know ye not that ye are the temple of God, and that the spirit of God dwelleth in you?" Baker preached ever after on this theme of inner divinity, urging all people to live in harmony with God and with each other regardless of their color or "so-called" race.

After several years of evangelism in the South, Baker moved to New York City in 1915 and, four years later, as the "Reverend M. J. Divine," he settled in Sayville, Long Island. Living with a few followers who pooled their funds, he distributed books on New Thought, which taught that everyone could enjoy earthly success by visualizing positive images and tapping an inner spiritual power. Disciples also strove for unity with God by renouncing carnal temptations such as tobacco, alcohol, drugs, and sexual relations.

During the 1930s Divine's free Sunday banquets attracted blacks from Harlem and Newark, New Jersey, plus a growing minority of whites. These interracial gatherings, however, contributed to his arrest in 1931 for "disturbing the peace," and his conviction the following June after a blatantly racist trial. But even before the verdict was overturned in January 1933, Divine found his messianic aura enhanced when, three

Religious leader Father Divine seated outside, wearing a favorite hat (date and location not known). (Credit: CORBIS/Bettmann.)

days after sentencing and censuring Divine, the judge suddenly died. Relocating to Harlem, Divine presided over a burgeoning movement, clustered in the northern ghettos but also featuring predominantly white branches in California and in several other countries.

Father Divine's network of "Peace Mission" centers held interracial services at a time when nearly all American congregations were segregated. Divine also used whites as secret emissaries to circumvent restrictive housing covenants and acquire homes, hotels, and beachfronts for his interracial following in northern white neighborhoods, including more than two thousand acres of choice property far from the city slums. The Peace Mission gained fame as well for launching thriving cooperative businesses. And in January 1936 Divine held a "Righteous Government Convention" that called for the abolition of segregation, lynching, and capital punishment, and urged an expanded government commitment to end unemployment, poverty, and hunger.

After 1940 the Peace Mission sharply declined in numbers and influence as the return of prosperity lessened its philanthropic appeal, and it evolved from a mass movement to a formal sect featuring half a dozen incorporated churches. In 1942 Divine left Harlem for Philadelphia, and four years later he announced a "spiritual" marriage to a twenty-one-year-old white disciple, thereafter known as Mother Divine. When Father Divine died in September 1965 after a long illness, disciples were stunned and saddened but not to the point of mass desertion. He had been largely out of public view for several years, during which time Mother Divine had prepared followers for the day when "Father will not be with us personally."

Since the late 1950s Mother Divine and her secretarial staff have administered the Peace Mission from a seventy-two-acre estate outside Philadelphia called Woodmont, which Father Divine proclaimed "the mount of the house of the Lord" on moving there in 1953. Disciples pay special homage to Woodmont's "Shrine to Life," a structure designed by Mother Divine; it surrounds a red marble crypt that holds the body of Father Divine. They believe that "Father" did not die, but rather cast off his mortal body to rule the universe through his spirit.

As the Peace Mission's membership has dwindled to perhaps a few hundred and as most of its properties have been sold off, it has accordingly reinterpreted its mission. During the 1930s the young, dynamic, and expanding movement boasted that it was fast converting the world, but today's members instead perceive themselves as a saving remnant, vigilant for the return in bodily form of their founding leader. Disciples have chosen to revere, rather than revive, Father Divine's earlier social activism; but within the Peace Mission's own centers Father Divine's vision of a chaste, integrated communal society endures.

See also CIVIL RIGHTS MOVEMENT; CULT; NEW THOUGHT; SECT.

BIBLIOGRAPHY

Harris, Sara, with the assistance of Harriet Crittendon. *Father Divine,* enlarged ed. 1971.

Hoshor, John. *God in a Rolls-Royce: The Rise of Father Divine: Madman, Menace, or Messiah . . .* 1936.

Parker, Robert Allerton. *The Incredible Messiah: The Deification of Father Divine.* 1937.

Watts, Jill. *God, Harlem U.S.A.: The Father Divine Story.* 1992.

Weisbrot, Robert. *Father Divine and the Struggle for Racial Equality.* 1983.

Robert Weisbrot

Feminist Spirituality

Feminist spirituality is a grassroots religious movement inside and outside established religions that re-claims the power, value, and dignity of women. It is a commitment to bringing about in oneself and in the world an alternative vision of justice and equality for all. It focuses on women's heritages, women's body as the locus of the divine, and women's work of replacing patriarchal, kyriarchal societies with equality for all. This empowering spiritual quest starts with women's search for meaning rooted in women's experiences. It is Earth-centered and embodied and oriented toward global justice. Feminist spirituality stands at the heart of human transformation, challenging accepted ways of knowing and being. It includes feminist knowledge, rites, religious practices, prayers, and beliefs.

The term "feminist spirituality" emerged during the second wave of the modern feminist movement in the United States in the 1970s. Feminists charged that Judaism and Christianity were sexist religions with a male God and male leadership that legitimized the superiority of men in family, religion, and society. They began to examine traditional arguments for female subordination, deploring the exclusion of women from the ministry, and rejecting teachings that denied women's selfhood. Some gathered in consciousness-raising groups to voice their own experience, critique patriarchal culture, and work to transform it. Some recovered a Goddess-centered religion that grounded women in a sacred, embodied self.

The 1980s saw this movement emphasizing inclusiveness, respecting the importance of differences and commonalities among women. It was challenged with and enriched by a diversity of voices, contents, methods, and perspectives, including those drawn from Judaism, Christianity, Islam, Buddhism, Hinduism, Native American traditions, and African cultures, as well as twelve-step programs, self-help programs, and the New Age movement. Diverse feminists began working to eradicate patriarchy and kyriarchy in all forms, including racism, classism, sexism, heterosexism, imperialism, ethonocentricism, and ageism.

Feminists with roots in established religions have searched for spiritual resources in their sacred texts and traditions. Jewish women recovered female images from the Torah, Talmud, and kabbalah; rediscovered women's prayers and poetry from the Diaspora; and reintroduced traditional women's rituals such as Rosh Chodesh (new moon). Christian women recovered the biblical and apocryphal figures of Sophia and Mary and worked for women's ordination. Catholic women retold stories of women's spiritual communities, created the women-church movement, and celebrated feminist Eucharistic meals. Protestant women sparked the Reimagining movement. Womanists reinterpreted the violence in the crucifixion of Jesus. Mujeristas gave voice to the struggles of women for liberation. Wiccan feminists abandoned established religions and revitalized the Goddess. Native American feminists restored memories of woman-centered and Mother-ritual-based cultures.

Although feminists hold a variety of beliefs about feminist spirituality, there is agreement about empowerment (healing) for women as the goal and reward, ritual as a tool of empowerment and a means of communication with the sacred, and nature as sacred.

Feminist spirituality groups exist in a variety of settings, from covens to sacred circles, women-church base communities to reimagining communities, living rooms to farmlands, city centers to country corners. Most are small, meet regularly, offer spiritual sustenance that institutional religions lack, raise feminist consciousness, provide community, facilitate women's spiritual search, and invite action for social justice. They often transcend religious and denominational boundaries. Typically, groups emphasize shared leadership, personal stories, equality, affirmation, and ritual celebration.

Spiritual feminists have uncovered and recovered female deities to symbolize female sacred power and mirror women as holy. Since Mary Daly wrote *Beyond God the Father* in 1973, declaring, "If God is male, then the male is God," feminists have publicly challenged exclusively masculine images of God and named female deities. They speak of the Great Mother, Goddess, Grandmother, Spider Woman, Corn Woman, Gaia, Sophia, and Mary. North American women have revived veneration of the ancient goddesses of Europe, the Near East, Native America, Shamanism, Buddhism, and Celtic mythology.

Feminists all over North America have created liturgies and rituals that honor women's experiences, communicate with the sacred, and empower women for personal and social transformation. They use symbols and stories, images and language, ritual elements and art forms that emerge from women's experiences. Women's life cycle rituals celebrate the holiness of women's bodies and the goodness of women's choices, commemorating menarche, partnering, reproductive choices, conception, miscarriage, abortion, childbirth, menopause, croning, and death. Healing ceremonies support women surviving rape, incest, domestic violence, addictions, breast cancer, hysterectomies, and HIV-AIDS. Wheel of the Year celebrations reinstate the sacredness of the ecological cycles of spring, summer, autumn, winter, and the four equinoxes. These ritual experiences are participative, circular, and body-centered. They provide a collective place where women's ways of knowing—thinking, feeling, reacting, living—become normative. They raise feminist consciousness and challenge humanity to achieve a global transformation toward justice.

See also BELONGING, RELIGIOUS; ECOFEMINISM; FEMINIST THEOLOGY; GOD; GODDESS; MARY; MASCULINE SPIRITUALITY; MATRIARCHAL CORE; MATRIARCHY; NAMES AND NAMING; NEW AGE SPIRITUALITY; NEW RELIGIOUS MOVEMENTS; ORDINATION OF WOMEN; PATRIARCHY; PRIESTESS; RELIGIOUS COMMUNITIES; SPIRITUALITY; WOMANIST THEOLOGY; WOMEN'S STUDIES.

BIBLIOGRAPHY

Christ, Carol P., and Judith Plaskow, eds. *Womanspirit Rising: A Feminist Reader in Religion.* 1979.

Eller, Cynthia. *Living in the Lap of the Goddess.* 1995.

Plaskow, Judith, and Carol P. Christ, eds. *Weaving the Visions: New Patterns in Feminist Spirituality.* 1989.

Winter, Miriam Therese, Adair Lummis, and Allison Stokes. "Feminist Spirituality." In *Defecting in Place.* 1994.

Diann L. Neu

Feminist Theology

Feminist theology examines the history, beliefs, and practices of religious traditions from feminist perspectives. More accurately termed "feminist theologies," the field encompasses a wide array of theoretical and experiential approaches to issues of sex and gender, as well as age, class, identity, and race. Feminist theologians have pioneered theories and methods in comparative religion, ethics, the history of religion, liturgy, religious philosophy, ritual, the sociology of religion, and textual interpretation.

Contemporary American feminist theologies are rooted in the nineteenth-century "first wave" of feminism, which sought both political and social equality for women. While much of this early feminist movement focused on emancipation and social welfare, a number of its leaders recognized that religious beliefs and practices also played a significant role in determining the status of women. They criticized the androcentrism (male focus) of biblical interpretation, religious leadership, and theological arguments used to justify the subordination of women.

This critique of religious androcentrism was taken up with the emergence of "second-wave" feminism in the 1960s and 1970s and provided a foundation for the new field of feminist theological inquiry. Pioneering feminist theologians exposed sexism in existing religious constructs. As with many other areas of feminist scholarship, this critical work was given expression in both academic and community settings. An important purpose of the work was (and continues to be) both to challenge and reconstruct intellectual paradigms and to effect feminist transformation of religious institutions.

In addition to the critical perspectives involved in seeking to eliminate androcentrism, early feminist theologians laid the groundwork for religious reforms and renewal that continue to the present. On a philosophical level, feminist theologies concerned with women's experience questioned and proposed new constructions of traditional views of divinity, human nature, revelation, salvation, and other religious categories. They sought to develop methodologies that valued feminine qualities of inclusivity and relationship. The reality and significance of lesbianism became a category of both inquiry and activism. New rituals and liturgy were created, rooted in distinctive female life-cycle events, such as menstruation and childbirth, as well as previously hidden areas, such as battering, incest, rape, and sexual abuse.

At the same time the work of other feminist theologians was based on a rejection of separate female and male human nature or spirituality. These theologians sought to transform religion by fully integrating women's teachings and experience into a common, egalitarian spiritual practice for women and men.

Feminist theological innovations also occurred within existing schools of contemporary religious thought, especially within liberation theology, a movement based on compatible values of the integration of theory and activism as well as an overriding concern with liberating social transformation. Feminist theologians were influenced by scholarship in other fields as they created new methods of textual analysis and historical interpretation.

Concurrent with attempts to integrate feminism into existing dominant traditions was a strain of feminist theology—or more accurately, thealogy (goddess study)—that rejected those institutions altogether in favor of new and re-created goddess-centered traditions. These thealogians emphasized an unbreakable link between the self- and social esteem of women and explicitly female images of the divine. They were also responsible for the growth of research into suppressed goddess imagery and traditions within androcentric religions.

By the late 1970s and early 1980s, American minority groups were asserting their voices within the field of religious studies, demanding greater recognition as distinctive groups whose historical, spiritual, and communal experiences remained unexpressed in the feminist theologies of the academy. These groups challenged others to incorporate a greater awareness of racism, classism, heterosexism, and anti-Semitism into their work as feminist theologians. Such concerns regarding diversity reflected discussion in the larger

feminist movements of the time and had an impact on feminist theologies in several ways.

One effect was the development of distinct strands of feminist theology based on differences of identity. By the early 1980s African-American feminists began to refer to themselves as "womanists," reclaiming and reinterpreting a distinctive cultural language to name a simultaneous female and black identity. Soon afterwards, Latina feminists coined the term *mujerista* to express a commitment to a perspective fully inclusive of their identities as both women and members of diverse Hispanic communities. In a similar manner, Asian Americans, Jewish Americans, Native Americans, and Muslim Americans have developed feminist theologies in which feminism is understood as interwoven in, rather than opposed to, their specific cultural identities.

A second direction brought about by an increased awareness of difference and diversity among women was that these issues themselves became the subject of feminist theological inquiry. As the 1980s progressed, the influence of deconstructionism, a movement critical of the notion of stable or singular identities, led to a questioning of whether there should or even could be any coherent explication of "female" experience. This critique demanded a more sophisticated analysis of the interplay among multiple, evolving, and competing forms of individual and group identities. It called into question the significance of work that assumed any fixed perspectives, including sex, race, and class. Early feminist theorists distinguished what they understood to be biologically determined sex (female or male) from socially constructed gender (femininity or masculinity). Now feminist theologians began to examine the fluidity of all these categories and develop an analysis of "gendered" power relations among men as well as women in religious contexts. Influenced by queer studies, feminist theologies have also challenged normative, static categories of sexuality and brought to light supressed homoeroticism within religious traditions.

No longer able to generalize about all women, feminist theologians have increasingly focused their work on specific women, historical and contemporary, and the particularities of their experience. This abandonment of the attempt to formulate a singular voice has allowed a renewed unity of purpose in which feminist theologies speak not for but with each other in a common enterprise.

See also ECOFEMINISM; GODDESS; INCLUSIVE LANGUAGE; LATINO TRADITIONS; LESBIAN AND GAY RIGHTS MOVEMENT; LIBERATION THEOLOGY; MASCULINE SPIRITUALITY; RELIGIOUS STUDIES; SEXUALITY; WOMANIST THEOLOGY; WOMEN'S STUDIES.

BIBLIOGRAPHY

Chopp, Rebecca S., and Sheila Greeve Davaney, eds. *Horizons in Feminist Theology: Identity, Tradition, and Norms.* 1997.

Christ, Carol P., and Judith Plaskow, eds. *Womanspirit Rising: A Feminist Reader in Religion.* 1979.

Gross, Rita M. *Feminism and Religion: An Introduction.* 1996.

Isasi-Díaz, Ada María. *Mujerista Theology.* 1996.

Sanders, Cheryl J., ed. *Living the Intersection: Womanism and Afrocentrism in Theology.* 1995.

Drorah O'Donnell Setel

Feng Shui

Feng shui is an ancient Chinese science of orientation premised on the belief that human habitation can be situated physically to take advantage of invisible currents of energy within the earth. This energy is called *qi (ch'i)*, and is that ineffable force affected by the pierce of the acupuncture needle. The human anatomy is a microcosm of the Earth, and the blood veins of one correspond to "dragon veins" of the other. When the ground is broken and the well is dug for a new house, or when the excavation for a tomb is conducted, such action taps into these dragon veins just like an acupuncture needle. Two different procedures for locating this geophysical qi began to develop as early as the Han dynasty (206 B.C.E.–220 C.E.). The *xingshi* or form school is based on the idea that water collects and stores qi while wind captures and scatters it. Feng shui means "wind and water," which is merely shorthand for the principle of "hindering the wind and hoarding the waters." The *liqi* or compass school, on the other hand, is based on the theory of the five phases of qi. This correlative system analyzes qi as a force that alternates between the poles of yin and yang as it progresses through five elemental phases. In the yang or productive phase, earth harbors metal, metal condenses water, water nourishes wood, wood feeds fire, and fire burns to earth. In the yin or conquest phase, earth dams water, water quenches fire, fire melts metal, metal cuts wood, and wood taps earth. These phases are correlated with the eight directional trigrams of the *Book of Changes,* and a person's year of birth is thought to correspond to a particular trigram. It is thus possible to avoid destructive qi by orienting dwellings or arranging rooms in productive directions.

A custom-made home in a planned community in Bellvue, Washington, is designed and situated in accordance with principles of feng shui. Such harmonious alignments are thought to bring good fortune and happiness. (Credit: AP/Wide World Photos.)

Feng shui became accessible to the English-speaking world only a hundred years ago when British missionary Ernest Eitel and Belgian missionary J. J. M. de Groot published their respective studies. But only in the past quarter century has the public at large discovered this ancient system. Chinese communities in the United States have always utilized their local feng shui masters, but owing perhaps to the popularity of Asian systems of thought in the era of New Age religion, every major city in America now has its own community of feng shui consultants. One of the earliest proponents in the United States was Thomas Yun Lin, who founded a temple for American Black Sect Tantric Buddhism in Berkeley, California, in 1986. His brand of feng shui dispensed with many of the traditional practices and relied instead on "intuition and mystical knowledge." The American Feng Shui Institute, founded by Master Larry Sang in Los Angeles in 1991, purports to transmit the scientific principles of feng shui without recourse to superstition. Two of its students, Elizabeth Moran and Val Biktashev, have recently collaborated, in consultation with Sang and Canadian master Joseph Yu, to write *The Complete Idiot's Guide to Feng Shui* (1999), the most comprehensive introduction to compass school feng shui currently available in English.

See also CHINESE-AMERICAN RELIGIONS; I CHING; NEW AGE SPIRITUALITY.

BIBLIOGRAPHY

de Groot, J. J. M. *The Religious System of China*, vol. 3, ch. 12. 1892; repr. in Derek Walters, *Chinese Geomancy*. 1989.

Eitel, Ernest John. *Feng-shui: or, The Rudiments of Natural Science in China*. 1873.

Feuchtwang, Stephan D. R. *An Anthropological Analysis of Chinese Geomancy*. 1974.

Field, Stephen L. "The Numerology of Nine Star Fengshui." *Journal of Chinese Religions* (Fall 1999).

Moran, Elizabeth, and Val Biktashev. *The Complete Idiot's Guide to Feng Shui*. 1999.

Walters, Derek. *The Feng Shui Handbook*. 1991.

Wong, Eva. *Feng-shui*. 1996.

Stephen L. Field

Financing Religion

During most of Christian history, churches were supported by taxes, land rents, and benefices. Throughout the Middle Ages, taxes and rents supported the institutions. This ended with the Napoleonic era, when most church lands in Europe were confiscated, and clergy came to be supported by governments.

In the American colonies, churches were supported by local governments until the late 1770s. In 1791 the First Amendment to the U.S. Constitution called for disestablishment of all churches and an end to government support. The new method of financing churches became pew rentals, which lasted throughout the nineteenth century. In the years 1900 to 1920 the system of stewardship appeals, pledges, and envelopes arose that is in use today. At present pledging is the major method of raising financial support in mainline Protestantism, and a combination of tithing and pledging is the major method in evangelical Protestantism. Roman Catholicism relies less on these methods and more on voluntary offerings.

Religious Giving in the 1990s

Most religious institutions today get their financial support from giving by members. In a 1993 study of congregations in five denominations (four Protestant groups and the Roman Catholic Church) in America, it was found that 89 percent of all income came through regular contributions from members. The rest came from bequests, income from investments, and small amounts from fees for programs, rental of building space, and fund-raising events (Hoge et al., 1996). Very few congregations receive support from their denominations.

A 1991 study estimated that 72 percent of the funds of religious congregations was used for current operating expenditures, 14 percent was spent on local capital outlays and savings, and 14 percent was donated to other organizations and individuals—usually denominational programs. This agrees with a 1993 study of five denominations in which 13 percent of funds was sent to mission and service programs outside the congregation. Other research demonstrates that this percentage declined gradually from the 1960s to today.

Denominational offices and programs are supported by payments from congregations. Every denomination has a required or suggested payment to regional and national synods, dioceses, and conferences. These offices in turn support seminaries, missionaries, publications, and so on.

Religion is the number one recipient of philanthropic giving in the United States. It receives an estimated 60 percent of all money given (Hodgkinson and Weitzman, 1996). The estimated total of contributions to religion was $44 billion to $49 billion in 1995. Most religious giving goes directly to local congregations, although in 1993 approximately 16 percent of all religious giving by individuals went to groups or causes outside of local congregations, most commonly to mission programs, social service programs, colleges, and seminaries.

The trend in overall religious giving to Christian churches in raw dollars has been moving upward at roughly the rate of inflation since the 1960s. But as a percentage of overall household income of church members, it has fallen gradually. A study of Protestant denominations in 1995 found that the percentage of household income given by members fell gradually from 3.1 percent in 1968 to 2.5 percent in 1992 (Ronsvalle and Ronsvalle, 1996). Catholic trends are largely unknown, since the Catholic Church never releases summary data on contributions.

Denominational Differences

The methods of handing contributions vary from denomination to denomination. Among Christian groups the Church of Jesus Christ of Latter-day Saints (commonly called Mormons) is unique; it requires that members contribute 10 percent of their household income if they are to be in good standing and receive an entrance pass to Mormon temples. Each Mormon member meets with the local clergyman once a year to discuss the member's giving during that year, and the clergyman decides whether to give the person a pass for entering a temple. Due in part to this procedure, Mormon giving is the highest of any Christian group. No other denomination requires giving 10 percent of income (called "tithing") and also checks up on each member once a year. A few other denominations require tithing for being a full member but without any checking up.

The mainline Protestant denominations (Episcopalians, Presbyterians, Lutherans, Methodists, United Church of Christ, Disciples of Christ, and some others) put less emphasis on tithing. They typically have a stewardship campaign in the autumn, during which they ask members to fill out pledge cards saying what they will contribute the following year. Virtually all churches provide envelopes to members so members' contributions can be confidential, yet the treasurer can add them up for the year and send the member an end-of-year receipt for income-tax purposes. Pledging is much less common in small churches in any denomination, since they are usually made up of only a few families who know each other well; thus their financial arrangements are informal. The evangelical Protestant denominations have higher percentages of members who tithe, so they rely less than mainline denominations on annual stewardship campaigns and pledging.

Religious giving in the Jewish community is different, largely because many American Jews see themselves as ethnically Jewish but not religious. Each metropolitan area in the United States has a Jewish federation, which organizes fund-raising. The 200 federations in operation in the United States in the 1990s resemble combined United Way campaigns in each city, and they collectively collect and disburse the vast bulk of Jewish charitable giving. The federations support over 1,000 Jewish organizations and causes, ranging from Jewish schools at all levels to community centers and study trips to Israel. The federations are the main planning and decision-making structure in the American Jewish community.

Synagogues are separate, and they are supported mostly by annual membership dues, which are seen by Jews as akin to school tuition, not as charitable giving. According to a 1990 survey, 41 percent of American Jews were affiliated with a synagogue, and affiliation entails paying annual set dues, typically in the range of $600 to $1,400 for a family. In a typical synagogue, two-thirds to three-fourths of the annual budget is covered by membership dues. In addition, synagogues ask for voluntary contributions and sponsor fund-raising activities. Total philanthropic giving by Jews, apart from synagogue membership dues, is high, estimated at about $1,600 per family in 1990 (Kosmin and Ritterband, 1991).

The amount of money contributed by members in various denominations differs widely, with some contributing five times as much as others. As noted earlier, the Mormons have the highest rate among Christian bodies, followed by several evangelical and pentecostal bodies, then followed by mainline denominations. The Catholic Church has a lower rate of contributions than the Protestant bodies. In 1993 a study estimated that per-household giving to one's congregation averaged $1,696 in the Assemblies of God, $1,154 in the Southern Baptist Convention, $1,085 in the Presbyterian Church (U.S.A.), $746 in the Evangelical Lutheran Church in America, and $386 in the Catholic Church. Other research shows that Mormon giving and Jewish giving are higher than any of these five.

Influences on Giving

The main explanation for the different rates of contribution is in four factors. First, different religious groups have different levels of personal participation, especially attendance and volunteering. Second, different groups attach different theological meanings to contributions, most importantly regarding whether God will reward the givers with spiritual benefits. Third, conservative and evangelical groups give a higher percentage of total household philanthropic giving to their churches and less to other causes; that is, their giving is more concentrated on the local church. Fourth, some denominations stress the obligation of tithing one's income, while others do not. Also, some nontithing groups stress making an annual pledge befitting the level of one's household income, while others do not. Groups that require tithing or annual pledging have higher levels of giving than others. In all of these causal factors, conservative and evangelical Protestant groups are highest.

Levels of giving by individual members are highly skewed, with a few members contributing the majority of funds in all churches. The formula applies in virtually all congregations that 20 percent of the households contribute 80 percent of the funds. Sometimes it is 25 percent contributing 75 percent.

Trends in the 1990s

The most important trend is that church members and synagogue members have an increasing antiestablishment mood, which weakens their commitment to national denominational structures. Thus decision-making is being made increasingly at the local level, less money is being sent to national offices, and national denominational structures are slowly shrinking. The trend has been present since the 1980s. The best guess is that future denominational structures will be less hierarchical and more voluntary.

A second trend is that young adults have weaker denominational loyalty than their elders, so that young adults shift denominations readily (especially within Protestantism and Judaism) and gravitate to local churches whose programs and leaders they like best. This makes financial bases of local churches more volatile and less stable than in the past.

A third trend is a clear growth in endowments for congregations. Although exact numbers are not known, it is clear that bequests, wills, and large gifts to congregations are higher today than ever. The same is true of many denominational programs, so that, for example, foreign missions in mainline Protestant denominations are often supported more than 50 percent by endowment income rather than by current contributions from members.

See also CHURCH OF JESUS CHRIST OF LATTER-DAY SAINTS; JUDAISM; MAINLINE PROTESTANTISM; ROMAN CATHOLICISM.

BIBLIOGRAPHY

Hodgkinson, Virginia A., and Murray S. Weitzman. *Giving and Volunteering in the United States, 1996.* 1996.

Hoge, Dean R., Charles E. Zech, Patrick H. McNamara, and Michael J. Donahue. *Money Matters: Personal Giving in American Churches.* 1996.

Kosmin, Barry A., and Paul Ritterband, eds. *Contemporary Jewish Philanthropy in America.* 1991.

Ronsvalle, John, and Sylvia Ronsvalle. *Behind the Stained Glass Windows: Money Dynamics in the Church.* 1996.

Dean R. Hoge

First Amendment.

See Freedom of Religion.

Focus on the Family

Focus on the Family (FOTF) is an international evangelical organization headquartered in Colorado Springs, Colorado; FOTF's mission is the "care and preservation of the home." Begun in 1977 as a twenty-five-minute radio broadcast by child psychologist James C. Dobson, Jr. (1936–) in response to permissive childrearing philosophies and perceived attacks on the traditional nuclear family, FOTF was part of the larger resurgence of "born again" Christianity in America that began with the presidency of Jimmy Carter. Today FOTF is a multiservice evangelical organization whose reach extends to seventy-two countries in twenty-six languages, with more than thirteen hundred workers and an annual budget of more than one hundred million dollars. Sociologically, one may interpret FOTF as an organizational hub for the contemporary evangelical subculture, providing resources that enable evangelical families to surround themselves with professionally informed but resolutely evangelical interpretations of parenting, marriage, counseling, health care, nutrition, decorating, cleaning, time management, and social/political issues, as well as supply their homes with an array of evangelical entertainment options, from music to radio dramas to cartoons to magazines.

At the center of FOTF's activities is its twenty-five-minute weekday radio broadcast, called *Focus on the Family, with Dr. James Dobson,* and its monthly companion magazine, by the same name, is mailed to every listener who contacts FOTF (four million now listed). (The latter is part of FOTF's elaborate fund-raising program, which also includes monthly fund-raising letters from Dobson, other mail requests, and on-air solicitations.) Topics covered on the FOTF weekday broadcast are mostly chosen by Dobson but aim for the following distribution: 40 percent on childrearing, 30 percent on marriage, 25 percent on "Christian living" (e.g., counseling, antipornography, spirituality), and 5 percent on public policy. While the latter may be the principal reason for Dobson's and FOTF's recognition among the general public, most of FOTF's broadcasts are concerned with the realm of home and family, with only occasional but strident forays into the public sphere. One of the broadcast's most frequent topics, for example, is child discipline. FOTF advocates spanking children—especially when children willfully disobey their parents. Yet FOTF reminds parents to balance "love and control," and to avoid spanking if they have a violent temper or a history of abuse. Another frequent FOTF topic is marriage relationships. FOTF holds that men and women are different because they were created differently by God—thus men are to be leaders and women are to be nurturers. Failure to recognize this, FOTF maintains, leads to "destructive" consequences for individuals, marriages, families, and the entire society.

In addition to its signature radio program and companion magazine, FOTF also produces subscription magazines tailored for teen boys (*Breakaway*, circulation 90,000), teen girls (*Brio*, circulation 170,000), preteens (*Clubhouse*, circulation 105,000), and children (*Clubhouse, Jr.*, circulation 82,000). These magazines are professionally edited and designed, and feature articles on celebrity evangelicals, on relationships, on leisure, and on remaining devout. The editors work zealously to communicate that fun and peer acceptance are not antithetical to evangelical faith. FOTF is also involved in building professional networks among evangelical physicians, attorneys, executives, teachers, counselors, and pastors. These networks provide FOTF with both advisers and audiences for its efforts to disseminate professionally informed advice from an evangelical perspective. Moreover, the involvement of these credentialed experts helps to convey professional, even "scientific," endorsement of FOTF's message, a factor in no small part responsible for FOTF's success in finding a following in a society whose bases for truth are as pluralistic as America's are.

Yet ironically, this very pluralism, which has allowed organizations such as FOTF to flourish, is viewed with deep suspicion by FOTF. This suspicion, in fact, animates many of FOTF's activities. It may also be its undoing, as evangelicals are themselves far more pluralistic than FOTF or its founder, Dobson, realize. While a majority of evangelicals would support the FOTF position on gender roles, for example, that percentage is dropping steadily, due to the rising acceptance of full equality for women among evangelicals. Similarly, evangelicals span the political spectrum, and while some cluster loudly around the Republican Party, more are suspicious of political activity because it detracts from the primary purpose of evangelization. The pluralism within evangelicalism, if not recog-

nized by FOTF, will eventually lead to FOTF's marginalization from the mainstream evangelical subculture. What is not likely to affect FOTF greatly is the departure of Dobson. By no means a charismatic figure, Dobson owes his success to his commitment to providing evangelicals with professionally informed advice on children and marriage—a commitment readily found among other professionally trained evangelicals.

See also DOBSON, JAMES C., JR.; EVANGELICAL CHRISTIANITY; JOURNALISM, RELIGIOUS; PSYCHOLOGY OF RELIGION; PUBLISHING, RELIGIOUS; RELIGIOUS RIGHT; TELEVANGELISM.

BIBLIOGRAPHY

Focus on the Family. "*Who We Are and What We Stand For.*" 1997.

Hailey, Mel. "The Role of Religious Organizations in Evangelical Political Activity: The Moral Majority and Evangelicals for Social Action." In *The Role of Religious Organizations in Social Movements,* edited by M. Yarnold, 1991.

Hunter, James Davison. *Evangelicalism: The Coming Generation.* 1987.

Moore, Jennifer. "Focus on the Family Keeps Close Tabs on Four Million Supporters." *The Chronicle of Philanthropy* (November 1, 1994): 43, 46.

Smith, Christian. *American Evangelicalism: Embattled and Thriving.* 1998.

Wilcox, Clyde, and Elizabeth Adell Cook. "Evangelical Women and Feminism: Some Additional Evidence." *Women & Politics.* 9 (1989): 27–49.

Timothy T. Clydesdale

Food

Historically food has been an important symbol reflecting the social and spiritual life of societies. The prevalence of food as a symbol of religious life has much to do with whether food is scarce or abundant for a given society. The Old Testament chronicles the wanderings of nomadic societies, which eventually find a homeland. Throughout the Old Testament food is generally a scarce resource, and consequently there is both symbolic and practical value placed on key foods that sustain life, such as water and bread and olive oil.

The scarcity of food and water creates a particular appreciation for the nature of the feast, which produced bonding and unity among peoples that were sometimes at odds with one another. Norms of sharing—which sustains life—were important, and the

A father and son, members of a Lubavitcher family living in the Crown Heights section of Brooklyn, New York, display kreplach, a traditional Jewish holiday treat that symbolizes God's mercy and is served in Jewish families during Yom Kippur. (Credit: AP/Wide World Photos.)

rule of hospitality is an important part of the Judeo-Christian tradition. In societies where there is an abundance of food, however, its symbolism changes greatly. While America in the twentieth century was not without periods of economic depression and food shortages, for the most part the last half of the century was typified by food abundance. In fact, the United States consumes per capita many times the amount of food consumed by most other countries of the world.

Developments in agricultural technology play an important role in shaping the character of a society. Nomadic societies were very equalitarian: almost all property was communal. As societies began to engage in domestic agriculture, there was an increase in the diversity of occupations and in economic inequality. Horticultural societies had a greater tendency to engage in wars. Transitions to industrial and postindustrial society have profoundly changed the way in which societies organize themselves (Lenski).

American society underwent profound changes during the twentieth century. The nature of all social institutions changed substantially over its last half: the family, education, the economy, and politics. These changes have had an impact on the way in which religion and religious beliefs are understood in America and have affected the relationship between food and culture.

Family

At the turn of the century America was primarily an agricultural society in which increasing urbanization was evident. Urbanization was viewed as problematic by many, aggravating what were perceived as the social ills of poverty, crime, and deviance. Early in the century the ideal typical family was the nuclear family, with extended family living nearby. Meals were the mainstay that coordinated family life and provided a break from the hard labor required to make a living. The norm of three square meals a day was almost an eleventh commandment. The second half of the century saw major changes in family life, eating habits, and consequently the role of food in society. Changing lifestyles, especially among middle-class Americans, led to an increase in dining out and to the flourishing of fast-food chains and their upscale equivalents. The advent of the microwave oven in the home contributed to an increased dependence on processed and ready-to-eat foods. Family schedules became more individualized, and the typical family dinner, where all gather together with attendant religious rituals, tended to give way to the fast-paced personal schedule of each family member. For many, family dining tends to be reserved for holidays and special occasions. While food continues to mark birthdays, weddings, and major cultural festivals, its specific religious significance has diminished. One might speak of the McDonaldization of society: The food system has become the exemplar of modern society's emphasis upon calculability, predictability, efficiency, and control, which stand in contrast to the religious emphasis upon the spiritual dimension of breaking bread together around a common table.

Hunger

America seems to rediscover hunger every twenty to thirty years. Each historical response of the society resulted in a slightly different moral and religious response to the issue (Poppendieck). All religious traditions reflect concern for the care and feeding of the poor. Since the early 1980s religious concerns about feeding the poor have found expression in increasing numbers of food pantries and soup kitchens staffed by volunteers. On an international scale religious concern over world hunger and famine has been reflected in efforts to highlight issues of sustainable agriculture in which people feel secure regarding the availability of food that is safe, nutritious, and equitably distributed (Tansey and Worsley). International groups emerging from theological concerns, such as Oxfam and Bread for the World, work to increase public awareness of food issues and to affect the public policy of nation-states.

Health and Nutrition

Since the 1960s there has been increasing awareness of the relationship between food and health. As with C. W. Post, Sylvester Graham, and John Harvey Kellogg in the nineteenth century, the concern over proper healthy eating has moral and religious connotations. Dieting programs and a group of businesses focused on nutritional supplements and health

A Benedictine nun from the Convent of Perpetual Adoration in Kansas City, Missouri, making communion wafers. (Credit: CORBIS/Ted Spiegel.)

concerns have developed into a major industry. Several writers have suggested that food, rather than sex, has become the center of a new contemporary morality in which people feel more guilty about their eating habits than their sexual indiscretions (Iggers). These changing cultural norms, reflecting in part the new position of women in contemporary society, have resulted in a high incidence of anorexia and bulimia, especially among affluent females.

Current Trends

The connection between food and religion is typified by diverse and sometimes conflicting emphases in contemporary society. Food in American society, as well as in other first-world countries, has a complex relationship to the way in which individuals and groups view themselves. In the last half of the twentieth century, social currents arose that connected food, religion, and self-understanding. Across America communities sponsored differing forms of ethnic food festivals that linked food, religion, and ethnic traditions. Kwanza, an emergent celebration that affirms African-American culture, links food, family, and religion. The increasing recognition of Cinco de Mayo has similar symbolic relevance for many Hispanic Americans.

The globalization of the food system will increasingly engender religious and ethical issues regarding food. The impact of biotechnology on what people eat and concerns over a food system facing demands from an increasing population and declining amounts of farmable land will become more prominent issues. There was recognition at the beginning of the twenty-first century that the experiences of hunger and malnutrition in rich and poor countries alike have more to do with the politics of distribution than with food availability. Food continues to be more than just what people eat; it is an expression of who and what they are.

See also COMMUNION; ECOSPIRITUALITY; GLOBALIZATION; KOSHER; VEGETARIANISM.

BIBLIOGRAPHY

Iggers, Jeremy. *The Garden of Eating: Food, Sex, and the Hunger for Meaning.* 1996.
Lenski, Gerhard, and Jean Lenski. *Human Societies: An Introduction to Macrosociology.* 1974.
Levenstein, Harvey. *The Paradox of Plenty: A Social History of Eating in America.* 1993.
Poppendieck, Janet. *Sweet Charity? Emergency Food and the End of Entitlement.* 1998.
Ritzer, George. *The McDonaldization of Society.* 1995.
Tansey, Geoff, and Tony Worsley. *The Food System: A Guide.* 1996.

Visser, Margaret. *Much Depends on Dinner: The Extraordinary History and Mythology, Allure and Obsessions, Perils and Taboos of an Ordinary Meal.* 1988.

C. Lincoln Johnson

Freedom of Religion

As their colonial experiment began in 1607, the English monarchy was striving for a modicum of uniformity in religious expression and practice. Instead, the nation was torn by theological conflict until the final decade of the century. In 1689, after almost two hundred years of bitter religious rivalry and persecution, the English Parliament passed the Act of Toleration, which retained the Church of England as the established religion and granted toleration to a wide range of Protestants.

In the seventeenth century, American colonial religious sects spread out along the coast like the refraction from a prism. In England there was one political system, over which warring factions fought to establish a version of Protestantism. In America each faction found room for its own form of establishment, colony by colony.

Each of the thirteen colonies reflected a portion of that spectrum without any politically effective community of dissent. Each colony established its own brand of Protestantism, wherein minorities were frequently persecuted. The Anglican Church in Virginia and Puritanism in Massachusetts reigned supreme until the middle of the eighteenth century. Rhode Island, under the leadership of Roger Williams, was a notable exception, with no establishment for several decades.

By 1775 English America sported thirteen distinct governing bodies, under control of Parliament, and each with a discrete religious establishment. Some were severely restrictive; others, more lenient. That picture changed for some states at the birth of the new nation, signaled by the adoption of various declarations of rights. Other states—Massachusetts and Connecticut, for example—continued a church establishment well into the nineteenth century. This was confirmed in a letter to President Jefferson in 1801 by several Baptist leaders in Danbury, Connecticut: "[T]herefore what religious privileges we enjoy (as a minor part of the State) we enjoy as favors granted, and not as inalienable rights. . . ."

The 1789 Constitution was silent on religion save for prohibiting religious tests for holding public office. Adoption of the First Amendment religion clauses created no consensus on the issues of religious freedom and establishment at the state level. Leaders in Connecticut and Massachusetts saw those clauses as a protection against federal interference with state religious establishments. In contrast, Virginian James Madison championed a federal mandate securing religious freedom and nonestablishment in state law. That sharp ideological division explains why the Senate refused to extend the First Amendment's guarantees to state laws, rejecting Madison's sound insight that it was in the states and local communities where religious freedom was most at risk. Not until after the ratification and incorporation of the Fourteenth Amendment did Madison's view finally prevail.

Throughout the nineteenth century and the first half of the twentieth, even though most states had adopted strong declarations on the rights of conscience, a *de facto* Protestant establishment most frequently ignored or reinterpreted its own constitutions to allow for political control by Protestants. After 1850 that hegemony slowly eroded in the face of the immigration of Roman Catholics and, by the close of the century, the growing American Jewish population. Nevertheless, state practices, particularly respecting emerging public schools, were consistently tilted toward the Protestants in most jurisdictions. It was not until 1928, with the nomination by the Democrats of Al Smith to run for president, that the nation as a whole had to confront the full implications of that nineteenth-century de facto establishment. Smith's defeat, while frequently attributed to his Roman Catholic faith, was the result of numerous other factors as well. But it put the nation on notice that the religious issue would not go away.

In the early 1940s the U.S. Supreme Court focused on several state actions that, guided by the Fourteenth Amendment, it determined were in violation of the religion clauses. Those early decisions focused on "free exercise"; however, in 1948, in its *McCollum* decision, the Court declared unconstitutional the teaching of religion by sectarian denominations in the public schools. The nation awakened to the fact that long-established religious practices in a vast number of public schools were at risk. In that same postwar era a new wave of national religious fervor emerged, fueled by television evangelist Billy Graham and by Bishop Fulton J. Sheen. They found support in the public piety of presidents Truman and Eisenhower. In the fifties the *McCollum* decision was modified as the entire issue was overshadowed in the public mind by *Brown* v. *Board of Education* and the civil rights movement of that decade.

In 1960 the nation turned a corner with the election of Roman Catholic John F. Kennedy. The new president was more staunchly committed to a clearly defined church/state separation than his two predecessors had been. The year after Kennedy took office, the Supreme Court issued its 1962 decision *Engel* v. *Vitale*, forbidding public-school-sanctioned prayers. A year later, in *Abington* v. *Schempp,* the Court extended *Engel* to cover Bible reading in public schools. President Kennedy was the voice of reason when he spoke to the public following *Engel:* "We have in this case a very easy remedy, and that is to pray ourselves." But reason was hardly the order of the day in Congress. Following the 1962 Court decision an angry House of Representatives voted unanimously to replace some of the stars on the wall above the Speaker's desk with "In God We Trust." A Missouri Democratic congressman opined that one of the ". . . by-products of our act today is that we have given perhaps not too directly, but in not too subtle a way, our answer to the recent decision of the U.S. Supreme Court. . . ."

As Congress responded with proposals to amend the Constitution to overturn the Court decisions, the weight of the National Council of Churches, several Roman Catholic clerics, and the Conservative and Reform Jewish communities was on the side of the justices. The term "Religious Right" had not yet emerged. The "mainline" churches and synagogues were instrumental in blunting attacks on the Court. There were, to be sure, sharp critiques of the "Warren Court" on church/state issues by conservative religious leaders, but all efforts to derail, by constitutional amendments, the impact of the religion clauses consistently foundered throughout the rest of the sixties and the seventies. In 1971 the Court created three criteria by which to judge whether the establishment clause had been breached. The "*Lemon* test" asserted that any statute must have a secular legislative purpose, it must not advance or inhibit religion, and it must not foster excessive government entanglement with religion. In the following years there were several Court decisions that denied public funding for religious institutions.

But there was a storm brewing. The seventies were the decade when television became a player in a drama that altered the church/state debate. Religious fundamentalists had begun, in the late sixties, to use the medium for preaching and fund-raising. Jerry Falwell was one of the earliest television preachers. Adhering to a position espoused by his fundamentalist forebears, he eschewed political action altogether. Enter the Supreme Court once more.

In 1973 the Court handed down its decision in *Roe* v. *Wade,* overturning state antiabortion laws. It was predictable that the Roman Catholic leadership would find the justices to be in serious error. What was not anticipated was Falwell's response. He immediately found himself in a quandary. Should he become a politically active preacher in light of what he saw as an outrageous attack on ethics and values? The answer was unmistakably affirmative. More than any-

thing else, that single decision by the Lynchburg Baptist preacher was to energize a large block of several million Americans, devoted to Christian fundamentalism, into becoming politically involved. Some six years later the Moral Majority began to take shape; it entered the national political fray in 1980.

With the election of Ronald Reagan that year a new political force moved onto the public stage just at a time when the mainline Protestants were seemingly suffering from an identity crisis. That force came to be called the "Religious Right," and it aided Reagan in his defeat of President Carter. From the beginning the Moral Majority, conceived by Paul Weyrich and Howard Phillips and headed by Falwell, urged amending the Constitution to allow public-school-sponsored prayer and demanded the overturning of the *Roe* v. *Wade* decision. Reagan's Supreme Court appointees included justices less impressed with the Jefferson/Madison model on church and state. Indeed, for the first time a "litmus test" for court appointees was created, focused on the two issues—prayer in schools and abortion.

Throughout the eighties powerful pressure from the leaders of the Religious Right was exerted on those two fronts, and in 1992 it seemed to be bearing fruit. Two Supreme Court cases appeared ideal as a means of keeping the promises by the Reagan-Bush administration. President Bush, to that end, instructed the Justice Department to contest the two cases: *Planned Parenthood* v. *Casey* (abortion) and *Lee* v. *Weisman* (school-sponsored graduation prayer). The Religious Right had reason to expect victory on two fronts. But in two 5–4 decisions in June 1992, the Court upheld *Roe* v. *Wade* and declared unconstitutional public-school-sponsored graduation prayers.

The surprising election of Bill Clinton in 1992 created a dilemma in the minds of many of the religiously motivated supporters of Reagan and Bush. In his first term President Clinton appointed two judicial moderates to the Court, Ruth Bader Ginsburg and Stephen Breyer. Further, Clinton lent the power of his office in opposing a constitutional prayer amendment offered by Representative Ernest Istook, who had the full support of House Speaker Newt Gingrich. In 1998 Istook's efforts resulted in a vote far short of the required two-thirds majority, and Madison's legacy seemed, for the moment, somewhat more secure.

The state of Religious Right political action in 1999 was less clear. In the spring, even as vouchers for religious schools was becoming a hot political and judicial topic, there was a strong signal that some leaders of the Religious Right, having almost nothing tangible to show for twenty years of intense political activity on behalf of their moral agenda, were thinking of returning to a pre-1980 approach in which political action would take second place to the moral and spiritual growth of communities of faith. Leaders such as Paul Weyrich, William Bennett, and Robert Bork were making sounds in that direction. The move was, it appeared, based on an evident failure to convince enough politicians that a political party platform should include a moral agenda predicated on a particular religious perspective. As the century closed, the founders' secular republic had weathered, once again, efforts to install a colonial model that would provide governmental preference for religious institutions.

See also ABORTION; CHURCH AND STATE; FALWELL, JERRY; FUNDAMENTALIST CHRISTIANITY; MORAL MAJORITY; PRAYER IN SCHOOL; RELIGIOUS PERSECUTION; RELIGIOUS RIGHT.

BIBLIOGRAPHY

Alley, Robert S. *School Prayer: The Court, the Congress, and the First Amendment.* 1993.
Swomley, John M. *Religious Liberty and the Secular State.* 1987.

Robert S. Alley

Freemasonry

Freemasonry is a worldwide fraternal order that insists on belief in God as a condition of membership. Masonry traces its roots to the formation of the first Grand Lodge in London, England, on June 24, 1717. The first American Lodge was chartered in Boston on July 30, 1733. George Washington was a Mason. Membership in the various branches of Masonry reached over four million through the mid-twentieth century, but declined to two and a half million by 1991. Masons are initiated through the Blue Lodge but can later become members of the York or Scottish Rites. Masonry has been popularized through the social impact of the Shriners, famous for their charitable efforts in children's hospitals and burn centers.

There has been considerable debate over whether Freemasonry is a religion. While the rituals contain religious language and moral themes, Masons are free to belong to any religion that affirms belief in God and are forbidden to discuss the topic of religion in Lodge meetings. Conservative Christian and secular writers continue to argue that Masons exercise enormous international power for evil purposes. Stephen Knight, a British journalist, created a storm with *The Brotherhood,* his political exposé of Masonry. His untimely death after the book's publication led to charges that he was murdered under orders from the Lodge. Fundamentalist critics Jim Shaw and Tom McKenney contend in *The Deadly Deception* that key Masonic symbols are sexual in nature and represent a revival of both pagan mystery religion and overt Satanic worship. Another critic, William Schnoebelen, alleges that Masons are involved in fifty thousand ritual murders every year in the United States.

Various Masonic scholars (Wallace McLeod, Art DeHoyos, and Brent Morris) have provided compelling arguments against such staggering claims. For example, while Masons are to care for fellow members, their oaths forbid them to break the law or harbor any criminal. Accusations about Masonic murders are strong in only one case, a famous one involving ex-Mason William Morgan. This New York resident was killed in 1826, probably at the hands of a few zealous Masons who were enraged by his betrayal of the fraternity.

Critics have often attacked Masonry over its alleged secret and bloody oaths. In fact, the rituals were made public as early as 1730 in Samuel Prichard's *Masonry Dissected.* Furthermore, Masons do not take the oaths literally, but borrowed them from military history as a symbolic way to assert the importance of loyalty and commitment to one's comrades. Increasingly Masons are asserting the independence of the rituals from overt religious meaning. Scottish Rite leaders are reworking some of the more contentious wording and dramatic acts that are employed in the various degrees.

The history of Masonry reflects something of the deeper currents in changing religious ideology in America. The earliest Masonic writings manifest a more explicitly Christian focus. Then, in the nineteenth century, the growing attention to the world's religious pluralism led Masons to downplay the Christian interpretation of Masonic rites. With the rise of secularism in the twentieth century, and with a greater sensibility to specific religious claims, most Masons are now very insistent that that the Lodge is not a church of any sort.

See also SECRET SOCIETIES.

BIBLIOGRAPHY

Leazer, Garg. *Fundamentalism and Freemasonry.* 1995.

James A. Beverley

Free Will

The issue of the nature of free will and whether humans possess it is one of the oldest in philosophy; and while it is a topic in philosophical metaphysics, it nevertheless has many obvious ties to moral theory and to theology. For if we do not possess free will, it would seem that we cannot be held morally responsible for the actions that we perform. People who can demonstrate that they literally had no choice in performing a wrong action will not be blameworthy for doing what they did. Furthermore, if humans are not free and hence not blameworthy for their morally wrong actions, then (arguably) a good God could not punish them for their sin, since to do so would be to forfeit God's claim to justice.

Central to most discussions of free will is the thesis of determinism. Although there are many possible varieties of determinism, what they all have in common is the idea that what has happened in the past makes what will happen in the future in some important respect *inevitable*. Some philosophers believe that, necessarily, if determinism is true there is no free will; those who hold this view are called *incompatibilists*. Incompatibilists come in two types: *libertarians* and *hard determinists*. The former reject all varieties of determinism and believe that humans at least sometimes act freely. The latter accept determinism (in one of its forms) and so conclude that there is no such thing as genuine free will. In contrast to both kinds of incompatibilists are those who believe that determinism does not rule out the possibility of freedom of the will; those who hold this view are called *compatibilists*.

Compatibilists claim that human free will is not threatened by determinism. The heart of their account of freedom is this: one is free when one is able to do what one wants to do. One is able to do what one wants to do when one is not compelled or constrained by factors external to oneself. Suppose, for example, that Steve is given the opportunity to go whitewater rafting on the Snake River. If he takes a moment to consider the potential dangers and to weigh them against the likely benefits (that is, the excitement and plain fun) of such an adventure, and if he decides that the great likelihood of great excitement and fun outweighs the rather slim chance of injury or death, and so chooses to take the trip, he has acted freely.

Similarly, if he decided that the payoffs of the trip really were not so terrific and that he would not enjoy the trip for his fear of drowning, and so declined the opportunity, we would also say that he had acted freely. On the other hand, if he went on the trip because his life would be threatened if he did not go, or if he was knocked unconscious and placed on the raft comatose, then we would say that his rafting was not free. The difference is that in these cases, his rafting is not the result of an uncompelled act of will but is instead produced by psychological or even physical manipulation. Or again, if he were not to go on the trip because he was tied up by thugs who were ransacking his cabin, then his not rafting would not be free.

The compatibilist asserts that what matters in these cases is that the action (or the inaction) is the result of the right kinds of causes—namely, relevant decisions and other psychological states of the agent. Even if determinism is true, the compatibilist will point out, some of our actions are produced by such decisions and states. That is, even if we are determined by our upbringing or genetics, or even by the will of God, to perform an action, if the immediate cause of that action is our will acting without the compulsion of external forces, then we are free. Although this perhaps sounds paradoxical, it seems to be coherent. Suppose, for example, that God wills that Katie attend City University and so he determines that she will in fact go there. If the way God brings about her matriculation is by giving her academic ability and an appropriate upbringing, then God will have determined both that she attend CU and also that she attend of her own free will. For she will be doing what she wants to do and she will not be compelled in any freedom-inhibiting way (as would be the case if, for example, her attendance there were the result of her being told that attendance anywhere else would mean the death of her parents).

Incompatibilists doubt that this account of freedom captures what is important in free will. Consider the case of the person with a psychological disorder so strong that she cannot control it and so she necessarily acts in accordance with it. Suppose that Jones is a kleptomaniac and simply is unable to resist stealing when the opportunity arises. If such persons are even possible, then we have an example of a person who would be acting without external compulsion, who would be doing "what he wants to do" and yet who would not be acting freely (since he cannot help stealing in those circumstances).

The incompatibilist thinks that no action is free if, at the time of the action, there is only one thing the agent could do. Freedom requires that at the time of an action, the agent is able either to perform that action or refrain from performing it. Nothing in the past can necessitate the agent's doing what she does if her action is free. This is the heart of the incompatibilist's account of freedom. Now we can see that if this is what freedom comes to, it is inconsistent with determinism, since determinism implies that the past has made only one future chain of events possible.

Let us bring the debate into a theological context; the issue here is generally referred to as the "omniscience and freedom problem." Traditional theology claims that God is all-knowing, or omniscient. Typically this is thought to entail that God has perfect foreknowledge—that is, that God knows what is going to happen before it happens, indeed, that God has always known what was going to happen. Now suppose that Elisa goes horseback riding on July 13. God always knew that Elisa would go horseback riding then. Even more, God's beliefs are infallible; God is not capable of being wrong. So God infallibly believed a thousand or a million or a billion years ago that Elisa would go horseback riding on July 13. But if God believed that then and God cannot be wrong, then it looks as though Elisa could not have refrained from riding then. If freedom requires being able to do otherwise than what you actually do, then it might seem as though God's foreknowing what we will do robs us of our free will. As with every aspect of the free-will issue, however, this question is extremely complex. Many philosophers and theologians believe that, appearances to the contrary notwithstanding, God's foreknowledge and infallibility are consistent with human freedom. One way of arguing this is by appealing to the notion of divine timelessness. If God is external to time, then God experiences all events in time eternally; so God does not *foresee* them per se but is rather aware of them as they happen (although all events in time are eternally laid before God). So, it is sometimes argued, God's perceiving eternally that Elisa will go horseback riding on July 13 does not necessitate her riding then any more than the present author's perceiving her riding as she rides necessitates her riding.

In the twentieth-century American theological and cultural landscape, all of the different camps in the free-will debate can be found, although they do not fly their respective flags explicitly. Roman Catholic theologians have generally argued from a libertarian perspective, emphasizing the importance of the believer's own will cooperating with divine grace to bring about salvation and sanctification. Among Protestants, Lutheran and Reformed denominations, which emphasize divine providence and sovereignty, typically express ideas consistent with compatibilist accounts of freedom. The concept of "predestination" prevalent in the Reformed tradition is nothing other than a species of determinism; indeed, it is sometimes called "theological determinism." Although it is now only the most conservative of American churches in this tradition that continue to preach predestination, some will go as far as to deny any kind of human freedom (seeing such freedom as being incompatible with divine sovereignty), thus making them hard determinists. On the other hand, Wesleyan denominations, such as Methodism, emphasize the freedom of the believer, specifically rejecting predestination. The emphasis they place on human agency strongly suggests a libertarian perspective.

It is somewhat more difficult to place recent, so-called "New Age" religions in the present debate.

Some possess a strongly individualistic strand and stress the importance of individual human decision making as opposed to the more corporate nature of institutional religion; these groups one would suspect to be sympathetic to libertarianism. Other New Age groups see the individual, whether he or she recognizes it or not, as fundamentally a player in a large, cosmic drama, individuality being essentially illusory. Such groups tend to be determinists and either deny human freedom or think it can be worked into the larger deterministic worldview.

See also DISPENSATIONALISM; EXISTENTIALISM; GOD; NEW AGE SPIRITUALITY; RELIGIOUS EXPERIENCE; THEISM.

BIBLIOGRAPHY

Fischer, John Martin, ed. *Moral Responsibility*. 1986.
Watson, Gary, ed. *Free Will*. 1983.
Zagzebski, Linda. *The Dilemma of Foreknowledge and Freedom*. 1991.

Thomas Senor

Fundamentalist Christianity

Fundamentalist Christianity is a form of Protestantism that is reactive to modernity and attempts to make a militant defense of "the fundamentals" of Christian faith. On occasion, observers call some Roman Catholic movements fundamentalist, but Catholicism allows for development in doctrine, something that true fundamentalists reject. Thus Christian fundamentalism is almost always Protestant. (The phenomenon does have its counterparts in Judaism, Islam, and other faiths.)

Christian fundamentalists, according to most proponents and scholars, list at least five fundamental teachings: the inerrancy of the Bible as well as literal understandings of the virgin birth of Jesus, of his sacrificial death, of his physical resurrection, and of his second coming. The stress is on the word "literal." Politician William Jennings Bryan, a pioneer lay fundamentalist, typically insisted on literalism because, he said, Christian liberals sucked the truth out of basic biblical teachings by calling them symbolic or allegorical.

Bryan was a major figure in the first generation of fundamentalism, which took shape early in the twentieth century, acquired its name from 1919 to 1920, and came to its first climax as an agent in disputes within the Presbyterian and Baptist Churches in the northern United States. In the course of time, fundamentalism came to be identified with the South,

Fundamentalist worshipers carry signs praising Jesus Christ at a revival meeting in San Francisco, California.   (Credit: © Rick Browne/Stock, Boston/PNI.)

but most of its origins and many of its members were in the North.

The word "fundamentalism" does not appear in encyclopedias of Christianity before the twentieth century. Of course, there were conservatisms, traditionalisms, and orthodoxies before that. But in 1920, Curtis Lee Laws, the editor of the Baptist *Watchman-Observer,* and his allies called for a new name for their new movement. They complained that ordinary conservatives would not do "battle royal for the Lord" as some fundamentalists would and did. Between 1910 and 1915 some conservatives published twelve volumes called *The Fundamentals,* and in 1919 others formed the World's Christian Fundamentals Association, but the new word did not come into common use until after 1920, in Baptist, Presbyterian, and other denominational battles.

Defeated in denominational conflicts over control of seminaries and mission boards, many fundamen-

talists left their church bodies to form new seminaries and denominations. The most prominent of these individuals was Princeton professor J. Gresham Machen, an intellectual formulator of the movement, who in 1935 helped found the Orthodox Presbyterian Church. That body suffered schism, as fundamentalist churches often do. In 1937, a leader of the split-off faction, Carl McIntire, formed the Bible Presbyterian Synod. Because none of these splintering bodies approached the visibility of the more moderate ones they left behind, most observers relegated fundamentalism to the backwoods of the Bible Belt, and cultural elites dismissed them as hillbillies, Holy Rollers, and rednecks. Meanwhile, the fundamentalists busied themselves fashioning Bible colleges, publishing houses, and radio broadcasting networks.

Fundamentalists regathered initiative by 1941, when under McIntire numbers of parties formed the fundamentalist American Council of Christian Churches. They did so in part to anticipate the formation of a more moderate organization in 1942, the National Association of Evangelicals.

Evangelicals, who insisted on a literal belief in the same fundamentals, declared themselves to be offended by the belligerence of fundamentalists, who, they thought, were driving people away from conservative Christianity. Meanwhile, independent movements of Pentecostals were also emerging. They, too, shared belief in the same fundamentals, but their stress on direct experience of the Holy Spirit made fundamentalists of the Bryan, Machen, and McIntire stripes nervous. How, they asked, could one be sure that there would be no change in fundamentalist doctrine if people claimed to be hearing fresh messages from the Holy Spirit?

After two more decades of relative obscurity, fundamentalism reemerged during and after the cultural crises of the 1960s to become a highly visible and often political force. Some fundamentalists—for example, those led by the Jones family that created and led Bob Jones University in Greenville, South Carolina—sternly rejected political engagement. But beginning in the late 1970s many others did a complete about-face. They had previously seen Christian participation in politics to be distracting and even sinful. Now it was sinful *not* to be political, said pastor, television evangelist, and university founder Jerry Falwell, a major leader of the new version. His faction argued that the churches and the culture had become so corrupt and tainted that only aggressive efforts by fundamentalists could withstand the evils and reform religion and culture. They organized the Moral Majority and later the Christian Coalition.

The resultant New Christian Right leaders were so effective at organizing that they drew more public notice than had liberal Protestants in their heyday decades at midcentury. The New Right gained credibility among many for its support of Ronald Reagan in 1980, and it became a factor in Republican Party politics through the rest of the century.

Fundamentalism is a reactive, more than a reactionary, movement. If it were reactionary, it would use Protestant tradition simply to keep its distance from anything called modern or representative of modernity. That is not the case. Instead, most scholars see fundamentalism as a modern movement. Its leaders and members, as they react to inimical forces, are at home with many of the instruments and actions of modernity. They have been masters of what to others typify modernization in technology: radio, television, the Internet, efficient distribution of mailed messages, and the like. Rather than run from encounters with modern movements that helped inspire them to be reactive, they have engaged them. Thus theories of evolution, which they perceived as assaults on the faith in the name of science, led many fundamentalists to develop what they called "Scientific Creationism" to counter evolution in the classroom.

If fundamentalists reacted against evolutionary accounts of the origins of the universe and of humanity, they also reacted against evolutionary visions of the goals of history. Among these were European Marxism and progressive American movements in politics, education, and the like. While secular social progressives counted on humans alone to bring in a new order, as in Marxism's "classless society," the Protestant advance guard spoke of "bringing in the kingdom of God."

The unfolding future will not be a kind of utopia produced by humans, said the fundamentalists. Instead, they prophesied imminent global catastrophe when Jesus Christ would return to enjoy a thousand-year reign that would mean bliss for the faithful. These apocalypse-minded fundamentalists favored teachings introduced from the British Isles at about the turn of the twentieth century by evangelist Dwight L. Moody and others. It was this expectation of a catastrophic end to history that helped lead earlier fundamentalists to withdraw from politics and social activism. Believers were to concentrate instead on keeping America strong (fundamentalists tend to favor a strong military and to demonize enemies of the United States as "evil empires") and winning converts quickly before Jesus came again. By the 1970s, however, many of them, without losing faith in the sudden end to ordinary history, saw or sought opportunities to reform the world while advancing the causes of conversion and moral living.

Political fundamentalism in the Moral Majority and the Christian Coalition did not and does not concentrate chiefly on economic issues. On its chosen front line, "social issues" predominate. It deals with urgencies that are close to the lives of people besieged by modern change and confused by pluralism or religious diversity and relativism, which find no absolutes as bases on which to live or rule.

Thus the newer political fundamentalism reacted against U.S. Supreme Court decisions in 1962 and 1963 that ruled against officially inspired prayer and devotional Bible reading in public schools. The 1973 *Roe* v. *Wade* decision by the Supreme Court, which ruled that a right to abortion was constitutional, then provoked the most galvanizing reaction. Henceforth, issues dealing with sexuality, gender, conception, family life, education, obscenity, and the like formed the agenda for activists. When identifying villains, they pointed to "secular humanists," religious liberals, corrupting elites in big and encroaching government, mass media, and education as Antichrist.

Fundamentalism, being a movement or a characteristic more than a definable church body, is a term rarely used in the names of congregations and denominations. The word does not always appear, for example, in metropolitan telephone book advertisements and listings of churches. Therefore it is difficult to determine how many fundamentalists there are either in the United States or in counterpart movements that rose as products of American missionary efforts around the world. Numbering is also difficult because many heirs of people who had chosen the name "fundamentalist" for themselves saw that it could create a stigma, and they did not like to be thus labeled. The leadership of the nation's largest Protestant group, the Southern Baptist Convention, bears all the marks that friends, enemies, and most scholars call fundamentalist. But most of these Baptists do not like the adjective, and it must be used with care.

If one includes the Southern Baptist Convention majority, the numerous small denominations that originated as break-offs from more moderate denominations, many television and political movements, and individual fundamentalists who stay in more moderate bodies, it is likely that there are twenty million to thirty million in the United States. This very rough estimate depends on definition, but it is a clear indicator that fundamentalism, while smaller than the more moderate evangelicalism, is a major factor and is likely to remain so in times of drastic change.

See also BAPTIST TRADITION; CHRISTIAN COALITION; CREATIONISM; EVANGELICAL CHRISTIANITY; FALWELL, JERRY; MORAL MAJORITY; RELIGIOUS RIGHT.

BIBLIOGRAPHY

Ammerman, Nancy. *Bible Believers: Fundamentalists in the Modern World.* 1987.

Carpenter, Joel. *Revive Us Again: The Reawakening of American Fundamentalism.* 1997.

Lawrence, Bruce. *Defenders of God: The Fundamentalist Revolt Against the Modern Age.* 1989.

Marsden, George M. *Fundamentalism and American Culture: The Shaping of Twentieth-Century Evangelicalism, 1870–1925.* 1980.

Marty, Martin E., and R. Scott Appleby. *Fundamentalisms Observed.* The Fundamentalism Project, vol. 1. 1991.

Sandeen, Ernest. *The Roots of Fundamentalism: British and American Millenarianism, 1800–1930.* 1970.

Martin E. Marty

Future of Religion

In the 1960s, many groups of intellectuals and social scientists attempted to foresee what the year 2000 would be like, and in retrospect many of their publications seem surprisingly insightful. Now that we have reached the milestone they envisioned, we can use their methods to discern the shape of things to come in religion. The American Academy of Arts and Sciences organized a Commission on the Year 2000 to debate the alternative futures that might result from current decisions. In the very first sentence of the commission's report, *Toward the Year 2000* (1968), Daniel Bell quoted St. Augustine as saying that time was "a threefold present: the present as we experience it, the past as a present memory, and the future as a present expectation." In *The Year 2000* (1967) Herman Kahn and Anthony Wiener offered a methodology for looking into the future, not in terms of religious prophecy or mindless extrapolation from present conditions, but by developing alternative scenarios with varying degrees of subjective probability.

The "surprise-free projection" is simultaneously the most precise but also the least interesting scenario. The null hypothesis must be that the future will be like the present. But we know that at present, certain religious denominations are growing while others are shrinking, so a surprise-free projection must extrapolate these rates of change into the future as well. The best projection is not merely a mechanical calculation from current rates, but also an application of the best available theories to understand qualitative changes. For example, the work of Roger Finke and Rodney Stark on the history of American denominationalism from 1776 to 1990 can provide insight into the dynamic equilibrium that has prevailed for many decades and that can be expected to continue indefinitely.

Scenario I: The Surprise-Free Projection

Throughout the twenty-first century, the landscape of religion in the United States changes only in small details. Highly liberal denominations such as the Unitarian-Universalists and the United Church of Christ will continue to lose membership, and some of these secularized organizations will merge. At the same time, moderate denominations become more liberal, conservative denominations become moderate, and new sects break off from all of them to replenish the supply of conservative denominations. Secularization and a low birthrate diminish the number of practicing Jews, but immigration from Islamic societies maintains a significant minority of non-Christian monotheists. Because the Judeo-Christian-Islamic tradition is securely embedded in the culture, successful new religious movements all belong to this lineage. The overall church membership rate stays constant, and religion remains influential in many spheres of life, including politics and personal morality.

Scenario II: Secularization

Higher education and an increasing reliance on advanced information technology in all kinds of work erode the plausibility of supernatural beliefs. Nonreligious institutions in society continue to take over functions formerly performed by churches. Discoveries in biology, astronomy, and sociology render traditional religious beliefs ever more anachronistic. Technical innovations such as human cloning and artificial intelligence shake religion to its very foundations. Intense religion persists only in social and cultural backwaters, and the surviving mainstream denominations promulgate an extremely vague faith that has few implications for daily life. As long as peace, prosperity, and scientific progress prevail, traditional religion gradually sinks toward extinction, although its death may take centuries to complete.

Scenario III: A Rift Between America and Europe

Samuel Huntington, a participant in the old Commission on the Year 2000, has recently argued that the cultural and historical divisions of the globe are too well established to be dissolved easily by worldwide modernization. In particular, he speculates that the division in Eurasia between Eastern Orthodox cultures and Western Catholic-Protestant cultures will persist for many centuries, but North America and Western Europe will be a unified culture, perhaps including a developed Latin America. Yet one could just as well argue that secularization in Europe and revival in America will cause the transatlantic ties to snap. Western Europe will become a pessimistic, atheistic culture with a static welfare state and a rigid bureaucracy. In contrast, the Americas will be a chaotic but creative society in which hundreds of Christian movements tumble over each other and where the Roman Catholic Church is simply the largest of the Christian denominations. Despite great similarities in technology and consumer fads, Europe and the Americas will have increasing difficulty understanding each other, and only tensions with the remainder of the world will prevent the irritations between them from escalating into overt conflict.

Scenario IV: Paganization

Throughout most of human history, organized religious power has been very local in nature, and large societies have contained many competing religious movements. For the better part of two thousand years, however, Christendom has been attracted by the idea that there should be a single church, with Jesus Christ himself for its leader, and at times an alliance with the state has given an effective religious monopoly to one sacred organization or another. Despite the efforts of the ecumenical movement, this dream has always been precarious in America, where traditions of religious freedom are strong. Secularization may erode the religious mainstream in coming decades until it ceases to exist, and religious urges will find their expression elsewhere. From L. Frank Baum's popular novel *The Wonderful Wizard of Oz* in 1900 through *Episode I* of George Lucas's *Star Wars* series in 1999, popular culture has increasingly legitimated non-Christian notions of the supernatural. As the twenty-first century progresses, for many people religion will become a homespun creation of local messiahs promulgating a diverse possible array of beliefs and practices.

Scenario V: The Rise of a New World Faith

In the nineteenth century, the United States produced at least four distinctive new religions: Christian Science, Mormonism, Seventh-Day Adventism, and Jehovah's Witnesses. It is hard to discern what major new religions were created in the twentieth century, although Scientology in 2000 is comparable in membership to some of those four in 1900. If religion is defined broadly, then psychoanalysis in all its variants is a vast new tradition that has not yet exhausted its potential. Scientology exemplifies religion housed in a single strong organization, which has long been the Christian ideal, whereas psychoanalysis exemplifies religion dispersed among a tangle of local guru-transmission lineages, as in Hinduism. If scientology and psychoanal-

ysis are accurate omens, the new American religion of the twenty-first century may owe no debts to the Judeo-Christian-Islamic tradition.

The mills of the gods grind exceeding slow, and barring major world catastrophe, we should not expect rapid transformation of American religion. Thus, probabilities favor the surprise-free scenario, although elements of the others may gradually intrude as the decades pass. In *Social and Cultural Dynamics* (1937), Pitirim A. Sorokin outlined a cyclical theory of cultural change that asserted that great civilizations arise in ideational form (stressing faith in spiritual reality), then gradually evolve into sensate form (stressing skeptical emphasis on material reality). He asserted that Western civilization had entered the late sensate phase, which could soon lead to catastrophic collapse, followed by a possible dark age in which a new faith would launch a fresh ideational civilization. Social scientists pay no attention to Sorokin's ideas today, yet should Western civilization imitate its ancient predecessors and fall, then by definition the surprise-free scenario would become useless and we would have to expect the rise of a new world faith. Just as the seeds of Christianity were sown three centuries before its conquest of the Roman Empire, so the long-term future of American religion may belong to tiny cults even now being born in obscurity.

See also BELONGING, RELIGIOUS; CIVIL RELIGION; ECUMENICAL MOVEMENT; FREEDOM OF RELIGION; MEGACHURCH; MILLENNIALISM; POPULAR RELIGION; POSTDENOMINATIONAL CHURCH; PREMILLENNIALISM; RELIGIOUS COMMUNITIES; RELIGIOUS STUDIES; SOCIOLOGY OF RELIGION; SPACE FLIGHT.

BIBLIOGRAPHY

Bainbridge, William Sims. *Dimensions of Science Fiction.* 1986.

Bainbridge, William Sims. *The Sociology of Religious Movements.* 1997.

Huntington, Samuel P. *The Clash of Civilizations and the Remaking of World Order.* 1996.

Martin, David. *A General Theory of Secularization.* 1978.

Stark, Rodney, and Roger Finke. *The Churching of America 1776–1990.* 1992.

Stark, Rodney, and William Sims Bainbridge. *The Future of Religion.* 1985.

Wuthnow, Robert. *The Restructuring of American Religion: Society and Faith Since World War II.* 1988.

William Sims Bainbridge

G

Gay Rights Movement.

See Lesbian and Gay Rights Movement.

Gender Roles

Gender roles are socially expected behavior patterns for men and women. For much of United States history, that pattern reflected patriarchal norms, both within individual religious denominations and in the larger society. Since the advent of the feminist movement, however, gender roles have become much more diverse and are continually evolving.

In the nineteenth-century United States, most churches endorsed the separation of male and female spheres. Paralleling women's exclusion from professions such as law or medicine, only men were allowed to be priests or rabbis. Women were expected to stay home, raise children, and submit to their husbands, who in turn were expected to support the family (though working-class husbands did not always meet this expectation). As the nineteenth century drew to a close, these roles began to change.

It is often assumed, especially by religious conservatives, that feminists are trying to adapt gender roles in religion to changes in secular society. This is not necessarily the case. In the nineteenth century, religious feminism preceded, or at least went hand in hand with, secular feminism. Many nineteenth-century feminists came from the ranks of church-based moral reform movements (e.g., temperance) that had begun to question their political exclusion. Because patriarchy had long served to legitimate feminism, nineteenth-century feminists saw it as essential to question the Bible (e.g., Elizabeth Cady Stanton's *The Woman's Bible*). And some Protestant churches ordained women before Congress gave women the right to vote.

It was not until the twentieth century that a significant gap emerged between gender roles in secular society and those in religious communities, and religious and secular feminists went separate ways. Legislative reform (e.g., the Nineteenth Amendment and Title 9) as well as economic and demographic changes (e.g., the move from an industrial to a service economy; birth control pills) have transformed the socially expected behavior patterns for men and women. Most Americans today reject female submission and the notion that a woman's primary role is motherhood. The majority of women do work outside the home, and the proportion of women in the professions is rapidly approaching that of men. Though a glass ceiling remains, women cannot, legally at least, be excluded from any leadership position—except, of course, the clergy. In contrast to feminist progress in American society at large, gender roles in religious institutions have changed very slowly, if at all.

In general, religious conservatives tend to reject changes in gender roles, while liberals support them. Mainline Protestants such as Congregationalists, Presbyterians, and Methodists, as well as Reform and Conservative Jews, allow women's ordination, while

275

Sherry Chayat, the first American woman to be granted the highest honor of Buddhist religious life, stands in the Zen Center in Syracuse, New York, after having received transmission in the Rinzai Zen sect. (Credit: AP/Wide World Photos.)

Roman Catholics, Evangelical Protestants, and Orthodox Jews do not. But if you look closer, the picture is not so simple.

First, women's ordination is not the only measure of equal gender roles. Evangelicals do not allow a woman to fill the position of head pastor yet permit female assistant pastors, outreach ministers, school principals, and so on. Given the rather unimpressive record of the mainline denominations in placing women in head pastorships, it is not clear how much more equal gender roles are in churches that permit women's ordination.

Second, different denominations cite different reasons and use different methods of regulating gender roles. It is primarily Evangelicals who, because of their preference for a literal interpretation of the Bible, have continued to idealize homemakers and submissive wives. Yet because most Evangelical churches per-

mit the use of contraception to regulate family size, women are able to pursue careers once their children are older. By contrast, though recent Roman Catholic teaching has emphasized the equality of husband and wife, the church's absolute prohibition of contraception, if followed, effectively limits most women's ability to choose a career other than motherhood.

Third, we need to distinguish between gender roles in different social contexts. In Orthodox Judaism, for example, women are excluded from full participation in the synagogue (seating is segregated, women do not wear prayer shawls, and women are not called up to the Torah), yet many of the central Jewish rituals (e.g., the Sabbath meal, the Passover seder) take place in the home, where women play an important role. Many conservative Christians and Jews believe that patriarchal gender roles apply only to church or synagogue, and insist on equal roles in the home and the workplace.

We also need to distinguish between official gender roles (what is taught by clergy and in religious literature) and operative norms (how people actually expect men and women to behave). In many Evangelical churches, official teaching prohibits women pastors, yet there are a number of charismatic women preachers who have founded new congregations with the encouragement of their local church. Although the Roman Catholic Church officially prohibits contraception, the majority of Catholics believe that one can be a good Catholic without obeying this teaching. As Mark Chavez has pointed out, patriarchal gender roles may act as a kind of symbolic boundary that serves more to distinguish religious conservatives from liberals than to affect actual gender roles.

Finally, gender roles are ultimately a matter of individual interpretation. If an Evangelical woman interprets submission as mutual, then she will not necessarily let her husband make all the decisions. If an Orthodox Jewish woman believes her exclusion from Talmud study is a matter of custom rather than law, she will lobby her rabbi to provide classes for girls and women—and increasing numbers of Modern Orthodox rabbis have complied.

If we consider religions outside the Jewish and Christian tradition, the picture becomes even more complex. Gender roles in Islam are considered highly patriarchal, yet Islam is poorly understood. Americans' understanding of Islam is based largely on media reports about countries such as Iran or Saudi Arabia, and it is assumed that immigrant Muslims will carry on similar practices. Yet the largest group of American Muslims is not immigrant but African American; and regardless of who its members are, their practices are determined by interpretation. The Qu'ran explicitly states that a man can have up to four wives (while a woman must be monogamous), that men can beat their wives if they are not obedient, and that women should cover the alluring parts of their bodies, especially when they go out in public. In the masjid (mosque), women are not permitted to be imams (prayer leaders), and women sit separately, behind the men. Yet as with Judaism and Christianity, many American Muslims do not take these teachings literally, so the official norms are not always the operative ones, and the roles men and women play depend on the social context they find themselves in. And just as Jewish and Christian feminists have achieved reform in some churches and synagogues, so Muslim feminists are making progress. They point out that the Qu'ran allows up to four wives, but only if the man can treat them all equally. Since no man is capable of this, Islam essentially requires men to be monogamous as well. Similarly, the Qu'ran does not specify which parts of the body must be covered. Although some Muslim women, especially new converts and immigrants from conservative Muslim nations, will cover their entire body, their hair, and part of the face, others wear modest Western-style clothing.

By contrast, Hinduism and Buddhism have acquired a reputation for more equal gender roles, but this is largely due to the New Age movement, which has reformulated Eastern religious ideas to suit American tastes (e.g., feminist spirituality groups celebrate Hindu goddesses but ignore the highly patriarchal Laws of Manu). The majority of Hindus and Buddhists in the United States are immigrants (from China, India, and Vietnam), and their gender roles tend to reflect those of the country of origin, which in most cases means that they will be fairly patriarchal. In an effort to reach out to non-Asian Americans, some Hindu and Buddhist sects have adapted gender roles to the more feminist ideal of the American context (a significant number of Zen centers are headed by women). For any immigrant religion, whether it is Hindu, Buddhist, or Muslim, adapting to more feminist gender roles may create tension with the desire to maintain a cultural tradition.

Finally, we must address the issue of gender roles in the new religions. Being outside the mainstream, new religions are freer to experiment with gender roles, and historically many of them have done so. Religious communes illustrate this, starting in the eighteenth century with the Shakers (who mandated that religious leadership be in pairs of male and females) and continuing in the nineteenth century with the Oneida Perfectionists (who shared sex as well as child-rearing responsibilities), and in the twentieth century with the Children of God (an Evangelical group that abandoned the traditional Christian emphasis on female virginity to gain converts through a practice they called flirty fishing). Experimenting may or may not result in equal gender roles. Both Mormons (who practiced polygamy in their early years) and the Unification Church (which sees marriage and family as a vehicle to salvation) are highly patriarchal. By contrast, twentieth-century Goddess spirituality (or Wicca) was created for the very purpose of developing a women-centered, nonpatriarchal religion.

See also BIRTH; BIRTH CONTROL; CLERGY; ECOFEMINISM; FEMINIST SPIRITUALITY; FEMINIST THEOLOGY; IMAM; MARRIAGE, CHRISTIAN; MARRIAGE, JEWISH; MASCULINE SPIRITUALITY; MATRIARCHAL CORE; MATRIARCHY; NEW AGE SPIRITUALITY; ORDINATION OF WOMEN; PRIESTESS; PRIESTHOOD; RABBINATE; WOMANIST THEOLOGY; WOMEN'S STUDIES; WORK.

BIBLIOGRAPHY

Chaves, Mark. *Ordaining Women: Culture and Conflict in Religious Organizations.* 1994.

Haddad, Yvonne Yazbeck, ed. *Muslims of America.* 1991.

Manning, Christel. *God Gave Us the Right: Conservative Catholic, Evangelical Protestant, and Orthodox Jewish Women Grapple with Feminism.* 1999.

Ruether, Rosemary, and Rosemary Keller. *Women and Religion in America,* 3 vols. 1981, 1983, 1986.

Williams, Raymond Brady. *Religions of Immigrants from India and Pakistan.* 1988.

Zikmund, Barbara Brown, Adair T. Lummis, and Patricia Mei Yin Chang. *Clergy Women: An Uphill Calling.* 1998.

Christel Manning

Generation X

Generation X, also known as the "Baby Buster" generation, refers to the group of Americans born between the middle to late 1960s and the early 1980s. The term "Generation X" first appeared as the title of a 1991 best-selling novel by Douglas Coupland. Often called "GenXers," members of this group are distinguished by their individualstic, anti-institutional approach to religion.

Although they are closer in style and outlook to Baby Boomers (their predecessor generation) than Baby Boomers are to their own predecessors, nevertheless GenXers have their own religious traits. As a whole they appear to be much less religious than their elders; however, GenXers have showed a tendency to express religiosity outside traditionally understood institutions and to blend popular culture with spirituality. Generation X is more conservative than its predecessors, placing considerable emphasis on individual responsibility; the True Love Waits campaign for premarital sexual abstinence has had wide appeal for younger GenXers.

Many churches and synagogues have developed special programs to appeal to GenX tastes. Sinai Temple, a Conservative synagogue in Los Angeles, has developed a monthly "Friday Night Live" service geared especially toward unaffiliated GenX Jews. At the same time, new congregations, such as New Song Church in Covina, California, and established ones, such as Congregation B'nai Jeshurun in New York City, have emerged to serve the GenX cohort. Successful GenX congregations, whether subgroups or independent organizations, share certain characteristics that distinguish them from other groups. First, the worship environment reflects a straightforward spiritual message and seeks to create an experience of intimacy, accountability, and authenticity. These themes reflect GenX preferences for one-to-one relationships and personal responsibility (rather than abstract notions of social or ethical obligation), as well as GenXers' concerns about how to make sense of the fragmentation and chaos that typify their individual and collective experiences of the late twentieth century.

Third, the ritualistic-liturgical structure is flexible, providing for a wide range of human-divine interactions. This often involves the use of contemporary popular music rather than traditional hymns, or the introduction of different media and worship styles, such as video or meditation. Moreover, successful GenX congregations provide for a certain degree of "big-tent" theology within the core structure of their guiding missions and visions, even when the core is more traditional or conservative than the congregation. Many religious GenXers reject labels, preferring to call themselves "nondenominational" Christians or "reconservadox" Jews (an amalgam of the words "reform," "conservative," and "orthodox"). They prefer a broad but uncompromising doctrinal approach that does not demand blind conformity in return.

Fourth, the organizational and social structures are flexible, providing for a wide range of interpersonal relations within the church. Often congregations are managed and led by a small professional staff, rather than by a committee of lay leaders or board of directors. GenX congregations seek to provide members with a wide variety of ways with which to engage one another inside the religious community, from small discussion and support groups to community service project teams.

Fifth, recognizing that many GenXers experience "church" or "temple" as mostly a weekend activity, successful GenX congregations try to accommodate both committed members and intermittent attendees. Often this is inherent in the organizational structure of the congregation, particularly when the congregation is a subgroup of an established organization that has been set up for outreach and membership-recruitment purposes. At the same time, GenX congregations attempt to reach GenXers where they are, and they recognize the vast variety of sources from which young people draw spiritual sustenance. Unlike their Baby Boomer predecessors, who are "church shoppers" and "seekers," GenXers often do not anticipate making an exclusive commitment to a single institution. Rather, they are "church hoppers" who attend, whether regularly or infrequently, different congregations that collectively reflect the complexity of their spiritual journeys.

See also NEW AGE SPIRITUALITY; NEW RELIGIOUS MOVEMENTS; SPIRITUALITY; TRUE LOVE WAITS.

BIBLIOGRAPHY

Beaudoin, Tom. *Virtual Faith: The Irreverent Spiritual Quest of Generation X.* 1998.

Cohen, Michael Lee. *The Twentysomething American Dream.* 1993.

Coupland, Douglas. *Generation X: Tales for an Accelerated Culture.* 1991.

Coupland, Douglas. *Life After God.* 1994.

Roof, Wade Clark. *Spiritual Marketplace: Baby Boomers and the Remaking of American Religion.* 1999.

Roof, Wade Clark, and J. Shawn Landres. "Defection, Disengagement, and Dissent: The Dynamics of Religious Change in the United States." In *Leaving Religion and Religious Life,* edited by Mordechai Bar-Lev and William Shaffir. *Religion and the Social Order.* Vol. 7. 1997.

Strauss, William, and Neil Howe. *Generations: The History of America's Future, 1584–2069.* 1991.

J. Shawn Landres

Globalization

Human history has been a process of integration in which social units progressively grew from the hunter-gatherer band, to the tribe, to the nation, and finally to a global socioeconomic unity. Simultaneously, fundamental human needs demand small-scale social organizations, so countervailing forces work against integration and toward societal differentiation. Religion feels pressure from both directions, so in the world today we see evidence of religious unification and of fragmentation. Globalization exposes people to all the great religious traditions of the world, but also encourages making choices and intensification or faith commitments.

A century ago it was still possible to believe that Christianity would soon become the one world religion. Although today Christianity claims the largest number of adherents, Islam is in a strong second place, and the penetration of Christianity into most regions of Asia has stalled. Christianization of the Americas was largely achieved through military force and immigration. Without these factors, success in other parts of the world has been quite limited. When the American Baptist martyr Adoniram Judson arrived in Burma in 1813, he gained essentially no converts at all from the dominant Buddhists, and only after six years of effort translating parts of the Bible into the local language did he gain his first converts, from peripheral groups. When Burma went to war with Britain, he was tortured despite his protestations that his own nation also had struggled against British imperialism. For many Burmese, Christianity was an unwarranted intrusion from an alien culture, and even today the nation remains largely inhospitable to religious colonialism.

Korea is a very different story. The period of rapid Christian conversion was also a time of dominance by Japan, so Christianity could be embraced as an ally in Korea's great national struggle, rather than rejected as an invader. Most importantly, many of the missionaries adopted a strategy—sometimes called the Nevius Plan—that respected local culture and society. Presbyterian missionary John Nevius arrived in China in 1854 and set up a mission station at Chefoo (Yantai), directly across the Yellow Sea from Korea. He immersed himself in every aspect of Chinese culture and often blended it with American ideas. For example, he improved the fruit of the Chinese pear by grafting, and he redesigned the passenger-carrying Chinese wheelbarrow for use on his frequent missionary tours. He relied on his Chinese assistants to spread the faith throughout their communities. By the time of his first visit to Korea, in 1890, his three-part evangelism plan had already influenced the work of Presbyterian missionaries there. First, native Christians and their churches should be self-supporting, rather than relying on material help from the United States. Second, they should recruit new members through active participation in the community. And third, they should limit construction of church buildings to structures of native architecture they could afford without U.S. contributions. Over the following decades, this strategy of self-reliance fostered the building of strong Presbyterian churches across Korea, and other denominations imitated the Presbyterian success.

Although we tend to think of the nineteenth century as the great period of American overseas missions, in fact far more missionaries are working today. The one undeniable revolution accomplished by these missionaries is the growth of Protestantism in Latin America. Rather than introducing a new tradition, the missionaries offer variety within the existing Christian culture, appealing to many constituencies in modernizing Latin societies, from oppressed peasants to the rising middle class. At the same time, Protestant evangelists are linking their converts into transnational denominations and increasing the diversity of religious groups in their nations. At the sectarian end of the denominational spectrum, one result is the emergence of a large number of autonomous, local groups in such North American traditions as Pentecostalism and Holiness, not to mention the indigenous but Protestant-influenced Spiritist tradition. Thus the result of Protestantization is a combination of globalization and localization.

The symbolic opening of America to foreign faiths was the World's Parliament of Religions held at the 1893 World's Columbian Exposition (world's fair) in Chicago. Among the Asian representatives who spoke at this well-publicized gathering were Hindus, Buddhists (including Zen), and a Jain. The star of the show was Vivekananda, a Hindu working for the amalgamation of the major world religions. Vivekananda subsequently toured several cities, establishing Vedanta in the United States.

Asian religious influences in the United States have gone through several stages in response to changing immigration restrictions, patterns of overseas travel by Americans, and indigenous U.S. cultural trends. The Theosophy movement, with all its offshoots, was created by Westerners who radically transformed Asian religious ideas as they introduced them to a public that was largely ignorant of authentic Asian beliefs. World War II and the subsequent occupation of Japan facilitated the importation of Zen Buddhism, which harmonized with the postwar intellectual milieu of the Beat and existentialist movements. Relaxation of immigration quotas in the 1960s made it easier for evangelists from Asian religions to operate in America. Westerners who possessed positive stereotypes of Eastern religion may have been especially open to these evangelists and may not even have realized that many of them represented deviant groups in their homelands. For example, the Hare Khrishna movement was a splinter of a radical sect in India, rather than representing the central traditions of Hinduism. Some imported movements were westernized to increase their appeal. For example, Transcendental Meditation is a diluted form of Hinduism that employs scientific metaphors and that has specifically targeted university students.

Ironically, when Western missionaries adapt mainstream Christianity to local conditions, they make it easy for local innovators to create radical sects. The Unification Church is a natural outcome of the Nevius Plan. Its founder, Sun Myung Moon, was the son of a Korean family that converted to Presbyterianism. He encountered Adventism, blended its ideas with traditional Korean spiritual concepts, and then sought to bring this Koreanized version of Christianity to the United States. Thus globalization inevitably creates many new religious movements that are amalgams of separate traditions. Whether or not the great world religions will ever successfully invade each other's territory, globalization increases the religious choices rather than uniting everyone in a single faith.

See also BELONGING, RELIGIOUS; CHURCH; CONVERSION; CULT; CYBER RELIGION; DENOMINATION; ECUMENICAL MOVEMENT; MISSIONARY MOVEMENTS; NEW RELIGIOUS MOVEMENTS; PROSELYTIZING; RELIGIOUS COMMUNITIES; SECT; SOCIOLOGY OF RELIGION; SYNCRETISM; TELEVANGELISM.

BIBLIOGRAPHY

Bainbridge, William Sims. *The Sociology of Religious Movements.* 1997.

Lofland, John. *Doomsday Cult.* 1966.

Paik, L. George. *The History of Protestant Missions in Korea, 1832–1910.* 1970.

Seager, Richard Hughes. *The World's Parliament of Religions.* 1995.

Siewert, John A., and Edna G. Valdez, eds. *Mission Handbook 1998–2000.* 1997.

Trager, Helen G. *Burma Through Alien Eyes.* 1966.

Tworkov, Helen. *Zen in America.* 1994.

William Sims Bainbridge

Glossolalia

The term "glossolalia" literally translates from the Greek as "to speak in tongues." It is an ecstatic religious practice found in early Christianity, sporadically throughout the history of Christianity, and in various other religious traditions. Its most significant form in late-twentieth-century America is found in the Protestant Pentecostal and charismatic traditions.

Pentecostalism developed, at the turn of the twentieth century, out of the Wesleyan Holiness tradition. In 1901 Bethel Bible College students of Charles Parham in Topeka, Kansas, spoke in tongues, which Parham interpreted as evidence of the Baptism in the Holy Spirit mentioned in the Book of Acts. News spread to William Seymour, a Los Angeles holiness preacher, and a series of revivals began in Seymour's Azusa Street Mission. The ongoing revivals, in which glossolalia was a central practice understood as the evidence of the Baptism in the Holy Spirit (and therefore of sanctification), were marked by distinct racial and gender egalitarianism (Seymour was African American, and there were several women leaders).

Strict Pentecostals believe that glossolalia is the evidence of the presence of the Holy Spirit in the life of a Christian and that, therefore, all true Christians speak in tongues. For this reason they typically belong to specifically Pentecostal denominations, such as the Assemblies of God or the International Church of the Foursquare Gospel. Sine the 1970s, however, glossolalia has spread into traditionally non-Pentecostal denominations, such as the Episcopal and Catholic churches. Charismatics regard glossolalia as only one of many "gifts of the Spirit," each of which is evidence of the Holy Spirit's presence in the life of a believer. For this reason they often remain in their non-"spirit-filled" churches and practice the gifts on their own or in smaller cell groups.

Charismatics typically understand two forms of glossolalia as derived from the New Testament: a prophetic form, which can be "translated," in which God communicates directly to his people; and a private devotional form, in which believers commune with God in a mystical way that is thought to transcend both reason and language. St. Paul rebukes Christians who "make a show of their gifts" and commands those with the "gift of tongues" to refrain from public practice of the prophetic form of glossolalia when there is no one present who has been given the "gift of interpretation." The devotional form, however, is commonly practiced in charismatic churches as part of prayer sessions or as part of musical worship of the church service.

The practice of glossolalia is typically combined with the practice of other "gifts of the Holy Spirit." In addition to the "gift of interpretation," there is also the ability to aid in miraculous healing, the gifts of "words of knowledge" and "words of wisdom" (the ability to know hidden things and/or to speak prophetically), and other nonecstatic gifts, such as the "gift of administrations" and the "gift of hospitality." Heavy emphasis is placed on avoiding the sin of pride in regard to having been given the gift of tongues.

See also BAPTISM IN THE HOLY SPIRIT; CATHOLIC CHARISMATIC RENEWAL; CHARISMATIC MOVEMENT; ECSTASY; PENTECOSTAL AND CHARISMATIC CHRISTIANITY.

BIBLIOGRAPHY

Balmer, Randall. *Mine Eyes Have Seen the Glory.* PBS video. 1992.

Neitz, Mary Jo. *Charisma and Community.* 1987.
Poloma, Margaret M. *The Charismatics Movement.* 1982.

Julie J. Ingersoll

Gnosticism

Defined most narrowly, gnosticism was an obscure Christian heresy that flourished in the first few centuries after Christ. Defined more broadly, as has become the custom, gnosticism, while still a long dead movement, antedated Christianity and even influenced it. There were Jewish and pagan as well as Christian varieties of gnosticism, and gnosticism might best be seen as a religion in its own right.

By this broader definition, gnosticism was the belief in a radical, irreconcilable dualism of immateriality and matter. Immateriality was divine and wholly good. Matter was irredeemably evil. The cosmic predicament was that pieces, or sparks, of divinity had become trapped in matter. Human souls lay trapped in bodies. (In tripartite gnosticism, an immaterial spirit lay trapped in the soul as well as the body.) Because the sparks were not merely trapped but hidden, liberation required the revelation to humans of their divinity. The cosmic goal was for all sparks to be extricated and returned to their immaterial home.

Gnosticism can be defined much more broadly still as a contemporary, not merely an ancient, movement. The dualism often lies entirely within human beings and not in the cosmos. It is the alienation of humans from their true selves. Or the dualism is political or social, between nations, classes, or races. The true self is not specifically immaterial, and the place in which it resides is not specifically the body. The alienation of humans from the world may remain, but the world is not specifically material, and no immaterial world beyond beckons. Ordinarily, there is no alienation from any divinity, for most brands of contemporary gnosticism are atheistic. Just as there is no world beyond or god beyond, so, as often as not, there looms no true self beyond. Contemporary gnosticism still requires a revelation, but the revelation can be that all that one knows of oneself and the world is all that there is to know.

Contemporary gnosticism need not even be radically dualistic. The dualism can be irenic. In radically dualistic gnosticism, ancient or modern, one's old identity is to be rejected for a new one. In irenic gnosticism, which is exclusively modern, one's new identity is to be harmonized with the prior one.

Modernity per se has been called gnostic. Others have identified postmodernism with gnosticism. Scores of writers and thinkers of the last few centuries have been labeled gnostic—for example, Goethe, Schleiermacher, Blake, Hegel, Byron, Marx, Conrad, Nietzsche, Yeats, Hesse, Toynbee, Heidegger, Sartre, Simone Weil, and Jung. Americans labeled gnostic include Emerson, Melville, Wallace Stevens, Walker Percy, Jack Kerouac, Philip K. Dick, and Thomas Pynchon. Harold Bloom has characterized American religion as gnostic. Admittedly, the application of the term *gnostic* can be loose. Only a few of the figures named, such as Jung, were even familiar with gnosticism, let alone deemed themselves gnostics. Individuals aside, there exist in the United States today self-professed gnostic groups with hundreds, perhaps thousands, of members. The biggest are the Ecclesia Gnostica and the Gnostic Association.

See also AGNOSTICISM; ATHEISM; BODY; NEW AGE SPIRITUALITY; REVELATION.

BIBLIOGRAPHY

Altizer, Thomas J. J. "The Challenge of Modern Gnosticism." *Journal of Bible and Religion* 30 (1962): 18–25.
Bloom, Harold. *The American Religion.* 1992.
Brooks, Cleanth. "Walker Percy and Modern Gnosticism." *Southern Review* 13 (1977): 677–687.
Eddins, Thomas. *The Gnostic Pynchon.* 1990.
Jonas, Hans. "Gnosticism, Existentialism, and Nihilism." In *The Gnostic Religion,* edited by Hans Jonas, 2nd ed. 1963.
Segal, Robert A., with June Singer and Murray Stein, eds. *The Allure of Gnosticism.* 1995.
Voegelin, Eric. *Science, Politics and Gnosticism.* 1968.

Robert A. Segal

God

Few concepts are as widely disputed as that of God. Therefore, it would be foolishness to write an article that purported to discuss simply the concept of God. So what follows needs a bit of refining. The focus of this philosophical article is the Judeo-Christian conception of God, which, broadly speaking, is the notion of God most widely accepted in the United States today. Of course, the concept of God within the American Jewish and Christian communities is not uncontroversial or monolithic either. Nevertheless there is a shared traditional conception of God that will be the focus of this essay.

Although the Judeo-Christian conception of God is several millennia old, its theological and philosophical development jumped by leaps and bounds in the medieval period. While St. Anselm of Canterbury (ca.

1033–1109 C.E.), lived during the latter part of this era, his crystallization of this conception of God (which owes a great debt to the writings of St. Augustine) is still widely regarded as its best statement.

In Chapter Two of his meditative work, *The Proslogion*, Anselm sets up his justly famous ontological argument for the existence of God by first offering a definition of the Being the existence of which he intends to prove. He defines God as "the being than which nothing greater can be conceived." Anselm believed that from this short definition one could derive all the attributes traditionally ascribed to God. In order to see how this is plausible, we will examine his formula a bit more closely.

The first thing to notice about Anselm's definition is that it does not claim that God is merely the greatest being that happens to exist; in Anselm's view, if that were the best that could be said, then that being would not be God. In order to be counted as God, the being must be such that we cannot conceive of anything greater. But what exactly does this mean? Is Anselm saying that God is the greatest being that humans can form a conception of? That would be problematic, since it would apparently limit God to the conceptual powers of human beings. Fortunately, this is not the way Anselm is to be understood. For consider the conception of a being that is the greatest conception we are able to construct, but which is nevertheless limited in ways that we are not capable of seeing. Would such a conception satisfy Anselm's definition? No, it would not. For if we have the concept of a being who surpasses the greatest being that we can conceive of (where "conceive" requires our having a somewhat detailed understanding of the relevant concept), then the concept of the being who is surpassed is *not* the concept of the being than which nothing greater can be conceived.

A second point about Anselm's definition: the notion of "greatness" at issue is not moral, and it is not greatness as power; nor is it greatness with respect to any particular characteristic, attribute, or ability. Rather it is what might be dubbed "overall metaphysical greatness." The more metaphysical greatness one has, the more power, knowledge, wisdom, goodness, and so on that one has.

Here is a way of understanding Anselm's definition that deviates a bit from his terminology but is closer to his intention: God is the greatest possible being. Anselm wanted his definition to explain why the idea of something being greater than God is nonsense. If the concept of God is the concept of the greatest possible being, then by definition nothing can be greater.

Earlier it was noted that Anselm believed that all the traditional divine attributes or properties could be derived from his terse definition; it is time to see why he thought this. The greatest possible being is the being that has the greatest possible combination of "great-making" properties. A great-making property is a property that it is intrinsically better to have than to lack. Let us take knowledge as an example. Is knowledge in general a great-making property? It would certainly seem so. A being that has knowledge is, other things being equal, greater than a being that lacks it. So knowledge is a great-making quality. But since one can have less or more knowledge, even if we know that the greatest possible being has knowledge, how do we know how much this being possesses? If we keep in mind Anselm's definition, this question has an easy answer. God is the most perfect being possible. How much knowledge would an unsurpassably great being possess? All that there is to have. So one who adopts Anselm's formulation of the concept of God will have reason for thinking of God as omniscient, or all-knowing.

Many of the traditional divine properties are relatively well known and can be discussed only briefly. In addition to omniscience, God is also believed to be omnipotent (all-powerful), omnibenevolent (all-good), and omnipresent (everywhere present). In distinction from most forms of pantheism, the Judeo-Christian God is regarded as personal. A personal being is a being with knowledge and a will, and who is capable of acting on them.

The Judeo-Christian conception of God also portrays the deity as being the sole creator of the universe and of all that it contains. God is thought to be immanent in creation (that is to say, involved with and to be found in it) and yet transcendent from it. According to the traditional Judeo-Christian model, God is not to be confused with creation; even taken as an entirety, creation is metaphysically distinct from God. If creation were to cease to exist tomorrow, God would remain largely unchanged. The insistence on the ontological distinction between Creator and creation is a major point of distinction between the God of theism and the God of pantheism. Also, the insistence on the immanence of God distinguishes theism from some forms of deism popular during the eighteenth-century Enlightenment. The deistic God was believed to be an absentee Creator who no longer had anything to do with the operation of the universe. This God is like a clockmaker who builds then winds a clock, which henceforth runs entirely on its own.

In addition to these more popularly known attributes, the classical Christian conception of God includes several components that are apparently in part the result of Greek philosophical influences during the formative period of Christian theology. We will briefly look at four. The first is the notion of divine timelessness. To say that God is timeless is not to say merely that God has always existed and will always exist; it is rather to say something about God's very mode of existence. Whereas beings that are "in time" move through it from moment to moment, the past being moments that are no more and the future being moments yet to come, a timeless God will experience every moment together in an eternal present. God's life is not divided into the past, present, and future but is had forever all at once. God's timelessness is supposed to follow from the Anselmian definition of the perfect being, since a being not bound by time is thought to be, other things being equal, greater than one that is.

A closely related component of the classical conception of God is that of immutability. To be immutable (as it is traditionally understood) is to be not only changeless but also without the possibility of change. The motivation for this was straightforward: if God is perfect, then any change is for the worse. So God would not change; furthermore, even the possibility of change is the possibility of ceasing to be perfect, and the greatest possible being would be incapable of ceasing to be perfect. Although this line of reasoning has been influential, it should be noted that it is not at all clear that perfection requires the inability to change.

The third classical property we will consider is divine simplicity. To be "simple" in this sense is to have no parts of any kind. The idea is that not only does God, being an immaterial being, not have physical parts, but God is without complexity of any sort. In particular, God does not even have distinct characteristics or properties; all God's properties are identical to each other and even to the very Being of God. Simplicity was thought to be a great-making property because a metaphysically simple entity could not possibly come apart or decompose; hence change and eventual nonexistence were impossible.

The final traditional metaphysical property we will here consider is divine impassability. Although there are many different understandings of this property, they all have in common the belief that God is not affected by what humans do. It is thought inappropriate for finite beings to have any power over God; hence, he is impassable. One further wrinkle in the notion of impassability is that it is generally thought to entail a lack of emotional life in God. If God reacted to what humans do with emotions of anger, jealousy, or even compassion, then humans are exerting influence or control over God. This is traditionally thought unbecoming of the Greatest Possible Being. Although God might behave in ways that suggest the emotions of anger, jealousy, or compassion, his behavior does not in fact reveal those underlying emotional states.

These four traditional properties (timelessness, immutability, simplicity, and impassability), although absolutely fundamental to the Christian conception of God in the Middle Ages, have come under heavy attack during the latter part of the twentieth century. First, regarding timelessness, many theologians and philosophers believe that a being outside of time would in principle not be able to act in the temporal world. In particular, there is the difficulty of how response to petitionary prayer is possible if God is aware of every event in the temporal world at once. For responding to prayer seems to require being aware that the petition was made and then acting upon it. But such a sequence of events is by nature temporal with some events that come before others in the series. Also, there are difficulties for Christian theism in squaring timelessness with the doctrine of the Incarnation. For this doctrine states that the Second Person of the Trinity became incarnated in the person of Jesus Christ. Yet being a human being, Jesus Christ was surely temporal. Timelessness, then, seems at odds with the cornerstone of Christian theology and thus is looked at with suspicion by many.

The doctrines of immutability and simplicity have also come under sharp attack in the latter part of this century. First, process theologians claim that change is an essential part of being; they flatly reject the Greek and early Christian notion that immutability is a metaphysical virtue. But even many philosophers and theologians who strive to remain more traditional than the process theologians in their understanding of divinity believe that the notions of immutability (as classically conceived) and divine simplicity should be altered or even jettisoned. From the philosophical side, the grounds for immutability seem suspect. For instance, an omniscient being would know that what is happening *now* is happening now and that what happened yesterday happened yesterday. But in order for such a being to have knowledge that keeps up with the facts, as it were, the being's mental life would have to undergo change. As for simplicity, it has been argued that there is little sense to be made of the idea that, for example, omniscience and omnipotence are identical, and even less to be made of the claim that God's very being is identical to a single property. This is a very obscure doctrine indeed.

While timelessness, immutability, and simplicity do not enjoy the acceptance they once did, it is the doctrine of divine impassability that has come under the most serious and sustained fire in the latter part of this century. While perhaps there is something to be said for the idea that God is so ontologically above humans that God is completely unaffected by human actions, when the full implications of this view are considered, it surely seems that the conception of

God that includes it will include some pretty undesirable features. For an impassable God is, it seems, a fundamentally uncaring God. For although God might behave toward humans as if God cares, the bottom line is that, if impassability is true, then God has nothing analogous to emotional states. Yet in recent years the theology of God as a suffering God, a God who loves creation so much as to enter into it and take on its burdens and hardships has been at the core of much of Christian theology in the United States and elsewhere.

There is little doubt that just as recent Christological trends have tended to stress the humanity and historicity of Jesus, recent work in theology has by and large been a move away from the conception of God as a timeless, immutable, metaphysically simple, impassable being like that imagined by Greek philosophers. (There are, however, notable opponents to the current trends; philosophers Norman Kretzmann and Eleonore Stump have been remarkably successful at meeting objections to these traditional attributes and at giving explications of them that are as clear as one could hope for.) Current theology emphasizes God's interaction with creation, God's concern for the poor and dispossessed (liberation theology speaks most strongly to this), and God's willingness to make humanity God's partners in the redemption of creation. While many theologians who stress this side of divinity are not particularly concerned with theological orthodoxy, there are many others who note that what might be regarded as the "metaphysical excesses" of the classical conception of God are not to be found in the ancient creeds of the church, or in the Scriptures.

Let us conclude by considering again Anselm's definition of God as the greatest possible being. Medieval scholars and many traditionalists since would argue that this conception of God grounds the notions of timelessness, simplicity, and impassability. Yet this is controversial. For example, one might think that the ability to enter into creation and intimately interact with creatures is a great-making property but that this property is inconsistent with timelessness. If that is right, then timelessness might not be a great-making property after all, and being in time is. Similarly, if being able to have genuine love and compassion for all persons is a great-making property and if this precludes impassability, then the latter is cast into doubt as a property that the greatest possible being would have. In short, then we can see the disagreement between those who accept the classical conception of God and those who accept more modern conceptions not as a dispute about whether Anselm's definition is right but rather a disagreement about how to flesh out the surprisingly flexible skeleton that Anselm has left us with.

See also AGNOSTICISM; ALLAH; ATHEISM; BUDDHA; DEATH OF GOD; DIVINITY; JUDEO-CHRISTIAN TRADITION; LIBERATION THEOLOGY; PANTHEISM; PROCESS THEOLOGY; RELIGIOUS EXPERIENCE; THEISM; TRANSCENDENCE; TRINITY.

BIBLIOGRAPHY

Brummer, Vincent. *Speaking of a Personal God: An Essay in Philosophical Theology.* 1992.
Moltmann, Jurgen. *The Crucified God: The Cross of Christ and the Foundation and Criticism of Christian Theology.* 1993.
Morris, Thomas V. *Our Idea of God.* 1991.
Pinnock, Clark, et. al. *The Openness of God: A Biblical Challenge to the Traditional Understanding of God.* 1994.

Thomas D. Senor

God, Death of.

See Death of God.

Goddess

Prayer has been addressed to the Mother of God in Roman Catholicism and Christian Orthodoxy and to God the Mother in Shakerism and Christian Science, but until the 1970s the Goddess was notably absent from the American religious scene. The second wave of the feminist movement in the 1960s sparked a renewed questioning of the part played by religion in shaping women's roles. In 1971 American theologian and philosopher Mary Daly argued that when God is imaged exclusively as male (Lord, King, Father, Son, He, Him), it follows that society will be male-dominated.

In 1974 the first issue of *WomanSpirit* magazine (published quarterly until 1984) began to document a grassroots women's spirituality movement that rejected the male God of inherited religious traditions, celebrating instead the female body; the Earth and its cycles of birth, death, and renewal; daring to name the divine power "Goddess." In 1974 archaeologist Marija Gimbutas published *The Gods and Goddesses of Old Europe* (later revised and reprinted as *The Goddesses and Gods of Old Europe*); with numerous illustrations and a vision of Paleolithic and Neolithic "Old Europe" as a Goddess-worshiping, egalitarian, ecologically balanced, and peaceful civilization, it became a kind of "sacred text" of the emerging Goddess movement. The year 1975 saw the publication of Z. Budapest's *Feminist Book of Lights and Shadows* (later revised as *The Holy Book of Women's Mysteries*); the Hungarian-born Budapest urged women to revive the pre-Christian European religion of the Great Goddess, which she called "Dianic Witchcraft" (for women only) and offered examples of contemporary rituals. Merlin Stone's *When God Was a Woman* (1976) popularized the thesis that "in the beginning God was a woman." In 1978 more than five hundred women celebrated "The Great Goddess Reemerging" at the University of Santa Cruz extension, where feminist thea-logian (from *thea*, "Goddess") Carol P. Christ presented what has since become a widely reprinted essay, "Why Women Need the Goddess," as the keynote address. *The Spiral Dance* by Starhawk (Miriam Simos) appeared in 1979, providing a ritually oriented feminist reinterpretation of European Witchcraft as the ancient religion of the Goddess (for women and men). The 1980s and 1990s saw the publication of scores of books and hundreds of articles, scholarly and popular, that uncovered the history of the worship of the Goddess in prehistoric times, connected the dominance of male gods with the rise of patriarchy, and argued that the return of the Goddess would promote women's equality and ecological survival. In 1997 Carol P. Christ published *The Rebirth of the Goddess,* the first full-fledged thealogy of the movement.

Though the above-named authors could be called "leaders" of the movement (Starhawk in particular has done extensive teaching in retreat groups called "witch camps"), the movement is for the most part non- (and anti-) hierarchical, arguing that priesthoods and "great man" and "guru" systems are hallmarks of patriarchy. The most common mode of initiation into the movement is through personal experience and reading, followed by experimentation with prayer and ritual, either alone or in small groups. Participants are encouraged to trust their own experience.

Z. Budapest and Starhawk adapted the ritual cycle of the contemporary Neopagan movement to emphasize the Goddess and women's concerns. Celebrations are commonly held on the new or full moon and at equinoxes and solstices, and on February 2 (Brigid's Day), May 1, August 1, and October 31 (Halloween). Rituals invoke the Goddess as the power inherent in the cycles of birth, death, and renewal and celebrate the connection of all beings in the web of life. In contrast to biblical religions, Goddess religion names the body, especially the female body, as sacred, accepts a life that ends in death, and finds healing energy in darkness as well as light.

In a typical ritual for the spring equinox, participants journey to a local park or wildlife refuge, bring flowers to make crowns, invoke the Goddess as life and renewal, meditate on whatever is being renewed in their own lives, pray for peace on earth, and share

a meal. At Halloween an altar might be created for ancestors (dead relatives, friends, and others) and the Goddess invoked as She to Whom All Return, while participants meditate on the gifts they have been given by the ancestors and on the connections between life and death.

Other rituals in the Goddess movement address women's life cycles, with rituals for menstruation, pregnancy, birth, abortion, menopause, and "croning," or becoming a wise old woman. These rituals have been created to counter the sense of shame with which patriarchal religion and culture shroud the female body. A typical menstruation ritual claims that "our blood is the blood of life."

The ethics of Goddess religion are based in the root metaphors of the earth and the body as sacred and all beings as connected in the web of life. Carol P. Christ offers nine touchstones of the ethics of Goddess religion: nurture life; walk in love and beauty; trust the knowledge that comes through the body; speak the truth about conflict, pain, and suffering; take only what you need; think about the consequences of your actions for seven generations; approach the taking of life with great restraint; practice great generosity; and repair the web. Participants in the Goddess movement have demonstrated for equal rights and reproductive rights for women, against the opening of the Diablo Canyon nuclear power plant, and for other environmental and social justice issues.

The Goddess movement is numbered in the hundreds of thousands (mostly women, but some men) in North America, Australia, New Zealand, and Europe. Because the movement has no central organization or membership lists and "Goddess/Neopagan" is not an alternative on census lists, estimates of numbers are guesses. Anthropologist Susan Starr Sered in *Priestess, Mother, Sacred Sister* (1994) cites the Goddess movement as one of a handful of religions worldwide created and led primarily by women. Inroads have been made into traditional religions: Unitarian Universalists acknowledge the predominately Goddess-oriented "Covenant of Unitarian Universalist Pagans" (CUUPS); Catholic, Protestant, and Jewish women are experimenting with female names for the divine, including "Sophia-Wisdom" and "Shekinah—She Who Dwells Within."

See also ALLAH; FEMINIST SPIRITUALITY; FEMINIST THEOLOGY; GOD; MAGIC; NEOPAGANISM; PRIESTESS; SOPHIA; STARHAWK; WOMANIST THEOLOGY; WOMEN'S STUDIES.

BIBLIOGRAPHY

Christ, Carol P. *The Rebirth of the Goddess.* 1997, 1998.
Eller, Cynthia. *Living in the Lap of the Goddess.* 1995.

Gimbutas, Marija. *The Language of the Goddess.* 1989.
Starhawk (Miriam Simos). *The Spiral Dance.* 1979, 1989.

Carol P. Christ

Graham, Billy

(1918–), evangelist.

Billy Graham was the most successful and influential evangelist and evangelical Christian leader of the twentieth century. He spoke in person to more than eighty million people in more than eighty countries, and he reached countless additional millions by means of electronic and print media. For most of the last half of the twentieth century he was consistently ranked among the most admired persons in America.

Born in Charlotte, North Carolina, William Franklin Graham attended Bob Jones University (briefly),

Florida Bible Institute, and Wheaton College in Illinois. He rose to prominence within evangelical circles as a field representative for Youth for Christ International during the mid-1940s. His stadium revivals, called "crusades," his *Hour of Decision* radio broadcast, and his astute use of television made him famous nationally and internationally during the 1950s. *Christianity Today,* which he founded in 1956, became America's most widely read serious religious journal and remains the flagship publication of American evangelical Christianity. He was the first Christian, Eastern or Western, to preach in public behind the Iron Curtain after World War II, and his repeated visits helped foster greater religious freedom in Communist countries.

Graham was a friend and occasional adviser to a series of presidents, from Dwight Eisenhower to Bill Clinton. These associations added to Graham's public image but also led to criticism. After the 1973 Watergate scandal made it clear that he had been manipulated by the president for political gain, the disillusioned evangelist became more cautious and sounded

The Rev. Billy Graham waves to the crowd in Ericsson Stadium in Charlotte, North Carolina, on Sunday September 29, 1996, on the last night of the 1996 Carolinas Billy Graham Crusade.   (Credit: AP/Wide World Photos.)

repeated warnings against the temptations and pitfalls that lie in wait for religious leaders who enter the political arena. He pointedly refrained from involvement in the Religious Right, the religiopolitical movement that began in the late 1970s.

Graham played a major role helping worldwide evangelicalism become an increasingly dynamic, self-confident, and ecumenical movement. In hundreds of his crusades, Christians of almost every stripe worked side by side with each other, often for the first time. In addition, the Billy Graham Evangelistic Association (BGEA) sponsored or underwrote a series of monumental conferences that drew thousands of evangelical leaders together and helped them gain a better sense of their own strength and formulate concrete plans for expanding their reach and influence. The 1966 World Congress on Evangelism in Berlin helped create a kind of third worldwide ecumenical force, alongside Vatican II and the World Council of Churches. A 1974 conference held in Lausanne, Switzerland, included far more non-Western delegates and called for greater attention to pressing social problems and to adapting the gospel to a variety of cultures. Two conferences in Amsterdam, in 1983 and 1986, provided 13,000 evangelists from more than 170 countries with intensive training in the practical aspects of itinerant evangelism. A third, even larger Amsterdam conference was planned for the year 2000.

In recognition of his achievements, Billy Graham has received the Presidential Medal of Freedom (1983) and the Congressional Gold Medal (1996), the highest honors these two branches of government can bestow on a civilian.

See also BORN AGAIN CHRISTIANS; EVANGELICAL CHRISTIANITY; JOURNALISM, RELIGIOUS; PUBLISHING, RELIGIOUS; TELEVANGELISM; YOUTH FOR CHRIST.

BIBLIOGRAPHY

Graham, Billy. *Just As I Am*. 1997.

Martin, William. *A Prophet with Honor: The Billy Graham Story*.

William Martin

Guru

A guru is a teacher or spiritual guide, particularly in Hindu, Sikh, or Tibetan Buddhist tradition. The word derives from a Sanskrit term that means "profound," "dense," or "heavy." However, a popular folk etymology for the term breaks it into its component syllables in order to propose that the distinctive function of the guru is to lead devotees or disciples from darkness (*gu*) to light (*ru*).

A religious guru usually offers individual and group instruction that supplements what can be found in published or otherwise publicly available sources of information. He or she is likely to serve devoted followers in some combination of capacities that are tailored to fit individual needs and that include the practical and the inspirational as well as the informative dimensions of teaching. Practical advice from a guru, as from a sports coach or similar adviser, is likely to extend into the areas of diet, relationships, patterns of work and rest, and personal religious practice. Inspiration may be conveyed by example from the way the guru lives, or from songs and stories the guru shares.

Many of the roles typically embodied by religious gurus in Hindu, Sikh, or Buddhist traditions are similar to the functions performed by spiritual directors or confessors in Roman Catholic Christianity. Gurus are what social theorist Max Weber called types of religious virtuosi. As such, a guru may offer more than one level of initiation to followers and may scale the pedagogical process to suit the various levels of initiates. In such instances, the teachings and practices fitted to a disciple at one level may be considerably different from those assumed to be appropriate for another level. Hence the guru and his or her community will be involved in secrecy as a consequence of organizing instruction around the varying levels or gradations of initiation.

A traditional Hindu text that has become universally popular in the modern world—the *Bhagavad Gītā*—exemplifies these themes. It is a classic model of the secret dialogue between a guru (Krishna) and a disciple (Arjuna), in this case prompted by a major crisis in the life of the disciple. In the space of eighteen short chapters, Krishna discloses to the perplexed Arjuna by means of speech and induced visions the esoteric (hidden or private) meanings of terms that are widely and popularly familiar within Hindu tradition, overlooked spiritual dimensions within himself, and the unforeseen profundity of his guru. Arjuna becomes transformed by the initiatory power of the conversation represented in the *Gītā*. Similar stories about guru-disciple encounters are an integral part of Hindu, Sikh, and Buddhist spiritual lore.

Spiritual traffic between India and North America over the last century brought many sorts of gurus to the New World. Some of them were more like bishops or popes than spiritual directors or confessors in their claims to spiritual authority. Others were attractively charismatic, and a few were so prone to excesses in their style of living and teaching that they generated public scandal. Moreover, several of the imported gurus designated Western successors. By the end of the twentieth century, the term and the phenomenon are well on the way to becoming indigenous aspects of American religion.

See also BHAGAVAD GĪTĀ; HINDUISM; SIKHISM; TIBETAN BUDDHISM.

BIBLIOGRAPHY

Bainbridge, William Sims. *The Sociology of Religious Movements.* 1997.

Feuerstein, Georg. *Holy Madness: The Shock Tactics and Radical Teachings of Crazy-Wise Adepts, Holy Fools, and Rascal Gurus.* 1991.

Isherwood, Christopher. *My Guru and His Disciple.* 1980.

McKean, Lise. *Divine Enterprise: Gurus and the Hindu Nationalist Movement.* 1996.

McLeod, Hew. *Sikhism.* 1997.

McWilliams, Peter. *Life 102: What to Do When Your Guru Sues You.* 1994.

Miller, Timothy, ed. *When Prophets Die: The Postcharismatic Fate of New Religious Movements.* 1991.

Narayan, Kirin. *Storytellers, Saints, and Scoundrels: Folk Narrative in Hindu Religious Teaching.* 1989.

Rawlinson, Andrew. *The Book of Enlightened Masters: Western Teachers in Eastern Traditions.* 1997.

Storr, Anthony. *Feet of Clay: A Study of Gurus.* 1996.

Tweed, Thomas A., and Stephen Prothero, eds. *Asian Religions in America: A Documentary History.* 1999.

Gene R. Thursby

H

Hare Krishna.

See International Society for Krishna Consciousness.

Hasidim

Hasidim—literally, "the pious" (singular, Hasid)—were originally followers of the teachings of Rabbi Israel Ben Eliezer (1700–1760), the Ba'al Shem Tov ("Master of the Good Name"), a charismatic healer, storyteller, and mystic. His contemplative and ecstatic teachings emphasized concern for ordinary people and perceiving the presence of divinity everywhere. Disciples later attracted followings of their own, which evolved into the Hasidic communities. By the end of the eighteenth century, Hasidic communities had formed throughout Eastern Europe, particularly in Ukraine, Galicia, and Poland. However, in Belarus and Lithuania, Hasidim met with strong resistance for promoting customs that deviated from the Ashkenazi norms and the fear that Hasidic emphasis on devotion, ecstasy, and charisma might lead to heresy and religious anarchy. By the nineteenth century, Hasidim and their opponents joined to make common cause against their mutual enemy, the European enlightenment and the forces of modernization. Hasidim had little interest in the United States before World War II. Most Hasidim who left the great Hasidic communities of Eastern Europe preferred to ascend to the Holy Land of Israel, where Hasidim began to settle in the 1760s. Very few Hasidic rabbis and their followers were among the early waves of Eastern European Jew-

ish immigration to the "Golden Land," which represented secularism and materialism. The Hasidic presence in American history really begins with the Nazi genocide of Eastern European Jewry, of whom a very high percentage were Hasidim. Most of the minority of Hasidim who survived the Holocaust regrouped in New York after the war. These survivors were shepherded by a few major surviving Hasidic rebbes. The most influential were Rabbi Joel Teitelbaum, the Satmar Rebbe, who united Hungarian and Romanian survivors in Williamsburg, Brooklyn; and Rabbi Joseph Isaac Schneersohn, the Rebbe of Lubavitch, whose followers, Chabad Hasidim, formed a community in Crown Heights, Brooklyn. In 1950, Schneersohn was succeeded by his son-in-law, Rabbi Menachem Mendel Schneerson, whose influence continued to guide Chabad Hasidim, even after his death in 1994.

Hasidim were extremely successful in rebuilding their communities and religious institutions in Brooklyn and later in upstate New York. The Rebbes of Satmar and Lubavitch were perceived as rivals, representing differing models for serving God in America during the second half of the twentieth century. The Satmar Rebbe was, on theological grounds, an ardent anti-Zionist. He had a large following in Jerusalem, but opposed secular Jewish government in the Holy Land. Satmar concentrated on rebuilding and developing its own institutions rather than on outreach. Chabad had historically been anti-Zionist, but once the state of Israel was founded, they became strong supporters of Israel and its institutions, gaining considerable influence among Israeli politicians and lead-

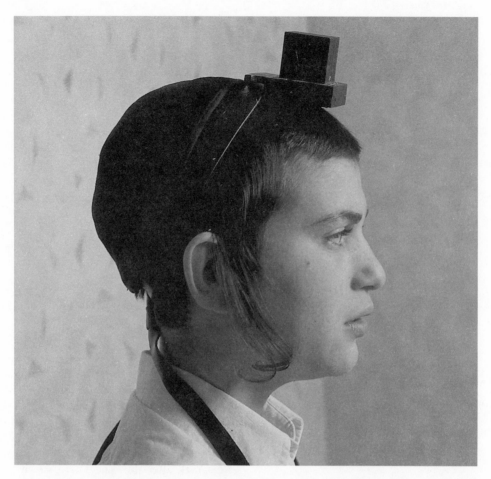

A Hasidic boy in Brooklyn, New York (ca. 1990), is wearing phylacteries, ready for morning prayer.   (Credit: CORBIS/Richard T. Nowitz.)

ers. Chabad Hasidim were also more integrated and conspicuous among various strata of the American Jewish community.

In the 1960s, Rabbi Schneerson began a vigorous and remarkably successful outreach program, aimed at returning American Jews to a more traditionally observant Jewish way of life. Chabad representatives were sent to communities wherever Jews lived. Emphasis was placed on reaching students at colleges and universities. This program was part of a larger mission to reach Jews in all parts of the world, especially the oppressed Jews in the Soviet Union. The project's success benefited from the strong financial support of members of the non-Hasidic American Jewish community, who were persuaded that Chabad Hasidism represented authentic traditional Judaism. A messianic dimension has always been part of Chabad teaching. However, this interest became increasingly important in Chabad during the 1980s, when many Chabad Hasidim began to publicly proclaim their leader, Rabbi Menachem Mendel Schneerson, as the messiah. While never explicitly affirming or denying

that he was the messiah, Rabbi Schneerson used messianic anticipation as a means of increasing fervor and dedication among his Hasidim. After his death, many Chabad Hasidim continue to believe in his messiahship, some even expecting his imminent resurrection. Some prominent Chabad leaders and opponents of Chabad in the general American Jewish community condemned these radical beliefs as heretical. While Chabad institutions continued to flourish, the central Chabad communities in Crown Heights and Israel have been rent by schism over the messianic status of their departed rebbe.

See also HOLOCAUST; HOLY LAND; JEWISH IDENTITY; JUDAISM; MESSIANISM; ZIONISM.

BIBLIOGRAPHY

Belcove-Shalin, Janet S. *New World Hasidism: Ethnographic Studies of Hasidic Jews in America.* 1995.

Mintz, Jerome R. *Hasidic People: A Place in the New World.* 1994.

Miles Krassen

Hawaiian Religions

Hawaiian spirituality today is founded on the religious practices of the time before the Hawaiian people had contact with the West. Hawaii was first populated some eight centuries ago by voyagers from what is now French Polynesia, at the end of a long migration eastward from the Southeast Asian mainland and then north and south across thousands of miles of ocean. They brought with them the worship of four great Polynesian gods—Kane, Ku, Lono, and Kanaloa—and innumerable lesser deities.

Traditional Hawaiian spirituality begins with the land, or *aina*. Land is a living thing, and all life force springs from the land. The life force in the land is related to that found in the sea, the winds, the rain, and other natural phenomena. In fact, for Hawaiians, all of creation is sentient, all is engaged in cocreation. All of what Westerners call living creatures and much of the landscape itself has life, consciousness, intention, emotion, and action. All beings—objects, animals, gods, and humans included—have greater or lesser amounts of *mana*, or spiritual power.

There is no radical disjunction between nature and humankind. Each aspect of nature—a rock, a volcano, a stream, a shark, the little fish called *humuhumu-nuku-nuku-apu-a'a*—is associated with a god or a goddess. The gods (*'aumakua* or *akua*) are also human ancestors, who have moved toward deity after death. The Polynesian *akua* Kane, who takes several dozen forms (*kinolau*), is the strongest life force, the giver of sunlight, fresh water, the wind, the rain clouds. People offer Kane prayers and *kapa* cloth, pigs, and *'awa* (a mild intoxicant). Ku is the god of war, of fishing, forests, rain, and canoes. He is the object of prayers for the harvest and also of human sacrifice. Lono, the god of peace, agriculture, and sport, is associated with wind and rain. He sponsors the *makahiki*, an annual four-month festival during which people refrained from war and did little work, but instead feasted and danced ritual *hula*. Those who prayed to Lono offered pigs, fish, and vegetables. Kanaloa, the fourth great god inherited from earlier Polynesians, is the less well-defined companion to Kane and is associated with the sea and fishing.

The most spectacular of the native Hawaiian akua and 'aumakua is Pele, goddess of the volcano, who often appears in the form of a beautiful woman. Other supernatural beings abound. For instance, the *menehune* are little people who preceded the Polynesians in the islands and are responsible for many of the very old stone walls and fishponds. Many went away when the Polynesians arrived, but some live on in the forests and come out at night to interact with spiritually sensitive individuals.

Before Western contact, Hawaiians arranged themselves in a strict social hierarchy. The *ali'i*, or chiefly class, played a special role in Hawaiian religion. It was from the ali'i class that *kahuna*, or religious experts, were selected. The land belonged to the akua and 'aumakua, and the ali'i were its guardians and caretakers, supervising the commoners. The ali'i maintained the *kapu* system, a set of religiously sanctioned regulations that maintained social hierarchy and order. Because they had more mana, they had more privilege, but also more responsibility for the social order.

Europeans and North Americans began to come to the islands in the 1770s with the explorations of Captain James Cook, who died in the islands after being taken for the god Lono. In the 1820s, Congregational missionaries from New England brought Protestant Christianity to Hawaii. They were followed by other missionaries: Catholics, Mormons, Buddhists, and representatives of other faiths. The New Englanders married into elite Hawaiian families, and the United Church of Christ is today the largest Protestant denomination in the islands.

While many Hawaiians are conscientious in their pursuit of these other faiths, the ancient beliefs and practices still animate daily life. A Mormon bishop tells of seeing Pele walking in the volcano Kilauea and of leaving an offering to protect his house from a lava flow. Catholic farmers pray to Lono for a bountiful harvest. A Buddhist plants a garden in his yard to protect his home with *ki* energy. A Methodist minister tells of her conversations with menehune. Congregationalists invite a kahuna to pray at the groundbreaking for their new church building. These are practitioners of varied religions, but all are also practitioners of native Hawaiian spirituality.

See also CREATION SPIRITUALITY; DIVINITY; ECOSPIRITUALITY; GOD; GODDESS; MATERIAL RELIGION; NATURE RELIGION; NEOPAGANISM; SPIRITUALITY.

BIBLIOGRAPHY

Beckwith, Martha. *Hawaiian Mythology.* 1970.

Cunningham, Scott. *Hawaiian Religion and Magic.* 1995.

Dudley, Michael Kioni. *Man, Gods, and Nature: A Hawaiian Nation I.* 1990.

Handy, E. S. Craighill, and Mary Kawena Pukui. *The Polynesian Family System in Ka'u, Hawaii.* 1972.

Kamakau, Samuel Manaiakalani. *Ka Pole Kahiko: The People of Old,* translated by Mary Kawena Pukui. 1964.

Malo, David. *Moolelo Hawai'i (Hawaiian Antiquities),* translated by Nathaniel B. Emerson. 1971.

Paul Spickard

Healing

Healing includes diagnosis of illness and various methods of curing. Human health is in a state of constant fluctuation and change. Any particular change is construed as follows: If waxing toward life, it is wellness; if waning toward death, it is illness. Healing is the negotiation between these two states. It attempts to increase life and wellness, but it is not always successful.

Issues of health and healing constitute a significant measure of the reality of everyday human existence. For humans to live, they must defend against illness and have strategies for responding to illness when it occurs; or the inverse—they must promote wellness as protection against the onset of illness. In almost all cultures, and throughout human history, healing has been inextricably related to religious concerns, themes, and practices. Whether part-time or full-time professionals, healers in most societies are religious specialists of some kind. Since health maintenance is a phenomenon that has religious dimensions, it represents a focal point for various beliefs, mores, practices, rituals, and observances. Examples include laying on hands, healing prayers, blessings, exorcisms, and purification practices. Many religions attempt to explain the causes and origins of illness. Some of these theories include spirit and demon possession, human Witchcraft, infractions of morality, or ritual offenses.

One reason why healing and religion have always had a historical relationship is that in dealing with illness they must also face the issues of suffering, pain, angst, and dying. Religion addresses these issues through establishing meaning, interpretation, and practices that are responses to suffering and death. Religious interpretive systems attempt to reduce the anxiety and fear associated with illness. In this context, illness has often been associated with sin. Religious healing attempts to accomplish curing through ritual, practice, and faith. Although modern empirical medicine can promote wellness and combat bodily pain and suffering, it does not always address the accompanying existential crises of human mortality.

Americans inherit a largely Judeo-Christian worldview, although indigenous and minority peoples have contributed significantly to contemporary health practices. The large influx into the United States of Asian peoples and ideas in the late twentieth century has also affected religious views and responses to health issues. Christian history is replete with images of healing as religious practice. As depicted in the Christian New Testament, Jesus is explicitly represented as a faith healer. One of his disciples, Luke, is identified as a doctor. A significant portion of the gospels' accounts record stories of healing.

American Christianity includes the practices of praying over the sick, laying on hands, and anointing with oil. These practices are rooted in the rituals of early Christians. These practices are also considered to convey forgiveness of sins, suggesting that sinfulness is connected with illness. Roman Catholics have maintained several rituals of healing and expiation of sin throughout their history, the rite of unction being one such expression of healing power through ritual. Early Protestants rejected formal rituals of healing, preferring informal practices such as praying and reading the Bible in times of sickness.

With the shift in recent decades of members away from mainline churches toward Evangelical and fundamentalist churches, several healing practices have gained increasing popularity: laying on hands and anointing with oil, as well as others. These "faith healing" practices occur throughout evangelicalism but are especially concentrated in Pentecostal and non-denominational charismatic churches. "Faith healing" is a term that generally refers to Christian practices of healing conceived as mediated through God's intervention, or through the power of the Holy Spirit. Faith healing practices include touching and laying on hands but also gesturing and other dramatic movements. With the growth of television evangelism, traditional "hands-on" healing is being supplemented by believers touching their televisions to receive healing. In some cases healing is received through television simply by viewing the ministry or by praying and reading the Bible while watching. Healing and evangelical TV ministries are a multimillion-dollar phenomenon in the United States today.

Another dimension of faith healing is represented by such groups as Christian Science. Christian Science is a movement, started in the nineteenth century, that rejects empirical medicine in favor of faith. This, and other such groups, do connect illness with sin. Christian Scientists conceive of empirical medicine as a challenge to God's authority and as a lack of faith. Jehovah's Witnesses do not adopt all the practices of other churches of this type but do reject the use of blood transfusions. Although some of the evangelical churches share similar attitudes, there is not as much consensus over whether faith replaces modern medicine or is a supplement to it.

Among some faith healing ministries, adherents accept and use modern medicine. Like more mainline denominations, many evangelicals do not see faith healing as a replacement for modern medicine, but instead accommodate their religious practices with visits to medical practitioners. No Christian institutions view empirical medicine as a substitute for faith,

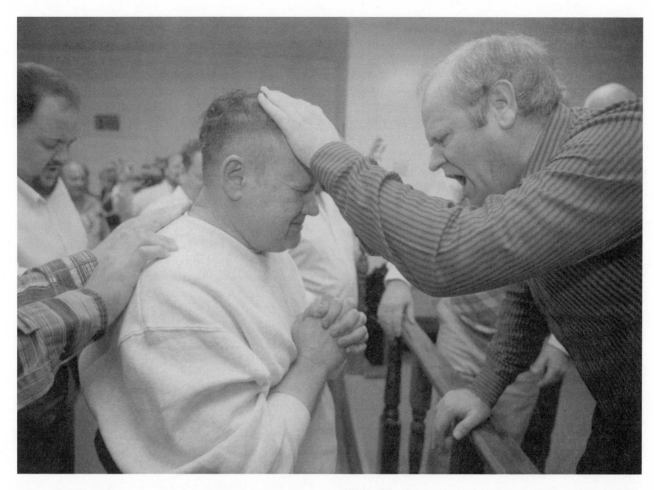

Rev. Carl Porter, minister of the Church of Lord Jesus Christ in Kingston, Georgia, lays hands on a congregant at a healing service on February 25, 1995.   (Credit: AP/World Wide Photo.)

prayer, and miraculous healing. Often modern medicine is understood as an instrument of God's healing work, as exemplified in prayer meetings at hospitals to guide the hands of a surgeon.

Religious healing has ethnic dimensions as well. Many minority groups have members who are suspicious of modern medicine. Reasons for this suspicion include a general distrust of majority culture institutions and practices and their eroding effects on ethnic traditions. Healing has a strong traditional place in the religious beliefs and practices of most Native Americans. Practitioners of Vodun (Voodoo) and Santería also figure among those who rely on religious approaches to illness.

A recent trend in religion and healing is the popularity of herbal and alternative medicine. Alternative medicine includes a host of practices with religious or pseudo-religious affiliations. Alternative medicine with religious valences includes aroma therapy, acupuncture, herbal healing, massage therapy, macrobiotics, biofeedback, Āyurveda, Chinese medicine, homeopathy, various exercise and dietary movements,

and others. All of these fields of practice tend to be holistic. They treat physical, psychological, and existential imbalance as illness. Their popularity is partially based on their respect for the human as a social and religious being and also as a physical organism. They also place significant emphasis on wellness—keeping people healthy and fit as a precaution against illness. In addition, they offer curing in response to illness.

Some of these traditions are modern imports; others developed in American religious history. In the nineteenth and early twentieth centuries, numerous groups appeared that can be loosely categorized as religious human potential movements. Mesmerists and Swedenborgians are two such examples that subsequently led to the development of more recent fields, such as chiropractic medicine. Swedenborgianism is a religion in which healing is the central religious practice. Herbal medicine has several streams of historical confluence: traditional European and African-American folk remedies, Chinese medicine, Native American botanical knowledge and theory, and South Asian Ayurveda. In many ways, theories of herbal medicine have been combined with empirical dietary research to increase sales of vitamins and minerals in the latter twentieth century. The long-standing links between religion and medicine are also seen in the popularity of vitamin and dietary supplements among some Evangelical Christian groups.

Modern medicine developed during the period of secularization and empirical science and has sometimes devalued religion and religious healing. Although there are still many fronts of contention between science and religion, some medical professionals consider religious practice and belief helpful to healing. In the 1990s the medical effects of religious practices and beliefs have begun to be assessed by the medical profession. Psychologists and therapists have studied how religious affiliation contributes positively to mental health. Some studies suggest that members of religious communities tend to suffer fewer personality disorders, such as depression. The use of Asian-inspired meditation methods has been shown to be helpful to sufferers of chronic pain or incurable disease. This field and its developing research are usually referred to as mind/body medicine. In a historical context this is not a new field, but instead a recognition by scientific medicine that some forms of religious practice and belief have transformative effects on immunity and general health. Many empiricists would not replace heart surgery with prayer, but they are beginning to recognize and study how prayer and meditation shorten the recovery time of patients.

See also ALTERNATIVE MEDICINE; CHRISTIAN SCIENCE; EVANGELICAL CHRISTIANITY; EXORCISM; HEALTH; HOLISTIC HEALTH; JEHOVAH'S WITNESSES; MIRACLES; NATURE RELIGION; PENTECOSTAL AND CHARISMATIC CHRISTIANITY; RITUAL; TELEVANGELISM.

BIBLIOGRAPHY

Albanese, Catherine L. *Nature Religion in America: From the Algonkian Indians to the New Age.* 1990.

Dayton, D. "The Rise of the Evangelical Healing Movement in Nineteenth-Century America." *Pneuma* (1982): 1–18.

Goleman, Daniel, and Joel Gurin, eds. *Mind Body Medicine: How to Use Your Mind for Better Health.* 1993.

Kinsley, David. *Health, Healing, and Religion: A Cross-Cultural Perspective.* 1996.

Kowalchik, Claire, and William H. Hylton, eds. *Rodale's Illustrated Encyclopedia of Herbs.* 1987.

McGuire, Meredith B. "Religion and Healing." In *The Sacred in a Secular Age,* edited by Phillip E. Hammond. 1985.

Jeffrey C. Ruff

Health

Health is a profoundly cultural concept. Prior to the seventeenth century, the Western world understood health in ways that mingled religious and medical perspectives. Religious explanations of disease (e.g., sin or spirit possession) as well as corresponding schemas for therapeutic intervention (e.g., confession or exorcism) have historically influenced Western attitudes toward health. However, the Scientific Revolution of the seventeenth and eighteenth centuries challenged these religious conceptions of health and disease. Scientific medicine focused solely on the material causes of disease, hoping to understand health without the interference of philosophical or religious ideas. This, of course, was itself a culturally conditioned attempt to understand health. It rested on faith in the rationalistic assumptions of the Enlightenment era, which confidently proclaimed scientific rationality to be the sole avenue toward meaningful knowledge. It should not be surprising that many Americans do not share this unreserved faith in materialistic science to understand all the complexities of human nature. Indeed, most Americans envision their lives as in some way participating in a sacred reality. And for this reason religious attitudes continue to influence many Americans' understanding of both physical and mental health.

The major religious traditions found in the contemporary United States have long histories of addressing matters of health and medicine. From biblical times to the present, rabbis, priests, and ministers have been concerned with issues related to the health of the body as well as the health of the mind and soul. The religious values taught by institutional religion influence the majority of Americans' attitudes toward sickness, sexuality, and lifestyle, including their attitudes toward such issues as birth control, abortion, and euthanasia. The biblical accounts of Jesus performing healing miracles supports ongoing belief in various forms of "faith healing" such as those that form the nucleus of the charismatic movement within Roman Catholicism or numerous Protestant pentecostal denominations. It should also be noted that church-supported hospitals can be found throughout the United States and that virtually every denomination has ordained clergy whose duties include pastoral care activities intended to heal, sustain, and guide individuals throughout the course of their lives.

Two religious denominations indigenous to American religious history warrant special attention for their persistent interest in the connection between spirituality and health. The Church of Christ, Scientist was founded by Mary Baker Eddy in 1879 with the principal task of demonstrating that health is a spiritual rather than a physical reality. Christian Science has profound faith that God has created all that is, and all that God creates is good. From this theological postulate it follows that sickness, pain, or evil are not creations of God and therefore do not exist in any real sense. These negative conditions are instead only the delusional appearance created by an erring, mortal mind. Because disease is considered to be rooted in a false conception, healing only requires that we replace spiritual ignorance with spiritual understanding. A second denomination that emphasizes the relationship between religion and health is the Seventh-Day Adventist Church. The church's founder, Ellen Gould White, received numerous visions and revelations in which she learned that healthful living is a moral and religious obligation. Declaring that "it is as truly a sin to violate the laws of our being as it is to break the Ten Commandments," Ellen White made concern with healthful living an essential element of preparing ourselves for the Second Coming of Christ. While interest in faith healing is part of the Seventh-Day Adventist heritage, more characteristic of the denomination is its concern with healthful diet. Strongly discouraging drinking, smoking, and meat-eating, Seventh-Day Adventists also support hospitals throughout the world in their efforts to make health reform an essential element of evangelical piety.

Some of the most interesting attempts to connect spirituality and health over the past few decades have occurred outside of established religious traditions in systems variously referred to as alternative medicine, holistic therapies, or New Age healing. Included among these health systems are chiropractic medicine, homeopathy, positive-thinking regimens, acupuncture, iridology, t'ai chi, yoga, Ayurvedic medicine, massage therapies, crystal healing, and various twelve-step recovery programs. Although their specific philosophies and practices differ, they are all concerned with healing the whole person and awakening our spiritual sensibilities. Taken together, these healing groups constitute an impressive expression of unchurched American spirituality. Most of these alternative healing systems draw a great deal of their vocabulary from Eastern religions and Western metaphysical philosophies. These belief systems envision humans as existing on many levels (or dimensions), including the physical, mental, and spiritual or astral levels. The healing techniques that these groups utilize seek to restore harmony and interconnection between and among these levels of selfhood. Such inner harmony is said to allow persons to become inwardly receptive to the "inflow" of healing energies that emanate from the spiritual or astral plane and restore health to the physical and mental dimensions of our lives.

According to the *New England Journal of Medicine,* those who become interested in these nontraditional conceptions of health are typically white, between ages twenty-five and fifty, and above average in education and income. Moreover, relatively few suffer from acute illness or refuse to consult medical doctors. What they most have in common is their interest in understanding health in ways that place them outside the intellectual boundaries of either scientific or religious orthodoxy—that is, adherents of these groups have found scientific materialism too confining. Scientific rationality has failed to provide them with an outlook on life that might disclose the ultimate meaning or significance of our lives. Biblical religion also strikes them as an inadequate guide to life. Most of those attracted to alternative healing philosophies are self-styled progressive thinkers and find scriptural religion too narrow and dogmatic. Holistic and New Age medical systems, on the other hand, invite people to explore the intimate correspondences and interconnections among the physical, mental, and spiritual levels of human existence.

There have been some theoretical developments within medical science that have made new connections between health and spirituality. Research in psychosomatic medicine has made it clear that it is not possible to make a complete separation between a patient's mind and body. Our personalities, inclusive of our beliefs and general world outlook, have a great deal to do with our overall health. Studies now indicate that religious belief is positively correlated with resistance to heart disease, stroke, and cancer. Continued research in the relationship between spirituality and health may well point the way to a reintegration of science and religion.

Psychotherapists have also given increased attention to the positive effects of religion on mental health. For many decades it was assumed that religion promoted superstition, dependency, and overall psychological weakness. Yet in recent decades studies have shown that religious belief is positively correlated with resistance to depression and suicide, avoidance of anxiety, and positive outcomes in substance abuse programs. Many psychotherapists have gone further and suggested that health should be understood as something more than the absence of disease. Full health, it is argued, should be considered as the capacity to sustain a lifestyle that is spiritual in the broadest sense of the term (i.e., including the abilities for creativity, self-renewal, empathy for others, spontaneity, and the subjective sense of fulfillment). This concern with understanding the nature of full psychological health accounts for the recent popularity of the psychological theories of Carl Jung. Jung proposed that the mind is by no means machinelike or wholly at the mercy of the outer environment. In his view, the mind is purposeful, spontaneously pushing toward wholeness and growth. Many Americans have found in Jung's work a "psychotherapeutic spirituality" that, while not religious in a traditional sense, is overtly spiritual in its emphasis on humanity's capacity for self-transformation. Many other psychological writers, such as Rollo May, Fritz Perls, Abraham Maslow, Carl Rogers, M. Scott Peck, and Thomas Moore, have also attracted sizable reading audiences who yearn for new understandings of the "further reaches" of human nature.

It appears that although Western science has attempted to separate considerations of the body from those of the human spirit, most Americans continue to view them as integrally related. The healing ministries of America's churches, alternative medicine, humanistic psychotherapy, and even recent research within scientific medicine are all evidence that American culture continues to support belief in the positive effect of religion on both mental and physical health.

See also ABORTION; ALTERNATIVE MEDICINE; BIRTH CONTROL; CHRISTIAN SCIENCE; EUTHANASIA AND ASSISTED SUICIDE; HEALING; HOLISTIC HEALTH; NEW AGE SPIRITUALITY; PSYCHOTHERAPY; QUANTUM HEALING; SEVENTH-DAY ADVENTISM; TWELVE-STEP PROGRAMS.

BIBLIOGRAPHY

Bregman, Lucy. "Psychotherapies." In *Spirituality and the Secular Quest,* edited by Peter Van Ness. 1996.

Fuller, Robert C. *Alternative Medicine and American Religious Life.* 1989.

Koenig, Harold. *Is Religion Good for Your Health? The Effects of Religion on Physical and Mental Health.* 1997.

Numbers, Ronald, and Darrel Amundsen, eds. *Caring and Curing: Health and Medicine in the Western Religious Traditions.* 1986.

Schumaker, John, ed. *Religion and Mental Health.* 1992.

Robert C. Fuller

Heaven

Belief in heaven, a place of eternal bliss after death, in which the redeemed experience the presence of God, has long been a part of Christian doctrine. Christians believe that Jesus' own death and resurrection provide fulfillment of his promise "I go to prepare a place for you. . . . that where I am you may be also" (John 14:3–4). The Nicene Creed and other early Christian confessions assert that Jesus "ascended into heaven from whence he shall come to judge the living and the dead."

Heaven was an important doctrine of the church in the Middle Ages, often linked with a belief in purgatory, an intermediate place for those not saintly enough to enter God's presence immediately, but not evil enough to go to hell. For many of the faithful, the eternal world was very near, linked through prayers for the dead and intercession by the saints.

The Reformation churches continued to emphasize the reality of heaven but rejected belief in purgatory and the saints, insisting that salvation be grounded *sola fide*—in faith alone as the sole criterion for heavenly citizenship.

Heaven is also closely related to the idea of the Kingdom of God, or the Kingdom of Heaven, a topic frequently addressed by Jesus. The Kingdom of God involves God's rule and reign in this world and the next. In this world the kingdom is always limited, a promise of things to come. In its future sense, the kingdom represents the ultimate victory of God over evil and suffering. When the kingdom comes in its fullness, then heaven is complete.

From the colonial era to the present, heaven has been an important emphasis of many American religious traditions. The contrast between the redeemed in heaven and the lost in hell was a frequent subject of evangelical preachers. Likewise, Catholic missioners (traveling priests) warned of the eternal consequences of sin and the loss of heaven. In a society where life expectancy was short and where infant mortality was high, the belief in heaven was a promise, not only of eternal life, but also of reunion with loved ones and friends lost too soon.

From the time of slavery, African-American Christians gave great attention to the promise of heaven. While whites often insisted that salvation changed only the slaves' eternal status, not their earthly condition, blacks understood heaven as a place of eternal redemption and justice. There, believers met Jesus "face to face," in liberation, peace, and deliverance. The promise of heaven was a powerful theme of African-American spirituals, evident in songs such as "Soon I Will Be Done with the Troubles of the World," "Swing Low, Sweet Chariot," and "Everybody Talking About Heaven Ain't A-going There."

Heaven was a continuing theme of nineteenth-century evangelical hymnody as well. Hymns included lyrics such as "When we all get to heaven, what a day of rejoicing that will be" and "In the sweet by and by, we shall meet on that beautiful shore." Shakers and other millennial groups believed that their communal societies were an earthly representation of the heavenly realm. They shared all things in common, practiced celibacy, created deep communal relationships, and communicated directly with the world to come through spirit songs and direct inspiration from those who had gone before them into "glory."

By the late twentieth century, many American Christians had minimized the idea of heaven, for a variety of reasons. First, some saw it as a doctrine of "pie in the sky by and by" sometimes used by political, economic, or religious establishments to keep certain exploited groups—slaves or laborers, for example—in their place. Second, theologians spoke less of the specifics of heavenly bliss than of the promise of hope that rested in God. Many challenged various expressions of popular piety that implied the immortality of souls, with a more Hebrew approach that stressed the wholeness of the person and the unity of body and spirit. The Greek idea of natural immortality was questioned in light of the idea that God alone is immortal and that eternal life for human beings is a gift from God. Third, movements for civil rights and other efforts at promoting social inequality called on people to work toward the experience of justice in the here and now, not in some deferred afterlife. Reformers such as Martin Luther King, Jr., did not reject the idea of heaven, but linked the promise of the kingdom with that of a "beloved community" that all Christians should work to bring about. Fourth, many who continued to affirm belief in an afterlife sought to distinguish it from a literal reading of symbolic language in the Bible, while suggesting that it was a state of union with God and the "communion of saints" of all the ages where justice, peace, and righteousness prevailed.

During the 1980s and 1990s popular attention to heaven and the afterlife captivated large segments of American culture inside and outside traditional religious boundaries. Numerous individuals published books recounting "near-death experiences" in which they claimed to have "crossed over" into eternity, returning, often with regret, to recount sensations of light, peace, and beauty. American popular culture witnessed a growing interest in angels and other spiritual beings, promoted in books, merchandise, and film. One such television series, *Touched by an Angel,* provided weekly stories of ways in which guardian angels visited and cared for persons in need. The death of popular heroes (e.g., Joe DiMaggio in 1999) provoked sentimental media speculation as to their heavenly entrance. The approaching millennium (the year 2000) increased speculation as to the possible return of Jesus Christ and the establishment of the Kingdom of Heaven. Global awareness raised many questions for Christians about the inhabitants of heaven and whether non-Christians would be allowed to enter. Some insisted that God's grace would welcome all—Jews, Hindus, Buddhists, Muslims, and other faithful people—while others feared that such "universalism" would destroy the uniqueness of the Christian witness. Through it all, numerous evangelical subgroups continued to proclaim traditional doctrines of heaven as the blissful abode of those who are truly "born again."

See also AFTERLIFE; ANGELS; DEATH AND DYING; GOD; HELL; NEAR DEATH EXPERIENCES; NIRVANA; SAINTHOOD; SALVATION.

BIBLIOGRAPHY

Kennedy, E. E. "Heaven and Hell." in *Dictionary of Christianity in America.* 1990.

King, M. L., Jr. *Strength to Love.* 1964.

McDannell, C., and B. Lang. *Heaven: A History.* 1988.

Bill J. Leonard

Heaven's Gate

Since the late 1940s, belief in unidentified flying objects (UFOs) and in human contact with aliens from outer space has become a widespread feature of American culture. Religious movements that base themselves on UFO beliefs have accompanied this broader cultural phenomenon, but for the most part these movements have existed at the fringes of American religious life. This relative isolation ended on March 27, 1997, when thirty-nine members of a UFO religion called Heaven's Gate committed mass suicide in the upscale San Diego suburb of Rancho Santa Fe.

Heaven's Gate was the latest name for a spiritual community that had pursued a neognostic path of spiritual transformation since the mid-1970s. The founders of the community were two Texans, Marshall Herff Applewhite (b. 1931) and Bonnie Lu Nettles (b. 1927). Applewhite, the son of a Presbyterian minister, had pursued successful careers as a stage performer and academician before losing his job in the music department at St. Thomas University in Houston because of an improper relationship with a student. Nettles was a married mother of four and a registered nurse when she met Applewhite in 1972. The pair soon came to believe that they were emissaries from a heavenly world called the Kingdom Level Beyond Human. Their mission was to collect those humans who were ready to undergo radical transformation into a higher stage of spiritual evolution. In this activity they believed they were recapitulating the mission of Jesus, who two thousand years earlier had called humanity to a higher evolutionary level without success.

After cutting ties with their families in Houston, Applewhite and Nettles drifted to the West Coast,

Marshall Applewhite, the leader of the Heaven's Gate cult.   (Credit: Reuters/NBC Reuters TV.)

where they began preaching a combinative belief system containing elements of Theosophy, Christian apocalypticism, and UFO lore. The couple claimed that, like the two prophets from the eleventh chapter of Revelation, they would be killed by their enemies, resurrected three days later on live television, and taken to heaven with their followers in a spacecraft. After successful recruiting drives in Los Angeles and southern Oregon in the mid-1970s, the nascent community numbered about 150 members and enjoyed a brief moment of national notoriety as Human Individual Metamorphosis, the "UFO cult." Members then went on a twenty-year odyssey, wandering through America's remotest campgrounds, living on handouts and inheritances, and gradually becoming a strictly controlled, high-intensity spiritual community with a distinct vocabulary of space-age metaphors and biblical references. Nettles, who claimed to receive the primary revelations for the group, died in 1985.

The community rejected all aspects of conventional human life—what they called "mammalian ways"—including family ties, individual careers, sexual relations, personal friendships, and drug and alcohol use. They believed that the world and its customs were under the control of malevolent space aliens called "Luciferians" and that only a complete renunciation of the world and the body would allow them to move on to the next evolutionary level.

After settling in Rancho Santa Fe, the community set up a successful computer business that specialized in website construction. In October 1996 Applewhite

began to predict an imminent "recycling" of the Earth. This "spading under" was necessary so the Earth could serve as a fresh garden for a future human civilization. The only chance to survive this cataclysmic event was to join the Heaven's Gate community and to prepare for rescue by a heavenly spacecraft. The appearance of the Hale-Bopp comet in early 1997 was interpreted as the sign that departure was imminent. Applewhite believed that hidden behind the comet was a spacecraft from the Level Beyond Human, coming to reap the "harvest" of those ready to graduate from Earth's school. On the night of their departure, the community's members drank a lethal cocktail of alcohol and barbiturates, lay down, and tied plastic bags around their heads. The evidence indicates that their mass suicide was planned carefully in advance and undertaken voluntarily in the belief that the moment of ascension was at hand.

The self-destruction of Heaven's Gate dramatizes the dangers faced by religious communities that embrace a worldview of radical perfectionism, utopianism, and apocalyptic world rejection.

See also Anti-Cult Movement; Cult; Cult Awareness Network; Extraterrestrial Guides; Religious Communities; Space Flight; Unidentified Flying Objects.

Bibliography

Balch, Robert W. "Bo and Peep: A Case Study of the Origins of Messianic Leadership." In *Millennialism and Charisma,* edited by Roy Wallis. 1982.

Balch, Robert W. "Waiting for the Ships: Disillusionment and the Revitalization of Faith in Bo and Peep's UFO Cult." In *The Gods Have Landed: New Religions from Other Worlds,* edited by James R. Lewis. 1995.

Phillip Charles Lucas

Hell

In Christian tradition the idea of hell concerns a place of eternal punishment for the wicked or the unredeemed. In some English translations of the Bible the Hebrew word *Sheol* is translated "hell," meaning the abode of the departed. In that case it refers to the place of the dead rather than a fiery realm of eternal damnation. In the New Testament, the Greek word *gehenna* is translated with the word "hell," referring to the place where the unredeemed receive punishment. In general, hell involves a complete separation from God for all eternity. Hell is also considered the abode of Satan, the Evil One. It is the ultimate end of the wicked, and the expression of God's wrath against sin and evil. Many early writings on hell, canonical and noncanonical, are found in apocalyptic literature. Daniel 12:1–3 is the earliest book to describe the rewards of the blessed and the punishment of the wicked. In Jewish literature, 2 Esdras provides extensive detail of the fates of the saved and the damned. In postapostolic Christian literature the Apocalypse of Peter provides frightening depictions of the terrors of the afterlife. The Book of Revelation offers an elaborate description of the end time, complete with a place of punishment seen as a lake of fire where torment is continuous in burning sulfur (14:9–11). Over time, hell became an elaborate doctrine in many Christian communions, made particularly poignant by Dante in his *Inferno* and John Milton in *Paradise Lost.* In its most basic sense in Christian tradition, hell is one of two destinations of human beings after death. Its inhabitants are cut off from God, love, and goodness, and, depending on the emphasis of specific Christian groups, forced to endure terrible forms of punishment.

In America, hell was a source of some debate from the Puritan period to the present. Some preachers, such as Jonathan Edwards (1703–1758), stressed the doctrine of a literal hell, full of fire and brimstone, as the destination of all who were not "in Christ." His most famous sermon, known as "Sinners in the Hands of an Angry God," provides one of the great rhetorical descriptions of hell in sermonic literature. Edwards's contemporary Charles Chauncy (1705–1787), pastor of First Church, Boston, rejected the idea of hell in favor of universal redemption and the benevolence of

the deity. These divisions continued into the twentieth century. Revivalism and evangelicalism tended to assert doctrines of a literal hell, though with varying emphases. Dwight L. Moody (1837–1899) attested to the reality of hell, but acknowledged that he gave more attention to the doctrine of eternal salvation than to damnation. Evangelist Billy Sunday (1862–1935), on the other hand, declared the dangers of a hell that could be escaped only through faith in Christ.

Contemporary American Christianity reflects similar approaches. Throughout the twentieth century, much classic liberalism rejected the idea of eternal punishment in favor of a theology of hope, worked for in this world, and the promise of eternal salvation for all (universalism). Conservative evangelicals generally affirmed a doctrine of eternal punishment, then varied as to their emphasis on the literal nature of a hell. They suggested that all persons who have not had "a personal experience with Jesus Christ" were bound for hell as a result of God's justice against sin. To challenge such an idea was to question the very essence of orthodox Christianity. Southern Baptist fundamentalists, for example, led a movement to promote biblical inerrancy (the belief that the Bible is inerrant in every issue it addresses), which involved a declaration of belief in "a literal, fiery hell." In other words, not only was hell a real place, but the doctrine of hell was a test of Christian orthodoxy. During the 1960s, a group of conservatives produced a film known as *The Burning Hell,* which visually depicted the agonies of the damned. It was widely circulated among Baptist and Pentecostal congregations as a tool for evangelism. Films on hell were simply a visual presentation of rhetorical descriptions that had long been characteristic of American revivalism. During the 1980s and 1990s some conservative churches emphasized the doctrine through dramatizations enacted in "Hell Houses," set up around the Halloween season and aimed at reaching young people with the dangers of eternal damnation, to bring them to Christian conversion. They included tableaus featuring demons, devils, and the damned in various scenes of hellish conditions. Other evangelicals minimized threats of hell in favor of greater emphasis on the rewards of heaven. Premillennialist doctrine (the belief that Christ will return before the thousand-year reign of God) suggests that at the Final Judgment the devil, his angels, and the unredeemed will be cast into the "lake of fire." The immediacy of that return is reason enough for evangelistic efforts to convert the "lost."

Some accepted the idea of divine judgment after death leading to the annihilation of the wicked—that is, unbelievers simply cease to be, while believers live eternally in the gracious presence of God. This belief in "soul annihilationism" is particularly prominent among Seventh-Day Adventists. Jehovah's Witnesses challenge the idea of a literal hell as inconsistent with the benevolent "fatherliness" of God. The Church of Jesus Christ of Latter-Day Saints (Mormons) promotes a belief that persons can escape hell by repenting after death, and by "proxy baptism" received on their behalf by living Mormons. Human events such as the Holocaust or the atomic bomb blasts at Hiroshima and Nagasaki led some to conclude that hell has an earthly dimension, evident in these and other actions that brought suffering to millions. Increasing globalism, pluralism, and interaction with other world religions raised serious questions about the nature of eternal punishment for those who were outside a particular religion or faith.

See also AFTERLIFE; APOCALYPSE; DEATH AND DYING; DEVILS, DEMONS, AND SPIRITS; EVIL; GOD; HEAVEN; SATANIC BIBLE; SATANISTS; SUFFERING.

BIBLIOGRAPHY

Brown, J. C. "Heaven and Hell." In *Dictionary of Christianity in America.* 1990.

Marsden, George. *Fundamentalism and American Culture.* 1980.

Russell, Jeffrey Burton. *The Devil: Perceptions of Evil from Antiquity to Primitive Christianity.* 1977.

                                        Bill J. Leonard

Heresy

Heresy is the denial by a member or members of a religious group of an officially held belief of that group. Churches and other religious organizations typically provide several things for their adherents. One is a code of conduct. Another is a set of worship practices. Another is a worldview. Heresy is a member's rejection of all or part of the worldview. Religious groups routinely regard rejection of their worldview as a threat and respond to it by rejecting the heretic.

Heresy would seem to be out of place in the modern world because modern people are trained to think for themselves and to decide for themselves what to believe. Indeed, the word "heresy" is from the Greek word *hairesis,* "choice," and choices are precisely what modern people are expected to make. In fact, however, religious groups, like all groups that endure for long periods of time, require boundaries, and these routinely include boundaries of acceptable beliefs. Groups in the modern world require bound-

aries as much as groups in the past. The need of churches and other religious groups for identity and boundaries comes into conflict with the need of individuals educated in the modern way to have the freedom to explore and embrace ideas that are in conflict with the ideas of the churches and other religious groups to which they belong, so the fact of heresy continues to occur today as much as in the past, even in groups who do not use the word "heresy."

Some religions have confronted many alleged heretics; others have not. For example, there have been almost no trials for heresy among American Jews and none at all among African-American Christians. On the other hand, there have been many trials for heresy among other American Christians. A possible account of these unexpected facts is that there are religious communities in which the community's practices are emphasized so strongly that if a member follows the practices, the community will ignore any deviant beliefs the member may have.

Those who defend heresy point out the priority of practice over beliefs: Love matters more than faith. Of course, that is itself a belief. They also point out that heresy is an expression of the responsibility of individuals to think for themselves; that today's heresy often becomes tomorrow's orthodoxy ("Christianity began as a Jewish heresy"); and that the treatment of heretics frequently has been morally outrageous. Those who oppose heresy point out that churches and religious groups have rights just as individuals do, and that heresy is cruel because it prevents people from receiving the help they need from the truth offered to them by their church or religious group.

The most famous charges of heresy in American religious history are among the earliest—namely, the witch trials at Salem, Massachusetts, in 1692. Their fame rests in part on the number of persons involved: More than one hundred people were jailed, thirteen women and six men were hanged, and one man was pressed to death for the practice of Witchcraft. New England Puritans understood Witchcraft to be a heresy and a sin. Since it involved using the devil's powers to do grave harm to others, it was also a crime and was punishable as such. Many modern people find it difficult to sympathize with the Puritans because these modern people do not believe in the possibility of Witchcraft. They find stories of modern heresy trials more understandable.

One of the most famous of these came two centuries after the trials at Salem. It was the trial of Charles A. Briggs, a professor of Hebrew and Old Testament at Union Theological Seminary in New York, then affiliated with the Presbyterian Church in the United States. Briggs, an ordained Presbyterian minister, was a proponent of critical study of the Bible and had been led by his studies to conclusions regarding the Bible and other subjects that were thought to be at variance with those of the Presbyterian Church. In 1892 he was accused of heresy, and in 1893 he was found guilty and suspended from the office of a minister in the Presbyterian Church. Union Theological Seminary was disaffiliated from the Presbyterian Church and kept Briggs as a faculty member.

Both the Salem witch trials and the trial of Briggs were formal heresy trials, but many churches and other religious bodies do not have organizational structures for the conduct of heresy trials. Baptists, for example, are organized so there is no body beyond local congregations that has the authority to try any person for heresy. Baptist associations and conventions can decide whether to accept and retain as members congregations with deviant beliefs or practices, but they have no authority to try either congregations or their members for heresy. As a result, the treatment of heresy among Baptists is informal rather than formal.

This in turn means that among Baptists and similar denominations it is almost always professors or other persons employed at denominational institutions who are tried for heresy. For example, in 1983 the Southern Baptist Theological Seminary refused to renew the annual contract of its longtime professor of theology, Dale Moody, because of Moody's beliefs about the revocability of salvation, and in 1993 the same institution dismissed theology professor Molly Marshall because of some of her views about God and the Bible. Neither Moody nor Marshall was formally tried for heresy, but each was dismissed from teaching because of allegedly deviant theological beliefs. When an accused heretic is a professor, issues related to heresy become entangled with issues of academic freedom, a freedom that is essential for the flourishing of institutions of higher education.

It seems unlikely either that heresy will disappear from American religions that embrace beliefs as part of their identity and boundaries, or that such religions will be able to maintain their identity and boundaries without from time to time exercising some form of discipline over alleged heretics.

See also CHURCH; CREEDS; CULT; DENOMINATION; DOGMATISM; FREEDOM OF RELIGION; RELIGIOUS PERSECUTION; SHUNNING.

BIBLIOGRAPHY

Berger, Peter. *The Heretical Imperative.* 1979.
Congregation for the Doctrine of the Faith. *Instruction on the Ecclesial Vocation of the Theologian.* 1990.
Noll, Mark A. *Between Faith and Criticism.* 1986.
Shriver, George H., ed. *Dictionary of Heresy Trials in American Christianity.* 1997.

Fisher Humphreys

Hermanas, Las.

See Las Hermanas.

Heschel, Abraham Joshua

(1907–1972), theologian, activist, and poet.

Rabbi Abraham Joshua Heschel symbolized traditional Judaism for many Jews and non-Jews from the 1950s through his death. He was born in Warsaw, Poland, and educated in Berlin, receiving a Ph.D. from the University of Berlin in 1933 and graduating from the Hoschschule für die Wissenschaft des Judentums (Advanced Institute for the Scientific Study of Judaism) in 1932. His earliest publications were love poems written in Yiddish, the language created out of Old High German and Hebrew and used by most Jews in Europe. Nevertheless, his thought and personality were peculiarly suited for the American setting. Soon after arriving in the United States in 1940 from Hitler's Germany to teach at the seminary for American Reform rabbis, the Hebrew Union College–Jewish Institute of Religion in Cincinnati, Ohio, he mastered English. His earliest publications in English (published between 1942 and 1951) exhibit poetic and expressive language. His greatest importance, however, lies in his ability to represent the theological, religious, and political ideals of many Jews of his time.

Many Jews feel torn between traditional and modernistic approaches to Jewish observance. Tension between adherence to past laws and dynamic adaptation to the present arises again and again in Heschel's writing, and he addresses the peculiar dilemma of American Jews, who are often drawn in two directions. His theological works provide a map to the inner struggle that characterizes many American Jews.

Many American Jews see themselves within a pluralistic setting in which differences among Jewish denominations or between Jew and non-Jew pale in the face of common concerns. Heschel's distinction between "theology" that focuses on divisive issues of specific beliefs and "depth theology" that plumbs the common human concerns of all religious souls helped ground that pluralism in a theoretical foundation. Heschel lived according to his principles. He counted among his friends leading Christian thinkers such as John C. Bennett, Daniel Berrigan, William

Sloan Coffin, and Reinhold Niebuhr. He conferred with Pope Paul VI in Rome concerning the Second Vatican Council statement on the Jews. He advocated cooperation among different religious groups. His final book, published posthumously, confirms his open pluralism by comparing the teachings of the Christian Søren Kierkegaard and the Hasidic rabbi Mendel of Kotzk (*A Passion for Truth*, 1973).

Heschel's final influence on the American community came from his ability to articulate a religiously based political activism. He addressed White House conferences, speaking on problems of youth (1960) and aging (1961). He spoke out at conferences on race and religion in Chicago (1963) and in New York (1964). He marched with Martin Luther King, Jr., at Selma, Alabama, in 1965. From 1966 until his death Heschel was an outspoken opponent of the American government's policies in Vietnam. The *New York Times* from 1965 onward frequently quoted his views on social and political concerns such as segregation, American policy in Vietnam, election preferences, education, and the Soviet Union's treatment of Jews. Many of his central ideas on these subjects are found in his book *The Insecurity of Freedom* (1966). Many Jews identified with the ideals he expressed.

See also BELONGING, RELIGIOUS; JEWISH IDENTITY; JUDAISM; KING, MARTIN LUTHER, JR.; NIEBUHR, REINHOLD; RABBINATE; RELIGIOUS COMMUNITIES; VATICAN II.

BIBLIOGRAPHY

Heschel, Abraham Joshua. *God in Search of Man: A Philosophy of Judaism.* 1955.

Heschel, Abraham Joshua. *The Insecurity of Freedom: Essays on Human Existence.* 1966.

Heschel, Abraham Joshua. *A Passion for Truth.* 1973.

Kaplan, Edward K., and Samuel H. Dresner. *Abraham Joshua Heschel: Prophetic Witness.* 1998.

Kasimow, Harold. *Divine-Human Encounter: A Study of Abraham Joshua Heschel.* 1979.

Daniel Breslauer

High Holy Days, Jewish.

See Jewish High Holy Days.

Hinduism

Of all the religions originating in Asia, Hinduism has the longest history in the United States. The Hindu tradition initially came to the country by way of books.

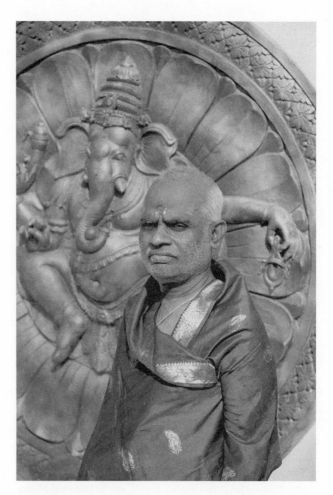

Hindu priest in Queens, New York. In the background is a depiction of the elephant-headed Hindu god Ganesha.   (Credit: CORBIS/Jacques M. Chenet.)

Orientalists translated Hindu scriptures into English in the late eighteen century, long before they turned their attentions to Buddhist translations. So when Transcendentalists such as Ralph Waldo Emerson and Henry David Thoreau mused about Asian religions in the 1830s and 1840s, they were for the most part musing about Hindu thought. Thoreau praised the "vast and cosmogonal philosophy" of the Bhagavad-Gita and fancied himself a yogi. Many of Emerson's essays and poems, including "Illusion," "Compensation," and "Brahma," were inspired by Hindu ideas. By the mid-nineteenth century, however, Buddhism had replaced Hinduism as the Asian religion of choice for American intellectuals. Theosophists Helena Blavatsky and Henry Steel Olcott formally converted to Buddhism in 1880, and the Boston Brahmins of the late nineteenth century were far more interested in Buddhist than in Hindu scriptures.

Hinduism's U.S. history changed dramatically when people, not just books, began to give voice to the tradition. Swami Vivekananda became the first Hindu missionary to the United States when he accepted an invitation to attend the World's Parliament of Religions, an interreligious congress held in Chicago in 1893 as part of the World's Columbian Exposition (World's Fair). By most accounts, Swami Vivekananda, a teacher of Advaita Vedanta, a monistic form of Hinduism that preaches religious tolerance and views Brahman (God) as equivalent to Atman (Self), was the most celebrated figure at the Parliament. His splendid British English and sharp intellect captured the imagination of the crowds and gave the lie to stereotypes about heathens from Asia. After the Parliament, Vivekananda lectured widely across the United States. In 1894 in New York City, he established the first of many Vedanta societies. He also paved the way for generations of Hindu gurus to come.

Like Vivekananda, Swami Paramahansa Yogananda came to the United States to attend an interreligious conference, in his case the International Congress of Religious Liberals, held in Boston in 1920 under the auspices of Unitarians, who since the nineteenth century had demonstrated a keen interest in monotheistic forms of Hinduism. Swami Yogananda also traveled across the United States, supporting himself as a lecturer. Unlike his predecessor, however, Yogananda did not return to his homeland. And instead of teaching Vivekananda's Advaita Vedanta philosophy, Yogananda spread the practice of "Kriya Yoga," which he promoted as the "airplane route" to God-realization. Yogananda established the Self-Realization Fellowship (incorporated in 1935), which swiftly replaced the Vedanta Society as America's largest Hindu organization.

Hinduism emerged on the public scene in the 1960s, when Maharishi Mahesh Yogi replaced Swami Yogananda as the most prominent guru in the United States. The Maharishi taught Transcendental Meditation (TM), a mantra-chanting practice that he and his followers insisted was secular rather than religious. Although the Maharishi arrived in the United States from India in 1959, he soon came to personify a wide array of Hindu teachers who immigrated after 1965. Sharing the Maharishi's spotlight was A.C. Bhaktivedanta Swami Prabhupada, whose International Society for Krishna Consciousness (ISKCON) and its Hare Krishnas brought a new style of Hindu practice—popular devotionalism—to the U.S. scene.

Hinduism was also represented by U.S.-born teachers, such as *Be Here Now* (1971) author Ram Dass and by Indian-born gurus such as Satya Sai Baba, who managed to obtain American followers without ever leaving India. After capturing the imagination of the rock group the Beatles in the 1960s, Hinduism achieved star status again in the 1990s through the well-publicized flirtations of pop stars Madonna and Sting with Yoga. As the century drew to a close, however, Buddhism (now in its Tibetan form) had once again replaced Hinduism as the Asian religion of choice among trendsetting Americans.

One reason for Hinduism's low profile was the relatively small size of the Indian immigrant community. Immigration from Asia to the United States was initiated by the Chinese, who first came following the discovery of gold in California in 1848. The Japanese came next, and they were followed by Asian Indians, who came in far fewer numbers and did not begin to arrive until the first decade of the twentieth century. All these pioneering Indian immigrants were called "Hindoos," but few actually practiced what we now call Hinduism. Most were Sikhs (practitioners of a distinct religious tradition that creatively combines elements of Islam and Hinduism), and roughly one-third were Muslims.

Like the Chinese and the Japanese who preceded them, Asian Indians were objects of racial and religious hatred. A series of anti-Indian riots broke out on the West Coast in 1907. In 1917 the U.S. Congress responded to popular complaints about the "Hindoo invasion" by including India in restrictive legislation that effectively cut off immigration from India and other "barred zones" until 1965. Hinduism itself came under attack in Katherine Mayo's *Mother India* (1927), which denounced the religion as both inhumane and sexist. In the 1970s, "anticult" activists focused their energies on "deprogramming" family members from ISKCON, and American feminist theologian Mary Daly revived the hostile spirit of Mayo's *Mother India* when she reduced the Hindu tradition to widow-burning in *Gyn/Ecology* (1978).

After the passage of less restrictive immigration legislation in 1965, immigration from Asia in general and India in particular boomed. The 1990 U.S. census counted 815,447 Asian Indians in the United States. Indians who arrived in the United States after 1965 differed significantly from the earlier immigrant cohort. In the early twentieth century, Indian immigrants came from rural areas and worked in the United States as agricultural laborers. Almost all were men, and many came from the Punjab region in northern India. In religion, Sikhism and Islam predominated. In the later period, nearly all were Hindus. Men and women came together with their families. They hailed from a wide variety of Indian regions, settled in urban rather than rural areas, and worked disproportionately in professional occupations. In studies conducted in the 1990s, these Indian Americans ranked exceptionally high in both education and income. Perhaps more than any other group of Asian immigrants, they lent plausibility to the now-contested "model minority" stereotype.

But they belied stereotypes about immigrants losing their distinctive religious beliefs and practices to meld into Judeo-Christian America. In fact, post-1965 immigrants from India appear, in many cases, to have become more rather than less religious after immigrating to the United States. In a country that was coming to value multiculturalism as much as it had once valued assimilation, being Hindu was becoming a way of crafting an American identity.

Thanks to this trend, combined with the social and economic successes of Indian Americans, the period from the mid-1970s to the end of the century was a bricks-and-mortar era characterized by temple building. In 1977, Hindus consecrated the country's first major Indian-style Hindu temples: the Sri Ganesha Temple (now called the Maha Vallabha Ganapati Devasthanam) in Flushing, New York; and the Sri Venkateswara Temple in Pittsburgh, Pennsylvania. In 1999, roughly 150 Hindu temples had been consecrated in the United States, and there was at least one in virtually every major U.S. city.

While these temples preserved many elements of Indian temple architecture, they added some American twists. Because Hindu families could initially afford to build only one temple in each urban area, U.S. temples tended to accommodate a wide variety of regional, linguistic, and sectarian differences. While in India even a small village could often accommodate separate shrines to key divinities such as Shiva, Vishnu, and Mahadevi, in U.S. temples those deities learned to get along. At Flushing's Sri Ganesha Temple, a model of this new ecumenism, at least thirty-two deities coexisted amiably, and members could be heard speaking Hindi, Gujarati, Tamil, and Bengali. American temples also distinguished themselves from their Indian forebears by carving out space for an array of social activities that in India would have taken place elsewhere. Hindu temples in the United States typically included sanctuaries for congregational worship (rare in India) as well as kitchens and meeting rooms for social functions and the education of children. Because many of these activities took place in temple basements, one scholar has referred to this development as "split-level Hinduism."

Several young Indian girls performing a traditional dance at the Hindu festival of Diwali in Seattle, Washington, ca. 1995.   (Credit: CORBIS/Dean Wong.)

At the end of the century, American Hinduism remained an ongoing experiment. Like members of other immigrant communities, American Hindus grappled with how to live in a diaspora as transnationals with loyalties to two countries. Student members of the vibrant Hindu Students Council (established in 1990) wrestled with how closely they should align themselves with the Vishwa Hindu Parishad (VHP), India's Hindu nationalist party. And parents struggled to inculcate in their children values that will help them succeed in a country whose business was business without jettisoning the spiritual and ethical values handed down to them by ancestors and in books.

See also BELONGING, RELIGIOUS; BHAGAVAD-GĪTĀ; CHAKRA; GURU; INTERNATIONAL SOCIETY FOR KRISHNA CONSCIOUSNESS; RELIGIOUS COMMUNITIES; TEMPLE; TRANSCENDENTAL MEDITATION; VEDANTA SOCIETY; YOGA.

BIBLIOGRAPHY

Fenton, John Y. *Transplanting Religious Traditions: Asian Indians in America.* 1988.

Jackson, Carl T. *Oriental Religions in American Thought: Nineteenth-Century Explorations.* 1981.

Jackson, Carl T. *Vedanta for the West: The Ramakrishna Movement in the United States.* 1994.

Jensen, Joan M. *Passage from India: Asian Indian Immigrants in North America.* 1988.

Tweed, Thomas A., and Stephen Prothero, eds. *Asian Religions in America: A Documentary History.* 1999.

Williams, Raymond Brady. *Religions of Immigrants from India and Pakistan: New Threads in the American Tapestry.* 1988.

Williams, Raymond Brady, ed. *A Sacred Thread: Modern Transmission of Hindu Traditions in India and Abroad.* 1992.

Stephen Prothero

Holiness Movement

The Holiness Movement arose within nineteenth-century Methodism in response to the sense that Methodists were neglecting their distinctive doctrine of Christian perfection. In 1839, Timothy Merritt began publishing *The Guide to Christian Perfection,* which became *The Guide to Holiness,* a periodical devoted to urging on American Methodists a second experience of grace. Advocates of the Holiness Movement maintained that the "grand depositum" John Wesley had bequeathed his followers was captured in the notion that the Christian life should be shaped by a sanctifying moment, a "second definite work of grace,"

which would replace the love of sinning with a love for God that would make sin distasteful. This was not sinlessness, and Wesley left some ambiguity about whether the change would be gradual or instantaneous. His American interpreters generally insisted that entire sanctification, or the "second blessing," would be manifested in an instantaneous transformation. The believer would testify to the experience, thus owning it and coming into accountability for its continuance.

While the Holiness Movement always had an interdenominational following, Methodists were its principle apologists and supporters. Prominent among them was Phoebe Palmer, the wife of a New York City homeopathic physician. A capable speaker and author, Palmer promoted taking the experience by faith. It required an act of full consecration, a "laying of all on the altar." The altar, she demonstrated by selective use of scripture, was Christ, and the altar "sanctified the gift." This combination of imagery from the Old and New Testaments gained a wide following and worked to make the second blessing more accessible.

Holiness teaching generally found wide acceptance in pre-Civil War Methodism, with prominent bishops advocating the message. Several small groups that affirmed two definite works of grace broke from the Methodist Church before the Civil War. Those who left had a combination of other quarrels with the denomination in addition to questions about holiness. They argued about things like lodge membership, free pews, church organs, and slavery. Objecting to the apparent growing prosperity and this-worldliness of Methodism, the Wesleyan Church and the Free Methodists created their own organizations. This early Holiness Movement sparked social reform and had vast interdenominational appeal. At Oberlin College, Charles Finney and Asa Mahan taught perfection by consecration and faith and enlisted their supporters to work to perfect American society as well as their souls. By mid-century, Christian perfection had become a prominent cultural theme.

After the Civil War, the Holiness Movement became increasingly marginalized from the centers of power of the church. The formation of the National Camp Meeting Association for the Promotion of Holiness in 1867 gave the movement institutional structure. From the 1880s, a succession of Holiness associations or leaders separated from the Methodist Episcopal Church, both North and South, to establish new religious associations. Such come-outism was not mandated by the church, although Methodist conferences sometimes found it necessary to issue calls for balanced views on the subject. Those who placed sanctification at the center of the religion seemed inclined to radical behavior as well as neglectful of other aspects of church doctrine and life. The Holiness Movement of the late nineteenth century tended to call Methodists to "old-time religion," as the denomination moved increasingly toward respectability and the social gospel.

While no single Holiness denomination emerged, the movement's energies produced the Salvation Army, the Church of the Nazarene, the Church of God (Anderson), the Holiness Church of California, the Fire-Baptized Holiness Association, the Pillar of Fire, the Church of God in Christ, and many more. Some of these early associations, like the Church of God in Christ, soon identified with the emerging Pentecostal Movement.

The Holiness Movement actively created and supported schools. For example, Olivet Nazarene University, Roberts Wesleyan College, Houghton College, Seattle Pacific University, Asbury College, and Asbury Theological Seminary are among those that have served the movement for many years. While the Holiness Movement since the mid-twentieth century is expressed primarily in denominations that have moved into membership in the National Association of Evangelicals, aspects of the movement's message retain transdenominational appeal. The academics, publications, and programs clustered around Asbury Seminary are one of its most enduring expressions.

The Holiness Movement molded particular forms of piety, shaped specific denominations, and provided devotional literature and hymns with appeal across denominations. Its later post–Civil War character played a role in the emergence of Pentecostalism. While a theological notion of Christian perfection stands at its core, it combines that notion with conservative evangelical predilections to find its niche in the religious scene.

See also EVANGELICAL CHRISTIANITY; METHODISM; PENTECOSTAL AND CHARISMATIC CHRISTIANITY; SALVATION ARMY.

BIBLIOGRAPHY

Dieter, Melvin. *The Nineteenth Century Holiness Movement.* 1998.

Jones, Charles, *The Holiness Movement.* 1974.

Smith, Timothy L. *Called Unto Holiness: Revivalism and Social Reform.* 1962.

Synan, Vinson. *The Holiness-Pentecostal Movement.* 1972.

Wacker, Grant A. "Travail of a Broken Family: Radical Evangelical Responses to the Emergence of Pentecostalism in America, 1906–1916" In *Pentecostal Currents in American Protestantism,* edited by Edith L. Blumhofer et al. 1999.

Edith L. Blumhofer

Holistic Health

Religion and medicine have been closely connected in almost every culture in world history. Indeed, both seek to move persons from a condition of brokenness to wholeness and to infuse them with a vitality for living. The Western scientific tradition, however, is nearly unique in that it operates on philosophical assumptions that separate the physical and the spiritual aspects of human life, concentrating only on the former. As a result, medicine has become increasingly technological, bureaucratic, and impersonal. The holistic health movement emerged as a reaction against modern medicine's abandonment of a philosophical vision that sees the interdependence of humanity's physical, mental, and spiritual natures. Its basic premise is that "every human being is a unique, holistic, interdependent relationship of body, mind, emotions, and spirit" (Belknap, Blau, and Grossman, p. 25). Advocates of holistic approaches to health are thus committed to a metaphysical interpretation of reality that goes well beyond the materialism of modern science and that frankly acknowledges the spiritual dimension of human well-being.

Holistic health encompasses a wide variety of beliefs and practices, ranging from the commonplace to the esoteric. Included in this category are such diverse practices as dietary systems, use of botanics or herbs, massage therapies, positive thinking programs, Eastern meditational disciplines, New Age color or crystal healing, and twelve-step programs. One introductory text explains that although holistic approaches to health are quite distinct from one another, they share a "reliance on treatment modalities that foster the self-regenerative and self-reparative processes of natural healing" (Otto and Knight, p. 3). This characterization of holistic medicine's distinctive outlook is important in that it echoes many of the philosophical themes rooted in nineteenth-century alternative medicine (e.g., Thomsonianism, hydropathy, Christian health regimens, mesmerism) as well as the tradition of "nature religion" in America. Holistic medical systems have faith in the beneficence and essentially progressive character of nature. This reverence for nature is matched by a belief in the fundamental dignity and sovereignty of the individual, especially over and against institutional authority. Holistic approaches to health are less invasive, concentrating on strengthening the individual's own system rather than assaulting it through surgery or heavy doses of pharmaceutics. And finally, holistic medicine pays attention to the attitudinal and even moral aspects of health, revealing its belief that health is but one aspect of a person's broader orientation to life. It is clear, then, that holistic health practices have gained widespread

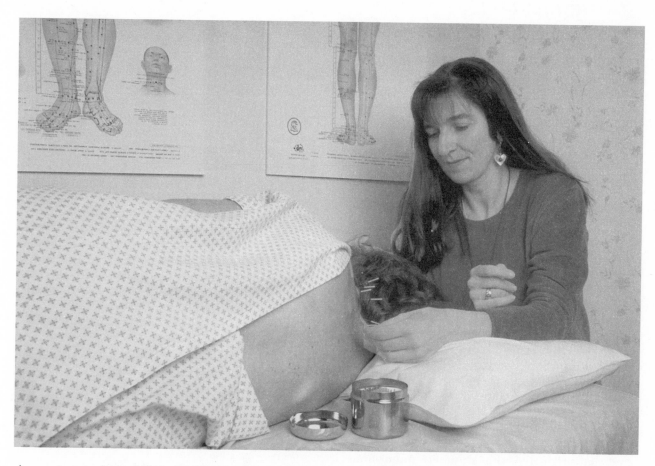

An acupuncturist in Missoula, Montana (ca. 1993), sticks a needle into the upper back of a patient. (Credit: © Bruce Hands/Stock, Boston, PNI.)

popularity not only for their therapeutic value but also for their ability to articulate important strands of American religious and cultural thought.

Following the lead of such influential American philosophers as Ralph Waldo Emerson and William James, holistic health systems espouse the view that every human being has untapped potential resources, and powers. Some holistic practices (particularly those that emphasize nutrition and exercise) seek to amplify the body's own natural healing process. Others, however, share Emerson's and James's more overtly metaphysical belief that certain mystical states of consciousness allow humans to become especially receptive to the inflow of a higher spiritual power. Thus some holistic health practices (particularly those that emphasize some form of meditation) seek to help people inwardly align themselves with resources and powers that are decidedly spiritual rather than physical.

Norman Cousins and Bernard Siegel were two of the late twentieth century's most widely recognized spokespersons for holistic healing. Cousins, former editor of *Saturday Review,* confronted a serious illness

for which medical physicians gave him a rather bleak prognosis. Cousins's autobiography recounts how he willed himself back to health through a deliberate regimen of optimistic and cheerful thinking. His lengthy remission brought a great deal of popular attention to the role of attitudinal factors in both creating and curing disease. Cousins attributed the mind's curative powers to the existence of the "life force" that drives organic life toward perfectibility. Cousins also hinted that this life force was metaphysical in nature and that mystical states of mind have the power to reveal the highest possibilities that humans can attain. Physician Bernard Siegel has been even more forceful in aligning holistic health practices with a decidedly metaphysical worldview. Siegel instructs cancer patients to read books on meditation and psychic phenomena so they might learn practical techniques for tapping into more-than-physical healing energies. According to Siegel, our unconscious minds are connected to the energy of God; hence any ailment can be healed.

Another example of the connection between holistic health and Americans' fascination with novel religious ideas can be seen in the five thousand nurses who have studied Dolores Krieger's technique of Therapeutic Touch. Krieger, who was a nursing instructor at New York University and a student of theosophical teachings, developed a healing technique predicated on the existence of a universal energy underlying all life processes. She claims that as long as an individual is continuously receptive to the inflow of this vital energy, which she refers to with the Hindu term *prana*, he or she remains healthy; illness ensues when some area of the body develops a deficit of *prana*. Using healing techniques highly reminiscent of nineteenth-century mesmerism, Krieger explains that healers can learn to become inwardly receptive to the flow of this spiritual energy into their own system and in turn impart it to others with the touch of their hands. New converts to Therapeutic Touch write that the philosophy behind this healing system opened them up to ideas and experiences that significantly enhanced their spiritual outlook on life. Persons who had been trained in nursing science become excited to read books on yogic meditation, Tibetan mysticism, and other techniques that might assist them in opening themselves to the flow of the universal power of wholeness.

Perhaps the most widely practiced form of holistic medicine is the twelve-step program of personal renewal that originated with Alcoholics Anonymous. AA's founder, Bill W., warned that people do not have the resources within themselves to bring about the kind of personal transformation necessary to heal profound cases of inner division. The key to such personal regeneration, he wrote, is "the feeling of being at one with God and man." Yet Bill W. was wary of organized religion. Knowing that many alcoholics are painfully conscious of their inability to live up to the moral absolutes associated with biblical religion, he instead sought to articulate a spiritual outlook that was free of dogmas and fixed traditions. AA's "twelve step" program is a unique blend of mysticism and self-help philosophy. Referring to itself as "spiritual rather than religious," it teaches people to develop a sense of inner connection with God while yet taking responsibility for their own decisions and actions.

Holistic approaches to health and healing are most prevalent among white Americans who are from twenty-five to fifty years of age and who have relatively more education and higher incomes. Few of these people, therefore, are attracted to these beliefs and practices because of ignorance or poverty. Indeed, it appears that one of the most vital functions performed by holistic health philosophies is that they introduce Americans to alternative visions of their spiritual potential. A 1978 volume titled *The Holistic Health Handbook* described dozens of holistic health systems, such as acupuncture, iridology, reflexology, t'ai chji, yoga, Ayurvedic medicine, and chiropractic medicine. Yet even the volume's Introduction suggests that "more important than the techniques is the expansion of consciousness they foster" (p. 13). It appears that many contemporary Americans are eager to explore ideas that fall just as far outside of conventional church religion as they do outside of conventional Western science. For this reason holistic health systems have succeeded in making spirituality a vital part of everyday life, even for those who feel disenfranchised with established religious institutions.

See also ALTERNATIVE MEDICINE; HEALTH; HUMAN POTENTIAL MOVEMENT; MACROBIOTICS; NATURE RELIGION; NEW AGE SPIRITUALITY; PEALE, NORMAN VINCENT; QUANTUM HEALING; TRANSCENDENTAL MEDITATION; TWELVE-STEP PROGRAM; YOGA.

BIBLIOGRAPHY

Belknap, Mary, Robert Blau, and Rosaline Grossman, eds. *Case Studies and Methods in Humanistic Medicine.* 1975.

Fuller, Robert C. *Alternative Medicine and American Religious Life.* 1989.

Gevitz, Norman, ed. *Other Healers: Unorthodox Medicine in America.* 1988.

The Holistic Health Handbook. 1978.

Kurtz, Ernest. *Not-God: A History of Alcoholics Anonymous.* 1991.

Otto, Herbert, and James Knight, eds. *Dimensions in Wholistic Healing.* 1979.

Robert C. Fuller

Holocaust

The word "holocaust" is derived from the biblical term "holocauston" (Septuagint) "for "burnt offering" made in sacrifice to God. The term—capitalized—began to be used by scholars in the late 1960s and early 1970s to refer to the death of approximately six million Jews at the hands of the Nazis during World War II. Two historical events in the 1960s brought Jews and Christians in America to reflect on its religious implications. For Jews it was the 1967 Arab-Israeli War (also known as the "Six-Day War"). For Christians it was the Second Vatican Council of the Roman Catholic Church (1962–1965) and its declaration concerning the Jews in the document *Nostra Aetate* (1964).

Before the 1967 war, the death of six million was too painful for most to speak of. To talk about it raised deep and troubling religious questions for traditional

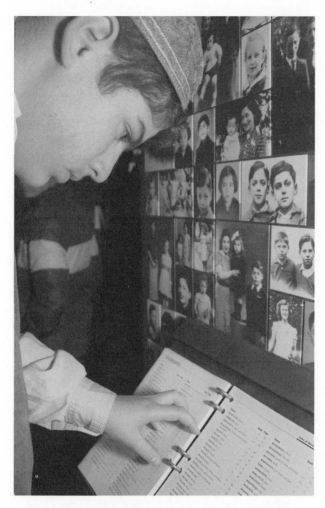

A fourteen-year-old boy searching for his great-grand-mother's name in a book listing Holocaust victims, at the Museum of Jewish Heritage in New York City, April 12, 1999.   (Credit: AP/Wide World Photos.)

Jewish identity: Where was God during the Holocaust? Why did God not rescue Jews from the Nazis, as he had rescued them from the ancient Egyptians? How can Jews continue to believe in the covenant of Sinai when God seems to have abandoned them to near-annihilation? Then the 1967 war seemed to repeat the threat of total annihilation but reverse the outcome. Against all odds, the Israeli Army overwhelmed the Arab armies who seemed to be intent on obliterating the Jewish state created by the United Nations in 1948. To many Jews the State of Israel became a symbol of God's saving presence in history, counterbalancing the devastation of the Holocaust. After this the Holocaust could be talked about and examined without leading to despair. Therefore the decades following the 1967 war gave rise to intense and unprecedented theological reflection by Jews on the Holocaust.

These reflections explored the crisis of Jewish identity created by the Holocaust and offered a variety of responses. For example, at one extreme the key author has been Richard Rubenstein, whose book *After Auschwitz* was published in 1966, on the eve of the 1967 war. For Rubenstein the covenantal God of Exodus died at Auschwitz. Jews must stop looking at history mythologically and expecting God to come and rescue them. However, this does not mean the end of Judaism; on the contrary, Jewish ritual and Jewish identity become more important, not less, as ways for Jews to sustain their identity in a hostile world.

In the middle, several Jewish authors responded to Rubenstein. These authors agreed with him that traditional pre-Holocaust Jewish identity was no longer viable, while disagreeing that this requires abandoning all belief in God. For example, Elie Wiesel chose instead to "wrestle with God." Putting God on trial, he accused God of being the one who broke the covenant, while Jews have chosen to remain faithful to it. Emil Fackenheim argued that God was present in history, even at Auschwitz. As proof he indicates that the persistence of Jews in affirming their identity after the Holocaust indicates that both secular and religious Jews seem to have heard a silent yet commanding voice from Auschwitz, commanding them to remain Jews so as not to grant Hitler a posthumous victory in his attempt to destroy Jews and Judaism. Irving Greenberg argued that Jews are tossed back and forth between belief and unbelief and are reduced to "momentary faith." In some moments the promise of the Sinai covenant sustains them, whereas in other moments Sinai is overwhelmed by the smoke and flames of Auschwitz, and faith seems impossible. What continues to give each of these authors hope is the rebirth of the State of Israel, giving rise to a shared theme of Holocaust and redemption.

Finally, at the other extreme one can find authors who deny that the Holocaust should have any impact at all on Jewish faith. Jacob Neusner, for example, argues that the focus on Holocaust and redemption through the rebirth of the State of Israel has led American Jews to embrace a superficial Jewish identity that requires nothing from them. He urges a return to the observance of the dual Torah of rabbinic Judaism.

The Holocaust creates a different sort of crisis of identity for Christians. For Christians the problem focuses on the role that the long history of Christian anti-Judaism played in supporting Nazi anti-Semitism, the high level of cooperation with the Nazis, and the lack of widespread Christian efforts to save Jews from the Nazis. For two thousand years Christianity taught that Jews were a people rejected by God for failing to recognize Jesus as the messiah and for orchestrating his crucifixion—a people superseded or replaced by Christians as God's new chosen people. But the Holocaust seems to have forced a reversal of those teachings. The Vatican II document *Nostra Aetate* was the first in Christian history to acknowledge the ongoing legitimacy of God's covenant with Israel. It also rejected all anti-Semitism, including Christian attempts to blame the Jews, as a people, for the death of Christ.

Some three and a half decades later, at the turn of the millennium, most of the major denominations of Christianity, both Catholic and Protestant, have issued official church proclamations acknowledging guilt for the history of Christian anti-Judaic teachings and for the moral failure of Christians during the Holocaust, and affirming the ongoing validity of the Jewish covenant. Indeed, it is one of the ironies of the Holocaust that precisely at the point when Jews are questioning the validity of the Jewish covenant, Christians, for the first time in history, are affirming it.

Three of the most important issues left unsettled by these official church declarations are: (1) how the "new covenant" of Christianity is related to the Mosaic covenant of the Jews; (2) how Christians can consider Jesus the messiah without claiming to "supersede" Judaism; and (3) how Christian ethics will need to be reformed. The first two questions are widely explored by contemporary Christian theologians. Protestant theologians such as Paul van Buren and A. Roy Eckhardt have argued for a one-covenant theory, whereas others, such as Catholic theologian John Pawlikowski, have argued for a two-covenant theory. Both groups have generally tended to look to Paul's letter to the Romans (especially chapters 9 to 11) for an alternative to the "myth of supersession." Paul suggests that gentiles are a "wild olive branch" grafted onto the natural olive tree of Judaism through their faith in Jesus. The one-covenant theorists generally read Paul as saying that Christianity adds nothing new except to extend the promises of Abraham to include the Gentiles, whereas the two-covenant theorists suggest that Christianity offers a new covenant that in various ways adds to and complements the Jewish covenant.

On the messianic question there has arisen a considerable theological consensus that Jesus is not the messiah of Judaism, at least not yet, for only when Jesus returns to create a new heaven and earth will he have fulfilled the messianic role. On this view, both Jews and Christians still await the coming of the messiah. It remains to be seen which of these positions, if any, the churches adopt into their official teachings in the new millennium.

Finally, the neglected question of the impact of the Holocaust on Christian ethics has been taken up by Protestant theologian Darrell J. Fasching. He criti-

cizes the traditional Christian ethic of obedience as playing into the hands of the Nazis and seeks to learn something from a dialogue with Jewish authors such as Elie Wiesel and Irving Greenberg about the Abrahamic *chutzpah,* or audacity (Genesis 18:25) to question all authority, even God if necessary, to avoid the kind of unquestioning obedience that made the Holocaust possible in the heart of Christendom.

See also ANTI-SEMITISM; JEWISH IDENTITY; JEWISH RENEWAL; JUDAISM; JUDEO-CHRISTIAN TRADITION; RELIGIOUS PERSECUTION; SECOND COMING; VATICAN II; ZIONISM.

BIBLIOGRAPHY

Fackenheim, Emil. *God's Presence in History.* 1970.

Fasching, Darrell J. *Narrative Theology After Auschwitz: From Alienation to Ethics.* 1992.

Pawlikowski, John T. *Christ in the Light of Christian-Jewish Dialogue.* 1982.

Rubenstein, Richard L. *After Auschwitz: Radical Theology and Contemporary Judaism.* 1966; 2nd ed., 1992.

van Buren, Paul. *A Christian Theology of the People Israel.* 1983.

Wiesel, Elie. *A Jew Today.* 1978.

Darrell J. Fasching

Holy Bible.

See Bible.

Holy Ghost.

See Trinity.

Holy Land

The concept of sacred space has held an important meaning for members of numerous religious traditions in America. However, in America the term "Holy Land" has been used almost exclusively by Christians and Jews to refer to the biblical Land of Israel, the modern geopolitical region of Palestine.

American interest in the biblical Holy Land goes back to the early European settlements in America. The New England settlers related to America as Canaan, and to themselves as the Sons of Israel, who had entered into a covenant with God and reached the promised land. English settlers gave their towns biblical names and looked on their experience as building the kingdom of God on Earth. The American-

Protestant understanding of the Holy Land shifted with the "rediscovery" of Palestine by Western nations in the early nineteenth century. American Protestants began traveling to Palestine as missionaries and explorers of the land. For many of those who adhered to a premillennialist messianic outlook, exploring and evangelizing in Palestine held a special meaning and remained high on their agenda. American missionaries labored in Palestine throughout the nineteenth and twentieth centuries, leaving their mark on the educational, medical, and cultural infrastructure of the country. A number of American groups motivated by messianic hopes settled in Palestine in the mid- and late nineteenth century, expecting to witness the events of the end times firsthand.

In the latter decades of the nineteenth century and the beginning of the twentieth, a new school of messianic hope, dispensationalism, strongly influenced American understanding of the Holy Land, particularly among the conservative evangelical segment of American Protestantism. For believers in the Second Coming of Jesus, Palestine, or modern Israel, is not only the historical site where Jesus taught, suffered, and was crucified, but also the place to which he will return to defeat Antichrist and establish his thousand-year reign on Earth. Accordingly, American evangelicals have taken special interest in the developments in Palestine and in the Jewish national movement. They have interpreted such events as the building of Jewish settlements in Palestine, the Balfour Declaration of 1917, and the establishment of the State of Israel in 1948 as "signs of the time," indicating that the messianic era is near, and that the events of the end times are beginning to unfold. The reading of current events in the Holy Land as the fulfillment of prophecy has been strongly enhanced by the Six-Day War of 1967 and its aftermath. The Israeli conquest of the historical parts of Jerusalem has stirred the messianic imagination and convinced many American premillennialists that the State of Israel has been established for a purpose, and that the time is near for the arrival of the Messiah. Leading American evangelists, such as Billy Graham, Jerry Falwell, Pat Robertson, and Hal Lindsey, have openly speculated on the connection between developments in the area and the messianic timetable.

The Mormon understanding of the Holy Land is similar to that of conservative Protestants. Like the Puritans, the Mormons have perceived America as the promised land and have expected the gathering of the Saints, the Sons of Israel of the tribe of Joseph, to take place in America. At the same time, the Book of Mormon describes a return of the Jews to Judea before the events of the end times begin. Mormon interest in Palestine remained strong throughout the nineteenth and twentieth centuries, and in the 1970s the Mormons built a center for Middle Eastern studies in Jerusalem. To establish their presence in the land and to secure the trust and cooperation of the Israeli government, the Mormons promised to refrain from evangelism, a concession they have rarely, if ever, made elsewhere.

For Roman Catholics, Palestine has traditionally been Terra Sancta, the Holy Land, an object of pilgrimage. Throughout the twentieth century, American Catholics have shown concern about the integrity of Catholic shrines and privileges in the Holy Land. From 1947 to 1949, Francis Cardinal Spellman of New York headed the worldwide Catholic demand for the internationalization of Jerusalem, Bethlehem, and Nazareth, towns holding special meaning for Christianity.

Similarly, Jews in America have looked on Palestine as the biblical land of Israel, their ancestral home. This became a subject of debate among nineteenth- and early-twentieth-century American Jews. Like the Puritans, many of them, including prominent Reform rabbis, declared America to be their Zion and eliminated prayers for the return of the Jews to Jerusalem from Reform liturgy. Zionism became an accepted component of American Judaism in the 1920s, following the ideological path of U.S. Supreme Court justice Louis Brandeis, who viewed the Jewish hope for the building of a national Jewish center in Palestine as going hand in hand with Jewish loyalty to America. American Jewish financial and political support for the building of a Jewish commonwealth in Palestine has been of great importance to the rise and survival of the State of Israel.

Palestine is also a holy land for the growing Muslim community in America, for whom Jerusalem is "the holy city." In addition to the three Abrahamic religions, a number of new religious movements influenced by Christian-Messianic notions also relate to Palestine as the Holy Land. One such group is the Raelians, who expect the arrival of the Messiah in a UFO in Jerusalem in the year 2035, to take his true believers to heaven.

The special relations that major American religious groups have with the Holy Land have influenced American attitudes toward the contemporary land of Palestine, including policies adopted by the U.S. government. Christian evangelical notions of the importance of Israel and its role in history have been particularly instrumental in the latter decades of the twentieth century in determining American financial, military, and political support for that country.

See also CHURCH AND STATE; CHURCH OF JESUS CHRIST OF LATTER-DAY SAINTS; DISPENSATIONALISM; EVAN-

GELICAL CHRISTIANITY; ISLAM; JEWISH IDENTITY; JUDAISM; MAINLINE PROTESTANTISM; PREMILLENNIALISM; ROMAN CATHOLICISM; SECOND COMING; ZIONISM.

BIBLIOGRAPHY

Ariel, Yaakov S. *On Behalf of Israel.* 1991.

Davis, Moshe. *America and the Holy Land.* 1995.

Davis, Moshe, ed. *With Eyes Towards Zion.* 1977.

Greenberg, Gershon. *The Holy Land in American Religious Thought, 1620–1948: The Symbiosis of American Religious Approaches to Scriptures' Sacred Territory.* 1994.

Grose, Peter. *Israel in the Mind of America.* 1983.

Handy, Robert T. *The Holy Land in American Protestant Life, 1800–1948.* 1981.

Yaakov S. Ariel

Holy Spirit.

See Trinity.

Home Schooling

Home schooling is the education of school-age children by their parents, rather than full-time attendance at a campus school. While only an estimated 15,000 children were home-schooled in the mid-1970s, the movement has grown at spectacular rates since then, especially among religious conservatives. This growth is at least in part due to the religious concerns of parents about their responsibility for training and educating their children, and their reservations about public schools. At a minimum, 750,000 to 1 million children are home-schooled. During the 1990s the number of children in home schooling more than doubled.

Though research on home schooling is limited, some tentative conclusions are possible. Regional studies find that home schoolers are primarily white, middle-class, well educated, and in occupations with considerable flexibility and autonomy. At least one-third are from conservative religious traditions, such as evangelical, pentecostal, or nondenominational religious organizations, and another 25 percent are from mainline religious organizations. Other studies also find that religious conservatives dominate the home-schooling movement.

The 1996 National Household Education Survey confirms that home schooling is much more likely among whites than nonwhites. And home schooling, not surprisingly, is associated with two-parent families in which parents work fewer than the average total hours outside the home. This makes sense, given that at least one parent—usually the mother—is home educating the children. Home-schooling parents have about the same level of education and income as non–home schoolers. Home schooling is least common in the Northeast and most common in the West. Home schooling is also more common in less residentially stable areas, perhaps because of the increased problems in public schools and reduced availability of church-related schools in these areas.

On average, home-schooling parents tend to be more religious—as measured by attendance at worship services—than non–home schoolers. At the same time, significant minorities of home schoolers do not attend religious services. These findings reflect two important sources of home schooling: (1) conservative Christians, who often opt out of public schools for ideological reasons; and (2) parents with a secular countercultural or "New Age" orientation who are likely to be primarily concerned with pedogogical issues.

Among churchgoing Protestants, pentecostals and charismatics are much more likely to favor nonpublic schooling over public schooling as the best strategy for Christians. And based on a 1996 nationally representative survey of churchgoing Protestants, fundamentalists and charismatics are more likely to send their children to nonpublic schools. Even after accounting for race, income, and education, the survey found that home schooling seems, unsurprisingly, more popular among evangelicals and fundamentalists than among theologically liberal respondents.

What are the academic results of home schooling? Most studies show that home-schooled children do as well as or better than their public school peers (Ray 1997), most likely because of the higher levels of parental involvement in the learning process.

Home schooling is not detrimental to the development of children's socialization skills. And home schoolers are not socially isolated, as many opponents fear. Home schoolers have developed an impressive social and organizational network, mitigating concerns that home schoolers are withdrawn from peers, community, and nation. In fact, alternative schoolers are actually more involved in civic life than public schoolers. Home-schooling organizations, which may involve coordinating field trips to local museums or to a jointly sponsored science class for home-school children, often cross the divide between conservative Christian parents and secular counterculturalist home-schooling parents.

Still, there are divisions within the home-schooling movement. Home-schooling organizations of conservative Christians tend to be hierarchical and formal-

A six-year-old boy in Littlerock, California, is instructed in phonics by his mother during a home schooling session on October 23, 1998.   (Credit: AP/Wide World Photos.)

ized, as opposed to the organization of secular countercultural groups, which tend to be decentralized and more informal. Also, attempts to organize home schoolers into a national constituency have often given way to separate home-schooling organizations, structured along conservative Protestant vs. secular-ecumenical lines.

Why do parents choose to home-school their children? Religion is a primary motive for many. But based on interviews with home-schooling parents, religious reasons are not the whole story. Home-schooling parents are not primarily driven by "secular humanism" in the public schools and generally do not demand that public schools become "Christian." In fact, some home-schooling parents are equally concerned about the teaching methods of other private schools. Nor are they attempting to unite home, school, and church into a tight web that keeps out the secular world.

Why choose home schooling? In addition to specifically religious reasons, a majority of home-schooling parents believe home schooling is a better method of education, that public schools are a poor learning environment, or that public schools are not academically challenging. About one-fourth of home-schooling parents also argue that the choice of home schooling depends on the needs of the child. Many conservative Protestants seem to move their children in and out of home schooling and other forms of schooling. Only a small minority take the position that the current organization of public schooling is radically wrong, or that home schooling is a responsibility of every Christian parent.

Many researchers interpret the home-schooling movement as a reaction to modernity and secularization. Home schooling is more likely in areas that have lost tightly knit communities and thus may be partly a response to the loss of moral order in the community. The growth of the state and of cultural diversity may lead to conflict between the organization and content of public education and the ideologies embodied in family and church. A result is a movement into alternative education, such as home schooling. Additionally, parents increasingly have the resources to take up home schooling successfully. Rising levels of education lead to a reduced sense that the "school knows best," and perhaps greater confidence in one's own ability to carry out the task of educating one's children.

Because of the demands of home schooling on parents, the rapid growth of the movement in the 1980s and 1990s may level off. But current signs point to continued growth in home schooling, especially among religious parents.

See also ATTENDANCE; CHURCH AND STATE; FUNDAMENTALIST CHRISTIANITY; HUMANISM; NEW AGE SPIRITUALITY; PRAYER IN SCHOOL; RELIGIOUS STUDIES; SECULARIZATION.

BIBLIOGRAPHY

Burns, Patrick. "A Profile of Selected Characteristics of Arizona's Home Schooling Families." Unpublished diss., Northern Arizona University. 1993.

Lines, Patricia. "Homeschoolering: An Overview for Education Policy Makers." U.S. Department of Education. Working Paper. 1997.

Lines, Patricia. "Homeschoolers: Estimating Numbers and Growth." U.S. Department of Education. Technical Paper. 1998.

Mayberry, Maralee, and J. Gary Knowles. "Family Unity Objectives of Parents Who Teach Their Children: Ideological and Pedagogical Orientations to Home Schooling." *Urban Review* 21 (1989): 209–225.

Ray, Brian. *Home Education Across the United States.* 1997.

Sikkink, David. "Public Schooling and Its Discontents: Religious Identities, Schooling Choices for Children, and Civic Participation." Unpublished diss., University of North Carolina at Chapel Hill. 1998.

Sikkink, David. "The Social Sources of Alienation from Public Schools." *Social Forces* 77 (1999).

David Sikkink
Michael O. Emerson

Homosexuality.

See Lesbian and Gay Rights Movement.

Hubbard, L. Ron.

See Scientology, Church of.

Humanae Vitae

On July 29, 1968, Pope Paul VI issued the encyclical "Humanae Vitae" ("On Human Life"), which reaffirmed the traditional teaching that artificial contraception opposed not only church law but also conflicted with reason and experience. Roman Catholic identity involves hierarchical authority, authoritative teaching, and organic continuity, including the foundations of Catholic moral reflection philosophically known as "natural law." However, Paul VI's teaching met with unprecedented public dissent from theologians and practical rejection by most married Catholics in the Western nations. The various national and regional conferences of Catholic bishops typically noted that the pope's teaching here, while authoritative, was not "infallible"—that is, required by faith alone. They taught that Catholics should follow the pope's teaching that "natural family planning" (ovulation, basal body temperature, or symptothermal methods) rather than artificial contraception was an ideal that made more transparent the complete gift of self that constituted the sacrament of marriage.

The reader of *Humanae Vitae* will find a rich and lyrical appreciation of the beauty of committed human love, highly influenced by the teaching of the Second Vatican Council (1962–1965), though the encyclical's public importance has been reduced to its ban on artificial contraception. *Humanae Vitae* immediately crystallized post–Vatican II debates about the interrelationships among papal and episcopal authority and the place of dissent in the church. The encyclical has also affected in complicated ways the church's post–Vatican II aspiration to contribute to the complex global dialogue about human rights, justice and poverty, and abortion.

In the Second Vatican Council the bishops abandoned the terms "primary end" (procreation) and "secondary end" (spousal unity) of marriage but left a review of the traditional teaching about contraception to a special commission that Pope Paul VI announced on June 23, 1964. In the context of media reports about the birth control pill and international conferences on population, there emerged a broad expectation that, as other dimensions of Catholic life were changing, so, too, would the magisterium's moral prohibition of *any* use of artificial contraception within marriage. The commission's majority finally came to agree with the conclusion that past teaching did not have to be read or interpreted in a way requiring an absolute prohibition of artificial contraception. Even its minority report, which Pope Paul VI finally adopted, conceded that moral reasoning alone could not sustain the ban. Contemporary defenders of *Humanae Vitae* as a litmus test of Catholic orthodoxy point to a contemporary "contraceptive mentality" of recreational sex leading to high rates of divorce, wife and child abuse, and increased abortion rates.

While the Catholic Church no longer directly impedes worldwide efforts at promoting contraception, many inside and even more outside the church contend, first, that *Humanae Vitae* detracts from the church's challenge to political elites who out of self-interest construe contraceptive ignorance, rather than extreme poverty, as the major cause of high fertility rates in poor nations; and second, that the encyclical blurs the church's more widely shared witness against characterizing abortion as a morally unproblematic means of birth control.

See also ABORTION; BIRTH; BIRTH CONTROL; DOGMATISM; ENCYCLICAL; PAPACY; RELIGIOUS STUDIES; ROMAN CATHOLICISM; SEXUALITY; VATICAN; VATICAN II.

BIBLIOGRAPHY

R. B. Kaiser, *The Politics of Sex and Religion.* 1985.

J. R. Kelly, "Catholic Sexual Ethics Since Vatican II" in *Religion and the Social Order,* edited by H. Ebaugh. 1991.

J. C. Schwarz, *Global Population from a Catholic Perspective.* 1998.

James R. Kelly

Humanism

Humanism is a philosophy of life without God. It maintains that reason is the best method for the discovery of truth, that the natural world of space-time is the only world that exists, and that the power to solve human problems lies mainly within human beings.

The first articulation of humanist principles comes from ancient Greece. Three Greek philosophers—Leucippus, Democritus, and Epicurus—proposed an atomic and materialistic view of reality that excluded the existence of supernatural power and supernatural gods. Epicurus founded a school in Athens that preserved this teaching. In the philosophy of Epicurus pleasure and happiness replaced both tradition and the will of the gods as the criteria for goodness and right behavior.

The triumph of Christianity in the Roman world led to the suppression of Greek philosophy, and especially Epicureanism. The victory of Islam in the East only aggravated this hostility. Humanism remained an "underground" philosophy in a triumphant Christian and Muslim world.

In the European Renaissance the word "humanist" appears. A "humanist" was a master of the secular texts of ancient Greece and Rome. These texts became an alternative to pious literature for European liberals who were weary of clerical dogmatism and intolerance.

By the eighteenth century the Renaissance had turned into the Enlightenment. Western Christianity had been weakened by division. Philosophers felt free to challenge the premises and institutions of religion. The rise of the scientific experimental approach to truth, reinforced by British philosophers such as Bacon, Locke, and Hume, undermined the authority of religious dogma and opened the educated public to the possibility of living without God.

In the nineteenth century, English philosopher John Stuart Mill and French philosopher August Comte defined classical humanism. Five principles were articulated:

1. The scientific and experimental method is the most reliable path to truth.
2. Reality and the natural world are one and the same.
3. The human struggle for survival takes place in the context of an indifferent universe.
4. Moral behavior leads to the greatest happiness of the greatest number.
5. Individuals have the right to be the masters of their lives.

Comte saw humanism as the religion of humanity. Mill saw humanism as a "natural religion." But their disciples generally viewed themselves as nonreligious.

Humanism in North America was identified with people who called themselves freethinkers. At the end of the nineteenth century dozens of freethinking and rationalist societies emerged in the major cities of the United States. Their agenda was to promote rational thinking and to oppose dogmatic religion. The charismatic spokesman of freethinking was Robert Ingersoll, a successful lawyer from Illinois who was viewed by many as the greatest orator in America. But Ingersoll directed his energies to personal enlightenment and not to the organization of a humanist movement.

In time there appeared two kinds of humanism: one religious and one secular. Religious humanists found their home in liberal religions. Many liberal Christians and Jews, who were either deists or pantheists or who no longer believed in a God who responded to prayer, saw themselves as humanists. Many members and leaders of the Unitarian movement openly promoted a nontheistic humanism, especially in the Midwest. John Dietrich of Minneapolis was their most prominent leader. In 1876 Felix Adler, the son of a distinguished Reform rabbi, established the New York Society for Ethical Culture, which taught ethics without God. Over the next fifty years a dozen similar societies were created all over America. In 1963 Sherwin Wine, a dissident Reform rabbi, founded the Birmingham Temple, which became the first congregation of humanistic Judaism. The new movement sought to blend humanism with secular Jewish culture.

Secular humanists avoided religious formats. While most of them joined no humanist organization, some of them organized local and national societies to provide humanist education through literature and lectures. Both the American Humanist Association and the Council for a Democratic and Secular Humanism were created for this purpose. Both secular and religious humanists cooperated in the issuance of two humanist manifestos and in the creation of a school for training humanist leaders, the Humanist Institute, in New York.

American humanism has been reinforced by the support of prominent American philosophers. Both the critical realism of Roy Wood Sellars and the pragmatism of John Dewey became important themes in American humanist thought.

In recent years political fundamentalists of the religious right have assaulted "secular humanism" as their chief enemy. Although exaggerating the power of humanism, the leaders of the assault have paid an unwilling tribute to the importance of humanism in America.

See also AGNOSTICISM; ATHEISM; DEATH OF GOD; ETHICAL CULTURE; GOD; JUDAISM; SECULARIZATION.

BIBLIOGRAPHY

Lamont, Corliss. *The Philosophy of Humanism.* 1965.
Lippmann, Walter. *A Preface to Morals.* 1929.
Russell, Bertrand. *Why I Am Not a Christian.* 1957.

Sherwin T. Wine

Human Potential Movement

The Human Potential Movement is the name for the movement of growth psychologies that flowered in the late 1960s and 1970s. Encounter groups, meditation, massage, and other practices were all enthusiastically advocated as ways toward actualization of "human potential." Although the primary language of the movement was that of humanistic and Gestalt psychology, especially the personality theories of Carl Rogers, Abraham Maslow, and Fritz Perls, the movement as popular expression of nontraditional spirituality eschewed scientific psychology's standards of verifiability and objective discourse. Instead, from its beginnings the Human Potential Movement's testimonies, enthusiasm, persuasive techniques, and styles of leadership were compared to religious movements—although the distance from "religion" as understood by its participants was very great.

The Human Potential Movement started at the Esalen Institute in Big Sur, California, where intense group experiences and an interest in the "farther reaches of human nature" (Maslow's phrase) combined with charismatic leaders, a beautiful secluded environment, and the ethos of the 1960s counterculture. The movement's primary theme is that humans are intended to grow, to develop an innate creative potential for freedom, spontaneous experiencing, expression of feeling, and altered states of consciousness. Blocks to growth lie in society and the internalization of its rules and restrictions. Western rationality and word-oriented knowledge also block the natural potential for experience in "the here and now." However, intense group experience, along with the expression of blocked emotions, can overcome these obstacles. Sexuality, mystical experience, and artistic creativity may all be unleashed once the repressions of social conditioning are undone.

While such ideas may have played a role in psychotherapies and educational reforms before the late 1960s, the Human Potential Movement actively popularized them. It expanded into venues such as weekend workshops, growth groups, and sensitivity training in many innovative (and therefore unregulated) situations. Centers for "growth" provided a combination of enjoyable recreation, intense emotional release, and "communitas," the ecstatic loss of individual boundaries within a group and outside one's ordinary structured workaday world. Openness to mystical states of consciousness, to some extent dependent on openness to using psychedelic drugs, was part of this movement's ethos.

The Human Potential Movement became a target for critics from several camps. Conventional psychotherapists objected to the claims of "growth" centers to offer "therapy." Political and religious conservatives warned against the movement's antinomianism and self-indulgence. Tales of people who went off to a weekend growth workshop and subsequently began lives of footloose and promiscuous "searching," leaving behind a trail of betrayals and unhappiness, cast doubt on the equation of all change with "growth." The political left found the rhetoric of the Human Potential Movement deceptive, since it promised solutions to life's problems within the self, ignoring society's structures. All of these criticisms eventually became focused on the "selfism" of the movement, and the era of its flourishing became known as the decade of "the me generation."

From the perspective of North American religion, the Human Potential Movement had several areas of influence. It offered a nontraditional spirituality with utopian hopes for an expansion of human nature's limits. Its goal was "putting the first man on earth," as one advocate prophesied. A "consciousness revolution" would lead to a complete new vision of what was possible for human beings, individually and collectively. Mystical experience, biofeedback training, and heightened ability to experience one's self were linked together. This transcendent promise for a future radically different from the technology-dominated, rationalistic present gradually coalesced into what is now called New Age Spirituality.

A second, less utopian, but much more pervasive effect was to make the language of "growth" and subjective experiencing so familiar and widespread that it became the "first language" of middle-class Americans. According to the influential critique *Habits of the Heart* (Bellah et al. 1985), this ideology of "expressive individualism" dominated the reasoning and values of Americans by the mid-1980s. People justify career moves, marital failure, and many other life changes using an imagery of "feelings" and "growth" without attending to beyond-the-self standards or loyalties.

The third relevant area of influence of the Human Potential Movement was the spread of its ethos, imagery, and practices into traditional religious environments. Small groups modeled on encounter groups became part of some mainline Protestant churches' activities. Language originating in the psychologies of the Human Potential Movement, such as Rogers's phrase "unconditional acceptance" (the idealized stance of the therapist toward the client), became appropriated within religious contexts very far removed from the Esalen Institute. Representing Christian goals as "growth" or as experiencing one's fullest potentials may have preceded the 1960s in the framework of liberal Protestant spiritualities, but the Human Potential Movement offered this language in a form less intellectually dry than earlier versions of it. Battles over its adoption and the involvement of churches with encounter and sensitivity groups anticipated the "culture wars" of the 1980s.

Retroactively, the Human Potential Movement's spectacular rise has been matched by its almost as quick disappearance as a separate "movement." There are several reasons for this decline. Interest in altered states of consciousness led to serious exploration of the practices and traditions of Asia, especially to engagement in serious Buddhist study and meditation. This led to training centers whose structure and language differed from the Esalen model. Another wing of the Human Potential Movement focused on alternative and adjunctive healing with a patient/healer relationship closer to that of traditional therapies than the formats advanced by the Human Potential Movement. The very success of the movement's language as the "first language" of so many Americans may have diluted any utopian claims it made for the promised growth to effect major changes. Also, an unbalanced vision of human nature, of how "self-actualization" may be linked to actual commitments, limits, and tragedies, may have left some participants chastened.

See also New Age Spirituality.

Bibliography

Back, Kurt. *Beyond Words: The Story of Sensitivity and the Encounter Movement.* 1972.

Bellah, Robert, et al. *Habits of the Heart: Individualism and Commitment in American Life.* 1985.

Havens, Joseph. "Gestalt, Bioenergetics, and Encounter: New Wine Without Wineskins." In *Religious Systems and Psychotherapy,* edited by Richard H. Cox. 1973.

Maslow, Abraham H. *The Farther Reaches of Human Nature.* 1971.

Rosenfeld, Albert, ed. "Mind and Supermind." *The Saturday Review* (February 22, 1975): 8–34.

Lucy Bregman

Human Rights

In 1776, the American Declaration of Independence asserted it was "self-evident" that human beings were "endowed by their Creator with certain unalienable Rights." Indeed, unless rights are based on the will of a supreme deity, it is hard to see what firm basis they can have. A primary aim of the Constitution of the United States, ratified in 1789, was to "establish Justice," and the reverence accorded this influential document has given it the quality of sacred law. But if a "right" is merely a special privilege granted to people within a particular corpus of laws, then there is nothing to prevent the government from rescinding it, and there is no justification for claiming the right outside the legal jurisdiction that enacted it. Social theorists from Thomas Hobbes (*Leviathan*, 1651) to

George Homans (*Social Behavior: Its Elementary Forms*, 1974) have attempted to derive principles of justice from the facts of human interaction and group life, yet by their very nature all these secular theories make justice highly contingent on immediate situations and therefore both narrow and mutable. Thus, to say that one has a particular "right" is a highly dubious rhetorical assertion of privilege unless the right has a religious basis.

At the same time, religion seems to be among the most potent forces limiting human rights. Repeatedly in human history, adherents of one religion have persecuted believers in another. At present, debates rage over the capacity of Islam to ensure women's rights. Some argue that it traps women in second-class status—for example, favoring sons over daughters in inheritance and making divorce far easier for husbands than for wives. On the other hand, it can be argued that the Qur'an conferred rights on women that they did not earlier possess in Arabian society, and that Islam can adapt to modern social and political conditions just as Christianity has done.

Seymour Martin Lipset has argued that Protestantism favors the development of democratic values more than Catholicism does, because Protestantism encourages individual responsibility. In contrast, Andrew Greeley has argued that Catholicism has a greater democratic potential because it considers the needs of the entire community. Perhaps the relation between religion and human rights is one of dynamic ambivalence. Belief in a supernatural power can serve either tyranny or liberty, depending on the historical circumstances. As Benjamin Disraeli said in his preface to *Lothair* (1870), "The divine right of kings may have been a plea for feeble tyrants, but the divine right of government is the keystone of human progress."

Pitirim Sorokin's classic theory of cultural transformation suggests that the concept of human rights belongs to an intermediate stage in the secularization process. Initially, according to Sorokin, each great civilization is born out of a period of chaos and barbarism, in a spasm of essentially religious creativity. A new ideational culture is established on a particular set of sacrosanct beliefs that consider reality to be fundamentally spiritual. Instead of rights, there are commandments that authoritatively tell humans how they should behave. As time passes, people turn away from spirituality toward materialism, and faith is gradually supplanted by rationality. In the midst of this historical process, people seek rationalizations such as natural rights to explain why the old customs still should be followed. Sorokin called this compromise idealistic, and belief in the existence of natural rights is a half-religious, half-secular idealism. Finally, the society becomes sensate, finding truth entirely in reason and the physical senses. God vanishes from the picture, and humans become the center of all moral judgment. Individual human desires supplant both commandments and rights as the ruling principle. For the sake of social stability, people may agree that individuals should avoid directly harming other individuals. But once the culture accepts the principle that humans may indulge their individual desires almost without limit, freedom begins to devour itself. Sorokin believed that any extreme sensate society was in grave danger of disintegrating into the chaos and barbarism out of which a new ideational culture might arise.

Americans reveal only lukewarm support for many civil rights when they respond to opinion polls such as the General Social Survey, which has measured the attitudes of a cross section of the population periodically since 1972. One standard question offers three choices to express the respondent's feelings about the Bible: (1) "The Bible is the actual word of God and is to be taken literally." (2) "The Bible is the inspired word of God but not everything in it should be taken literally, word for word." (3) "The Bible is an ancient book of fables, legends, history, and moral precepts recorded by man." Among those who have a literal interpretation of the Bible, more than half (56.6 percent) feel that antireligious books and films should be outlawed. Remarkably, even about one of eight people (12.9 percent) who feel the Bible is just a book of fables also would ban books that attack religion.

The following table gives percentages of people who hold thirteen different rights-related opinions, for each of the different feelings about the Bible. Four items on freedom of speech reveal a consistent tendency of biblical literalists to support this right less often than others do. Support for giving homosexuals the right to marry each other is weak in all groups but weakest among literalists, and the same is true for legalization of marijuana, which might be a step toward the right to decide freely what one smokes, eats, or injects into one's body. Opposition to abortion can be couched as a "right to life" position. Although there is widespread support for some kind of "right to die," the euthanasia item still shows significant religious differences. The right to legal due process would be compromised if it were legal to imprison a person merely on an anonymous tip that he or she was planning a crime. The majority want to deny legal immigrants the immediate right to government assistance such as Medicaid, food stamps, or welfare, but opposition is greatest among literalists. The question about racial intermarriage was asked in 1989, and it is surprising at this late date that significant opposition was found. The right of people to exclude a particular group from their neighborhood is clearly not

Table. Percentage of Americans Holding Various Rights-Related Opinions

Options	Feelings About the Bible		
	Literal	Inspired	Fables
Books and films that attack religions should be banned by law.	56.6%	26.3%	12.9%
People who want to overthrow the government by revolution should be allowed to publish books expressing their views.	49.2%	70.3%	80.4%
An admitted Communist should be allowed to make a speech in the community.	45.7%	71.8%	81.8%
A person who advocates doing away with elections and letting the military run the country should be allowed to make a speech in the community.	45.2%	66.7%	75.0%
An admitted homosexual should be allowed to make a speech in the community.	59.1%	83.7%	88.5%
Homosexual couples should have the right to marry.	5.6%	12.8%	25.1%
Marijuana should be made legal.	12.0%	19.5%	41.3%
It should be possible for a pregnant woman to obtain a legal abortion if the woman wants it for any reason.	23.6%	44.9%	66.8%
Euthanasia should be allowed by law if the patient and his family request it.	55.7%	74.6%	86.4%
If police get an anonymous tip that a man without a criminal record is planning to break into a warehouse, they should be allowed to detain the man overnight for questioning.	42.8%	31.1%	28.4%
Immigrants who come from other countries to the United States legally should be eligible immediately for government assistance.	27.0%	32.6%	47.1%
The law should allow marriages between blacks and whites (white respondents only).	46.2%	70.4%	81.7%
White people have a right to keep blacks out of their neighborhoods if they want to, and blacks should respect that right (white respondents only).	32.3%	18.3%	16.0%

widely supported today, but nearly a third of white biblical literalists affirm it. Much statistical research has examined whether lower support for many civil liberties might really be the result of some other factor, such as low education or region of the country, but these religious effects generally survive statistical controls and thus are probably accurate.

Considerable evidence suggests that religion can encourage respect for the rights of others, but only in certain ways. For example, rates of property crimes such as larceny (but not of homicide) are lower in parts of the United States where church membership rates are high. Research on juvenile delinquency suggests that religion does not instill respect for rights in isolated religious individuals but has a powerful effect by sustaining a communitywide moral order. In communities where churches are weak, delinquency is just as common among religious teenagers as among nonreligious ones. But where the churches are strong, religious teenagers are far less likely to be delinquent. Thus the relationship between religion and human rights is too complex to take for granted, and only careful scientific research can determine the circumstances under which religion promotes rather than compromises human freedom.

See also ANIMAL RIGHTS; CIVIL RIGHTS MOVEMENT; ETHICAL CULTURE; ETHICS; HUMANISM; LESBIAN AND GAY RIGHTS MOVEMENT; MATERIAL RELIGION; RELIGIOUS PERSECUTION; SECULARIZATION.

BIBLIOGRAPHY

Davis, James A., and Tom W. Smith. *General Social Surveys, 1972–1996: Cumulative Codebook.* 1996.

Esposito, John L. *Women in Muslim Family Law.* 1982.

Finlay, Barbara. "Right to Life vs. Right to Die: Some Correlates of Euthanasia Attitudes." *Sociology and Social Research* 69 (July 1985): 548–560.

Greeley, Andrew. *The Catholic Myth.* 1990.

Lipset, Seymour Martin. "The Social Requisites of Democracy Revisited." *American Sociological Review* 59 (1994): 1–22.

Mayer, Ann Elizabeth. *Islam and Human Rights.* 1991.

Sorokin, Pitirim A. *Social and Cultural Dynamics.* 1937.

Stark, Rodney, and William Sims Bainbridge. *Religion, Deviance, and Social Control.* 1996.

William Sims Bainbridge

Hutterian Brethren.

See Bruderhof.

I

I Ching

The *I Ching,* or *Yi Jing,* is one of the oldest books in the history of religious thought, but it was not until the seventeenth century that it attracted the attention of Western scholars, most notably the German mathematician Gottfried Wilhelm Leibniz (1646–1716), the inventor of the binary number system. Only in the twentieth century have mainstream thinkers such as C. G. Jung, the father of modern psychotherapy, regularly consulted the *Book of Changes.* In the past twenty years, catching the wave of the New Age movement, the *I Ching* has become the focus of various occult and pseudo-scientific thought systems.

Early History and Structure

Historical events mentioned in the earliest layers of the *I Ching* depict the period just prior to and following the founding of the Zhou dynasty (1046–249 B.C.E.). First known as the *Zhou Yi,* its earliest rendition was a series of sixty-four six-line omen texts and prognostications, which most likely originated in the sacred ritual of oracle bone divination—a tradition dating from Neolithic times. When rulers were not confident of their own ability to decide issues of great import (battles, wedding dates, journeys, etc.), they resorted to divination by scapulimancy (reading cracks in heated bones), or by casting lots using the stalks of the yarrow plant. The latter technique generated random numbers that would then correspond to a particular oracle in the *Zhou Yi.*

As the Zhou dynasty waned and as the power of the nobles began to eclipse that of the king, the use of yarrow stalk divination, originally a royal prerogative, permeated virtually all of literate society. This familiarity led to ever-increasing use of the text for rhetorical rather than religious purposes, and much of the original oracular import was forgotten. It was an age of collapsing social norms, and new schools of thought began to develop to account for the apparent degradation of society. As proponents of these incipient philosophies wrangled in the intellectual centers of the day, ancient texts such as the *Zhou Yi* were newly scrutinized. The debates eventually resulted in a compendium of ten commentaries, or "Wings," which attempted to picture the *Zhou Yi* as a coherent system of thought and not merely as a book of divination. The ten commentaries were attached to the sixty-four omen texts, and the book was canonized as the *I Ching* in 136 B.C.E.

In addition to the textual content of the *I Ching,* each of the sixty-four omen texts is accompanied by a linear configuration known as a *gua,* or hexagram. Each hexagram is a matrix of six solid (yang) and/or broken (yin) lines, which are perceived as dynamic, not static, and thus susceptible to change. Ordered change—the reversal of polarity—occurs in the alternation of yin and yang lines across each hexagram, corresponding in nature to the alternation of day and night, summer and winter, etc. Random change is manifested in the chance appearance of a particular hexagram when cast, which corresponds to the fortuitous occurrence of ominous events in nature. Time is a factor of change and is a function of both alternation and progression, just as day and night alternate as the seasons progress. In the stalk-casting ritual, as the hexagram develops from the bottom upward (reflecting organic growth), each line captures a possible development in the world outside the diviner. So the chance appearance of a given line in a given position, which results in a given omen, is equivalent to a real-life transformation or occurrence of a supernatural event. The hexagram omen, as such, is a microcosmic model of a unique moment in the life of the inquirer.

The *I Ching* in the West

The seventeenth and eighteenth centuries in Europe witnessed a search by the Figurists for a cosmic correspondence of the many cultures, religions, and sciences of the world under the supremacy of Christianity. At this time the Christian thinker Leibniz was attempting to combat Cartesian materialism by postulating a binary number system that represented creation *ex nihilo* (0) by God (1). A Jesuit missionary in Beijing discovered a numerical correspondence between the sixty-four hexagrams of the *I Ching* and Leibniz's binary system, which prompted Leibniz to claim that the former was an ancient Chinese "prefiguring" of the latter. Jung drew upon this history for his theories, concentrating on, among other things, astrology, magic, alchemy, quantum physics, relativity, ESP experiments, and, of course, the *I Ching*. In the foregoing account of *I Ching* structure we can see ample reason why Jung cited it as venerable proof of his synchronicity—the acausal correlation of subjective psychic states with objective events in the material world. The book intrigued Jung because he believed it was based on the inquirer's capacity to find in a specific *I Ching* omen a corollary to his own inner psychological state. While this may be an appropriate assessment of the modern function of the oracle, the Zhou dynasty kings believed the spirits of their dead ancestors were answering their questions through the medium of *I Ching* omens. The only way the original process of *I Ching* divination can coincide with Jung's notion of synchronicity is if the latter is based on a religious psychology, which is the opinion of some modern scholars (Faber 1998).

Something like the Figurist ideal seems to be the driving force behind any number of New Age systems of thought that make liberal use of *I Ching* structures. Many of these compare the sequence of sixty-four hexagrams to the sixty-four codons of the DNA genetic code, a correlation discussed by Katya Walter in her *Tao of Chaos* (1994). Most notable of these pseudo-scientific systems is Terence and Dennis McKenna's "Timewave" theory, revealed in their book *The Invisible Landscape* (1975). In this scheme, time is a complex of wave hierarchies composed of physical and psycho-logical energies that combine like hexagram lines. The Timewave will peak in the year 2012, which (coincidentally) is the time of the "Omega Point of Planetary Awakening" predicted by José Arguelles in his book *Earth Ascending* (1984), and the end year of the Mayan calendar. Arguelles's mix of Mayan myth, DNA sequences, and *I Ching* hexagrams is called "holonomics." Taking us full circle back to the Figurists is Joe E. McCaffree, a diffusionist who believes that the Chinese and Indian cultures were influenced by the older and superior Hebrew culture. In particular, he believes that the *I Ching* and the Torah are essentially the same book, and his *Bible and I Ching Relationships* (1982) is an attempt to prove his theory.

While these thought systems do not as yet constitute religious orders, there is one defunct American group inspired by the *I Ching* that flourished in the 1970s. Called the Great Brotherhood of God, it was founded by Cecil Frederick Russell (1893–1987), a disciple of the famous occultist Aleister Crowley (1875–1947), and was patterned after Crowley's Argenteum Astrum, the Order of the Silver Star. Crowley himself was an adept of the *I Ching*, and his writings contain interpretations of the hexagrams. According to one of its initiates, the study and practice of the principles of the *I Ching* were fundamental components of the Brotherhood. The order taught that the casting of hexagrams was the result of "superconscious Intelligences" communicating through the text of the *I Ching*. However, one of its leaders, Louis T. Culling (d. 1973), would have agreed with Jung, believing it was the "supraconscious" mind of the inquirer that spoke through the omen texts. His translation and study of the *I Ching* is called *The Pristine Yiking* (1989). Partly as a result of its association with Crowley and his adherents, in some Christian circles the *I Ching* is regarded as inherently occult and therefore heretical. Professor Jung Young Lee wrote his *Embracing Change* in 1994 to correct this misunderstanding.

See also ASTROLOGY; CHINESE-AMERICAN RELIGIONS; FENG SHUI; NEW AGE SPIRITUALITY; OCCULT, THE.

BIBLIOGRAPHY

Richard J. Smith assisted me in locating some of the sources that were consulted for this article. His forthcoming work will be the definitive analysis of "global" uses of the *I Ching*, including its contemporary use in the United States.

Faber, M. D. *Synchronicity: C. G. Jung, Psychoanalysis, and Religion.* 1998.

Girardot, Norman J. "Ritual Combat During the 'Babylonian Era of Sinology.'" *The Oracle* 2, no. 8 (1999): 8–24.

Smith, Richard J. *Fortune-Tellers and Philosophers: Divination in Traditional Chinese Society.* 1991.

Wilhelm, Richard, tr. *The I Ching; or, Book of Changes.* Rendered from Wilhelm's German into English by Cary F. Baynes. Foreword by C. G. Jung. 1961.

Stephen L. Field

Icons

Icons are religious images painted on wood in the Byzantine manner and used extensively in Eastern Orthodox Christianity, both in private homes and in the liturgical celebrations of the churches. The widespread use of icons is a distinctive mark of Eastern Orthodoxy all through the world, in both its Greek and its Slavic forms, and also in the Oriental churches such as the Coptic and Ethiopian communions, all of which are now represented in American religious life.

Early Christianity was ambivalent about religious paintings. The emperor cult and the practice of depicting savior gods in late antique art led to a deep suspicion among many Christian theorists that depictions of Christ should not be permitted at all. Regardless of this, however, Christian art began to flourish at an early date, as the funerary paintings in the catacombs can demonstrate, and by the fourth century the practice of depicting Christ both as a young man and as an imperial judge was gaining ground. Earliest forms of Christian art, particularly visible in Rome and Egypt, are characterized by the late antique style of Roman "realist" painting; but by the sixth century, when icons had developed a distinctive form and a much wider popularity among Christians, some distinctive "nonrealist" traits were emerging that were to be fixed by later church laws.

At this period, iconic art focused on figures of Christ, the Virgin Mary, some of the Apostles, and the martyr-saints whose shrines were becoming more popular. Icons were still largely a private matter, and the surviving panels are mostly of portable size. Very little survives from before the ninth century, as during this period a large reaction against the popularity of icons among Eastern Christians was taking place. This, the so-called iconoclastic crisis (from the Greek word for the smashing of icons), was one of the most severe internal disruptions to the life of the Christian East in the Byzantine period. Several emperors denounced Christian devotional painting as "idolatrous." The ensuing conflict led to a radical reassessment of the importance of art and culture in Christian worship practice.

Eastern theologians answered the charge by elaborating a theory of Christian art. The icon or image

A shop in Miami's Little Havana district displaying religious icons—sculptures of Jesus Christ and the Virgin Mary. (Credit: Jose Azel/Aurora/PNI.)

was painted to be a focus of Christian worship. The Christian was not worshiping the icon itself, but the figure depicted. Thus, if the image was venerated (typically with a deeply reverential bow, or with an offering of incense before it), then the worship such devotion represented would pass directly to the person depicted within the image: whether it was Christ, the Virgin, or one of the saints. The icon became, therefore, a primary medium of Christian worship. These theologians (named iconodules, or venerators of icons) created a technical vocabulary of worship, distinguishing among important concepts such as adoration, worship, veneration, and reverence. They accused their iconoclastic accusers of not having sufficient intellectual subtlety, or tolerant humility, to recognize a genuinely Christian theology of culture. And they argued that to advocate the smashing of icons was nothing short of blasphemous. The theological argument of the iconoclasts that the spiritual God cannot be depicted in material form was answered by iconodules arguing that since the Incarnation God has indeed been embodied in Christ, so he now can be depicted in graphic form. The practice of iconography was, therefore, allied with the expression of a strong doctrine of divine Incarnation, and this remains true in Orthodoxy today.

The iconodule theologians, and Eastern Christians as a whole, defended the practice of venerating icons, and to this day it is a very marked feature of Orthodox religious practice. The Western Church never elaborated a doctrine of religious art in the same intense manner. The West preferred to approach art in a pedagogical, intellectualist fashion. Thus religious art existed in churches to serve a teaching function. In the East, by contrast, the icon existed to fulfill a doxological function. Art was not to be looked at for didactic reasons but to be experienced as a medium of prayer.

Accordingly, Orthodox icons are functionally used: They are kissed in church celebrations, carried in processions, laid over people for purposes of blessing, incensed, and so forth. It is unusual for an Orthodox home to be without several icons, and the churches will have many, not least the large icons that separate the altar area, or sanctuary, from the main body of the church. This screen (iconostasis) usually holds life-size figures of Christ, the Virgin, John the Baptist, and the patron saint of the church.

In the course of the twentieth century, with a large Orthodox presence accumulating in North America, icons again became much more familiar to Western Christians, and they are once more becoming popular across a wide range of churches other than the Orthodox.

See also COPTIC ORTHODOX CHURCH; EASTERN ORTHODOXY.

BIBLIOGRAPHY

Limouris, G. *Icons: Windows on Eternity.* 1990.

McGuckin, J. A. "The Theology of Images and the Legitimation of Power in Eighth-Century Byzantium." *St. Vladimir's Theological Quarterly* 37, no. 1 (1993): 39–58.

Rice, D. T. *Icons and Their History.* 1974.

Weitzmann, K. *The Icon.* 1978.

John Anthony McGuckin

Identity Christianity

Identity Christianity (IC) is a theological stew composed in equal parts of hackneyed linguistics, conspiratology, pyramidology, and UFO lore. Seasoned with apocalyptic urgency and right-wing politics, it is topped with a rich layer of British Israelism. Emerging from the crucible of American religious experimentation, Los Angeles, in the 1940s, the mother church moved to Idaho, where its paramilitary arm, the Aryan Nations, was organized in the 1970s. Independent groups broke away because of personal jealousies, tactical disagreements, and theological disputes. Most of these are located today in the Rocky Mountain and Pacific Coast states. During the 1980s and 1990s these became seedbeds of terrorism. The violence was partly attributable to successful recruitment efforts by IC missionaries of disaffected white youths and prison inmates.

IC is manicheistic. It sees the world as divided into good and evil, represented by Aryans and Jews, respectively. Black people ("muds") are viewed as quasi-human pawns in the Jewish One World conspiracy, together with "liberal dupes," "Reds," environmentalists, and feminists. What constitutes a Jew is a matter of heated debate. Nonracist ICs argue that the title applies to any members of the "satanic cult," Judaism, regardless of their race. IC racists disagree, insisting that regardless of their nominal faith, Jews are Khazars, an Asian folk supposedly descended from the mating of Shelah (the mongrel son of Judah) and the "red-skinned" Edomites. The Edomites themselves are considered to be the product of Esau (the losing competitor to Jacob-Israel for God's favor) and the "hooked-nosed" Hittites. Other IC racists maintain, simply, that the Jew is the "spawn of Satan," born from Eve's cohabitation with the Serpent. In this theory, the father of the Jews is Cain, history's first murderer.

Identity Christianity is so called because the "true" identity of the Aryan people is considered Israel. Hence the Bible is theirs; God's promise that Israel will rule the earth is theirs. Jesus Christ is not a Jew, but theirs, an Aryan. After being released from capture by the Assyrians, the story goes, the ten lost tribes of Israel migrated over the Caucasus Mountains—hence their racial type, Caucasian. Eventually they settled in various European countries, many of which today allegedly bear their names: Denmark (Denmark), the tribe of Dan; Jutland, Judah; Spain (Cadiz), Gad; and so on. Some ICs claim that America is the home of Manasseh, Ephraim's (Britain's) twin; others argue that it will be the final gathering place for all of Israel at the end of time. Elaborate archaeological data, etymologies, numerologies, and biblical promises are cited to buttress these claims.

IC doctrine is disseminated through underground media consisting of books, taped sermons, videos, and shortwave radio broadcasts. Some IC churches also sponsor conventions such as the Aryan World Conference, where cross-burnings are conducted, along with weapons and tactics training and evangelism. While the number of active IC congregants is minuscule, those who access its media range in the tens of thousands.

See also BRITISH ISRAELISM; DOGMATISM; FUNDAMENTALIST CHRISTIANITY; KU KLUX KLAN; RELIGIOUS RIGHT; SURVIVALISM.

BIBLIOGRAPHY

Aho, James A. *The Politics of Righteousness.* 1990.

Barkun, Michael. *Religion and the Racist Right.* 1994.

James A. Aho

Imam

Since the word "imam" has a long and complicated history in Muslim society, it is not surprising that its meaning and conceptualization should undergo some development when Islam is transferred to the North American milieu. Meaning "leader" or "master" in its early Arab form, it took on important new meanings with the historical evolution of Muslim civilization. Thus, in Sunni tradition, the imam is associated with community leadership of a ritual kind, while in Shi'ism, the Imam (always capitalized) takes on transcendent dimensions. Within Shi'ism there are obvious differences in understanding the roles associated with the imam, depending on whether we are referring to Twelver Shi'ism as represented by the majority religion of Iran, or Isma'ili tradition, whose religious head is the Aga Khan. These differences continue among Muslim immigrants.

At the same time, there has been an evolution of the imam of the local mosque brought about by the North American experience. For example, two important influences have been the rise of powerful African-American Muslim groups and the pressure of congregational structures within American culture. There are four principal areas of modification: educational, programmatic, official, and developmental. While most of these changes are found within Sunni organizations and African-American Muslim groups, they have also had an impact on Shi'a structures. While given different names, the functions are developing whatever the religious focus of the group.

Educational changes are most noticeable with regard to the leadership itself. In present-day North America, mosques are self-consciously taking an active and involved role in community life, and the need to have an educated leadership to appeal to the educational levels of members is having its effect. This is particularly evident where second- and third-generation immigrants have moved into positions of responsibility; these leaders have insisted that mosque personnel reflect their own educational levels. In some mosques, imams are also called on both to address the educational requirements of a college-educated clientele and to provide intellectual and cultural background for the practice of Islam for their children. One of the ongoing responsibilities is the teaching of Arabic, the liturgical language of Islam. Management, educational, and psychological counseling skills are also in high demand. These needs have encouraged a more educated leader within the mosque community.

Early leadership among immigrant communities arose from among immigrants themselves or from imams trained in schools "back home." Bringing imams to North America required sufficient financial commitment to pay salaries and provide housing, a situation that was difficult to sustain in the first half of the twentieth century. Several Middle Eastern countries subsidized organizations for this purpose. On the other hand, among the early Black Muslim masjids, missionary imams were supported by Elijah Muhammad's organization; once established, they were primarily dependent on family and converts for financial assistance. As Islam has matured in North America, some communities have set a benchmark amount for leading families to contribute so that religious organizations and mosques can be placed on fiscally solid ground. In keeping with North American expectations of "results" for payment, the imam has had to develop skills to meet expectations. At the same time, the demand for greater social and religious abilities has spawned a culture of workshops, seminars, and weekend retreats designed to address specific Islamic issues. In some cases, advanced schools have been set up on an ad hoc basis to address these sophisticated requirements for imams.

Muslims in North America have had to face the difficult task of dealing with a society whose values often conflict with those of traditional Islam. Moreover, mosque communities function in line with the congregational norm in North America: Religious institutions are entirely a matter of personal, not state, interest. Without a Muslim culture to sustain it, the mosque community must sustain itself, and this makes the local mosque much more a center of personal and religious continuity. The result is that programs aimed at maintaining and enhancing Islam shift to the mosque and its personnel. Imams must carry out training sessions for children and other young people, organize and staff family enrichment programs, promote Islam among converts, and develop community spirit. In these tasks the imam functions much as a minister or a rabbi in a Christian or a Judaic congregation. Promotional activity for Islam in general or the local mosque in particular is an added programmatic dimension of the imam's work.

Most religious jurisdictions in North America have an official face—that is, they represent to the public, to the media, and to the institutional culture distinctive attitudes and ideas. The official charged with this responsibility, reflecting the expectation of ministers in the population at large, is the imam. He (there are no female imams) must present the views of the group in public forums and in interactions with various charitable, educational, and political organizations; hence the requisite that the imam be highly articulate in English, and perhaps also (in some locales) in French and Spanish. Moreover, high-profile African-American Muslim spokespersons have established the expecta-

An imam leads his followers in afternoon prayer at the Assadiq Foundation's City of Knowledge School in Pomona, California, on Saturday, December 19, 1998, the eve of the holy month of Ramadan. (Credit: AP/Wide World Photos.)

tion that Muslim leaders be able to handle themselves in interviews with radio and TV personnel. Preaching, traditionally associated with the *ùlama* (scholarly class) in Muslim countries, has shifted to the mosque environment in North America, and likewise may be the responsibility of the imam. Interreligious dialogue is another task normally assigned to the imam. Finally, the imam is now crucially involved in ceremonial aspects of social life, such as marriages and funerals, which bring Muslims into the public eye, and peoples from other faiths into contact with Muslims. The role of mediator and interpreter of the tradition has rested on him.

Finally, the imam in North America has had to marshal support for developmental issues, such as the construction of Islamic schools, the formation and care of halfway houses for prisoners, and housing and support for broken families. Without the close family system found in traditional Muslim society, the mosque community, lead by the imam, has had to provide a surrogate network for the sustenance of community life. Thus, where families have traditionally been the foundation for marriage counseling and encouragement, in some cases that responsibility has shifted to the mosque community and professional help. Indeed, it is more the case that religious people will seek such assistance through sympathetic imams

rather than in secular counseling services. Moreover, the mobility of North American society has meant that the elderly may not live in the vicinity of their families. Mosques have therefore had to step in with programs to sustain the retired and the elderly, a responsibility that ultimately comes to bear on the imam and his sensitivity to problems of an aging society.

In short, the function of the imam within both indigenous and immigrant Islamic communities in North America has evolved perceptibly from the notion of leader and traditional ritual specialist originating in Islamic countries, reflecting the new and different cultural situation of Islam on this continent. More and more, the imam in North America is becoming a religious professional, befitting a sophisticated Islamic society with its own distinctive character in the religious landscape.

See also CLERGY; ISLAM; MINISTRY; MOSQUE; NATION OF ISLAM; PRACTICE; PREACHING; RITUAL; SEMINARIES.

BIBLIOGRAPHY

Madelung, W. "Imama." In *The Encyclopedia of Islam,* 2nd ed., vol. 3, edited by B. Lewis, V. L. Menage, C. Pellat, and J. Schacht. 1971.

Madelung, W. "Imamate." In *The Encyclopedia of Religion,* vol. 7, edited by M. Eliade. 1987.

Waugh, Earle H. "The Imam in the New World: Models and Modifications." In *Transitions and Transformations in the History of Religions,* edited by F. Reynolds and T. M. Ludwig. 1980.

Waugh, Earle H. "Muslim Leadership and the Shaping of the Umma: Classical Tradition and Religious Tension in the North American Setting." In *The Muslim Community in North America,* edited by E. H. Waugh, B. Abu-Laban, and R. Qureshi. 1983.

Earle H. Waugh

Immanence.

See Transcendence.

Implicit Religion

The concept of implicit religion originated in Britain in the 1960s, as an alternative to the assumption by the secularization thesis that the decline in organized religion was leading to the elimination of all experience of the sacred. The concept hypothesized that the understanding of secular life would be assisted if the possibility was entertained that it might contain, within itself, its own kind of religiosity. Indeed, the phrase that was originally used, "secular religion," expressed the sense of paradox that the suggestion encapsulated in 1967.

Three empirical tests of the concept's heuristic utility were undertaken (Bailey 1997). Since 1978 the Network for the Study of Implicit Religion has held three series of academic conferences, religious education courses, and church study days, which have no doubt helped to popularize the phrase. Also, since 1997 the Centre for the Study of Implicit Religion and Contemporary Spirituality has been located at Middlesex University in London. However, the more general recognition of the concept is presumably part of the general shift toward seeing the religious as a type of being human, rather than religion as a discrete kind of human behavior.

Thomas Luckmann's concept of "invisible religion" is almost identical to that of implicit religion and was also put forward, though in a much more developed way, in 1967. Robert Bellah's "civil religion" (1967) can be seen as another example of a similar hypothesis as far as societal behavior is concerned. The attention that has increasingly been given, since the 1960s, to "values" and culture, "ethos" and spirituality,

and that which is commonly said to be "implicit" in public or private life generally, can be seen as directing attention to particular aspects of the overall phenomenon of implicit religion.

Implicit religion has been defined in terms of "commitments," or "integrating foci," or "intensive concerns with extensive effects." The first description in particular suggests that the concern is with all levels of consciousness. The second description in particular suggests that the concern is with all widths of sociality. The third description in particular suggests that the religious elements in life (conscious or unconscious, individual or social) may not be fully integrated, but they must be reciprocally related to the secular. This use of the phrase to describe the core of a way of life chimes in with popular usage, certainly in the United Kingdom ("her real religion is her children"), and with the medieval monastic *religio,* from which the modern term presumably derives (rather than from the classical Latin).

Experience shows the need to add three caveats to the three definitions. First, implicit religion does not mean "implicit Christianity"—or an implicit form of any other religion that has so far been named. Indeed, no relationship (developmental, structural, or evaluative) is posited as existing between any particular form of implicit religion and any particular explicit religion. Second, any particular form of implicit religion is no more assumed to be a good thing than is any particular form of explicit religion. Indeed, as with explicit religion, religiosity is seen as a dimension of human beings (like sexuality, or spirituality and physicality) that therefore calls for study and understanding first, and only if necessary for evaluation subsequently. Third, implicit religion insists that (in advance of empirical study) anything *may* be sacred; this is a million miles away from saying that *everything is* sacred. So the core concern may be rather more focused than in studies of explicit religion.

See also CIVIL RELIGION; SPIRITUALITY.

BIBLIOGRAPHY

Bailey, E. I. *Implicit Religion in Contemporary Society.* 1997.

Bailey, E. I. *Implicit Religion: An Introduction.* 1998.

Bellah, R. N. "Civil Religion in America." *Daedalus: Journal of the American Academy of Arts and Sciences* 96, no. 1 (1967).

Luckmann, T. *The Invisible Religion.* 1967.

Edward I. Bailey

Inclusive Language

Inclusive language represents language intended to refer impartially to all people. In particular, it represents language that affirms women as well as men. Words such as "humanity," "humankind," and "people" convey a greater sense of impartiality than the generic usage of "man" and "mankind." The latter words are thought, more and more, to represent only males. Thus inclusive language refers to any words, phrases, and concepts that affirm both men and women, refusing to ignore or marginalize women in any way.

Why use inclusive language? For some it is merely a matter of clarity. Less confusion occurs when men are referred to as men; women are referred to as women; and men and women together are referred to as people. There are other reasons, of course, why Christians advocate inclusive language. It may involve loving others as yourself (Mark 12:31). It may also involve justice, advocating language that reflects the equal worth of all people, which was established by the creation of both men and women in the image of God (Genesis 1:27) and affirmed among those who are one in Jesus Christ (Galatians 3:28). For reasons such as these, an increasing number of Christians modify their language in ways that fully include women as well as men.

Mutual Respect

Although inclusive language usually involves references to men and women, it is considered more far-reaching. Sometimes inclusive language is described as bias-free language because it does not want to exclude or discriminate against anyone, regardless of gender, race, culture, nationality, or religion. The final purpose of inclusive language is to be nondiscriminatory toward all people, not just women. A special principle lies at the heart of inclusive language: mutual respect. Mutual respect has regard for the value of all people and how we relate to them.

Concern over inclusive language increased among Christians during the 1970s in the wake of the modern feminist movement. Feminists think that male-linked language serves to stereotype and oppress women. Words, after all, can define and shape who we are and who we want to become. So, it is argued, language reflective of a patriarchal society needs to be changed. Patriarchy represents a view of society in which men have authority over women, subordinating them through male-dominated practices and institutions in the family, church, and culture as a whole. Although patriarchy seems to represent the status quo in scripture, Christians increasingly think that scripture advocates greater recognition of the equality of men and women. Thus our language should reflect the equal affirmation of women, not only in the words we use but also the ways we describe them.

Language About God

Some Christians question the adequacy of male-linked language in reference to God. Since both men and women are created in God's image, God is thought to transcend male and female imagery. Although God is usually portrayed as a male in scripture, these Christians use generic terms in their references to deity—for example, God, Creator, and Spirit. They may not reject biblical language about God, but they discourage such usage in contemporary dialogue.

Other Christians think that God-talk should be changed radically. Because male-oriented language in reference to God may be thought to legitimize patriarchy, all male imagery of God should be eliminated, including male references to Jesus Christ. In some instances, it is argued that women, at least, need to re-image God as Goddess. This female imagery for deity is considered necessary in countering the repressive patriarchy of historic Christianity.

Opponents

Some Christians oppose the use of inclusive language. A common reason has to do with the pragmatic question of whether centuries of male-linked language, generically understood, need to be changed. The requisite modification of pronouns, nouns, and other ideas about women is considered difficult and sometimes awkward-sounding. Thus inclusive language is considered a nonissue, a view which is reinforced by the widespread failure of society to use it.

Another reason for opposing inclusive language stems from those who support a biblical basis for patriarchy. In reaction against inclusive language, these Christians consider it an accommodation to feminism. They argue that greater care should be taken in order to affirm women, but it should not occur at the expense of rejecting the biblically mandated hierarchy of creation (e.g., Genesis 2). Fidelity to the plain and obvious teachings of scripture should supersede Christian beliefs and practices influenced by feminism.

Spread of Inclusive Language

Christians increasingly consider inclusive language an important part of their belief and practice, at least with regard to their references to men and women. They incorporate it into their thoughts, speech, publications, and worship. Christian lectionaries, liturgy, hymnody, choruses, and other worship aids commonly use inclusive language. Several biblical translations also use inclusive language, the most notable being the New Revised Standard Version, published first in 1989.

Most Christians who use inclusive language consider it a matter of conscience. It is not merely a matter of political correctness to think seriously about how language serves to include or exclude others, perhaps trivializing or discriminating against them. Instead responsible phraseology should be used to promote inclusiveness.

See also FEMINIST THEOLOGY; GENDER ROLES; GOD; GODDESS; MATRIARCHY; PATRIARCHY; THEISM.

BIBLIOGRAPHY

Dumond, Val. *The Elements of Nonsexist Usage.* 1990.

Hardesty, Nancy A. *Inclusive Language in the Church.* 1987.

Kimel, Alvin F., ed. *Speaking the Christian God.* 1994.

Thorsen, Don, and Vickie Becker. *Inclusive Language Handbook.* 1998.

Don Thorsen

Indigenous Peoples, Religions of.

See Native American Religion.

International Society for Krishna Consciousness

Standing at the forefront of the contemporary emergence of Eastern religions in North America, the International Society for Krishna Consciousness was the first of the Asian religious groups to form in the wake of the changes in 1965 in the U.S. immigration laws allowing more Asians to immigrate to the United States. The society was founded by A. C. Bhaktivedanta Swami Prabhupada (1896–1977), who in the mature stage of his life was responding to the admonition of his teacher to bring the popular Bengalee Vaiṣṇava Hinduism, as taught by the Guadiya Mission, to the West. His arrival coincided with the coming of age of the baby boom generation and the emer-

A Hare Krishna devotee in San Francisco, California, 1982, sits on a cloth and intones a chant, the words of which are displayed on the placard next to him.   (Credit: CORBIS/Vince Streano.)

gence of the psychedelic street people subculture in America. He spoke directly to the subculture participants, offering them a means of getting high through meditation and chanting rather than taking drugs, and the overwhelming majority of people who joined were former drug users.

Swami Prabhupada taught a form of Vaiṣṇava practice that had been spread through Bengal by Chaitanya Mahaprabhu (1486–1534) and that offered freedom from this world's situation through adoption of the renounced life as a *sanyassin*, devotional service in a temple setting, and the chanting of the Hare Krishna mantra. The mantra was repeated as a prayer to Krishna, the Supreme Deity conceived as a personal God. When done while dancing and accompanying music, chanting lifted the believer into a transcendent consciousness.

Youthful male believers shaved their heads and adopted the saffron robe identifying themselves as monks. Devotees lived communally in Krishna temples; and supported the work of translating, printing, and distributing the books of their teacher through begging on the streets and in airports. In the early 1970s their lifestyle became one of the major targets of parental criticism, and the society was branded as a "cult." During the 1980s the society was one of the groups facing multiple deprogrammings and a major court case that threatened to wipe out much of the movement when it resulted in a multimillion-dollar judgment for brainwashing a member (later overturned on appeal). In the midst of the anti-cult controversy, the movement suffered from the defection of one of its more conservative gurus, Swami Bhaktipada, who had oversight of the centers in West Virginia and Ohio. Swami Bhaktipada became involved in illegal activities and was eventually convicted for ordering the death of an ex-member.

Through the 1980s and 1990s, as the brainwashing controversy was laid to rest in the courts, the movement spread internationally under the guidance of the Governing Body Commission, which had assumed authority in the movement following Swami Prabhupada's death, and a set of new gurus who assumed spiritual authority in different parts of the globe. Their support in North America was greatly expanded by the adherence of thousands of first-generation Indian Americans who found in the Hare Krishna temples the best representation of their religion in the West.

With their first-generation problems behind them, and with centers in more than sixty countries, the Krishnas have found their place in America's multireligious landscape.

See also ANTI-CULT MOVEMENT; BELONGING, RELIGIOUS; BRAINWASHING; CHANTING; CONVERSION; CULT; CULT AWARENESS NETWORK; FREEDOM OF RE-LIGION; GURU; HINDUISM; MEDITATION; MUSIC; NEW RELIGIOUS MOVEMENTS; PROSELYTIZING; RELIGIOUS COMMUNITIES; TRANSCENDENCE; TRANSCENDENTAL MEDITATION.

BIBLIOGRAPHY

Bromley, David G., and Larry D. Shinn, eds. *Krishna Consciousness in the West.* 1989.

Prabhupada, Swami A. C. Bhaktivedanta. *Bhagavad-Gita As It Is.* 1972.

Shinn, Larry D. *The Dark Lord: Images of the Hare Krishna in America.* 1987.

J. Gordon Melton

InterVarsity Christian Fellowship

InterVarsity Christian Fellowship (IVCF) is an interdenominational, evangelical parachurch organization promoting personal spiritual and intellectual development on American college and university campuses. Founded in England in 1877, IVCF came to Canada in 1928. With the support of Chicago industrialist Herbert J. Taylor, IVCF established an American branch in September 1941 under the leadership of C. Stacey Woods. Opening with chapters on forty-six U.S. campuses, IVCF had more than five hundred chapters by the early 1950s—growth enhanced by its absorption of the Student Foreign Missions Fellowship (1945) and the Christian Nurses' Fellowship (1948). From the 1960s through the late 1990s IVCF fluctuated between seven hundred and nine hundred campus chapters, with active membership ranging between twenty thousand and thirty thousand students. Over the years, its massive Urbana Missionary Conference has been its most important activity. Held every third year over the Christmas vacation at the University of Illinois, it has continued the traditions of the Student Volunteer Movement and other evangelical youth mission organizations. In the 1990s the Urbana conferences attracted an average of nearly twenty thousand students.

Along with groups such as Campus Crusade for Christ and the Navigators, IVCF played an important role in establishing a visible evangelical presence on American campuses in the post–World War II era. IVCF is unique among these groups, however, in that its enduring British heritage has emphasized the life of the mind over pragmatic revivalism. As a result, IVCF, with its publishing arm, InterVarsity Press (founded in 1948), has been a consistent advocate for an intellectually engaged evangelicalism. In this role it has done much to foster a thoughtful approach to contemporary intellectual, cultural, and social questions not only within InterVarsity's constituency but within the wider evangelical subculture as well.

See also CAMPUS CRUSADE FOR CHRIST; EVANGELICAL CHRISTIANITY; JESUS MOVEMENT; NAVIGATORS; YOUTH FOR CHRIST.

BIBLIOGRAPHY

Hunt, Keith, and Gladys Hunt. *For Christ and the University: The Story of InterVarsity Christian Fellowship of the U.S.A., 1940–1990.* 1991.
InterVarsity Christian Fellowship. Collection 300, archives of the Billy Graham Center, Wheaton College, Ill.
Woods, C. Stacey. *The Growth of a Work of God.* 1978.

Larry Eskridge

Islam

Islam is the religion of Muslims. The word, which literally means "submission," signifies that human beings should, instead of taking the path of confrontation with God, surrender to his will and accept him as the lord and master of their lives. It also means "peace," and this meaning is related to the first in that submission to God is supposed to bring peace to human beings in this life and the next. Islam is ordinarily associated with the name of the seventh-century Arabian prophet Muhammad. However, it claims to have been the religion of all prophets—even those who preceded Muhammad. What is meant is that all prophets taught submission to God and promised peace as a result of that submission.

Muhammad

Muhammad (ca. 570–632), who was born in Mecca and belonged to its ruling tribe, Quraysh, began preaching Islam after receiving his first revelation in 610. The message criticized Arab idolatry and called for a return to the religion of Abraham, whom the Arabs acknowledged both as their great ancestor and as their religious and spiritual leader. The Quraysh were at first indifferent but became concerned, even alarmed, upon noticing that Muhammad was gaining dedicated converts. Though undeterred by the Quraysh's persecution of them, the Prophet and his followers migrated to Medina, to the north, when an opportunity of establishing a foothold in that wartorn city presented itself. In Medina the Muslims became the dominant element and, after a series of battles with the Quraysh, conquered Mecca in 630, two years before Muhammad's death. In a short time almost all of Arabia embraced Islam. Muhammad is regarded as the last prophet and is believed to have lived an exemplary life, which Muslims try to emulate.

Sources

The fundamental sources of Islam are two—the Qur'an, the name by which the collective revelations of Muhammad are known; and Muhammad's *sunna*, or exemplary conduct. Broadly speaking, the Qur'an is the source of dogma, whereas the sunna furnishes details of Islamic praxis in its ideal form. The sunna is available to us in the form of *hadith*, which consists of Muhammad's sayings and actions as transmitted by Muhammad's companions. A clear distinction is made between the Qur'an, the Word of God; and hadith, the word of Muhammad. Hadith, however, is essential to the exposition and understanding of the Qur'an. The Qur'an and hadith are the two principal sources of Islamic law, though analogy (precedent-based reasoning) and consensus (scholarly agreement on the solution to a given problem) are also recognized as being important.

Beliefs

Islam is often presented as a complete code of Islam—which is to say that Islam contains not only a belief system but also commandments pertaining to all spheres of practical life. Islamic dogma consists of three major beliefs: monotheism (there is only one God), prophecy (a series of persons were chosen by God to convey his message to humankind), and the afterlife (human beings will be resurrected, judged, and sent to Heaven or Hell depending on their performance in this world). Belief in angels and scriptures is also enjoined. But the first—belief in angels as creatures and servants of God—can be taken as a corrective to the idolatrous Arabs' view of them as God's daughters and thus subsumed under monotheism, whereas the second—that scriptures were revealed to some of the prophets—can be regarded as a supplement to the belief in prophecy. Called the Articles of Faith, these beliefs are often expounded in great detail by Muslim theologians but are essentially simple, which accounts for their enduring appeal. They are summed up in the Islamic Testimony: There is no god but God, and Muhammad is His messenger.

Rituals

Islamic religious practice takes the form of four main rituals, called the Pillars of Islam (the Islamic Testimony, on which they are grounded, is regarded as the fifth Pillar). They are: prayer (to be performed five times a day in a prescribed manner), fasting (during Ramadan, the ninth month of the Islamic lunar calendar), welfare due (mandatory charity, to be given

Muslims observing afternoon prayer on October 6, 1995, at the Islamic Cultural Center of New York, the largest mosque in Manhattan.   (Credit: AP/Wide World Photos.)

once a year according to a certain formula), and pilgrimage (performed at the Kaʿbah in Mecca at least once in one's lifetime). Taken together, the rituals will be seen to involve bodily exertion, spiritual and mental concentration, and expense of time and money; they call for serious commitment by the individual. But they also have a social and egalitarian dimension. In prayer, for example, rich and poor Muslims stand shoulder to shoulder behind a prayer leader who is not a priest and who may belong to any social class. Likewise, the welfare due seeks to help the poor and the needy in society.

Disciplines of Knowledge

As the fundamental text of Islam, the Qur'an had to be studied carefully. Preoccupation with the Word of God led to the rise of the discipline of Qur'an exegesis, with a large number of commentaries—some comprehensive, others specialized—being produced. Focus on the legislative and doctrinal material in the Qur'an gave rise to the sciences of law and theology (and the latter in turn to the rise of philosophy), whereas the spiritual teachings of the scriptures paved the way for mysticism. Since Muhammad was believed to have lived an ideal life worthy of emulation by Mus-

lims and expounded the Qur'an through his words and actions, the fields of *sira* (Muhammad's biography) and hadith were developed both as aids to understanding the Qur'an and as possessing intrinsic importance and value. Interest in the life of the Prophet soon grew into an interest in the lives of other distinguished persons and in the careers of nations, and so biography and historiography were developed. Finally, the Qur'anic exhortation to study nature as the handiwork of God and as containing signs and evidence of the glory and mercy of God provided an impetus to the growth of natural sciences. The Islamic religious, social, and natural sciences are thus informed by a certain orientational and conceptual unity that ultimately derives from the Qur'an.

Major Issues in Islamic Thought

One issue each from theology, philosophy, and mysticism will be cited. A principal concern of the Muslim theologians was to explain the scope of human freedom in view of the divine omnipotence stressed in the Qur'an. Most theologians, while conceding that human freedom is necessary to meaningful moral behavior in this world and also to reward and punishment in the next, were inclined to accept a more or less predestinarian view, although a strong libertarian undercurrent has always been present. In philosophy Muslim thinkers sought to harmonize Islamic faith with Greek thought, but they ran into difficulties on such issues as the eternity of the world and were severely criticized by the orthodox for selling Islam short. In mysticism a reaction against legalism and formalism led many sensitive people to draw on the spiritual sources of the religion to have a more personal experience of God. Overall, Muslim intellectuals have tried to realize the ideals and norms of a monotheistic religion in different areas of thought and life.

Spread of Islam

After its establishment on the Arabian peninsula, Islam spread quickly outside. Iran, Iraq, and Syria were conquered early, as were parts of Central Asia, and successful military operations were mounted in North Africa, Spain, and India. Muhammad was succeeded by four caliphs (632–661), whom the Sunnites reverently remember as the "rightly guided caliphs" (cf. the Shi'ite view below). They were followed by the Umayyad (661–750) and 'Abbasid (750–1258 and later) dynasties. But more remarkable than the physical expansion was the acculturation of the large numbers of new converts. For example, Arabic became the *lingua franca* of the Muslim world—almost all of the primary sources of Islam, no matter where produced, are in Arabic—and possession of knowledge of the Qur'an and hadith gave anyone a position of respect in society. Likewise, well-defined rituals and values arising out of a set of simple beliefs imparted a basic unity of thought and approach in the theoretical and practical domains of life; and an essentially egalitarian society, by facilitating physical mobility, social interaction, and intellectual advancement—especially in cosmopolitan areas—opened up new opportunities, making Islam a desirable choice for the non-Muslim citizens. Today there are more than fifty countries, mostly in Asia and Africa, with substantial numbers of Muslims. Most Muslims are not Arabs (Arabs form only about 20 percent of the world Muslim population). In the modern period, until a few decades ago, large parts of the Muslim world were under colonial domination, and their economic and political systems have been heavily influenced by those of the colonizing countries. Problems of poverty, illiteracy, and oppressive political and economic structures plague many Muslim countries, but there are signs that a general reawakening, with a definite Islamic component, is occurring in many places. In many countries young Muslims are trying to rediscover their Islamic roots; the demand for Islamic literature—both classical and modern—is high; and a determination to implement Islamic law is noticeable.

Sunnites and Shi'ites

Islamic society was not without its problems, though. An early split was to have profound theological and political consequences. The Shi'ites (literally "partisans") believe that prophets are succeeded by infallible leaders and guides known as *imams*. The largest Shi'ite sect believes in a series of twelve imams beginning with 'Ali, Muhammad's cousin and son-in-law and fourth caliph after him, and ending with an imam who went into a state of occultation in the 870s but who is expected to make a triumphal return at the end of time. Most Shi'ites reject the caliphate of the first three of the rightly guided caliphs and interpret Islamic history differently from the Sunnites. Twelver Shi'ism has become a powerful political force in Iran since the 1979 revolution there.

Islam in America

The Muslims in America number about six million. They can be divided into two categories, indigenous and immigrant. In the 1930s Elijah Muhammad founded the Nation of Islam, criticizing the whites as devils and preaching a black supremacist doctrine. Malcolm X, a prominent member of the party, made the pilgrimage to Mecca, where he saw the Islamic egalitarian principle at work. Upon his return he renounced allegiance to Elijah Muhammad and supported mainstream Islam; he was assassinated in suspicious circumstances. After Elijah Muhammad's death in 1975, his son Warith Deen Muhammad gradually brought the Nation of Islam into mainstream Islam, although a group under Louis Farrakhan clung to the old philosophy; this latter group is not regarded by most Muslims as holding the right views.

The immigrants came to America in several waves. The early decades of the twentieth century saw the arrival of many Arab workers in the automotive and steel industries. In the middle decades students arrived, and then professionals, both groups representing a wider spectrum of the world Muslim population. Today the immigrant Muslims can be divided into two main groups—those from Arab countries and those from the Indian subcontinent. On the whole, the immigrants have been quite active in building mosques, schools, and Islamic centers. With their strong educational background and diversified vocational expertise they are relatively more resourceful and have taken the initiative in launching Islamic projects. But whether indigenous or immigrant, the American Muslims have several common problems. There is, for example, the issue of integration: To what extent may they assimilate to mainstream American society without losing their religious identity? There is also concern about giving the younger generation an Islamic education that is meaningful in the American context. Media coverage of Islam and Muslims is usually negative, and stereotypes abound. Several Muslim organizations now monitor anti-Muslim portrayals in literature, films, and public and private institutions, and some progress has been made in this regard.

See also ALLAH; FARRAKHAN, LOUIS; IMAM; ISLAMIC CIRCLE OF NORTH AMERICA; ISLAMIC SOCIETY OF NORTH AMERICA; MALCOLM X; MECCA; MOSQUE; MUHAMMAD, ELIJAH KARRIEM; MUHAMMAD, WARITH DEEN; MULLAH; MUSLIM BROTHERHOOD; MYSTICISM; NATION OF ISLAM; QUR'AN; RITUAL.

BIBLIOGRAPHY

Esposito, John L. *Islam, the Straight Path,* 3rd ed. 1998.

Haddad, Yvonne Yazbeck, and Adair T. Lummis. *Islamic Values in the United States: A Comparative Study.* 1987.

Watt, W. Montgomery. *The Formative Period of Islamic Thought.* 1973.

Wormser, Richard. *American Islam: Growing Up Muslim in America.* 1994.

Mustansir Mir

from Afghanistan to Bosnia. Its Muslim Alert Network closely monitors anti-Muslim activities and literature. But while it has a strong outreach program, it also emphasizes personal piety: Its members, who are expected to perform da'wah for at least a certain numbers of hours every week, are required to adhere strictly to the Islamic code of behavior in their personal life and public dealings.

The ICNA is deeply influenced by the work and writings of Abu'l A'la Mawdudi (d. 1979), the founder of the Jama'at-i Islami (Islamic Party) of Pakistan (and India), and is controlled mainly by Pakistanis. It is governed by a constitution and is run by elected officials. It is headquartered in Jamaica, New York.

See also ISLAM; ISLAMIC SOCIETY OF NORTH AMERICA; JOURNALISM, RELIGIOUS; PRISON AND RELIGION; PUBLISHING, RELIGIOUS.

BIBLIOGRAPHY

Barazangi, Nimat Hafiz. "Islamic Education in the United States and Canada: Conception and Practice of the Islamic Belief System." In *The Muslims of America,* edited by Yvonne Yazbeck Haddad. 1991.

Johnson, Steve A. "Political Activity of Muslims in America." In *The Muslims of America,* edited by Yvonne Yazbeck Haddad. 1991.

Mustansir Mir

Islamic Circle of North America

The Islamic Circle of North America (ICNA) is a Muslim organization that evolved in the early 1980s from the earlier Circle of Friends. The ICNA's declared aim is to invite all people—Muslims and non-Muslims—to submit to the will of God by accepting him as the sole sovereign and by implementing his commandments in all spheres of life. Thus it is essentially a *da'wah* (missionary) organization. In presenting its message it seeks to make full use of modern communications technology: It employs multimedia resources to disseminate information about Islamic religion and culture. Aimed at general audiences, the audiovisual materials produced by it explain the teachings of Islam, present the Islamic viewpoint on issues affecting Islam and Muslims, and document major events involving Muslims in modern times. A variety of ICNA websites provide online information about Islam, and a toll-free telephonic service answers questions about Islam. ICNA is active in prisons, distributing Islamic literature among inmates and helping converts in the practice of their religion. It has mounted a series of relief efforts for Muslims in need,

Islamic Society of North America

The Islamic Society of North America (ISNA) is a large umbrella organization of Muslims in North America. Established in 1982–1983, the ISNA grew out of the Muslim Students Association (MSA), which had been founded in 1963 to help the growing immigrant Muslim student population preserve their identity and practice their religion in a non-Islamic environment. Unlike the MSA, the ISNA aimed at organizing the larger Muslim groups across North America. Boasting a membership of several thousand, the ISNA today includes and coordinates the activities of the MSA and many other organizations. It has an ambitious social and educational program: It seeks to help local communities establish mosques, schools, and student houses; owns a publishing house that produces Islamic literature for use at all levels; puts out a periodical, *Islamic Horizons,* and several professional journals; holds annual conventions in major cities where eminent scholars from the Islamic world are invited to speak; arranges seminars and workshops for teachers and Islamic workers; and arranges study groups and other programs for youth. It has established financial institutions to enable Muslims to make investments in accordance with Islamic economic principles. Finally, it tries to create political awareness among Muslims to enable them to play an effective role in the political process. The ISNA is governed by a constitution and is administered by elected officials. It is headquartered in Plainfield, Indiana.

The ISNA's significance lies not only in that it represents a developed stage of organized Muslim activity in America and Canada, but also in that it has begun to produce a new crop of Muslim leaders, activists, and professionals who, with their distinctive experiences and perspectives, will influence the coming generations of Muslims in North America and also will help to determine ways in which Islam and Muslims are perceived in the West.

See also ISLAM; ISLAMIC CIRCLE OF NORTH AMERICA; JOURNALISM, RELIGIOUS; MOSQUE; PUBLISHING, RELIGIOUS.

BIBLIOGRAPHY

Ahmed, Gutbi Mahdi. "Muslim Organizations in the United States." In *The Muslims of America,* edited by Yvonne Yazbeck Haddad. 1991.

Johnson, Steve A. "Political Activity of Muslims in America." In *The Muslims of America,* edited by Yvonne Yazbeck Haddad. 1991.

Nyang, Sulayman. "Islamic Society of North America." In *Oxford Islamic Encyclopedia of the Modern Islamic World,* edited by John J. Esposito. 1995.

Mustansir Mir

J

Jackson, Jesse

(1941–), minister, politician, and civil rights activist.

The Reverend Jesse Jackson was born Jesse Burns in Greenville, South Carolina. He was raised as a Baptist. His mother, Helen Burns, was a domestic and beautician, while his father, Noah Robinson, was a married neighbor. Two years after Jesse was born, his mother married Charles Jackson, who adopted her son in 1957. Jackson later described his struggle to overcome the prejudice he faced because of his out-of-wedlock birth as an important motivating factor in his success.

A star high school athlete in Greenville, Jackson then attended North Carolina Agricultural and Technical State College in Greensboro on a football scholarship. During his years in Greensboro, Jackson became active in the civil rights movement and organized sit-ins at segregated local facilities.

After his graduation in 1964, Jackson entered the Chicago Theological Seminary, where he studied for two years. Meanwhile, he joined the Southern Christian Leadership Conference (SCLC), a nonviolent civil rights organization. His leadership talents attracted the notice of the Reverend Dr. Martin Luther King Jr., SCLC's leader, and in 1966 King selected Jackson to lead the Chicago branch of Operation Breadbasket, an SCLC program that used boycotts of various companies to secure better jobs and living conditions for African-Americans. Jackson succeeded so well that in 1967 he was made Operation Breadbasket's national director.

In June 1968, two months after King was assassinated in Jackson's presence in Memphis, Tennessee, Jackson was ordained as a Baptist minister in the National Baptist Convention, U.S.A. Although he did not take up a pulpit, his language and oratorical style borrowed heavily from black religious tradition. Similarly, his acute concern for social injustice and economic disparity was a direct outgrowth not only of his personal experiences but of that black church tradition of social reform. After Dr. King's death, Jackson's relationship with SCLC became strained, and in 1971 he left SCLC and founded Operation PUSH (People United to Save Humanity), which combined black economic empowerment with educational achievement and inculcation of self-esteem. He remained director of PUSH until 1984.

On October 30, 1983, Jackson, long a Democrat, took his religiously inspired social activism one step further by announcing his candidacy for the Democratic nomination for the presidency of the United States. Early in 1984, before the first primaries were held, Jackson gained national visibility when he personally negotiated the release of Robert Goodman, from Syria, a captured U.S. military pilot. As the presidential campaign went into full swing shortly thereafter, Jackson organized his campaign around what he called a "rainbow coalition" of progressive and disfranchised groups. Although his campaign was hindered by lack of funds, logistical troubles, and Jackson's much-publicized, seemingly anti-Semitic slur against New York City as "Hymietown," he finished a strong third for the nomination and boosted Democratic voter registration efforts. Four years later, Jack-

337

Rev. Jesse Jackson gives the eulogy for his father, Noah Lewis Robinson, on Sunday, February 2, 1997, at Tabernacle Baptist Church in Greenville, South Carolina.   (Credit: AP/Wide World Photos.)

son again ran for president as a Democrat, even as the evangelical leader Pat Robertson was seeking the presidency as a Republican. Although Jackson failed to be nominated, he received seven million votes and over twelve hundred delegates and gained widespread praise for his oratory at the Democratic National Convention.

During the 1990s Jackson actively campaigned for jobs and equal rights for African-Americans. He pursued numerous other activities, including a television show in 1991 and an unsuccessful bid to assume leadership of the National Association for the Advancement of Colored People in 1994. In 1999, a year after President Clinton selected Jackson as his spiritual adviser following revelations of Clinton's affair with Monica Lewinsky, Jackson earned both praise and criticism when he met with Serbian dictator Radovan Milosevic to negotiate the release of three American soldiers captured during NATO air strikes in Yugoslavia.

See also AFRICAN-AMERICAN RELIGIONS; ANTI-SEMITISM; KING, MARTIN LUTHER, JR.; SOUTHERN CHRISTIAN LEADERSHIP CONFERENCE.

BIBLIOGRAPHY

Frady, Marshall. *Jesse Jackson: A Biography.* 1996.

Hertzke, Allen D. *Echoes of Discontent: Jesse Jackson, Pat Robertson, and the Resurgence of Populism.* 1993.

Jackson, Jesse. *Straight from the Heart.* 1987.

Reynolds, Barbara. *Jesse Jackson: The Man, the Myth, the Movement.* 1975.

White, Jack. "The Trouble with Jesse." *Time* (May 17, 1999).

Greg Robinson

Jainism

The Jaina religious tradition originated in northern India. It emphasizes the observance of nonviolence (*ahimsa*) to purge the soul (*jiva*) of karma. The ultimate goal of Jainism is to achieve liberation (*kevala*) from rebirth. Many Jainas engage themselves in the businesses of trade, publishing, and jewelry. Two early teachers, Parsvanatha (ca. 800 B.C.E.) and Mahāvīra, the Jina (ca. 450 B.C.E.) organized large congregations of nuns and monks. Mahāvīra, a contemporary of the Buddha, emphasized the observance of nonviolence, truthfulness, not stealing, sexual restraint, and nonpossession.

Jainism first came to America when Virchand Raghavji Gandhi spoke at the 1893 World Parliament of Religions in Chicago. In 1933, Champat Rai Jain presented a talk on "Ahimsa as the Key to World Peace" at a meeting of the World Fellowship of Faiths. A handful of Jainas came to the United States from India and East Africa in the 1950s and settled in America. Through the World Jaina Mission, a few Americans of European descent converted to Jainism at this time.

Two factors contributed to a sharp rise in the number of Jainas in America during the 1960s. In 1965 the Asian Exclusion Acts of the 1880s and 1920s were overturned by legislation that allowed greater numbers of nonwhites to become permanent residents and citizens. Kenya and Tanzania expelled large numbers of South Asians in 1967 and 1968; many of these were Jaina merchants. In 1971, all Indians were required to leave Uganda during the repressive regime of Idi Amin. Many Jainas left for England, and some of them then proceeded to the United States.

Throughout the 1960s and 1970s, Jainas often teamed with Hindus to create worship spaces to serve both religions. The Jain Center of New York was established in 1966, and the first Jaina-only temple was opened by the Jain Center of Boston in 1973. The Jaina teacher Muni Sri Chitrabhanu opened the Jain Meditation International Center in New York in 1975, and Acarya Sushi Kumarji established Siddhacalam, a Jaina ashram in the Poconos (in northeastern Pennsylvania) in 1983. The Jain Society of Southern California established a Jaina temple and library in 1986. The largest Jain temple complex in America, established by the Jain Society of Chicago, was dedicated in 1993. Other temples can be found in Washington, D.C., in New Jersey, in Richardson, Texas, in Toronto, and in other cities. Every two years the Jaina community convenes a major convention sponsored by the Federation of Jaina Associations in North America. Surveying event attendance and temple rosters, Bhuvanendra Kumar estimates that between sixty to one hundred thousand Jainas live in North America.

Jaina holidays include Mahāvīra Jayanti, the birthday of the Jina, which occurs in March or April, and Paryusan, a special seven-day fast observed during late August. The Nammokkara Mantra, the primary Jaina prayer, ideally chanted twice each day, pays homage to the Jinas, the liberated souls, the teachers, the leaders of religious orders, and to the nuns and monks who have taken vows of nonviolence. The two Jaina denominations, the Svetambara and Digambara, both look to Umasvati's *Tattvarthasutra* (ca. 100 C.E.) as the authoritative text on Jaina philosophy, cosmology, and ethics. The Jaina community in North America publishes three journals: the *Jain Study Circular* (New York), *Jain Digest* (various cities), and *Jinamanjari* (Toronto).

The Jaina tradition has attracted interest from the animal rights movement, and many Jainas have become involved with vegetarian societies. Web sites, newsletters, teacher training, and a variety of community events for young people seem to indicate that the Jaina community, which has survived for nearly three millennia as a minority tradition in India, will continue to thrive through successive generations in North America.

See also ANIMAL RIGHTS; HINDUISM; KARMA; PACIFISM; VEGETARIANISM.

BIBLIOGRAPHY

Dundas, Paul. *The Jains.* 1992.

Jaini, Padmanabh S. *The Jaina Path of Purification.* 1979.

King, Noel, and Surendra Singhvi. "Jain Studies in the West." *Jinamanjari,* 9, no. 1 (1994): 56–63.

Kumar, Bhuvanendra. *Jainism in America.* 1996.

Umasvati. *Tattvartha Sutra: That Which Is,* translated by Nathmal Tatia, with the combined commentaries of Umasvati, Pujyapada, and Siddhasenaguni. 1994.

Christopher Key Chapple

Japanese-American Religions

This article is not about Japanese religions in America, but about Japanese-American religions. That is an important distinction. There is much writing about Japanese religions in America—about Zen Buddhism, Soka Gakkai, etc.—and those religions have a prominent public profile, including celebrity believers. These faiths have tens of thousands of adherents, but their adherents are mainly European Americans (along with a few African Americans and others). This article, rather, is about the religious experiences of Japanese Americans.

The Japanese-American population is now four and five generations removed from Japan. The main period of immigration from Japan came between the first importations of workers to Hawaiian plantations in the 1880s and the U.S. government's abrupt cutoff of Asian immigration in 1924. The majority of those immigrants, like other Japanese of the Meiji era, carried a mixture of Buddhist, Confucianist, and Shinto religious beliefs and practices. Shinto, an amorphous blend of nature-oriented religious expressions, identifications, stories, and quasi-deities that had long existed in Japan at the folk level, was codified by the government into a national cult in the last third of the nineteenth century as a prop to a growing national identity.

Most Japanese immigrants, called Issei, had some familiarity with this religious field. But they had a more articulate sense of Buddhism as a formal religion with doctrine and institutions. Confucianism was the religio-philosophical system that underlay the patriarchal, extended Japanese-American family structure. As such, it may be seen as foundational to all Japanese-American religious experience, for it was in the family, not in formal communal institutions, that most religious activity and expression resided.

Most Japanese-American families in the immigrant generation (and many in succeeding generations) kept a *butsudan,* or home shrine or alcove. In these sacred spaces, believers would light incense, contemplate the Dharma, remember deceased loved ones, and recite prayers and the name of the Buddha. Families had recourse to formal religious institutions for weddings, funerals, and other ceremonial occasions. Yet though a majority bore the Buddhist label gladly, that did not mean regular activity at a formal religious institution. By the early twentieth century there were Buddhist temples in every city with a significant Japanese population, and a few Shinto shrines in places, such as Honolulu, with heavy concentrations of Issei. Buddhist priests (almost always missionaries from Japan rather than American-born, even today) were reckoned by all to be community leaders.

A Japanese-American woman dressed in traditional garb (a quilted kimono and a large cloth headdress), holding a horse-headed rod in a ceremony at the Japanese Village in Anaheim, California. (Credit: © John Running/Stock, Boston/PNI.)

A significant minority of the immigrants had become Christians in Japan and chose to emigrate in part because they perceived the United States to be a Christian nation. Many more became Christians in America. Indeed, Christian missionaries were very active in Japanese immigrant communities, where they provided English classes, lessons in American social behavior, health care, employment referrals, and other practical services along with spiritual tutelage. Thus they won many converts.

Many Issei adopted Christianity partly because they saw it as part and parcel of becoming American, or at least of succeeding in America. Some historians emphasize a Japanese nationalist role for Protestant Christianity in the years before World War II—fully as much as Buddhist institutions, they say, Issei Christian institutions abetted Japanese nationalism in the diaspora. Whatever its political role, Christianity appealed to some Issei more than Buddhism because they saw Christianity as an activist religion rather than a fatalistic one, and thus better suited to the American cultural scene.

By the 1930s, Christian and Buddhist institutions had come to assume similar shapes in Japanese American communities. Each called itself a "church," each had Sunday school and regular worship services, each sponsored youth groups and basketball teams and women's societies. All these activities took place in a racially segregated environment; except for a few Christian missionaries, all the participants were Japanese Americans.

The Japanese-American second generation, or Nisei, came of age during World War II. Nearly as many of them were Christians as Buddhists. There were even more Christians in those places where Japanese Americans were relatively better integrated into the non-Japanese population. There were comparatively more Christians in the Pacific Northwest than in California and more in California than in Hawaii, where the Japanese community was dense and tied together by Buddhist institutions in a way that did not occur on the continent. Shinto as a formal religious expression declined after the first generation, although a residual link with nature remained in the popular Japanese-American consciousness.

In the concentration camps in which the U.S. government imprisoned Japanese Americans during World War II, Buddhism was suppressed and came to be viewed by many as an expression of resistance to government oppression. This further impelled the more assimilationist elements of the American-born population toward Christianity. In the postwar period, many Nisei fled identification with Japan and things Japanese and sought to merge into the white middle class. As they did so, some moved from Buddhist to Japanese-American Christian churches. Others left institutional religion altogether or sought places in white congregations. Private, family worship and a Japanese-derived sense of spirituality (self-discipline, contemplation, harmony with nature, devotion to the family) continued informally even as formal linkages changed.

Today Buddhism is barely a majority religious identity among Japanese Americans. The Japanese-American variety is quite different from the Buddhisms best known to non-Japanese Americans. White forms of Buddhism, particularly Zen, concentrate on individual meditation and enlightenment. The most populous variety of Japanese American Buddhism, Jodo Shinshu, is a more populist religion, stressing ritual recitation of the name of the Amida Buddha, ethical living, community, and the goal of achieving the western Pure Land in a future life.

Families with both Christian and Jodo Shinshu ties have been characterized by adherence to Japanese ethical values or attitudes that some call religious. Most prominent among them are *on* (obligation), *giri* (duty), *shikataganai* (acceptance of things beyond one's control), *enryo* (restraint), *gaman* (endurance), and *arigatai* (gratitude). All these together spur hard work, concern for the collectivity, and suppression of individualistic tendencies—values that have contributed to material and social success for the Japanese-American population at large.

One remarkable development in Christianity has been the growth, since the 1970s, of a pan-Asian American religious identity. This has paralleled the Asian-American movement in politics and education, wherein formerly distinct Asian peoples such as Chinese, Filipinos, Koreans, and Japanese have banded together under an umbrella identity to pursue common political goals. In religions this has given rise to pan-Asian American churches, Japanese-American ministers in Chinese-American churches and vice versa, writings on Asian-American rather than ethnically distinct theologies, and so forth.

The dominant social trends of the current Japanese-American generation are dispersal, middle-class status, assimilation toward white America, and intermarriage. It has reached a point where, outside Hawaii, hardly a Japanese family lives within walking distance of another, and a majority of Japanese Americans marry non-Japanese. In that climate, pan-Asian-American Christianity may become the dominant expression of Japanese-American religiosity, for the long-term maintenance of ethnically discrete institutions and practices seems unlikely.

See also BELONGING, RELIGIOUS; BUDDHISM; CHINESE-AMERICAN RELIGIONS; CONFUCIANISM; CONVERSION, DHARMA; KOREAN-AMERICAN RELIGIONS; PRACTICE; RELIGIOUS COMMUNITIES; RITUAL; SOCIOLOGY OF RELIGION; SOKA GAKKAI; ZEN.

BIBLIOGRAPHY

Hayashi, Brian Masaru. *"For the Sake of Our Japanese Brethren": Assimilation, Nationalism, and Protestantism among the Japanese of Los Angeles, 1895–1942.* 1995.

Kashima, Tetsuden. *Buddhism in America.* 1977.

Matsuoka, Fumitaka. *Out of Silence: Emerging Themes in Asian American Churches.* 1995.

Prebish, Charles S., and Kenneth K. Tanaka, eds. *The Faces of Buddhism in America.* 1998.

Tuck, Donald R. *Buddhist Churches of America: Jodo Shinshu.* 1988.

Yep, Jeanette, et al. *Following Jesus without Dishonoring Your Parents.* 1998.

Yoo, David. *Racial Spirits: Religion and Race in Asian American Communities.* 1999.

Paul Spickard

Jehovah's Witnesses

Otherwise known as the Watchtower Bible and Tract Society, Jehovah's Witnesses are one of the largest, and among the most prominent, of sectarian movements arising out of Christianity in the nineteenth century.

With approximately 5.5 million followers worldwide and almost a million adherents in America alone, Jehovah's Witnesses are popularly known for their fervent opposition to war and military service and to important medical procedures such as blood transfusions, skin grafts, and organ transplants. They also gained notoriety throughout the twentieth century with their predictions of Armageddon, the final battle between God and the legions of Satan, and the end of the world.

The phrase "Jehovah's Witnesses" is taken from the following passage in the Book of Isaiah: " 'You are my witnesses,' says [Jehovah]." (Isaiah 43:10, Revised Standard Version). The word "Jehovah" derives from an early English transliteration of the Hebrew title for the Deity. The word today is generally rendered by Biblical translators and scholars as "Yahweh," but Jehovah's Witnesses hold that the earlier pronunciation is accurate. Moreover, they maintain that "Jehovah" is the one, true, proper name for the Deity. Jehovah's Witnesses reject a number of the main tenets of orthodox Christianity, specifically the doctrine of the Trinity and the belief that Jesus was equal with God. Instead they look upon Jesus as an incarnation of the Archangel Michael, a created being.

The movement that later became known as Jehovah's Witnesses began with a Bible fellowship in Pennsylvania founded by Charles Taze Russell (1852–1916) shortly after the Civil War. These early "Russellites" radically reinterpreted traditional Protestant doctrine in light of what they took to be the proper interpretation of Scripture. Incorporated in the 1880s as Zion's Watch Tower Bible and Tract Society, the movement had grown by the advent of World War I to a sizable sect of Christianity. The sect adopted the name Jehovah's Witnesses in 1931 to avoid confusion with other Bible-based associations.

Jehovah's Witnesses, as in the Protestant faith, recognize the twin sacraments of baptism and the Lord's Supper. However, they only celebrate the Lord's Supper once a year as a "memorial" to Christ's death. The memorial service, which has attracted as many as

A Jehovah's Witness member giving out the Watchtower *magazine outside the New York City Jehovah's Witnesses headquarters.*   (Credit: CORBIS/Robert Maass.)

eleven million people on a global scale at any given time, usually coincides with the Jewish holiday Passover.

Jehovah's Witnesses uphold the same strict posture as fundamentalist Christian groups concerning the infallibility of Scripture, the condemnation of abortion, the status of women, and the prohibition of homosexuality and sexual relationships apart from marriage. But they are even more rigorous when it comes to observing what they consider "pagan" celebrations such as Christmas, Thanksgiving, and the Fourth of July. Jehovah's Witnesses can be excommunicated for certain practices or observances that are an accepted part of modern, secular society. Jehovah's Witnesses do not have a weekly Sabbath.

The leadership and governance structure of Jehovah's Witnesses is distinctive among twentieth-century religious movements. Those who belong to Jehovah's Witnesses are not called "members" in the normal sense of the term, but "pioneers" and "publishers." The distinction between these two groups is based on the amount of time each spends going door to door

involved in the pursuit of evangelism. There is no formal ministry or clerical hierarchy. All Jehovah's Witnesses are expected to proselytize. The most intensive practitioners are the "pioneers." "Regular pioneers," the organization's elite, commit to a minimum of one thousand hours per year of spreading the word. At the low end, "publishers" spend about one hour a week.

The congregations of Jehovah's Witnesses are known as Kingdom Halls. Kingdom Halls are under the leadership and authority of elders and "overseers." Groups of twenty congregations are termed "circuits." Circuits are contained within districts, which are included within branches and zones. The supreme headquarters for Jehovah's Witnesses is in Brooklyn, New York.

Besides the reading of Scripture, the worship and evangelism of Jehovah's Witnesses is built around articles in their *Watchtower* magazine.

Jehovah's Witnesses sponsor missionary activity in almost every nation on Earth and recently have been especially active in the former Soviet Union, where they have reportedly made about a hundred thousand converts. After the Russian parliament passed legislation in 1997 restricting recruiting efforts by "nontraditional" religious groups, prosecutors in that country targeted Jehovah's Witnesses in particular. Jehovah's Witnesses also have clashed with both religious and political authorities over their recruitment policies in the State of Israel.

The theology of Jehovah's Witnesses centers on their unique brand of eschatology. They believe that Armageddon is close at hand, and have predicted its arrival on various occasions, including the years 1914, 1918, 1920, 1925, 1941, and 1975. The failure of these predictions to prove true has been an ongoing source of tension between Jehovah's Witnesses and the rest of American Christianity. According to Jehovah's Witnesses' beliefs, Christ returned in 1914 and was enthroned as King of Kings and Lord of Lords but his kingdom remains invisible and is peopled by the 144,000 members of the elect mentioned in the Book of Revelation. In addition, Jesus' enthronement resulted in the expulsion of Satan from Heaven and his fall to Earth, unleashing the woes of the twentieth century.

World War I forced Jehovah's Witnesses to confront the issue of obedience to the state. They were pacifists from the outset, and the war experience prompted a hardening of their views on the relationship between believers and the government. Jehovah's Witnesses not only refuse to support war, even indirectly, they also will not salute the flag or take loyalty oaths. Their overtly "unpatriotic" attitudes have made them objects of fierce persecution in many different countries and principals in numerous court tests of the meaning of religious freedom in the United States.

Various critics and ex-members in recent years have wrongly labeled Jehovah's Witnesses a "cult." These accusations are usually in response to the demanding system of administration, doctrine, and morality that Jehovah's Witnesses exercise over their flock. Cults as a rule are focused on the charismatic leadership of a single individual, or small cadre of individuals. The historical strength of Jehovah's Witnesses, on the other hand, has been their ability to mobilize advocates at the grassroots level without reliance on any "cult of personality."

The rapid expansion of Jehovah's Witnesses, both inside and outside the United States, can probably be explained by its message concerning the surety of redemption for those caught up fearfully in the apocalyptic currents of the twentieth century. Within the United States the movement has spread rapidly among both white and African-American populations. As old social and economic orders crumble, especially in the Third World, the appeal of Jehovah's Witnesses will most likely continue to accelerate.

See also APOCALYPSE; CHRISTIAN SCIENCE; CONSCIENTIOUS OBJECTION; ESCHATOLOGY; FUNDAMENTALISM; MISSIONARY MOVEMENTS; PROSELYTIZING; TRINITY.

BIBLIOGRAPHY

Beckford, James A. *The Trumpet of Prophecy: A Sociological Study of Jehovah's Witnesses.* 1975.

Penton, M. James. *Apocalypse Delayed: The Story of Jehovah's Witnesses.* 1986.

Carl A. Raschke

Jesus Freaks.

See Born Again Christians; Jesus Movement.

Jesus Movement

Jesus Movement is a theologically conservative, experience-based Christian youth movement that emerged from the late 1960s counterculture. Diverse and largely unorganized, the movement's adherents came from both the "hippie" counterculture and the ranks of evangelical church youth. Popularly referred to as "Jesus Freaks" ("freak" being the countercultural slang term for one's enthusiasms) by those in the larger youth culture, the movement's early adherents called themselves "Street Christians." However, "Jesus People" quickly became the preferred term, and the movement itself became known as the Jesus Movement.

No development of the late 1960s could have been more unexpected—or seemed more incongruous—than the Jesus Movement's mixture of the counterculture and evangelical religion. However, there were a number of parallels between the two subcultures. The hippies' interest in mysticism and their fondness for spontaneity and emotional expression found a natural affinity in the forms of pentecostal theology and worship. Rock music, which played a central role in the counterculture, traced many of its musical and emotional roots to the black and white churches in the South. Evangelical views on man's sinful nature resonated with many young people's growing disillusionment with the physical and psychological pathologies of permissive sex and drug use. And evangelicalism's primitivist tendencies, association with rural America, and outsider status dovetailed nicely with the countercultural mind-set, even as the evangelical proclivity for the apocalyptic mirrored hippie perceptions of modern America.

The Jesus Movement first appeared in the San Francisco area where, as early as 1965, young bohemian converts associated with the First Baptist Church in Mill Valley, California. With the help of a group of local pastors they established the "Living Room" coffeehouse in the hippie enclave of Haight-Ashbury during the 1967 "Summer of Love," making contact with thousands of young seekers and runaways. However, the movement's early stronghold developed in the Los Angeles area. There, several youth-oriented congregations, such as Calvary Chapel in Costa Mesa, the First Presbyterian Church of Hollywood's Salt Company coffeehouse, and Southern Baptist youth worker Arthur Blessitt's "His Place" on the Sunset Strip achieved considerable success among countercultural youth. While these most successful examples of the nascent movement had direct links to mainstream evangelicalism, other groups emerged in the Los Angeles area that represented a smaller but very visible authoritarian and cultic branch of the Jesus Movement. Chief among these was (Moses) David Berg's radically countercultural Children of God, and Tony and Susan Alamo's separatist Alamo Christian Foundation.

During 1969 and 1970 the Jesus Movement continued to expand through such groups as John Higgins's "House of Miracles" (later "Shiloh") network of communes and Berkeley's Christian World Liberation Front (CWLF). But the movement was also increasingly in evidence outside California. In the Pacific Northwest, Linda Meissner's "Jesus People Army" established several communal homes and coffeehouses in Seattle, Spokane, Yakima, and Everett, Washington, and in Vancouver, British Columbia. Similar efforts appeared in Cincinnati, Atlanta, Toronto, and upstate New York.

In 1971 the Jesus Movement became a national cultural phenomenon in the wake of their discovery by the nation's leading periodicals and broadcast networks. Triggered in part by the controversy surrounding the November 1970 release of the rock opera *Jesus Christ Superstar,* secular media interest in the movement centered on the cultural dissonance in the combination of hippie music and fashions with the "old-time religion." But the Jesus Movement also made for an upbeat, reassuring "youth angle" after several years' worth of stories about youthful rebellion, the drug culture, and radical politics. Coverage in the secular media triggered an immediate outpouring of articles and books within evangelical circles pointing to the Jesus Movement as evidence of a national revival and the enduring social and cultural relevance of conservative Christianity.

With media exposure the Jesus Movement exploded during 1971 and 1972, fueled by a flood of evangelical youth eager to identify with the movement. Existing groups such as the Shiloh communities and the Children of God attracted numerous recruits, while hundreds of new communes, fellowships, and coffeehouses sprang up across North America. Binding the sprawling movement was its adaptive use of popular culture. Jewelry, posters, buttons, and bumper stickers emblazoned with slogans and symbols provided both a visible means of self-identification and advertisement of their Christian commitment. Underground "Jesus Papers" such as *The Hollywood Free Paper* and the CWLF's *Right On!* enjoyed regional and, at times, national circulation within the movement. Most important, however, was "Jesus Music," a hodgepodge of folk, pop, gospel, country, and rock styles that served as a ubiquitous vehicle for worship, evangelism, and entertainment. Through exposure on the coffeehouse and festival circuit, a growing market arose for recordings by popular Jesus Music singers and bands such as Larry Norman, Randy Matthews, Love Song, and the 2nd Chapter of Acts.

Probably the high-water mark of the Jesus Movement was Campus Crusade for Christ's Expo '72. Held in Dallas in June 1972, the event attracted eighty thousand young people for music, seminars, and evangelistic training. While "Godstock"—as it was dubbed by the secular media—was a convincing demonstration of the Jesus Movement's strength and its appropriation by the evangelical mainstream, it was the Jesus Movement's last hurrah in the national spotlight. After Explo, secular media lost interest, and by mid-1973 the movement faded from the religious press as well. Nonetheless, the dwindling Jesus Movement persisted at the grassroots level until about 1976. Its disappearance partly reflected the fact that many adherents were growing older and pursuing educational, vocational, and personal decisions that took them away from the movement. More significant, however, was the changing nature of the youth culture. As the counterculture receded and as new musical styles (disco, punk, new wave) entered popular culture in the mid- and late '70s, the Jesus Movement style was increasingly out of step with the times. The up-and-coming cohort of evangelical youth, attracted to new music, clothing, and hairstyles, was primed for a new way to relate to the emerging—and rapidly segmenting—youth cultures.

While the Jesus Movement came to an end, its impact on the evangelical subculture was profound. A number of parachurch organizations (such as Jews for Jesus and Christ is the Answer Ministries), the multimillion-dollar contemporary Christian music industry, and some of America's fastest-growing denominations in the last part of the twentieth century (including Calvary Chapel, Hope Church, and the

Vineyard), trace their roots directly to the Jesus Movement. On a more general level, the informality of the Jesus Movement's music and worship has, to one degree or another, altered the practices of nearly all evangelical churches and paved the way for the phenomenon of the "seeker-friendly" church embodied in congregations such as Willow Creek Community Church of South Barrington, Illinois. Clearly, however, its most important impact was on the youth scene. The Jesus Movement served as a bridge back to the American mainstream for many of the countercultural youth who joined the movement in the '60s and '70s. For participating evangelical youth the movement provided a way to negotiate the boundaries between family religious loyalties and their peer group and, as such, was the means by which many maintained their religious identity during their adolescence. Indeed, evangelicalism's adaptation of the Jesus Movement was the culmination of a trend (one that had begun with the 1940s Youth for Christ movement) that gradually accepted the idea of an evangelical equivalent to the larger youth culture.

See also BELONGING, RELIGIOUS; CAMPUS CRUSADE FOR CHRIST; CHILDREN OF GOD; EVANGELICAL CHRISTIANITY; INTERVARSITY CHRISTIAN FELLOWSHIP; JEWS FOR JESUS; NAVIGATORS; NEW RELIGIOUS MOVEMENTS; POSTDENOMINATIONAL CHURCH; RELIGIOUS COMMUNITIES; RELIGIOUS EXPERIENCE; YOUTH FOR CHRIST.

BIBLIOGRAPHY

Di Sabatino, David. *The Jesus People Movement: An Annotated Bibliography and General Resource.* 1999.

Ellwood, Robert S., Jr. *One Way: The Jesus Movement and Its Meaning.* 1973.

Enroth, Ronald M., Edward E. Ericson, Jr., and C. Breckinridge Peters. *The Jesus People: Old Time Religion in the Age of Aquarius.* 1972.

Eskridge, Larry. "One Way: Billy Graham, the Jesus Generation, and the Idea of an Evangelical Youth Culture." *Church History* 67, no. 1 (1998):83–106.

Richardson, James T., Mary White Stewart, and Robert B. Simmonds. *Organized Miracles: A Study of a Contemporary, Youth, Communal, Fundamentalist Organization.* 1979.

Larry Eskridge

Jesus Seminar

The Jesus Seminar is a group of New Testament scholars organized in California by Robert Funk in 1985. The initial purpose of the seminar was to apply critical methods to determine what Jesus "really said," as against what is attributed to him in the Christian gospels. The biennial meetings focused on particular sayings attributed to Jesus in ancient gospels, canonical and noncanonical. Votes were taken on the sayings' authenticity, using colored beads dropped into a box: red, indicating that Jesus undoubtedly said this; pink, indicating that Jesus probably said something like this; gray, indicating that Jesus did not say this, though the idea or ideas contained in the saying may reflect something of Jesus' own; and black, indicating that Jesus did not saying anything like it. Each color was assigned a rating (red = 3; pink = 2; gray = 1; black = 0), and the results were tabulated to achieve a "weighted average."

Results of the seminar's work were published in 1993 as *The Five Gospels,* containing an introduction, a new translation of, and commentary on the Gospels of Matthew, Mark, Luke, John, and Thomas (the only noncanonical gospel that is fully extant, in a Coptic version). The sayings attributed to Jesus are printed in the respective colors, and reasons are given in the commentary why the sayings are so colored. Only 18 percent of the recorded sayings of Jesus are regarded as authentic, rated either red or pink.

The seminar's methodology reflects results of critical New Testament scholarship developed over the past two hundred years, which the seminar wishes to make available to the public. The following "pillars of scholarly wisdom" guide the approach taken: (1) the distinction between the historical Jesus and the Christ of faith; (2) preference for the Synoptic gospels (Matthew, Mark, Luke) over John as sources for the historical Jesus; (3) the chronological priority of the Gospel of Mark; (4) the hypothetical source "Q" used independently by Matthew and Luke; (5) the "liberation of the noneschatological Jesus" from previous scholarship; (6) the contrast between an oral culture and a print culture; and (7) the "burden of proof" on those who argue for authenticity. Pillar 5 is not widely accepted by other scholars. The seminar's rejection of the general consensus that Jesus' message was dominated by eschatology (end-time expectation) results in a picture of Jesus as a "secular sage." Jesus as a Jewish prophet proclaiming the imminent "Kingdom of God" is a feature of the 82 percent of the Jesus tradition that is rejected by the seminar as inauthentic.

The next item on the seminar's agenda was to determine what Jesus of Nazareth really did and what was done to him. The approach taken was the same as for the earlier work. The results were published in 1998 as *The Acts of Jesus.* The combined number of red and pink events (authentic deeds) constitute 16 percent of the total events studied.

Thus the Jesus Seminar regards most of what is reported about Jesus in ancient sources as fiction. As might be expected, the pronouncements of the Jesus Seminar have been widely attacked, especially by Fundamentalist Protestants.

See also BIBLE; ESCHATOLOGY; RELIGIOUS STUDIES.

BIBLIOGRAPHY

Funk, Robert W., Roy W. Hoover, and the Jesus Seminar. *The Five Gospels: The Search for the Authentic Words of Jesus.* 1993.

Funk, Robert W., and the Jesus Seminar. *The Acts of Jesus: The Search for the Authentic Deeds of Jesus.* 1998.

Pearson, Birger A. "The Gospel According to the 'Jesus Seminar': On Some Recent Trends in Gospel Research." In *The Emergence of the Christian Religion,* edited by Birger A. Pearson. 1997.

Birger A. Pearson

Jewish High Holy Days

Also known as the Days of Awe or Ten Days of Repentance, the High Holy Days, beginning on 1 Tishri (September to early October) with Rosh Hashanah, the Jewish New Year, and ending on 10 Tishri with Yom Kippur, the Day of Atonement, have their biblical origins in Numbers 29:1–11 and Leviticus 16:29–34. Many American Jews who are not otherwise particularly observant participate in synagogue worship during these sacred days. Unlike other Jewish holidays, the High Holy Days have little connection to nature or Jewish history. Rather, they are a time for individual reflection on the past year, for seeking forgiveness, and for communal prayers of repentance. Jews wish others a happy New Year, and a good inscription in the divine book of judgment, based on the belief that God examines humanity on Rosh Hashanah and enters individuals for life or death; the final decision remains suspended until Yom Kippur. During Elul, the month preceding the High Holy Days, numerous special prayers and rituals culminate in Selikhot, a midnight service of penitential invocations the Saturday night before Rosh Hashanah.

Rosh Hashanah is also known as Yom HaDin, the Day of Judgment, and Yom HaZikaron, the Day of Remembrance, indicative of the account-taking and spiritual resolution characterizing the entire ten-day period. Most American Jews observe Rosh Hashanah for two days (as do Jews worldwide), although some Reform Jews celebrate only one day. Rosh Hashanah observance encompasses domestic ritual, including a festive meal at which apples are dipped in honey in hopes of a sweet New Year, and synagogue worship, on the evening Rosh Hashanah begins and during the two days of the holiday. This season's uniqueness is emphasized in the synagogue by white vestments for the Holy Ark and the Torah, as well as by distinct prayer melodies. Liturgical language incorporating poetic passages stresses God's sovereignty, human repentance, and divine judgment and forgiveness. Rosh Hashanah worship includes varied soundings of the *shofar,* the ram's horn, which invokes the revelation on Mount Sinai (Exodus 19:19), metaphorically summons the congregation to repentance, announces the advent of divine judgment, and reminds worshipers of the messianic age that will be ushered in by the shofar's blast. On the afternoon of the first day of Rosh Hashanah, many Jews observe the custom of *tashlikh* ("casting off") at a body of running water, symbolically throwing their sins away in the context of a brief worship service. Shabbat Shuvah ("Sabbath of Penitence"), between Rosh Hashanah and Yom Kippur, is built around the theme of *teshuvah* ("repentance"), based on the traditional prophetic reading from Hosea 14.

Yom Kippur, extending from sunset to sunset, is marked by physical abstinence for adults, including no food or drink, no displays of luxury or physical adornment, and no marital relations. These prohibitions reinforce the supremacy of prayer and repentance over any other human need on this day. Yom Kippur ritual takes place entirely in the synagogue; just as the synagogue vestments are white, so some people wear white robes, symbolizing the efficacy of repentance (Isaiah 1:18). The initial evening service, beginning at sunset, is named for the introductory prayer, Kol Nidre ("all vows"), which cancels personal commitments unfulfilled during the past year. Liturgical themes stress the enormity of human transgressions but affirm that repentance is possible and that God will grant forgiveness. Litanies of human infractions and moral violations are recited in the plural, reflecting the communal nature of this day of judgment and redemption. Since Judaism insists that divine clemency is possible only when harmony has been restored between people, it is considered essential for individuals to ask forgiveness prior to Yom Kippur from all those they may have treated badly, knowingly or unknowingly, and to compensate for wrongs.

Worship throughout the day of Yom Kippur recalls ancient rites of expiation undertaken by the high priest when the Temple stood in Jerusalem and invokes the prophet Isaiah's call for a sincere return to God and God's laws. An afternoon memorial service (Yizkor) remembers deceased family members as well as martyrs from various epochs in Jewish history. Yom Kippur concludes after sunset with the Ne'ilah ser-

A Jewish person wearing a white shawl blows a shofar horn at Rosh Hashanah. (Credit: © Bill Aron/ PhotoEdit/PNI.)

vice, which ends with a final declaration of faith and one long blast of the shofar, followed by hopes for ultimate redemption and peace for all humanity. The Yom Kippur greeting is "May you be sealed for good" [in God's book of judgment]. Families and friends often gather at the end of Yom Kippur to break the fast with a light meal.

See also JEWISH IDENTITY; JEWISH OBSERVANCE; JUDAISM; LITURGY AND WORSHIP; PRAYER; SYNAGOGUE; TEMPLE.

BIBLIOGRAPHY

Agnon, Samuel Joseph. *Days of Awe: A Treasury of Traditions, Legends and Commentary on Rosh Hashanah, Yom Kippur and the Days Between.* 1965.
Dosick, Wayne. *Living Judaism: The Complete Guide to Jewish Belief, Tradition and Practice.* 1995.
Ross, Lesli Koppelman. *Celebrate! The Complete Jewish Holidays Handbook.* 1994.

Judith R. Baskin

Jewish Identity

Contemporary discussions of religious identity in modern times have focused on cultural hybridity, synthetic, and constructed formations of identity. However, the question of Jewish identity within Jewish communal institutions and across religious communities has remained within the context of *halakhah,* or religious law. This definition states that a Jew is anyone born of a Jewish mother. The main source for this definition is located in the Talmud's statement that "Your son by an Israelite woman is called your son, but your son by a non-Jew is not called your son, but her son" (b. *Kiddushin* 68b). Thus the son or daughter of a Jewish mother and a non-Jewish father is a Jew, while the son or daughter of a Jewish father and a non-Jewish mother is not a Jew. The halakhic definition also does not admit any possibility of ever abandoning one's Jewish identity. This is based on the Talmud's equally forceful statement that "a Jew, even if he has transgressed, remains a Jew" (b. *Sanhedrin* 44a). Jewish identity is a category of radical exclusivity. Once one is in the defined category there is said to be no escape from it. A Jew may cease practicing Judaism, may completely assimilate into the surrounding society, shun Jewish society, or even convert to another religious tradition, but he or she remains by the halakhic definition a Jew.

A minority opinion has been argued from time to time suggesting that the child of a non-Jewish father and a Jewish mother is not Jewish. Most recently in 1960 this position was argued by a rabbi of the Haifa rabbinic court on the basis of a conflict of opinions concerning the status of a child born of a Jewish mother and a non-Jewish father (b. *Kiddushin* 75b). One opinion takes the position that the child has the status of a *mamzer,* or bastard. The other opinion, which is accepted as authoritative, recognizes the child as *kasher,* or legitimate. The vast majority of halakhic authorities conclude that the word *kasher* in the second opinion means that the child assumes the genealogical status of his mother. The rabbi sought to bolster his argument by citing another text in which the term *kasher* appears to be the antonym of the term *mamzer,* signifying that the child does not bear the stigma of bastardness (*Tosafot* to b. *Yevamot* 16b). While the rabbi acknowledged the preponderance of opinion that the child of such a union is Jewish, he suggested that the child's status is not clear-cut. The "Jewishness" of the mother does not automatically guarantee that the child is deemed to be Jewish in the eyes of *halakhah,* he reasoned. In a case where the father is a non-Jew, the child is accorded the halakhic status only if he "conducts himself as a Jew." If he does otherwise, he is deemed to be a non-Jew. The child of a Jewish mother and a non-Jewish father may thereby elect to acquire the halakhic status of being a Jew. He is deemed Jewish if he or she is raised as a Jew and conducts himself or herself accordingly. Such a child is not required to undergo the ritual of conversion. However, a child of a Jewish mother and a non-Jewish father who is not raised as a Jew is understood to have renounced his option to assimilate his or her Jewish identity. For many halakhists this argument is out of the question, and they reiterate that personal status is contingent only upon parentage and cannot be determined by any subsequent behavior.

Halakhah determines Jewish identity on the basis of a symbolic family in which matrilineal descent is the critical element. This is not a racial definition of identity. A convert to Judaism is accorded the same halakhic status as an individual born of a Jewish mother. The conversion ritual then constructs a mythological lineage that binds the convert to the primordial Jewish parents, Abraham and Sarah. But the central question remains: when did this definition of identity arise? The traditions of the Hebrew Bible and ancient Israel suggest that patrilineal descent determined inheritance and identity. The halakhic definition of Jewish identity has been in place since late antiquity, and it is often argued that it arose in the wake of the disastrous Jewish revolts against Rome at the end of the first century and the beginning of the second century of the Common Era, when both the religious and political Judaean leadership had to confront issues of the legal status of the offspring of forced sexual unions between Jewish women and non-Jewish men.

The creation of the modern state of Israel complicated this definition of Jewish identity. In 1950, the Israeli Knesset, or parliament, approved "The Law of Return," which gave Jews immediate citizenship. The halakhic definition, it appeared, became the definition of citizenship, at least for the Jews of the new state. There have been a series of challenges to this formulation of citizenship. Perhaps the most celebrated case was that of Brother Daniel. Brother Daniel had been born Oswald Rufeisen in Poland, in 1922. His parents were Jews, and he was given a traditional Jewish education. He was active in the Zionist youth movement, and after completing his secondary education in 1939, he completed two years of training in preparation for immigration to Palestine. In June 1941 he was caught by the Gestapo and imprisoned at the beginning of the German-Russian phase of the war. He escaped and secured a certification that he was a German Christian. He became a secretary and interpreter at the German police station in the district capital of Mir. There he was instrumental in passing on information about German plans to destroy the

Mir Ghetto. Many of the Jews in the ghetto escaped because of his actions.

When Rufeisen's identity was discovered, he was arrested. During his interrogation he confessed that he was helping the Jews because he himself was Jewish. He was imprisoned again, escaped a second time, and found his way to a Catholic convent, where he stayed for nearly two years before leaving to join a Russian partisan group. There he was suspected of being a German spy and was sentenced to death. Just as he was about to be executed, one of the Jews he had saved from the Mir Ghetto joined the partisans and testified to his true identity. He was subsequently given a Russian decoration for his service with the partisans.

While in the convent in 1942, Rufeisen converted to Catholicism and at the end of the war in 1945 became a priest, entering the Order of the Carmelites and taking the name of Brother Daniel. He chose this order deliberately because they had a chapter house in Palestine. During the Israeli War of Independence, he sought permission several times from his superiors to immigrate to Palestine. In 1958 he received permission to travel to Israel and to reside there permanently. Upon arriving in Israel, he sought an immigration certificate and an identity card as a Jew under the Law of Return. This was rejected and he pursued the matter to the Israeli High Court of Justice, which in 1962 ruled in favor of the state's rejection of his claim to Jewish identity. The court reasoned that actions that are antithetical to Judaism, irrespective of *halakhah,* are antithetical. The rabbinical court's law was essentially different from the secular law of the state and its understanding of who was a Jew for purposes of citizenship. Brother Daniel was hence not a Jew and could not claim citizenship under the Law of Return.

A series of additional cases have followed in the 1960s and 1980s involving whether it is possible to claim cultural identity as a Jew, the authority of non-Orthodox rabbis to supervise conversion, and the Jewish identity of immigrants from Ethiopia and the former Soviet Union. These bitterly divided secular and religious Israelis. In an unprecedented move, Prime Minister Benjamin Netanyahu sought in 1997 to widen his support among the extreme orthodox members of his coalition government by proposing unambiguously to amend the Law of Return so that only Orthodox rabbis would have the power to supervise conversion. The culture war between those Israelis who were either secular or non-Orthodox and the Orthodox moved from an Israeli issue to an issue involving Jews in the Americas and in Europe where the non-Orthodox constitute the majority of the Jewish populations. The prime minister sought to defuse the crisis by appointing a special committee headed by Finance Minister Ya'akov Neeman. In 1998 the committee proposed a compromise in which non-Orthodox rabbis would help to prepare potential converts. While being acceptable to many non-Orthodox leaders, the compromise was rejected by the Orthodox rabbis and parties who were vehemently opposed to even the smallest recognition of non-Orthodox religious leadership.

Non-Orthodox Jews in the United States, increasingly troubled by the high rates of intermarriage within their communities, have sought to expand the halakhic definition to include recognition of children of Jewish fathers and non-Jewish mothers as Jews. In 1983 the American Reform movement's Central Conference of American Rabbis voted to extend Jewish identity to a child of an intermarried couple (either a Jewish father or a Jewish mother) as long as there is nothing in the parents' home or in the child's education that would negate Judaism. The rabbis qualified their ruling by stating that the child would be considered Jewish if he were circumcised, had a Hebrew name, engaged in Torah study, had a *bar* or *bat mitzvah,* and was confirmed, all acts showing a personal and positive commitment to Judaism.

See also DIVORCE, JEWISH; JEWISH OBSERVANCE; JUDAISM; MARRIAGE, JEWISH.

BIBLIOGRAPHY

Abramov, S. Zalman. *Perpetual Dilemma: Jewish Religion in the Jewish State.* 1976.

Bleich, J. David. *Contemporary Halakhic Problems.* Vol. 2. 1983.

Cohen, Shaye J. D. *The Beginnings of Jewishness: Boundaries, Varieties, Uncertainties.* 1999.

Forster, Brenda, and Joseph Tabachnik. *Jews by Choice: A Study of Converts to Reform and Conservative Judaism.* 1991.

Samet, Moshe. "Who Is a Jew? (1978–1985)." *Jerusalem Quarterly* 37 (1986): 107–139.

Silberman, Charles. *A Certain People: American Jews and Their Lives Today.* 1985.

Richard Hecht

Jewish Observance

Judaism and Christianity include both beliefs and practices, but beliefs are central to Christianity while practices are central to Judaism. Thus if asked to identify the core of their faith, devout Christians would undoubtedly point to the belief that Jesus is the Christ; indeed, even if they were raised as Christians and are no longer Christian, they would say that they held this belief at one time but not now. Religious Jews asked the same question, on the other hand, would indubitably cite the commandments *(mitzvot)* embedded in Jewish law *(halakhah)* as the central feature of Judaism even before they mention God, who presumably commands them, or Jewish peoplehood or Torah—and long before they would mention Jewish beliefs about the Messiah or life after death. The Torah itself stipulates, by traditional count, 613 commandments, and each of them is a demand either to do something or to refrain from doing something; none of them, with the possible exception of the first sentence of the Decalogue, is a commandment to *believe* something or *deny* something else—except as those are expressed in practice (e.g., idolatry). Thus Jewish observance is, from the very beginning, central to Judaism.

Because of the separation of church and state in the United States, with its resulting freedom of religion, Americans do not think of religious demands as legal requirements. Religion in America, in other words, is voluntary. Moreover, religion in America covers primarily ritual and family matters; other issues are left to civil law.

That is definitely not the understanding of classical Judaism, according to which Jewish law is a full, legal system. Jewish legal texts therefore include not only laws about prayer, holidays, other rituals, marriage, and divorce, but also landlord-tenant relations, contracts, judicial procedures, and criminal matters. It also includes as legal obligations a number of duties that Americans would classify as merely moral, such as the duty to give charity to the poor and the duty to help someone who is drowning. Thus the scope of Jewish law is as wide as that of any other legal system—and, in some respects, wider.

The means of enforcement used by Jewish law also parallel those of other legal systems. During most of their history, Jews lived in semiautonomous Jewish communities in which Jewish law was enforced by Jewish authorities and backed up by the non-Jewish government. The Enlightenment changed that, but it was not until 1945 that the majority of the world's Jews lived in countries governed by Enlightenment principles. In the four centuries before then, most Jews lived in eastern Europe and the eastern Mediterranean, where the old, corporate system of government prevailed. Thus it is only since 1945 that most of the world's Jews have settled their disputes in the government's courts. Moreover, ultimately, religious Jews believe, Jewish law is enforced by God. Thus from the perspective of classical Jewish texts and Jewish practice over the ages, Jewish observance is anything but voluntary.

Now, though, almost all of the world's Jews live in free, democratic countries where religious strictures are not enforced by the government. Orthodox Jews—comprising about 7 percent of America's Jews—believe that Jewish law as it has come down to us is nevertheless required of Jews by God. Conservative Jews—approximately 38 percent of America's Jews—believe that, too, but they understand Judaism historically and therefore believe that the content of Jewish law may and should change over time, just as it has historically. However, most of traditional Jewish law is to be conserved (hence the name "Conservative"), and the burden of proof is on those who wish to change it. For Conservative Jews, it is the community, led by its rabbis, that decides which laws to add, modify, or delete; in contrast, for Reform Jews, comprising 42 percent of America's Jews, it is the individual who determines what he or she will observe—although, according to Reform ideology, only after duly studying the tradition. In practice, while the various movements' synagogues and schools follow the ideological position of their respective movement, individual Jews are generally eclectic in their own personal observance. In all denominations of American Judaism, but especially in Conservative and Reform Judaism, new observances marking the lives of women have been introduced in the twentieth century, especially in the past few decades.

Because the ultimate authority for Jewish observance is God, the scope of Jewish observance has been extremely wide, including even how to tie your shoes in the morning and how often a man has to offer to engage in sexual relations with his wife. This broad scope of Jewish law is one factor that marks it as a distinctly religious legal system: It shapes a person's relationship not only to the other members of the community, but also to other human societies, to nature, and to God.

Furthermore, while the classical tradition sees all of the demands of the tradition as one seamless web, moderns typically see some aspects of Jewish observance as primarily ritual in character and other parts as primarily moral. So, for example, Jewish law demands (not just suggests) observance of the Sabbath and dietary laws just as much as it demands honesty in business and respect for others. Moreover, some parts of Jewish law, such as the laws of personal injury and contracts, are, from the perspective of the Jewish tradition, part of Jewish observance rather than a separate set of criminal and civil concerns to be handled by the government. Precisely because Judaism has not differentiated Jewish law into these various categories, the moral aspects of life very much influence the ritual, criminal, and civil elements of Jewish law. That is why the Hebrew word for Jewish observance or Jewish law, *halakhah*, actually encompasses more than moderns usually have in mind when they use words like "observance" and "law." The etymological root of *halakhah* is the Hebrew verb "to go," and so *halakhah* is the way to go in life. It includes moral demands, civil and criminal law, rituals, and family law, and all of these aspects of *halakhah* are inspired and motivated by the loving relationship, or Covenant, that Jewish observance forms with the Jewish People and with God.

See also DIVORCE, JEWISH; FREEDOM OF RELIGION; JEWISH IDENTITY; JUDAISM; MARRIAGE, JEWISH; TORAH.

BIBLIOGRAPHY

Dorff, Elliot, and Arthur Rosett. *A Living Tree: The Roots and Growth of Jewish Law.* 1988.

Jacobs, Louis. *The Book of Jewish Practice.* 1995.

Klein, Isaac. *A Guide to Jewish Religious Practice.* 1979.

Orenstein, Debra, ed. *Lifecycles: Jewish Women on Life Passages and Personal Milestones,* 2 vols. 1994.

Elliot N. Dorff

Jewish Renewal

In the late 1960s and early 1970s cataclysmic social changes in the United States brought about marked shifts in the Jewish community as well. The civil rights and black power movements heightened awareness of the importance of group identity, solidarity, and meaning. Young Jews, influenced by these domestic developments and by the events surrounding the Six-Day War in Israel, began to revitalize Jewish religious life. Seeking new forms to replace the synagogue, they organized *havurot*, small groups for studying, praying, and socializing together. Although occasionally linked to synagogues, these groups rejected institutional structures such as buildings and professional staffs. Their gatherings were informal and participatory, and they focused on intergenerational experiences. The *havurah* movement remains today a loose confederation of many of these groups. Eschewing institution building, they are coordinated by a national committee that sponsors an annual summer institute.

Building on the havurah movement's commitment to intimacy and participation, Rabbi Zalman Schachter and his followers started B'nai Or (Sons of Light). B'nai Or was organized in the style of the havurah but had a particular religious slant toward what came to be defined as neo-Hasidic Judaism, focusing on the celebratory, joyous, and life-affirming aspects of prayer and ritual and on the Jewish mysticism of kabbalah and Hasidism. Schachter's group also experimented with Eastern mystical traditions and their connections to Jewish mysticism. The teachings of Abraham Joshua Heschel, Martin Buber, and Schachter himself were foundational to B'nai Or. The group held regular prayer services in Philadelphia, and its influence spread as Schachter's teachings became known across the United States and Canada. An annual summer retreat brought adherents together to experience Schachter's charismatic teaching, singing, and prayer and to apply the meditative and spiritual teachings of Sufism and other Eastern traditions to Jewish prayer life.

In 1987, under growing feminist influence, B'nai Or underwent a name change to P'nai Or (from Sons of Light to Faces of Light). Although from its inception accepting of equality for women, P'nai Or grew to be the spiritual home of many women and men who wanted to build a renewal of Judaism based on the insights that Jewish feminists had begun to unearth about Judaism's patriarchal nature. In keeping with its focus on the spiritual, much of the feminist contribution of P'nai Or has been to rewriting liturgy and working toward an ecofeminist approach to the environment.

The environmental focus was also important to another leading thinker associated with Jewish renewal, Arthur Waskow. Waskow is known for his work on peace and justice issues and as a leading proponent of using the midrashic methods of storytelling and interpretation to reinvigorate contemporary Jewish connections to ancient texts. Waskow was the founder of the Shalom Center, a group that was founded to provide a Jewish voice to the antinuclear movement in the 1980s and that continued to work on environmental causes and other peace and justice issues.

In 1993 P'nai Or and the Shalom Center merged to create ALEPH: Alliance for Jewish Renewal. ALEPH publishes a quarterly journal, *New Menorah*. It sponsors Elat Chayyim, a Jewish retreat center in upstate New York, where Waskow is in residence and where Schachter teaches. The Jewish Renewal Life Center in Philadelphia provides yearlong programs of study. There is now a network of Jewish Renewal communities, including forty havurah and synagogue affiliates in the United States and Canada. Schachter runs a Spiritual Eldering Institute based in Colorado. ALEPH also coordinates a process for ordaining rabbis.

The Jewish Renewal movement as it exists today has gained many adherents and created institutions to support its growth. Its focus is on renewing Jewish connection to God, understood to be an immanent presence in the world. Jewish history is seen as a series of renewed encounters with God (with the Buberian caveat that those encounters have been "in eclipse"). Prayer is central to Jewish renewal and incorporates chant, meditation, dance, storytelling, and psychological encounters with Torah texts. It incorporates learnings from other spiritual paths, especially forms of Buddhism, Sufism, and New Age Spirituality. It welcomes those who have been marginalized in Jewish life: women, gay men and lesbians, converts, and those who have never been involved in Jewish life but who are seeking new avenues of spiritual expression.

See also BUDDHISM; CIVIL RIGHTS MOVEMENT; HASIDIM; JEWISH IDENTITY; JEWISH OBSERVANCE; JUDAISM; KABBALAH; NEW AGE SPIRITUALITY; SUFISM; SYNAGOGUE; TORAH.

BIBLIOGRAPHY

Petsonk, Judy. *Taking Judaism Personally.* 1996.
Schachter-Shalomi, Zalman. *Paradigm Shift.* 1993.
Waskow, Arthur. *These Holy Sparks.* 1983.

Rebecca T. Alpert

Jews for Jesus

The term "Jews for Jesus" has been used since the early 1970s to designate Jews who have embraced the Christian faith yet retained their identity as Jews. The original group that formally carries the name "Jews for Jesus" was founded in 1970 in San Francisco by Moishe Rosen, a missionary of the American Board of Mission to the Jews. The new organization evangelized Jews who were influenced by the counterculture, adapting its evangelization messages and manners to the style of the new generation. Members of the group wore jeans and T-shirts, grew their hair, and embraced the musical trends of the day. Jews for Jesus also gave expression to the new emphasis in American culture on searching for one's roots and ethnicity. It advocated the idea that Jews did not have to give up their identity as Jews, but rather could rediscover themselves as Jews at the same time as they embraced Jesus as their savior. The missionary organization has used Jewish symbols, names, and expressions in its missionary literature. Jews for Jesus also has emphasized its support for the State of Israel and has called its musical band "The Liberated Wailing War." Starting out as a local group in the San Francisco Bay Area, Jews for Jesus has grown to become one of the largest missions in the nation, with branches outside America as well.

In its theology and style, Jews for Jesus has become part of a larger movement of Jewish Christians that came about in the 1970s and 1980s. Often calling themselves messianic Jews, such communities have promoted the idea that Jews who embrace Christianity should not assimilate into the Christian culture or join regular churches, but instead should retain their Jewish heritage and create their own communities. Jewish-Christian congregations differ as to the amount of Jewish tradition they choose to retain. The more "traditionalist" communities have introduced Arks and Torah scrolls into their assemblies, their members wear yarmulkes during services, and they celebrate Jewish holidays such as Chanukah and Purim. All Jewish-Christian congregations celebrate Passover, and most have chosen to conduct their prayer meetings on Friday nights or Saturday mornings. The notion that they have transcended the historical boundaries between Judaism and Christianity, overcoming old, seemingly irreconcilable differences and injuries to amalgamate the Christian faith with Jewish ethnicity, has served as a source of energy and a sense of mission for the movement's members. By the late 1990s there were more than two hundred congregations in America, as well as dozens more in Israel and throughout the Jewish world, and the movement is growing.

Jews for Jesus, and the movement of Jewish believers in Jesus in general, have advocated the faith and values of the conservative evangelical segment of Christianity. As such, they point to a great amount of adaptability by evangelical Christianity in its relation to the cultural choices of the baby boom generation. They also reflect the growing appreciation by this segment of Christianity for Jews as the object of biblical prophecies and as a nation destined to regain its old status as the Chosen People.

See also CONVERSION; ECUMENICAL MOVEMENT; JEWISH IDENTITY; JEWISH OBSERVANCE; JUDAISM; JUDEO-CHRISTIAN TRADITION; NEW RELIGIOUS MOVEMENTS; PRACTICE; PROSELYTIZING; RITUAL.

BIBLIOGRAPHY

Ariel, Yaakov S. "Counterculture and Mission: Jews for Jesus and the Vietnam Era Missionary Campaigns." *Religion and American Culture* 9, no. 2 (1999).

Feher, Shoshonah. *Passing Over Easter.* 1998.

Lipson, Juliene G. *Jews for Jesus: An Anthropological Study.* 1990.

Pruter, Karl. *Jewish Christians in the United States: A Bibliography.* 1987.

Rausch, David A. *Messianic Judaism: Its History, Theology and Polity.* 1982.

Rosen, Moishe, and William Proctor. *Jews for Jesus.* 1974.

Yaakov S. Ariel

Jihad

Jihad is the endeavor or struggle to establish and defend Islam. The struggle can take several forms. In a military context it becomes armed struggle and is the one meant in the Qur'an when reference to fighting between Muslims and non-Muslims is made. Many verses in the Qur'an exhort Muslims to fight courageously and to be willing to sacrifice their wealth and lives (9:41, 88; 61:11). Those who fight "in the way of God" are called *mujahidun* and are promised great reward in the hereafter (4:95); God has made a "deal" with the believers whereby He has bought their wealth and lives in exchange for paradise (9:111). Those who die in battle are called martyrs, though they are not to be thought of as dead: "Do not call them dead; they are living, in the presence of their Lord, and are being given sustenance" (3:169). Technically, such jihad is termed *qital.* For it to be valid, qital must be religiously justifiable. For example, *jihad* cannot be waged to convert non-Muslims to Islam, to gain personal glory, or to enhance national pride. But it may be waged, for example, to combat aggression or to fight tyranny. Muhammad and his followers in Medina were permitted by the Qur'an to fight because they had been turned out of their homes in Mecca and had been "wronged" (22:40). The Islamic legal code prohibits wanton destruction of life and property during war and guarantees certain rights to the enemy.

The Qur'an also speaks of "jihad in God" (29:69), an elliptical expression for the endeavor to find and determine ways to serve God with a view to winning His pleasure: "Those who endeavor [*jahadu*] in Us—We will certainly guide them to Our ways." Such jihad is to be understood as the effort to bring one's whole life into accord with the will of God. It calls for a deep commitment to discipline oneself through constant self-examination, and it is probably because of the rigorous demands it makes on one that the Prophet termed this jihad against one's baser self greater than qital, the external jihad against an enemy, for, unlike the latter, it involves fighting against the part of oneself that incites one to evil (called *an-nafs al-ammarah* in Qur'an 12:53). This is the jihad Muslim mystics frequently speak of and try to engage in.

Qur'an 4:76 says that those who believe in God fight in His way, whereas those who disbelieve in Him fight in the way of the *taghut* (those who rebel against God). Muhammad is reported to have said that speaking the truth in the presence of a tyrant is the greatest form of jihad. Scriptural and prophetic statements like these have led Muslims in the past, and particularly in modern times, to view resistance to or fighting against political oppression and social injustice as jihad. Such statements were, for example, frequently cited in Iran in the late 1970s during the anti-Shah movement.

See also ISLAM; MECCA; QUR'AN.

BIBLIOGRAPHY

Dajani-Shakeel, Hadia, and Ronald H. Messier, eds. *Jihad and Its Times*. 1991.

Osman, Fathi. *Jihad: A Legitimate Struggle for Human Rights*. 1997.

Mustansir Mir

Jones, Jim

(1931–1978), cult leader.

Jim Jones was the leader of an unconventional Christian movement, the People's Temple, in the United States, and founder of a cooperative agricultural community, Jonestown, in the South American jungles of Guyana that ended in mass suicide on November 13, 1978. In the American media, Jonestown became emblematic of the dangerous, coercive, and brainwashing "cults" that allegedly threatened American mainstream society. As he was demonized in the popular imagination, Jim Jones emerged as the model of the crazy, criminal cult leader in America.

Jones, a white minister, was born in Indiana and drew attention during the mid-1950s to Pentecostal faith healing, social service, and racial integration. After reporting a vision in 1967 of an imminent nuclear war, Jones moved his ministry to northern California, where he gained formal affiliation with the Disciples of Christ and attracted a large, primarily African-American following. In sermons during the early 1970s Jones attacked what he regarded as a false notion of God as a transcendent person. He derided such a notion by ridiculing the deity of conventional Christianity as the Sky God, the Mythological God, the Spook, or the Buzzard. However, Jones proclaimed a genuine God, which he identified as love. Citing Karl Marx, Jones declared that divine love was a social system in which each according to their ability gave to each according to their need. For Jones, God was socialism—"God Almighty, Socialism"—a principle of divine love that he claimed to exemplify by being the Christ, the divine socialist in a body.

While his sermons celebrated the Soviet Union, China, and Cuba as utopias of Divine Socialism, Jones identified the United States as a domain of evil. "Any system that fights against socialism is against God," he declared. "So who is fighting against socialism? You are sitting in the midst of the anti-God system: American capitalism." Depicting American capitalism as a racist, fascist, and oppressive system, Jones informed his congregation that "America's system is representative of the mark of the Beast and America is the Antichrist." In these terms Jones worked out his novel

Rev. Jim Jones, the leader of the People's Temple. (Credit: CORBIS/Roger Ressmeyer.)

form of Christianity on the international battlefield on which capitalism confronted communism during the Cold War. In this apocalyptic scenario, Jones proposed a new understanding of the messianic age that would result in the Kingdom of God, the reign of Divine Socialism on earth.

During the mid-1970s, however, former members, who called themselves Concerned Relatives, began a media campaign to expose alleged brainwashing, financial corruption, torture, and child abuse within the People's Temple. Under pressure from this negative media attention, Jones led about a thousand of his congregation to Guyana, which he regarded as a congenial black socialist country in South America, to found the community of Jonestown. In November 1978, however, when the community was visited by a congressional delegation that included journalists and Concerned Relatives, Jones led more than nine hundred of his followers in what he called "revolutionary suicide." Understood as a blow against their principal enemies—the U.S. government, the media, and former members—mass suicide appeared to many in Jonestown as a way of redeeming a human identity from the dehumanizing pull of American capitalism, racism, and oppression through a single superhuman act. Although many at Jonestown hoped that their deaths would awaken the conscience of America, media coverage of the community, which was headlined by both *Time* and *Newsweek* as the "Cult of Death," reinforced and revitilized anticult stereotypes. As more than one anticult activist concluded, "All cults lead to Jonestown."

See also ANTI-CULT MOVEMENT; BRAINWASHING; CHURCH AND STATE; COMMUNES; CULT; CULT AWARENESS NETWORK; FATHER DIVINE; PENTECOSTAL AND CHARISMATIC CHRISTIANITY; PEOPLE'S TEMPLE; PSYCHOLOGY OF RELIGION.

BIBLIOGRAPHY

Chidester, David. *Salvation and Suicide: An Interpretation of Jim Jones, the People's Temple, and Jonestown.* 1988.
Hall, James. *Gone from the Promised Land: Jonestown in American Cultural History.* 1987.

David Chidester

Jonestown.

See Jones, Jim; People's Temple.

Journalism, Religious

Religion has been a subject of interest to the American news media ever since secular newspapers began to be published in the American colonies. The journalistic tradition of raising religious hackles is almost as old, dating from the early 1720s, when Boston's clerical establishment found itself under assault by the independent and iconoclastic *New England Courant*, published by James Franklin with the help of his younger brother Benjamin.

Although a comprehensive history of secular news coverage of religion has yet to be written, it is broadly the case that religion has been considered most newsworthy to the extent that it has played a role in public life in general and in politics in particular. For example, contention over the status of Connecticut's Congregational religious establishment elicited more coverage of religion in the *Connecticut Courant* between 1800 and 1818 than in the decades before or after.

It was James Gordon Bennett, the founding editor of the *New York Herald*, who in the 1830s led the American press into the promised land of religion coverage. Bennett, a Scotsman by birth and a liberal Roman Catholic by faith, was the first editor of a secular newspaper to devote space to the yearly meeting held in New York by denominational bodies and parachurch groups devoted to women's rights, temperance, and the abolition of slavery. He sent reporters out to report what the city's preachers were saying. Most notoriously, he happily assailed any religious activity or pronouncement that did not meet his standards— whether the Episcopalians' lavish Christmas decorations, the antiliberal pronouncements of the Vatican, or the histrionics of itinerant evangelists.

Urban revivals, notable public events that promised widespread moral and social reform, became a staple of religion reporting in the nineteenth century. Leading clergy began to write for the newspapers, sometimes via widely syndicated columns. The Sunday newspaper, though criticized as a desecration of the Lord's Day by some pastors, became a place for edifying religious prose. The *Atlanta Journal,* for instance, featured facing Sunday columns by the Methodist bishop of Georgia and the pastor of Atlanta's First Baptist Church.

Beginning in the twentieth century, major metropolitan dailies grew increasingly sensitive to the religious diversity of their increasingly diverse readership, and increasingly reluctant to involve themselves in religious controversy. Free listings of religious services gave way to paid advertising, resulting in the creation of the "church page," which typically included listings of church activities and friendly articles on ecclesiastical affairs. Although efforts were made to enhance the professionalism of religion editors and reporters, religion increasingly became a backwater—covered as a service for readers but hardly a priority for news executives. Stories with significant religious dimensions—the civil rights struggle, for example—typically fell outside the religion "beat."

The situation began to change in the early 1990s, for reasons at least in part commercial. The recession of the late 1980s jolted the American newspaper industry into an intense preoccupation with long-term declining circulation; one response was to beef up religion coverage in hopes of attracting new readers. Some editors strengthened their religion coverage as a species of public relations—to convince the large churchgoing public that the newspapers were not out of step with its values.

At the same time, journalists did not fail to recognize the growing public role of religion in the United States and around the world. After a quarter century, political Islam and the American Christian Religious

Right proved to be phenomena of considerable staying power. Quite apart from "fundamentalist" politics, a heightened sense of the importance of "values" in society and an interest in the way religious institutions might contribute to social welfare led the American news media to turn greater attention to religious subject matter. Dozens of newspapers expanded their church and religion pages into freestanding "faith and values" sections. Religion was routinely featured on covers of American newsweeklies. Public Broadcasting had a weekly religion news show, *Religion and Ethics Newsweekly,* airing on more than two hundred channels. By the end of the millennium, religion coverage was enjoying unprecedented popularity in the American news media.

To understand how the American news media treat religion, it is useful to think in terms of certain moral attitudes that govern how religion stories are formulated. These attitudes, called "topoi" (singular, "topos"), embody basic ideas about the nature of religion that derive from the Western religious tradition, resulting in religion stories that "make sense" in American culture. The following list of topoi is not meant to be exhaustive, but does mark out the basic territory within which most religion coverage takes place. Each topos should be understood as pointing, explicitly or implicitly, to one or another antitopos, moral opposites also capable of generating news stories.

Good Works

Doing good is a basic characteristic of religion as it is understood in Western religion. Religion coverage has always been replete with stories of religious people and institutions helping the poor, ministering to the sick, and offering relief to those who have suffered natural disasters. Although there are important American Christian traditions—notably within evangelical Protestantism—that have emphasized saving souls over good works, the news media tend to embrace an attitude more associated with the Social Gospel. Antitopoi of good works may be religiously inspired evildoing, hypocrisy (see below), false prophecy (see below), or simply doing nothing for the least among us.

Tolerance

Legal and political issues involving the First Amendment's ban on religious establishments and protection of religious free exercise are too varied and complex to be handled journalistically simply within the context of "separation of church and state." Instead, church-state issues tend to be handled in terms of the topoi of tolerance and intolerance. Tolerance is always good and intolerance bad; opposition to political candidates because of their religious faith is always

frowned upon. The debate is likely to be over who is truly tolerant/intolerant. Conservative Christian activists may be portrayed as religiously intolerant, yet they seek to have themselves portrayed as objects of secularist intolerance.

Hypocrisy

The American news media warmly embrace the special antagonism shown by the Western prophetic tradition toward those who fail to practice what they preach. The televangelist scandals of the late 1980s, and cases of pedophilia by Catholic priests prompted an extraordinary amount of news coverage. In the pedophile cases, the violations of law were generally serious, but such was not the case when it came to the activities of Jim and Tammy Faye Bakker and Jimmy Swaggart. The latter should serve as a reminder that hypocrisy is not in itself a crime, but rather a moral defect the news media feel impelled to expose as a matter cultural tradition.

False Prophecy

If the topos of hypocrisy points to those who fail to adhere to the moral standards they profess, the topos of false prophecy concerns those whose professed norms are themselves considered wrong. News coverage of the Mormons in the nineteenth century was preoccupied with the issue of polygamy and the importance of showing its evils. Similarly, much coverage of new religious movements, or cults, in the latter part of the twentieth century has gone forth under the topos of false prophecy. True prophecy, the antitopos, governs coverage of exemplary religious leaders like the evangelist Billy Graham, the Catholic nun Mother Teresa (cf. good works), and the Anglican archbishop Desmond Tutu of South Africa.

Inclusion

Inclusion is a topos related to tolerance but specifically concerned with the recognition of unfamiliar or previously disfavored religious groups. The Mormons, first subjected to "false prophecy" treatment, in due course were deemed to merit coverage as a worthy religious group meriting full acceptance in American society. Since inclusion is primarily a topos of domestic applicability, complications may occur when the religious group in question includes significant numbers of coreligionists abroad. For example, because "inclusion" does not govern coverage of Islam outside the United States, Muslims in America have taken offense at how their religion is characterized in foreign reporting. In response, the American news media have taken special pains to provide "positive" (i.e., inclusive) coverage of Muslim communities in the

United States when there are "negative" (i.e., exclusionary) stories of violence perpetrated by Muslims abroad.

Supernatural Belief

It is often asserted that the news media have a difficult time with religion because journalism is about proving facts, and religion is about faith that is beyond proof. This is especially likely to be the case when the religious subject matter at hand has to do with the miraculous or the supernatural. Yet religious traditions are far from uninterested in empirical demonstration—witness the Roman Catholic Church's insistence on proof of miracles to canonize a saint. And journalism often seeks not demonstrable evidence but sources prepared to assert that something happened. For this reason, the topos that governs coverage of supernatural events is the faith of the believers; belief is the story, whether it has to do with a miraculous healing or an apparition of the Virgin Mary. The contrary topos is justified disbelief—showing the alleged miracle to be a fraud or a delusion. The latter, however, generally requires a good deal of careful investigation and so is far rarer.

Declension

The decline of religion has been a theme in Western religion since Moses found the Golden Calf, and in America almost since the Puritans landed on Plymouth Rock. New (or allegedly new) religious phenomena, whether cults or megachurches or New Age practices or religion "shopping," are commonly seen as evidence of spiritual decline from an earlier age of traditional ("old-time") faith and practice. To be sure, the opposite topos, of religious revival, periodically comes to the fore. The prevailing cultural inclination, however, is to see decline.

See also CATHOLIC WORKER; PRACTICE; PSYCHOLOGY OF RELIGION; PUBLISHING, RELIGIOUS; RELIGIOUS STUDIES; SOCIOLOGY OF RELIGION; WISDOM LITERATURE.

BIBLIOGRAPHY

Hoover, Stewart. *Religion in the News: Faith and Journalism in American Public Discourse.* 1998.
Olasky, Marvin. *Prodigal Press: The Anti-Christian Bias of the American News Media* 1988.
Silk, Mark. *Unsecular Media: Making News of Religion in America.* 1995.

Mark Silk

Journeys and Journeying

Many a religious or spiritually oriented person has claimed to be a "seeker" on a kind of sacred quest to find truth and the meaning of life. Such a quest is considered to be part of what "the religious life" entails. Thinking of oneself as "spiritual" means that one follows a spiritual path through a life informed by a certain metaphysical and ethical perspective toward whatever concept of salvation or enlightenment one might imagine.

A quest often involves a journey, since one has to travel in some manner away from the unenlightened condition toward the goal of the spiritual path. The journey may be literal or metaphorical, with both exterior and interior dimensions. But it is important to note what the term *quest* fundamentally entails. A "quest" involves a question or questions. A spiritual questor is, by definition, seeking answers to the great existential questions of life, such as the source and nature of our existence, the presence and nature of the divine, the purpose of our own embodied life in this world, and so on. One has to journey toward the answers to these questions since, fundamentally speaking, one does not possess these answers in the current "placement"; if one did, one would not be seeking the answers.

If such a religious seeker happens to find satisfying answers to these questions, then his or her spiritual path might be said to become less a quest as such, and more a translation of the implications of those answers into a manner in which to live day to day life spiritually. One journeys through the spiritual life, enjoying a sustained sense of communion with the sacred, more so than toward a goal to be reached in some transcendental locus or future condition. In either case the religious life involves a journeying. This dimension of spirituality has been well represented in world religions with rich traditions of ritual journeys and pilgrimages. In many cases the life of the founder or great exemplar of a religion is viewed as a journey on a spiritual path, and each stage of that journey is ritually reenacted by adherents of the faith.

Such a journey or pilgrimage can be seen in the core myths or sacred stories of most, if not all, of the world's great religions. In Judaism, for example, the journey of the progenitor, Abraham, from Ur of the Chaldees toward a "promised land" that God agreed to bequeath to him and his descendants is retold ritually and venerated as the founding of the peoplehood and faith of Israel. Then the descent into slavery in Egypt and the delivery from out of the house of bondage by the mighty, outstretched arm of the Lord becomes the bedrock myth of the Jewish experience, ritually reenacted in the annual celebration of the Passover.

The history of the Jewish people has been precisely a journey, a prodigious walkabout out of ancient Babylon to the promised land, into the Diaspora, and then a sojourning in nearly all the lands of the world's nations, from northern Europe to Spain, through the Arab lands, and all the way to India, China, and faraway America. The history of the people is an absolutely central element in the Jewish faith. The "chosen people" have been led by their God on a great walkabout through his creation. The manner in which they should walk this noble path has been clearly laid out in remarkable detail by the law that God gave to his people. A life as lived by the holy commandment of the Torah is precisely the essential spiritual journey for the observant Jew, as God's word comes to pervade every aspect of life.

Similarly, in the Christian tradition, the journey of God's son into the embodied condition of humanity in this world becomes the initiatory movement in the unfolding of God's plan for his creation. Once the Savior advented into the world, the scant three years of his sacred mission could be said to have been a kind of walkabout from Nazareth to the Sea of Galilee, through Palestine, culminating in the journey to Jerusalem and ultimately to Golgotha and beyond, through hell and up to resurrection to gain the highest seat at the right hand of power next to the Lord in heaven. This foundational myth becomes the model for Christian life, put into practice as an aspiration to achieve the Christ-like life. The ritual of the Eucharist, or Lord's Supper, reenacts the sacred meal of the Last Supper, transformed by Jesus from the sacred meal of the old covenant commemorating the Passover—the journey to salvation—into the journey of the new covenant, through Christ's self-sacrifice to atonement with God. Each stage of His journey is reenacted in the ritual of the Stations of the Cross.

Later developments in Protestantism authored new versions of the spiritual journey of the Christian life in the visioning of the pilgrim's progress toward religious freedom in America, the new promised land. The journey toward Manifest Destiny brought the faithful to the frontiers of that promised land, as also the journey of Joseph Smith brought his Latter-Day Saints to a hopeful new place marked out by God.

In Islam, journeying is of the essence of the faith as well, as the dawn of the era of the faithful is itself dated from the hegira, or hijra, the flight of Mohammad to Medina in the year 621. His subsequent return to Mecca, cleansing of the holy temple, the Ka'ba, and adoption of the pre-Islamic ritual pilgrimage, the hajj, became the foundation for one of the more important Islamic rituals, and one of the five duties of life required of every Muslim who is capable of it—the ritual pilgrimage to the Ka'ba in Mecca. Likewise, Mohammad's mystical "night journey," or "celestial journey," the mi'raj, from Mecca to Jerusalem at the Dome of the Rock and from there to heaven, becomes a core element of the faith. Each Muslim who earns his or her place in heaven is promised to experience a reenactment of the mi'raj upon dying.

In the Hindu tradition, the journey to the sacred waters of the Ganges is ritually enacted every year. To bathe in its sacred waters is parallel to a cleansing baptism that one can enjoy many times through life. Pilgrimages by the faithful to holy sites and shrines occur all over India, making up the very lifeblood of the Hindu spiritual path. The great religious and philosophical traditions of India are based on the concept of the inner journey of the ego consciousness through its dissolution into the "great self" or "god-self" in the journey toward enlightenment and moksha, the liberation from the suffering of life. The ultimate journey in this religious tradition is the journey out of the condition of illusion, which mistakenly perceives a separateness, back to Godhead, the true native condition of the soul.

Likewise in Buddhism, the spiritual journey is also well represented. The religion's founder, Siddhartha Gautama, began his own spiritual journey with the "great going forth" into the city of his birth to witness its joys and pain for the first time, and the subsequent "great renunciation" as he formally took up the religious life. That life involved the continuous journeying over some five years to learn from the various teachers authoring new avenues of spirituality across northern India, culminating in Siddhartha's own achievement of enlightenment under the Bodhi tree at Bodhgaya. The long years of his mission as a spiritual teacher then began, during which he traveled widely across north India. The sites where Buddha taught and had experienced the stages of his own spiritual path became pilgrimage sites for Buddhists from all parts of the world. Visiting these sites might represent outward expressions of the essential inner journey for the adherent of Buddhism, through many lifetimes in samsara toward enlightenment into nirvana. Buddha's grand journey through millions of lifetimes ultimately to reach his birth as Siddhartha is recounted in dozens of Jataka stories, helping to make up the mythology of the new religion. Many hundreds of these lifetimes are depicted in bas-relief sculptures at one of the most extraordinary religious pilgrimage sites, the Buddhist temple of Borabudur on the island of Java.

A most unusual shrine, the temple is built around a small mountain. With no actual rooms inside and no ceiling, the building is composed of a long spiral corridor onto the walls of which have been sculpted scenes from the former lifetimes of Buddha. As the pilgrim travels ever higher on the spiral, he or she is meant to experience the spiritual evolution of Buddha toward higher and higher consciousness. Toward the top of the hill the walls fall away, as Buddha approached the lifetime when he would reach enlightenment, and the pilgrim steps out into the open air. The pilgrim might notice that there was never any ceiling along the path. Had one been able to wrest one's attention away from the intricacies of each lifetime's minutiae, the overarching light was always present—symbolically, enlightenment was available at any point. The journey around the tip of the mountain brings the pilgrim to the culminating point, the serene Buddha statue seated on the very summit representing the lifetime of Siddhartha Gautama, the one who reached Buddhahood. A ritual pilgrimage like this truly captures the various dimensions of spiritual journeying, as one has to journey to Borabudur in Java, and then travel the path upward toward the summit, while one externalizes the interior journey toward higher consciousness and ultimately to realization of Buddhahood.

The Tibetan form of Buddhism has added yet another expression of the spiritual journey in the great tradition of the *Tibetan Book of the Dead,* the "Book of the Great Awakening on the Death Plane." This fascinating religious classic of the eighth century C.E. depicts the journey through death as a means for achieving enlightenment. Traditionally, on the occasion of a death, the Buddhist priest, the lama, would return to the home of the recently departed every day for the forty-nine days of the predicted experience of the "bardo," the state "between two" lives on the path toward rebirth. The lama would ritually recite each chapter of the *Book of the Dead* to the dead one on his journey. The book envisions the whole process of death and rebirth as a grand spiritual journey through the different "lokas," or locations, of the life energies of the cosmos.

This text is a highly developed example of the way in which most religious traditions consider death to involve a great journeying into and through the realm of the afterlife. This mysterious journey even earned a specific title in ancient Greek religion—the *nekyia,* or death journey, such as the one Odysseus undertook in the eleventh book of the *Odyssey* to consult the shade of Teiresias the Seer.

Farther east in traditional China, the dominant religions provide followers with ritual journeys. In the case of Confucianism, the Li, or complex ritual system, governed every aspect of human interaction in one of the world's most highly ritualized societies, classical China. The Li provides the patterns for maintaining a spiritual course through life and onward into the spirit realm once one passes and becomes an ancestor spirit.

And in the Taoist tradition, the follower seeks to course through life putting oneself in accord with the natural changes from yin to yang. The Taoist flows with the changes and might follow a lifestyle like that exemplified by Chuang Tzu, the third-century B.C.E. follower of the founder of Taoism, Lao Tzu, a philosopher traditionally placed in the sixth-century B.C.E. Chuang Tzu describes a life of "aimless wandering" coursing down the rivers and streams of life, enjoying the changes as they occur. This is a kind of spiritual journeying as the Taoist seeks to attain the hub of the Tao, the still center of balance around which the changes continue to revolve.

Later, the Taoist tradition developed ritual pilgrimages to temples that were purposely built in areas very difficult to access, to prove the worthiness of the adept in his quest to gain the power, the "teh" of the Tao (or way of life). This power brought extraordinary abilities as the adept sought to access the ethereal energies of the universe. In the journey through the famous Shao Lin temple, the adept would have to endure countless rigorous ordeals, as his mettle was tested in challenge after terrifying challenge. Many dozens died at some point along the way, as the mysterious temple built into a mountainside connecting to underground tunnels is said to be littered along the way with the bones of those who never made it. This temple site was the original parent of all the martial art traditions of China, which later spread to Korea and Japan and from there to the world at large.

Similarly, in the Japanese Shinto tradition, pilgrimages rest at the very core of the religion. *Shinto* is a term taken over from Chinese. It is the "way" or "Tao" of the "shen," the spirits, known in Japanese as the *kami.* Pilgrimages to their sacred shrines make up the very lifeblood of Japanese spiritual traditions. The sacred climb up the slopes of Mount Fuji is a goal to which all spiritually minded Japanese aspire. In these pilgrimage/ordeals the adept earns the teh, or power, of the spirit realm.

And in shamanic and indigenous traditions across the world, the faithful go on vision quests, such as those embodied in the spiritual traditions of the Plains Indians of North America, and walkabouts, as in the traditions of the aboriginal Australians. The native seeks to live life altogether by "walking in a sacred manner." Practices of shamans around the world include the essential ritual journey to the spirit realm, the "celestial journey" to the "astral plane," to traffic with spirits, shepherd the dead, seek lost souls, and learn secret cures for various ailments. The famous experience of out-of-body travel is one of the long recognized spiritual arts of shamans in all lands. Here again, the essential religious experience is precisely a journey.

Considering all these examples from religious traditions across the world, one begins to wonder whether these traditions are not viewing life itself as a kind of spiritual journey. The religious life is precisely a life path sanctified by ritual journeying. According to the Swiss psychologist C. G. Jung (1875–1961), one of the primary functions of religion is precisely to offer the believer a ritual means to follow some version of the "hero's journey," the mythical name for the psychological process that Jung termed "individuation." This concept of the hero's journey was picked up by the American mythographer Joseph Campbell (1907–1987) and popularized in his first great work *The Hero with a Thousand Faces*. In this book Campbell lays out the various stages of the hero's journey, though the specifics of these stages may vary in different cases. A thousand stories across the world have depicted this grand archetypal journey, which Jung and Campbell suggest stands as a metaphor for the interior journey of the ego consciousness through the unconscious, ultimately to reach a state of wholeness, or psychic integration—the goal of the Jungian system.

Campbell posits three large stages on the hero's journey, with more specific ones within these categories. The first stage involves the "initiation to the quest," wherein the adept first receives the "call of destiny," or the "mission statement," which lays out the task being required of him or her. The hero or hera (i.e., heroine) then experiences a shock, and a "separation from the ordinary," as the sacred quest is accepted and begun.

The second great stage involves the Journey itself. A mentor is located and the "descent into the underworld of the adventure" begins. The hero or hera gathers a set of companions, each of them representing a significant aspect of the psyche. The group travels together, encountering daemons and strange threshold guardians. They are put through tasks and ordeals, as the coveted title of "hero" must be won by a truly heroic effort. During the trial, courage is found and exhibited and many transformational moments are experienced. Dragon slaying of some type may occur. The quest culminates in the *nekyia*, or journey into death, symbolic of ego-sacrifice, followed by the triumphant resurrection of a changed consciousness. The hero or hera comes upon and wins the treasure, or boon.

The third stage involves the hero's return to society as a transformed being. The higher self has been forged during the journey and it is this which returns bearing the boon as a gift to all humanity. This entire journey of the hero is viewed in the works of Jung and Campbell as being emblematic of an inner journey toward wholeness. It is the ego-self who sets out on the quest, its mythical name being "hero" or "hera." The mentor and various personages encountered and incorporated along the way represent the subpersonality fragments of the deeper consciousness, integrated together eventually to achieve a state of wholeness. This culminating scene is imaged nicely in the final scenes of the great hero sagas of our own day. In *The Wizard of Oz*, for example, Dorothy (ego/hera) travels to Oz (the unconscious) and wakes up from her great dream at the end of the story surrounded by representative versions of each of the fragmentary elements she has incorporated on her journey.

Likewise, in the science fiction film series *Star Wars*, the final scene of the great hero journey of Luke Skywalker in a galaxy far, far away, pictures him surrounded by all the personalities who have shared his journey. Each of these personages, Han Solo, Princess Leia, Obi Wan Kenobi and the others, represents aspects of the great self, which Luke incorporates, aspects such as the embraced shadow element, the anima, the wise old man and so on. In the case of Dorothy's friends, the Scarecrow, Tin Man, Lion, Toto, and the Wizard of Oz, they each represent deeper aspects of Dorothy's consciousness, which she incorporates as she moves from the focus of the small ego-self into the perspective of the great self. Through the journey she incorporates into herself her masculine side, her animus, brain power, courage, wisdom aspect, and so on. A similar mythic perspective of the hero's journey can be applied also to the famous journey, or trek, through our own galaxy, as projected forward into the twenty-third and twenty-fourth-centuries in the popular version of modern mythology known as *Star Trek*.

These are powerful stories that exemplify the hero's journey, the pathway toward individuation to achieve psychic balance and wholeness, a word related to the word "health." The question becomes whether individuation is ever finally truly achieved by real men and women engaged in their own hero and hera journeys through the tasks and trials of everyday life. Would achieving wholeness then result in a kind of stagnation? Genuine examples of full psychic integration may be rare enough in any case. One imagines that there would always be a new quest looming before the self-actualized soul. There are always new boons to win to aid humankind in its grand, collective journey toward realization of its vast potential. New challenges will always beckon the true hero or hera to take up yet another great spiritual journey.

See also ARCHETYPE; BUDDHISM; CAMPBELL, JOSEPH; DREAMS; HINDUISM; ISLAM; MECCA; MYTH; NEW AGE SPIRITUALITY; PILGRIMAGE; QUEST; RITES OF PASSAGE; SHAMANISM; SPIRITUALITY; TAOISM; VISION QUEST.

BIBLIOGRAPHY

Campbell, Joseph. *The Hero with a Thousand Faces.* 1956.

———. *Myths to Live By.* 1972.

———. *The Power of Myth.* 1982.

Eliade, Mircea. *Shamanism, Archaic Techniques of Ecstasy.* 1951.

Evans-Wentz, W. Y. *The Tibetan Book of the Dead.* 1960.

Jung, Carl G. *Aion: Collected Works.* Vol. 9, part 2. 1959.

———. *The Archetypes and the Collective Unconscious: Collected Works.* Vol. 9, part 1. 1959.

———. *Psychology and Alchemy.* 1953.

Neihardt, John. *Black Elk Speaks.* 1932.

Smith, Huston. *The World's Religions.* 1991.

Turner, Victor, and Edith Turner. *Image and Pilgrimage in Christian Culture, Anthropological Perspectives.* 1978.

Sharon L. Coggan

Judaism

Judaism is the world's oldest monotheistic faith and traces its historical beginnings to the covenant established by God with the biblical Abraham, Sarah, and their descendants almost four thousand years ago. This covenant was later renewed and elaborated upon at Mount Sinai through the revelation of the Torah: divine teachings issued as commandments that are incumbent upon Jews of every generation.

Judaism, as it had been understood and lived for much of the last two thousand years, is largely a rabbinic creation, based on the teachings of the Hebrew bible as interpreted by rabbinic sages of the first few centuries before and after the common era. It further developed during the Middle Ages and modern era and, through changes and additions to its laws and customs, continues to develop today. There has never been one creed or specific set of beliefs to which all Jews have adhered. Nonetheless, the three components or "symbolic structures" of God, Torah, and Israel, referring to the land of Israel and the entire Jewish people, have been central to Judaism since its inception.

Jews and Judaism in America

Out of a total Jewish population of twelve million (less than 0.2 percent of the world's population), approximately 5.8 million Jews live in the United States today.

While this number represents slightly more than 2 percent of the U.S. population, it makes the United States home to the largest Jewish community in the world. Given the voluntary nature of religious and ethnic identification in the United States, it is also the most diverse.

The first Jews to settle in America arrived in New Amsterdam, the unofficial capital of the Dutch colony of New Netherland, in September 1654. Just as their Spanish and Portuguese ancestors had fled to South America hundreds of years before, so these twenty-three Brazilian Jews came to America seeking physical protection and religious freedom. Like many Jews in Brazil, they had sided with the Dutch in their earlier, successful struggle to take Brazil from the Portuguese, hoping to gain the kinds of religious rights already enjoyed by the Jews of Holland. When Brazil was recaptured, all those who had openly sided with the Dutch fled, the twenty-three Jews who eventually sailed to New Amsterdam on the *Ste. Catherine* among them.

Soon after their arrival, however, Governor Peter Stuyvesant requested permission from the directors of the Dutch West India Company to expel such "hateful enemies and blasphemers of the name of Christ." Had a second, more outspoken group of Jewish settlers not launched their own counterappeal, he might well have succeeded. Nonetheless, Stuyvesant issued a number of regulations that remained in effect throughout Dutch rule: Jews could not build synagogues (though by 1756, at the order of the Dutch West India Company, he was forced to let Jews worship in private homes); they could not build a ritual bath or have their own ritual slaughterers (kosher butchers); and they could neither vote, hold office, open shops for retail trade, nor serve in the colony's militia. Consequently, by the beginning of the eighteenth century, when it appeared that New Netherland would soon fall into British hands, most of the Jews of the colony left, having failed to gain religious, political, or economic equality under the Dutch and unsure as to what their situation under the British would be. While some sought greater freedoms elsewhere in America, many set sail for the Netherlands or for other Dutch colonies in the West Indies where, without Stuyvesant, the local Jewish population could live more freely, and more fully, as Jews.

By 1700, there were about 250 Jews in America; by 1776 that number had increased to 2,500, no more than 0.1 percent of the colonial population. Most of the early immigrants were traditionally religious *Sephardim*—Jews of Spanish and Portuguese descent. Settling in such major seaport cities as New York City, Newport, Philadelphia, Charleston, and Savannah, many found work in areas related to shipping and

A Jewish family celebrating the seder on March 22, 1989, in San Francisco, California.   (Credit: CORBIS/ Roger Ressmeyer.)

international trade. They built synagogues and *mikvaot* (ritual baths), purchased land for use as cemeteries, supervised the slaughter and preparation of meat, created mutual aid societies, and assumed communal responsibility for the religious education of their children. In each of the congregations they established, worship was in accordance with the liturgical customs of Sephardic Jews. Given the small size of pre–Revolutionary War Jewish communities, it is perhaps not surprising that throughout the eighteenth century, those Jewish immigrants of Central European origin (*Ashkenazim*) who settled in these cities, joined already existing Sephardic congregations rather than establishing synagogues of their own.

As early as 1730, the number of Ashkenazic Jews in America surpassed that of the Sephardim. This imbalance became even greater during the nineteenth century. Between 1830 and 1880, as the general population of America dramatically increased, almost 250,000 Jews immigrated to the United States, most from Central Europe. Unlike their eighteenth-century counterparts, the majority came with their families. Educated and primarily middle class, they were eager to take advantage of the many economic, political, and social opportunities that America offered and to build a new life in a country they soon considered to be home. Part of the attraction of America was its "newness." With neither a centuries-old history of anti-Semitism nor ghetto walls to serve as reminders of the medieval status of Jews as outsiders, and without an established church to formally identify them as "religious dissenters," America seemed to be filled with unlimited possibilities. Indeed, with religious affiliation voluntary and freedom of religion guaranteed in the Bill of Rights, nineteenth-century Jewish immigrants saw America as offering them the unique opportunity to fully integrate into American society, as individuals and as Jews.

Coming to the United States during a period of great, geographical expansion, they spread out more widely than had earlier Jewish immigrants, in search of new places to settle and new economic opportunities. While many followed earlier patterns of Jewish immigration, settling in the north and southeast, a significant number joined the mid-nineteenth-century American migration to the west and southwest. Thousands put down roots in such pre-existing areas of Jewish settlement as New York, Philadelphia, Baltimore, and Charleston, establishing their own, German Jewish congregations, while others created new and vibrant German Jewish communities in such cities as Albany, Pittsburgh, Cincinnati, and (after the Louisiana Purchase of 1803) New Orleans and St. Louis. By the end of the century, sizeable and enduring German Jewish communities had been created in cities like Atlanta, Louisville, Indianapolis, Chicago, and San Francisco as well.

By the 1850s, those who came to America from Germany included a number of ordained rabbis. Most of them were committed to moderate, if not radical, religious reform as a means of both adapting Judaism to the modern world and accommodating Judaism to America. Instigating liturgical and theological change in synagogues throughout the United States, leaders of America's nascent Reform movement soon created a network of organizations and institutions that facilitated Reform Judaism's influence and growth. Most notable were three national institutions established by Rabbi Isaac Mayer Wise: the Union of American Hebrew Congregations (1873), with which over one hundred synagogues were affiliated by 1880; Hebrew Union College, America's first rabbinical seminary, located in Cincinnati (1875); and the Central Conference of American (Reform) Rabbis (1889). (In 1950, Hebrew Union College merged with Rabbi Stephen Wise's Jewish Institute of Religion in New York City. Today, HUC-JIR has campuses in New York, Cincinnati, Los Angeles, and Jerusalem, and includes among its programs a Graudate School and Schools of Sacred Music and Education.)

Reform Judaism's overwhelming popularity began to decrease by the 1890s, as hundreds of thousands of Eastern European Jews began to arrive in America. Escaping the waves of anti-Semitic violence first set in motion after the assassination of Czar Alexander II, a great many of the 1,250,000 Eastern European Jews who arrived between 1881 and 1914 had abandoned Judaism long before coming to America. Most who remained traditionally religious were willing to make certain accommodations in ritual observance, yet few, if any, were willing to declare all of them "inessential," as had the Reformers. For most Eastern European Jewish immigrants and their children, a Judaism stripped of such ethnic elements as the use of Hebrew and distinctive prayer garb in communal worship; the dietary laws; and holidays and prayers reflecting an ongoing, emotional attachment to the land of Israel was no longer Judaism. Even if they *had* been attracted to the Reform movement, they would not have received a warm welcome, for most German Jewish immigrants and their children had little if any desire to worship alongside of poor, uneducated, and not yet Americanized Jews who threatened their own, successful integration into American society.

Almost all of the congregations established by the new immigrants were Orthodox. A great many of them were tiny, impoverished congregations where immigrants worshiped and socialized with other traditionally religious Jews who came from the same area or town. Among the more religiously devout were thousands who identified themselves as *hasidic* (though *Hasidism* primarily grew in the United States after World War II). They, like those immigrant rabbis who joined the newly created Association of American Orthodox Rabbis (*Agudath Ha-Rabonim*), opposed the Americanization of Judaism, a stance maintained by the association even today. On the other hand, a significant number of immigrants and their children were attracted to a more modern form of Orthodoxy. While modern Orthodoxy, like Hasidism, has experienced greatest growth since 1945, earlier organizations and institutions facilitating its success include the Isaac Elchanan Theological Seminary in New York City (1897); the Rabbinical Council of the Union of Jewish Congregations of America, created by Elchanan Seminary graduates as a modern alternative to the *Agudas HaRabonim*; Yeshiva College (1928, chartered as a university in 1945) and Yeshiva's Stern College for Women (1954). They also include Young Israel, a movement that, by the 1920s, introduced greater decorum and the use of English into traditional Jewish worship and sponsored public lectures aimed at attracting young, well-educated Jews to Orthodoxy.

The religious movement that proved most successful in attracting Eastern European Jewish immigrants and especially, their children, was Conservative Judaism, with its emphasis on Jewish peoplehood and its dual commitments to tradition and change. Established by a number of prominent, traditional rabbis in direct response to the radical universalism of Reform and the parochialism of Orthodoxy, it began in Januay 1887 with the opening of the Jewish Theological Seminary of America in New York City. Reorganized in 1902 under the leadership of Rabbi Solomon Schechter, the seminary soon boasted a distinguished faculty, a library, and a Teachers Institute to prepare lay people for careers in Jewish education. Established in 1909, the Teachers Institute was ably led for over fifty years by Rabbi Mordecai Kaplan, one of the seminary's first ordinees, who later founded American Judaism's fourth major religious movement: Reconstructionism.

From 1902 until his death in 1915, Solomon Schechter laid a philosophical and organizational foundation for Conservative Judaism that remains today. He helped initiate the establishment of the Rabbinical Assembly (of Conservative Rabbis); instigated the creation of the movement's congregational arm, the United Synagogue of America (now known as the United Synagogue of Conservative Judaism) in 1913; and in numerous essays, books, and lectures, expounded an understanding of Judaism that offered an all-embracing concept of Jewish peoplehood as *Klal Yisroel* (translated by Schechter as "Catholic Israel"). He unabashedly proclaimed a love for the land of Israel, as Judaism's spiritual and cultural home, and viewed religious observance within the context of a rabbinic, legal system (*halakhah*) that contained within it the mechanisms for change.

Contemporary Concerns and Developments

According to a 1990 population survey conducted by the Council of Jewish Federations (CJF), more than 50 percent of American Jews who religiously identify themselves as Jewish do not belong to a synagogue. Included among the unaffiliated are those who confuse, or conflate, Judaism with Jewishness (Jewish ethnic and cultural identity); those whose observance is limited to such family-oriented holidays as Chanukah and Passover, attending synagogue on the Jewish High Holidays and, perhaps, fasting on Yom Kippur; and those who *are*, in fact, affiliated Jews, though they are not members of religious congregations. Actively supporting such seemingly secular Jewish organizations as those involved in communal fund-raising, Jewish education, social service, support for Israel, or the fight against anti-Semitism, may not appear to be religiously motivated. Yet, as Jonathan Woocher convincingly argues in his book *Sacred Survival* (1986), such involvement is, in fact, an expression of a "civil Judaism" rooted in a distinct, Jewish religious sensibility and a passionate commitment to the survival of Jews, Judaism, and Jewish moral values.

Among the 41 percent of American Jewish households with current synagogue affiliation, 43 percent are affiliated with the Conservative movement; 35 percent with Reform, 2 percent with Reconstructionism, and 16 percent with Orthodoxy. The remaining 4 percent, who listed their affiliation on the CJF survey as "other" or "don't know," presumably belong to a Jewish religious fellowship (*havurah*) or group that is not affiliated with American Judaism's four major denominations. Included among them are those within the Jewish Renewal movement, a loosely organized, international network of *havurot* (fellowship members) that see themselves as part of a larger Jewish alliance committed to the healing and transformation of one's self, one's communities (both local and national), and the world. Particular concerns of this movement include mysticism, feminism, and ecology. Historically rooted in the American Jewish counterculture of the 1960s, its popularly acknowledged spiritual elder is Rabbi Zalman Schachter-Shalomi, founder of ALEPH: [The] Alliance for Jewish Renewal. While the number of those self-identifying as Renewal Jews is relatively small, its progressive political and religious agenda continues to reach a wide Jewish audience through books and publications such as *Tikkun*, founded and edited by Michael Lerner, and *New Menorah* and *The Shalom Report*, published by Arthur Waskow's Shalom Center, now a division of ALEPH. In addition to special events and presentations throughout the country, ALEPH offers courses, holiday programs, and spiritual retreats at Elat Chayyim, its retreat center in upstate New York.

Contemporary Concerns and Developments

Reform Judaism

While Reform Judaism continues to place greatest emphasis on Judaism as a religion whose essence is ethical monotheism, the last few decades have witnessed a greater appreciation for rituals and observances long dismissed by the movement as old-fashioned, if not obsolete. *The Centenary Perspective*, issued by the Central Conference of American Rabbis (CCAR) in 1976, counterbalanced Reform's long-held universalistic hopes with a particular focus on Jewish survival. Without mandating a specific code of behavior, the perspective insisted that Jewish living does not just mean living an ethical life but engaging in activities "which promote the survival of the Jewish people and enhance its existence." Suggested activities included creating a Jewish home, observing the Sabbath and holy days, engaging in private and public worship, and making a serious commitment to Jewish study. At its May 1999 convention in Pittsburgh, the CCAR adopted a new statement of principles. Re-identifying those activities suggested in the 1976 perspective as modes of living to which the Reform movement was *committed*, it also affirmed the importance of Hebrew knowledge and of religious obligations, some long observed by Reform Jews, others demanding renewed attention. While the creation of ARZA (The Assocation of Reform Zionists of America) in 1967 signaled a radical departure from the movement's early anti-Zionism, the 1999 perspective, addressing itself to all Reform Jews, went even further. It described love for the Jewish people as a *mitzvah* (religious obligation), affirmed Reform's commitment to the State of Israel, and encouraged immigration to Israel (*aliyah*), acknowledging the unique opportunities for Jewish living that it affords.

Yet despite what some have heralded, or decried, as Reform's return to tradition, the movement continues to support ideas and activities that reflect an ongoing adaptation to modernity. As the 1999 perspective makes clear, Reform Judaism remains firmly committed to egalitarianism. This is reflected in the movement's early obliteration of sex-differentiated religious roles; the ordination of women as rabbis (since 1972); women's investiture as cantors (since 1975), and the recent creation of gender-inclusive liturgies. Reform's most radical break with tradition remains the CCAR's Patrilineal Discent Decision of 1983. In contrast to rabbinic law's insistence that in cases of mixed marriage, religious status follows that of the mother (matrilineality), the CCAR maintained that such offspring are Jewish if *either* parent is a Jew and *if* he or she is religiously raised and self-identifies as Jewish. Moreover, having long accepted interested gay and lesbian Jewish congregations as members of the Union of American Hebrew Congregations, and more recently, qualified gay and lesbian Jews into the Reform rabbinate (1990), the movement continues to see itself as an inclusive community, open to different kinds of families "regardless of their sexual orientation," including those who have converted or intermarried, who are committed to creating a Jewish home.

Conservative Judaism

Having emerged as a movement driven less by ideology than by specific actions in reaction to the extremes of Orthodoxy and reform, Conservative Judaism long refrained from promulgating any ideological platforms or perspectives. Indeed, as some sociologists have observed, the lack of a clear-cut ideology may well contribute to Conservatism's wide appeal. At the very least, it helps explain why there remains less uniformity in religious attitudes and behavior among Conservative synagogues, and between Conservative clergy and laity, than in other Jewish religious movements (though the increasing use of the movement's recently published prayer book, *Sim Shalom*, has helped promote greater liturgical uniformity among congregations). It also helps explain what Ismar Schorsch, chancellor of the seminary, described as the "admirable and intriguing" tension lying beneath the surface of the movement's first collective statement of principles, *Emet ve'Emunah* (*Truth and Faith*), issued by lay and rabbinic leaders in 1988.

Recognizing the difficulty of effecting change within the framework of *halakhah*, the Rabbinical Assembly's Law Committee has long maintained that its decisions are not binding, giving Conservative pulpit rabbis far greater power in establishing congregational religious policy than that exercised by rabbis serving other types of congregations. It has also prompted the movement to put difficult issues on hold, sometimes "indefinitely," including the recently debated question of whether or not to admit openly lesbian and gay Jews into the Conservative rabbinate. Because the spectrum of those self-identifying as Conservative Jews is fairly large, the long-standing concern that the movement might split was realized following the seminary's 1983 decision to admit women into its rabbinical program and the subsequent ordination of Amy Eilberg in 1985 (soon thereafter, women were admitted into the seminary's School of Sacred Music, invested as cantors, and after a protracted struggle, gained entry into Conservatism's professional cantorial association as well). Opposed to these decisions, a small but vocal group of Conservative rabbis and lay people formed their own Union for Traditional Conservative Judaism. Still small in number, the group (now known as the Union for Traditional Judaism), no longer identifies with the Conservative movement, thus ending the split initially caused by their departure.

Reconstructionism

More so than any other American Jewish movement, Reconstructionism remains closely tied to the thought of one individual: Mordecai Kaplan (1881–1983), a Conservative rabbi whose emphasis on Judaism as an ongoing, ever-changing religious civilization created by the Jewish people, led to the establishment of a small, yet vibrant movement whose date of origin is considered by some to be 1922 (with Kaplan's assuming leadership of the Society for the Advancement of Judaism in New York City), by others, 1934 (the publication date of his monumental *Judaism as a Civilization*). Its major organizations and institutions currently include the Reconstructionist Rabbinical College (RRC) in Wyncote, Pennsylvania (first opened in Philadelphia in 1968); the Reconstructionist Rabbinical Association; and the Federation of Reconstructionist Congregations and Havurot. Decisions reached by other Jewish movements after years of debate and dissension have been arrived at more easily, and with far less fanfare, by Reconstructionist leaders. Such decisions have included the ordination of women as rabbis (women were admitted to RRC from its inception), the ordination of openly gay and lesbian Jews, and the acceptance of patrilineal descent. Reconstructionist prayer books of the 1940s deleted references to the election of the Jewish people, God as a supernatural miracle worker, and a future messianic redeemer. Its newer liturgies, including the Sabbath and holiday prayer book published in 1994, have "remained faithful to these principles," while including formerly deleted prayers as liturgical options. Other recent liturgical changes include the use of gender-inclusive language, poems and prayers written by contemporary Jewish men and women, and new, theologically diverse, metaphors for God.

Orthodoxy

The term "Orthodoxy" applies to Jews who strive to live in accordance with God's teachings as revealed in Judaism's sacred texts and codified by rabbinic sages. It does not, however, refer either to a unified movement or a single religious community. Thus, for example, concerns and trends within modern Orthodoxy are very different from those within Hasidism, while Hasidism itself does not refer to a single group of Jews, but rather to a number of different religious communities, each with its own leaders, beliefs, and particular religious concerns.

Since the 1970s, some of the most visible developments within modern Orthodoxy have concerned the religious roles and education of women. There has been a proliferation of traditional women's prayer groups, created by Orthodox women as a means of participating more fully in public worship. Such groups meet once or twice a month, most often on Shabbat morning, and conduct a full service, with the exception of prayers for which a *minyan* (prayer quorum) is needed. Since men are not present, participants are *halakhically* permitted to lead prayers, recite the Torah blessings, and read from the Torah scroll. While strong opposition to these groups continues, they continue to receive the guidance and support of Orthodox rabbis like Rabbi Emanuel Rackman, who believe that to seek more Jewish responsibility is not anti-*halakhic* but, to the contrary, claims *halakhah* as "the birthright of all Jews." Since February 1997, over a thousand women, and some men, have attended annual conferences on feminism and Orthodoxy in New York City. The interest and excitement they have generated, along with the development of new educational programs, growing demands to remedy *halakhically* sanctioned injustices against women, and, since December 1997, the hiring of a female "congregational intern" to serve as pastor, teacher, and counselor at Manhattan's Lincoln Square Synagogue, demonstrate that even among Jews who accept *halakhically* based, gender-distinctive roles, a growing number are actively seeking to raise women's legal status, while creating new opportunities for women to participate more knowledgeably, and more fully, in communal religious life.

Hasidic Jews continue to live in tightly knit, pietistic communities, bound together by their strict adherence to Jewish law; devotion to the rebbe (the charismatic leader of a particular, Hasidic dynasty or group); distinctive dress, customs, and educational institutions; a unique sense of history; and, to as great a degree as possible, isolation from "outsiders" (including other Jews) and from the modern world. Political and ideological disagreements continue to engender hostility among Hasaidic communities, including rabbinical supervision of *kashrut* (the proper observance of Judaism's dietary laws); political recognition and support of the modern State of Israel (still opposed by some Satmar Hasidim); and outreach to nonobservant Jews (a major effort of Lubavitcher Hasidim since the 1960s). Finally, there continues to be disagreement over the immanence of messianic redemption. By the early 1990s, many Lubavitchers were heralding their rebbe, Menachem Mendel Schneerson, as the messiah. Since Schneerson's death in 1994, most Lubavitch Jews have accepted this belief, some denying his death, others awaiting his physical resurrection.

See also ANTI-SEMITISM; BAR MITZVAH AND BAT MITZVAH; CHANUKAH; CRYPTO-JUDAISM; DIVORCE, JEWISH; HASIDIM; HESCHEL, ABRAHAM JOSHUA; HOLOCAUST; HOLY LAND; INCLUSIVE LANGUAGE; JEWISH HIGH HOLY DAYS; JEWISH IDENTITY; JEWISH OBSERVANCE; JEWISH RENEWAL; JEWS FOR JESUS; JUDEO-CHRISTIAN TRADITION; KABBALAH; KAHANE, MEIR; KAPLAN, MORDECAI; KIPPAH; KOSHER; LESBIAN AND GAY RIGHTS MOVEMENT; MARRIAGE, JEWISH; MENORAH; MIDRASH; MIKVEH; MYSTICISM; ORDINATION OF WOMEN; PASSOVER; RABBINATE; RELIGIOUS PERSECUTION; SABBATH; SCHECHTER, SOLOMON; SHAVUOT; SHIVAH; SYNAGOGUE; TALMUD; TORAH; ZIONISM.

BIBLIOGRAPHY

Cardin, Nina Beth, and David Wolf Silverman, *The Seminary at 100: Reflections on the Jewish Theological Seminary and the Conservative Movement.* 1987.

Kaplan and Us: A 60th Anniversary Symposium. Special Issue of *The Reconstructionist: A Journal of Contemporary Jewish Thought and Practice.* 60, no. 2 (Fall 1995).

Meyer, Michael A. *Response to Modernity: A History of the Reform Movement in Judaism.* 1988.

Mintz, Jerome R. *Hasidic People: A Place in the New World.* 1994.

Neusner, Jacob, ed. *Understanding American Judaism: Toward the Description of a Modern Religion.* 2 vols. 1975.

Sachar, Howard M. *A History of the Jews in America.* 1992.

Seltzer, Robert M., and Norman J. Cohen, eds. *The Americanization of the Jews.* 1995.

Sorin, Gerald. *Tradition Transformed: The Jewish Experience in America.* 1997.

Umansky, Ellen M., "Jewish Women's Religious Lives in the United States in the Nineteenth and Twentieth Centuries," in *Jewish Women in Historical Perspective*, edited by Judith R. Baskin, 2nd ed. 1998, pp. 337–363.

Wertheimer, Jack, ed. *The American Synagogue: A Sanctuary Transformed.* 1987.

Woocher, Jonathan S. *Sacred Survival: The Civil Religion of American Jews.* 1986.

Ellen M. Umansky

Judeo-Christian Tradition

The Judeo-Christian tradition (JCT) is a concept that has played a shifting role in the construction of American religious identity since the eve of World War II. Originally invented to designate connections between Judaism and Christianity in antiquity, "Judeo-Christian" began to be used to signify the common religious inheritance of the West by left-wing authors in the 1930s—a time when "Christian" had become a political code word for fascism and anti-Semitism (e.g., the Christian Front of Father James Coughlin). Liberal Protestants and Catholics in particular stressed the existence of the Judeo-Christian tradition to indicate their spiritual solidarity with the threatened Jewish population of Europe.

During World War II, "Judeo-Christian" was taken up by liberal intellectuals as an umbrella term to designate the religious dimension of the Allied cause. But as a shibboleth, the term fully came into its own in the early years of the Cold War, when it was employed by pastors, politicians, and pundits to mobilize the spiritual forces of America against the "godless Communist" foe. As Daniel Poling, president of the Military Chaplains Association of the United States, asserted at the association's 1951 convention, "We meet at a time when the Judeo-Christian faith is challenged as never before in all the years since Abraham left Ur of the Chaldees." The following year, in a speech before the Freedoms Foundation, President-Elect Dwight D. Eisenhower declared, "Our form of government has no sense unless it is founded in a deeply felt religious faith, and I don't care what it is. With us, of course, it is the Judeo-Christian concept but it must be a religion that all men are created equal."

Besides functioning in Cold War political discourse, the JCT was imbued with theological substance by Reinhold Niebuhr and his neo-orthodox associates, who regarded Christianity as deriving more from "Hebraic" than from "Hellenic" influences. They saw the JCT less in terms of specific articles of faith or moral ordinances than as a common view of the flawed nature of humankind and an embrace of the prophetic critique of human institutions and idolatry of all sorts. This outlook was criticized by some Roman Catholics, who rightly saw it as bound up with the neo-orthodox critique of Catholic natural-law philosophy. For their part, some Jewish writers assailed the JCT for, as they felt, subordinating Jewish distinctiveness to a larger, essentially Christian reality. Not until the late 1960s, however, did the JCT come in for sustained cultural criticism.

In *The Myth of the Judeo-Christian Tradition* (1969), novelist and editor Arthur Cohen asserted that the only tradition shared by Jews and Christians was one of mutual enmity; indeed, he went so far as to charge proponents of the concept with laying the groundwork for Nazi anti-Semitism. At about the same time, voices from the contemporary American counterculture were blaming the JCT for afflicting the world with Western spiritual imperialism and conventional bourgeois morality. But while the JCT, like other emblems of the American Cold War consensus, took its lumps during the Vietnam War era, within a few years it had discovered new friends, this time in the emergent Christian Religious Right.

Beginning in the late 1970s, the Reverend Jerry Falwell's Moral Majority organization made extensive use of Judeo-Christian language as part of an effort to present itself as an organization of religious believers of different faiths rather than simply of evangelical Protestants. During the Reagan presidency and on through the 1990s, "Judeo-Christian" (now often embedded in the phrase "Judeo-Christian ethic") became a standard rhetorical feature of American social conservatism, even as the Moral Majority was succeeded by the seemingly less religiously inclusive Christian Coalition as the Religious Right's premier membership organization. Rhetorically, the phrase became interchangeable with "traditional family values." Substantively, its twin pillars often seemed to be opposition to abortion and to homosexual rights. Where once the enemy had been communism, now it was secularism or, according to some, secular humanism.

As it did duty on the conservative side of America's *fin-de-siècle* culture wars, the JCT lost its capacity to stand for the country's common religious heritage. This was not only the result of its appropriation by the Religious Right. Given greater awareness of the presence of Muslims, Hindus, Buddhists, Sikhs, and other religious communities within American society, the idea that the United States was a "Judeo-Christian" country was felt to be as exclusionary as "Christian" had seemed after World War II. The Western religious tradition itself had to be characterized in a way that included Muslims; in some ecumenical religious circles "Judeo-Christian" began to be replaced by "Abrahamic"—a term expressing the common ancestry of Judaism, Christianity, and Islam in the patriarch Abraham of the Hebrew Bible.

But even as its use as an umbrella term was undermined by greater awareness of religious diversity, the JCT was gaining a new degree of intellectual respectability. In comparison with other world religions, Judaism and Christianity could more easily be recognized as possessing common features, and religion scholars could increasingly be found unself-consciously referring to "the Judeo-Christian tradition" in articles for academic journals. Thus, after two millennia of Judeo-Christian history and a half century of popular usage, the JCT seemed to have established itself as a useful concept outside the realm of world and domestic politics.

See also CHRISTIAN COALITION; CULTURE WARS; ECUMENICAL MOVEMENT; JUDAISM; MORAL MAJORITY; NIEBUHR, REINHOLD; RELIGIOUS COMMUNITIES; RELIGIOUS RIGHT; RELIGIOUS STUDIES.

BIBLIOGRAPHY

Silk, Mark. *Spiritual Politics: Religion and America Since World War II*. 1988.

Mark Silk

Jung, Carl Gustav.

See Archetype; Dreams; Myth.

K

Kabbalah

Kabbalah (literally, the "received tradition") is the general term for Judaism's mystical tradition. Scholars acknowledge that such a tradition existed from at least the early centuries of the common era, and the earliest written texts go back to about the fifth century C.E. Important older texts include the Sefer Yetzira (ca. eighth century), the Bahir (eleventh century), the Zohar (thirteenth century), and the writings of a circle of mystics of Sfat, Israel (sixteenth century). In Renaissance times some Christians became interested in Kabbalah, and in the late nineteenth century, theosophical groups sometimes included studies of Kabbalah in their research into the world's traditions.

Originally Kabbalah was a highly secretive aspect of Judaism, confined to adult, married males who had devoted themselves to study and had already mastered the sacred texts of Torah and Talmud. With the founding of Hasidism, a pietist movement of Eastern Europe in the eighteenth century, the teaching of mystical concepts became more widespread, though in contexts still dominated by male teachers. In modern times, rabbis and teachers educated in the Hasidic movement have been responsible for most of the revival of interest in Kabbalah. In the 1940s and 1950s the writings of Martin Buber and Abraham Joshua Heschel, both from Hasidic backgrounds, popularized some of the stories and teachings of Hasidic masters. Since the 1970s, such teachings have become available to a larger public, still primarily Jewish, but extending in recent years to non-Jews as well.

While different versions of the teachings come from different sources, the principal tenets of Kabbalah are fairly clear: The world we see, and everything in it, is a purposeful manifestation of an infinite God, and thus everything in creation has within it a divine spark or soul. However, God intentionally concealed the divinity within each entity, so that it is the work of human beings to uncover and clearly reveal that divine essence. This work constitutes the individual and collective purpose of existence.

In particular, Kabbalists since at least medieval times have envisioned the divine as manifesting itself through ten channels of energy, known as *sefirot*, from the Hebrew word for "number." These are usually known, in English translation, as Crown, Wisdom, Understanding (alternatively, Wisdom, Understanding, and Knowledge), Loving-Kindness, Discipline, Beauty, Victory, Glory, Foundation, and Kingship. The first three are spiritual and intellectual qualities, the next six are character attributes relevant to our emotional and physical expression, and the last is the ultimate manifestation of these in the world. By working to perfect oneself in these qualities a person can become a pure channel for divine energy and thus help to perfect the world.

Different sorts of groups disseminate these teachings. Among Orthodox Jews the best-known groups are the Hasidic sects of Lubavitch and Breslov. Lubavitch is also known by the acronym Chabad, in which the C, B, and D are taken from the Hebrew words for the three upper sefirot, Wisdom, Understanding, and Knowledge. Both groups emphasize the study of teachings of their particular spiritual leaders—in the case of Chabad a lineage of seven rabbis from late-eighteenth-century Russia until the early 1990s, and in the case of Breslov one rabbi, Nachman of Breslov, who lived in the Ukraine in the late eighteenth and early nineteenth centuries. Chabad teaches a more intellectual contemplation of concepts leading to intimacy with the divine, while Breslov emphasizes the pouring out of the heart in a personal relationship to God. Both encourage Jews to observe the traditional commandments, as transmitted through mainstream rabbinic tradition, while deepening their understanding of the mystical meanings of those commandments. They have helped fuel the *baal teshuvah* (returnees to Judaism) orthodox revival movement.

Another important channel of Kabbalistic teachings has been the Jewish Renewal movement. Beginning in the late 1960s, two charismatic rabbis, both from the Chabad tradition, separately inspired a new generation of Jewish youth. Rabbi Zalman Schachter-Shalomi, a brilliant scholar of contemplative, musical, and philosophical aspects of Judaism, encouraged followers to incorporate into Judaism elements of other religious and ethical traditions, notably Hindu meditative techniques and environmental ethics. Rabbi Shlomo Carlebach, an outstanding composer and singer, inspired Jews all over the world to infuse tradition with emotion. Both helped establish new Jewish communities and encouraged Torah observance without requiring it. Their students have helped bring mystical teachings to a larger audience and have also contributed to the baal teshuvah movement.

In general, the emphasis in contemporary Kabbalistic teachings is on personal and community development through study, self-examination, and moral improvement. Study typically includes the Bible, interpreted in its symbolic more than its historical or practical dimensions; ethical texts; and Kabbalistic or Hasidic inspirational material. Self-examination involves frequent inventory of one's behavior and personal relationships, working toward more positive attitudes in all aspects of life and adopting a broad perspective of loving-kindness and forgiveness toward all beings. Ultimately the goal is to recognize the unique purpose that each person has in life, the preciousness of one's connection to God, and the interconnectedness of all beings in the framework of the divine purpose for all human life. While most traditional teachers focus primarily on the student's awareness of the relatedness of all Jews and the purposes of the Jewish people, many of the newer teachers see the message of Judaism, as understood through Kabbalah, as relevant to all human beings.

Kabbalah differs from other contemporary mysticism in certain emphases and tendencies. First, it in-corporates Judaism's traditional emphasis on living in the ordinary world. Kabbalists do not normally withdraw from the world or practice asceticism, but look to the ordinary structures of Jewish life for their disciplines. This tends to be the case even if the practitioners do not accept all the traditional laws—for example, those in the Jewish Renewal movement generally use a modified form of dietary laws, with a preference for vegetarianism. Second, whereas some forms of mysticism have one standard method of meditation, Kabbalistic traditions offer a variety of types of meditation and prayer. The traditional Jewish prayer book is recognized as a text that encodes many mystical meanings in the ordinary prayers. Third, Kabbalah views each individual as a potential channel for the divine, depending on the extent to which a person has cleared himself or herself of ego-centeredness. Each can "draw down" godly influence into himself or herself, and "elevate" each area of life through this influence. Thus humans are cocreators with God. Finally, Kabbalah emphasizes the collective aspect of human existence: All souls come from one source; all are intricately interconnected; and each individual is a unique part contributing to the whole.

See also DIVINITY; HASIDIM; HESCHEL, ABRAHAM JOSHUA; JEWISH OBSERVANCE; JEWISH RENEWAL; JUDAISM; MEDITATION; MYSTICISM; PRAYER; RABBINATE; TALMUD; TORAH.

BIBLIOGRAPHY

Aaron, David. *Endless Light: The Ancient Path of the Kabbalah to Love, Spiritual Growth, and Personal Power.* 1997.
Cooper, David. *God Is a Verb.* 1997.
Kaplan, Aryeh. *Inner Space: Introduction to Kabbalah, Meditation, and Prophecy.* 1990.
Silberman, Neil. *Heavenly Powers: Unraveling the Sacred History of the Kabbalah.* 1998.

Tamar Frankiel

Kahane, Meir

(1932–1990), rabbi, activist.

Meir David Kahane was born in Brooklyn on August 1, 1932, to a family of rabbis. He was killed by an assassin on November 5, 1990, in New York City. For some, Rabbi Kahane was a leader, philosopher, activist, and teacher. For others, he was a racist and a nuisance. Undoubtedly he was a very influential Jew, and he helped change the Jewish conscience in both America and Israel.

Rabbi Meir Kahane, founder of the Jewish Defense League, delivers a typically fiery speech in Brooklyn, New York, October 1985. (Credit: © Frank Fournier/Contact Press Images/PNI.)

He graduated from Brooklyn College in 1954, and studied at Brooklyn's Mirer Yeshiva, from which he received his rabbinic ordination in 1956. He graduated from New York Law School and thereafter obtained a master's degree in international relations from New York University. He served as a rabbi in New York in the 1960s and wrote for the *Jewish Press.*

Rabbi Kahane founded the Jewish Defense League (JDL) in 1968, to combat the growth of anti-Semitism. At that time, Jews of such communities as Crown Heights and Williamsburg (in Brooklyn) were easy targets of hoodlums. He believed that it was the duty of Jews to protect one another. "Never again," said Kahane, would hoodlums kill Jews without getting killed. But the JDL also fought for Soviet Jews by engaging in demonstrative tactics that succeeded in highlighting the plight of millions of oppressed Jews behind the Iron Curtain. At times Kahane's tactics resulted in his arrest.

The JDL moved the issue of Soviet Jewry to the front pages. Thanks to Kahane's efforts, Russian Jews started to flow out by the hundreds and then the thousands. But as Rabbi Kahane said, "More than what we did for Russian Jewry was what they did for the young and lost American Jewish youth who finally had a Jewish cause to fight for . . . and they did that which their parents never did for their Jewish brothers and sisters who perished during the Holocaust."

Rabbi Kahane demanded that Jewish funds go for Jewish causes, primarily for Jewish education, and he fought against assimilation among Jewish youth. Established American Jewish organizations opposed him. They preferred quiet diplomacy as a means to help Soviet Jews. Kahane was sure that such tactics would not save the Jews of Russia.

American officials of the Nixon administration, such as U.N. ambassador Charles Yost, met with Kahane to dissuade him from disrupting Soviet artistic performances in America because they were afraid that Soviet-American reconciliation efforts would be damaged. "Three million Jews in Soviet Russia are being ripped from us now," said Kahane, "and it is our obligation to break any and every law to save them! We Jews have a hang-up. It's known as respectability. When President Roosevelt told us that he could not bomb the railroads leading to Auschwitz, we were respectable. And six million Jews died. It's time to bury respectability, before it buries us."

In 1971 Kahane immigrated to Jerusalem, Israel. Menachem Begin, leader of the Herut Party, offered Kahane a seat in Parliament, but he refused, since Herut was not a religious party. In 1984 Kahane formed an independent party, Kach, and proposed that Israel annex the territories taken in 1967 and establish Jewish settlements there. Some called him a racist. He made no apologies for his views. "Judaism is not Thomas Jefferson, and the Middle East is not the Midwest." He said on May 11, 1980, "There will never be peace between Jews and Arabs."

In 1984 he was elected to the Knesset (the Israeli Parliament). Just before the 1988 elections, polls predicted that Kach would receive as many as 14 of the 120 Knesset seats in Parliament. Parliament banned Kach from running for office, and the Israeli Supreme Court upheld this move. Both major Israeli parties (Likud and Labor) condemned Kahane. He was the first Jew in Israel to be held under administrative detention without charges or due process, something that until then was reserved for terrorists.

In 1987 he founded the Yeshiva of the Jewish Idea to train Jewish leaders capable of responding to the challenges facing Israel and the Jewish people. The yeshiva aimed to educate rabbis and scholars to spread the teaching of the Torah. On November 5,

1990, Kahane was assassinated by an Egyptian American. Some still believe that Kahane contributed to the survival of Jewish identity in both the United States and Israel.

See also ANTI-SEMITISM; BELONGING, RELIGIOUS; HUMAN RIGHTS; JEWISH IDENTITY; JEWISH RENEWAL; JUDAISM; RELIGIOUS COMMUNITIES; RELIGIOUS PERSECUTION; ZIONISM.

BIBLIOGRAPHY

Friedman, Robert I. *The False Prophet.* 1992.

Kahane, Meir. *Never Again: A Program for Survival.* 1972.

Kahane, Meir. *Uncomfortable Questions for Comfortable Jews.* 1987.

Herbert Druks

Kaplan, Mordecai

(1881–1993), rabbi, activist.

Mordecai Kaplan, an American rabbi, an ideologue, and the founder of Reconstructionism, sought to integrate Judaism with the fundamental values of American civilization. Liberal yet Zionist, Kaplan believed that Judaism had to change so it could function in a democratic society. He was born in Lithuania, was educated in New York City, and lived most of his life in the United States. He was passionately Jewish and passionately American.

The traditional education he received mostly from his father gave Kaplan a solid grounding in classical rabbinic texts. His own graduate studies at Columbia University, where he concentrated on sociology, led him to formulate a religious ideology that emphasized the link between religion and experience. Although the perfection of the individual might be the aim of religion, Kaplan believed that this goal could be achieved only within the context of a community. He held that for Judaism to survive in the secular culture of the modern era, Jews must have more in common than their religion. Throughout the ages Judaism as the evolving religious civilization of the Jewish people bound them together into a vital organic entity. A vigorous Jewish life in America could be brought into being, he maintained, only with the creation of new institutions appropriate to a democratic, technologically advanced society. Kaplan had a vision of the expanded synagogue as the vehicle for the survival of Jewish civilization.

Kaplan became a major force in American life through his training of rabbis and teachers from 1909 to 1963 at the Jewish Theological Seminary of America, the center of Conservative Judaism in America. In 1922 he established the Society for the Advancement of Judaism (SAJ) in New York City to implement his ideology. In 1934 he published *Judaism as a Civilization,* in which he set the Jewish people, their past experience, and their present welfare at the center of his conception of Judaism. The Torah (Hebrew scriptures), revelation, and God were all explained in terms relating to Jewish peoplehood. Kaplan's openness to ritual experimentation lead to the first bat mitzvah (female confirmation) when his daughter Judith turned 12½ in 1922.

Kaplan's productivity was overwhelming when we consider that many of his books were written when he was in his seventies and eighties. In addition to his published works, he was a prodigious diarist, having produced a journal amounting to twenty-seven volumes. An intense workaholic with a very full schedule, he included among his activities teaching rabbis at the Jewish Theological Seminary, writing, lecturing throughout the country at synagogues and colleges, and functioning as rabbi of the SAJ.

Kaplan was criticized by many groups throughout his career. Traditional Jews considered him heretical because he altered the liturgy and rejected belief in a supernatural deity who performed miracles and intervened in the historical process. Secular universalists saw his nationalism (Zionism) as regressive, and some liberal religious thinkers believed that he reduced Jewish life to community values, completely omitting the spiritual element of Jewish civilization.

It is true that Kaplan rejected traditional theism in favor of process theology. Nevertheless, he affirmed the belief that the divine is experienced in the positive forces of the universe that aid human beings individually and collectively in their search for salvation (e.g., life abundant). Kaplan was no atheist, and the quest for the divine was invariably part of his religious life. His belief in group life as the vehicle for the spiritual quest eventually lead to the establishment, in 1968, of Reconstructionism as a Jewish denomination, with a rabbinical school of its own in Wyncote, Pennsylvania.

Mordecai Kaplan was vigorous and productive well into his nineties. The fact that he died in 1983 at age 102 means that in a literal sense he lived through virtually the whole saga of the American Jew in the twentieth century though he moved to Israel shortly before his death. He will be remembered primarily as the principal theologian of cultural integration within the American Jewish community and as the founder of Reconstructionism.

See also BELONGING, RELIGIOUS; HERESY; JEWISH IDENTITY; JUDAISM; PROCESS THEOLOGY; RABBINATE;

RELIGIOUS COMMUNITIES; RELIGIOUS STUDIES; SOCI-OLOGY OF RELIGION; ZIONISM.

BIBLIOGRAPHY

Kaplan, Mordecai. *The American Judaism of Mordecai M. Kaplan.* 1990.

Kaplan, Mordecai. *The Future of the American Jew.* 1948.

Kaplan, Mordecai. *The Greater Judaism in the Making.* 1960.

Kaplan, Mordecai. *The Meaning of God in Modern Jewish Religion.* 1937, 1962, 1994.

Kaplan, Mordecai. *A New Zionism.* 1955.

Scult, Mel. *Judaism Faces the Twentieth Century: A Biography of Mordecai M. Kaplan.* 1993.

Mel Scult

Karma

The term "karma" is derived from the ancient Sanskrit language and carries an idea that is centrally important in the major religious traditions that come from India. The basic idea is that action (karma or karman) has consequences. The Hindu, Buddhist, and Jain traditions share this assumption. To whatever extent one is capable of intentional and willful action, one is responsible for it and eventually will experience its consequences. The general assumption in the notion of karma is that whatever action you intend or actually carry out will reflect your present character and will determine your future destiny to an extent that you may not be able to anticipate at the time when you entertain or perform the act itself. In short, the idea of karma places a very high value on the cultivation of careful and consistent patterns of thought and behavior.

In the traditional religions of India, the context for taking account of karmic patterns of acts and consequences is greatly extended because of a second and closely related idea. This is the idea of rebirth or reincarnation. It affirms that any living entity is at most only a link in a longer and larger chain of life that extends far into the past and future. Although a living person may seem to be exclusively the product of a unique human birth that happened just a few years ago, from the perspective of karma and rebirth that person is a contemporary manifestation of earlier life-forms and a step on the way to later forms of life that are integrally connected to the present one. Although hardly anyone claims to remember his or her previous births or is capable of predicting future ones, the fact that a few rare people display or seem to display such powers is convincing to many Hundus, Buddhists, and Jains, who believe that every form of life is part of a universal karmic process that does not uniquely privilege humans over others.

The idea of karma, only sometimes combined with the notion of reincarnation, has been part of American religious thinking since the New England Transcendentalists, who were inspired by the religions of India and discussed the *Bhagavad Gītā*, which is the Hindu text best known to modern people. The work of the Theosophical Society, which had headquarters in America and in India and which contributed to the revival of Hinduism and Buddhism in South Asia during the colonial era, as well as the several visiting lecturers from Asia who came to the United States to speak at the first World Parliament of Religions in Chicago in 1893, did much to spread the idea. From World War I through the 1960s, this-worldly or ethical notions of karma were spread by the influence of great practitioners of civil disobedience such as Mahatma Gandhi and Martin Luther King, Jr. Since the late 1960s, new religious movements and new immigrants from Asia have begun to make the idea of karma seem to be part of the American cultural fabric. Although Columbus did not find India, in time the karmic process brought India to America.

See also BUDDHISM; HINDUISM; JAINISM; KING, MARTIN LUTHER, JR.; NEW RELIGIOUS MOVEMENTS; REINCARNATION; THEOSOPHICAL SOCIETY.

BIBLIOGRAPHY

Conser, Walter H., Jr., and Sumner B. Twiss, eds. *Religious Diversity and American Religious History: Studies in Traditions and Cultures.* 1997.

Ellwood, Robert S., ed. *Eastern Spirituality in America.* 1987.

Keyes, Charles F., and E. Valentine Daniel, eds. *Karma: An Anthropological Inquiry.* 1983.

Miller, Timothy, ed. *America's Alternative Religions.* 1995.

Neufeldt, Ronald W., ed. *Karma and Rebirth: Postclassical Developments.* 1986.

O'Flaherty, Wendy Doniger, ed. *Karma and Rebirth in Classical Indian Traditions.* 1980.

Tull, Herman W. *The Vedic Origins of Karma: Cosmos as Man in Ancient Indian Myth and Ritual.* 1989.

Tweed, Thomas A., and Stephen Prothero, eds. *Asian Religions in America: A Documentary History.* 1999.

Gene R. Thursby

Kierkegaard, Søren.

See Existentialism.

King, Martin Luther, Jr.

(1929–1968), minister, civil rights leader, and activist.

Born into a black Baptist family in Atlanta, Georgia, King, the most influential civil rights leader and clerical activist in American history, was descended from two notable religious figures: His maternal grandfather founded the Ebenezer Baptist Church in Atlanta in 1895, and his father became pastor of that church in 1932. Admitted at fifteen to Morehouse, an elite black college in Atlanta, King decided to become a minister after hearing scholars such as Benjamin E. Mays, the president of Morehouse, depict religion as a potential force for social change.

King became ordained at his father's church in 1947, and after earning a B.A. in sociology from Morehouse in 1948, he entered Crozer Theological Seminary in Pennsylvania. King graduated from Crozer in 1951 and began his doctoral study at Boston Univer-

The Rev. Dr. Martin Luther King gives a sermon at Ebenezer Baptist Church in Atlanta, Georgia, in April 1964.   (Credit: CORBIS/Flip Schulke.)

sity's School of Theology. In 1954 King accepted the pastorate of Dexter Avenue Baptist Church in Montgomery, Alabama. The following year he earned his doctorate, and soon afterward he unexpectedly assumed a new role as social activist that would increasingly dominate his life.

In December 1955, the arrest of a black woman, Rosa Parks, for refusing to yield her seat on a bus to a white man, led blacks to organize a boycott of the offending bus company and to choose King as their leader. The boycott triumphed in December 1956, aided by a U.S. Supreme Court ruling that overturned segregation laws for public transportation. King emerged as a national figure, in part a tribute to his eloquent definition of the campaign as a struggle, not against whites, but against injustice.

The protest in Montgomery set the pattern for King's later campaigns by fusing mass action with expressly spiritual ideals. Among the diverse sources of King's thought was the transcendentalist Henry David Thoreau, whose essay "On Civil Disobedience" in 1849 declared, "In a society where anyone is imprisoned unjustly, the proper place for a just man is also a prison." King also cited the early-twentieth-century minister of the "Social Gospel," Walter Rauschenbusch, who insisted that achieving justice, even more than personal piety, was the key to salvation. From the hard-edged neo-orthodox theologian Reinhold Niebuhr, King recognized that evil may not always be healed by love alone. Above all, King embraced the tenets and techniques of the Hindu ascetic Mohandas Gandhi, whose readiness to go to jail for breaking unjust laws, together with acts of nonviolent mass resistance such as marches and boycotts, had helped end British colonial rule in India.

In 1957 King created a network of activist southern ministers known as the Southern Christian Leadership Conference (SCLC). From 1960 to 1965 he led or endorsed virtually every major nonviolent challenge to segregation throughout the South. In the spring of 1963 King's nonviolent demonstrations in Birmingham were met by police beatings and attack dogs, images of which shocked the American public into support for black civil rights. On August 28, 1963, King voiced his dream of racial brotherhood in religious imagery that culminated with his invoking "the old Negro spiritual, 'Free at last, free at last, thank God almighty, we are free at last.'" In March 1965 King led the last great campaign of the nonviolent black protest movement, a march from Selma to Montgomery, Alabama, that sparked passage of the powerful Voting Rights Act of 1965.

King's last years were marked by leadership of a widening circle of protests against racism, poverty, and war, which he saw as interrelated injustices. The flaring of ghetto riots persuaded him that the nonviolent protest movement had to shift its focus to aid the mass of ghetto blacks. His increasing activity in the northern ghettos after 1965 accompanied growing doubts about an economic system that he felt "often left a gulf between superfluous wealth and abject poverty." King also became a sharp critic of American involvement in Vietnam, which he charged had caused untold devastation and diverted resources from compelling domestic tasks. King spent his final months aiding a strike by impoverished sanitation workers in Memphis, Tennessee, where he was slain by a white racist named James Earl Ray on April 4, 1968.

King was neither the first nor the most militant African-American apostle of nonviolent resistance. But his matchless eloquence, honed by years of northern graduate training and southern Baptist preaching, inspired both blacks and whites with a vision of racial harmony that rested equally on the Judeo-Christian ethic and the American democratic creed. King inspired as well by personal example, as he braved arrests, threats, FBI surveillance and harassment, and ultimately martyrdom in pressing his reform causes. Throughout, he shared his faith in the triumph of freedom, equality, and peace despite all obstacles, proclaiming, "The arc of the moral universe is long, but it bends toward justice."

See also CIVIL RIGHTS MOVEMENT; JUDEO-CHRISTIAN TRADITION; NIEBUHR, REINHOLD; PRISON AND RELIGION; SOUTHERN CHRISTIAN LEADERSHIP CONFERENCE.

BIBLIOGRAPHY

Branch, Taylor. *Parting the Waters: America in the King Years, 1954–1963.* 1988.

Branch, Taylor. *Pillar of Fire: America in the King Years, 1963–1965.* 1998.

Garrow, David J. *Bearing the Cross: Martin Luther King, Jr., and the Southern Christian Leadership Conference.* 1986.

King, Martin Luther, Jr. *Stride Toward Freedom: The Montgomery Story.* 1958.

King, Martin Luther, Jr. *Where Do We Go from Here: Chaos or Community?* 1968.

King, Martin Luther, Jr. *Why We Can't Wait.* 1964.

Lewis, David Levering. *King: A Biography,* 2nd ed. 1978.

Oates, Stephen B. *Let the Trumpet Sound: The Life of Martin Luther King, Jr.* 1982.

Robert Weisbrot

Kippah

The kippah (Hebrew; plural, kippot), or yarmulke (Yiddish), is a head covering worn by observant Jews

Two Jewish boys, wearing a kippah, or yarmulke, on their heads, read from the Haggadah during a Seder. (Credit: CORBIS/Roger Ressmeyer.)

to demonstrate their humility before and fear of God, whose name is usually spelled "G-d." Whereas in some faith traditions—notably Christianity—one uncovers one's head to show respect (usually in a house of worship), the reverse is the case in Judaism, where an uncovered head is seen as a sign of arrogance.

The kippah does not have its origins in Jewish law, but its use has been a nearly universal practice since gaining popularity in the thirteenth century. Among American Jews, wearing the kippah varies according to one's level of observance and one's denominational affiliation. Orthodox and other traditional Jews wear the kippah at all times, except in bed, whereas Conservative Jews usually wear a kippah only during prayer services. Among Reform and Reconstructionist Jews, wearing a kippah is always optional, even during prayer services.

Among Orthodox Jews, the kippah is worn only by men, although women are under similar religious obligations to cover their heads. Since the late 1960s, however, some non-Orthodox women, seeking to overcome gender-based differences and inequities in Jewish traditions, have chosen to wear a kippah, though generally only while praying. They also wear a tallit, or prayer shawl. This trend has contributed to a general increase in ritual practice during Reform congregational services.

Disputes over the right to wear a kippah have been at the core of a number of church-state controversies, the most famous of which was resolved by the U.S. Supreme Court in *Goldman* v. *Weinberger* (1986). S. Simcha Goldman, an Orthodox rabbi and captain in the U.S. Air Force, appealed lower court rulings that confirmed the Air Force's right to prohibit him from wearing a kippah when he was in his military uniform and on duty indoors. Goldman claimed that this prohibition was an unconstitutional infringement of his First Amendment right to free exercise of religion. In a five-to-four decision written by William Rehnquist, the Supreme Court held that the First Amendment does not prohibit the military from establishing its own regulations regarding uniforms; therefore the Air Force had the authority to restrict Goldman's wearing of his kippah. Dissatisfaction with this decision, as well as with other decisions that seemed to give the government greater authority to regulate or restrict religious practices, led to the enactment of the Religious Freedom Restoration Act in 1993.

See also BELONGING, RELIGIOUS; CHURCH AND STATE; FREEDOM OF RELIGION; JEWISH IDENTITY; JEWISH OBSERVANCE; JUDAISM; MENORAH; RELIGIOUS COMMUNITIES; RELIGIOUS FREEDOM RESTORATION ACT.

BIBLIOGRAPHY

Chabad-Lubavitch. "The Significance of the Skull Cap (Yarmulke): Some Aspects of the Jewish Practice of Covering the Head." 1991.

Jacob, Walter, ed. *New American Reform Responsa.* 1992.

Lauterbach, Jacob Zallel. *Studies in Jewish Law, Custom, and Folklore.* 1970.

J. Shawn Landres

Koran.

See Qu'ran.

Korean-American Religions

As the millennium turned, nearly a million Americans had Korean ancestors. This makes Korean Americans the third-largest Asian-American group after Chinese and Filipinos. Many Korean Americans are Buddhists; more are Christians. In both cases, Korean-American religion is inflected with a marked degree of ethnic nationalism.

The first Koreans who came to U.S. territory did so between 1902 and 1905, when approximately seven thousand laborers came to work on Hawaiian plantations. Within just a few years they had begun to spread out across the North American continent. They formed Christian churches early, first in Honolulu (1903) and Los Angeles (1904), and then across the United States. Racial bars to Asian immigration kept the number of Korean Americans tiny for two generations. Large-scale immigration from Korea did not come until after the 1965 immigration act removed the tight, racially motivated national origins quotas. Soon more than twenty thousand Koreans were coming to America each year, most of them relatively well-educated members of the middle class.

Christianity is more common among Korean Americans than in any other Asian-American ethnic group. That stems partly from Korea's history under Japanese colonialism. In many Asian countries, Christianity was long identified with European and American colonialism. But in Korea the colonizing power was Japan. Christian missionaries, particularly Protestants, showed themselves willing to identify with the Korean people to the point that some were imprisoned by the Japanese. Their resistance to foreign aggression against Korea won the hearts of many Koreans, who became converts to Christianity. Today, about 70 percent of Korean Americans are Christians. The majority of them are mainline Protestants of a somewhat evangelical bent.

One finds many expressions of Korean nationalism in Korean-American religion. The pre–World War II Korean nationalist movement was built mainly not in Korea but in the diaspora, and churches were among the primary places for meeting and planning. In recent decades, dozens of charismatic pastors have emerged in Korea or in Korean communities in America. Many have spread the notion of special revelation by God to Korean Christians such as themselves, a sense of special destiny to spread their version of the gospel.

Beginning with the first generation in Hawaii, Korean-American Christian churches have been centers for community organizing, and Korean-American communities have been led by the pastors. Churches have been agents for the preservation of Korean culture, through language classes, through the use of the Korean language in services, through maintaining Korean festivals, and through ever reiterating the importance of the family. Some would say that Korean-

American churches have been instruments for the perpetuation of patriarchy in the diasporic population.

One remarkable development in Christianity has been the growth, since the 1970s, of a pan–Asian-American religious identity. This has paralleled the Asian-American movement in politics and education, wherein formerly distinct Asian peoples such as Chinese, Filipinos, Koreans, and Japanese have banded together under an umbrella identity to pursue common political goals. In religion this has given rise to pan–Asian-American churches, ministers from one Asian ethnic group leading churches of another ethnic group, writings on Asian-American rather than ethnically distinct theologies, and so forth.

Yet this Asian-American lumping has worked differently for Korean Americans than for the other Asian-American groups. Korean ethnic identity has been less fully subsumed than, say, Chinese or Japanese identity under the Asian-American rubric. If one reads a book or hears a speech on "Asian-American theology" by a Chinese American or a Japanese American, one will witness blended characteristics and qualities in the theology—some Chinese references, some Japanese, some American. If one reads or hears a similarly labeled book or speech by a Korean American, one will almost surely see Korean ethnic imperatives and cultural characteristics written onto the entire Asian-American group. For example, one noted theologian locates the heart of an Asian-American theology in *han* suffering, a distinctly Korean cultural expression. This would make little sense to most Chinese or Japanese Americans and can hardly be said to stand for all of Asian Americans. This expanding of Korean concepts to stand for all Asian Americans may be related to that nationalistic sense of mission, of the essentialness for others of Koreanness writ large, that undergirds much Korean-American spirituality.

As Korean America enters its second adult generation since the 1965 immigration law, some trends are clear. Members of the one-and-a-half generation (those born in Korea but raised in the United States) and the second generation are less tied to the all-Korean churches and other ethnically segregated institutions than are their parents. Yet by far the majority still are Protestants. Scarcely a major college campus lacks a Korean Christian club, and many chapters of such evangelical parachurch organizations as InterVarsity Christian Fellowship and Campus Crusade for Christ have come to be dominated by Koreans and other Asian Americans.

See also Belonging, Religious; Buddhism; Charismatic Movement; Chinese-American Religions; Conversion; Evangelical Christianity; Japanese-American Religions; Practice; Religious Communities; Sociology of Religion.

Bibliography

Kim, Jung Ha. *Bridge-Makers and Cross-Bearers: Korean-American Women and the Church.* 1997.

Matsuoka, Fumitaka. *Out of Silence: Emerging Themes in Asian American Churches.* 1995.

Park, Andrew Sung. *Racial Conflict and Healing: An Asian-American Theological Perspective.* 1996.

Prebish, Charles S., and Kenneth K. Tanaka, eds. *The Faces of Buddhism in America.* 1998.

Yep, Jeanette, et al. *Following Jesus without Dishonoring Your Parents.* 1998.

Yoo, David. *Racial Spirits: Religion and Race in Asian American Communities.* 1999.

Paul Spickard

Koresh, David

(1959–1993), charismatic religious group leader.

Born Vernon Wayne Howell, David Koresh was the charismatic leader of a Seventh-Day Adventist sect called the Branch Davidians between 1985 and 1993, and is best known for defying federal authorities in a

David Koresh, the leader of the Branch Davidian cult, who died in a standoff with federal officials in Waco, Texas, in April 1993. (Credit: REUTERS/HO/Archive Photos.)

standoff that ended in a fiery assault by the FBI that killed eighty-four people. Vernon Howell was born out of wedlock to Bonnie Clark in Houston in 1959. He was raised in the Adventist Church and often listened to radio and television evangelists. He reportedly memorized entire sections of the Bible and even lectured classmates. In 1981, at age twenty-two, he joined the Mount Carmel Branch Davidian community outside Waco and endeared himself to the group's prophetess, Lois Roden. The prophetess later announced that the mantle of leadership would pass to Vernon rather than to her own son George, who suffered from Tourette's syndrome and was given to violent outbursts. After Lois's death, a leadership crisis ensued. Most of the Davidians sided with Howell, but George Roden forced them off the property at gunpoint. Howell later retook the property in 1988, when he paid more than sixty thousand dollars in back taxes owed the county. Just prior to this incident Howell had traveled to Israel, where he received a vision. He came back radically changed, taking a new name, David Koresh. "Koresh" was the Hebrew name for Cyrus, a divinely sanctioned conqueror of Babylon, the empire that oppressed God's people.

Koresh envisioned himself in a messianic role, leading believers into an apocalyptic confrontation with the "world" (the biblical archetype of which was Babylon) and, ultimately, salvation. His teachings revolved around the doctrine of the Seven Seals. Koresh believed he was the seventh messenger spoken of in the Bible, who was to open the Seven Seals. According to Revelation 11:15, this messenger appears shortly before the end time to prepare the way for Christ's return. One controversial aspect of this teaching was that this same messianic figure was to be the perfect mate for all female adherents. Herein a new lineage of God's children would be created from his seed. These children would constitute the twenty-four elders who rule during the millennium. Hence Koresh took a number of women as "spiritual wives," some of whom were under legal age. Reports of sexual abuse arose, leading to investigations by authorities and fueling demands for intervention. When a report of firearms violations was filed with the Bureau of Alcohol, Tobacco, and Firearms (ATF), the investigation culminated in a raid on the Davidian community. A shoot-out ensued, and four ATF agents and six Branch Davidians were killed. The FBI's Hostage Rescue Team (HRT) took command of the standoff for the next fifty-one days, but negotiations stalled after the first week, prompting the HRT to launch a gas assault on the barricaded group. The remaining cult members, including Koresh himself, then set themselves on fire, a mass suicide. Subsequent congressional investigations found that both the FBI and the ATF acted irresponsibly and with excessive force. For many politically disenfranchised Americans, Waco became a symbol of government abuse and Koresh a defiant hero.

See also Anti-Cult Movement; Apocalypse; Branch Davidians; Cult; Seventh-Day Adventism.

Bibliography

Dick, J. Reavis. *The Ashes of Waco*. 1998.

Tabor, James D., and Eugene V. Gallagher. *Why Waco? Cults and the Battle for Religious Freedom in America.* 1995.

Wright, Stuart, A., ed. *Armageddon in Waco: Critical Perspectives on the Branch Davidian Conflict*. 1995.

Stuart A. Wright

Kosher

"Kosher"—from the Hebrew *k-sh-r*, meaning "right," "fit," or "proper"—commonly refers to the system of laws (kashrut) that governs the eating practices of traditional Jews. The kosher, or kashrut, system originates in three sets of biblical regulations: (1) the division of all animals into "pure" and "impure" (and hence permitted and prohibited) categories (Leviticus 11 and Deuteronomy 14); (2) the prohibition against "cooking a calf in its mother's milk" (Exodus 23:19, Exodus 34:26, and Deuteronomy 14:21); and (3) restrictions on the manner in which animals may be slaughtered and the prohibition against consuming blood (Leviticus 17). Jewish eating customs developed little beyond their biblical foundation in the postbiblical centuries, as both Jewish (Philo) and pagan authors attest. In fact, the only Jewish dietary practice commonly noticed or mentioned by non-Jewish authors is the abstention from pork.

The early rabbis (first to the sixth centuries C.E.) did much to transform the biblical eating system. Particularly notable was their establishment of rules pertaining to the separation of meat and dairy products. In rabbinic practice, soon accepted by all of Israel, *all* meat was to be separated from *all* dairy products, and a variety of symbolic separations were instituted to protect against transgression. Among these was a period of waiting between the consumption of meat and dairy products. During the early Middle Ages, there was much debate about how long a period of waiting was required—from an hour or less to six hours. The latter, more stringent custom was accepted by most European communities by the late Middle Ages.

Modern reformers saw the dietary regulations as outmoded. They understood that one of the central consequences—indeed, the underlying motivation—

A rabbi immerses a pot in boiling water, to make it kosher for use in Passover food preparation, at the Elmora Hebrew Center in Elizabeth, New Jersey, Monday, April 1, 1996. Passover begins at sundown on Wednesday. An assistant prepares food in the background at right. (Credit: AP/Wide World Photos.)

of kashrut was to maintain the separation of Jews from their non-Jewish neighbors. Desiring to become full citizens of the modern world, these reformers rejected kashrut altogether. Many modern Jewish stories depict the eating of prohibited food as the first act of rebellion by Jews wishing to enter the modern world. As modern attitudes spread, particularly among the offspring of immigrants to America, the observance of kashrut declined, and neighborhoods that once were home to dozens of kosher butcher shops saw one after the other close. Jews moving to new suburban neighborhoods often did not demand similar sources for kosher food.

Though many Jews abandoned the laws they found restrictive, most did not want to abandon their Jewish identity altogether, and, as in the past, eating customs continued to distinguish Jews from their neighbors. Characteristic of a new compromise were "kosher-

style" restaurants, establishments that served only kosher meat—though they also served dairy products—and featured foods attractive to the Eastern European Jewish palate.

After World War II, many religious Jews resettled in America and sparked a resurgence of interest in the practice of kashrut. In recent years, as some Jews have returned to traditional practices, this trend has increased. As a consequence, though the actual percentage of Jews observing kashrut has continued to decline, the demand for—and availability of—kosher foods has increased. Reflecting this development is the plethora of sophisticated new kosher restaurants in cities such as New York.

Also characterizing the contemporary scene is the development of "alternative" forms of kashrut. These include "eco-kashrut"—demanding respect for the environment in the production of foods—and "Jewish" vegetarianism, motivated by the belief that the world described in Genesis 1–2, in which humans were not permitted to consume animals, is one we should aspire to re-create.

See also ECOSPIRITUALITY; FOOD; JEWISH IDENTITY; JEWISH OBSERVANCE; JUDAISM; VEGETARIANISM.

BIBLIOGRAPHY

Grunfeld, Isidor. *The Jewish Dietary Laws.* 1972.
Welfeld, Irving. *Why Kosher?* 1996.

David Kraemer

Ku Klux Klan

Ku Klux Klan (KKK) is a name that has been claimed by many unrelated racist, anti-Semitic groups in the United States from the Reconstruction era after the Civil War to the present. The strongest period of the KKK was during the 1920s, when the membership of male and female chapters totaled approximately three million, largely in the northern and midwestern states. Earlier and later waves of the Klan, based more exclusively in the rural South, have been much smaller, with memberships numbering in the thousands. In the latter decades of the twentieth century the Klan has become a declining segment of organized racism in the United States, losing membership to neo-Nazi and other white supremacist groups but also increasingly allied with these groups.

Over time, Klans have varied considerably in their relationship to organized religion. The large 1920s Klan recruited heavily from among the members, and sometimes the clergy, of conservative Protestant denominations, especially Baptists and Methodists. This Klan preached virulent anti-Catholicism, along with anti-Semitism and white supremacism, mobilizing its adherents in support of a white, Protestant nation by claiming that Catholics and Jews represented a threat

A group of klansmen, wearing their robes and hoods, stand in front of a burning cross at Stone Mountain, Georgia, September 5, 1971.   (Credit: CORBIS/Bettmann.)

to Christian morality and American values. Anti-Semitism was nurtured by Klan propaganda portraying Jewish leaders in the entertainment field as corrupting the morals of Protestant youth. To foment anti-Catholic sentiment, Klan chapters featured sensationalistic speakers claiming to be ex-nuns and former priests who could reveal loathsome secrets of Catholicism and distributed a forged "Knights of Columbus Oath" purporting to reveal Catholic designs to torture non-Catholics.

In later waves of the Klan, anti-Catholic rhetoric generally waned, while anti-Semitism became more central. Although some Klans continued to disparage Catholics, others, including the influential group headed by David Duke in the 1970s, welcomed Catholics as members. In contrast, anti-Semitism in the Klan deepened. This is exemplified in the distribution of the forged document *Protocols of the Elders of Zion,* allegedly a Jewish plan for world domination. Anti-Semitism has served as a basis for alliances between Klans and other white supremacist organizations, especially neo-Nazi and Christian Identity groups such as the Church of Jesus Christ Christian, which argues that Aryans are the lost children of Israel. Some Klan organizations have become so deeply intertwined with the self-proclaimed "churches" of Aryan supremacism that Klan leaders have also served as Christian Identity ministers.

Throughout its history the Ku Klux Klan has been denounced by many religious organizations, including most Protestant denominations. Yet Klan practices mimic, often in distorted forms, the symbols and rituals of Christianity. This is most obvious in the burning cross, logs shaped into a Christian cross and set ablaze to terrorize minority group members; in ritualized practices such as Klan baptism; and in the ceremonial use of altars and texts. Christian imagery also exists in the names of many Klan organizations, such as Christian Knights of the KKK and the Assembly of Christian Soldiers.

See also ANTI-SEMITISM; CIVIL RIGHTS MOVEMENT; IDENTITY CHRISTIANITY; SECRET SOCIETIES.

BIBLIOGRAPHY

Blee, Kathleen M. *Women of the Klan: Racism and Gender in the 1920s.* 1991.

Chalmers, David M. *Hooded Americanism: The History of the Ku Klux Klan.* 1987.

Kathleen M. Blee

L

Las Hermanas

Las Hermanas, the first national organization of Chicana/Latina Roman Catholics in the United States, was organized in 1971 to challenge overt discrimination toward Spanish-speakers in the church and in society at large. Influencd by the politics of mass protest, religious Chicana women mobilized during a time of intense social upheaval worldwide. The national ethnic movements of the 1960s and 1970s, fighting for civil rights and self-determination; modern American feminism; anti–Vietnam War protests; Latin American liberation movements; and Vatican II all contributed to a milieu of social unrest and radical transformation. As politically conscious religious women, members of Las Hermanas brought the ethnic and gender struggles of the era into the religious realm. Through direct involvement in the Chicano movement, the organization expanded the ministerial role of the U.S. Roman Catholic Church, bridging civil rights and religious concerns. Membership grew in the first nine months from two hundred to nine hundred, representing twenty-one states, expanded to include Puerto Rican and Cuban-American women, and by 1976 membership included laywomen. Their class and ethnic diversity has earned them recognition as a highly creative and successful effort for solidarity in a diverse Latina/Latino reality.

Between 1971 and 1985 Las Hermanas influenced the policy decisions of major ecclesial bodies such as the National Conference of Catholic Bishops/United States Catholic Conference (NCCB/USCC), the Leadership Conference of Women Religious (LCWR), and the Secretariat for Hispanic Affairs of the USCC. Their concerns included institutional representation for the Spanish-speaking, culturally sensitive ministries, educational programs, employment practices, and women's ordination—in short, spiritual and political needs of Spanish-speaking Catholics in the United States. Members also participated actively in the Chicano movement, including student protests for educational rights, the farmworkers' struggle for labor rights, and widespread community organizing. Their activism represents the first time that Chicana/Latina religious leaders systematically challenged both public and private institutions to address ethnic, gender, and class discrimination.

Las Hermanas quickly developed national and international alliances with other groups, including the National Association of Women Religious (NAWR), Padres Asociados para Derechos Religiosos, Educativos y Sociales (PADRES), and the Latin American Conference of Religious Congregations (CLAR), organizations also concerned with justice and social change. PADRES, an organization of Chicano clergy, mobilized in 1969 and collaborated with Las Hermanas for a number of years. Together they provided the primary leadership of the U.S. Latino Catholic Church from the early 1970s to the mid-1980s.

A specifically feminist agenda did not shape the organization until 1976; however, early on Las Hermanas espoused feminist ideas. Experiencing the limitations of a "sanctified" hierarchical and male-dominated church made these women particularly aware of the forces of patriarchy. Community-centered consciousness and shared leadership, characteristic of

383

Chicana feminists, describe their early activism. Since 1980 Las Hermanas has focused specifically on issues affecting grassroots Latinas, including moral agency, reproductive rights, sexuality, and domestic abuse. Annual conferences, retreats, and newsletters articulate issues integral to the daily lives of many Latinas. In the process they have articulated a spirituality and a theology rooted in the Mexican/Cuban/Puerto Rican Roman Catholic faith but shaped by their experiences as feminists. Las Hermanas provided the "seedbed" for the production of *mujerista* theology, a blending of feminist concerns and liberation theology.

The women of Las Hermanas, both religious and laity, defy longstanding stereotypes depicting Latina Catholics as apolitical, asexual, passive bearers of their faith, for in the legacy of Las Hermanas, living one's faith also means living one's politics. The organization currently faces financial constraints yet continues to have a national membership dedicated to the empowerment of grassroots Latinas.

See also CIVIL RIGHTS MOVEMENT; FEMINIST SPIRITUALITY; GENDER ROLES; LATINO TRADITIONS; LIVED RELIGION; ROMAN CATHOLICISM; VATICAN II.

BIBLIOGRAPHY

Díaz-Stevens, Ana María. "Latinas and the Church." In *Hispanic Catholic Culture in the U.S.: Issues and Concerns,* edited by Jay P. Dolan and Allan Figueroa Deck. 1994.

Isasi-Díaz, Ada María. *Mujerista Theology.* 1998.

Medina, Lara. "*Las Hermanas:* Chicana/Latina Religious-Political Activism, 1971–1997." Ph.D. diss., Claremont Graduate University, 1998.

Ruiz, Vicki L. *From Out of the Shadows: Mexican Women in Twentieth-Century America.* 1998.

Lara Medina

Latino Traditions

Identity is rooted in tradition and particularly in a sense of peoplehood (Shils 1981). Christianity among the American peoples was first brought from Iberia, a European meeting place for Visigoth, Muslim, Jewish, and Christian religious traditions, and this mixing or cultural *mestizaje* continued with Native American customs (Elizondo 1992). As it had done in the Europe of Franks, Goths, and Celts, the agricultural cycle shaped the way these "adopted" celebrations became Christian, providing local variations to a religious calendar (Stevens-Arroyo and Díaz-Stevens 1993). Latino religious traditions have inherited a Catholic matrix

that carries over into a cultural identity that Latino Protestants, Evangelicals, and Pentecostals also share. Within the United States there is a growing diversity of Latino traditions owing to the migrations from Mexico, Central America, South America, and Cuba.

Latino traditions can be described by referring to an agricultural cycle. Planting begins in early February and is initiated by the feasts of the Purification of Mary (Nuestra Señora de la Candelaria) and of St. Blaise. Fire and light are associated with Candlemas, which along with the feast of St. Blaise contains elements of the Roman Lupercalia. Fasting continues during the forty days of Lent, but the last days of Lent are characterized by intense attention to vicarious identification with the sufferings of Christ. Good Friday, with its emphasis on fasting and redemptive power, sometimes supplanted Easter Sunday in the focus of Christian piety. The *penitentes* of New Mexico scourged themselves publicly on Good Friday in reparation for sins, much as the members of Seville's *cofradías* (confraternities) show contrition. The Feast of the Finding of the Holy Cross (May 3) coincides with the month dedicated to the Blessed Virgin Mary, and both feasts allow for the introduction of femininity into festivals of spring. These include various processions and other religious gatherings, often with young women assuming important roles, in which a statue of Mary is elaborately adorned and crowned with flowers or a prominent cross on a home altar is similarly decorated.

Summertime feasts include St. John the Baptist (June 24) and Our Lady of Mount Carmel (July 16), of relevance to maritime settlements, and various forms of bathing and blessing of waters. The Feast of St. James the Apostle (July 25) has rich roots in Iberian practice, where this feast reenacted symbolically the centuries-long wars between Christians and Moors (Foster 1960; Benavides 1995), and has assumed similar customs in the Americas.

Harvest is observed with prominent feasts such as St. Michael the Archangel (September 29), St. Francis of Assisi (October 4), Our Lady of the Rosary (October 7), and St. Rafael Archangel (October 24), matching particular autumn agricultural practices to a saint's day. The feasts of All Saints (November 1) and All Souls (November 2) carry resonances of Mesoamerican rites for communication with the dead, particularly in Mexican-influenced areas.

In addition, each town has its patron saint, so that the village would often add the *fiestas patronales,* a week of festivities not unlike medieval feasts that symbolically united the different classes in a common Christian belief and practice (Díaz-Stevens 1990). Civic, religious, and even ribald elements—parades, processions, and carousing—were put into stark con-

Three Kings Day (January 6) is celebrated with this parade in New York's East Harlem on January 6, 1997. (Credit: AP/Wide World Photos.)

junction that celebrated the community as much as the saint's life and works. In the Americas these fiestas preserved their popular character, adding Native American or African traditions to the Iberian matrix, much as had occurred in Europe's ancient religions. The baroque epoch in which Latin American popular religiosity was established fixed a pattern of simultaneous interiority and public display for religion that has survived in today's Latino traditions (Stevens-Arroyo 1998), which demonstrate communitarian characteristics inseparable from an interiorized devotionalism.

The special mixture of public and personal is perhaps most clear in the important cycle of Christmas. For Latinos, Christmas generally begins with the Feast of Our Lady of Guadalupe (December 12). The cycle climaxes on the second Sunday of January, called "Bethlehem's Octave," which features the Feast of the Three Kings or Epiphany. The Christmas cycle features distinctive music and special foods, making it the richest segment of Latino popular religiosity. The sixteenth-century Spanish missionary use of miracle plays or *actos sacramentales* has significantly enriched many of these celebrations, especially in areas influ-

enced by Mexican customs. Perhaps the most well known of these traditional Christmas plays is *La Pastorela*, which has been celebrated in San Antonio, Texas, since the beginning of the twentieth century (Flores 1995). A less formal version of these plays is the *posadas*. The entire village is involved in a dramatic reenactment of the journey of Joseph and Mary to Bethlehem, where Jesus was born. The subsequent public party includes the breaking of the *piñata* in a public place so that children receive their first Christmas gifts from the community rather than from "Santa Claus." In the Caribbean the processions from house to house are centered on a tradition of celebrating the journey of the Three Kings or Magi. Jovial processions or *parrandas* go from house to house singing *aguinaldos* and asking for a gift. Members of the different households would join in so that by the end of the evening members of the whole community had gathered together in singing and merrymaking. The final stop on Christmas Eve is the parish church for the midnight Mass, or *la misa del gallo*.

Christmas Day itself is marked by a meal for the extended family. Among Mexican and Central Americans, meat is diced and spiced in a stew, added to cornmeal (*tamales de maiz*), while among Puerto Ricans and other people of Caribbean heritage the meat is added to mixtures of ground plantain and green bananas or yuca (*pasteles de plátanos* or *de yuca*). The preparation segregates men from women. Thus popular religion often depends on food offered in ritual cuisine. While these elements are ludic and seemingly divorced from sacred celebration, they are essential to the communitarian nature of the religious celebration (Díaz-Stevens and Stevens-Arroyo 1998).

The Feast of the Holy Innocents (December 28) bears many similarities to the medieval Feast of Fools. In places where it is still observed, children carry mock spears imitating the soldiers of King Herod attempting to kill Jesus. The children are provided with the power of political authority in a ludic representation of how the poor view the government's police.

The Feast of the Epiphany or Three Kings Day on January 6 is the traditional time of giving gifts to children. Freshly cut grass is placed in a box underneath the bed, and in the morning gifts are found in the box as testimony from the grateful kings. The three visitors are depicted as combining the three major racial groups in Latin American history: white (European), yellow (Taíno), and black (African).

Personal and familial experiences are also part of Latino traditions. The rites of passage usually involve reception of the Christian sacraments. In the Catholic world, most of these rites of passage are accompanied by the recitation of the rosary (Elizondo 1975). Moreover, the public recitation of the rosary usually begins with imaginative introductions or glosses that use poetry to connect biblical events to individual needs in the *rosario cantao,* or sung rosary, which is a lively and animated event.

Christians generally believe that Baptism is required to enter Heaven. Immediately upon birth, the midwife commonly sprinkled holy water on the child, sometimes reciting the Latin formula for the sacrament. Baptism in the church incorporates into a family the *compadre* and *comadre,* who are godparents. Called *compadrazgo* (Elizondo 1975), the obligation on the adults makes them the equivalent of brothers and sisters. Birthdays and holidays such as Christmas necessitate gift-giving between those spiritually related by Baptism as if they were blood relatives.

The first Holy Communion was another occasion for family social celebration, adopting some of the trappings of a wedding. The function of Christian maturity, fulfilled by Confirmation in other, more settled places, was supplemented for female children through *la quinceañera,* a custom of formally presenting or introducing young daughters to society. In many places the wedding ceremony includes the ancient Iberian custom of *las arras,* coins symbolic of the groom's commitment to support his new bride. As with virtually every culture in the world, marriages are accompanied by huge family parties with food, music, dancing, and other ways of integrating two families.

Care for the sick often relies on a healer or *curandera,* who also possesses a wide repertoire of prayers, *pases* or ritualistic gestures, sprinkling of holy water, anointing and massages with oils, and extracts of herbs. If both the curanderas' medicine and that of doctors fail, then the *rezador/a* (a communal prayer leader) is asked to pray over the ill person, asking divine intercession for a cure or preparing for death. Sometimes a person would make it known that he or she would not die until a specific matter was settled between himself or herself and another person. After death, the deceased is dressed in a special attire called *la mortaja,* and the wake proceeds with both prayers and family reminiscences. For burial, a simple wooden box is sought, and the closest of kin carry the remains of the dear one to the town church and cemetery, where the priest or minister officiates at the last ceremonies. The mourners comfort one another for an additional eight days of prayers. Every year the day of death is commemorated by an anniversary *velorio* (wake), to which a *rezador/a* and the friends and family are invited back.

The closest members of the family often are expected to mourn the person's departure for a period of time. Sometimes widows, orphans, mothers, or other relatives would vow to clothe themselves in black or not to cut their hair for the rest of their lives.

These are called *promesas,* from the Spanish word for "promise." But promesas need not be connected to death and oftentimes are not. A promesa (or a *manda,* among Mexican Americans) may be made to ask for any special blessing or in thanksgiving for one received. Connected to promesas is yet another custom—the wearing of medals or scapulars. In ways that seem unique to Latinos, religion in the barrios of the United States nurtures the revitalization of old traditions and the creation of new ones.

See also ANTHROPOLOGY OF RELIGION; BELONGING, RELIGIOUS; PATRON SAINTS AND PATRON-SAINT FEASTS; QUINCEAÑERA, LA; RITES OF PASSAGE; RITUAL; SACRAMENTS.

BIBLIOGRAPHY

Benavides, Gustavo. "Syncretism and Legitimacy in Latin American Religion." In *Enigmatic Powers,* edited by Anthony M. Stevens-Arroyo and Andrés Pérez y Mena. 1995.

Díaz-Stevens, Ana María. "From Puerto Rican to Hispanic: The Politics of the *Fiestas Patronales* in New York." *Latinos Studies Journal* 1 (1) (1990): 28–47.

Díaz-Stevens, Ana María. 1993. *Oxcart Catholicism on Fifth Avenue.* 1993.

Díaz-Stevens, Ana María, and Anthony M. Stevens-Arroyo. *Recognizing the Latino Resurgence in U.S. Religion: The Emmaus Paradigm.* 1998.

Elizondo, Virgilio. *Christianity and Culture.* 1975.

Elizondo, Virgilio. *The Future Is Mestizo.* 1992.

Flores, Richard R. *Los Pastores: History and Performance in the Mexican Shepherd's Play of South Texas.* 1995.

Foster, George W. *Culture and Conquest: America's Spanish Heritage.* 1960.

Shils, Edward. *Tradition.* 1981.

Stevens-Arroyo, Anthony M. "The Evolution of Marian Devotion Within Christianity and the Ibero-Mediterranean Polity." *Journal for the Scientific Study of Religion* 37 (1) (1998): 50–73.

Stevens-Arroyo, Anthony M., and Ana María Díaz-Stevens. "Religious Faith and Institutions in the Forging of Latino Identities." In *Handbook for Hispanic Cultures in the United States,* edited by Felix Padilla. 1993.

Ana María Díaz-Stevens

LaVey, Anton Szandor

(1930–1997), cult leader.

Born Howard Stanton Levey, Anton Szandor LaVey was founder and high priest of the Church of Satan. As a teenager he became fascinated with occult pow-

Anton Szandor LaVey, High Priest of the Church of Satan, stands at the entrance to his church, wearing an elaborate satin cape and a shirt with pentagram, March 4, 1967. (Credit: CORBIS/Bettmann.)

ers, and in the late 1950s he began giving lectures at his home on vampires, cannibalism, and lycanthropy (werewolves). On April 30, 1966—the occult holiday of Walpurgis Night—he shaved his head, donned a black robe, and announced the formation of the Church of Satan with members of his weekly group. The news media readily accepted this eccentric character into the pantheon of counterculture figures in San Francisco. In the first year LaVey performed a satanic wedding, a satanic funeral, and a satanic baptism of his own daughter, Zeena. In 1969 LaVey published *The Satanic Bible* (which has sold nearly a million copies), in which he postulated "no difference" between "white" and "black" magic, asserting that all practitioners seek the attainment of self-aggrandizement. The book contained "Nine Satanic Statements," a diabolical equivalent of the Ten Commandments. The eighth statement succinctly summarized the church's philosophy: "Satan represents all of the so-

called sins, as they all lead to physical, mental, or emotional gratification." LaVey wrote two other books, *The Compleat Witch* (1970) and *The Satanic Rituals* (1972). He was also an occult adviser/consultant to the movie industry. Interest in the Church of Satan declined in the late 1970s, and by the time LaVey died in 1997, he was facing bankruptcy proceedings. The legacy of LaVey's church exceeds any measurable impact in terms of the numbers of its adherents. Even at its peak, membership was never more than five hundred.

See also CULT; DEVILS, DEMONS, AND SPIRITS; MAGIC; OCCULT, THE; SATANIC BIBLE; SATANISTS.

BIBLIOGRAPHY

Alfred, Randall H. "The Church of Satan." In *The New Religious Consciousness*, edited by Charles Y. Glock and Robert N. Bellah. 1976.

Richardson, James T., Joel Best, and David G. Bromley, eds. *The Satanism Scare*. 1991.

Victor, Jeffrey. *Satanic Panic: The Creation of a Contemporary Legend*. 1993.

Stuart A. Wright

Lazaris

Lazaris is the name given to a nonphysical entity who speaks through the body of Jach Pursel (1947–). Pursel has been channeling Lazaris since 1974. The name "Lazaris" is also used to describe the organization and the phenomenon as a whole. Lazaris describes himself as a "spark of consciousness" beyond our physical and causal planes. He is "working with" people on this planet to reach the next evolutionary step. Pursel and his two partners run a lucrative business based in Orlando, Florida, called Concept:Synergy, which markets Lazaris's wisdom in the form of tapes and seminars.

In 1974 Pursel, a Michigan insurance executive, became, reluctantly at first, what is known as a "full trance, objective" channel. "Objective" means that Lazaris is not a part of Jach's consciousness; "full trance" means that he is not conscious when Lazaris speaks through him. Lazaris's teachings include predictions, prophecies, healing techniques, and pronouncements concerning the nature of the universe, an eclectic mix common to much of the New Age.

Pursel set up a nonprofit foundation to promote Lazaris's teachings, but in the late 1970s he changed this to a for-profit corporation and in 1980 he relocated to Marin County, California. In the 1980s, as the so-called New Age movement began to attract the attention of mainstream media, Concept:Synergy took on a higher profile. In 1986 the organization began to mass-market Lazaris tapes and books through mail order and New Age bookstores. Pursel moved his headquarters to Rodeo Drive in Beverly Hills, while Lazaris became publicly associated with celebrities. Pursel even channeled Lazaris in front of a live audience on the Merv Griffin and Mike Douglas talk shows. Since 1989, when Pursel relocated to Florida, Lazaris has kept a lower profile.

People interact with Lazaris via a regular schedule of seminars conducted in hotel meeting rooms in five cities (Los Angeles, San Francisco, Orlando, Atlanta, and Newark), a website (www.Lazaris.com), and occasional one-on-one phone consultations. A Lazaris seminar may be two, three, or four days, plus individual evening sessions. A day will begin with Pursel going into a trance and Lazaris speaking on a predetermined subject, leading a guided meditation, and sometimes taking questions from the audience. Topics range from how to release negative ego to how the star Sirius affects our lives. Typically, two hundred or three hundred people attend each session, and the average cost is $500 per person, exclusive of meals or accommodations. By maintaining a core group of devotees, using word-of-mouth advertising, and avoiding the scandal that has tainted other successful channels, Lazaris is today one of the most enduring and financially lucrative of all channels.

Concept:Synergy does not keep statistics about its clientele, so no demographic data exist. But in general, Lazaris devotees are mainly of the baby boom generation (though younger and older cohorts are not uncommon), middle-class and overwhelmingly white. Like much else in the New Age, Lazaris, both the entity and the organization, has never called itself a religion. Concept:Synergy is a for-profit, taxpaying corporation. Anyone is welcome to attend any or all of the seminars, paying on a straight fee-for-service basis.

See also CHANNELING; NEW AGE SPIRITUALITY; NEW RELIGIOUS MOVEMENTS.

BIBLIOGRAPHY

Klimo, John. *Channeling.* 1987.

Pursel, Jach (Lazaris). *Lazaris Interviews.* 2 vols. 1988.

Elijah Siegler

Legalism

Legalism is the attempt to apply precise laws and rules to determine all our actions and decision-making. Le-

galists exercise these rules and laws despite the various contexts in which we may find ourselves. At the heart of legalism is an assumption that there are objective standards that we can apply in the same way to all kinds of actions without regard to context or consequence. Therefore, there are rules prescribed for every conceivable occasion in which we must make a choice in our actions. Those who are legalists follow the laws and rules in every situation. The letter of the law is more important than the spirit of the law. Some ethical systems have worked out very detailed rules of conduct, but most will always allow some flexibility according to the demands of the situation.

Judaism, Roman Catholicism, Protestantism, and all major Western religious traditions have legalistic impulses. The postexilic Maccabean and Pharisaic leadership of ancient Judaism lived by the written law, or Torah, and the oral law, or halakhah. Historically, the Torah is based on God's revelation to Moses at Mount Sinai and was the expression of God's will for the nation of Israel; it is found in the Pentateuch (the first five books of the Old Testament: Genesis, Exodus, Leviticus, Numbers, and Deuteronomy). Today Torah is any expression of God's will. Halakhah is the body of teaching that sought to apply the law to all life situations and provide instructions for decision-making and behavior. Today Reform and Conservative branches of Judaism have moved away from legalism, but Orthodox Judaism remains legalistic.

Roman Catholicism bases its legalism on natural law. It tends to sketch ethical rules by applying human reason to the facts of nature and to the lessons of historical experience. This leads to the belief that there are universally agreed upon and valid natural moral laws by which one can live one's life. Roman Catholics have responded to legalism by developing casuistry that is the application of ethical rules to specific cases to guide one's conduct or conscience.

Although most forms of Protestantism rarely develop intricate systems of law, they have often resorted to an unyielding insistence on moral rules. Whereas Roman Catholics have relied on natural law, Protestants have relied on Scripture to develop their legalism. Protestant legalism, then, is based on the words and sayings of the law and the prophets, the evangelists, and the apostles of the Bible. Within Protestantism, sexual morality tends to elicit legalism more than any other area of human behavior. In all forms of religious legalism there is the possibility that an elaborate system of exceptions and compromises to the rules is developed to try to account for every situation and to respond to the need for compassion and the differing circumstances in people's lives.

See also BIBLE; CREEDS; ETHICS; FUNDAMENTALIST CHRISTIANITY; JUDAISM; MAINLINE PROTESTANTISM; ROMAN CATHOLICISM; SEXUALITY; TORAH.

BIBLIOGRAPHY

Katz, Jacob. *Divine Law in Human Hands: Case Studies in Halakhic Flexibility.* 1998.

Provost, James H., and Knut Walf, eds., *From Life to Law.* 1996.

Ulstein, Stefan. *Growing Up Fundamentalist: Journeys in Legalism and Grace.* 1995.

Emilie M. Townes

Lent

Mentioned in some of the earliest known Christian documents, this season has always been connected with the celebration of Easter. The term is taken from the Middle English word *Lenten,* and concepts surrounding it are also perforce associated with spring or the vernal equinox. References as early as the third century C.E. mention a period of penitential anticipation of Easter, often associated with a convert's preparation for baptism, which would be administered on Easter Eve. In earliest times these periods of fasting, prayer, and self-sacrifice are mentioned as lasting no more than one or two days. But by 325 the Council of Nicaea substantially regularized Lenten observances in its fifth canon by referring to a common denominator of forty days. That number drew on Old Testament precedent as well as the example of Jesus' fasting in the wilderness before starting his earthly ministry. Eastern Orthodox references to this time frame use the word *tessarakoste,* while Latin churches use *quadragesima* for the same purpose.

The actual number of days during which Lent is observed differs between Eastern and Western churches. For those following the Latin tradition, Lent begins on Ash Wednesday and extends through the subsequent forty days, including Saturdays and Sundays, to end with Holy Saturday and its last services before celebrating Christ's resurrection. Orthodox Lent, on the other hand, begins on Pure (or Clean) Monday and also includes forty fast days, but since fasting cannot be observed on a Saturday or a Sunday, the season embraces a longer period of time. In prior centuries there were many strict rules about fasting during Lent. People were admonished to eat only one meal a day, only in the evening. Then they were warned against consuming any meat, fish, eggs, butter, or alcohol. Eastern Orthodox traditions continue to perpetuate quite rigorous strictures on diet to the present day. In the West, however, such rules were more often relaxed, beginning notably in the ninth century, when church leaders began allowing people to eat earlier in the day. In contemporary times, beginning with

Roman Catholic priests placing ashes on the foreheads of church members at St. Peter's Church in Chicago on Ash Wednesday, February 17, 1999, at the beginning of Lent. (Credit: AP/Wide World Photos.)

World War II and continuing the practice thereafter, most Western churches have dispensed with solemn Lenten fasting altogether except for Ash Wednesday and Good Friday.

In today's America, those churches whose liturgical calendars include Lent are flexible and realistic about rules of observance. There is a general emphasis on developing a penitential attitude in believers, and people are allowed considerable freedom in choosing what will engender a proper spirit within each individual. Many continue to observe Lent by denying themselves, abstaining from certain foods or activities during the season. Others try to develop a more reverential perspective by embracing some new activity, teaching themselves how worship and practical behavior can reinforce each other. But whether viewed positively or negatively, expressed through denial or extra effort, Lent has always received its main importance as a period that points ahead to the resurrection of Jesus Christ. In preparing for baptism, a convert anticipates the reward of first communion on Easter Day. Penance and prayers by those already baptized seek to renew and increase an appreciation of Holy Week, with its nadir at Good Friday and its triumphant vindication three days later.

See also ADVENT; CALENDARS; EASTER; EASTERN ORTHODOXY; FASTING; MAINLINE PROTESTANTISM; ROMAN CATHOLICISM.

BIBLIOGRAPHY

Mitchell, Leonel L. *Lent, Holy Week, Easter, and the Great Fifty Days.* 1996.

O'Shea, William J. *The Worship of the Church: A Companion to Liturgical Studies.* 1957.

Henry Warner Bowden

Lesbian and Gay Rights Movement

As gay men and lesbians became a visible presence in American society in the late 1960s, they began to confront their relationship to religious organizations. Organized religion, and ancient Jewish and Christian Scripture in particular, has been understood as a leading source of opposition to gay and lesbian rights. Gay men and lesbians have challenged that perspective, arguing that the references to gay sexuality in the Bible arose in a different context from the world we know today of committed gay and lesbian relationships. They have created their own religious organizations and demanded the right to participate openly and equally in Jewish and Christian (and to a lesser extent Buddhist, Hindu, Native American, and Is-

lamic) communities in the United States and internationally.

The Universal Fellowship of Metropolitan Community Churches (MCC) is the oldest and largest independent gay and lesbian religious organization. It was founded in Los Angeles in 1968 by the Rev. Troy Perry, a Pentecostal preacher who had been defrocked when his homosexuality was revealed. MCC churches have two sacraments (baptism and communion) and six rites (membership, holy union, funeral, laying on hands, blessing, and ordination). The worship styles and theological orientations of the more than three hundred churches vary according to the background and interests of minister and parishoners, but all MCC member churches subscribe to the idea that "Scripture does not condemn loving, responsible homosexual relationships."

The Unity Fellowship Church Movement was founded in Los Angeles in 1985 by Bishop Carl Bean. Unity has congregations in several large cities. Unity churches are open to all Christians and to all gay, lesbian, bisexual, and transgendered people and their allies. The leadership of Unity is predominantly African American, and its worship style is similar to that found in other black churches in the United States.

The first gay synagogues started in Los Angeles and London in 1972, and in New York in 1973. These synagogues formed the nucleus for the World Congress of Gay, Lesbian, and Bisexual Organizations, which was founded in 1980 and which now consists of more than fifty synagogues and groups worldwide. Most of the gay and lesbian synagogues have joined either the Reform or the Reconstructionist movement, although some remain independent. Their worship styles are eclectic, as members and rabbis represent various Jewish religious backgrounds, from Orthodox to secular.

In the late 1990s the American Catholic Church was founded in Baltimore by the Most Rev. Lawrence Harnes. The church follows Roman Catholic teachings but accepts clergy whatever their marital status, gender, or sexual orientation. Its forerunner was the Eucharist Catholic Church, which was organized in Atlanta in the 1940s and which ministered particularly to gay men.

Virtually all organized religious groups have had to respond to gay and lesbian demands for inclusion. Responses have varied. Some groups seek to convert gay men and lesbians to heterosexuality. Some organizations welcome openly gay individuals if they remain celibate. Many support civil rights but refuse religious rights, such as ordination and same-sex unions. In every denomination that has not embraced gay and lesbian rights there is an organized group engaged in a struggle for equality and acceptance.

Some individual congregations define themselves as welcoming, whatever the stance of their national organization. Some denominations have embraced gay and lesbian people as equal members of laity and clergy.

Evangelical Christian groups have for the most part rejected demands of gay and lesbian people for inclusion in their churches and are the leading sponsors of groups to convert them to heterosexuality. But there are many groups of gay evangelicals, including the National Gay Pentecostal Alliance, Good News, Evangelical Anglican Church in America, and the Faith Temple in Washington, D.C., organized by the Rev. James Tinney, a black gay evangelical. These groups seek acceptance of gay relationships based on the argument that it is God's will that they were created gay and Christian.

The Catholic Church has affirmed love and welcome for gay men and lesbians if they remain celibate. Dignity, the largest national lay movement of Catholic gay men, lesbians, and their families and friends, was founded in 1973 and has grown to include seventy-five chapters in the United States. They demand the right to worship openly as lesbians and gay men within the church; refuse celibacy, since they are denied the right to marry; and advocate change in the church's teaching about gay and lesbian relationships. Other groups, such as Courage, which was founded in the 1980s, accept Catholic teachings about celibacy for gay men and lesbians but encourage open participation of gays in the Catholic Church.

Orthodox and Conservative Jewish groups have not welcomed openly gay men and lesbians into their midst, although the Conservative movement has gone on record as supporting civil rights for gay men and lesbians and deploring antigay violence. A group of women who call themselves Orthodykes explore their desire to remain committed to traditional Judaism as lesbians.

Other groups that have not welcomed openly gay and lesbian participation also have groups of gay men and lesbians within their ranks who support and advocate rights. These include AXIOS, an organization for Eastern and Orthodox Christians; Affirmation, a group for gay and lesbian Mormons; the Seventh-Day Adventist Kinship, a group to promote understanding; Emergence International: Christian Scientists Supporting Lesbians, Gay Men, and Bisexuals; Honesty, a Southern Baptist group; and the Brethren/Mennonite Council for Lesbian and Gay Concerns.

Some Christian denominations are deeply divided on the acceptance of gay men and lesbians. These groups have welcoming churches as well as organizations to support gay men and lesbians. These include

A male gay couple exchange vows at the Episcopal Church of the Atonement in Fairlawn, New Jersey, on June 21, 1998.   (Credit: AP/Wide World Photos.)

the Episcopal group Integrity, Presbyterians for Gay and Lesbian Concerns, Lutherans Concerned, the Association of Welcoming and Affirming Baptists, and Cornet, the United Methodist Covenant Relationships Network. There are some ordained gay and lesbian clergy who have been allowed to remain in congregational service after coming out, and many who serve in other capacities. Same-sex unions are commonly performed although not officially sanctioned. Gay men and lesbians are active and equal members of welcoming or reconciling congregations. Yet each of these denominations also includes congregations and individuals who adamantly oppose the inclusion of gay men and lesbians, and ministers have lost their positions if they have come out as gay or performed same-sex-union ceremonies. Acrimonious battles have been fought over this issue, often coming to no resolution.

The United Church of Christ, the Unitarian Universalist Church, the Society of Friends, and Reform and Reconstructionist Judaism have been the most accepting of gay men and lesbians. The first openly gay ordination in the United States took place under the auspices of the United Church of Christ, which ordained the Rev. William Johnson in 1972. All the groups ordain gay and lesbian clergy, support equality of membership in congregations, and allow clergy to perform same-sex unions. (Reform Judaism has yet to make a decision about the latter.)

Religious groups outside the Jewish and Christian traditions have also had to deal with this issue in the American context. The Hartford Street Zen Center in San Francisco is openly gay, and Buddhism in general tends toward toleration of gay and lesbian sexuality. GAI, Gay American Indians, incorporates issues of spirituality into its work, as does Trikone, a group of lesbian and gay South Asians. Most Goddess religions are strongly gay-affirmative. While Islam does not support open expressions of gay and lesbian sexuality, there is great tolerance for private relationships.

Because much of the acceptance of gay men and lesbians in religious circles is predicated on the notion that sexuality is based on nature rather than on choice, and on choosing either celibacy or committed relationships, bisexuality has been slow to find acceptance in religious circles. Yet there is a growing support for bisexual concerns, and some gay-lesbian groups (Jewish, Christian Science, Unitarian Universalist) have added "Bisexual" to their names. But the world of religious support for gay men and lesbians has been slow to incorporate support for bisexual and transgendered people.

See also CHASTITY; CIVIL RIGHTS MOVEMENT; CLERGY; HUMAN RIGHTS; MARRIAGE, CHRISTIAN; MARRIAGE, JEWISH; METROPOLITAN COMMUNITY CHURCH; PRIESTHOOD; UNITY.

BIBLIOGRAPHY

Comstock, Gary David. *Unrepentant, Self-Affirming, Practicing: Lesbian/Bisexual/Gay People Within Organized Religion.* 1996.

Cooper, Aaron. "No Longer Invisible: Gay and Lesbian Jews Build a Movement." *Journal of Homosexuality* 18 (1989–1990): 83–94.

Hartman, Keith. *Congregations in Conflict: The Battle over Homosexuality.* 1996.

McNeill, John. *The Church and the Homosexual.* 1976.

Perry, Troy D., and Thomas L. P. Swicegood. *Don't Be Afraid Anymore: The Story of Reverend Troy Perry and the Metropolitan Community Churches.* 1990.

Rebecca T. Alpert

Liberation Theology

Liberation theology is a variegated Christian movement—present, in one form or another, in most major denominations and regions of the world—emphasizing the Christian obligation of active, practical solidarity with the poor and oppressed, and with their struggles against poverty and oppression.

The term and its synonym "theology of liberation" began to be used in about 1969—in Spanish, Portuguese, and English—by Protestant and Roman Catholic theologians throughout the Americas.

Several foundational texts of liberation theology—the Peruvian Gustavo Gutiérrez's *A Theology of Liberation*, the U.S. American James Cone's *Black Theology and Black Power*, and the Brazilian Rubem Alves's *A Theology of Human Hope*—appeared almost simultaneously, independently of each other, at the end of the 1960s.

Origins

The language of liberation has gained currency since early in the 1960s across the world, among groups and movements such as political, union, and community organizers; democratic and socialist movements; and guerrillas against colonial rule. Movements of oppressed peoples to free themselves from the yoke of colonialism (Vietnam, Mozambique, Puerto Rico), military dictatorships (Cuba, Philippines, Zaire), capitalism (Tanzania, Chile), racism (South Africa, the U.S. civil rights movement), or communism (Czechoslovakia, Poland) often identified their thrust with the term "liberation"—as in the many fronts of national liberation of Africa, Asia, and the Americas in the 1960s.

The Christian churches—especially in Third World countries and in the United States—found themselves increasingly challenged by these movements of liberation. First, this was because these movements frequently saw and denounced the churches as tools of domination in the hands of the oppressors. Second, it was because a growing minority of church members were participating in such movements, taking time and energy away from church work, and, most significantly, provoking confrontations with the powers that be—which often led their pastors to disavow them. Last but not least, it was because a growing number of churches experienced a steady drain of youth and working-class members toward the liberation movements, such members rarely finding support to reconcile their religious faith with their commitment to liberation movements, and thus frequently distancing themselves from organized religion or rejecting religion altogether.

Christian Responses

These challenges provoked disparate reactions from church leaders, theologians, and activists—depending on their background, allegiances, outlooks, and so on. Some churches, religious orders, congregations, denominations, individual church leaders, and lay activists took a militant, antiliberationist stance, seeing in any liberation movement a sign of the Antichrist, and justifying the use of armed violence to eliminate such movements (e.g., the Anti-Communist Alliance of Argentina). Most congregations, pastors, religious thinkers, and activists, however, tended either to avoid the matter altogether—as if it didn't have any important bearing on their lives—or to develop some modest form of attention and succor to the poor, but with little to no patience for those understanding poverty as a result of systemic oppression, as an unjust social product urgently demanding social reform.

In some places in the Americas, nonetheless, a few Christian voices began to integrate—in action as well as in thought—a consistent commitment to those liberation movements, and a deep, reflective Christian faith accompanying that commitment. Ironically, part of the impetus behind this integration came from the churches' call of "going to the poor" (getting to know them firsthand by living with them, as them, and in service to them), to counter and preempt the growth of communism among the poor—and of Protestantism as well, in the case of the Latin American Roman Catholic Church. Heeding that call, however, frequently put missionaries, clergy, and lay church activists in a novel, shocking predicament: one that elicited among many not only a radical questioning of the prevalent explanations of and responses to the reality of poverty, but also, more decisively, a critique of the churches' actual place, role, and self-understanding in an unjust, oppressive world.

Crucial catalysts of such processes were Pope John XXIII's and the Second Vatican Council's summons for an humbler, serving church (1961–1965); the progressive ecumenical (Protestant) World Council of Churches–sponsored network ISAL (Iglesia y Sociedad en América Latina); the radical writings and tragic death of the Colombian Roman Catholic priest Father Camilo Torres (1966), spurring *camilista* groups of Christian socialists across Latin America; and the many groups of lay and clergy arising in similar directions all over the Americas.

U.S. Beginnings

The civil rights movement (under the leadership of the Reverend Dr. Martin Luther King, Jr.), the United Farm Workers (with the Roman Catholic pacifist labor organizer César Chávez at its forefront), and the antiwar movement all contributed to create in the United States, in the 1960s, an environment propitious for the development of indigenous theological movements connected with these novel struggles for liberation. Moreover, U.S. missionaries to Latin America (such as Maryknollers and Quakers) often brought back to the United States—besides significant firsthand accounts of the troubling associations between, on the one hand, Latin American oppression, and, on the other, U.S. public and private agencies—news about the emerging theological quests and responses amid poverty and oppression south of the border.

Thus, from the 1960s on, a wide array of liberation theologies—such as African American, Hispanic, feminist, pacifist, Asian American, Native American, ecofeminist, and gay-lesbian—emerged in the United States. In all of them, at least originally and indirectly, there is a certain influence of both African American and Latin American liberation theology. Despite all the obstacles and reactions against liberation theologies, these continue to flourish, multiply, and grow across the United States.

The Defining Features

One of the key traits of all liberation theologies is a recognition that theology is, as Gustavo Gutiérrez likes to put it, a "second moment." Life, including faith, is first—at both the community and the individual level. Theology follows life, as a human effort to understand God's presence and God's demands amid real life.

Each and every liberation theology, while recognizing a somewhat universal yearning for liberation, underscores the particularity of its own attempt—an attempt stemming from the unique experiences of oppression and the specific struggles for liberation of a singular segment of humankind—to grasp God's reality and guidance in the concrete lives of the human community.

Simultaneously, liberation theologies are very critical of theologies claiming universal validity and speaking for humanity as a whole: more often than not, elite theologies stemming from—and either blurring or aggrandizing—the particular experience of an elite minority.

Liberation theologies all put a strong emphasis on praxis—conscious, transformative action of human communities. Theology is not an end in itself; it is a means for a community of believers to orient their real, day-to-day lives in relation to one another and with other people. Thus liberation theology is not what is important; what is key is the actual liberation from oppressive structures and practices. The value of liberation theology, if any, resides in its becoming a useful means for that actual human liberation.

Thus, more than a new set of scriptures, structures, dogmas, or theological concerns, liberation theologies are experiments in collective, dialogical rethinking of the traditional scriptures, church structures, dogmas, and theological themes from within or in service to the specific struggles for self-liberation of a particular oppressed community. Part of such work is deconstructive (examining which power dynamics underlie certain interpretations of scripture, of church structures, etc., and analyzing what consequences such interpretations have). A crucial part of it, however, is constructive: building an understanding of God, scripture, salvation, etc., that makes sense of the lives, pains, and anger of specific oppressed persons and peoples; that contributes to their healing; and that empowers them to struggle to free themselves from such oppression and its deleterious effects.

See also CIVIL RIGHTS MOVEMENT; MAINLINE PROTESTANTISM; ROMAN CATHOLICISM; SOCIOLOGY OF RELIGION; SUFFERING; VATICAN II; WORLD COUNCIL OF CHURCHES.

BIBLIOGRAPHY

Berryman, Phillip. *Liberation Theology.* 1987.
Gottwald, Norman K., ed. *The Bible and Liberation.* 1983.
Novak, Michael. *Will It Liberate?* 1986.
Smith, Christian. *The Emergence of Liberation Theology.* 1991.
Torres, Sergio, and John Eagleson, eds. *Theology in the Americas.* 1976.

Otto Maduro

Life After Death.

See Afterlife.

Liturgy and Worship

It could well be said that the years since 1965 have been, in America as well as in much of the rest of the religious world, a time of unprecedented liturgical change—indeed, upheaval. One could probably go farther to suggest that for Christian churches at least, there has not been such a time since the Reformation of the sixteenth century in Europe and successive "aftershocks" in other places in the centuries that followed.

The roots of this thirty-five year period of liturgical change can be found in two seemingly disparate movements. The more obvious is a series of scholarly and highly "traditional" efforts in many Roman Catholic, Anglican, and Protestant churches dating back almost exactly one hundred years before 1965. In England, Scotland, and Continental Europe, during the late nineteenth century, attempts began to return to earlier worship patterns. There was a renewed interest by Protestants and Anglicans in practices advocated by such sixteenth-century Protestant reformers as John Calvin, Huldrych Zwingli, and John Knox. There was also a revived interest in seventeenth-century Puritans, eighteenth-century Methodists, and in elements of sixteenth and seventeenth-century English worship. In the Roman Catholic Church, the impact of the sixteenth-century Counter-Reformation was challenged in the late nineteenth century with a revived interest in the high Middle Ages and later an appeal to the Patristic era. In the twentieth century, supportive developments in biblical studies (the so-called "Higher Criticism"), ecumenism (as in the World Student Christian Federation and the World Council of Churches), and neo-orthodoxy in the Reformed and Lutheran Churches combined to encourage this liturgical movement, which rapidly crossed the Atlantic to North America. The transatlantic move significantly changed certain of these traditions, particularly in the Roman Catholic Church, where there was added an urban, societal dimension very much under the influence of the Benedictine community's publication of a new journal, *Orate Fratres,* founded by Virgil Michael in 1926 and later to become *Worship.* This is an important connection in relation to the second set of influences on liturgical renewal in America.

This other set of influences may be described as social and cultural. The assassinations of the Kennedy brothers and of Martin Luther King, Jr., in the United States signaled a new form of countercultural consciousness, the civil rights movement, which produced its own very powerful liturgies: processionals ("marches"), hymns (freedom songs and African-American spirituals), symbols (handclasps), martyrs (such as those just named and others), sacred sites (the bridge at Selma, Alabama; and the Lincoln Memorial, where King gave his stirring "I have a dream" speech), and the emergence of black churches (Methodist, Baptist, and Pentecostal) as seminal social forces. Next there arose another paraliturgical form of social and ritual consciousness, the anti–Vietnam War thrust and the related "flower children" youth movement symbolized by Woodstock. This, too, developed its own cultic patterns. Inevitably all of these cultic/cultural developments influenced the churches' culture and cult as embodied centrally in their liturgies.

What has come to characterize liturgical life worldwide in the Protestant, Anglican, Roman Catholic, and Eastern and Oriental Orthodox churches in the several decades since 1965 may be even more pronounced in these churches in the United States. To a lesser extent one might also describe in the same way developments in Judaism, even though significant differences in cultural contexts would have to be addressed.

For many, the word "liturgy" brings to mind elaborate rituals and complex, fixed ecclesiastical texts and traditions. The Greek antecedents of the word, however, would seem to suggest a broader meaning. The two Greek stem words *laos* ("people") and *ergon* ("energy") combine to provide its usual translation, "the work of the people," or "that which the people do." This demonstrates the difference between the more narrow but common concept—ritual activity largely in the hands of the clergy—and the broader concept of the recurring activity of the whole people of God.

In 1965, the Roman Catholic Church's Vatican Council II completed its work. Its initial deliverance, *Sacrosanctam Concilium,* was approved overwhelmingly by the council on November 23, 1963 (movingly and perhaps significantly, the day after the assassination of President John F. Kennedy). That document set off a virtual chain reaction of reformed liturgies, not only in the Roman Catholic Church but also throughout the Protestant world, since many of those churches recognized in its provisions much of their own earlier reformations from the sixteenth century forward. All aspects of liturgical action—textual, architectural, ritual, aesthetic, musical, and catechetical (having to do with baptism)—illustrate this astonishing, almost tectonic set of shifts.

How then can the shape of these liturgical changes be described? The description will refer to three basic traditions: Protestant–Anglican–Roman Catholic, Orthodox-Oriental, and Jewish. In each case the crucial areas of liturgical change will be analyzed as the Sunday/Sabbath service, language and participation, and music and ritual.

Protestant–Anglican–Roman Catholic

Whereas for centuries the Protestant/Catholic "standoff" has been evidenced by an emphasis on reading and preaching the scriptures on the Protestant side as opposed to an emphasis on the celebration of the Mass on the Catholic side, with the Anglicans (Episcopalians) not surprisingly moving to one side or the other and sometimes both, it is now increasingly agreed by both sides that the normative Sunday service should include both Word and Sacrament on a weekly basis, and in that order. This idea is not yet shared by the Baptists, other free churches, or the so-called megachurches.

As a result of the Catholic Church's Vatican Council II, the worldwide body of Catholic English-speaking churches rapidly shifted from Latin to a modern form of English (prepared and proposed by a consultative body of bishops known as the International Commission on English in the Liturgy, founded in 1963), effectively "leapfrogging" the classic Elizabethan English of many, if not most, Protestant churches. The effect of this was to impel U.S. Protestant churches to revise their texts from that older English into more modern forms, which was done under the guidance of ecumenical bodies that have always included Roman Catholic, Anglican, and Protestant representatives, namely the Consultation on Common Texts (founded in 1964) and more recently an international group, the English Language Liturgical Consultation (founded in 1985). *The Worshipbook* (1970) of the Presbyterian churches was the first officially sponsored attempt to make such a linguistic shift, although George MacLeod's Iona Community had pioneered in this respect ever since its founding in 1938. This move immediately provided for a much more vocal and understandable level of participation by the laity. This goal is nicely expressed in a phrase from the Roman Catholic *Constitution on the Sacred Liturgy* as "full, conscious, and active participation in liturgical celebrations" (para. 14). And behind this goal there lies an even deeper aspect of liturgical change in these late decades of the twentieth century, a sense that worship is basically a communal event rather than an occasion for individuals to meditate or simply express their personal, individual piety and receive personal support and encouragement.

Inevitably this shift in language and participation, as well as revisions of structure, required new musical forms, from folk to pop to hymns and chants. This became particularly evident due to the equally surprising ecumenical adaptation of the new Roman Catholic Order for Scripture Reading at Sunday Mass (*Ordo Lectionum Missae,* 1969 and 1981), a three-year cycle. Throughout Protestant and Episcopal churches in the United States (and now internationally), by virtue of the work and influence of the consultation just named, this impulse has resulted in a large corpus of hymnody to complement and encourage the ecumenical adaptation of the Roman Catholic system and now known as *Revised Common Lectionary* (1992). At the ritual and aesthetic levels it can only be briefly suggested that just as the Catholic side has simplified and declericalized its ceremonial aspects, so the Protestant side has taken on the use of symbols, symbolic gestures, and ceremonial behavior such as vestments, color, and movement.

Orthodox-Oriental

Orthodox-Oriental churches have been more reluctant to move in any of the ways just described—perhaps for reasons of ethnic identity, overlapping jurisdictions not always being in close touch with each other, and a high degree of conservative consciousness regarding the divine liturgy (Sunday). The lower level of participation in the above-mentioned ecumenical-liturgical movements can also be attributed to ancient disputes with Roman Catholicism and Orthodox nonacceptance of Protestant bodies. However, in the 1990s there was considerable effort to translate the liturgy into various forms of English, and especially to encourage the vocal and sacramental participation of the laity. Music and architecture were also involved. This is largely true in the Orthodox Church of America (in which the Russian church is the principal party in that it is self-governing in the United States), followed by the Greek Orthodox Archdiocese of North America, which also participates in the Orthodox Church in America and its related Standing Committee of Orthodox Bishops.

Jewish

Differing pictures emerge from the three major associations of synagogues: Orthodox, Conservative, and Reform.

Orthodox Judaism is fairly fixed in the Hebrew language and liturgical forms inherited from various European communities. On the other hand, Reform Judaism, which largely abandoned most of that in favor of a kind of American inculturation (much of which understandably resembled American mainline Protestantism), seems now to be actively recovering more traditional liturgical practices, for both synagogue and domestic use. The centrist Conservative synagogues seem also to be moving in the same direction, though this is not as drastic, since this community has always maintained the use of some Hebrew and traditional ceremonies and calendrical observances. Here, too, there is a growing interest in providing catechetical and liturgical materials for interfaith marriage, known as *teschuvah*.

Many of the Jewish and Christian communities in the late twentieth century in the United States have taken massive and remarkably similar strides to recover much that is authentic in their own traditions from earlier centuries, and not because "old" is necessarily "best," but rather because tradition itself is a living and changing experience of adaptation. Many of these communities' adaptations are in fact conscious responses to changing cultural structures, but also in the context of their own historic cultic context. Just as life is always the context of liturgy at its best, so also it is the deepest conviction of these religious traditions that liturgy must always be the primary context for the life and practice of believers.

See also BELONGING, RELIGIOUS; CHANTING; CIVIL RIGHTS MOVEMENT; COMMUNION; MINISTRY; MUSIC; PRACTICE; PRAYER; PREACHING; RELIGIOUS COMMUNITIES; RITUAL; ROCK MASSES; SOCIOLOGY OF RELIGION; SPIRITUALS; VATICAN II.

BIBLIOGRAPHY

Austin, Gerard, ed. *Eucharist Toward the Third Millennium.* 1998.

Davies, Horton, *Bread of Life and Cup of Joy.* 1993.

Hoffman, Lawrence, and Bradshaw, Paul F., eds. *The Making of Jewish and Christian Worship.* 1991.

Pecklers, Keith, S.J. *The Unread Vision: The Liturgical Movement in the United States of America.* 1998.

Saliers, Don E. *Worship as Theology: Foretaste of Glory Divine.* 1994.

Spinks, Bryan D., and Iain R. Torrance, eds. *To Glorify God: Essays on Modern Reformed Liturgy.* 1999.

West, Fritz. *Scripture and Memory: The Ecumenical Hermeneutic of the Three-Year Lectionaries.* 1997.

White, James F. *A Brief History of Christian Worship.* 1993.

Horace T. Allen, Jr.

Lived Religion

The term "lived religion" denotes an approach to the question of what religion is as it exists in society or in a social field. From this perspective, religion is understood as doing, or practice, but in a distinctive sense. In the collection of essays *Lived Religion in America: Toward a History of Practice,* ed. David D. Hall (1997), where this approach is pursued programmatically by historians and sociologists, practice signifies something more than mere doing: it refers to the forms of action by and through which any tradition, "church," or community works out the nature and boundaries of what it is to be religious.

Thus defined, this approach has three main aspects: (1) Lived religion understood as practice is a means of acknowledging the differences that so often open up between official doctrine or norms of behavior and what adherents of a religion or a church actually "do." Historians of lived religion take for granted that religious actors—be these clergy or laity, "professionals" or amateurs—adapt, appropriate, resist, or improvise in response to regulating, systematic, or formalized constructions of what constitutes religion. Rather than censoring such differences or excluding them as nonreligious, the historian of lived religion seeks to map these processes and especially to explore how the relation between the official and the unofficial is always being negotiated. (2) Lived religion as practice is a means of recognizing that religious actors behave in patterned ways. Practice is not random or aimless but takes on a structure or shape that we commonly designate as "ritual." Accordingly, the historian of lived religion is interested in every aspect of worship and liturgy—that is, what happens inside those spaces that receive official designation as the approved sites for religious practice. But the rituals that occur outside or on the margins of that space are no less interesting: church suppers, family reunions, saints' days. Mother's Day, healings, gift-giving, pilgrimages to shrines, to name but some of the many possibilities. The centrality of ritual in the description of lived religion is paralleled by the importance of ritual theory, especially as rethought by Catherine Bell in *Ritual Theory, Ritual Practice* (1992), where ritual is recast as "ritualization" (that is, always open-ended and in process). (3) Lived religion is about the framework of meaning that is embedded within any given practice. The chapter in Robert Orsi's *The Madonna of 115th Street* (1985), "The Meanings of the Madonna of 115th Street," where he explicates the multiple, overlapping, even contradictory meanings of a symbol, exemplifies a mode of analysis that connects practice to the play of meaning.

What then is practice? As I have suggested in *Lived Religion in America* (p. xi), it "encompasses the tensions, the ongoing struggles of definition, which are constituted within every religious tradition and which are always present in how people choose to act religiously. Practice thus suggests that any synthesis is provisional." Not only is this perspective of great importance in understanding contemporary religion; it can also yield new understandings of the past.

See also LITURGY AND WORSHIP; PRACTICE; RITUAL; SOCIOLOGY OF RELIGION.

BIBLIOGRAPHY

Orsi, Robert. *Thank You, St. Jude: Women's Devotion to the Patron Saint of Hopeless Causes.* 1996.

Peacock, James L., and Ruel W. Tyson, Jr. *Pilgrims of Paradox: Calvinism and Experience Among the Primitive Baptists of the Blue Ridge.* 1989.

David D. Hall

Love

There is rich history of attempting to define love and its scope. Ultimately there is no one definitive interpretation of love. Generally, love involves a strong feeling of affection, care, and desire. This has prompted a centuries-old debate on the relationships among love, charity, desire, and friendship.

Traditionally for some, love is equated to the New Testament Greek word *agapē,* and it is sometimes equated to the Latin translation of agapē, *caritas,* or charity. Anders Nygren (1953) drew a sharp distinction between agapē and caritas because he believed that charity combines the desire and longing of *erōs* with the spontaneity and gratuity of agapē. This was, for Nygren, a distortion of the Christian theme of agapē. Beyond religious contexts, charity often refers to benevolence and philanthropy, as it is a response to human needs.

Others make distinctions among agapē, erōs, and *philia.* Historically for Christians, love is considered the primary characteristic of God's nature and is also seen as the ultimate expression of Christian faith and action. In the New Testament, the most common words for love are philia and agapē. Philia denotes friendship and affectionate mutual regard for those with whom one is closely connected—biologically or emotionally. Agapē denotes God's unmerited love for humanity or the love humans have for each other that is shaped by God's love for humanity. Agapē has often been seen as a love that flows toward another, whatever the goodness or lovability of that person or persons. Eros is not found in the New Testament; however, many see it as indicating a passionate desire that loves for the person or the object's ability to satisfy one's own needs.

Theologians such as Augustine and Thomas Aquinas suggest that agapē is similar to a passionate love for God. For them, there is a place for ardent friendship that flows from our relationship with God. In the contemporary era, theologians such as Mary E. Hunt have expanded this interpretation. Hunt considers the friendships between women. For her, the love found in these friendships prompts a drive for unity that does not mean that either party loses her uniqueness as an individual. Rather, this unity generates something new that is greater than and beyond the two individuals.

Until recently, Christian theology and ethics argued that God's love is best represented by agapē. Roman Catholicism appeals to the personal relations with the Trinity (Father/Son/Holy Spirit or Creator/Redeemer/Sustainer) as a way to emphasize unity and community as the essential features of love. Margaret

Farley, a Roman Catholic theologian and ethicist, finds that human love is characterized by the equality found in the relationship within the Trinity. Protestantism appeals to the death of Jesus on the cross for sins of humanity and often stresses self-sacrifice as the distinctive feature of love. Some Protestant theologians, such as Beverly Wildung Harrison, caution that the death of Jesus on the cross should not be seen as his desiring death. Rather, Harrison argues that Jesus accepted death as a consequence of his persistent love for humanity.

This overview merits a closer examination of the debate on the nature of love. Within this debate are concerns about the compatibility of self-love with other forms of love, the importance of self-denial, the possibility of truly loving those beyond one's immediate family or intimate relationships, and the possibility of love that is completely objective. In the twentieth century, Nygren helped to focus this debate in *Agapē and Eros* (1953). For Nygren, agapē prohibits all self-regard or self-centeredness, for Christians must love as God loves. Because Nygren believed that only God can really love objectively, people are only able to love others without seeking personal gain to the extent to which they are routes through whom God works.

Nygren's position parallels the philosopher Søren Kierkegaard's *Works of Love* (1847). Kierkegaard contrasted Christian love with the love between man and woman or between friend and friend. For him this latter form of love is selective and focuses only on particular people or persons. This kind of love between humans is only a disguised form of self-love (how Nygren depicts erōs) that will ultimately fail over time. Christian love, for Kierkegaard, does not choose its object but goes out to all and is a duty that will not fail and will withstand the shifts of time and circumstances.

Nygren was partially supported by others, such as Karl Barth. In his *Church Dogmatics* (IV/2), Barth agrees with Nygren's distinction between agapē and erōs. However, he disagrees with Nygren's refusal to admit that it is possible for humans to have love toward God. Barth points to the way in which Jesus approved the love Mary Magdalene showed him when she washed his feet with oils and when he chastised the disciples when their actions and ideas were legalistic rather than demonstrating love toward others. For Barth one cannot follow Jesus and God obediently if one does not love them. Love, then, is the foundation for the Christian life, and the freedom to love God and others is the gift God gives humanity through Jesus Christ. Ultimately Barth considers Kierkegaard too legalistic and Nygren too pessimistic.

In recent years the notion that genuine love must involve self-sacrifice and a rejection of self-concern has been challenged by Gene Outka and others. The most outspoken critics of this understanding of love are found among those representing various liberation theologies (e.g., Latin American, black, womanist, Asian American, feminist). The largest body of work has been generated by feminists who are particularly critical of the idea of love as self-sacrifice.

Generally, the major drawback these thinkers see in equating love with self-sacrifice is that this often reinforces social inequality. When one makes self-sacrifice such a high, if not primary, virtue, this gives powerful religious validation to oppressive and destructive behaviors and situations (e.g., sexual abuse, domestic violence, unjust economic systems). Those who lack power and status in society have no incentive to seek equality when the religious ideal is altruistic self-sacrifice. The danger is that self-sacrifice becomes an end in itself rather than as a means to create more just and loving relationships among people.

Another drawback in equating love with self-sacrifice is that this fails to emphasize the relational character of love. Feminist theologians such as Barbara Hilkert Andolsen, Margaret Farley, and Beverly Wildung address this by arguing that self-love is not morally negative. In fact, for them, situations of self-sacrifice are often indications that oppressive behavior and attitudes are present. They make an important distinction between self-sacrifice and self-abnegation. Farley, in particular, notes the difference between *justifiable* self-sacrifice and *faithless* self-abnegation. She insists that justifiable self-sacrifice is that which confers actual benefits on others. Its aim is universal human dignity, which is found in mutual relationships based on love and justice.

These theologians define love as mutuality between people that calls for openness and vulnerability for all parties. Farley is clear that love (agapē) is full mutuality that is found in genuine equality between men and women. This mutuality is marked by loving relationships. Harrison agrees with Farley about the radical nature of mutuality and points out that most of humanity is unable to maintain the openness and vulnerability that this love demands.

The nature of erōs has also been reinterpreted in more recent years. Writers such as Audre Lorde focus on the nature of the erotic, particularly in women. For her, the erotic is a resource that is deeply female and spiritual. It is a kind of knowledge that is intuitive and nonrational. Ultimately it is powerful because it is the creative energy to feel and to be fully present, body and soul, in all that we do and experience.

On a larger scale erōs means that humanity has at its disposal the power that comes from sharing deeply all of life and living. Rather than relying on self-sacrifice or self-abnegation to create loving relationships, erōs opens our capacity for joy and gives us a way to scrutinize how we create our social relationships. This will allow us to realize our deepest emotions and feelings and relate to one another passionately. This now passionate relationship is not confined to sexual emotions but encompasses all emotions. All of who we are is brought to bear in this form of erōs. Ultimately erōs in this sense seeks an intimate and lasting form of mutuality that recognizes and affirms just and loving relationships in humanity and the larger social order.

There is little doubt that the debate about the nature of love will be unending. At stake is our understanding of how we see ourselves as humans and how we behave in relation to others and the world around us. As this shifts with our various circumstances and the environments they produce, we will gain new insights, rediscover old paradigms, and reform our behaviors to signal the ways in which we believe we must relate to each other in caring ways.

See also BIBLE; ETHICS; FEMINIST SPIRITUALITY; FEMINIST THEOLOGY; LEGALISM; PSYCHOLOGY OF RELIGION; TRINITY; WOMANIST THEOLOGY.

BIBLIOGRAPHY

Andolsen, Barbara Hilkert. "Agape in Feminist Ethics." *Journal of Religious Ethics* 9, no. 1 (1981): 69–83.

Farley, Margaret. *Personal Commitments: Beginning, Keeping, Changing.* 1986.

Gremillion, Joseph, ed. *The Gospel of Peace and Justice: Catholic Social Teachings Since Pope John.* 1980.

Hunt, Mary E. *Fierce Tenderness: A Feminist Theology of Friendship.* 1992.

Nygren, Anders. *Agapē and Erōs: A Study of the Christian Idea of Love.* 1953.

Outka, Gene. *Agapē: An Ethical Analysis.* 1972.

Emilie M. Townes

Lubavitcher Movement.

See Hasidim.

Lutheran Churches

The Protestant Reformation emerged in sixteenth-century Europe out of a century of efforts to reform Roman Catholicism. Its Lutheran phase began in 1517 with Martin Luther's public criticism of penitential practices promoting indulgences and good works for the forgiveness of sins. Luther emphasized faith in a gracious God who forgave sin solely for the sake of Jesus Christ. Sinners are made right with God, he insisted—"justified by grace alone"—through faith alone without penitential works. Basing his reform on biblical doctrines, Luther emphasized the primacy of scripture in norming faith and practice. He reformed the Latin Mass using these three principles, promoting worship in the vernacular so God's word rightly preached could be heard, and the sacraments rightly administered could be received by faith. For Luther, the Christian was simultaneously sinner and justified, caught in daily struggle between the power of sin and God's justifying word. Lutheran ethics emphasized good works of neighborly love that follow faith but that do not merit salvation.

The Lutheran reformation spread these core beliefs from Lutheran Saxony throughout churches in northern Germany and Scandinavia. They were professed publicly before Emperor Charles V in the Augsburg Confession (1530). Public accountability for the faith that is confessed remains a hallmark of Lutheran churches. Key confessional documents include Luther's *Small and Large Catechisms* (1529) and the "Formula of Concord" (1577), which resolved issues arising after Luther's death in 1646 regarding predestination, the relationship between faith and works, the use of the law as a scriptural norm in religious life, and the "Real Presence" of Christ in the Eucharist. These four "confessions," Philip Melanchthon's "Apology" for the Augsburg Confession, two Luther treatises, and three ecumenical creeds were published together as *The Book of Concord* (1580).

The Lutheran confessions guide American Lutheranism today and provide an evangelical voice in ecumenical councils. Other Christians sometimes describe Lutheranism as quietist. This criticism originated with pietist Lutherans who restructured Lutheran theology in the eighteenth century by emphasizing "sanctification." They insisted on converted lives devoted to biblical study, prayer, and good works. Because of reform-minded missionary work among European immigrants in North and South America, Asia (especially India), and eventually Africa, Lutheran pietism has strongly influenced the church in America.

Perhaps half of all Lutheran immigrants have remained loyal to the church of their fathers and mothers. The earliest immigrants, from Sweden, Germany, and the Netherlands, formed Lutheran congregations in America, welcoming pastors sent by state churches and pietist institutions. Lutheran emphases on the priesthood of the baptized and the office of ministry fostered lay-controlled congregations with strong pastoral leadership. Later immigrants, from the Baltics, Scandinavia, Eastern Europe, and the indigenized Lutheran churches in Africa, the Carib-

In a service at St. John's Lutheran Church in Normal, Illinois (1988), a pastor blesses several congregants who have come before him.   (Credit: CORBIS/Philip Gould.)

bean, and Central and South America, built on these foundations while increasing membership diversity. Today there are 20,000 congregations in the United States with a baptized membership above 8.6 million. They show strong signs of member satisfaction and denominational loyalty. Lutheran adherents have increased to more than 70 million worldwide, making up the largest body of Protestant churches today.

Lutheran congregations have consistently grouped themselves into larger organizations (synods), reflecting different national, ethnic, and confessional traditions. Their congregational representatives and pastors gather periodically to conduct joint church business. Lutherans borrowed this polity from British Protestants rather than importing European models of episcopacy. Twenty-four general synodical bodies were reported by the U.S. Census of 1906. Two conciliar bodies—the National Lutheran Council (1918) and the Lutheran Council in the U.S.A. (1958)—assisted synods in joint military chaplaincy and social ministry while encouraging synodical mergers. Elected leaders, both politically skilled and theologically astute, have guided these developments over 250

years—Henry Melchior Muhlenberg, eighteenth-century Lutheran patriarch; nineteenth-century synodical founders Samuel Simon Schmucher, Charles Porterfield Krauth, Tuve N. Hasselquist, and C. F. W. Walther; and twentieth-century leaders in church mergers and council work James R. Crumley, Jr., Franklin Clark Fry, Frederick H. Knubel, Kent S. Knutson, William Kohn, Ralph Long, David W. Preus, Jacob A. O. Preus, and Hans Gerhard Stub.

After a century of mergers, nineteen separate Lutheran church bodies remain today, still separated by ethnic or confessional differences. These include three major Lutheran bodies—the Evangelical Lutheran Church in America (ELCA—5.2 million members), the Lutheran Church, Missouri Synod (LCMS—2.6 million members), and the Wisconsin Evangelical Lutheran Synod (WELS—410,000 members). Consolidation has significantly reduced minor differences among these major groups of Lutherans. The use of common worship services has further encouraged Lutheran unity, often preceding the merger of participating bodies and thereby demonstrating the principle that worship shapes belief. Yet major confessional differences continue to play a crucial role in shaping twentieth-century Lutheranism.

Conservative Lutherans (including LCMS and WELS) subscribe to the entire *Book of Concord* as well as other statements of faith, including a key belief in biblical inerrancy. A "third use" of the law suggests the importance of biblical literalism in defining other issues, including women in church and society, and norms for sexual ethics. Suspicious of worship's power to shape belief, conservatives shun intercommunion, limiting worship to the like-minded. Such theological precisionism can generate controversy. Though yoked together in the synodical conference, WELS broke fellowship with an increasingly moderate LCMS during the liberal 1960s, charging it with doctrinal laxity and "unionism." Subsequently the LCMS divided into conservative and moderate factions over biblical inspiration and inerrancy. The majority forced out a small contingent of liberalizing moderates—5 percent—devoted to modern biblical criticism. They withdrew, forming the Association of Evangelical Lutheran Churches (AELC) in 1976, making possible the LCMS's subsequent move to the right.

Moderate Lutherans allow intercommunion among Lutheran bodies subscribing only to the Augsburg Confession with its insistence on the Gospel rightly preached (i.e., justification) and the sacraments rightly administered ("Real Presence"). They also rely on biblically derived statements of faith and practice, but less as norms and more as guides for ethical deliberation. The key issue of biblical inerrancy has shaped intercommunion among them as well. The new American Lutheran Church (ALC), formed in 1960, was committed to further mergers among conservative bodies (including the LCMS) embracing biblical inerrancy. The Lutheran Church in America (LCA) was formed in 1962 from more liturgical and ecumenically minded Lutheran groups. Committed to merging distinct Lutheran traditions into new confessional bodies, the LCA embraced modern biblical scholarship and social advocacy. The ALC rejected merger overtures from the LCA until AELC leaders, believing survival impossible after their break with the LCMS, issued "A Call to Lutheran Union" in 1978, proposing a merger of all three bodies. Their joint publication of *The Lutheran Book of Worship* (1978)

The edifice of the Georgetown Lutheran Church in the Georgetown section of Washington, D.C., is made of stone masonry.   (Credit: CORBIS/Lee Snider.)

gave strong incentive to the formation of the ELCA in 1988. The result was a major new Protestant church body with confessional differences resulting in internal issues about episcopacy, the office of ministry, liturgical development, and sexual ethics, all still to be resolved at the end of the century.

Today the LCMS and the WELS continue a separatist tradition of conservative Lutheranism with modest ecumenical agendas of cooperation and dialogue among Lutheran bodies. Given this posture, the ELCA has effectively run out of partners for further merger talks. It retains an active ecumenical agenda with major Protestant and Roman Catholic church bodies. Old questions about justification, "Real Presence," and episcopal authority remain live issues. Now they are also discussed in an ecumenical context with a tendency to blur a Lutheran confessional identity. Lutheran conservatives and moderates are at different places along the spectrum of American denominations and offer alternative visions for the future of Lutheranism in denominational America. How each survives in a changing religious marketplace will influence the history of American Lutheran churches in the twenty-first century.

See also CONGREGATION; CONVERSION; DENOMINATION; DOGMATISM; MAINLINE PROTESTANTISM; ROMAN CATHOLICISM.

BIBLIOGRAPHY

Gritsch, Eric W. *Introduction to Lutheranism.* 1994. Lueker, Erwin L., ed. *Lutheran Cyclopedia,* rev. ed. 1987.

Nelson, E. Clifford, ed. *The Lutherans of North America,* rev. ed. 1980.

Piepkorn, Arthur Carl. *Profiles in Belief,* vol. 2. 1978.

Wiederaenders, Robert C., ed. *Historical Guide to Lutheran Church Bodies of North America,* rev. ed. 1998.

Robert F. Scholz